The Union Cavalry in the Civil War

$450 CASH IN HAND.

ENLIST AT ONCE, AND AVOID A DRAFT.

JOIN A VETERAN REGIMENT.

THE 1st NEW YORK CAVALRY

The oldest Volunteer Cavalry Regiment in the U.S. Service,
and whose reputation is excelled by none.

TOTAL BOUNTY:

TO VETERANS, $777; TO ALL OTHERS, $677.

HEADQUARTERS:

600 BROADWAY.

Lieutenants A. C. HINTON and G. S. POINDEXTER,
RECRUITING OFFICERS.

STEPHEN Z. STARR

The
Union Cavalry
in the
Civil War

VOLUME I
From Fort Sumter to Gettysburg
1861–1863

Louisiana State University Press
Baton Rouge

Copyright © 1979 by Louisiana State University Press
All rights reserved
Manufactured in the United States of America
Design: Patricia Douglas Crowder
Typeface: Linotype Primer
Composition: G&S Typesetters, Inc.
Printing: Thomson-Shore, Inc.
Binding: John Dekker & Sons, Inc.

LIBRARY OF CONGRESS CATALOGING IN PUBLICATION DATA

Starr, Stephen Z
    The Union Cavalry in the Civil War.

    Bibliography: p.
    Includes index.
    CONTENTS: v. 1. From Fort Sumter to Gettysburg, 1861–1863.
    1. United States. Army. Cavalry—History—Civil War, 1861–1865. 2. United States—History—Civil War, 1861–1865—Campaigns and battles. I. Title.
E492.5.S7   973.7′41   78–26751
ISBN 0–8071–0484–1 (v. 1)

to
T. Harry Williams
with admiration, affection, and gratitude

Contents

viii

Illustrations

Maps

Preface

GLAMOR WAS THE WORD FOR THE CAVALRY WHEN THE Civil War broke out. The middle years of the nineteenth century were a time of overripe romanticism. Otherwise sober men, a generation or two removed from an utterly unromantic frontier, saw the cavalry through the eyes of Sir Walter Scott and themselves in the role of the mailed knight wielding a saber, with its fine-sounding French name, the "arme blanche," the true weapon for man-to-man combat, unlike the impersonal, unwieldy, plebeian musket of the lowly infantryman. Beyond argument was the immense superiority of a man riding a steed—not a mere horse—into battle, over the heavily laden footsoldier, slogging his dreary way through ankle-deep, viscous mud.

Precious few of these gaudy visions survived the realities of the first few months of a cavalryman's exposure to the service. The steed turned out to be an untrained, unmanageable scarecrow, requiring an inordinate amount of care; except on parade, the saber generally stayed in its rusty scabbard, since much of the fighting was on foot. And the yellow cavalry trim on jacket and trousers became tarnished and blackened with dirt and the smoke of campfires.

   In no time at all, the glamor evaporated. In its place came a
life of hardship impossible to realize fully a hundred and twenty
years later, compounded of exposure, filth, an unspeakable diet,
medical care primitive even by the standards of the day, disease,
disability, and death. For those who survived the hazards of mere
existence in the army, there were the additional hazards of skirmish and battle, magnified by derisory training and inexperienced
or downright poor leadership. On the home front, however, the
glamor of the cavalry led a charmed life. In the postwar years especially, the story of the cavalry in the Civil War acquired a halo
of romance and became the object of a never-ending fascination,
fueled by a stream of books glorifying the more spectacular deeds
and personalities, both real and idealized, of the cavalry on both
sides, and decade after decade, this fascination has continued to
flourish.
   The purpose of the present study is to describe the cavalry and
its military role in the Civil War as realistically as the mass of
surviving records, official and personal, will allow. For obvious
reasons—*ars longa, vita brevis* holds true for the reader as well
as the author—the protagonist is the northern cavalry, and the
southern cavalry is considered only to the extent needed to present a rounded picture.
   I have been living with the Federal cavalry for fifteen rewarding years. In my mind, as in the minds of the men I write about,
the cavalry glamor went up in smoke long ago, to be replaced by
a two-fold vision that this study endeavors to express. First is the
intellectual fascination of observing the emergence from the
slough of despond of a misunderstood, misused, untrained, and
inept branch of the service and its development through a process
of sheer pragmatism, of unarticulated ideas bubbling up from below, into the cutting edge of the Federal armies. In the last year
of the war, when attrition, the discharge of time-expired veterans,
and other factors caused a steady deterioration in the quality of
the Federal infantry, particularly in the East, the blue cavalry
came into its own, well led, equally skillful whether fighting on
foot or on horseback, battlewise, tough, true veterans, fighting
men of superb quality. The second aspect is primarily emotional:
an unbounded admiration for the men—boys, many of them, six-

teen, seventeen, and eighteen years old—of the Federal cavalry. Not all of them were heroes by any means; the cavalry had its share of deserters, cowards, malingerers, thieves, misfits, the stupid, the drunkards, and the shirkers, and they were to be found in every rank, but it is impossible to live with these men in spirit without an ever-growing respect for their hardihood and dedication.

It needed a true nobility of spirit (an expression most cavalrymen would have laughed at) for a regiment of cavalry to vote in the 1864 presidential election, as did the 2nd Ohio Cavalry, 201 for Lincoln and 4 for McClellan, and to glory in having done so. Their vote was a deliberate expression of their determination to see the war fought to a finish. They well knew when they cast their ballots that if the war was to continue, they themselves would have to bear the brunt of the fighting and the dying.

Partly because of my admiration for these men and partly because of my personal predilections, I have endeavored to tell the story of the Union cavalry primarily in terms of its personnel, from general to latest-come recruit, and have done so whenever possible in their own words. The campaigns, battles, and tactical developments are indispensable, and I hope I have done them justice, but I believe, and hope readers will agree, that more than a hundred years after Appomattox, the men behind these events and trends—who they were, how they lived and died, what they experienced, how they behaved, what they said and thought—are no less important, and as worthy of study, as the events themselves.

This history of the Union cavalry in the Civil War will appear in three volumes. The present volume covers the beginnings of the northern cavalry—how it was raised, organized, officered, equipped, and trained—and it is followed by the story of its operations up to and including the battle of Gettysburg. The second volume will deal with cavalry operations in the East, on both sides of the Blue Ridge, from July, 1863, to General Lee's surrender at Appomattox. The third volume will cover cavalry operations west of the Alleghenies, from the beginning to the end of the war.

At the sacrifice of the chronological and geographic unities, I have deemed it helpful for the reader to begin the story with the Federal cavalry at the apogee of its effectiveness, with James Harrison Wilson's Selma Campaign in the Spring of 1865, an all-cavalry operation that demonstrates vividly the high level of competence the Union cavalry reached after a long, slow, and frequently painful process of development.

I am grateful for the help I have received from the staffs of the National Archives and Records Service, the Library of Congress, the Cincinnati Historical Society, the Public Library of Cincinnati and Hamilton County, and the Kansas State Historical Society. I acknowledge with thanks the permission of the Cincinnati Historical Society to quote extensively from the unpublished reminiscences of Sergeant Roger Hannaford, 2nd Ohio Cavalry. I am indebted to Miss Robin Martin for the skillful preparation of the maps and would be grossly remiss if I failed to acknowledge the benefit to myself, and more especially to my readers, of the lady-like but firm bludgeoning I have received from the editorial staff of the Louisiana State University Press, the Mesdames (perish the Ms's) Jarrett, Hall, and DiPiero.

My special and most cordial thanks are due to Professor Jay Luvaas, Allegheny College, and Dr. Thomas Thiele, both of whom have read the present volume in manuscript and suggested changes that have greatly improved it. And I owe a special debt to my good friend, William H. Wright, sworn enemy of indirect discourse and superfluous verbiage, for trampling on and demolishing most (but due to authorial obstinacy, not all) of my finest flowers of rhetoric.

And before and above all these, I am grateful for the presence and patient encouragement of my dear wife. She, more than I, has earned an honorary membership in the Grand Army of the Republic. Much as she disapproves of wars and battles, this is intended to be *her* book.

The Union Cavalry in the Civil War

INTRODUCTION

Climax in Alabama

IN JANUARY, 1865, JAMES HARRISON WILSON, TWENTY-seven years old, spare, hard-faced, a neatly trimmed moustache and beard emphasizing the prominence of his jaw, wore the twin stars of a major general on the shoulder straps of his uniform. He was commanding officer of the Cavalry Corps of the Military Division of the Mississippi. Two years before, Assistant Secretary of War Charles A. Dana had written of him, "His leading idea is the idea of duty, and he applies it vigorously and often impatiently to others. In consequence he is unpopular among all who like to live with little work. But he has remarkable talents and uncommon executive powers, and will be heard from hereafter."[1] Graduated sixth in the forty-one-member West Point Class of 1860, the outbreak of the Civil War found Wilson stationed at Fort Vancouver on the Columbia River, as a second lieutenant in the Corps of Topographical Engineers. Ordered East in July, 1861, he served on General Thomas W. Sherman's staff in the Port Royal Expedition. In November, 1862, he joined General Ulysses S. Grant's staff as chief topographical engineer and inspector general. By

1. Charles A. Dana, *Recollections of the Civil War* (New York, 1898), 73.

his own account (Wilson did not lack a generous appreciation of his own military sagacity) it was he who suggested to Grant the daring and ultimately successful plan to capture Vicksburg by crossing the Mississippi well below the city and investing it from the east.

In October, 1863, Grant asked that Wilson be promoted to brigadier general and given a cavalry command, for which Grant thought he possessed "uncommon qualifications."[2] The promotion was duly made, but Wilson remained on Grant's staff until the following January, when Dana had him assigned to Washington as chief of the Cavalry Bureau, to "get the . . . Bureau into order and honesty. . . . It is a question of saving millions of money and rendering the cavalry arm everywhere efficient."[3] In a whirlwind tour of duty of ten weeks, Wilson reorganized the scandalously lax system of inspecting horses purchased for the cavalry, put the fear of God into defaulting horse contractors, and, what was of far more lasting importance, had the seven-shot Spencer carbine, which he rightly called "by all odds the most effective firearm of the day," adopted as the standard cavalry firearm.[4]

For the first three years of the war Wilson held a succession of staff appointments with ever-increasing credit. He had friends and admirers in high places, in the army as well as the government, and he cultivated them all assiduously. He had not, however, commanded troops in the field, but the opportunity to do so now came his way. His tour of duty as head of the Cavalry Bureau ended on April 7, 1864, and he was given command of the Third Division of the Cavalry Corps of the Army of the Potomac.

The condition of the division when Wilson assumed command, a scant four weeks before the start of the Wilderness Cam-

2. *The War of the Rebellion: A Compilation of the Official Records of the Union and Confederate Armies* (128 vols.; Washington, D.C., 1880–1901), Ser. I, Vol. XXX, Pt. 1, p. 73; hereinafter cited as *Official Records*. Unless otherwise indicated, all citations are to Series I.

3. *Ibid.*, Vol. XXXII, Pt. 2, pp. 115–16.

4. Thomas F. Thiele, "The Evolution of Cavalry in the American Civil War, 1861–1863" (Ph.D. dissertation, University of Michigan, 1951), 66. In the course of the war, the national government bought nineteen different makes of cavalry carbines; in point of popularity with cavalrymen, the Sharps ranked after the Spencer, but it was a single-shot weapon and fired an easily damaged paper cartridge.

paign, would have daunted anyone with less than his abundant supply of self-confidence. Made up of seven (later nine) regiments and parts of two others, with a nominal strength of over 7,000 men, the division mustered a mere 3,436 present for duty, and of these 744 were dismounted and another 378 had horses that had been condemned as unserviceable. Its camps were badly located and poorly policed, "its equipment and clothing nearly used up, and its heterogeneous collection of carbines dirty and out of order."[5] Most of the division was on picket duty, covering a line twenty-eight miles long. Few of the officers bothered to attend stable call, and routine duties were performed so fitfully that Wilson ordered "one colonel in arrest and . . . admonish[ed] the rest that radical improvements must be made at once if they would save themselves from a similar fate."

Wilson's troopers and two batteries of horse artillery crossed the Rapidan at Germanna Ford shortly after midnight on May 4, as the spearhead of the advance of the army into the Wilderness. From that day until its transfer to the Shenandoah Valley three months later, the division was almost constantly in action, protecting the flank of the infantry as it moved forward, step by bloody step, to Spotsylvania, across the North Anna, the Pamunkey, Totopotomoy Creek and the James, to the defenses of Richmond and Petersburg.

Wilson had firm ideas on the way cavalry should be used and was not at all reluctant to express them; his chief, the hard-bitten, bullet-headed Philip Sheridan, fortunately shared those ideas, but only once during the entire campaign was the cavalry used the way they thought it should be. The entire corps of three divisions marched and fought as a unit in Sheridan's raid to Richmond, in the course of which it administered a stinging defeat to the cavalry of General Lee's army at Yellow Tavern and killed its commander, "Jeb" Stuart.

Wilson's performance in this, his first command, was no more than adequate, even allowing for the fact that he was not a cavalryman by training and had never before commanded troops in combat. In his only independent operation, a raid to break up the

5. This and the quotation which follows are from James H. Wilson, *Under the Old Flag* (2 vols.; New York, 1912), I, 372–73.

Richmond & Danville, Southside, and Petersburg & Weldon rail-roads south and west of Petersburg, he came close to losing his entire division. A thorough job was done of breaking up the rail-roads, but on its return to base the division ran head on into Con-federate cavalry, backed by a full division of infantry, and was badly mauled, escaping with the loss of all its guns, nearly all its wagons and ambulances, and nine hundred men killed, wounded, or taken prisoner.

In his reminiscences, Wilson contends at great length that the blame for the near-disaster of his division lay at Sheridan's door.[6] Some of his men, however, held Wilson himself to blame. Roger Hannaford, a trooper in the 2nd Ohio Cavalry, wrote that "in the opinion of every man who survived the raid . . . Genl Wilson's name was a stench in their nostrils and . . . ever afterward . . . he was held in very little repute, and as a consequence our Div[ision] was looked upon as the poorest in the whole Cav[alry] Corp[s] or in fact the whole Army; so true it is that confidence in your Com-mander is necessary to the success of any body of men."[7] This is a comment to recall in connection with Wilson's subsequent per-formance at Nashville and in the Selma Campaign.

At the beginning of August, 1864, Wilson and his division were relieved of duty with the Army of the Potomac and sent to join Sheridan in the Shenandoah Valley, where Jubal Early had established himself after his raid to the outskirts of Washington. Sheridan was given the Valley command with orders to "follow [Early] to the death." Wilson's division, with that of General A. T. A. Torbert, also transferred from the Army of the Potomac, and twenty-five hundred horsemen from the Department of West Virginia under General W. W. Averell, made up Sheridan's caval-ry. On his way to the Valley, Wilson stopped at the Cavalry Depot at Giesboro, Maryland, to refit his division, obtain horses for its dismounted men, and exchange its miscellany of inferior firearms for a uniform issue of Spencer carbines. Six weeks later, on Sep-tember 19, Wilson led the advance of the bulk of Sheridan's army across Opequon Creek and his men fired the opening shots in the

6. *Ibid.*, I, 468–69, 489–521.
7. Roger Hannaford (2nd Ohio Cavalry), "Reminiscences" (MS in the Cincinnati Historical Society, Cincinnati, Ohio), 98(d)–99(a).

ensuing battle, a smashing victory for Sheridan, and "the first battle of the war," Wilson wrote, "in which the cavalry was properly handled in cooperation with the infantry, and in which it played the decisive part."[8] Three days later Early was defeated again, even more disastrously, at Fisher's Hill and retreated to Harrisonburg with the Federals at his heels. There, on September 30, Wilson was ordered to turn over his division to the flamboyant George Custer and report to General Sherman in Atlanta, to reorganize and command the cavalry of Sherman's military division. To give Wilson the requisite rank for his new post, he was brevetted major general.

Wilson's new appointment came about as a result of a revealing exchange of telegrams between Grant and Sherman. Grant wired Sherman on September 22, "It has seemed to me that you have during your [Atlanta] campaign suffered for want of an officer in command of cavalry, whose judgment and dash could both be relied on."[9] Grant was nearly right. Sherman had conducted the campaign under the constant menace to his communications of the redoubtable Nathan Bedford Forrest. Largely because of its inability to deal with that untaught genius, Sherman had no confidence in his cavalry and even less in its principal officers. The story may be apocryphal, but he is reported to have said to General W. L. Elliott, one of his chiefs of cavalry, "Elliott, why in the hell don't you do something? If you can't do anything else, get out and hunt up an old wagon that is stuck in the mud . . . and bring it in."[10] Understandably, therefore, Sherman replied to Grant, "I do want very much a good cavalry officer to command. . . . My present cavalry needs infantry guards and pickets, and it is hard to get them within ten miles of the front. . . . I do want a man of sense and courage to manage my cavalry, and will take any one that you have tried."[11] It is to be noted that this dis-

8. Wilson, *Under the Old Flag*, I, 557.
9. *Official Records*, Vol. XXXIX, Pt. 2, p. 238.
10. Benjamin F. McGee, *History of the 72nd Indiana Volunteer Infantry of the Mounted Lightning Brigade* (Lafayette, Ind., 1882), 395.
11. *Official Records*, Vol. XXXIX, Pt. 2, p. 442. Sherman's own handling of his cavalry left much to be desired. A good judge has termed it "not impressive. Though he possessed four divisions, he never employed them as a whole. Instead he used them individually, usually one on each

consolate message was sent when the war was well into its fourth year. Wilson was chosen for the post, and Grant's notification to Sherman ended with the prediction, "I believe Wilson will add 50 per cent. to the effectiveness of your cavalry."[12]

The newly promoted major general stood in no danger of being overwhelmed by the burden of living up to General Grant's high estimate of his powers. But what he found when he reported for duty with Sherman shook even his ample self-confidence. There were in the military division no fewer than seventy-two regiments of cavalry and mounted infantry. This, nominally, was a force of nearly eighty thousand men, but the aggregate number actually present and equipped was not quite ten thousand rank and file, and even this fragment was scattered over a distance of four hundred miles or more, from Atlanta in the east to Memphis in the west, with outlying regiments and detachments as far north as Knoxville and Nashville. In one respect, however, Wilson was fortunate. After the briefest of conversations, Sherman told him to draft his own instructions; he was to give himself the authority to organize the cavalry of the military division with himself in command and with full power "to make such dispositions and arrangements as [he] might think best for getting the largest possible force into the field and inflicting the greatest possible amount of damage upon the enemy."[13]

Wilson's first act was to relieve from duty (a euphemism for "get rid of") the chiefs of cavalry of Sherman's three armies. Two of the victims, George Stoneman and Benjamin Grierson, may have deserved a better fate, but they had too much rank and seniority to be comfortable subordinates to a major general on whose brevet the ink was hardly dry. Next, Wilson called in all details and detachments, most of which were serving as ego-buttressing decorative escorts to army and corps commanders, and sent them to their regiments. Dismounted men and convalescents were re-

---

flank, and one, or two, in reserve. Consequently, when he ordered some big effort . . . the cavalry wholly failed him." Alfred H. Burne, *Lee, Grant and Sherman* (New York, 1939), 88.

12. *Official Records*, Vol. XXXIX, Pt. 3, p. 64. The choice (as between Wilson and General A. T. A. Torbert) was actually made by Sheridan.

13. *Ibid.*, 414–15; Wilson, *Under the Old Flag*, II, 12.

turned to their regiments from remount camps, depots, and hospitals as far afield as Chicago, St. Paul, and Vicksburg, and every regiment was assigned to a brigade, and every brigade to a division.

Wilson was greatly hampered in these operations by a lack of reliable records. "No one," he wrote, "pretended to know how many men were actually with the colors nor how many horses were available or could be gotten together for service. Even the chiefs of cavalry were ignorant as to the number of mounted and dismounted men, the number and kinds of arms, equipments, and remounts required, or where they were to be had."[14] The horses, arms, and equipment that could be collected in a hurry had to be given to the division that was to make the March to the Sea with Sherman, under the command of Judson Kilpatrick, whom Sherman himself selected for the post with the remark, "I know Kilpatrick is a hell of a damned fool, but I want just that sort of a man to command my cavalry on this expedition."[15] Wilson was to remain in Tennessee and proceed with his work of reorganization and reequipment. His cavalry, when fully organized, was to be a part of the army General George H. Thomas had been given to oppose the northward march of Confederate General John B. Hood's hard-bitten, veteran Army of Tennessee, forty thousand infantry plus ten thousand cavalry under the ever-dangerous Forrest. Thomas was given three small corps, a total of twenty-seven thousand men. He eked out these inadequate forces by arming the civilian employees of the Quartermaster and Commissary Corps in Nashville to man the city's fortifications and by forming a "division" out of the convalescents, the weak, the lame, and the halt whom Sherman weeded out of his army and sent back to Chattanooga. He also received about seven thousand reinforcements from the North, mainly in the form of newly raised regiments. For cavalry he had the five thousand troopers Wilson was able to collect in a hurry, many of them without horses, adequate arms, or equipment. Fortune, however, favored Thomas. Hood delayed for a month starting his march for Tennessee, his subordinates bungled a nearly perfect opportunity to cut off and de-

14. Wilson, *Under the Old Flag*, II, 26–27.
15. *Ibid.*, II, 13.

stroy General John M. Schofield's corps at Spring Hill, and he himself chose to fight the totally needless battle of Franklin, with its frightful toll of six thousand Confederate casualties. Had it not been for these delays and errors, all Tennessee and Kentucky would have been at Hood's mercy, with incalculably grave consequences for the fortunes of a war-weary Union.

For five days, from November 27 to December 1, Wilson, with but forty-five hundred mounted men, protected the flanks of Schofield's and General David S. Stanley's corps, as they made a successful fighting withdrawal from Columbia, Tennessee, to Nashville.[16] On December 2, the Federals were safely within the Nashville defenses, a southward-facing arc with its ends anchored on the Cumberland River, above and below the city. The Confederates had also reached Nashville and were building breastworks and redoubts on a roughly L-shaped line four miles long, with its apex pointing toward the center of Thomas' position and following the crests of the hills south of the Federal lines.

The Atlanta and Wilderness campaigns had demonstrated time after time, notably at Kennesaw Mountain and Cold Harbor, that frontal assaults against steady troops who had had even a few hours in which to throw up breastworks of fence rails and logs banked with earth, either failed disastrously or succeeded only at a terrible cost to the attackers. Now, at Nashville, both sides had the protection of well-sited and well-fortified lines, and both commanders knew that a direct attack on the enemy would probably result in a bloody repulse. Thomas, in any case, was not yet ready to move. One of his three corps, the XVI, had just arrived from Missouri, and General James B. Steedman's "Provisional Division" from Chattanooga did not reach Nashville until the night of December 1.[17] Wilson's cavalry, its strength reduced to

16. "During . . . the operations between Pulaski and Nashville . . . the cavalry were never seen by me. They were far in front or on the flank, doing all the 'seeing' for me, giving me information of vital importance in respect to the enemy's movements. . . . I believe no cavalry ever performed that important service more efficiently. At no time during that short campaign did I suffer any inconvenience from lack of information that cavalry could possibly give." John M. Schofield, *Forty-Six Years in the Army* (New York, 1897), 227.

17. Steedman's division was "a hybrid of six brigades from four different corps made up of fragments from 200 . . . regiments. A large pro-

three thousand by a campaign lasting barely two weeks, needed time to rest and refit as best it could in the intervals of patrolling the fords across the Cumberland above and below the city.[18]

Thomas was gravely concerned about the menace to his flanks and rear posed by Forrest's "at least 12,000" cavalry.[19] Also, from the beginning of the campaign, he had set himself the objective of not merely defeating, but of destroying, Hood. To protect himself from Forrest and destroy Hood, Thomas needed a powerful cavalry of his own. Wilson had the men, but on December 2 barely three thousand of them were mounted, and many of these had horses so weakened and broken down by the campaign in wintry weather from Columbia back to Nashville as to be nearly useless. To get additional horses in a hurry, Thomas obtained permission to "seize and impress" them wherever they could be found.[20] Armed with this authority, Wilson's quartermasters and troopers collected seven thousand horses in Tennessee and Kentucky within a week. A clean sweep was made as far north as Louisville of every animal capable of carrying a man. Streetcar horses, dray horses, and carriage horses were seized, including an expensive pair belonging to Vice-President-elect Andrew Johnson; livery stables were emptied, and a circus that had the misfortune to be in Nashville at the moment lost every horse it owned.[21]

His mounted troops increased to ten thousand in this drastic

---

portion were unfit for duty. Twenty-five per cent of them were scarcely convalescent. Fifty per cent were recruits. . . . There were no ambulances or wagons. Some of these troops were not armed until the evening of . . . [December] fourteenth. Some of the recruits were untrained. Many were unable to speak or understand English." F. F. McKinney, *Education in Violence: The Life of George H. Thomas and the History of the Army of the Cumberland* (Detroit, 1961), 404. See also *Official Records*, Vol. XLV, Pt. 1, pp. 880–82.

18. *Official Records*, Vol. XLV, Pt. 1, p. 1181. Colonel Horace Capron's brigade, for example, 1,200 strong at the start of the campaign, was down to 411 men and 267 serviceable horses by November 30.

19. *Ibid.*, Pt. 2, p. 70.

20. *Ibid.*, 18.

21. *Ibid.*, 139. "The general impressment of horses by the military [in Louisville] is so oppressive that we cannot think it meets with your [*i.e.*, Stanton's] approbation. All horses are taken without regard to the occupation of the owner or his loyalty. Loaded milk carts, drays and butcher's wagons are left in the street, their horses seized."

but effective fashion, Thomas was ready to deal with Hood and issued his orders for an attack on the morning of December 10, but "a terrible storm of freezing rain" on the evening of the ninth made all movement on the hilly terrain impossible, and the orders had to be canceled.[22]

In an access of folly, Hood had sent Forrest with two divisions of cavalry to destroy the Nashville & Chattanooga Railroad east of Nashville and to attack the Federal garrison at Murfreesboro. Forrest was still absent on this senseless errand on the fourteenth, when the weather turned mild. The sheet of ice covering the hills around Nashville melted, and Thomas assembled his corps commanders to give them their orders for the attack to be made the next day. Steedman's division, which included several regiments of blacks who had never been under fire, were to pin down the Confederate right, and the IV Corps was to pin down Hood's center. The main attack, against Hood's left, which had the protection of a stone wall and five carefully sited redoubts, each housing a battery of artillery supported by infantry, was to be made by Wilson's cavalrymen on foot, backed by the infantry of the XVI Corps.

On the morning of the fifteenth, in midwinter darkness, Thomas' army was aroused at four o'clock to prepare for battle. Two hours later, Steedman launched his attack. Wilson's three divisions, led by Edward Hatch, R. W. Johnson, and Joseph F. Knipe, plus John T. Croxton's unattached brigade and the infantry of General A. J. Smith's XVI Corps, were deployed south of the Union fortifications, in a line facing generally southeast. Delayed by a heavy fog that blanketed the field, they moved forward at eight o'clock as a gigantic scythe, pivoting on their left. Brushing aside Hood's flank guard, they overwhelmed the five redoubts, one after the other. The left of the Confederate line, overlapped

22. General Jacob D. Cox, who was there, wrote later, "The slopes in front of the lines were a glare of ice, so that movement away from the roads and broken paths could be made only with the greatest difficulty and at a snail's pace. Men and horses were seen falling whenever they attempted to move across country. A man slipping on the hillside had no choice but to sit down and slide to the bottom, and groups of men in the forts and lines found constant entertainment in watching these mishaps. . . . manoeuvers were out of the question for nearly a week." Jacob D. Cox, *Military Reminiscences of the Civil War* (2 vols.; New York, 1900), II, 352–53.

by more than a mile and taken in reverse, was driven in rout from the shelter of the stone wall. If Hood had not brought Cheatham's infantry around from the right flank to reinforce his left, the Federals would have been across his lifeline, the roads back to Franklin, and his army would have been trapped and forced to surrender. As it was, he escaped by the thinnest of margins. Driven back nearly three miles, he was saved as much by the early darkness and the exhaustion of Wilson's troopers as by the desperate resistance put up by his own men.[23]

During the night, Hood's engineers laid out a new defense line on the Overton Hills. His tired troops had little time to entrench before daylight brought a resumption of the Federal attack. Thomas' orders for the second day called for a repetition of the scheme that had been so effective the first day—a holding attack by the Union infantry on the Confederate right and center, to be followed by an all-out attack on Hood's left by the cavalry, again fighting dismounted. Again the plan worked to perfection. By four o'clock in the afternoon, Shy's Hill, at the apex of Hood's L-shaped line and the anchor of his position, had been pounded to pieces by the Federal artillery and overrun by the infantry. By that time also, Wilson's cavalrymen, advancing over the rough terrain in a line a mile and a half long, had gotten behind the southern end of the Confederate position and were approaching the Franklin Pike, the sole escape route to the south still open. It was a rainy, dark day, and had it not been for the early nightfall and the fierce resistance put up by Hood's rear guard, which kept the Federals away from the pike, his entire army would have been bagged. As it was, he lost nearly all his artillery and trains, three thousand men killed and wounded, and forty-five hundred taken prisoner. It was clear to everyone that the power and drive of Wilson's cavalry had been the decisive factor in the overwhelming Union victory.

The pursuit of Hood's beaten army by the compact mass of Wilson's nearly ten thousand mounted troops, interrupted by the

23. "The boys, unused to marching on foot, had now charged for nearly a mile and were so completely exhausted as to be unable to move faster than a slow walk." Lyman B. Pierce, *History of the Second Iowa Cavalry* (Burlington, Iowa, 1865), 144.

rain and the night, was resumed at dawn on the seventeenth. Two days later Forrest rejoined Hood. His three thousand cavalrymen, together with nineteen hundred infantry—the remnants of eight brigades—fought off the Federals in an epic rearguard action. Under unbelievably grim conditions, Forrest saved the wreck of what had been the proud Army of Tennessee. There was a hard frost nearly every night, and during the day heavy rains alternated with storms of snow and sleet. Every stream was out of its banks, the fields were knee-deep in mud, and the roads were hardly better.[24] Many of the Confederate infantry were barefoot, and since the retreat led through country that had been picked clean of food and forage on Hood's march north, his men and animals alike were on starvation rations. The seventy-five-mile pursuit mercifully ended on Christmas Day, when the Confederate infantry began crossing the Tennessee River. Forrest and the rear guard followed three days later. In the pursuit, the Federals had captured eight thousand more prisoners, and the road south from Nashville was littered with the wreckage of Hood's wagons and equipment. A mere ten thousand ragged, starving scarecrows, "a shattered debris of an army," remained of the fifty thousand men who had begun the campaign six weeks before.[25]

In January and February, 1865, the Nashville Campaign having ended, Wilson's cavalry corps was encamped on the north bank of the Tennessee River, at the southernmost point of its great swoop through Alabama. The camps were located at Waterloo and Gravelly Springs, where the borders of Alabama, Mississippi, and Tennessee meet. The command now numbered twenty-seven thousand rank and file, most of them veterans.[26] The loss

24. Wilson, *Under the Old Flag*, II, 160. With doubled teams of twelve mules, it took twelve hours to move an army wagon loaded to half its capacity six miles. J. W. Morton, Forrest's twenty-year-old chief of artillery, wrote that "the suffering of soldiers on both sides were [sic] indescribable. The coating of ice on the road gave way to mud, and the continued rainfall froze on the guns and pistols, making it agony for the numb fingers to fire them." J. W. Morton, *The Artillery of Nathan Bedford Forrest's Cavalry* (Nashville, 1909), 287.

25. *Official Records*, Vol. LII, Pt. 2, p. 808.

26. Wilson, *Under the Old Flag*, II, 165. However, in *Official Records*, Vol. XLIX, Pt. 1, p. 354, he reported twenty-two thousand men, and horses for sixteen thousand of them.

of horses in the pursuit of Hood had been enormous—five thousand in thirteen days—but by the middle of February the wastage had been more than made good, and Wilson had mounts for twenty thousand of his men. The camps were at the head of steamboat navigation, and the corps received all the supplies it needed from the depots on and beyond the Ohio, but before the supply system was fully organized and reserve stocks accumulated, ice in the river halted shipments, and for a few days in late January the men were on short commons. On Sunday afternoon, January 29, as Wilson rode through the camps of Colonel R. H. G. Minty's brigade, he was greeted by the aggrieved troopers with cries of "Hard Tack! Hard Tack!" Wilson promptly demonstrated his disapproval of such unmilitary behavior by ordering the entire brigade to fall in, and he kept them standing in line for eight hours.[27]

In other ways, too, Wilson made it plain that the free and easy ways of western cavalry did not meet with his approval. He kept the men busy from daybreak to nightfall with drill, inspections, reviews, dress parades, patrols, and picketing.[28] His large and efficient staff, which made certain that his frequent, all-embracing, detailed orders were fully carried out, endeared neither itself nor Wilson to the officers and men of the command. There was much stress on stricter discipline, starting with the division and brigade commanders who were not only ordered to be present at all drills and reveille roll calls and to "inspect the camps of their commands three times a day to see that the daily routine of camp duties are properly performed," but were also to certify daily "on honor" that

27. Thomas Crofts, *History of the Service of the Third Ohio Veteran Volunteer Cavalry* (Toledo, 1910), 187.
28. *Ibid.*, 187; McGee, *History of the 72nd Indiana*, 511; P. S. Michie, *The Life and Letters of Emory Upton* (New York, 1885), 135. "The cavalry . . . had practical proofs of the belief of its generals in the value of military training and discipline. The government of the corps was made step by step more careful and rigid. Infractions of discipline were promptly, and sometimes conspicuously, punished. . . . All the men not actually on other duty were every day put through drills, inspections and instruction regardless of the bad weather. The closest attention was given to the care of the camps, horses and equipments. . . . It was hard work, and so much more strictly required than before that many found it very irksome." William F. Scott, *The Story of a Cavalry Regiment: The Career of the Fourth Iowa Veteran Volunteers* (New York, 1893), 426.

they had done so.[29] The policing of camps, the cleanliness of kitchens, the wearing of regulation headgear by the men and of chevrons by the noncommissioned officers, all these and more were the subject of orders.[30] At the same time, however, Wilson saw to it that the men's worn-out clothing and their defective and damaged arms and equipment were replaced.[31] Above all, he made sure the horses were properly taken care of; he ordered stables built for them, and they had their full quota of feed even when the men were on half-rations.[32]

There was grumbling in the ranks, doubtless laced with comments of a hoary antiquity about the commanding general's ancestry. The historian of the 72nd Indiana Mounted Infantry reported:

General Wilson came to us from the Army of the Potomac and brought with him much of the "grand review" style of that army; that of itself was enough to prejudice all Western soldiers against him, for if there was anything Western troopers did hate, it was anything that was done for mere style. . . . But added to this love of show, he seemed to study just how to keep every soldier in his whole army on duty every day. . . . we had general orders from General Wilson read to us every morning, and upon almost every conceivable subject . . . just as though we had been in the service almost three years and yet did not know how to make ourselves comfortable and keep clean. . . . But after all

29. 2nd Michigan Cavalry, Regimental and Company Order and Letter Books, General Orders No. 6, January 25, 1865, in Record Group 94, National Archives. Hereinafter cited as 2nd Michigan O&L Books.

30. For example, 7th Pennsylvania Cavalry, Regimental and Company Order and Letter Books, Circulars dated February 9 and February 26, 1865, in Record Group 94, National Archives. Hereinafter cited as 7th Pennsylvania O&L Books. The need for such orders is illustrated by a letter written by Lieutenant Colonel Horace N. Howland, 3rd Ohio Cavalry, who "found some of the sentinels sitting on stumps, others on the ground paying very little attention to what was going on or to their duties and very poorly instructed. The camp . . . was very poorly cleaned and parts of which [sic] was in a very filthy condition and with little or no policing done." 3rd Ohio Cavalry, Regimental and Company Order and Letter Books, letter dated February 19, 1865, in Record Group 94, National Archives. Hereinafter cited as 3rd Ohio O&L Books.

31. 2nd Michigan O&L Books, Special Field Orders No. 6, January 14, 1865, in RG 94, NA.

32. Ibid. See also 3rd Ohio O&L Books, General Orders No. 35, March 6, 1865, in RG 94, NA.

was said and done, when we broke camp in the spring, we were no better prepared for the campaign than when we went into camp.[33]

On the other hand, numerous regimental histories and individual troopers' reminiscences testify to the high morale, and indeed, high spirits, of the entire command, as it waited for the spring rains to end and the roads to dry, to start on the campaign that everyone knew was in preparation at General Wilson's headquarters.[34] E. N. Gilpin of the 3rd Iowa Cavalry, the winter of his discontent forgotten, was to write a short time later, "We are masters of the situation. . . . I do not believe there is an army in the world that surpasses these divisions, that now march in compact, well-balanced columns, men and horses in perfect form; disciplined, well officered, sure of themselves. It would be impossible to stampede them, and it would require awful carnage to convince them that they were not invincible."[35]

Morale such as this is no accident. It results from an exceedingly subtle reaction between two main elements: the confidence of the led in their leaders, and the habit of success. The cavalry knew that *they* had won the battle of Nashville. As for confidence, it was evident to the men in the ranks that Wilson, for all his addiction to spit and polish and his fussiness, and despite (or because of) his brash ways, knew what he was about and had the will to victory in him. Moreover, he was singularly fortunate in his subordinates. One of them, General Emory Upton, Wilson himself selected to command the Fourth Division.

Upton, a native of New York, graduated eighth in the forty-five man West Point Class of 1861 and was twenty-five in the

33. McGee, *History of the 72nd Indiana*, 511–12.

34. Scott, *Story of a Cavalry Regiment*, 425; William L. Curry, *Four Years in the Saddle: History of the First Regiment Ohio Volunteer Cavalry* (Columbus, 1898), 213.

35. E. N. Gilpin, "The Last Campaign: A Cavalryman's Journal," *Journal of the United States Cavalry Association*, XVIII (1908), 655. Another trooper wrote that Wilson's command "was a model of organization, hardened by drill, veteran by experience, and confident in themselves and their leaders. It was an inspiration to belong to it." Charles D. Mitchell, "Field Notes of the Selma Campaign," in Military Order of the Loyal Legion of the United States (hereinafter cited as MOLLUS), Commandery of Ohio, *Sketches of War History, 1861–1865* (7 vols.; Cincinnati, 1888–1910), VI, 176.

spring of 1865. A student at Oberlin before entering the Military
Academy, he had taken strong abolitionist convictions to West
Point with him. He had been colonel of a New York infantry regiment and was promoted to brigadier general for his superb conduct in the fighting at Spotsylvania and in the attack on the Mule
Shoe. After being transferred to the Shenandoah Valley in the
summer of 1864, Upton showed his understanding of leadership
in the battle of the Opequon; knocked off his horse by a shell
fragment and ordered by Sheridan to the rear to have his badly
wounded leg attended to, Upton refused, had a tourniquet applied
to his leg, and, carried about on a stretcher, continued to lead his
brigade until the battle was won. He reported for duty at Gravelly
Springs as soon as his leg healed. Called by Wilson "the best all-
around soldier of his day," Upton earned the even more flattering
admiration of the enlisted men of his division.[36] One of these wrote
that "every one who met . . . [Upton] felt the influence of his zealous spirit," and wrote another, "Upton has captured his division
. . . they know he is a brave man and a skillful general. Their
hearts are with him . . . and they all want to yell when they see
him riding down the line."[37]

Upton was the best of a strikingly able set of commanders of
divisions and brigades. E. M. McCook of Ohio, Eli Long of Kentucky, and Edward Hatch of Iowa, commanded the First, Second,
and Fifth Divisions, respectively. Several of the brigade comman-

36. Wilson, *Under the Old Flag*, I, 181; others of Wilson's adjectives
for Upton were "peerless" and "incomparable." In Grant's Wilderness
Campaign, Upton's regiment, the 121st New York Infantry, lost in action
twenty-three of its twenty-six officers. James H. Wilson, "The Cavalry of
the Army of the Potomac," in *Papers of the Military Historical Society of
Massachusetts*, XIII (1913), 55. Benjamin Grierson had been assigned to
the command of the Fourth Division, "but failing to use due diligence in
assembling and preparing it for the field, he was replaced by . . . Upton,
an officer of rare merit and experience." *Official Records*, vol. XLIX, Pt. 1,
p. 354.

Hereinafter, the word "Cavalry" will be omitted, in the text as well as
in the notes, from the names of mounted regiments, unless it is needed to
avoid confusion. Thus, we shall speak of the 1st New York, 4th Iowa, etc.,
but of the 4th Kentucky Cavalry, to distinguish it from the 4th Kentucky
Mounted Infantry.

37. Scott, *Story of a Cavalry Regiment*, 357; Gilpin, "The Last Campaign," 636.

ders, notably E. F. Winslow in the Fourth Division, J. T. Croxton and O. H. LaGrange in the First, and R. H. G. Minty in the Second, were cavalrymen of outstanding ability.[38]

One aspect of the daily drilling was of particular importance. All the troops in the command had been trained in the relatively simple single-line cavalry tactics developed by Union General Philip St. George Cooke (who happened also to be the father-in-law of the most glamorous of Confederate cavalrymen, "Jeb" Stuart) and adopted by the Union army in the first year of the war to replace the traditional but more complicated two-rank "Poinsett" or "1841" tactics. Wilson decided that single-line tactics were not suitable for cavalry combat in hilly, heavily wooded country. Allowing for normal intervals, a twenty-four hundred-man brigade made a line nearly a mile and a half long under the Cooke system, making effective control of a mounted action virtually impossible at the brigade or division level and difficult even at the regimental level. In Wilson's view, tight control from the top was essential to success in a mounted action, and to make such control more feasible he introduced the two-rank system.[39] For dismounted action, however, he retained the single-rank formation, which made the change more palatable for his conservatively minded men.

The purpose of all the drill and preparation was an entirely new kind of campaign Wilson had in mind. Captain Dennis Hart Mahan, whose theories of the art of war had shaped the thinking of a whole generation of West Pointers, had laid down that "the arm of cavalry by itself can effect but little; and in many circum-

38. McCook was one of eight brothers—four of whom became generals—who served in the Union army; three of the eight, as well as their father, Major Daniel McCook, lost their lives in the war. Whitelaw Reid, *Ohio in the War: Her Statesmen, Her Generals and Soldiers* (2 vols., Cincinnati, 1868), I, 875. Five sons of Major Daniel McCook's brother also served in the Union army. Colonel Robert H. G. Minty, Anglo-Irish by birth, served for five years in the British army before coming to America. He was successively major in the 4th Michigan, lieutenant colonel of the 3rd Michigan, and colonel of the 4th Michigan. He was brevetted brigadier general and major general and was twice voted the thanks of Congress. Ella Lonn, *Foreigners in the Union Army and Navy* (Baton Rouge, 1951), 228–29.

39. 2nd Michigan O&L Books, Special Field Orders No. 6, January 14, 1865, in RG 94, NA. See also Donn Piatt and H. V. Boynton, *General George H. Thomas* (Cincinnati, 1893), 595–96; Scott, *Story of a Cavalry Regiment,* 427.

stances, does not suffice even for its own safety. . . . It can neither attack nor hold a post without the aid of infantry."[40] As late as the spring of 1863, General William S. Rosecrans sent out his cavalry supported by strong bodies of infantry, so that his horsemen "might never be completely demoralized by a complete whipping" and to have the footsoldiers at hand to "finish the fight the cavalry had begun."[41] Wilson was convinced that cavalry was capable of a more decisive role than this. Having led cavalry armed with the Spencer, he reasoned that large bodies of men, possessing the overwhelming fire power their Spencers gave them, called "cavalry" for convenience, but using horses merely to make them mobile in the highest degree, could, without the aid of infantry, fight their way through any opposition, and if need be, could even occupy territory. Cavalry raids had been staged by both sides throughout the war against the enemy's lines of communication and supply, but they had been mere hit-and-run affairs. Wilson's concept was far more ambitious; it was nothing less than a cavalry invasion: a raid raised to a higher power. Even before the battle of Nashville had demonstrated a hitherto unsuspected potential of the cavalry, he had written his friend John Rawlins, Grant's chief of staff, "Cavalry is useless for defense; its only power is in a vigorous offensive; therefore I urge its concentration south of the Tennessee and hurling it into the bowels of the South in masses that the enemy cannot drive back."[42]

In July, 1863, Quartermaster General Montgomery C. Meigs had ended a long, mournful letter to General Rosecrans on the insoluble problem of supplying horses to the cavalry faster than it could destroy them, with the advice, "Rely more upon infantry than upon cavalry, which taxes the Treasury and exhausts the resources of the country."[43] The infantry put it more succinctly, with derisive shouts of "Charge, Chester, charge!" and others much

40. Dennis Hart Mahan, *Advanced Guard, Outpost and Detachment Service of Troops, with the Essential Principles of Strategy and Grand Tactics* (New York, 1863), 39.

41. Alonzo Gray, *Cavalry Tactics as Illustrated by the War of the Rebellion* (Fort Leavenworth, Ks., 1910), 70.

42. *Official Records*, Vol. XXXIX, Pt. 3, p. 443.

43. Allan Nevins, *The War for the Union: The War Becomes Revolution, 1862–1863* (New York, 1960), 476.

less printable, to the accompaniment of roars of laughter, when the inept, ineffectual Federal cavalry of the early years of the war ambled past them on their sorry nags. In his tour of duty with Grant, his brief assignment as head of the Cavalry Bureau, and his discussions with Sherman, Wilson had seen and heard enough of the mishandling of cavalry by army commanders who had no confidence in the mounted arm and would not have known how to use it even if they had. He, on the other hand, had a high opinion of the military potential of properly organized and armed cavalry under strong leadership, and he was confident that he could supply that leadership.

The question of what operation Wilson should undertake next had come up for discussion shortly after the pursuit of Hood ended. On January 21, Sherman suggested that twenty-five thousand infantry and Wilson's cavalry be sent to central Alabama to capture Tuscaloosa and Selma and to destroy at Selma the largest arsenal and foundries the Confederacy possessed, outside of those in Richmond.[44] But Schofield's XXIII Corps was sent East, and in mid-February Grant ordered Thomas to plan a cavalry demonstration against Tuscaloosa and Selma with five thousand men, as a diversion to help General E. R. S. Canby's campaign to capture Mobile.[45] Thomas visited Wilson's headquarters on February 23 to discuss Grant's order, and Wilson easily persuaded him to enlarge its scope. Wilson wrote, "I convinced him that a 'demonstration' . . . would be useless waste of strength and, if permitted to go with my whole force into central Alabama, I would not only defeat Forrest . . . but would capture Tuscaloosa, Selma, Montgomery and Columbus, and destroy the Confederacy's last depots of manufacture and supply and break up its last interior line of railroad communications."[46] Grant approved the enlarged plan Wilson had persuaded Thomas to endorse and directed in addition that in carrying out the operation, Wilson be allowed "the latitude of an independent commander."[47] Thus, Wilson not only received

44. *Official Records*, Vol. XLV, Pt. 2, pp. 621–22.
45. *Ibid.*, Vol. XLIX, Pt. 1, pp. 708–709.
46. Wilson, *Under the Old Flag*, II, 180–81; see also *Official Records*, Vol. XLIX, Pt. 1, p. 355.
47. Wilson, *Under the Old Flag*, II, 181.

permission to make the campaign on his own terms, but also, still only twenty-seven, he became, and still remains, the youngest army commander in American history.

Wilson's Third Division was with Sherman in Savannah. At the beginning of February he was ordered to send another—he chose the Seventh—to General Canby and was also ordered to leave the Sixth Division behind, to protect middle Tennessee.[48] He had four divisions left, but had horses enough to mount something less than three full divisions: E. M. McCook's First, Long's Second, and Upton's Fourth, which totaled 14,000 men, 12,500 of whom were mounted.[49] The three divisions were made up of twenty-three regiments, all but one of which hailed from the western states. The exception was the 7th Pennsylvania, which, having done its soldiering in the West from 1861 on, could have claimed to be a western regiment by adoption.[50] Of the twenty-two others, four were from Iowa: the 3rd, 4th, 5th and 8th; four from Ohio: the 1st, 3rd, 4th and 7th; and two from Michigan: the 2nd and 4th. Also present were the 98th and 123rd Mounted Infantry from Illinois, and the 4th, 6th and 7th Cavalry and the 4th Mounted Infantry from Kentucky. From Indiana came the 4th Cavalry, the 17th and 72nd Mounted Infantry, and a battalion of the 2nd Cavalry. The roster was completed by the 1st Wisconsin, and the

48. *Official Records*, Vol. XLIX, Pt. 1, p. 354.

49. *Ibid.*, 342. The exact numbers were 4,096 in the First Division, 5,127 in the Second, 3,923 in the Fourth, 334 in the 4th United States, and 211 in the Battalion of Pontoniers, for a total of 13,691. *Ibid.*, 403–404.

50. Few cavalry regiments on either side had a more distinguished record than the 7th Pennsylvania. On May 5, 1862, in association with the 1st Kentucky, it had given John Morgan a thorough drubbing at Lebanon, Tennessee. A year later, in the Tullahoma Campaign, it charged and overran a Confederate battery at Shelbyville, Tennessee; General D. S. Stanley wrote of the latter exploit, "On the part of the Union soldiers there can scarcely be instanced a finer display of gallantry than the charge made by the 7th Penna. Cavalry. . . . To face a battery ready loaded and waiting, supported on either flank by riflemen, to ride at the muzzles and guns and through them, is no baby's play, and this was done by a regiment of Pennsylvania blacksmiths." David S. Stanley, *Personal Memoirs of Major-General David S. Stanley, U.S.A.* (Cambridge, Mass., 1917), 148–49. See also the two histories of the regiment: Thomas F. Dornblaser, *Sabre Strokes of the Pennsylvania Dragoons in the War of 1861–1865* (Philadelphia, 1884), *passim*; and William B. Sipes, *The Seventh Pennsylvania Veteran Volunteer Cavalry* (Pottsville, Pa., n.d.), *passim*.

10th and a battalion of the 12th from Missouri. Three six-gun batteries, Battery I, 4th United States Artillery, attached to the Fourth Division; the Chicago Board of Trade Battery, attached to the Second; and the 18th Indiana Battery, attached to the First, made up the artillery.[51] The two Illinois and two Indiana regiments of mounted infantry, constituting the First Brigade of the Second Division, were the four regiments of the Lightning Brigade, formerly commanded by Colonel John T. Wilder and entitled to rank with the Iron Brigade and the Stonewall Brigade among the premier fighting units of either army.[52]

It will be noted that with the exception of Battery I of the 4th United States Artillery, the three divisions were made up wholly of volunteers. Moreover, one of the three commanders of divisions, five of the six commanders of brigades, and twenty-five of the twenty-six commanders of regiments and batteries were volunteers also.[53]

Far more than six or eight weeks of drill would have been required to effect a major change in the military character of Wilson's volunteers. Veterans for the most part of from two to four years of service, they had become inured to hardship and had learned to accept as inevitable the failures and inadequacies of the army supply system. By Regular Army standards, they were unorthodox and informal to a degree, from the private who preferred a cheery "Howdy, Colonel" to the regulation salute, to the colonel who, unable to get Spencer cabines for his men through proper channels, bought them directly from the manufacturer and gave in partial payment his personal notes guaranteed by his hometown bankers.[54] But the volunteers' rampant and sometimes

51. *Official Records*, Vol. XLIX, Pt. 1, 402–403.
52. The Lightning Brigade has the further distinction that one of its men, B. F. McGee of the 72nd Indiana Infantry, wrote one of the most delightful (and, alas, one of the longest) of the seventy-odd Union cavalry regimental histories.
53. After Eli Long, a Regular officer who had transferred to the volunteer service, was wounded at Selma, and Minty took his place in command of the Second Division, two of the three divisions were commanded by volunteer officers, Upton being the only Regular. Minty's place in command of his brigade was taken by another volunteer, Colonel Horace N. Howland of the 3rd Ohio. *Official Records*, Vol. XLIX, Pt. 1, p. 403.
54. The colonel who bought Spencers for his men was John T. Wilder,

dangerous individualism had its compensatory virtues; when they had learned the elements of soldiering, they became self-reliant and flexible. They developed the ability to take care of themselves under the most unfavorable circumstances and the willingness to make do with what they could get if they could not get what they wanted. And they had started with the ability to learn quickly whatever *they* decided was worth learning. With all this went an amazing variety of skills. For example, the commander of the Lightning Brigade, Colonel A. O. Miller, was a physician in civil life. A trooper in the 3rd Iowa reported, "Our fellows can do anything, from running a locomotive to a prayer meeting; they are masons, stokers, lawyers, farmers, engineers, store-keepers, shoemakers, horse-doctors, gamesters."[55]

Good officers and good weapons: Wilson's troopers had both. It would be difficult to overstate the boost in morale produced by the Spencer carbine, with which all these regiments were now armed.[56] It is the one Civil War topic on which testimony is virtually unanimous. Wilson himself wrote that with the Spencer, "Green regiments, that you couldn't have driven into a fight with the old arms, became invincible"; George Custer stated, "I attrib-

---

commanding officer of the Lightning Brigade. S. C. Williams, *General John T. Wilder* (Bloomington, Ind., 1936), *passim.* In no other army in modern times would the 72nd Indiana have made the change from infantry to the mounted service, not on the strength of an army order, but because the enlisted men voted in favor of doing so. But when the cavalry uniform was issued to the regiment, the men cut the yellow cavalry trim off their jackets and the yellow stripes off their trousers, so that they would not be taken for cavalry; they wanted it known that they belonged to a distinctive branch of the service, namely the mounted infantry. McGee, *History of the 72nd Indiana*, 108–109.

55. Gilpin, "The Last Campaign," 626.

56. In order to reach that point, Wilson had to take Spencers away from some of the regiments of the Fifth and Sixth Divisions and give them to the units that were to make the Selma Campaign. Before the campaign began most regiments of the Corps also received the light and serviceable "Light Cavalry Saber, Model 1860," thirty-five inches long and with a curved blade, as a replacement for the "Heavy Cavalry (Dragoon) Saber, Model 1840" and the "Ames Contract of 1833" saber, both of them ponderous, nearly straight weapons, forty-one and thirty-nine inches long, respectively, which, together with similar imports from Europe, had been issued to the cavalry in the first two years of the war. Stephen Z. Starr, "Cold Steel," *Civil War History*, XI (1965), 145–46.

ute . . . [the] success [of the 5th Michigan at Gettysburg] in a great measure to the fact that this regiment is armed with the Spencer . . . which . . . is in my estimation, the most effective firearm our cavalry can adopt."[57] Even more meaningful are the opinions of the men who had to use the gun. B. F. McGee of the 72nd Indiana Mounted Infantry testified that the Spencer "to our mind, was so nearly perfect that after using it for two years, our brigade had not a single change to suggest." W. F. Scott of the 4th Iowa wrote, "To have a carbine of better range and of more certain shot than any other gun they knew, from which seven shots could be fired without loss of time . . . was of striking value in heightening the self-confidence and improving the morale of the cavalry. From that time on to the end of the war . . . [the] regiment . . . expected to win, and even acquired a sort of habit of looking upon every approaching fight as a 'sure thing'."[58] And finally, Sergeant James Larson of the 4th United States declared, "Best of all, the premium General [Sooy] Smith promised us for our part in the Mississippi campaign—a brand new Spencer carbine for every man in the regiment. We were proud of them. . . . [They] were to us our medals of honors, our Spencer carbines."[59]

57. Wilson, "Cavalry of the Army of the Potomac," 84; Custer quoted in [Frederick Whittaker], *Volunteer Cavalry: The Lessons of a Decade* (New York, 1871), 172.
58. McGee, *History of the 72nd Indiana*, 121; Scott, *Story of a Cavalry Regiment*, 283.
59. James Larson, *Sergeant Larson: 4th Cavalry*, ed. A. L. Blum (San Antonio, 1935), 240. James Larson's dicta carry special weight because his story is prefaced by a sworn affidavit to attest that "the following 'memoirs' contain true and correct statements of everything related herein, and . . . everything related therein is done so without any exaggeration whatever." Some troopers complained of the weight of the Spencer, but the only dissent known to the present writer on the superiority of the Spencer is that of General Basil Duke, C.S.A. He wrote, "It has been the verdict of every officer of the Western Confederate Cavalry with whom I have talked upon the subject, and it certainly has been my experience, that those Federal cavalry regiments which were armed with the breech-loading guns did least execution. . . . the very fact of having to load his gun will make a soldier comparatively cool and steady . . . while if he only has to stick in a cartridge and shoot . . . he will fire fast but he will fire wildly. . . . Morgan's command . . . were loud in describing the terrific effect of the Spencer . . . [but] subsequently . . . met the troops carrying Spencer rifles with more confidence than those armed in any other way." Basil W. Duke, *A History of Morgan's Cavalry* (Bloomington, Ind., 1960), 176–78.

The officers—their military virtues and vices—are a far more complex story than that of the Spencer carbine. By the early months of 1865, the great majority of those who had entered the service as officers in 1861 and 1862 were gone—killed, dead of disease, disabled, resigned, or forced out of the service for incompetence or misconduct. In the spring of 1865 most of the lieutenants and captains, and even an appreciable proportion of the field-grade officers of the cavalry, were men who had started in the ranks. To cite one example: every officer of the 4th Kentucky Mounted Infantry in the Selma Campaign, with the exception of the colonel and the lieutenant colonel, had come up through the ranks.[60]

By the fourth of March, Wilson's preparations were complete and he was ready to start, but his camps were north of the Tennessee River, then in flood, and he was unable to cross. The waters receded sufficiently by the eleventh to allow the crossing to begin, and a week later the entire command was encamped south of the river; on March 21 orders were issued for the march to begin the next morning.[61] Reveille on the twenty-second was at half past three. Soon the fires were alight, the aroma of coffee and frying bacon filled the air, and the horses were feeding. At five o'clock, as the cloudless eastern sky began to lighten with the promise of a bright spring day, the bugles blew "boots and saddles," and regiment after regiment filed out of camp. In many, perhaps most, of the earlier campaigns of the war, both northern and southern, the objectives and timetable of the campaign were common gossip in camp and in the newspapers for days or weeks beforehand. The Selma Campaign was a refreshing exception to this casual disregard of security. Not until the day of departure did the rank and file learn that Selma was to be their first objective.[62] For Wilson's

60. R. M. Kelly, Thomas Speed, and Alfred Pirtle, *The Union Regiments of Kentucky* (Louisville, 1897), 312.

61. Just after crossing the Tennessee, the 3rd Iowa received from the Sanitary Commission a shipment of cabbage, potatoes, and sauerkraut. "They also sent us compressed cakes which . . . our mess cook calls 'desecrated vegetables.' We have boiled, baked, fried, stewed, pickled, sweetened, salted it, and tried it in puddings, cakes and pies; but it sets all modes of cooking at defiance." Gilpin, "The Last Campaign," 623.

62. McGee, *History of the 72nd Indiana*, 525; Lewis M. Hosea, "The

veterans, the "romance" of war had gone up in smoke long ago; nevertheless, after three months in camp they were in high spirits and happy to be on the move once again.[63]

Selma, situated on the north bank of the Alabama River, was about 180 miles as the crow flies southeast of Wilson's point of departure. For the first 90 miles the roads ran through hilly, wooded, sparsely populated country that had been fought and marched over repeatedly by both sides and was bare of food and forage. To get fourteen thousand men and sixteen thousand horses and mules through these barrens required careful planning. Wilson's orders required every mounted man to carry five days' rations, one hundred rounds of ammunition, a pair of horseshoes, and twenty-four pounds of grain for his horse; two hundred and fifty supply wagons started with the expedition, guarded by the fifteen hundred dismounted men commanded by Captain Richard C. Rankin, 7th Ohio, who were to be mounted as fast as suitable horses were captured for them along the way; the wagons carried twenty days' supply of sugar, fifteen of salt, and forty-five of coffee, plus eighty rounds of ammunition per man for the entire command and forage for the horses and draft animals. As fast as the wagons were emptied they were to return in groups to the Tennessee River, for Wilson did not want his march impeded any longer than necessary by a string two miles long of slow-moving wagons.[64] Finally, pack mules carried a five days' supply of hardtack, plus a ten days' supply each of coffee, sugar, and salt.[65] The fifty-five days' supply of coffee was Wilson's concession to the hu-

---

Campaign of Selma," in MOLLUS, Commandery of Ohio, *Sketches of War History, 1861–1865* (7 vols.; Cincinnati, 1888–1910), I, 80.

63. McGee, *History of the 72nd Indiana*, 525; Mitchell, "Field Notes of the Selma Campaign," 178.

64. Wilson's report on the campaign details the sugar, salt, coffee, and ammunition carried in the wagons, but makes no mention of forage for the draft animals. He knew that his army would need six to eight days to traverse an area entirely destitute of forage. Given the meticulous planning of the entire operation and Wilson's concern for keeping his animals in good condition, it may be assumed that he did not fail to provide enough forage to get them through the barren stretch. *Official Records*, Vol. XLIX, Pt. 1, p. 356.

65. Wilson planned for a sixty-day campaign, but expected to replenish his supplies of sugar and salt by captures from the enemy.

man weaknesses of his men; he knew that so long as they had their coffee, hot, strong, and sweet, they would retain their good humor and their willingness to put up with other deprivations and hardships.

To enable him to cross the unfordable streams that flowed across his line of march, Wilson took with him a train of thirty fully equipped pontoons, escorted by a battalion of the 12th Wisconsin. But he was determined not to allow his column to be weakened or the number of animals requiring to be fed increased by hauling excess baggage. Each brigade was allowed one, and only one, wagon to haul medical stores and the irreducible minimum of officers' baggage, and each regiment was allowed one pack mule for the same purpose. This was a far cry from the early months of the war, when it was not uncommon for a single regiment to impede its movements with a tail of as many as three or four dozen heavily loaded wagons.[66]

Wilson's meticulous planning down to the last coffee bean and cartridge was fully justified, for his opponent was to be the ever-dangerous Nathan Bedford Forrest. In January, Forrest had been given command of all the cavalry in Mississippi, east Louisiana, and west Tennessee. In February he was promoted to lieutenant general, a richly merited step up in rank, but one which he no doubt would have been glad to exchange for a few thousand well-armed and well-mounted reinforcements. After the most strenuous efforts to round up deserters, stragglers, and recruits, he was able to muster a mere ten thousand men and lacked the means to employ his well-tested method of dealing with the Yankees—"Get 'em skeered and keep the skeer on 'em."[67] By the middle of February, Forrest and his department commander, General Richard Taylor, had decided that Selma was likely to be Wilson's target and prepared as best they could to intercept him. Forrest's headquarters and most of his troops were at West Point, Mississippi, a short distance west of the Alabama line. Facing the possibility of cavalry raids from the Gulf and from west Tennessee in addition to the threat posed by Wilson, Forrest remained at West Point, but an-

66. Gray, *Cavalry Tactics*, 143, quoting General Orders No. 160 of October 18, 1862; see also McGee, *History of the 72nd Indiana*, 40.
67. Morton, *Artillery of Forrest's Cavalry*, 181.

ticipating the likelihood of having to move east in a hurry he had bridges built over the Tombigbee and Black Warrior rivers, ration dumps established on the roads eastward from West Point, and the trees blazed to mark the routes to Tuscaloosa and Selma.

Forrest expected Wilson to conduct a conventional cavalry raid, a duplicate of those he himself had led so often and so successfully in the past, and his opinion was shared by General Taylor.[68] Neither of them realized that they were about to face not a raid but an invasion. They did not know that there was nothing of the knight-errant about Wilson, that he had a coldly calculating, businesslike approach to the conduct of war, with no room in it for a mere raid which by its very nature was incapable of exerting any lasting effect on the enemy's ability to keep on fighting.

In keeping with the precise planning of the entire operation, Wilson gave each of his divisional and brigade commanders a detailed statement of his objectives, with the routes to be followed as far as Selma, the timetable, and the scope and degree of discretion each of them was to be allowed to depart from the overall plan, precisely spelled out. To confuse Forrest and keep him off balance as long as possible, the three divisions were to march on divergent routes. This precaution, however, proved unnecessary. With a huge area to try to protect, Forrest had to remain where he was until he was certain that Wilson was the only, or the most immediate, threat. On March 27, he learned that Wilson was on the move, and he directed his command to march by way of Tuscaloosa to Montevallo, about 50 miles north of Selma, to intercept the "raiders." As a result, Wilson met no opposition in the first 130 miles of his march and was able to cover the distance in ten days, notwithstanding that all but the last dozen or so miles "was extremely difficult and toilsome, country rough and barren, roads bad, streams swollen, and approaches treacherous."[69]

---

68. Taylor telegraphed General R. E. Lee on March 27, "A raid [is] advancing from the North and another from Northeast Alabama toward Selma and Montgomery. . . . My intention is to meet and whip these detached columns before they can advance far into the country or unite with each other." *Official Records*, Vol. XLIX, Pt. 1, p. 419.

69. *Ibid.*, 350. General Croxton, whose brigade escorted the train, reported, "March 23 . . . toiled with [the train] from daylight to dark, using almost all the brigade to carry it along. Made four miles." And again,

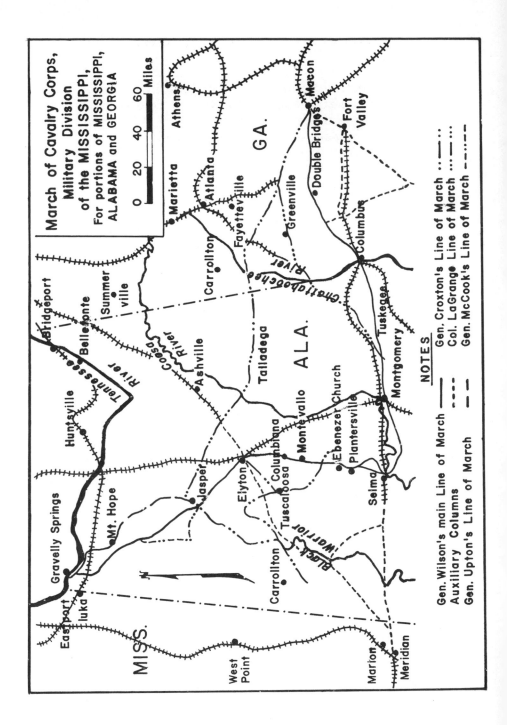

March of Cavalry Corps,
Military Division
of the MISSISSIPPI,
For portions of MISSISSIPPI,
ALABAMA and GEORGIA

0 20 40 60 Miles

NOTES

Gen. Wilson's main Line of March ———
Auxiliary Columns ————
Gen. Upton's Line of March ————

Gen. Croxton's Line of March —··—··
Col. LaGrange Line of March —···—···
Gen. McCook's Line of March —·—·—

GA.

ALA.

MISS.

Tennessee River

Coosa River

Chattahoochee River

Black Warrior

Bridgeport
Bellefonte
Summer ville
Huntsville
Gravelly Springs
Eastport
Iuka
Mt. Hope
Jasper
Carrollton
West Point
Marion
Meridian
Selma
Montgomery
Tuscaloosa
Elyton
Columbiana
Montevallo
Ebenezer Church
Plantersville
Tuskegee
Columbus
Greenville
Fort Valley
Macon
Double Bridges
Athens
Marietta
Atlanta
Fayetteville
Carrollton
Ashville
Talladega

At the "poor, insignificant" village of Elyton, now the city of Birmingham, the work of destruction began. Upton's division destroyed four iron works, five collieries, and other valuable property. When the division following Upton's went into camp that evening, "the sky was red for miles around, caused by the fires . . . [of] burning cotton gins, mills, factories, etc."[70]

Between Elyton and Montevallo the road crossed the Cahawba River. There was no bridge, and General Philip D. Roddey, stationed with his small division below Montevallo to intercept Wilson, had had the ford thoroughly blocked. Hence the Federals had to detour to Hillsboro, where there was a railroad trestle three hundred (or by another account, nine hundred) feet long and one hundred feet high over the river. To make the crossing the track north of the bridge was torn up and the ties, "8 feet long, 10 to 12 inches in diameter and flattened just a little on two sides" were laid crosswise on the bridge, as close together as possible. "As . . . [the ties] were not very straight, there were numerous cracks where a horse's foot would drop through. . . . it was with the utmost difficulty that we got . . . [the horses] started across it. Col. Miller . . . ordered the brigade to dismount . . . and in no case to let the horses stop for a moment, nor let a vacant space occur between them, lest there should be a balk and the whole column . . . [be] tumbled off into the river. . . . Allow three feet for the width occupied by each horse, and you see the men had to walk on the ends of the ties and also on the outside of the stringers. . . . We want to tell you there were times while crossing that bridge when we drew our breath very short and thanked God when we were over."[71]

Having learned from his scouts on March 30 that Forrest had left West Point and was marching toward Tuscaloosa, Wilson ordered Croxton to leave the column with his sixteen hundred-man

---

"Marched a distance of twenty-eight miles. . . . This was one of the hardest day's marches in the campaign. The roads were in terrible condition, and I was compelled to cut new roads, corduroy old ones, build bridges over swamps, and use my command to carry wagons and ambulances along." *Ibid.*, 419.

70. McGee, *History of the 72nd Indiana*, 534.
71. *Ibid.*, 535–36.

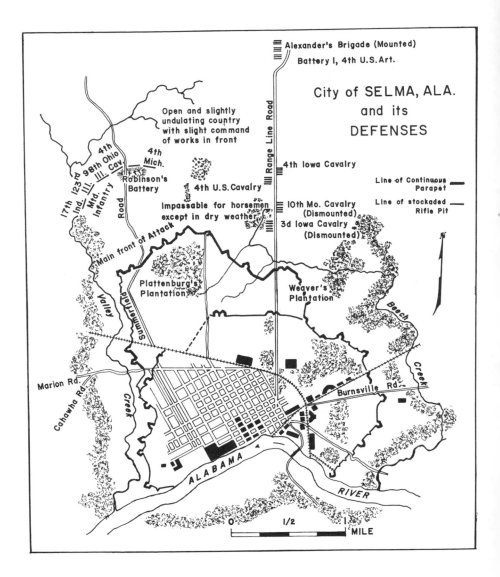

City of SELMA, ALA. and its DEFENSES

Alexander's Brigade (Mounted)

Battery I, 4th U.S. Art.

Open and slightly undulating country with slight command of works in front

4th Ohio

123d Ill.

98th Ill. Cav.

4th Mich.

Robinson's Battery

4th U.S.Cavalry

Impassable for horsemen except in dry weather

17th Ind. Mtd. Infantry

Range Line Road

4th Iowa Cavalry

Line of Continuous Parapet

Line of stockaded Rifle Pit

10th Mo. Cavalry (Dismounted)

3d Iowa Cavalry (Dismounted)

Road

Main front of Attack

Plattenburg's Plantation

Weaver's Plantation

Valley

Summerfield

Beech Creek

N

Marion Rd.

Cahawha Rd.

Creek

Burnsville Rd.

Creek

ALABAMA

RIVER

0   1/2   1 MILE

brigade, march to Tuscaloosa as rapidly as possible, "destroy the bridge [over the Black Warrior River], factories, mills, university . . . and whatever else may be of benefit to the rebel cause," and rejoin the corps south of Montevallo.[72] (The phrases "as rapidly as possible," "with the greatest possible celerity," "with the utmost spirit and rapidity," "at once," occur repeatedly in Wilson's orders, but contrary to the ways of some other commanding officers of Union cavalry as late as 1863 and 1864, he expected them to be taken literally, and his subordinates, left in no doubt that he did, acted accordingly.) On the evening of the thirty-first, at Trion, Croxton learned that the Confederates had passed through Tuscaloosa earlier in the day and were camped for the night only two miles away; indeed, Croxton found himself squarely between General William H. Jackson's division and Forrest's artillery and trains, which had remained in Tuscaloosa for the night. Faced with an unexpected situation, Croxton ignored his orders for two days and tried to badger Jackson into an engagement in order to prevent him from continuing his march, which, if Forrest's plans had worked out, would have brought him down on Wilson's rear while Forrest, with the rest of his forces, attacked Wilson in front. After a skirmish with Croxton on April 1, Jackson marched away, but not until he had informed the commander of the Tuscaloosa militia that he had attacked and dispersed Croxton's brigade, which, he said, "is scattered in the mountains and cannot again be collected. Assure the fair ladies of Tuscaloosa that the tread of the Vandal hordes shall not pollute the streets of their beautiful city."[73] Alas for General Jackson! No sooner had he marched away than Croxton and his "Vandal hordes," who had not been scattered in the mountains, occupied beautiful Tuscaloosa, and their tread did pollute its streets.[74]

72. *Official Records*, Vol. XLIX, Pt. 1, p. 419.
73. C. C. Andrews, *History of the Campaign of Mobile, Including the Cooperative Operations of Gen. Wilson's Cavalry in Alabama* (New York, 1867), 261.
74. The subsequent adventures of Croxton's brigade are a saga in their own right. When it left Tuscaloosa on April 5 after destroying "the foundry, factory, two niter works, the military university [and] a quantity of stores, and supplied the command with all the rations . . . [it] could carry," Wilson had already captured Selma and was about to march east. He

Meanwhile, on the evening of March 30, Wilson had reached Montevallo. More iron works, rolling mills, and collieries went up in flames and smoke, but when the corps resumed its march the next day, it found Roddey's division, Edward Crossland's small brigade, and D. W. Adams' few hundred infantry and militia drawn up across the Selma road and preparing to attack. Upton, who had the lead, deployed his two brigades and attacked first, "with guidons unfurled and the trumpets sounding the charge," and with the guns of his battery of Regulars in close support.[75] The Confederates were driven back and, when they tried to make a stand some distance behind their original position, were driven back once more. The Federals bivouacked that night fourteen miles south of Montevallo. The Confederate loss had been small, probably fewer than a hundred men, but the Federal gain had been immeasurably greater. They had met and beaten back, they thought, the fearsome Forrest himself and had thereby "gained . . . a moral supremacy . . . which they never lost. They had fairly 'got the bulge on Forrest.'"[76] Or, in the words of another witness, "Forrest's army was the only army in the department that amounted to anything, and we had met it and defeated it, and now we felt that we could just go where we pleased and do anything Uncle Sam wanted us to do."[77]

---

moved so rapidly that Croxton, whose march was delayed repeatedly by rain-swollen streams, did not catch up with him until May 1, at Macon, Georgia. From March 30 to May 1, Croxton wrote, "We marched 653 miles, most of the time through mountainous country so destitute of supplies that the command could be subsisted . . . only by the greatest efforts, swimming four rivers, destroying 5 large iron works (the last in the cotton States), 3 factories, numerous mills, immense quantities of supplies, capturing 4 pieces of artillery and several hundred small arms, near 300 prisoners, rejoining the corps, the men in fine spirits and the animals in good condition." *Official Records*, Vol. XLIX, Pt. 2, p. 424. The brigade had to ford or swim so many streams that the men called the march "Croxton's naval expedition."

75. Wilson, *Under the Old Flag*, II, 208; *Official Records*, Vol. XLIX, Pt. 1, pp. 357–58.

76. Wilson, *Under the Old Flag*, II, 209. Actually, Forrest did not arrive on the scene until ten P.M., after the fight was already over. John A. Wyeth, *That Devil Forrest: Life of General Nathan Bedford Forrest* (New York, 1959), 528–29.

77. McGee, *History of the 72nd Indiana*, 543. See also Hosea, "The Campaign of Selma," 90.

The skirmish—for it was little more than that—at Montevallo was the prelude to two days of an almost continuous running fight. It began shortly after dawn on April 1 with a piece of phenomenal good fortune for Wilson. Upton's troopers captured one of Forrest's couriers; the dispatches the man carried were at once delivered to Wilson and as a result, he wrote, "I now knew exactly where every division and brigade of Forrest's corps was, that they were widely scattered and that if I could force the marching and the fighting with sufficient rapidity and vigor, I should have the game entirely in my hands."[78] Jackson was entirely out of it, and General James R. Chalmers' division, still west of the Cahawba River, could be prevented from crossing and kept out of the way by destroying the bridge at Centerville, a mission entrusted to and successfully accomplished by Colonel Oscar H. LaGrange's brigade. Thus Forrest, positioned across the Selma road at Ebenezer Church, six miles north of Plantersville, had only some three thousand men at hand to try to block two full divisions of nearly nine thousand Federals, all armed with Spencers.[79]

With his fine instinct for terrain, Forrest deployed his men at Ebenezer Church in a naturally strong position which they improved with barricades of fence rails and slashings of pine trees. His right and center were protected by the swampy bottoms of Mulberry Creek and Bogler's Creek, his left was on a high, wooded ridge, and his six guns dominated the roads on which the Federals were expected to advance. All morning, Long's division on the right and Upton's on the left had been driving off the small groups of cavalry Forrest had sent forward to harass their march. Long, with the 72nd Indiana Mounted Infantry in the van, was the first to reach Bogler's Creek and at once drove in Forrest's skirmishers. Then the four-company saber battalion of the 17th Indiana Mounted Infantry, led by gigantic Lieutenant Colonel Frank White, rode forward in a charge directly at the center of the Con-

78. Wilson, *Under the Old Flag*, II, 211.
79. According to Wyeth (*That Devil Forrest*, 530), Forrest had only two thousand men; according to Wilson (*Under the Old Flag*, II, 215), he had "something like five thousand." In his official report (*Official Records*, Vol. XLIX, Pt. 1, p. 359), Wilson credits Forrest with "about 5,000." Piatt and Boynton (*General George H. Thomas*, 609) state that Forrest had between three and four thousand men.

federate line, where Forrest had stationed himself with his head-quarters flag, his staff, an escort company of seventy-five men, and two companies of Crossland's Kentuckians.[80] In the ensuing melee, Federal sabers against Confederate revolvers, Captain J. D. Taylor of the Hoosiers, swinging his saber, rode directly at Forrest and slashed his arm repeatedly before Forrest was able to turn in his saddle and gun him down. When Forrest, his arm still in a sling, met Wilson a few days later, he said (perhaps less grammatically), "If that boy had known enough to give me the point of his saber instead of its edge, I should not have been here to tell you about it."[81]

Before Long could deploy the rest of his division to support the two Indiana regiments, the Fourth Division rode up on his left. Without bothering to reconnoiter, Upton threw forward a strong dismounted skirmish line and sent two regiments, mounted, to charge the Confederate right flank. Heavily attacked in front and flank, Forrest was driven from the field with the loss of three of his six guns and about four hundred men, most of whom were taken prisoner. He was pursued toward Selma as long as there was light to see.[82]

It was a jubilant crowd of Federals that went into bivouac that evening at Plantersville, within nineteen miles of Selma. As Sergeant James Larson of Wilson's escort described the scene,

The trees covered with foliage are lit up from under by the numerous campfires scattered here and there over hundreds of acres and the

80. A former member of the 17th Indiana Mounted Infantry wrote after the war that the "Lightning Brigade was only partially armed with sabers (usually the two flank companies) and of course always prepared to fight on foot . . . and at the same time was equally efficient in mounted movements, excepting a general saber charge, and yet one of the most daring, gallant and effective saber charges . . . in the Department of the Cumberland during the war was made by four companies of the 17th Indiana . . . at [Ebenezer] Church." George I. Robinson, "With Kilpatrick Around Atlanta," in MOLLUS, Commandery of Wisconsin, War Papers (3 vols.; Milwaukee, 1891–1903), I, 201.
81. Wilson, Under the Old Flag, II, 217; Wilson describes Taylor as a "mere stripling." Wilson and Forrest met under a flag of truce ostensibly to discuss an exchange of prisoners.
82. Seeing the guns, belts, cartridge boxes, blankets, coats, and hats that Forrest's men discarded in their flight, a waggish member of the 3rd

colors and shades of the leaves are changed to various hues as they are moved by the night breeze to and from the rays of light. Then the irregularity in the formation of . . . camp adds another charm to the scene and gives the camp a gypsy-like appearance. There is no rule as to where the horses shall be tied or the fires built or the men spread their blankets. Hence the horses are tied promiscuously among the trees where they are munching their feed. The campfires, in like manner, are built here and there among the trees and the men are lying about on their blankets or busying themselves with cooking. In fact, the camp has the appearance of a pleasure excursion, a picnic party.[83]

In his old age Wilson wrote of the atmosphere of that evening in words that, after the lapse of nearly a half century, recapture the exhilaration of success; "Every officer and soldier who participated in . . . [the action] was satisfied with himself and the part he had played. There was neither hesitation nor laggards that day. Even the horses seemed carried away by the 'noise of the captains and the shouting.' The foraging parties brought in plenty of provisions . . . and a more joyful bivouac was never had by hungry and tired soldiers. All were full of hope for the morrow."[84]

While the men ate, smoked, talked, and rested, the young major general gave thought to the problem he would face the next day. The Selma fortifications were known to be exceptionally strong, and they would be defended by Forrest and his men. It was to be expected that Forrest would be in greater strength than he had been at Ebenezer Church, for he would have under him the Selma militia and would certainly have urged Chalmers and Jackson to exert the last ounce of energy to reach Selma the next day. But once again, Wilson was greatly favored by fortune. Early in the evening, one of Upton's patrols captured a British engineer named Millington, who had worked on the Selma defenses and obligingly drew for Upton "an accurate pencil sketch of the trace and profile of the works and of the topography in front and rear

---

Iowa, which led the pursuit, called out that the "Rebels" were "too fast for their goods." Gilpin, "The Last Campaign," 635.

83. Larson, *Sergeant Larson*, 173.

84. Wilson, *Under the Old Flag*, II, 219. Wilson was seventy-five when *Under the Old Flag* was published. He died at age eighty-eight, the last survivor of his West Point class.

. . . together with the number and position of the guns."[85] The sketch was at once sent to Wilson.

Forrest, his clothing and horse stained with blood from his slashed arm, reached Selma on Sunday morning, April 2. Chalmers and Jackson had not arrived, but he was able to collect between three and six thousand troops to man the fortifications.[86] Armstrong's brigade held the left, Roddey the right, and the infantry and local militia the center. Forrest, with his escort and Crossland's Kentuckians, stationed himself behind the center. To assemble the Selma militia, Forrest ordered every male capable of firing a gun to turn out, regardless of age. No one was to be excused; the orders were "fight or swim; into the works or into the river."

The Selma fortifications were not the hastily thrown-up fieldworks that had become a familiar feature of Civil War combat.[87] They had been planned and built with great care to take advantage of the terrain. The main line of works, shaped like an in-

85. *Ibid.*, 219. According to Piatt and Boynton, Millington "had been employed in planning and constructing the fortifications of Selma." *General George H. Thomas*, 605.

86. Forrest had "little more than one-third" of Wilson's nine thousand men, according to Robert Selph Henry, *"First with the Most" Forrest* (New York, 1944), 432. In his official report, Wilson credits Forrest with seven thousand men, including the militia of Selma and the surrounding country, but writes in his autobiography that Forrest had, "according to the best accounts we could get, from five to six thousand men, cavalry, artillery, infantry and militia." *Official Records*, Vol. XLIX, Pt. 2, p. 361; *Under the Old Flag*, II, 235.

87. The Selma fortifications are described, with minor differences in detail, in McGee, *History of the 72nd Indiana*, 551–52; Wilson, *Under the Old Flag*, II, 121–22; Scott, *Story of a Cavalry Regiment*, 447–48; Joseph G. Vale, *Minty and the Cavalry: A History of Cavalry Campaigns in the Western Armies* (Harrisburg, Pa., 1886), 429–30; and in Wilson's official report, *Official Records*, Vol. XLIX, Pt. 1, 360–61. McGee, who had seen the fortifications of Louisville, Nashville, Chattanooga, and Atlanta, pronounced those at Selma the strongest of them all. He walked over the ground over which Long's men attacked, and wrote, "As we looked over the ground, we were filled with astonishment and wonder. How in the world did our men succeed in reaching the main line at all? It seemed to us that if a single line of our brigade had been behind this embankment we could have annihilated any army in the world that had attempted to storm the works." McGee, *History of the 72nd Indiana*, 559. For a map of the Selma defenses, see *The Official Atlas of the Civil War* (New York, 1958), Plate LXX, No. 4.

verted letter "U" with the closed end pointing northwest, began at
the Alabama River upstream from the town and ran in a six-mile
arc to the river just below it. The western face of the works was
protected for its full length of two miles by the swampy and wooded bottoms of Valley Creek; its eastern face was similarly protected by the marshy bottoms of Beech Creek and its tributaries.
The apex of the "U," a little over three quarters of a mile long,
faced a stretch of open fields six hundred yards wide. Lacking the
natural defenses of the east and west faces, this stretch of the
works was made exceptionally strong. The fortifications at this
point consisted of a two hundred-yard deep abattis "of trees
dragged in as closely together as they could be laid side by side,
limbs all left on and sharpened at the point . . . sticking out . . .
like the quills of a thousand porcupines."[88] Inside the abattis was
a row of cheveaux de frise, backed by several rows of short stakes
driven into the ground and connected with wire. Next, and still
fifty yards in front of the main line of works, was a stockade, six
to eight feet high, built of pine trunks sharpened to a point at the
top. Then came the main line of earthworks, consisting of a ditch
eight feet wide and eight feet deep, with steeply sloping sides and
a row of sharpened stakes planted in the bottom. The soil exca-
vated from the ditch was used to build an embankment eight feet
high, its outer face forming with the inner face of the ditch a continuous slope sixteen feet high and "so steep that to climb it was
almost impossible."[89] On the inner side of the embankment was
a fire step for the defenders. At irregular intervals, redans and
bomb-proof revetments were built into the embankment, each one
sited to enable the riflemen manning it to enfilade the ditch and
its approaches. Finally, twenty-four large bastions, each with a
platform and embrasures for artillery, projected from the embankment. Four of the bastions and two redans were located in the
short stretch of the works at the apex of the "U."[90]

Wilson's orders called for the march on April 2 to begin at
5:30 A.M. Long, whose Second Division was the stronger by two
regiments, was to make his approach from the northwest, via the

88. McGee, *History of the 72nd Indiana*, 551–52.
89. *Ibid.*, 552.
90. Scott, *Story of a Cavalry Regiment*, 448.

Summerfield Road, and was to attack the apex of the "U." Upton and the Fourth Division were to take the Range Line Road, to the left of Long's route. When he reached Selma, Upton was to deploy a picked force of three hundred men, cross the Beech Creek swamps, and attack the eastern face of the fortifications which, because of the protection of the swamps, was expected to be lightly held. Long was to launch his attack when he heard the gunfire on Upton's front. On the way south from Plantersville, Wilson rode stirrup to stirrup with Long and his brigade commanders in turn, showed them Millington's sketch, made sure they understood his plan for the attack, and "dwelling upon the results of failure and disaster ... emphasized ... that the works must be carried at no matter what cost."[91] Having reached Selma, and after a hasty inspection of the fortifications, Wilson decided to wait until dark to attack.

Behind the shelter of a low ridge, Long lined up his regiments in a shallow arc, with the 17th Indiana Mounted Infantry on the right, and then, in order, the 123rd and 98th regiments of Illinois Mounted Infantry, the 4th Ohio, the 7th Pennsylvania, and the 4th Michigan.[92] The attack was to be made on foot, with 1,550 officers and men in a single line and nearly shoulder to shoulder. Normally when cavalry fought on foot, every fourth man remained behind as a horseholder; on this occasion, however, only every eighth man stayed out of action. To support the attack, Long posted the six guns of the Chicago Board of Trade Battery on a rise of ground near the Summerfield Road. His pack animals and led horses were in the rear, guarded by four companies of the 72nd Indiana Mounted Infantry.

As Long was getting into position, "frequent reports" were brought to him that "rebel cavalry, estimated at from 500 to 1,000 men," were skirmishing with the 72nd Indiana detachment in the

91. Wilson, *Under the Old Flag*, II, 224.
92. It is impossible to list with complete confidence the regiments that participated in Long's assault. The list in the text is the author's attempt to reconcile the contradictions and discrepancies in the official reports of Wilson, Long, Minty, Miller, and Vale, the reports of the regimental commanders, and the accounts of the regimental historians, including McGee of the 72nd Indiana Mounted Infantry, Crofts of the 3rd Ohio, Dornblaser and Sipes of the 7th Pennsylvania, Wulsin of the 4th Ohio, and lastly, Vale, in *Minty and the Cavalry*. Wulsin is Lucien Wulsin, *The Story of the Fourth Regiment Ohio Veteran Volunteer Cavalry* (Cincinnati, 1912).

rear.[93] The enemy was the van of Chalmers' division, which had at last arrived, but too late to help Forrest on his side of the fortifications where he needed added strength. Long sent back five more companies of the 72nd Indiana to help their comrades and decided on his own initiative to launch the attack on the fortifications at once, without waiting for Upton or darkness. It was now just five o'clock on a clear, mild spring day, and still broad daylight. The signal was given, and the 1,550 men, led by Long himself and his two brigade and six regimental commanders, went forward at a run. They had six hundred yards of open ground to cross to reach the abattis, with "no trees, no bushes, no logs, no rocks, behind which to take shelter."[94] The works before them were held by Forrest's strongest and most reliable unit, the fourteen hundred men of Armstrong's brigade, and when the Federals, their Spencers blazing, came in sight, they were met by a sheet of fire from fourteen hundred muskets and twenty guns firing canister. But Long's men were not to be stopped. Long himself fell, with a severe scalp wound, and so did the Second Brigade commander, Colonel Miller, shot through the leg. Colonel George W. Dobb of the 4th Ohio was killed, Colonel Charles C. McCormick of the 7th Pennsylvania and Colonel Jonathan Biggs of the 123rd Illinois fell, badly wounded. Their men went on. A corps of pioneers, carrying axes, ran ahead and hacked passageways through the abattis and the stockade. The men negotiated the ditch and the rampart behind it by climbing on each other's shoulders. Corporal John H. Booth of the 4th Ohio was the first into the works and was killed instantly. There was a brief scuffle with revolvers, carbines, and clubbed muskets, as more and more of the Federals leapt over the ramparts or climbed through the gun embrasures, and then the Confederates broke and ran. In a furious action lasting barely twenty minutes the Second Division had broken through the strongest section of the defenses, but the cost was heavy. Four officers and thirty-eight men were killed and 270 were wounded.[95] The 7th Pennsylvania's loss in killed and wounded was a stagger-

---

93. *Official Records*, Vol. XLIX, Pt. 1, p. 438.

94. Dornblaser, *Sabre Strokes of the Pennsylvania Dragoons*, 211.

95. Wilson, *Under the Old Flag*, II, 228. In his two official reports, however, Wilson gives different casualty figures—46 killed and 200 wounded in one report, and 40 killed, 260 wounded, and 7 missing in the other. *Official Records*, Vol. XLIX, Pt. 1, pp. 351 and 361.

ing 25 percent; the 4th Ohio lost fifty-two officers and men, nearly 22 percent of those engaged.

As soon as Upton heard the firing on Long's front, he realized that Wilson's orders to wait for darkness no longer held, and without waiting for new orders or asking questions he led his three hundred men forward with a rush through the swamp and carried the works in his front. At the same moment, Wilson, mounted on his gray charger Sheridan, followed by his bugler and an orderly carrying his red battle flag displaying the two stars of a major general, led his staff and his escort of Regulars, all with sabers drawn, in a headlong charge down the Range Line Road, straight into the gap in the fortifications through which the road ran. Behind them came the 3rd and 4th Iowa and the 10th Missouri. The defenses of Selma were now breached at three points, and every man of the attacking force was pressing forward as fast as his own or his horse's legs could carry him.

A little less than a mile behind the line of works that had been breached by Long's division there was a second line of redoubts, connected by a partially completed line of earthworks. It was now quite dark, but despite the darkness and the chaos of defeat, Forrest, Buford, Armstrong, and Adams collected a few hundred men to make a stand in this second line and even managed to break up the charge of the 4th United States. But these few stalwarts were overwhelmed by the flood of bluecoats closing in on them from all directions, and eventually they broke and ran. Nothing was now left to check the Federals, who poured into the town by every street and lane.

A common feature of every campaign involving the cavalry in the first four years of the war, especially on the Union side, was the immense loss of horses, due far more to ignorance, carelessness, neglect, and abuse than to enemy action. Campaign after campaign ended with a third or a half of the participating cavalrymen trudging along on foot, notwithstanding that dozens or hundreds of horses had been taken from farmers along the way to replace broken-down animals.[96] But in this respect too, as in

96. One example of dozens that might be cited: the 7th Pennsylvania began the Atlanta Campaign with 919 horses. At its end, four and a half months later, they had 560, 42 of them replacements captured en route, making a wastage of 401, or 44 percent. Losses in earlier years of the war,

many others, the Selma Campaign differed from those that had
gone before. There were many officers in the Union cavalry who
knew as much or more as Wilson did about the care of horses; he
was exceptional only in making sure that the knowledge was fully
utilized. Many of his orders before and during the campaign dealt
with the care of horses, and in this area too he saw to it that his
orders were obeyed to the letter and not emasculated on their way
down the chain of command. Officers were required to make certain that the horses were carefully saddled to prevent sore backs.
To spare the animals as much as possible, the men were required
to dismount and lead them at regular intervals throughout the
day, and to do so always when the road ran up or down a steep
hill. Going faster than at a walk, except in action, was strictly
forbidden. Cast shoes had to be replaced at once, and the horses
had to be groomed daily under the supervision of the officers.

The result can be seen in the obviously surprised comment of
several regimental historians that the condition of the animals was
as good at the end of the campaign as it had been at the beginning.[97] Nevertheless, there had been losses, due largely to the generally poor quality of the horses supplied to the corps in January
and February. But two thousand horses were captured at Selma,
the mounts of those of Forrest's cavalrymen who had been taken
prisoner or of those who, when the rout began, were unable to
reach their horses and escaped on foot.[98] The best of the captured
animals were given to the dismounted men or used to replace the
weakened or diseased horses of the command. This left a surplus
of about five hundred animals. To make sure that they did not
fall into the hands of the enemy after his departure, Wilson ordered them shot and the carcasses thrown into the Alabama River.

Wilson remained in Selma for a week, and when he left the
main object of the expedition was accomplished; the Selma arsenal, with all its shops, foundries, machinery, and magazines,

---

even when there was no active campaign on foot, were frequently as great,
or even greater. Gray, *Cavalry Tactics*, 162–63.

97. For example, Mitchell, in "Field Notes of the Selma Campaign,"
188, stated, "Both men and horses . . . are in better condition than when
we started." See also Gilpin, "The Last Campaign," 656.

98. Wilson's prisoners at Selma numbered 150 officers and 2,700 men.
Forrest himself escaped. Wilson, *Under the Old Flag*, II, 235.

was totally destroyed.[99] Selma, however, was not the end of the campaign. Wilson captured Montgomery without a fight on April 12, and as any other officer would have done in his place, he made an impressive affair out of his entry into the first capital of the Confederacy:

With perfect order in column of platoons, every man in his place, division and brigade flags unfurled, guidons flying, sabers and spurs jingling, bands playing patriotic airs, and the bugles now and then sounding the calls, the war-begrimed Union troopers, batteries, ambulances and wagons passed proudly through the city. Not a man left the ranks, not a loud word was uttered, and not an incident happened to hurt the feelings of the . . . people. . . . Five brigades, not far from twelve thousand troopers, were in that column passing in review, as it were, before the ladies and gentlemen of the city.[100]

The Stars and Stripes were raised over the state house, which was visited by a few of the more thoughtful or curious troopers, one of whom wrote in his diary, "Visit the deserted Capitol and the echoes of my footfalls in its twilight corridors sound uncanny. I seek the Senate chamber, where Davis was inaugurated, but the play is over, lights out, and the curtain down. The air is fresher outside, and I turn away."[101]

Winslow's brigade of Upton's division had a hard fight to capture Columbus, Georgia; the men attacked on foot, in the dark, shouting "Selma! Selma!," but aside from this fight and another at West Point, Georgia, there was no longer any opposition, and the march of the corps turned into a delightful excursion, an experience to be recalled with nostalgia in the postwar years. "For us the road will always be memorable, winding over hills and mountains, through dark forests and green valleys, past cotton fields and plantations, with barns and clustering cabins, by rich cities, along

99. The corps remained in Selma long enough to issue "Vol. I, No. 1" of the *Yankee Cavalier*, in which "the people of this benighted region" were informed "that the Union still exists, and unless they 'repent and believe' very soon they will forever be damned. Subjugation is as sure to follow the track of Uncle Samuel's victorious armies as daylight is sure to follow the track of 'Old Sol,' unless . . . the people throw down their arms and fling themselves into the arms of 'Old Uncle Abe'. . . . The people of Selma . . . should understand that the old humbug . . . that 'Yanks won't fight' is played out." McGee, *History of the 72nd Indiana*, 567–68.
100. *Ibid.*, 251.
101. Mitchell, "Field Notes of the Selma Campaign," 188.

shores of rivers, and by the margin of brooks half hidden in flow-ers and grasses, past quiet villages and hamlets, beneath the bright blue sky that bends with magic in it above the Sunny South."[102] There, too, was the sight of "new trees and plants . . . [the] magnolia, live oak, juniper . . . Spanish moss," and the be-havior, no longer a novelty but still strange, of the hundreds of Negroes of all ages and both sexes, who followed the column to freedom.[103]

Not until his corps reached Macon did Wilson receive trust-worthy information that Generals Lee and Johnston had surren-dered and that the war was ended. His campaign too was at an end, except that some of his regiments participated in the pursuit and capture of Jefferson Davis. With that task accomplished, Wilson could give thought to the meaning and lessons of the cam-paign. He had gone into the mounted service with the conviction that "the great fault in our cavalry system had . . . been overwork in detachments and the absence of instruction, organization, and uniformity of equipment."[104] The command he had received from Grant, and the free hand the skeptical Sherman had given him, provided him the opportunity to test the validity of his theories. In January, 1865, he had under him the largest cavalry command of the Civil War, and when he led his fourteen thousand men south on March 22, he had a force that was concentrated, reason-ably well instructed—by experience, if nothing else—and uni-formly equipped with the best firearm of the war. And he supplied it with leadership of superior quality, that of a far-seeing com-manding officer who knew what he wanted to accomplish and left as little as possible to chance. General Richard Taylor, a good judge, wrote after the war, "General Wilson['s] . . . soldierly quali-ties are entitled to respect; for of all the Federal expeditions of which I have any knowledge, his was the best conducted."[105]

102. Gilpin, "The Last Campaign," 656.
103. Mitchell, "Field Notes of the Selma Campaign," 184.
104. *Official Records*, Vol. XLIX, Pt. 1, p. 355.
105. Richard Taylor, *Destruction and Reconstruction* (New York, 1879), 220. A British historian writes that Wilson's Selma Campaign "was one of the most remarkable cavalry operations of the war, for . . . it was not a mere raid or dash, but an invading army determined to fight its way through. . . . It is certainly . . . one of the most extraordinary affairs in the history of the cavalry service." G. T. Denison, *A History of Cavalry* (Lon-don, 1913), 386.

Wilson's reputation would be far higher, and deservedly so, if his Selma Campaign had occurred earlier against more powerful opposition, and if it had not been overshadowed by the dramatic events in Virginia and North Carolina in the closing weeks of the war. Wilson himself was well satisfied with what he and his command had accomplished. He wrote his friend Adam Badeau on April 22, "I have the best cavalry and the best cavalry officers in America," and he recommended for promotion Upton ("the best general of cavalry I ever saw"), Long, Winslow, Alexander, Minty, Miller, and LaGrange.[106]

The Federal cavalry, its men and its leaders, needed nearly four years of preparation, much of it of the most painful character, to acquire the ability to make a campaign like that which produced the capture of Selma and Columbus. And too, the Federal high command needed these four years to become aware of the tremendous potential of its mounted troops when properly used. Sheridan in the East and Wilson in the West demonstrated for all to see the capabilities of the kind of cavalry that four years of war had brought into being. But this cavalry did not get its chance until the war was nearly over. If there had been vision in high places it might not have taken four years to make possible General Upton's remark that until the capture of Selma and Columbus, he had had no idea what cavalry could do; having been present at both, he was certain that nothing short of the ocean could stop them.[107]

---

106. James P. Jones (ed.), "'Your Left Arm': James H. Wilson's Letters to Adam Badeau," *Civil War History*, XII (1966), 241.

107. Wilson's losses for the entire campaign were 13 officers and 86 enlisted men killed, 3 officers and 559 enlisted men wounded, and 7 officers and 21 enlisted men missing, for a grand total of 725. Wilson, *Under the Old Flag*, II, 239–94. It would not be proper to close this account of the Selma Campaign without recording that the Congressional Medal of Honor was awarded to thirteen men who took part in it. No less than eight of those honored belonged to the 4th Iowa, two were members of the 3rd Iowa, two of the 17th Indiana Mounted Infantry, and one of the 4th Kentucky Cavalry. *Official Records*, Vol. XLIX, Pt. 1, p. 504; Wilson, *Under the Old Flag*, II, 253.

I

Prelude to War

"ALL [WAS] SMILES, JOY, AND GOOD FELLOWSHIP" IN
Charleston, South Carolina, in November, 1861.[1] The state legislature had just fixed the date for the election of delegates to a
convention that everyone knew would take South Carolina out of
the Union. On December 20, the convention, in session in Charleston, voted unanimously to adopt an Ordinance of Secession. Overnight, war between North and South, theretofore mere bombast
in the mouths of extremists, ceased being inconceivable.

The menace of war came upon an utterly unmilitary nation
of thirty-one million people. The size of the American military
establishment would have delighted the most devout pacifist of
that or any other day. On December 31, 1860, the Regular Army
had a paper strength of 18,093 of all ranks; its actual strength
was 16,367 officers and men.[2] With legislative prescience not unmatched in later times, just nine days before passage of the South
Carolina Ordinance of Secession the United States Senate ap-

1. Augustus B. Longstreet, quoted in Allan Nevins, *The Emergence of
Lincoln* (2 vols.; New York, 1950), II, 321.
2. Emory Upton, *The Military Policy of the United States* (Washington, D.C., 1904), 225.

proved a resolution directing its Committee of Military Affairs to investigate the possibility of reducing bloated military expenditures.[3] Of the 198 companies of infantry, artillery, and cavalry composing the minuscule army, 183 were stationed in 79 posts and forts on the frontier; 15 manned 23 arsenals and guarded the Canadian border and the Atlantic Coast. The War Department, housed in a nondescript building near the White House, had a staff of 90 civilian employees in Washington (34 of whom resigned during the secession crisis), and another 168 in outlying depots and stations.[4] Housed in the War Department building were the eight bureaus that administered the army. These were headed in 1860 by officers who, with one exception, had been in the service since the War of 1812 or earlier, and one of whom, Colonel George Gibson, had held the post of quartermaster general for forty-two years.[5] The professional head of the army was the venerable Lieutenant General Winfield Scott, seventy-four years old and in failing health.

Included in General Scott's command were five regiments of mounted troops: the 1st and 2nd Dragoons, organized in 1833 and 1837, respectively; the Regiment of Mounted Riflemen, organized in 1846; and the 1st and 2nd Regiments of Cavalry, organized in 1855 under the regime of Secretary of War Jefferson Davis, formerly a lieutenant in the 1st Dragoons.[6]

The mounted service of the army had been a stepchild of the military establishment from the start. In the Revolutionary War, good American cavalry under competent leadership had opposed Colonel Banastre Tarleton's dragoons in the Carolinas, but after Yorktown there were no mounted troops in the army until 1808, when Congress authorized the formation of a regiment of "light dragoons." A second dragoon regiment was authorized in January, 1812, but both these regiments were ordered disbanded three years later, and for the next eighteen years the army was again

3. A. Howard Meneely, *The War Department, 1861: A Study in Mobilization and Administration* (New York, 1928), 27.
4. Allan Nevins, *The War for the Union: The Improvised War, 1861–1862* (New York, 1959), 194.
5. Meneely, *The War Department, 1861*, p. 108.
6. The 3rd Dragoons were authorized in 1847, but the regiment was disbanded at the close of the Mexican War. Gray, *Cavalry Tactics*, 5–6.

without a mounted component.[7] A major objection in congressional eyes to the establishment of a cavalry force was its high cost; an appropriation of $300,000 had been required to recruit, equip, and mount the ten companies, nine hundred officers and men, of the 2nd Dragoons.[8] Not until the edge of settlement reached the plains did Washington concede, albeit reluctantly and with a tight hold on the purse strings, the need for mobile troops to deal with the Plains Indians.

During the first seventy years of the Republic, the mounted arm not only suffered from an Anglo-Saxon legislative body's ingrained fear of a standing army, but had special handicaps of its own to overcome. The Corps of Engineers could point to its usefulness; engineer officers built many of the internal improvements dear to the hearts of congressmen. The artillery manned the fortifications which were the visible means of defense against the navies of the Old World. The infantry had at least the virtue of being economical. The cavalry was not only expensive to raise and maintain, but it also seemed quite useless. The resultant feeling of grudging acceptance by Congress is evident even in the formal language of legislation: "There shall be raised and organized, under the direction of the President . . . one additional regiment of dragoons or mounted riflemen. . . . The President . . . may disband the said regiment whenever, in his opinion, the public interest no longer requires their service."[9]

The United States Army, in the absence of mounted troops that might have developed a native cavalry tradition, sought to acquire one by importation from Europe. In the first few years of

7. President Jackson was authorized in June, 1832, to raise "Mounted Volunteers for the Defense of the Frontier." Under this authority, six hundred Rangers were recruited, each of whom was required to furnish his own horse and weapons and was paid one dollar per day. Experienced cavalry officers being unavailable, officers for the "Mounted Volunteers" were detailed from the infantry. Thiele, "The Evolution of Cavalry," 10–11.

8. T. F. Rodenbough (ed.), *From Everglade to Canon with the Second Dragoons* (New York, 1875), 18.

9. In an access of economy, Congress voted in 1842 to unhorse the 2nd Dragoons, who were to serve thereafter as infantry. Two years later, however, Congress yielded to popular clamor from the West and gladdened the hearts of the regiment by voting to remount the Dragoons. Thiele, "The Evolution of Cavalry," 17–18.

its existence, the 1st Dragoons, organized by Colonel Henry Dodge and Lieutenant Colonel Stephen Watts Kearny, lacked even a uniform drill; nearly every company had its own system of tactics, invented or developed for it by the company commander, who was generally a transplant from the infantry. Some progress toward uniformity came about through the establishment in 1835 of the Cavalry School at Carlisle Barracks. Then, in 1839, Philip Kearny and two of his fellow lieutenants were ordered by Secretary of War Joel Poinsett to go to France and enroll in the Royal School of Cavalry at Saumur, to "perfect themselves in the theory and practice of the great French Cavalry service and upon their return work out a system of Cavalry Tactics for the Dragoons modeled on the French system which Poinsett thought the best in Europe, 'but so modified as to fit the needs of the United States Dragoons'."[10] Returning to the United States in the fall of 1840, Kearny and his colleagues wrote a *System of Cavalry Tactics* which was issued by the War Department in February, 1841. Known familiarly as the "Poinsett Tactics" or the "1841 Tactics," the *System* was for the most part a translation of the French cavalry manual, and it served for twenty years as the bible of the United States mounted troops.

After the start of the Crimean War, the then secretary of war, Jefferson Davis, sent another delegation of army officers abroad to study "the practical working of the changes which have been introduced of late years into the military systems . . . of Europe." One of the members of the mission, Captain George Brinton Mc-Clellan of the 1st United States Cavalry, made a special study of the Russian and the Austrian cavalry. One product of his investigations was the McClellan saddle, modeled upon the Austrian pattern, which remained the official saddle of the United States mounted troops until the end of its horse-cavalry days.[11] Another

10. On the basis of Kearny's Mexican War record, General Scott called him "the bravest man I ever knew and a perfect soldier." J. K. Herr and E. S. Wallace, *The Story of the U.S. Cavalry, 1775–1942* (Boston, 1953), 56. For Poinsett's instructions to Kearny, see Thomas Kearny, *General Philip Kearny* (New York, 1937), 49. Kearny, then a brigadier general of volunteers and commanding a division in the Army of the Potomac, was killed in the battle of Chantilly on September 1, 1862.

11. James S. Hutchins, "The United States Cavalry Saddle, McClellan

of McClellan's importations was the not entirely impractical idea that some of the Plains Indians might be excellent raw material for irregular cavalry on the Russian Cossack model. The idea was actually tried in the Civil War; the 1st Texas Cavalry, whose name makes a strange showing on the roster of *Union* cavalry regiments, was made up mostly of Comanche Indians under white officers.[12]

What may be called the Modern Age of European cavalry doctrine began in the Thirty Years' War, with the innovations introduced by King Gustavus Adolphus of Sweden. He increased the mobility of his horsemen by relieving them of their heavy body armor, keeping only a light breast and back plate for cuirassiers; he armed each cavalryman with a long sword and two pistols and taught them to work with the infantry in battle, posting them in masses on the flanks of his footsoldiers. The next major step forward came under Frederick the Great. The commanders of his cavalry, Seydlitz and Zieten, drilled the Prussian mounted troops to work in unison, as regiments and brigades, and took great pains to inculcate in their officers the values of aggressiveness and the initiative, which they rightly considered the twin keys to a successful cavalry. One of Frederick's regulations warned that "any cavalry officer awaiting an attack will be cashiered," and another declared, "All attacks are to be made without firing, and the last 200 yards at the gallop."[13]

Cavalry reached the pinnacle of its glory under Napoleon, who

---

Pattern, Model 1857, in Tojhusmuseet, Copenhagen," *Saertryk af Vaabenhistoriske Aarboger*, XVI (1970), 146–62.

12. George B. McClellan, *European Cavalry* (Philadelphia, 1861), 115. On General J. W. Davidson's November to December, 1864, raid to destroy the Mobile & Ohio Railroad, the 1st Texas cavalrymen were detailed as foragers and caught enough steers with their lassoes to keep the four thousand-man expedition supplied with beef. Thomas W. Smith, *The Story of a Cavalry Regiment: "Scott's 900," Eleventh New York Cavalry* (New York, 1897), 190. The 1st Texas experiment was not an unqualified success; "complaint was made . . . that no dependence could be placed on the . . . [regiment] as they deserted at every opportunity, taking with them their horses and accoutrements." Ella Lonn, *Desertion During the Civil War* (New York, 1928), 97. There were Indian regiments, more or less regularly enrolled, serving on both sides in the Trans-Mississippi area during the Civil War.

13. Evelyn Wood, *Achievements of Cavalry* (London, 1897), 243.

had a high opinion of its value. He used with great success his regiments of chasseurs—lightly armed men, slight of build and mounted on light, active horses—to screen the movements of his own armies and to discover and keep watch on the movements of the enemy. Larger men, in helmet, breastplate, and backplate, mounted on large, powerful horses, were the famed and feared cuirassiers, whose charge was intended to sweep all before it. Believing firmly in the value of mass action, Napoleon grouped his regiments of cuirassiers into brigades and divisions, and eventually into army corps, which he used with devastating effect in his battles, hurling against the enemy infantry, previously shaken by his artillery, masses of as many as twelve thousand horsemen.

In addition to his chasseurs and cuirassiers, Napoleon had twenty-one regiments of dragoons. These were a compromise between the light and heavy cavalry, sufficiently active to replace, at need, the light cavalry as the eyes of the army, and sufficiently heavy to employ on occasion the shock tactics of the cuirassiers. They had a further important skill, peculiar to themselves; being armed with a carbine in addition to the saber, they could when necessary dismount and fight on foot and, in fact, were trained to do so. They were not mounted infantry, troops whose function was to fight on foot and for whom the horse was merely a means of rapid locomotion between fights; they were true cavalry, fighting as such whenever possible. But when the tactical situation demanded it, the dragoons dismounted and were ready to defend ground or to attack on foot. Under certain circumstances, for example in fighting Spanish guerillas, the dragoons performed outstandingly effective service. Several of Napoleon's generals of cavalry, most notably Joachim Murat, who began life as the son of an innkeeper and rose to the dignity of a Marshal of France, King of Naples, and brother-in-law of the emperor, became resplendent figures of legend, and it was one of Napoleon's cavalry officers who made the classic remark that the function of cavalry in war was to lend tone to what would otherwise be nothing but a vulgar brawl.[14]

14. In the same spirit is the inscription on a portrait of Dante in the Cavalry Club in London. It reads, "The Divine Poet—Dante Alighieri—Lieutenant of Guelph Cavalry—Battle of Campaldino, 1289."

A straight line of development, reaching its culmination under Napoleon, had made the massed charge against enemy infantry the prime tactical function of cavalry. When the United States went to Europe to shop for a cavalry tradition, it was this concept which it imported as the cavalry ideal; the principle that the "efficiency of . . . [cavalry] resides in the power of its shock" became official American doctrine.[15] It was taught at West Point, dutifully committed to heart by class after class of cadets, and utterly ignored in practice as soon as they came up against the realities of frontier service. As Confederate General Richard Ewell, former captain in the 1st United States Dragoons put it, in his years of service on the plains "he had learned all about commanding fifty United States dragoons, and forgotten everything else."[16]

It would have been difficult, if not impossible, to collect at any time after 1833 enough American cavalrymen in one place to deliver what a European officer would have recognized as a cavalry charge, or even to train these men to do so. The 1st Dragoons, for example, at the end of 1848 had three companies stationed in New Mexico and Arizona, three in California, and one each at Forts Scott, Leavenworth, Washita, and Snelling.[17] The 2nd Dragoons, with headquarters in Utah, had individual companies scattered from Kansas in the east to Oregon in the west.[18] In the Mexican War, a single squadron of the 2nd Dragoons under Captain Charles A. May made a gallant charge against a Mexican battery at the battle of Resaca, but this was an exceptional event. The norm of service on the frontier against the Plains Indians provided few, if any, opportunities for a saber charge; the service was dull, frequently dangerous, and seldom the pathway to distinction or

15. Mahan, *Advanced Guard*, 34.

16. Taylor, *Destruction and Reconstruction*, 37. Cavalry tactics were taught at West Point from 1837 on. Sidney Forman, *West Point* (New York, 1950), 177. In June, 1839, a sergeant and five troopers were transferred from Carlisle Barracks to West Point, the Quartermaster's Department supplied 12 horses, and instruction in riding was given the cadets thereafter. Edward C. Boynton, *History of West Point* (New York, 1871), 226.

17. Albert G. Brackett, *History of the United States Cavalry* (New York, 1865), 124.

18. Moses Harris, "The Union Cavalry," in MOLLUS, Commandery of Wisconsin, *War Papers* (3 vols.; Milwaukee, 1891–1903), 344.

glory. The effect on officers was the opposite of stimulating; General Richard Taylor wrote after the Civil War, "Take a boy of sixteen from his mother's apron strings, shut him up under constant surveillance for four years at West Point, send him out to a two-company post upon the frontier where he does little but play seven-up and drink whiskey at the sutler's, and by the time he is forty-five . . . he will furnish the most complete illustration of suppressed mental development of which nature is capable."[19]

Nevertheless, when the 1st and 2nd Cavalry were organized in 1855, the best officers in the service eagerly sought assignment to the two regiments, and their original roster of officers reads like a Civil War roll of honor. Five, including Robert E. Lee, Albert Sidney Johnston, and Joseph E. Johnston, became full generals in the Confederate army; George B. McClellan and George H. Thomas became army commanders for the Union and E. Kirby Smith and John B. Hood for the Confederacy, and more than thirty altogether, including William J. Hardee, Earl Van Dorn, George Stoneman, John Sedgwick, Richard Garnett, J. E. B. Stuart, and Lunsford Lomax, became corps, division, or brigade commanders in the two armies.

The low estate of all branches of the Regular Army was largely due to the unshakeable faith of the American people in the minuteman tradition. George Washington's declaration that the militia was a "destructive, expensive and disorderly mob," and the equally emphatic and unfavorable verdict of General-in-Chief Scott, based on his experience in three wars, that volunteers were an endless source of trouble and embarrassment to their commanders, undisciplined, fractious, and too often cowardly, were conveniently ignored.[20] In the eyes of Congress and of the people at large, the militia was the palladium of the Republic.

There was, however, little in the state of the militia in the decades between the War of 1812 and the Civil War to justify this

19. Quoted in Dabney H. Maury, *Recollections of a Virginian* (New York, 1894), 229.
20. Washington is quoted in H. Wager Halleck, *Elements of Military Art and Science* (New York, 1863), 147; on another occasion he said, "To place any dependence upon militia is, assuredly, resting upon a broken staff." Scott is quoted in C. W. Elliott's, *Winfield Scott: The Soldier and the Man* (New York, 1937), 718–19.

comfortable article of faith. In the northern states the story was much the same everywhere. The militia was either nonexistent, or it was an object of contempt and ridicule. The permanent military establishment of Indiana consisted of a quartermaster general and an adjutant general, each of whom had a stipend of one hundred dollars per year and whose troops existed only on paper, Indiana having disbanded its militia in 1834. For many years the state failed to requisition for the militia the allowance of weapons it was entitled to receive from the Federal Government, nor did it own any cartridges, knapsacks, canteens, or tents; except for a few hundred flintlock muskets, Indiana owned no military materiel of any kind.[21]

In Iowa, it had become a pleasant legislative tradition that the annual report of the Committee on Military Affairs to the legislature should be a mock-heroic performance, to provide an entertaining interlude amidst the labors of the general assembly. There were no laws on the statute book to provide for the enrollment and organization of the militia, and the few companies that had been organized and were kept in existence by private initiative obtained their arms from the state through a process of having the captain of each company file a bond with the governor "for their safe keeping and return," the captain having obtained a similar bond in his own favor from the members of his company.[22]

The four hundred men in the five companies of the Pennsylvania militia, the first to arrive in Washington after the fall of Fort Sumter, brought with them a total of thirty-four muskets and no ammunition. In Vermont, the militia was similarly inactive:

The state had ceased to make appropriations for the support of the militia. The "June trainings" had become a joke and most people believed that all need of military arts and munitions was soon to be ended by the approaching end of all wars. . . . All State laws requiring the enrolled militia to do military duty . . . had been repealed. . . . The uniformed companies had one by one disbanded; and in 1856 there . . . had not been for ten years, even the semblance of a military organization. . . . The military property of the State in January, 1861,

21. Catharine Merrill, *The Soldier of Indiana in the War for the Union* (2 vols.; Indianapolis, 1866–69), I, 7.
22. Cyril B. Upham, "Arms and Equipment for the Iowa Troops in the Civil War," *Iowa Journal of History and Politics*, XVI (1918), 3–6.

consisted of 957 muskets . . . 503 Colt's pistols, described by the Quartermaster General as "of no practical use whatever"; and 104 tents.[23]

In Ohio the militia was alive, but hardly well:

> The militia of Ohio, known as the corn-stalk militia, was . . . crude and absurd. . . . Each county contributed a division and was commanded by a grand officer with a magnificent staff. . . . Each of the townships furnished a company. The only uniformed persons were the general staff, colonels, and some few of the colonels' staff officers. Captains were distinguished by a great tin or brass plate tied in front of their beaver hats, usually with a tall red plume erect from the plate. . . . This, with a stout, crooked sword with black leather scabbard, made the panoply of a captain. The lieutenants were lucky if they possessed a sword. The privates wore their best Sunday suits. They were expected to carry a gun and many had squirrel rifles or shotguns, but guns were heavy things to tote so many substituted canes or cornstalks. . . . The pageant [of the annual muster] well repaid the rustic audiences and gave them something to talk about for the next six months.[24]

The day after his appointment to command the Ohio militia, General McClellan visited the state arsenal in Columbus to see what it contained. He found a few boxes of rusted, damaged smoothbore muskets, and in a large heap in one corner a pile of mildewed artillery harness. And that was all.

Of the 130,000 men in Wisconsin liable for service in the militia, 1,993 were actually enrolled for duty. The state "enjoyed the benefits of a militia law to a sufficient degree to permit the Adjutant General . . . to draw his annual salary [and] his stationery, and to enable him to make a report of the number of men subject to military duty, and the condition and whereabouts of a few hundred rusty guns, which were in the hands of a score of independent companies, whose duty it was to ornament the occasion of a 4th of July, or some other gala day."[25]

There were only a few companies of mounted militia in the North, the best known, perhaps, being the celebrated First Troop

23. G. G. Benedict, *Vermont in the Civil War* (2 vols.; Burlington, Vt., 1886–88), I, 9–12.
24. Stanley, *Personal Memoirs*, 13.
25. E. B. Quiner, *The Military History of Wisconsin* (Chicago, 1886), 48. The state's inventory of cavalry weapons consisted of 101 pistols, 80 "musketoons," and 40 sabers.

of the Philadelphia City Cavalry, which had had a distinguished record in the Revolutionary War. The Nittany Valley Company of Independent Dragoons, another Philadelphia unit, was armed with broadswords and horse pistols furnished by the state, but the members themselves bought and paid for their "handsome uniforms" and tack, which were in little danger of being soiled by use, inasmuch as the troopers met for drill no more than three or four times a year. When they did, "the crowd of spectators looked with admiration upon . . . [them], giving expression to their enthusiasm by huzzahs . . . loud and long. When the command was given to fire a volley . . . the scene beggar[ed] description. Women shrieked, children cried, the horses stood on their hind feet and pawed the air, and as the cloud of smoke lifted from the scene of confusion, more than one horseman was seen on the ground readjusting his accoutrements."[26]

The South had a greater fondness for peacetime soldiering and for soldiering in general than did the North. The predominantly agricultural economy and the presence of slave labor allowed the wealthier white males of the southern and border states more leisure than was common in the North. Thus, membership in a gaudily attired militia company, especially in a cavalry company, the exuberance of whose uniforms was limited only by the imaginations and pocketbooks of the members, was a cherished adjunct of a southern gentleman's way of life, equally satisfying to his romantic leanings, his gregariousness, and his taste for conviviality.[27] Hence the militia south of the Mason-Dixon line was considerably more numerous in proportion to the total white popula-

26. Dornblaser, *Sabre Strokes of the Pennsylvania Dragoons*, 9–10.
27. See also George C. Eggleston, *A Rebel's Recollections* (Bloomington, Ind., 1959), 58–59, describing a mounted company of Virginia militia: "A fine body of men, who spent three or four days each month partly in practicing a system of drill which . . . is as yet wholly undreamed of by any of the writers upon tactics, and partly in cultivating the social virtues over that peculiar species of feast known as a barbecue." The uniform of the Little Fork (Virginia) Rangers was "beautiful and conspicuous." It consisted of blue caps, "red cut-away jackets with yellow stripes across the front, and white trousers"; in winter, black trousers with red stripes down the seams replaced the white trousers. Woodford B. Hackley, *The Little Fork Rangers: A Sketch of Company "D" Fourth Virginia Cavalry* (Richmond, Va., 1927), 26.

tion, and in a far more efficient state, than was the moribund militia of the northern states. It is noteworthy that in response to the president's call for mounted regiments to serve in the Mexican War, Arkansas, Kentucky, and Tennessee each sent one regiment, Missouri and Texas each sent two, but there were none from the states north of the Ohio River.[28]

When the secession crisis came, the five mounted regiments of the Regular Army were far from the scene of action, scattered in driblets over the huge area from the Mississippi River to the Pacific and from the Canadian border to Mexico. Moreover, these regiments were officered largely by southerners, many of whom, placing loyalty to their states ahead of their allegiance to the national government, resigned their commissions.[29] Four of the five colonels, T. T. Fauntleroy, W. W. Loring, Robert E. Lee, and Albert Sidney Johnston, went with their states, as did three lieutenant colonels, G. B. Crittenden, William J. Hardee, and W. H. Emory. Many more officers of lesser rank—J. E. B. Stuart, John B. Hood, Richard S. Ewell, Fitzhugh Lee, Earl Van Dorn, E. Kirby Smith, and Joseph Wheeler, to mention only the most prominent —were to make their mark in the service of the Confederacy. Other cavalry officers, notably George H. Thomas and Edwin V. Sumner, left the cavalry to command brigades or divisions of infantry for the North.[30]

This, then, was the state of the cavalry at the outbreak of the Civil War. The national government had at its disposal five (to which it was shortly to add a sixth) regiments of mounted troops. By an Act of Congress of August 3, 1861, the six regiments were organized into a single, uniform mounted arm, to be known thenceforth as "Cavalry." The 1st and 2nd Dragoons became the 1st and 2nd Cavalry, the Regiment of Mounted Riflemen became

28. Brackett, *History of the United States Cavalry*, 60.
29. For example, of the 25 West Point graduates who were officers in the 2nd United States Cavalry in 1860, 17 were southerners. Thomas B. Van Horne, *The Life of Major-General George H. Thomas* (New York, 1882), 12. Of the approximately 900 officers of the Regular Army, 269 resigned to join the South and 26 were dismissed because they had joined the Confederate army. William A. Ganoe, *The History of the United States Army* (New York, 1942), 250.
30. Brackett, *History of the United States Cavalry*, 211.

the 3rd Cavalry, the 1st and 2nd Cavalry were renumbered and became the 4th and 5th Cavalry, and the new regiment became the 6th Cavalry.[31] With the exception of a few companies, the five existing regiments were stationed far from the eastern seaboard and were needed to hold in check the Indians of the West and Southwest.[32] All but a handful of the enlisted men remained with the colors, but many of the most experienced and capable officers departed. Apart from these regiments of Regulars, the national government could count on only a few ill-equipped or unequipped, and largely untrained, companies of mounted militia, whose utility in war was questionable.

Those officers of the Regular cavalry who remained faithful to the Union had been indoctrinated in the European cavalry tradition. They believed that a minimum of one, or even two or three years of training were needed to produce an efficient trooper.[33]

31. *Official Records*, Series III, Vol. 1, p. 403. The August, 1861, re-organization was bitterly resented by officers and men alike, and morale suffered. The oldest of the renamed and renumbered regiments had been in existence a mere twenty-seven years; nevertheless, all five regiments had developed a powerful sense of identity and regimental pride. The Dragoons and the Mounted Rifles were especially bitter, because they lost not only their distinctive names but also had to give up the colors that distinguished them from other branches of the service—orange for the Dragoons and green for the Mounted Rifles—and had to change over to the cavalry yellow. The War Department orders reorganizing the mounted regiments gave the Dragoons and Mounted Rifles permission to wear their distinctive colors until their existing uniforms wore out. The depth of their attachment to their uniqueness is attested by the fact that some of these uniforms acquired a miraculous durability, and the orange and green stripes and trim were still to be seen as late as 1865.

32. In the decade 1850–1860, there had been twenty-two distinct Indian wars. With the departure of most of the Regulars to the East, the Indians began plundering the settlements, farms, and wagon trains. Their attacks and raids became so constant and serious that in the Dakota Territory alone, some five thousand settlers abandoned their homes and farms. W. D. Sloan, "Iowa Cavalry—Sixth Regiment," *Civil War History*, III (1957), 189.

33. The argument for one year of training is made in Harris', "The Union Cavalry," 350; Frank W. Hess calls for one year "with the very best system of instruction and under the best instructors," in "The First Cavalry Battle at Kelly's Ford, Va.," *First Maine Bugle, Campaign III, Call 3* (1893), 7; Herr and Wallace, *The Story of the U.S. Cavalry*, 118, believe two years of training is required; and Nevins, in *The Improvised War*, 274, calls for three years' training.

They believed, further, that, as Captain George B. McClellan put it, "The strength of cavalry is in the spurs and sabre," that is, in the mounted charge.[34] If any of them, either as a group or as individuals, were troubled by the patent divergence between official doctrine and their own daily experience in the West, they kept their misgivings to themselves.[35] They were, to be sure, members of a most conservative and most authoritarian profession, in which expressions of heretical notions did not meet with encouragement. It is clear that none of these cavalry officers was sufficiently unorthodox to wonder, or daring to ask, whether the dramatic improvement in infantry firepower in the thirty years preceding the Civil War might not have made the traditional cavalry charge a deadly anachronism. It was suspected in 1861, notably by General Scott, that the broken, wooded terrain of Virginia would dictate major departures from European cavalry practice, but there was no theorist to predict the nature and extent of these departures, nor, until the war was already in its third year, did anyone come forward to propose workable alternatives to a doctrine that was equally inapplicable to modern conditions of weaponry and to the special conditions, both human and topographic, of the American Civil War.[36]

In an army which in 1861 had only two serving officers, both in their seventies, who had ever commanded in the field a military unit as large as a brigade, no one had any firm grasp on the technique of an effective combination of cavalry with the other

34. George B. McClellan, *Regulations and Instructions for the Field Service of the United States Cavalry in Time of War* (Philadelphia, 1861), 13. In fairness to McClellan, it should be added that a few pages earlier (p. 9) he had written, "The nature of cavalry service in the United States being quite different from that performed by any in Europe, we ought not to follow blindly any one system, but should endeavor to select the good features, and engraft them upon a system of our own."

35. As late as 1863, after two years of war had demonstrated beyond question that European shock tactics were totally unsuited to American conditions and had been rendered suicidal by modern infantry weapons, Confederate General Joseph Wheeler, an officer in the Regiment of Mounted Riflemen in the "Old Army," wrote, "The charge is the decisive action of cavalry." Joseph Wheeler, *A Revised System of Cavalry Tactics for the Use of the Cavalry and Mounted Infantry, C.S.A.* (Mobile, 1863), Pt. II, p. 66.

36. Carl B. Schurz, *Reminiscences of Carl Schurz* (2 vols.; New York, 1907–1908), II, 230–31.

arms.[37] Nor was there any indication that anyone had grappled with the fundamental question of what the primary mission of the cavalry in a modern war should be. Was its main function mere tactical support of infantry and artillery in battle, together with the traditional scouting and protective duties, or in addition or as an alternative to these might it not have the capability of fulfilling an independent strategic role of its own?

37. The two septuagenarians were Generals Scott and John A. Wool.

II

The Noise of the Captains

FROM THE ENACTMENT OF THE SOUTH CAROLINA ORDI-
nance of Secession, followed by the secession of six more southern
states and the formation of the Confederacy, almost to April 12,
1861, none but the congenital pessimists expected a war, and
none but the fire-eaters and hotheads wanted it. Not until years
later was the adjective "inevitable" attached to the war that began
with the firing on Fort Sumter, an "act of rash emotionalism" and
thus a fitting expression of the atmosphere of histrionics, bombast, and threats in the South that, as much as anything, made
the war "inevitable."[1] For five months, from Abraham Lincoln's
election to the presidency to within a few days of April 12, the
national government protested its pacific intentions and was careful to make no preparations for an eventuality it wanted above
all to avoid.

The bombardment of Fort Sumter ended all hesitations in
Washington. Three days later, on April 15, President Lincoln issued a proclamation that declared the existence in seven southern
states of "combinations too powerful to be suppressed" by the civil

1. The quoted phrase is from Nevins, *The Improvised War*, 73.

machinery of the government and called "forth . . . the militia of the several States . . . to the aggregate number of seventy-five thousand, in order to suppress said combinations and to cause the laws to be duly executed."[2] The next day, the War Department sent telegrams to the governors of the states that had not seceded to notify them of the number of regiments each was to furnish in response to the president's call; a total of ninety-four regiments were called for, seventeen from New York, six from Pennsylvania, and on down the list to one each from the smaller and the newer states. The call was spurned with varying degrees of rhetorical indignation by the governors of the border states, but the northern governors, riding a tidal wave of popular enthusiasm, called upon the militiamen of their states to assemble and organize to avenge the insult to the flag.

Governor John A. Andrew of Massachusetts, more farsighted than his colleagues, had begun in January to provide his militia with arms and equipment and had them drilling nightly. By the evening of April 15, four Massachusetts regiments had orders to be in Boston the next day, and before nightfall on the seventeenth, all four, and not just the two the War Department had asked for, were on their way to Washington. Governor Samuel J. Kirkwood of Iowa, like Lucius Quintus Cincinnatus of an earlier day, was doing his spring plowing when the War Department telegram requesting a single regiment of Iowa troops was delivered to him. He exclaimed to the messenger, "Why, the President wants a whole regiment of men! Do you suppose I can raise as many as that?" Within two weeks he had ten thousand men clamoring to be accepted and was wiring Washington, "For God's sake send us arms! We have the men."[3] And so it was throughout the North.[4]

Within a few weeks from April 15, Washington was crowded

2. *Official Records*, Series III, Vol. I, pp. 89–90.
3. Carl Sandburg, *Abraham Lincoln: The War Years* (4 vols.; New York, 1939), I, 221. See also Upham, "Arms and Equipment for the Iowa Troops," 11.
4. A typical situation: Robert H. Milroy, of Rensselaer, Indiana, later a major general of volunteers, in the predawn darkness of April 15, when news of the surrender of Fort Sumter arrived, had the courthouse bell rung, paraded the town with fife and drum, and had a full company signed up before breakfast. Indiana needed only eleven days to raise the six regi-

with an army of eager and enthusiastic militia, their training and equipment varying from poor to none.[5] In the West, George B. McClellan, commanding the Department of the Ohio, was preparing to invade West Virginia with an army of twenty thousand. Lack of cavalry components, however, left a conspicuous gap in the composition of these armies. The troops in Washington, grown by July to an army of thirty-six thousand under Irvin McDowell, were to fight and lose the battle of Bull Run with a cavalry component of a mere seven companies of Regulars. Posted on the right of the Federal line of attack at the start of the action, portions of the cavalry were sent to serve as escort and couriers for Generals McDowell, David Hunter, and Samuel P. Heintzelman and to support various batteries; when the Federal attack collapsed and turned into a rout, the seven companies covered the disorderly retreat.[6] McClellan, operating in mountainous, heavily wooded country, in which cavalry for scouting would have been of great value, could get none assigned to him by the War Department; his repeated requests for mounted troops were fruitless.[7] He obtained a few companies of mounted militia by appealing directly to the governors of the states of his department, but not until July did General Scott at last give him permission to muster in a solitary company of volunteer cavalry from Ohio for three years' service.[8]

---

ments requisitioned from the War Department; they were organized, formed into a brigade, and ready to march by April 27. Merrill, *The Soldier of Indiana*, 26, 15.

5. A "well informed journalist" wrote on May 15 that of the thirty thousand volunteers in Washington by that date, no more than two thousand would have been recognized as soldiers by a British or French general —nor, he might have added, by General Scott. Nevins, *The Improvised War*, 171.

6. Brackett, *History of the United States Cavalry*, 212. The seven companies were two of the 1st Cavalry, four of the 2nd, and one of the 2nd Dragoons. In command was Major Innis N. Palmer, 2nd Cavalry; his report on Bull Run is in *Official Records*, III, p. 393. Prior to the battle, General McDowell, in the absence of sufficient cavalry for scouting, had to rely on his engineer officers, on deserters, and on rumor for information about the enemy. Thiele, "The Evolution of Cavalry," 239.

7. Charles D. Rhodes, *History of the Cavalry of the Army of the Potomac* (Kansas City, Mo., 1900), 6; see also *Official Records*, III, 194, 211, 674, 742.

8. *Official Records*, III, 195, 208, 762; see also Thiele, "The Evolution of Cavalry," 33.

Until July 21, when the defeat at Bull Run was turned into a rout by the cry "The Black Horse Cavalry are coming!" the War Department wanted no volunteer cavalry.[9] Offers to supply mounted troops, including those from the governors of Indiana, Minnesota, Iowa, and Pennsylvania, were endorsed by Secretary Simon Cameron, "Accept no cavalry."[10] Under a law enacted in 1803, the president could call out the militia for not more than ninety days; hence the reluctance of the War Department to accept units that could not be adequately organized, equipped, or trained before the end of their brief period of service, is understandable.[11] But the unwillingness to accept volunteer cavalry was again in evidence when the president called for 42,034 volunteers to serve for three years or the duration of the war; the War Department orders issued the next day specified that these new formations were to consist of thirty-nine regiments of infantry and but one regiment of cavalry.[12] This flew in the face of Dennis Hart Mahan's dictum that the right proportion of cavalry to infantry was one to three in a "champagne," and one to five in "broken or mountainous country."

After a hard struggle with the War Department, Governor Richard Yates of Illinois obtained permission on May 30 to enlist

9. Captain James H. Stevenson, who arrived in Washington the day after the battle, talked with many of the men who had been in it. "These men," he reports, "astonished the crowd of eager listeners with some of the most marvelous stories of the prowess of the 'rebels.' . . . The Black Horse Cavalry were like demons mounted upon fiery dragons, and their swords fearful to think of." James H. Stevenson, "Boots and Saddles": A History of the First Volunteer Cavalry of the War, Known as the First New York (Lincoln) Cavalry (Harrisburg, Pa., 1879), 37–38.

10. For example, Official Records, Series III, Vol. I, p. 77.

11. "This was the time when many who ought to have known thought the war would be an affair of ninety days." Benjamin W. Crowninshield, A History of the First Regiment of Massachusetts Cavalry Volunteers (Boston, 1891), 4.

12. General Orders No. 15 in Official Records, Series III, Vol. I, pp. 145–46, 151–54. The men enlisted for the cavalry regiment were to furnish their own horses and tack, for the use of which they were to receive fifty cents per day. Also, in a compromise with democratic principle, it was specified that one third of the officers were to be appointed by the colonel from among the sergeants; the other two thirds were to be elected by the men. On May 3, the War Department also ordered the addition of eight infantry regiments and one regiment each of artillery and cavalry to the Regular Army, the last being the 3rd (later renumbered the 6th) United States Cavalry.

five companies of cavalry. When it became known that he had this authorization, ten companies, each with political backers, clamored to be mustered in, and Yates wrote to Secretary Cameron in pleading tones, "Now, Mr. Cameron, please do get General Scott to accept my ten cavalry companies. We want to be fully ready to take the starch out of the Missouri secession cavalry."[13] In June, Indiana was requested to enlist two companies of cavalry, and one of these was organized by Captain James R. Bracken. Men who were too late to join Bracken's company were offering from ten to two hundred dollars to take the places of men who had had the good fortune to be accepted.[14] The president himself ordered the acceptance of an Iowa regiment of cavalry—the 1st Iowa—made up of previously organized militia companies bearing such warlike names as the Hawkeye Rangers and the Black Plume Rangers. It was also due to presidential pressure on the War Department that volunteer cavalry regiments were accepted from Kentucky and Indiana.

One factor contributing to the War Department's unfriendly attitude toward volunteer cavalry was the desperate shortage of equipment and weapons. Lieutenant Colonel James W. Ripley, chief of the Ordnance Bureau, later reported that at the outbreak of the rebellion the government owned only 4,076 cavalry carbines, 27,192 pistols, 16,933 sabers, and 4,320 sets of horse accoutrements, nearly all of which were needed for the Regular cavalry.[15] The high cost—between five hundred thousand and six hundred thousand dollars in 1861—to equip and mount a cavalry regiment, the higher salaries of cavalry officers, and the number of artificers—blacksmiths and saddlers—needed to keep a cavalry regiment in the field also militated against the acceptance of mounted units. But the hostility to volunteer cavalry had deeper roots, as evidenced by the circumstances surrounding the formation of the 1st New York (Lincoln) Cavalry.

Carl Schurz, a veteran of the German revolutionary movements

---

13. *Ibid.*, 272.
14. Merrill, *The Soldier of Indiana*, 76.
15. Thiele, "The Evolution of Cavalry," 62. Ripley was an "infirm, incompetent veteran . . . whom the press soon dubbed Ripley van Winkle." Nevins, *The Improvised War*, 351.

of 1848, was active in Republican politics and was a man of influence among the many thousands of German immigrants in the United States. He was in Washington to solicit a diplomatic post from the new administration when an idea came to him.[16] He reasoned that the new armies would need an efficient body of cavalry. There was no time to train to the requisite level of competence men totally without experience. But in New York City and vicinity there were hundreds of able-bodied men of military age who had served in cavalry regiments in Germany, "and who had only to be armed and put upon horses to make cavalrymen immediately fit for active service." To lead them, a sufficient number of "experienced cavalry officers trained in the Prussian army or some other German army" were also available. Schurz was confident that he was well enough known in German emigré circles to be able to organize a regiment out of these materials. He explained his idea to the president, who liked the scheme and sent Schurz to Secretary Cameron to make the necessary arrangements. Cameron's reaction was favorable also, but he thought it best to obtain General Scott's sanction as well and sent Schurz to the general to get it.

Scott's first question, after Schurz had finished his explanation, gave a good indication of his attitude. His face assuming "a look of stern and somewhat impatient authority," he asked whether Schurz had had any experience in organizing and training mounted troops. Schurz replied in the negative, whereupon the crusty old general remarked that he had already deduced that to be the case. In his opinion, he went on, the war would be short and would be over long before any volunteer cavalry could be sufficiently trained to be able to take the field.[17] Moreover, he said, "The theater of war would be in Virginia, and the surface of Virginia was so cut up with fences and other obstructions as to make operations with large bodies of cavalry impracticable." The Regu-

16. The story of Schurz's scheme, his interviews with Lincoln, Cameron, and Scott, and the quotations in this paragraph and the next are from *Reminiscences of Carl Schurz*, II, 229–31.

17. These were strange words from the author of the "anaconda strategy." Perhaps, having decided that he wanted no volunteer cavalry and resenting the time he had to waste with a meddling amateur, Scott was not particularly choosy about the reasons he gave Schurz.

lar cavalry he already had, he added, was ample for the needs of the army, and Schurz's regiment would be superfluous. Schurz returned to Cameron and the president with his report and both of them told him that Scott "was taking too narrow a view" of the situation; they overrode the objections of the professional head of the army and authorized Schurz to go forward with his scheme.[18]

It is instructive to follow the fortunes of Schurz's regiment as it struggled to come into being. As one of the earliest off the mark, and with a complex parentage, the travails of the 1st New York were more severe and more unusual than those of most other cavalry regiments, but they illustrate perfectly the state of innocence and confusion in which the North went to war.

While Schurz was making the rounds of the offices in Washington, the following advertisement appeared in the New York *Tribune* of April 16:

WANTED: A Captain of Cavalry
The Cavalry Department of the Northern army is, without a doubt, the one most lacking in efficiency. To supply this flagrant need is the desire of several gentlemen of this city, two of whom have in the handsomest manner offered to supply horses and equipments for the first fifty volunteers who shall be unable to mount and equip themselves. All that is needed now to effect an organization is a competent leader, and to any one sufficiently well versed in tactics to command such a troop, a superb horse, half brother to the celebrated Patchen, and a full suit of regimentals, will be guaranteed.[19]

18. Schurz's authorization to proceed, given him on May 1, read as follows: "To the Governors of the Several States: I have authorized Col. Carl Schurz to raise and organise a volunteer regiment of cavalry. For the purpose of rendering it as efficient as possible he is instructed to enlist principally such men as have served in the same arm before. The Government will provide the regiment with arms, but cannot provide the horses and accoutrements. For these necessaries we rely upon the patriotism of the States and the citizens thereof and for this purpose I take the liberty of requesting you to afford Colonel Schurz your aid in the execution of this plan." *Official Records*, Series III, Vol. I, pp. 140–41. Implicit in this document, or at least in the discussions leading up to it, is a colonelcy for Schurz. As will be seen later, Schurz did not consider himself restricted to the recruitment of men with previous cavalry experience.
19. William H. Beach, *The First New York (Lincoln) Cavalry* (New York, 1902), 9. Another member of the regiment has a different account of the origin of these companies. He writes that "an eccentric gentleman, who had sold jewelry in Maiden Lane, thinking the government might need an extra regiment or so of cavalry before the war ended, had inserted

So many responded to the advertisement that the sponsors called a meeting, which was attended by 150 applicants. A committee was formed and active recruiting began under the management of men "connected with wealthy and prominent families."[20] In a short time, enough recruits to form four companies had signed the rolls and the solicitation of votes by and on behalf of candidates for the lieutenancies and captaincies in the four companies was in full swing.[21]

Bayard Clark, formerly a colonel of cavalry in the Regular Army and later a member of Congress, volunteered to go to Washington to persuade the War Department to accept the four companies. His reception by Cameron was as frosty as possible. The secretary, Clark reported, "refused authority to raise the regiment, was undecided as to the necessity that would arise for cavalry, had his prejudices, and so had General Scott. The latter, Cameron said, had no faith in volunteer cavalry; it was a very expensive arm of the service; it would open an immense field for fraud and corruption. . . . We could not always depend on the country we advanced into for forage, and the necessity of a supply large enough for the animals would so increase the trains as not only to impede the movements of the army, but to quadruple the cost of transportation, and render it extremely dangerous to advance far beyond its depots."[22]

Schurz, meanwhile, having received Cameron's authorization to recruit his regiment of German veterans, heard that several companies of cavalry were forming in Philadelphia. He decided to stop there on his way to New York, to try to enroll these units in his regiment. His salesmanship was anything but low-keyed. He announced that since his regiment was the only one the government had agreed to accept, the Philadelphians' only chance of

---

in the Herald an advertisement, proposing a meeting . . . for the purpose of considering measures to raise a regiment of volunteer cavalry." F. Colburn Adams, *The Story of a Trooper* (New York, 1865), 6.

20. Beach, *First New York (Lincoln) Cavalry*, 10.

21. The "Act to authorize the employment of volunteers" of July 22, 1861, which provided for the first call of three-year volunteers, specified that company officers (lieutenants and captains) were to be elected by their men and were in turn to elect the field-grade officers.

22. Adams, *The Story of a Trooper*, 21–22.

getting into the army as cavalry was to join up with him. He inti-
mated that if they joined his regiment, they would have "the right
to a major, and also a voice in the appointment of other field and
staff officers."[23] The success of his persuasion was minimal, for
only the partly formed "Philadelphia Light Cavalry" company accepted the invitation.

This company had an interesting history. James E. Stevenson,
former sergeant in the 1st United States Dragoons, noticed one
day an advertisement in a Philadelphia newspaper for "a person
competent to instruct a troop of cavalry in the United States tactics."[24] He offered his services and took charge of a score of troopers, "all fine-looking young men, dressed in French cavalry uniforms, wearing sabers and revolvers, and mounted on fine horses,"
which they rode and managed in expert fashion. The troop took
possession of an unused race course near Germantown and began
serious training under Stevenson's direction. There was dismounted drill in the morning, mounted drill in the afternoon,
guard duty at night, and Regular Army discipline was enforced.
Nevertheless, the young men had a pleasant life:

Hundreds of ladies and gentlemen in carriages and on horses, came
to witness the mounted drills . . . the ladies waving their handkerchiefs and the gentlemen cheering when we performed any evolution
which excited their admiration. . . . it was an animating sight to be-
hold the grandstand filled to overflowing with young ladies, the elite
of society . . . their beautiful faces radiant with pleasurable excitement, as they witnessed the dashing horsemanship of the gallant
young troopers. . . . We generally went through the saber exercise in
open order, in front of the stand, so that the ladies might be enabled
to watch the different individuals as they executed the cuts, thrusts
and parries, at the word of command.

But the Philadelphia Light Cavalry, as the troop called itself, did
not fare equally well in the more important task of attracting

23. Stevenson, *"Boots and Saddles,"* 14.
24. This and the quotations which follow are from *Ibid.,* 10–15. Stevenson reports, "We occasionally gave exhibition drills, for the purpose of
exciting the young people present to join us; and as nothing of the kind
had ever been seen by the people of these parts, our horsemanship and
manoeuvers elicited unbounded applause. The young troopers would frequently electrify the assemblage with a stirring chorus of patriotic song;
after which we were sure to have a large increase of visitors." *Ibid.,* 16.

enough recruits to bring their numbers up to the minimum needed to form a company. Their drillmaster reports that they "rode all over the country, among the farmers' sons, in quest of recruits, and visited the towns and villages in several counties adjoining Philadelphia, where we heard of mounted 'Home Guards' to see if we could induce any of them to join us. Our gay uniforms, flashing sabers and prancing chargers were universally admired, and many patriotic young men would fain have joined us, but the conditions imposed by the government were thought too hard to be complied with." Their recruiting efforts a failure, the troop decided to disband, but a few of them, led by Stevenson, joined a squadron of two companies that Captain W. H. Boyd was assembling, entirely at his own expense. This squadron took over the promise of the Philadelphia Light Cavalry to join Schurz's regiment.

On his arrival in New York after his Philadelphia visit Schurz communicated with Frederick von Schickfuss, who had had an honorable record as a cavalry officer in Germany, and arranged to have him begin recruiting former cavalrymen of German extraction. Within a short time von Schickfuss had enough men for four companies. They were generally spoken of as "Germans," and indeed, the majority of them were of German birth, but there were numerous veterans of the Polish and Hungarian wars of independence among them, and one recruit was reputed to be "closely connected with the royal family of Russia. For some misdemeanor he had been obliged to leave his own country. Under an assumed name, he enlisted as a private in Company E."[25]

The four companies von Schickfuss raised were less than half the number Schurz needed, but now he learned of the four "American" companies whose application to be accepted had been urged without success by Colonel Clark.[26] The obvious community of interests between the two groups provided the basis of an agreement. Schurz called on the "Americans," and invited them to join his regiment. They were inclined to accept, provided they were given

25. Beach, *First New York (Lincoln) Cavalry*, 27.
26. The "Americans" had a sizeable contingent of men of English, Scottish, and Irish birth, "wild, turbulent fellows . . . who gave a good deal of trouble to their officers." Stevenson, *"Boots and Saddles,"* 56–58.

a fair share of the regimental offices. Schurz offered them the right to elect the major of their battalion, as well as the posts of regimental quartermaster and regimental surgeon. The "Germans" too were to elect their own major, and the remaining field and staff officers were to be appointed by Schurz. Agreement was reached on this basis, and the union of the eight companies was effected.

But now a fresh complication arose. Schurz received word from Washington that he had been appointed United States minister to Spain. Hence the regiment, still lacking four companies, had to find a colonel as well. Lieutenant George D. Bayard of the Regular Army, then serving as an instructor at West Point, was suggested as a possibility, and he was offered the post. He was unable to accept and recommended that the offer be made to Captain Joshua T. Owen, also of the Regular Army and a fellow instructor at West Point. Owen was receptive, but explained that he could not accept unless he was granted leave of absence from his regiment. It was thus decided that Lieutenant Ezra H. Bailey, a member of the regiment-to-be, should go to Washington and obtain it for him.

In Washington, Bailey was unable to gain admittance to see the adjutant general, who was too busy to meet with him, and was likewise turned away at General Scott's office.[27] He waited until after office hours and followed the general to his home, where he was eventually admitted. Bailey explained his errand; not surprisingly, the general "seemed to be in a bad humor" and told him flatly that an officer of the Regular Army would not be released to serve with volunteers. The general "didn't believe in volunteer cavalry anyhow . . . and then it would take longer to get . . . [volunteers] ready for efficient service than it would to put down the rebellion."

A crestfallen Bailey left "the august presence with hanging head and drooping spirits." Strolling along, trying to think of something he could do, he found himself in front of the White House. On an impulse, he walked in and asked to see the president, "trusting vaguely that something advantageous to his mission would be the result." Admitted to Lincoln's office, Bailey told

27. Bailey's visit to Washington is described in *Ibid.*, 21–23; the quotations in this and the next paragraph are from that source.

the president his difficulties. The harassed chief executive replied with a smile, "I can't see why you should have so much difficulty about getting a colonel. Why, I could supply you with a hundred, from Illinois alone, inside of a week." He urged Bailey to return to New York and continue the search for a qualified officer and promised to order the acceptance of the regiment as soon as it was fully organized.

When Bailey reported on the outcome of his journey to Washington, someone suggested that the colonelcy be offered to Philip Kearny. This was done, but Kearny declined the offer and recommended for the post Andrew T. McReynolds of Grand Rapids, Michigan, whom he had known as a captain of cavalry in the Mexican War. The officers and most of the men met to discuss McReynolds' qualifications and voted to tender him the colonelcy. McReynolds accepted, and Schurz formally endorsed over to him, as if it had been a negotiable instrument, his letter of authorization from Secretary Cameron.

The regiment, not yet in being, now had a colonel chosen by itself, but even yet its troubles were not over. It was deemed desirable to obtain official ratification of Schurz's transfer of his commission, and a delegation of officers headed by McReynolds went to Washington for that purpose.

Arriving in Washington [on June 12] the officers called upon the President. He referred them to the secretary of war. The secretary . . . [said that] there was no need of proceeding further in the raising of the regiment, or of raising any cavalry whatever, as the war would be over in ninety days. . . . they went again to see the President . . . [who] listened to the statement of their affairs and then endorsed the papers: "Hon. Secretary of War: Please say to Col. A. T. McReynolds that when he will present the cavalry regiment according to the within authority, they will be received under him as they would have been under Col. Schurz." . . . With this the delegation returned to the secretary . . . [who] lost his temper, and . . . declined to do anything more in the matter without the approval of General Scott. The general was so pressed with business that it was difficult to see him . . . [but] the delegation . . . obtained an audience long enough to secure a brief note from the general approving the acceptance of . . . [the] regiment . . . the secretary had not expected this. But he could not disregard it, and he gave a qualified approval . . . "on condition that the whole regiment be at Washington . . . by the first day of August."[28]

28. Beach, *First New York (Lincoln) Cavalry*, 20–22.

Higher authority was not the only source of the regiment's troubles. Recruits were coming in a satisfactory rate, including a full company raised in the Syracuse area and another from Colonel McReynolds' home town in Michigan. The regimental camp was pleasant and the weather propitious. The men, as yet without uniforms or arms, were subjected to a minimum of drill and discipline and enjoyed a life that, by general agreement, was a "big picnic."[29] But there were unpleasant incidents involving officers "whose unfortunate habits led them into difficulties," and others "who considered an enlisted man a proper subject for abuse and profanity." One such officer was handed a document, "numerously signed, and not expressed in the most elegant and courteous phraseology," to inform him that he was not fit to associate with patriots and gentlemen, and that his presence was a detriment to the regiment.[30] More serious was the quarrel that inevitably broke out between the "Americans" and the "Germans," arising from an insulting remark made by one of the former to one of the latter. It was all McReynolds could do to prevent open warfare between the two groups. The incident led to the decision to remove the Americans to a separate camp; "Bellevue Garden was chosen, and very soon the Americans were under canvas on the banks of the East River, where they enjoyed good bathing and plenty of fresh air."[31]

Another military organization, made up largely of Germans and calling itself "Lincoln Greens," was encamped near the Germans of the Lincoln Cavalry. The latter decided that the Lincoln Greens were poaching on the name of *their* regiment. Taunts and insults were exchanged and the ill-feeling between the two groups grew.

One day there were sounds of war in the usually quiet precincts of Elm Park. A lager beer saloon, close by, was the focus of excitement, and the representatives from Hungary, Germany, Poland, Prussia and Austria were in a perfect frenzy. Men and officers were seen buckling on their sabers and pistols, and hastening to the scene of the uproar, and soon there was a regular pitched battle going on between the rival parties, who each claimed "Lincoln" as their patron. . . . not much harm was done after all. . . . several Teutons on both sides were slight-

29. *Ibid.*, 29.
30. *Ibid.*, 27.
31. Stevenson, *"Boots and Saddles,"* 29.

ly wounded, and there was a lively foot race as our Germans demoralized their enemies and pursued them across the fields into their own
camp.[32]

These were distractions from the more serious business of filling up the ranks and getting each company mustered in when it
reached the prescribed minimum. This process created problems
whose solution called for ingenuity, guile, and a lack of scruple.
The uncertainties and delays that beset the early days of the regiment caused numerous desertions; the more impatient patriots,
afraid that the rebellion would be crushed before the Lincoln Cavalry took the field, departed to join regiments with better prospects
of getting into the war while it lasted. Consequently, when a company thought to be ready for muster found itself a few men short
of the minimum, there was a lively hunt for recruits to fill up the
deficit; if that failed, "There were instances where a few men
would be borrowed for the purpose of standing in the ranks and
answering invented names until the muster could be completed,
when they would be allowed to return to their own companies. It
was reported that in a few cases good wages were paid to outsiders
for taking part in this brief service."[33]

Mustering officers were under orders not to pass any recruit
"who is in years apparently over forty-five or under eighteen, or
who is not in physical strength and vigor," specifications which
left much to be desired from the standpoint of precision, and
mustering officers were anything but strict in applying them.
Nevertheless, men were at times rejected.[34] When this happened
to Captain Boyd's two companies in Philadelphia, reducing their
numbers well below the minimum, Boyd "went off to Camden,
N. J., after a squad of recruits he had heard of there."

These he had to purchase from those in charge of them, and being
short of cash, he gave his gold watch in payment. He had parted with
a valuable horse a short time before for a similar purpose. Some of
those fellows got away from him before he got them to a place of safekeeping, but a sufficient number remained to warrant . . . appearing
before the mustering officers again. . . . [They] began to reject again,
and the Captain, fearing another failure, sent several trustworthy men

32. *Ibid.*, 32.
33. Beach, *First New York (Lincoln) Cavalry*, 25–26.
34. *Official Records*, Series III, Vol. I, p. 68.

to procure temporary substitutes. This they did by offering a few dollars apiece to some laboring men, telling them that they would be allowed to skedaddle as soon as they got mustered in. The ruse worked well, and soon the roll was completed and the troop mustered in.[35]

After its painful birth, the 1st New York (Lincoln) Cavalry, as it wished to be known, was at last ready, or nearly so, to join the army. Other cavalry regiments had the good fortune of coming into being in more conventional ways, if, indeed, the adjective "conventional" can be used to describe any activity connected with the Civil War in its early stages, for the armies were raised in a country in which, in the words of a European visitor, there was "a horror of all trammels, systems and uniformity."[36]

Within a few days after April 12 it became apparent that the understaffed, overworked, and routine-ridden War Department, headed by a secretary whose administrative skills it would be flattery to call modest, was unequal to the task of dealing with the multitude of massive and complex problems demanding instant solutions. The able and ambitious secretary of the treasury, Salmon P. Chase of Ohio, stepped into the breach. He inspired the May 3 call for 42,034 volunteers to serve for three years, and if he had had his way, the call would have been for 65,000 men. He was then directed by the president to recommend a plan for organizing the new levies. His two military advisers, W. B. Franklin and Irvin McDowell, recommended that the new three-year regiments be apportioned among the states on the basis of their congressional representation, that they be made part of the Regular Army and given national numerals, that their officers be nominated by the governors and commissioned by the president, and that each regiment be made up of three battalions, one of which was to remain at a base camp to receive and train recruits, so that the two battalions in the field could always be kept up to full strength with trained men. From the standpoint of military efficiency, the scheme had everything to recommend it, but its adoption in the United States of 1861 was a psychological and political impossibility. The "national numerals" was perhaps the principal

35. Stevenson, "Boots and Saddles," 34–35.
36. Auguste Laugel, The United States During the Civil War, 1861–1865 (Bloomington, Ind., 1961), 179.

stumbling block. Chase rejected the whole plan with the remark that he would "rather have no regiments raised in Ohio than that they should not be known as Ohio regiments."[37]

The rejection of the Franklin-McDowell proposals meant that the new regiments would be raised under a system that had worked far from well in the Revolutionary War, the War of 1812, and the Mexican War and was to creak and groan under the demands of a war fought on a vastly greater scale than any that had gone before. The price in wasted lives and treasure was enormous, but Chase was undoubtedly right in his view that the people would not have accepted the idea of a national army divested of local ties. Hence the Union army in the Civil War was made up almost entirely of regiments whose identity was established by the name of the state from which they came, and the number they received by virtue of their chronological position among the regiments of cavalry supplied by their respective states. Many of these regiments had sizeable out-of-state components; for example, the 7th Kansas had three full companies and parts of two others recruited in Illinois, and one company recruited in Ohio. There were two Indiana companies in the 9th Illinois, and men from Indiana, Iowa, and Michigan in the 8th Illinois. The 5th West Virginia had companies from Ohio and Pennsylvania; the 5th Iowa had Missouri, Minnesota, and Nebraska companies; the 2nd New York was made up of men from New York, New Jersey, Connecticut, Vermont, Pennsylvania, and Indiana, and, as has been mentioned, the 1st New York contained companies from Michigan and Pennsylvania. Nonetheless, each of these regiments was firmly identified with the state whose name it bore.[38]

The reluctance of the War Department to accept volunteer

37. Nevins, *The Improvised War*, 169; see also Upton, *The Military Policy of the United States*, 233.
38. The 1st New York (Lincoln) Cavalry was originally intended to be known as the 1st United States Volunteer Cavalry and was to be a volunteer regiment in the Federal service, with no state affiliation. In keeping with the decision that volunteer regiments were to be identified with the states in which they were raised, the regiment was assigned to New York, but it was first necessary to settle a controversy with the governor of Pennsylvania, who claimed it for his state on the strength of Captain Boyd's two companies from Philadelphia. Stevenson, *"Boots and Saddles,"* 61–62.

cavalry having evaporated in the aftermath of the battle of Bull
Run, there were thirty-one such cavalry regiments in the Union
army by August 31, another nineteen by December 1, and by the
year-end, a mere five months after the battle, no fewer than
eighty-two regiments of cavalry—nearly ninety thousand mounted
troops—had been mustered into the Federal service.[39] Aside from
the 1st New York, a few units forced on the War Department in
June and July, and the single regiment authorized by the May 3
call, all these regiments were raised in response to two successive
calls, on July 2 and August 4, each for three hundred thousand
men.

  With many variations in detail, the inception of the eighty-
two regiments followed a fairly uniform pattern. A citizen who in
his own estimation enjoyed sufficient local prominence to attract
recruits solicited from the governor of his state, or the secretary
of war, or the president, authority to raise a regiment of cavalry,
or in some cases was asked by the governor to do so. More often
than not political considerations were a factor in the quest for and
the granting of these authorizations. The colonelcy of a regiment,
which either explicitly or implicitly was to be the reward of success, had a present value in prestige and an even greater future
value in political coin, that no colonel-to-be, however patriotic,
was likely to ignore.[40] Politics was clearly the basis of the authorizations granted to supporters of the administration in Congress to raise one or more regiments, which they in turn parceled
out among their loyal constituents back home.[41] When it is remembered that at first enlistment was on a wholly voluntary basis
—bounties and the draft came later—and that the government
lacked not only the powers of compulsion but even the propagan-
da apparatus that combined with compulsion to produce the men
for the armies of World Wars I and II, it will be evident that a

  39. Russell F. Weigley, *Quartermaster General of the Union Army: A
Biography of Montgomery C. Meigs* (New York, 1959), 256; Upton, *The
Military Policy of the United States*, 438.
  40. Upton, *The Military Policy of the United States*, 166.
  41. Examples are Senator Benjamin F. Wade (2nd Ohio), Senator Ira
Harris (6th New York), Congressman F. W. Kellogg (6th and 7th Michigan), and Senator John Sherman (Sherman Brigade, including a battalion
of cavalry).

politically oriented system was the only means the government had at its disposal to raise the armies it needed. And whatever the theoretical and practical weaknesses of the system, it did produce 2,700,000 men for the Union armies before the war ended.[42]

But like every other activity in what Allan Nevins has justly called an improvised war, the raising of regiments proceeded in an atmosphere of chaos. The president, secretary of war, favored members of Congress, and governors of loyal states all granted authorizations to raise regiments, and each of these powers and principalities acted with such a blithe disregard for the others that regiments of infantry and cavalry, and batteries of artillery were raised, or failed to be raised, in a disorganized welter of conflicting jurisdictions, competition, exaggerated claims and promises, and downright mendacity. On August 21, 1861, Governor Andrew Curtin of Pennsylvania, driven to desperation, wrote the president that he had been requested by the War Department to raise ten regiments and was trying to raise them in competition with fifty-eight individuals who also had authority from Washington to raise regiments in his state. The result, he wrote, was confusion and delay, not a single one of the sixty-eight potential units having succeeded in filling its ranks.[43] Curtin and several other governors, from motives that were partly disinterested and partly political, objected bitterly to the president and the secretary of war granting commissions to raise regiments to individuals who then competed for recruits with the governors' appointees. As a result of these protests, Lincoln, with his ever lively sense of political realities, agreed in 1862 that Washington would thereafter grant such commissions only with the approval of the governors concerned.

The key figure in the recruitment of a regiment was the gentleman who had been given the authority to undertake the project, the entrepreneur whose standing in the community, together with his ingenuity, drive, and competence determined the success of

42. Thomas L. Livermore, *Numbers and Losses in the Civil War in America, 1861–1865* (Bloomington, Ind., 1957), 1. Livermore's exact number is 2,668,000, not counting 230,000 militia and "emergency men" serving for short periods.

43. Meneely, *The War Department, 1861*, pp. 211–12.

the recruiting effort. In this context, the word "competence" was not thought of in any military sense. With few exceptions, an individual's supposed ability to command a regiment, or even his physical ability to bear up under the hardships of field command, did not appear to enter into the decision of whether to grant him recruiting authority. The essential qualification, aside from the right political connections, was the candidate's ability to persuade the authorities that he could attract enough recruits to make up a regiment.

Governors John Andrew of Massachusetts and Edwin D. Morgan of New York were exceptionally careful in selecting candidates for colonelcies, but even they made some egregious mistakes. Other governors were much less careful and issued recruiting commissions to the manifestly unfit, doing so at times on frivolous grounds. To cite only one example, Charles W. Doubleday was made colonel of the 2nd Ohio because "he had acquired some miltary experience while serving as a member of a filibustering expedition against Nicaragua."[44]

Judged by its results, the system was not an unqualified success. It could and did produce colonels like the

retired merchant of New York, filled with the vanity of wearing the uniform, who spent twenty thousand dollars to raise a regiment of cavalry, of which he was, of course, commissioned colonel. His camp was near us; he was never there. . . . he displayed his uniform continually on . . . Pennsylvania Avenue and in the barrooms of the great hotels. He was present at all the receptions at the White House, at all the evening parties of the ministers, always most attentive to the wives of the high officials and of the senators. Radically incompetent of commanding his regiment, much less of leading it into battle, but sustained by the double power of money and of political influence, he was nominated brigadier-general.[45]

And F. Colburn Adams, himself a member of the 1st New York, wrote after the war that "colonels' commissions were given, and men authorized to raise regiments of cavalry who had never mounted a horse; who were physically as well as mentally unfit to be soldiers. . . . I have known not less than a dozen colonels of cavalry loitering about the streets and hotels of Washington for

44. Luman H. Tenney, *War Diary* (Cleveland, 1914), IX.
45. Regis deTrobriand, *Four Years with the Army of the Potomac* (Boston, 1889), 89.

weeks and months, not one of whom gave the slightest thought to his men."[46]

Colonel William Halstead, a prominent member of the New Jersey bar and a man of considerable political eminence, "was approaching his seventieth year, and scarcely possessed the strength and endurance requisite to fulfill the arduous duties of his new profession. But he . . . certainly proved that he possessed the ability to raise . . . [a] regiment."[47] In August, 1861, Halstead received authority to raise what was to become the 1st New Jersey; within a month, ten full companies of the regiment were encamped in Washington. To raise a regiment in a month was one thing, but to command a thousand men, few of whom had any notion of the ABC's of soldiering, or even of the demands of life in camp, was well beyond Colonel Halstead's capabilities. The historian of the regiment describes the result:

The commanding officer had never had an opportunity of studying the complicated discipline of camp life, or the proper manner of meeting its requirements. . . . The most ordinary precautions of sanitary police were neglected, and the accumulating filth of the camp, festering in the scorching sun . . . [combined] with the pestilential damps that exhaled at nightfall from . . . [Rock Creek] and the [Potomac] river. . . . Drill . . . there was little, and that little almost a voluntary matter with officers and men; and there was no distinct authoritative announcement of duties, no promptly enforced penalty for disobedience. . . . The colonel . . . becoming ill from the effect . . . of camp life, took a sick leave, and retired for a time to Washington.[48]

The officers and men of the 10th New York, commanded by Colonel John C. Lemmon, were divided by "the most intense partisan warfare" into pro- and anti-Lemmon factions, the latter openly declaring their intentions of ousting the colonel from his position, on the grounds of incompetence and old age.[49] The ignorance or incompetence of a Colonel Halstead or a Colonel Lem-

46. Adams, The Story of a Trooper, 28–30. Adams does not explain what he himself was doing in Washington to enable him to observe the dozen colonels of cavalry who were absent from their regiments.

47. Henry R. Pyne, The History of the First New Jersey Cavalry (Trenton, 1871), 2.

48. Ibid., 19–20.

49. Noble D. Preston, History of the 10th Regiment of Cavalry, New York State Volunteers (New York, 1892), 21.

mon were responsible for more fatalities among their men than were the bullets and sabers of the enemy. Fortunately for the Union, and even more fortunately for the men in the ranks, the Halsteads, Lemmons, and political colonels were in a minority. At the opposite end of the scale were men like Colonel Lemuel B. Platt of the 1st Vermont. In the summer of 1861, Platt proposed to Governor Erastus Fairbanks that he be given authority to raise a regiment of cavalry. In the absence of a state law permitting the levying of mounted troops, the governor referred Platt to Washington. Platt called on Secretary Cameron and, in reply to the secretary's question about the extent of his military experience, explained that many years before he had attended a three-day militia muster and had passed two of those days in the guardhouse. In his direct New England manner, he told Cameron that he did not consider himself qualified to train and command the regiment, but that he would guarantee to raise it in forty days. Greatly impressed by Platt's candor, Cameron handed him a colonel's commission and the needed authorization. In forty-two days from that date, the 1st Vermont was at Camp Ethan Allen in Burlington, fully organized, officered, uniformed, and mounted on the Morgan horses for which the state was famous. Platt had kept his part of the bargain and resigned when the regiment was about to take the field.[50]

There was, too, the colonel of an unidentified Maine regiment, who, ordered to appear before an examination board, requested the privilege of making a statement to the board.

He was a large, heavy man, about sixty years of age, manifestly unfit for active service, which he frankly admitted. But he was a man of influence in his state, and had raised and taken command of his regiment as a patriotic duty. He declared that forty years ago military work was his delight, that he loved to train with the militia, to wear the uniform, and prance about on horseback to the sound of martial music; but actual war was a different thing, for which he frankly confessed himself entirely unprepared. . . . He added frankly that he was too old to learn, and proposed to send in his resignation at once, if the board would suspend proceedings and save him from further humiliation by recommending its acceptance.[51]

50. Benedict, *Vermont in the Civil War*, II, 533–34.
51. Wilson, *Under the Old Flag*, I, 78–79. The function and operations of examining boards will be described later in the text.

William McLaughlin, who recruited and commanded the cavalry battalion of the Sherman Brigade of Ohio, was a veteran of the Mexican War, more than seventy years old in 1861, "but his ardent patriotism induced him to enter the field. . . . The hardships and privations of active service proved too much for his physical endurance, and six months after leaving Ohio he died."[52]

There were many like Platt, the nameless Maine colonel, and William McLaughlin. Whatever they lacked in military qualifications, they made up for in patriotism and zeal. In their origins and personalities, they represented all the variety of American life. Abel D. Streight of the 51st Indiana Mounted Infantry was a publisher; Benjamin H. Grierson of the 6th Illinois was a teacher of music, band conductor, piano tuner, composer and arranger, painter, poet, and songwriter and joined to these cultural accomplishments a profound distrust of horses. Charles Jennison of the 7th Kansas was a physician, John Goddard of the 1st Maine a lumberman, Mexican War veteran Edward C. Williams of the 9th Pennsylvania was a bookbinder, and FitzHenry Warren of the 1st Iowa had been first assistant postmaster general and was an associate editor of the New York *Tribune*. Not surprisingly, the law and politics, in many cases joined in the same individual, had the largest number of representatives. Indeed, a cynical reporter for the New York *Times* wrote of these gentlemen, from the rank of colonel on down, "Each colonel comes into the field expecting to run for Congress, each Captain has his eye upon a seat in the state legislature, each lieutenant is looking forward to the hour when he can appeal to the patriotism of the public for the position of justice of the peace, constable, pound master or something."[53]

One of the more unusual representatives of the breed of lawyer-politician turned colonel-of-cavalry was Frank Wolford of the 1st Kentucky. Known to his men as "Old Meat-Axe," Wolford had

---

52. Wilbur F. Hinman, *The Story of the Sherman Brigade* (Alliance, Ohio, 1897), 44, 839.

53. Bruce Catton, *Grant Moves South* (Boston, 1960), 398. There was, however, at least one reversal of the quest of a colonelcy as a stepping stone to political office. James S. Jackson of Kentucky resigned his seat in the U.S. House of Representatives, obtained authorization from the president to recruit a regiment of cavalry, and raised and commanded the 3rd Kentucky. R. M. Kelly, Thomas Speed, and Alfred Pirtle, *The Union Regiments of Kentucky* (Louisville, 1897), 133.

served as a private in the Mexican War. He was inordinately addicted to speechmaking, which frequently took the form of three- and four-hour harangues. Utterly contemptuous of the outward trappings of rank, Wolford's usual "uniform" was an old red hat and a brown jeans coat, and his face was normally "undefiled by water or razor." He also had tactical ideas that were distinctively his own, being credited, perhaps unjustly, with such commands as "Huddle up," "Scatter out," and "Git up and git"; he "cared but little for prescribed forms in manoeuvering his men, so he got them in shape to suit himself."[54]

Wolford was not the only odd fish who refused to allow the exalted status of a colonel of cavalry to inhibit the expression of his individuality. John Goddard of the 1st Maine issued orders to his regiment prohibiting the use of profanity and followed this up with the announcement that he would not recognize any commissioned or noncommissioned officer who had not signed a temperance pledge.[55] The German-born colonel of the 15th Pennsylvania, which contained several companies of his compatriots, limited his official functions in camp to holding special reviews of the German companies and making patriotic speeches to them in their mother tongue.

In a class apart were the officers of the Regular Army who managed to overcome the opposition of the adjutant general's office and were permitted to accept commissions as colonels of volunteer cavalry, and men who had resigned from the Regular Army before the war, but reentered the service when offered the colonelcy of a volunteer cavalry regiment. Richard H. Rush, formerly a captain of artillery in the Regular Army, recruited and commanded the 6th Pennsylvania, known for a time as Rush's Lancers. Cavalry Lieutenant George D. Bayard, after declining the colonelcy of the 1st New York, was allowed to become colonel of the 1st Pennsylvania. Cavalry Captain Gordon Granger

54. Eastham Tarrant, *The Wild Riders of the First Kentucky Cavalry (Union)* (Louisville, 1894), 61, 31. See also Hambleton Tapp, "Incidents in the Life of Frank Wolford, Colonel of the First Kentucky Union Cavalry," *Filson Club History Quarterly*, X (1936), 82–99.

55. Edward P. Tobie, *History of the First Maine Cavalry* (Boston, 1887), 20–21.

became colonel of the 2nd Michigan, and on his promotion to brigadier general was succeeded in the command of the Michigan regiment by infantry-quartermaster Captain Philip Sheridan. Captain Josiah H. Kellogg, 1st United States Cavalry, was given leave of absence from his regiment to become colonel of the 17th Pennsylvania. Lieutenant C. H. Tompkins, 2nd United States Cavalry, became colonel of the 1st Vermont.[56] Captain Albert G. Brackett, also of the 2nd United States Cavalry, recruited and commanded the 9th Illinois, which was intended originally to be a "national" regiment, under the name of the "First Western Cavalry."[57] Lieutenant James B. Swain, U.S.A., raised and commanded the 11th New York. Other Regulars were commissioned colonels of volunteer regiments made up of previously organized companies of militia. Among these were Captain Washington L. Elliott of the 3rd United States Cavalry, Robert Williams, former instructor of cavalry tactics at West Point, and T. M. Bryan, Jr., colonels respectively of the 2nd Iowa, 1st Massachusetts, and 18th Pennsylvania.[58]

56. While still a lieutenant in the 2nd United States, Tompkins led one of the earliest cavalry scouts of the war. Sent with a fifty-man detachment to reconnoiter the neighborhood of Fairfax Court House, Virginia, he proceeded to attack the Confederates in the town itself and came away with five prisoners. His report is in *Official Records*, III, 60. General McDowell endorsed his report with the comment, "The skirmish has given considerable prestige to our regular cavalry in the eyes of our people and of the volunteer regiments, but the lieutenant acted without authority and went further than he knew he was desired or expected to do.... He has been so informed by me ... and whilst in the future he will not be less gallant, he will be more circumspect."

57. Edward A. Davenport, *History of the Ninth Regiment Illinois Cavalry Volunteers* (Chicago, 1888), 14–15.

58. At Governor Andrew's request, General Scott asked the secretary of war to grant Robert Williams leave from the Regular Army so he could accept the colonelcy of the 1st Massachusetts. Cameron, aware of Andrew's political power, granted the request despite the adjutant general's endorsement, "Adjutant General protests and opposes." Crowninshield, *A History of the First Regiment*, 41. An interesting instance of a Regular Army officer trying to become colonel of a volunteer cavalry regiment is related by a member of the 5th Michigan. In the spring of 1863, the regiment being stationed in Virginia, "a very young man, with long flaxen hair, came to our camp and staid several days with us, trying to get our officers to petition Gov. Austin Blair to appoint him Colonel of our regiment, but we all declined to sign such a petition, as we considered him too young." Samuel

Having raised a regiment, or having been appointed to the command of one, what lay ahead for the newly commissioned colonel? In most cases he had first to tackle the arduous job of getting the regiment organized and equipped. Then came the task, for which colonels commissioned from civil life were prepared either poorly or not at all, of training the regiment to some semblance of military skill and discipline. And then, after he took the field at the head of an inadequately prepared and poorly armed regiment, came the manifold trials and hardships of campaigning and the strains of administration, plus the hazards of illness, wounds, capture, defeat, and death. But with all the work, the risks, adversities, and frustrations, came also the chance for success and fame, and the satisfactions described beautifully by one of the best and most articulate members of the fraternity, Colonel George E. Waring, Jr., of the 4th Missouri:

It is a pleasant thing to be a colonel of cavalry in active field service. . . . To be the head of the brotherhood, with the unremitted clank of the guard's empty scabbard trailing before one's tent door day and night; with the standard of the regiment proclaiming the house of chief authority; with the respectful salute of all passers, and the natural obedience of all members of the command. . . . living in this atmosphere, one almost feels the breath of feudal days coming . . . to brush his cheek, whispering to him that the savage instinct of dead sires has not been, and never will be, quite civilized out of the sons. And then the thousand men, and the nearly million that they cost, while they fill the cup of the colonel's responsibility nearly to overflowing and give him many heavy trials—they are his own men; their usefulness is almost of his own creation, and their renown is his highest glory.[59]

Harris, *Personal Reminiscences* (Chicago, 1897), 17. The flaxen-haired young man was Staff Captain George A. Custer.

59. George E. Waring, Jr., *Whip and Spur* (Boston, 1875), 40–41. The 4th Missouri, recruited mainly in St. Louis, was known originally as the Fremont Hussars. Colonel Waring and his adjutant were "Americans," but the rest of the officers and a great majority of the enlisted men were of German birth. Hence the regiment was generally known as the "*Vierte Missouri.*" The lieutenant colonel, Gustav von Helmrich, had been a cavalryman in Germany for twenty-eight years before coming to America. Lonn, *Foreigners in the Union Army*, 109–10.

III

Assume the Port of Mars[1]

HAVING RECEIVED AUTHORITY TO RAISE A REGIMENT OF cavalry, the newly commissioned colonel went into action. He had to raise the regiment with reasonable promptness, under the penalty of forfeiting the glory and perquisites of the colonelcy. Thus, when three prospective colonels tried simultaneously to raise the 14th, 15th, and 18th Illinois, and none of them was able to attract within the allotted time the minimum number of recruits needed to form a regiment, the state consolidated the three partial regiments to form the 14th Illinois, and two of the colonels-to-be lost their commissions.[2]

Like any good executive, the expectant colonel began by enlisting the assistance of gentlemen of lesser stature than his own to do the actual work of finding and signing up recruits. The more fortunate colonels did not have to search for assistants; especially in the first year of the war, they had merely to choose the most promising among the many who applied and indeed clamored for

1. For the successive stages of the Table of Organization of a volunteer cavalry regiment, see the Appendix.
2. W. L. Sanford, *History of the Fourteenth Illinois Cavalry and the Brigades to Which It Belonged* (Chicago, 1898), 11–12.

authority to raise companies.[3] But even when the colonel had to find recruiting agents and persuade them to work for him, the process was commonly a straightforward business proposition. It was clearly understood that commissions in the regiment would be the reward of performance and that rank would be proportionate to the number of men each recruiter brought to the rendezvous.[4] In at least one case, the 3rd Indiana, the arrangement was openly advertised and clearly spelled out:

Any company of fifty-two men will be accepted and mustered with a First Lieutenant, and if they fail to fill up within a reasonable time, they will be consolidated with other parts of companies . . . . parts of companies will be accepted with a view to making such consolidations:
> For forty-five men, a Captaincy.
> For thirty-five men, a First Lieutenancy.
> For twenty-five men, a Second lieutenancy.[5]

The candidates for these lesser commissions, like the colonels and the enlisted men, came from all walks of life. The colonel and lieutenant colonel of the 3rd Indiana were lawyers; one of the majors had been a midshipman in the navy, then a newspaper editor, thereafter a lawyer and, when he decided to try his hand at the trade of cavalry officer, was employed as a clerk in a government bureau in Washington. As civilians, the line officers of the regiment had been farmers, teachers, tailors, livery stable keepers, steamboatmen, and merchants, and one of the captains "had been a minister in a Methodist church . . . while his orderly sergeant was a storming Universalist preacher who never hesitated to combat the theology of anyone, regardless of rank, whose theology conflicted with his peculiar views."[6] Among the officers of the 1st

3. Hinman, *Story of the Sherman Brigade*, 36.
4. J. H. Kidd, *Personal Recollections of a Cavalryman* (Ionia, Mich., 1908), 38; "there were four of us whose commissions hinged upon getting a minimum number of men into camp within fifteen days." Colonel Chris Miller, commissioned by Governor Morton to raise the 72nd Indiana (later Mounted) Infantry, in turn issued three or four recruiting commissions for each of the ten companies, to men ambitious to become officers in the regiment. McGee, *History of the 72nd Indiana*, 7.
5. Thomas S. Cogley, *History of the Seventh Indiana Cavalry Volunteers* (Laporte, Ind., 1876), 47.
6. William N. Pickerill, *History of the Third Indiana Cavalry* (Indianapolis, 1865), 10.

Iowa were "quite a number" of the "noted and talented politicians of the State"; and in this regiment, as in many others, lawyers, judges, orators, and stump speakers held a disproportionately large share of the captaincies and lieutenancies. And since even local prominence was usually a plant of slow growth, many of these gentlemen were rather old to make the change from a swivel chair, law books, and the comforts of home to the rigors of life in the field at the head of a group of daredevil cavalrymen. When the 9th Ohio was first organized the captains of three of its companies were forty-eight, fifty-eight, and fifty-nine years old, respectively; all three were "prominent men at home who had organized their companies through their influence and offered to take the field with their men."[7] This was doubtless an extreme case, but there is abundant evidence to show that in the first two years of the war, many officers of volunteer cavalry regiments were too old to stand up under the physical strain of service in a branch of the army that called for above average endurance and hardihood.

Nevertheless, the aged came forward eagerly. So did thousands of younger men. No doubt their motives for doing so were as various as their origins and personalities. Unquestionably, a sincere and rather self-conscious patriotism actuated the great majority. The Union, in its barely seventy years of existence, had become the object of an almost mystic devotion, and its preservation was a sacred duty to thousands who joined the colors. Willard Glazier of the 2nd New York wrote his sister, "When our country is threatened with destruction by base and designing men . . . it becomes her sons to go to her rescue and avert the impending ruin. The rebelling South has yet to learn the difference between the *true principles* of the Constitution, and the *delusion* of 'State rights.' . . . I shall return to my studies as soon as the Rebellion is put down and the authority of our Government fully restored, and not until then."[8]

Others had less exalted motives. They joined because their

7. William D. Hamilton, *Recollections of a Cavalryman of the Civil War After Fifty Years* (Columbus, Ohio, 1915), 82–83.
8. J. A. Owens, *Sword and Pen, or, Ventures and Adventures of Willard Glazier* (Philadelphia, 1889), 119.

acquaintances and friends were joining, or from ambition, for adventure, or merely to escape a nagging wife or a dull job. When
they chose the cavalry over the artillery or the infantry, it was
more often than not out of sheer romanticism, there being a glam-
or about the cavalry in the popular mind that the other branches
of the service did not have—the yellow sash, the yellow stripe
down the trouser seam, the yellow trim on jacket and cap, a
charger to ride, the strident cavalry bugle calls. All this had an
irresistible attraction for a generation brought up on Harry Lorre-
quer's *Charles O'Malley, the Irish Dragoon,* and on Sir Walter
Scott's romances, as popular in the North as they were in the
South. "[T]here hung about the cavalry service," one of the historians of the 1st Maine has written, "a dash and an excitement
which attracted those men who had read and remembered the
glorious achievements of 'Light Horse Harry' . . . and of 'Morgan's
Men' in the revolutionary war. . . . men who had read much in history or in fiction, preferred the cavalry service."[9] In a more practical way, the historian of the 1st Massachusetts thought that men
chose to be officers or soldiers in the cavalry because it was considered an elite corps, and "men preferred to enlist in that branch
. . . because the would-be trooper preferred riding to walking, with
perhaps an idea that at the end of the march his horse would be
put up at some peripatetic livery stable."[10] Equally persuasive for
many was the compliment implied by the invitation to raise or
join in raising a company for a regiment of cavalry.

Some, finally, became cavalry officers by accident. One such
was William D. Hamilton, who, having raised a company for an
infantry regiment, was asked by Governor David Tod to transfer
his allegiance to the 9th Ohio. "I thanked the governor," Hamilton
wrote, "but said these men were recruited for the . . . Infantry . . .
and . . . they might refuse to go. 'Not very likely,' replied the governor, 'as all boys like to ride horseback.' 'Besides,' I said, 'I know
little about the cavalry service, and have a poor opinion of it.'
'You know a horse when you see one?' he asked with a twinkle in
his eye. 'I was brought up on a farm,' I said. 'That is as much as

9. Tobie, *First Maine Cavalry,* 3–4.
10. Crowninshield, *A History of the First Regiment,* 9.

any of them can say,' he replied. This . . . explains how I became a cavalryman."[11]

In addition to selecting recruiting agents, the colonel was also expected to provide the primitive publicity of the day, to make it known that a cavalry regiment was in process of formation and was looking for recruits. "Cards" and "puffs" in the newspapers were an obvious and widely used vehicle, but the crowning glory of the publicity campaign was the gaudy recruiting poster, adorned with a drawing of a fully equipped cavalryman, armed to the teeth and riding a prancing thoroughbred, affixed to every roadside tree, telegraph pole, fence, covered bridge, and building, "setting forth in seductive phrase the superior advantages offered to those who would enlist in the ranks of [the X Cavalry.]"[12] A colonel who announced that his regiment would be fully uniformed, equipped, and mounted at an early date had a great advantage in attracting recruits, and the claim was frequently made, often with little foundation in fact.[13] Fortunately for those who put forth such placards, they were not under oath and were at liberty to substitute hopes for reality.[14] There were no penalties for exaggeration or even downright mendacity, and so "burning placards were posted in the villages offering inducement in the way of proposed equipment that would have made every man a port-

11. Hamilton, *Recollections of a Cavalryman*, 41.
12. Hinman, *Story of the Sherman Brigade*, 36. "We got some immense posters printed, and among other inducements offered by our company was the experience of future officers, one gained in a foreign service, the other on the field of Bull Run." Josiah M. Favill, *The Diary of a Young Officer* (Chicago, 1909), 42 ff.; quoted in Henry Steele Commager (ed.), *The Blue and the Gray: The Story of the Civil War as Told by Participants* (2 vols.; Indianapolis, 1950), I, 72.
13. Samuel L. Gracey, *Annals of the 6th Pennsylvania Cavalry* (Philadelphia, 1868), 34.
14. One candidate for a captaincy, recruiting a company for the 17th Pennsylvania, had his own posters printed. He based his appeal for recruits on his ownership of Black Warrior, which had won all its races in northeastern Pennsylvania. A third of his poster was taken up "by a big wood cut of the 'Black Warrior' going at his best gait . . . [and thus] there was the further natural consequence—the sporting element rallied to his call." James Albert Clark, "The Making of a Volunteer Cavalryman," in MOLLUS, Commandery of the District of Columbia, *War Papers, No. 70* (Washington, D.C., 1907), 9.

able arsenal. The recruit, in imagination, saw himself bristling with death and desolation, mounted on an Arabian barb, breathing flame as he bore his rider to victory. All this was in strong contrast to the pitiful equipment that was at first in reality issued."[15]

The candidates for captaincies and lieutenancies had to invest more than just their time and energy. They were expected to bear some or all of the expenses of the recruiting campaign, aided in some cases by contributions from the colonel or from well-to-do and patriotic friends.[16]

The methods used to attract recruits were of every possible variety. J. H. Kidd, aspiring to a commission in the 6th Michigan, of which he later became colonel, held war meetings in country schoolhouses; dubious about his own oratorical talents, he took along a friend who was a good speaker. The friend attended to the oratory while Kidd himself was ready with blanks for the recruits to sign. "These meetings," reported Kidd, "were generally well attended but sometimes it was difficult to induce anybody to volunteer."[17] Samuel Harris was more ingenious, or had better luck, in raising a company for the 5th Michigan. He went to a county fair, buttonholed every likely looking young farmer, and had 117 recruits signed up in two days.[18] Charles Lothrop recruited a company for the 1st Iowa in the following manner:

Thinking my services might be of some little value, I commenced the formation of a company. A drum and fife were brought into requisition. The streets were duly paraded. The usual ragtag and bobtail of followers and boys trooped after the music. A company roster was made out and freely signed. Merchants, lawyers, doctors and artisans all seemed anxious to join. Meetings were held, patriotic speeches

15. Simeon M. Fox, "The Story of the Seventh Kansas," *Transactions of the Kansas State Historical Society, 1903–1904* (Topeka, 1904), 17–18.
16. For example, the 7th Pennsylvania. Sipes, *The Seventh Pennsylvania*, 2. See also deTrobriand, *Four Years with the Army of the Potomac*, 89, and Stevenson, *"Boots and Saddles,"* 33. The cost of raising the 6th Pennsylvania was underwritten by friends of Colonel Richard Rush, who had been authorized to raise the regiment. Gracey, *Annals of the 6th*, 20–21.
17. Kidd, *Personal Recollections*, 40.
18. Harris, *Personal Reminiscences*, 10. Harris was promised the first lieutenancy of the company if he succeeded in getting enough men for it.

were delivered in which sixty to ninety days were allowed to completely annihilate our Southern neighbors and drive what few of them were left back into the Union. . . . a telegram came notifying me to hold my company in readiness to report . . . at a moment's notice. Then came consternation . . . a general stampede and back-out of so large a number of would-be soldiers that it nearly depleted our company. But by the heroic efforts of those really in earnest the company was made up again.[19]

There was considerable rivalry among the recruiters to fill up the rosters of their companies as promptly as possible, for it was customary to number the companies from A to M (by old army custom the letter J was not used) in the order of their arrival at the camp of rendezvous or of their readiness to be mustered in with their ranks filled. The men took a strange pleasure in belonging to Companies A or B rather than L or M, but more importantly, the line officers' initial seniority in their respective ranks depended on the "seniority" of their companies.

In a special category were the numerous officers of foreign extraction in the Union cavalry. Wiliam H. ("Bull Run") Russell wrote that there were "daily arrivals in Washington of military adventurers from all parts of the world. . . . Garibaldians, Hungarians, Poles, officers of Turkish and other contingents . . . surround the State department and infest unsuspecting politicians with illegible testimonials in unknown tongues."[20] Some queer fish were recommended by Washington to the states for commissions, lest, as Secretary of State William Seward said, "some really good man should get among the rebels."[21] But a surprisingly large number of the foreigners who were commissioned in the cavalry made fine records, and in addition they generally brought with them a pleasing dash of color and eccentricity.

Captain, later Lieutenant Colonel Frederick von Schickfuss of the 1st New York, was a model officer, "prompt, approachable and gentlemanly. He was up and out on the grounds at reveille. He supervised affairs. As often as practicable, he called out the

19. Charles C. Lothrop, *A History of the First Regiment Iowa Cavalry Veteran Volunteers* (Lyons, Iowa, 1890), 27.
20. William H. Russell, *My Diary North and South* (2 vols.; Boston, 1863), II, 273.
21. *Ibid.*

entire available command and drilled it in person, and the various evolutions skilfully performed were enjoyed by the men as well as by the commander himself. His wife, a comely, cheery woman, heartily respected, shared his life in the camp."[22] The senior captain of the 4th Missouri, Captain Count von Gluckmannsklegge, was in the opinion of his colonel "in many respects the most accomplished officer" in the regiment; "his life had been passed in the profession and he had only left his position of major in a Bavarian regiment of Uhlans to draw his sabre in defense of 'die Freiheit' in America. . . . He was . . . a man of keen worldly shrewdness and of quick judgment—qualities which . . . may have been sharpened by long practice in those games of chance with which it has not been unusual for European officers to preface their coming to . . . America."[23]

Lieutenant Colonel Count Louis Palma di Cesnola of the 11th New York (later colonel of the 4th New York), the "beau ideal of a light cavalryman" in the eyes of his subordinates, had left the university to volunteer for service in the Sardinian army in the Austro-Sardinian War of 1859. Promoted to major for bravery in the battle of Novara, he served in the Sardinian army until he came to America in 1860.[24] Joseph Kargé, lieutenant colonel of the 1st New Jersey, came to America after escaping from the prison in which he was serving a sentence for his participation in the Polish revolution of 1848.[25] He held the regiment together when it was nearly wrecked by the incompetence of its colonel. Temporarily in command when the latter became involved in difficulties with the War Department, Kargé "set to work to make

22. Beach, *First New York (Lincoln) Cavalry*, 59.

23. Waring, *Whip and Spur*, 40–41.

24. Smith, "*Scott's 900*," *Eleventh New York*, 242. See also Lonn, *Foreigners in the Union Army*, 242. Another officer of the 11th New York, Baron von Alvensleben, "the vagrant scion of a very distinguished Prussian family," turned up in camp after the regiment was fully organized. "Where the baron obtained the [shoulder] straps in our regiment we never made out, but one day he joined us . . . a full-fledged second lieutenant. As the gallant baron could not speak a word of English, his stay with us was short." *Ibid.*, 19.

25. Lonn, *Foreigners in the Union Army*, 243. The regimental historian, on the other hand, states that Kargé had been an officer in the "Prussian service." Pyne, *First New Jersey Cavalry*, 21.

soldiers out of the officers and men. . . . Officers grumbled and soldiers swore, but still the routine was inexorably carried on; and before long all awoke to the consciousness that they had never been so comfortable since their first enlistment. In the five weeks of this *regime*, a soldierly spirit was implanted in the men, which preserved its vitality through all the ensuing trouble."[26]

One of the most colorful officers on the Union side was Percy Wyndham, who became colonel of the 1st New Jersey in February, 1862, after Colonel Halstead left the service. "Young, dashing, handsome, every inch a soldier," Wyndham, son of a captain of cavalry in the British army, was sixteen when he fought in the Students' Corps in Paris in the Revolution of 1848. Later in the same year he secured transfer to the French navy, with the rank of ensign of marines. He resigned in 1850 and obtained a commission in a British artillery regiment, which he left two years later to become a lieutenant in a regiment of Uhlans in the Austrian army. In May, 1860, he took service under Garibaldi, and so distinguished himself by his gallantry that within two months he was promoted to major and given command of a regiment; three months later he was promoted to lieutenant colonel and given command of a brigade. He was knighted on the field by King Victor Emmanuel and made a Chevalier of the Military Order of Savoy. A year later, "the lure of active combat . . . was so strong that he obtained leave of absence for twelve months and came to . . . [America] to offer his services to the Union cause."[27]

Endowed with one of the most luxuriant moustaches in either army, Wyndham showed his quality on the morning of August 30, 1862, at Second Manassas. Brigaded with the 1st Pennsylvania, the 1st New Jersey was posted behind the left of the Union line, directly in the path of Longstreet's tremendous and decisive attack on the left wing of the Union army. The regimental historian writes:

Suddenly there was a roar that shook the solid earth beneath us, and the air around was filled with all imaginable missiles. Shell, round shot and spherical case tore through the ranks in a terrific crossfire. . . . As Wyndham wheeled his men, preparatory to the retrograde,

26. Pyne, *First New Jersey Cavalry*, 23–24.
27. Lonn, *Foreigners in the Union Army*, 294.

some of the troopers betrayed undue haste to come around. Instantly, he ordered them to the right about, and marched them toward the fire that had excited them. Then he halted, and made them a few remarks. Twirling his long moustache, he informed them that he objected to confusion and disorder and disliked their manner of performing the late evolution; that if the next attempt was not more satisfactory, he would be forced to keep them drilling under fire until they had learned the proper way in which a wheel should be performed. . . . The wheel the next time was performed as if on parade, and, without a waver, the column passed steadily through the fire to its position. The ground was pitted with musket balls by this time, but the twirl of that long moustache was more formidable than a rifle.[28]

Alfred Nattie Duffié, graduate of St. Cyr, had seen active service with the French army in Algeria and Senegal, the Crimean War, and the Franco-Sardinian War against Austria before he came to America in 1860. He entered the Union army as a captain in the 1st New Jersey, transferred to the 2nd New York with the rank of major, and in the spring of 1862, Governor William Sprague appointed him colonel of the 1st Rhode Island over the heads of the lieutenant colonel and the three majors of the regiment, all of whom promptly resigned. A full-fledged mutiny was narrowly averted, but the governor's courageous act was the making of the regiment, for within a few months Duffié transformed it from "pitiable inefficiency" to "one of the best and most dependable."[29] Regis deTrobriand, with perhaps some partiality for a fellow Frenchman, reported that when he visited Duffié, he "found him in his tent, surrounded by his officers, to whom he was . . . giving a lesson in tactics. We visited his camp . . . where everything breathed the air of order and cleanliness, and a care for the least details of the service. The horses were in good con-

28. Pyne, *First New Jersey Cavalry*, 107–108. Wyndham had been taken prisoner in a skirmish before Second Bull Run, but escaped and resumed command of the regiment. He was badly wounded in the battle of Brandy Station on June 9, 1863, and resigned his commission a month later. He served again on Garibaldi's staff in 1866–1867 and after further adventures was killed in a ballooning accident in India.

29. Frederick Denison, *Sabres and Spurs: The First Regiment Rhode Island Cavalry* (Central Falls, R.I., 1876), 102–105. The quotation is from Lonn, *Foreigners in the Union Army*, 208.

dition, the men appeared finely and the equipments were irreproachable."[30] Duffié's main handicaps as a commander of a regiment of American volunteers were an excessive addiction to parades, pomp and pageantry, and the issuance of congratulatory orders of an overblown floweriness.[31] And, like Colonel Wolford of the 1st Kentucky, Duffié was greatly given to oratory; his eloquence was marred, but not inhibited, by his strong French accent and his lack of familiarity with American idiom.

Indeed, it was a rare regiment of cavalry that did not have among its officers one or more veterans of a foreign army. Five officers of the 11th New York had been commissioned or noncommissioned officers in British cavalry regiments, a sixth had served in the Austrian army, and a seventh in the Sardinian army.[32] Lieutenant George Johnson of the 3rd Pennsylvania had been a noncommissioned officer in a British cavalry regiment and was wounded in the charge of the Light Brigade at Balaclava. The senior major of the 1st Vermont, W. D. Collins, was former sergeant of artillery in the British army; this, together with his horsemanship, made him a man of note in the regiment and an oracle of military wisdom, a distinction that came easily in the early months to any veteran of a European army, whatever his former rank or branch of the service may have been.

There were adventurers and charlatans among the foreign officers, and many more who could not make the adjustment from the caste-ridden rigidities and the pomp and circumstance of European armies to the casual anarchy of American volunteers. But those who learned to adapt their military knowledge to American conditions, and their manners and methods to suit American tastes and prejudices, became valuable officers. They

30. deTrobriand, *Four Years with the Army of the Potomac*, 338.
31. A sample of Duffié's congratulatory orders: "Again it is my proud privilege to congratulate you upon your admirable appearance, drill and discipline as a regiment." 1st Rhode Island Volunteer Cavalry, Special Order No. 11, January 16, 1863, in Regimental and Company Order and Letter Books, Record Group 94, National Archives. Hereinafter cited as 1st Rhode Island O&L Books.
32. Smith. *"Scott's 900," Eleventh New York*, 12. Two other officers of the regiment had served in the Regular Army.

made a great contribution to a service in which no more than a tiny minority had any knowledge of the tricks of the trade that were not to be found in the manuals, but were essential for a cavalryman to know. The historian of the 1st Ohio tells the following story of how his regiment, in its first campaign, forded the Duck River in Kentucky:

We had never had any experience in swimming our horses and when we started into the stream marching by fours and as the horses began to swim the fours were soon broken, and just at this time our attention was attracted by an officer standing on the bank . . . shouting . . . "Do not break the fours." We did not know what reason there was for this, but we endeavored to keep our fours together the best we could, and soon learned that this was the only safe way to ford a stream by swimming horses, as in that manner the horses support each other and they can swim much easier and it is more safe for the men than to become scattered.[33]

The man on the riverbank was not one of their own officers but Colonel August Willich, late of the Prussian army.

In the summer of 1861, Henry Wilson of Massachusetts, chairman of the Senate Military Affairs Committee, proposed that the Regular Army be broken up and its younger officers be assigned to train and lead regiments of volunteers. Said Wilson, "this army of ours is paralyzed toward the head. Your ablest officers are young captains and lieutenants; and if I wished today to organize a heavy military force, such as we are calling into the field . . . I would abolish the [Regular] army as a first act, and I would then take officers . . . and place them where their talents fit them to go, without reference to the ranks they occupied in the old regiments."[34] McClellan and General John Charles Fremont shared Wilson's opinion. An act of Congress passed on July 29, 1861, authorized the general-in-chief to allow officers of the Regular Army to accept commissions in volunteer regiments.[35] There was certainly merit in the idea from the standpoint of military efficiency, and the war might have been shortened and thousands of lives saved if it had been adopted. But the proposal missed the crucial fact that the volunteer officer, commissioned, however

33. Curry, *Four Years in the Saddle*, 31.
34. Quoted in Nevins, *The Improvised War*, 192–93.
35. Meneely, *The War Department, 1861*, p. 195.

mistakenly, from civil life, was essential to the success of the recruiting system, which would probably have collapsed if the incentive of commissions for those who were willing to spend their
time and money to recruit men for the army had been totally or
partially removed. The War Department, in any case, anxious to
preserve the Regular Army intact, blocked whenever possible the
transfer of Regular officers to the command of regiments of volunteer cavalry, and in some cases actually ordered officers who
were already serving as colonels or lieutenant colonels of volunteers to return to their regiments in the Regular Army to serve as
captains or lieutenants. So strong was this prejudice that as late
as 1864 General George Meade tried to block such a transfer, with
the remark that "a lieutenant of engineers was of more importance than a colonel of volunteers."[36]

Despite the opposition of the adjutant general's office, a sizeable number of Regular Army officers managed in one way or another to obtain transfers to the volunteers. A fairly common and
eminently sensible arrangement was for a colonel commissioned
from civil life to compensate for his own lack of military knowledge by enticing a Regular officer, preferably of the cavalry, to
become lieutenant colonel of his regiment and assume the responsibility of whipping it into shape. Lieutenant Colonels Thomas
Hight of the 1st Maine, Thomas Drummond of the 4th Iowa,
D. A. Murray of the 3rd Ohio, and W. H. Ingerton of the 13th
Tennessee are examples. They came as strangers into units whose
members were often schoolmates, neighbors, and friends and
were given a task calling for firmness and severity. Their lives
were no bed of roses, as Colonel Ingerton, for one, discovered.
The historians of the 13th Tennessee relate,

Col. Ingerton . . . was a model officer. . . . He was a thorough disciplinarian, the man of all others needed. . . . But there was . . . a great
prejudice in the minds of our officers and men against serving under
a regular officer; and especially having him promoted over our native
officers that we had known all our lives. Much feeling was aroused in

36. Upton, *The Military Policy of the United States,* 236. Upton does
not give the name of the lieutenant in question. The transfer was made
despite Meade's opposition, and Upton adds that the unnamed officer had
command of a cavalry brigade within six months, and of a division within
a year. In all probability, the officer was Ranald Mackenzie.

the Regiment and violence threatened if Ingerton remained. Col. Ingerton remained cool and . . . told the officers . . . he did not desire to remain with them if it was not satisfactory and made a proposition to the officers that he would remain a month, and if at the end of that time he was not satisfactory to them, he would resign. . . . He at once addressed himself to the drilling and disciplining of the Regiment; all recognized his ability and nothing further was ever heard of his resigning. . . . [He] soon won the confidence of officers and men; and though he was untiring in drill and discipline, and some times harsh in dealing with negligent, or inefficient officers and men, he won the admiration and affection of the Regiment.[37]

Most officers of volunteer cavalry had to submit themselves to election when the regiment was formally organized, the captains and lieutenants being chosen by the enlisted men of their companies, and the majors and lieutenant colonel by the lieutenants and captains. In most cases, the election of line officers was a formality, it being generally understood that the men would cast their votes for those who had recruited them. There were occasional surprises, however, when the troopers took the bit in their teeth and made unexpected choices, occasionally bestowing shoulder straps on men who had had some military experience, either in the Regular Army or the militia.[38] To avoid such contretemps, the more forward-looking recruiters began their canvassing early and obtained firm pledges of support from their men before the regiment was organized.

Many a regimental election was conducted in the same atmosphere of hoopla and skullduggery, and with the same troublesome results, as the elections for state and local offices "back home."

37. Samuel W. Scott and Samuel P. Angel, *History of the Thirteenth Regiment, Tennessee Volunteer Cavalry, U.S.A.* (Philadelphia, 1903), 142–43.

38. *Ibid.*, 117. See also Smith, "Scott's 900," *Eleventh New York*, 12. One must cross the lines for the most amusing instance of a prospective officer making sure of his election. He administered the following oath to the men who enlisted in his company: "You solemnly swear to obey, fight for and maintain the laws of the Confederate Government and the Constitution, and support John W. Dean for captain of this company." Benjamin LaBree, *Camp Fires of the Confederacy* (Louisville, 1898), 213. The 1st Kentucky carried democracy to its ultimate limit by electing even its noncommissioned officers. Tarrant, *Wild Riders of the First Kentucky*, 11.

The 1st New Jersey enjoyed for a time the luxury of having two lieutenant colonels, both claiming to have been legally elected, and each having a loyal and vocal faction of supporters.[39] The officers of the 2nd Ohio were directed in September, 1861, to elect a successor to Colonel Charles W. Doubleday, who resigned after organizing the regiment. They were informed that if they failed to reach a unanimous choice, the governor would appoint a Regular Army officer to command them. The ensuing election resulted in the choice of Major Henry Burnett for colonel, whereupon the defeated candidate, Major George G. Miner, protested to the governor that Burnett owed his election to "underhanded work." Evidently there was substance in Miner's charge, for one of the troopers noted in his diary, "Officers and men full of wine and champagne at Burnett's expense."[40] Burnett's election was subsequently declared void, and August V. Kautz, a West Pointer and a veteran of the Mexican War, was appointed to the colonelcy.

From the standpoint of military efficiency, the election system had little to recommend it, for in the main, officers were elected for reasons that had little to do with their qualifications for a most demanding occupation. Nearly every regimental historian could have echoed the comment of William F. Scott of the 4th Iowa, that the result of the system "was more or less vicious and demoralizing. . . . it caused a fever of ill-feeling or discontent, presented a serious obstacle to the improvement of discipline, prevented the development of that esprit de corps which is of such

39. Pyne, *First New Jersey Cavalry*, 20.
40. Tenney, *War Diary*, 31. In September, 1862, Major Miner was promoted to lieutenant colonel of the 7th Ohio. Charles A. Webster of the Independent Loudoun Rangers (U.S.A.) used a more direct method to get himself elected first lieutenant of his company. Taking advantage of the temporary absence of his captain, "he called the company in line and declared the office [of first lieutenant] vacant, and announced his candidacy, and concluded by saying, 'All in favor of Webster for 1st lieutenant step two paces to the front,' when nearly the entire company stepped to the front; he declared himself elected." When the captain returned, "he was furious, and declared the election a usurpation of both military and civil rights." Briscoe Goodhart, *History of the Independent Loudoun, Virginia Rangers* (Washington, D.C., 1896), 78–79.

great value among soldiers, and put upon mere personal popularity that premium which should have been the reward of capacity and courage."[41]

Some colonels had the political skill and the hardihood to see to it that their own choices were elected as officers, but any interference in the accepted democratic process had its dangers, as Colonel Williams of the 1st Massachusetts discovered. All the companies of his regiment had elected their officers and expected to elect the field-grade and staff officers as well. Before they could do so, however, Governor Andrew appointed Williams colonel, and one of his own aides lieutenant colonel of the regiment. "When the two colonels appeared on the field, the company officers, who had expected that the field officers would be chosen from among their own number, were astonished and dissatisfied, and this feeling soon spread among the men. In consequence, a mutiny broke out. . . . Williams was not the man to stand any insubordination. Energetic action followed, and this trouble culminated in the wounding of one man and the dismissal of many officers by the colonel."[42] Colonel Rush of the 6th Pennsylvania was more fortunate; he was permitted to appoint all the officers of his regiment, with no recorded objections from his men. Generally, however, the men's right to elect their officers was so much a time-honored part of the militia-volunteer system that most colonels accepted it, or at least tolerated it, until well into the war and in some cases to the very end. As the war progressed, however, it became more and more the rule to fill vacancies in the commissioned ranks not by election but by the promotion on merit of men selected by the colonel.

Some governors defied the democratic principle and built up political capital by issuing lieutenant's or captain's commissions to well-connected applicants from civil life, who then turned up unannounced, uniformed and shoulder strapped, to face the consternation and disgust of their new colleagues. Company I of the 4th Illinois voted to secede from the regiment and join the 8th Illinois when Governor Yates sent them a second lieutenant of his own choice. It took all of Colonel T. Lyle Dickey's diplomatic skill

41. Scott, *Story of a Cavalry Regiment*, 21.
42. Crowninshield, *A History of the First Regiment*, 42–43.

and the departure of the luckless lieutenant to restore peace.[43] Simeon Fox of the 7th Kansas, a regiment that acquired several officers in this manner, wrote that "the first selection of officers [elected by the men] was not always a success. . . . But I will say this method produced better results than would have [been] obtained from a direct independent appointment by the governor, and this opinion is abundantly sustained by the character of the appointments he later imposed upon us from civil life. Two of his appointments did make good. . . . All the rest went down to oblivion through forced resignation or the sentence of a court martial."[44]

But before there could be officers of cavalry there had to be cavalrymen for them to command. In a few cases, colonels-to-be wanted only recruits of a certain type, and their recruiting agents were directed to accept no others. The 17th Pennsylvania was to be made up entirely of "country boys." The recruiters for the 1st Maine had the more difficult assignment of enlisting "only men of superior intelligence . . . none but sound, able-bodied men . . . of correct morals and temperate habits, active, intelligent, vigorous and hardy."[45] Generally, however, and especially when cavalry recruiters had to compete with equally ambitious and persuasive recruiters for the artillery and infantry, men were signed up with no questions asked.

The practice, and perhaps the necessity, of accepting all comers regardless of qualifications brought thousands into the cavalry who should have been rejected because of age, lack of physical fitness, or a total ignorance of horsemanship. By law, recruits had to be eighteen years old or older to enlist without parental consent, but this limitation was regularly ignored. Every cavalry regiment

43. P. O. Avery, *History of the Fourth Illinois Cavalry Regiment* (Humboldt, Ill., 1903), 47.

44. Simeon M. Fox, "The Early History of the Seventh Kansas Cavalry," *Sixteenth Biennial Report of the Board of Directors of the Kansas State Historical Society* (Topeka, 1909), 118. In May, 1862, as a result of political shenanigans, Fox's regiment had four colonels in command simultaneously. One was appointed by the governor of Kansas, one by the lieutenant governor, one by the War Department in Washington, and one by the major general commanding the Department of Kansas.

45. Henry P. Moyer, *History of the 17th Regiment Pennsylvania Volunteer Cavalry* (Lebanon, Pa., 1911), 25. Tobie, *First Maine Cavalry*, 3.

had in its ranks boys of seventeen, sixteen, fifteen, and even younger, who lied about their age and were passed by complaisant or careless mustering officers. The 13th Tennessee had "not less than two hundred soldiers under the age of 18 years; some below 16. These were all placed on the rolls at 18."[46] Boys of sixteen and seventeen, and one who was three months short of his fifteenth birthday, all of them claiming to be eighteen or nineteen, were accepted for the cavalry battalion of the Sherman Brigade, but, says the brigade historian, these youngsters had to be of "robust appearance" to be mustered.[47] Ways were found to get even the less "robust" accepted. Private Sewell Babcock of the 15th New York was not only under age, but of a short stature as well. So, "while the [mustering] officers were going through the preliminaries, Babcock, who was in the rear rank, with the aid of some of his comrades, built a little mound of earth, covered it with grass, and stood on it. He passed."[48] George H. T. Springer was fourteen when he was mustered in as a trooper in the 7th Kansas in September, 1861. He received an honorable discharge four years later, in September, 1865, a mature veteran of eighteen. A parent whose underage son enlisted without his consent could obtain the boy's discharge by civil process, and more than one hard-bitten cavalryman of fifteen or sixteen experienced the humiliation, much to the entertainment of his temporary comrades, of being snatched from the ranks by an irate father armed with a writ of habeas corpus.[49]

At the opposite end of the scale from the youngsters were the patriarchs. In General Sheridan's opinion, an ideal cavalry regi-

46. Scott and Angel, *History of the Thirteenth Regiment,* 259.
47. Hinman, *Story of the Sherman Brigade,* 795.
48. Chauncey S. Norton, *"The Red Neck Ties,"* or, *History of the Fifteenth New York Volunteer Cavalry* (Ithaca, N.Y., 1891), 15. There were cases of mere children attaching themselves to a cavalry regiment. Wayland Halderman, aged twelve, ran away from his home in Cincinnati, "joined" the 12th Ohio, was allowed to stay, and distinguished himself in a fight with "Sue Mundy's" guerillas at Lebanon, Kentucky; he was the only one mounted when the fight began, fired the first shot, and having a good horse, "was one of the foremost pursuers." Frank H. Mason, *The Twelfth Ohio Cavalry* (Cleveland, 1871), 52.
49. Stanton P. Allen, *Down in Dixie: Life in a Cavalry Regiment in War Days* (Boston, 1888), 27–28. Allen was fourteen when he enlisted in

ment would have been made up only of bachelors from eighteen to twenty-two years old. But especially in the first year or two of the war, every cavalry regiment had numerous troopers who were in their late thirties, with some in their forties and even fifties. Private Daniel Ellsworth of the 7th Kansas was seventy when he enlisted in 1861, and unlike many a younger man, he served faithfully to the end of his three-year term of enlistment. Company C of the 1st Kentucky numbered among its enlisted men "Colonel" Avery, "a wealthy old man about eighty years of age."[50]

General Sheridan's ideal cavalryman was to weigh not more than 130 pounds. The less exacting specifications of the 1st Maine, which was quite exceptional in having any, called for men weighing not less than 125 and not more than 160 pounds. But every regiment, including the 1st Maine, had its share of men who would not have been out of place in one of Napoleon's regiments of cuirassiers.[51] The 17th Pennsylvania had a contingent of "great, brawny, half-wild fellows . . . muscular woodsmen, bear hunters in the deep wilderness"; Companies A and E of the 2nd Michigan were made up of "large men, mostly from the lumber mills and camps of the Saginaw Valley . . . Stalwart lumbermen, who looked as if they would be equally at home with rifle, pistol,

---

the 21st New York. He was snatched from the ranks by his father and was further humiliated by a full report of the incident in his hometown newspaper. Three months later, still short of his fifteenth birthday, he ran away from home again and, claiming to be twenty-one, enlisted in the 1st Massachusetts. This time his parents gave up and allowed him to remain in the army. Governor Andrew, reviewing the recruits for the regiment before they left for camp, remarked that some of them seemed "rather young." One of the officers replied that "the cavalry uniform makes a man look younger than he is." *Ibid.*, 96. Alonzo B. Pennington and John Allison, both under age, were removed from the 7th Kansas by their fathers.

50. Tarrant, *Wild Riders of the First Kentucky*, 14.

51. A knowledgable cavalryman writing after the war gave it as his opinion that "Men whose weight runs from 130 to 150 pounds are best adapted for the requirements of American cavalry." William H. Carter, *Horses, Saddles and Bridles* (Baltimore, 1900), 160. Nevertheless, "men were enlisted from all walks of life, with no reference to capability. No selection was even made according to size and weight . . . and the men ranged from pygmy to giant; and there was never any authority for changing them . . . into other branches of the service, according to fitness." Crowninshield, *A History of the First Regiment*, 5–6.

saber or axe."[52] The strain on an overworked, half-starved horse of having to carry a "great bear hunter, six feet six inches tall, with his huge frame in proportion," or any of his oversized fellows, plus their weapons, ammunition, and equipment, requires no comment.

Even less excusable than the recruitment of men whose size and weight should have barred them from service in the cavalry, and leaving it to disability or death to weed out many who should not have been accepted in the first place, was the derisory physical examination of recruits, and in the case of regiments mustered in before August 3, 1861, the absence of any physical examination whatever.[53] The 1st Kentucky had been on active service for two and a half months before it was mustered in, without the formality of a physical examination. The recruits of the 8th Illinois marched single-file between the mustering officers and the surgeon; if "any defect was noticed, they were stopped and examined, and if a sufficient cause presented itself, rejected."[54] The men of the 51st Indiana Mounted Infantry "worked their arms, wriggled their fingers, champed their teeth, and marched back and forth, to satisfy the mustering officers of their soundness."[55] Clearly, "physical examinations" like these, or that of another regiment which resulted in the rejection of one man out of eighty, had little value in weeding out the unfit.[56] The men themselves recognized that a major cause of the large number of deaths and discharges for disability decimating every regiment within the

52. 17th Pennsylvania: Clark, "Making of a Volunteer Cavalryman," 9–10; 2nd Michigan: Marshall P. Thatcher, *A Hundred Battles in the West, St. Louis to Atlanta: The Second Michigan Cavalry with the Armies of Mississippi, Ohio, Kentucky and Cumberland* (Detroit, 1884), 22–23.
53. Upton, *The Military Policy of the United States*, 424.
54. Abner Hard, *History of the Eighth Cavalry Regiment, Illinois Volunteers* (Aurora, Ill., 1868), 36.
55. William R. Hartpence, *History of the 51st Indiana Veteran Infantry* (Indianapolis, 1894), 6.
56. The regiment was the 7th Pennsylvania. Dornblaser, *Sabre Strokes of the Pennsylvania Dragoons*, 17. The following describes the physical examination of Company A, 1st Ohio: "A sleepy-looking man called the Captain to him, took hold of his left hand, lifted his arm over his head, and with a peculiar twist that made the bones crack, brought it down to his side; then the right arm in the same way. He then raised his hat brim and looked into his eyes, examined his teeth, felt his body to see if he

first few months after its organization, was the lack of an adequate physical examination of recruits.[57]

As was only natural in an army drawn from a nation still predominantly agricultural, half or more of the cavalrymen, particularly those serving in border state and western regiments, came from the farm. The 1st Ohio, 9th Illinois, 1st Kentucky, most of the Indiana, Iowa, and Wisconsin regiments, and even those raised in the western counties of Pennsylvania and New York, were manned largely by farmers and the sons of farmers. Every regiment, however, had representatives of many other vocations and trades. Company K of the 1st Maine was made up of seafaring men, and the Michigan regiments had whole companies of lumbermen. The chronicler of the 8th Illinois relates that his regiment contained "men of all callings and vocations; men who could perform almost any labor that occasion might require; could build railroads, run engines, publish newspapers, manage flour or saw mills, build carriages or repair almost any kind of machinery, and during the course of the war these various accomplishments found opportunity for usefulness. Neither were the fine arts and professions without their representa[tives]."[58] A newspaperman who accompanied a cavalry regiment in the Appomattox Campaign described it as "composed of laborers and artificers of every possible description. There were blacksmiths, moulders, masons, carpenters, boatbuilders, joiners, miners, machinists, riggers and ropemakers. They could have bridged the Mississippi, rebuilt the Tredegar Iron Works, finished the Tower of Babel, drained the Chesapeake, constructed the Great Eastern, paved Broadway, replaced the Grand Trunk railroad, or tunneled the Straits of Dover."[59]

wore a truss, and our Captain had passed his medical examination. . . . Each man, as his name was called, stepped forward and went through the same examination. . . . Five men were rejected, two of whom were given a second trial at the Captain's request and passed. Samuel L. Gillespie ("Lovejoy"), *A History of Company A, First Ohio Cavalry* (Washington Court House, Ohio, 1898), 11.

57. William P. Lloyd, *History of the First Reg't. Pennsylvania Reserve Cavalry* (Philadelphia, 1864), 12.

58. Hard, *History of the Eight Cavalry*, 36.

59. George A. Townsend, *Rustics in Rebellion* (Chapel Hill, N.C.,

When the Mississippi Marine Brigade, a hybrid waterborne cavalry organization, built its winter quarters near Vicksburg in the fall of 1863, "Plenty of good cypress timber was obtainable up the Yazoo and details . . . were sent after it. A good sawmill was near the camp, which the Marines were permitted to run. . . . Persons in the regiment competent to run this mill were found and designated for this special duty. . . . Carpenters competent to boss the construction of the buildings were also found within the regiment. . . . When [the buildings] were completed, stoves were in demand to warm them. There was a foundry in Vicksburg which the Marines were permitted to use, and plenty of huge shells, fired from Union guns during the siege, lying around loose. A canvas[s] of the regiment was again made, pattern makers and molders discovered . . . and large stoves, each with the name of the company and the regiment upon it, were cast and put together."[60]

The 5th New York may well hold the record in the variety of the skills and trades of the troopers in its ranks. Its 1,064 officers and men represented 126 different trades and occupations, including acting.[61]

Groups of college students left their books and enlisted in cavalry regiments; nine from Oberlin College joined Company H of the 2nd Ohio and eight from Washington College (now Washington and Jefferson) the 15th Pennsylvania. Company B of the 18th Pennsylvania was made up mainly of students from Allegheny College. An independent company, the "College Cavaliers," made up of Dartmouth College students with a few additions

1950), 63. Townsend does not identify the regiment in question. In the Union army as a whole, 48 percent of the men were farmers, 29 percent artisans, 16 percent laborers, 5 percent "members of commercial occupations," and 2 percent professional and miscellaneous. E. J. Copp, *Reminiscences of the War of the Rebellion* (Nashua, N.H., 1911), 531.

60. Warren D. Crandall and Isaac D. Newell, *History of the Ram Fleet and the Mississippi Marine Brigade in the War for the Union on the Mississippi and Its Tributaries* (St. Louis, 1907), 450.

61. J. O. Buckeridge, *Lincoln's Choice* (Harrisburg, Pa., 1956), 90. The 156 men who served in Company C of the 9th Pennsylvania represented thirty-six different trades and occupations. John Rowell, *Yankee Cavalrymen: Through the Civil War with the Ninth Pennsylvania Cavalry* (Knoxville, Tenn., 1971), 23.

from Norwich College in Vermont, served creditably in the Shenandoah Valley in the summer of 1861.[62]

The men in any given regiment usually came from a relatively small area, three or four counties, or a single congressional district. Seven of the ten companies of the 12th Illinois Mounted Infantry came from Henry County, Illinois. In eight of the ten companies of the 1st Vermont the company was composed of men from a single county. On the other hand, it was not unusual for a regiment, especially one raised in the first year of the war, to contain companies from two or three states, or even more.

It may be assumed that the percentage of foreign-born in the cavalry was not appreciably different from the 18 percent in the Union army as a whole. Regiments raised in the larger cities, especially those on the eastern seaboard, had the highest percentage of men born abroad; the 4th New York, 3rd New Jersey, 4th Missouri, and 3rd Ohio were known as German regiments, and the 2nd, 3rd, and 4th Wisconsin had numerous all-German companies. The 9th New York grew out of an unsuccessful attempt to form a lancer regiment made up entirely of Polish immigrants familiar with the weapon. The 5th New York, besides the record number of occupations represented in its ranks, may also hold the record for cosmopolitanism; it had in its ranks troopers hailing from nineteen different foreign countries.[63]

If there was a common denominator for the men and boys of the Union cavalry, it was their lack of ability to ride or take care of a horse.[64] In the North, unlike the South, horses were driven,

62. Tenney, *War Diary*, ix; Charles H. Kirk, *History of the Fifteenth Pennsylvania Volunteer Cavalry* (Philadelphia, 1906), 17; S. B. Pettengill, *The College Cavaliers* (Chicago, 1883), 5. The College Cavaliers were a ninety-day unit. When the troopers from Dartmouth were mustered out on October 1 and returned to college, they learned that they were expected to take the year-end examinations which they had missed by enlisting. Their captain thereupon persuaded the president of Brown University to accept the entire Dartmouth contingent if they were expelled for refusing to take the examinations. The Dartmouth faculty learned of this arrangement, caved in, and waived the examination. Pettengill, *College Cavaliers*, 90.

63. Buckeridge, *Lincoln's Choice*, 90.

64. A British authority quoted by Crowninshield, *A History of the First Regiment*, 10, stated, "The men ... intended for cavalry service should be selected with the utmost care ... and should, above all, be chosen from those who have been accustomed to horses from their youth ... who love horses, and are capable of taking care of them. ... from

not ridden. The extent of the riding skill even of most boys raised on northern farms was to sit bareback on the broad rump of a plow horse as it ambled back to the barn after a day's work in the fields. Regimental historians are nearly unanimous in testifying to their fellow troopers' lack of riding skills. The historians of the 3rd Pennsylvania state that most members of their regiment "had not been astride a horse until they were mustered into the United States service. . . . Many of them showed much more fear of their horses than they ever did afterward of the enemy. The wild fumbling after mane or saddle strap, the terror depicted on some faces when the commands 'trot' or 'gallop' were given, are a lasting source of amusement." They quote an unidentified contemporary as saying, "it seemed that the qualifications of a recruit for the cavalry might be summed up in this: he neither knows how to groom, feed, water or ride his horse, and is afraid of him." [65] In the 15th New York, "scarcely one out of a hundred men . . . ever rode a horse . . . and to witness their attempts to mount and go through the evolutions was amusing to say the least." [66]

Not until too late did cavalry recruits learn that the infantryman had only himself to look after, but not so the dashing trooper; "the company must first put up the picket rope and then the horse must be watered, fed and groomed. . . . Then [the trooper] unsaddles, gets his coffee . . . and is ready to lie down an hour after the infantryman is asleep. In the morning, if the cavalry are to move at the same hour [as] the infantry . . . they must have reveille an hour earlier than the infantry, to have time to feed, groom and saddle their horses." [67] Even the patriotic and idealistic Cavaliers from Dartmouth and Norwich learned that having to care for their horses was more of a chore than they had anticipated; they had not understood, they said, that they were expected to be

---

other men than these, it is difficult, almost impossible, to form a good cavalry. What . . . can be expected of a stocking manufacturer, or a linen weaver, who considers a horse a wild beast?"

65. Regimental History Committee, *History of the 3d Pennsylvania Cavalry* (Philadelphia, 1905), 200.

66. Norton, *"The Red Neck Ties,"* 17.

67. Curry, *Four Years in the Saddle*, 24.

stable boys; and to feed, water, and groom their horses did not accord with their ideas of the "pomp and circumstance of glorious war."[68]

In the course of the war, numerous regiments were converted from infantry to cavalry or mounted infantry; the 41st Massachusetts Infantry became the 3rd Massachusetts, the 4th Wisconsin Infantry the 4th Wisconsin, the 4th Tennessee Infantry the 1st Tennessee, the 2nd West Virginia Infantry the 5th West Virginia, the 12th New York Infantry the 15th New York, the 3rd New Hampshire Infantry the 3rd New Hampshire Mounted Infantry, the 33rd New York Infantry became the 1st New York (Veteran), and the 34th Ohio Infantry, the 8th Ohio. The entire Lightning Brigade was made up of regiments that had served as infantry until, given the opportunity to change to the mounted service, the men elected to do so.[69] Only one instance is recorded of a regiment declining an offer to convert to cavalry. This oddity was the 75th Indiana Infantry.

The units with the most serious teething troubles were commonly those which, having been raised as cavalry, were threatened with conversion to infantry. Volunteer cavalrymen, most of them avid readers of newspapers, knew that Senator Henry Wilson introduced a bill in January, 1862, to reduce the volunteer cavalry establishment to fifty regiments; Senator William Fessen-

---

68. Pettengill, *College Cavaliers*, 27.

69. The historian of the 3rd Massachusetts called it a "wonderful transformation . . . a very surprising but agreeable change." James K. Ewer, *The Third Massachusetts Cavalry in the War for the Union* (Maplewood, Mass., 1903), 79. The transformation of the 4th Tennessee Infantry into the 1st Tennessee Cavalry was the fulfillment of a "long cherished hope." W. R. Carter, *History of the First Regiment of Tennessee Volunteer Cavalry in the Great War of the Rebellion* (Knoxville, Tenn., 1902), 59. Colonel Alfred Gibbs of the 130th New York Infantry "received papers from Washington to the effect that if the regiment would furnish half the horses needed, the transfer to cavalry might be made. The regiment . . . quickly pledged the horses, and a dispatch was forwarded to Washington accordingly. . . . [Some time later] the circumstance which above all . . . aroused the regiment to a high pitch of enthusiasm and rejoicing, was the welcome announcement that the long talked-of and hoped-for transfer from infantry to cavalry had been made." James R. Bowen, *Regimental History of the First New York Dragoons* (N.p., 1900), 85–89.

den of Maine went Wilson one better by proposing that the reduction be to twenty regiments.[70] No one knew if, when, or on whom the axe would fall if these cuts came into effect. Many cavalry regiments—most of them still struggling with preparations for active service—felt threatened with disbandment, or with the alternative of accepting transfer to the infantry. In most such cases the men's reaction was violent. The rumor that the 6th New York would have to serve as infantry or be disbanded caused the men to "positively decline" to serve as footsoldiers; faced with a similar choice, so did the troopers of the 10th New York.[71] The 8th New York, aroused by a rumor that the regiment would be converted to infantry, let it be known that they had enlisted to serve as cavalry "and the government could not make them fight on foot"; many of them promptly deserted.[72] Even a temporary change in the status of the 22nd Pennsylvania from cavalry to infantry, to deal with a sudden emergency, caused a reaction of "intense disgust," "loud protests," and a wave of desertions.[73]

70. Once the floodgates holding back the formation of volunteer cavalry units had been opened, so many came into being that the War Department was unable to equip them, as will be shown in the next chapter. General McClellan asked the War Department in November, 1861, not to muster in any more cavalry regiments because there was not enough equipment for those already in the service. At the same time, the paymaster general, asked to suggest ways in which the cost of the war could be reduced, proposed the elimination of regimental bands and a reduction in the number of cavalry regiments. Thiele, "The Evolution of Cavalry," 34–35. It was under these circumstances that the War Department considered disbanding some cavalry regiments and converting others to infantry.

71. Committee on Regimental History, History of the Sixth New York Cavalry (Second Ira Harris Guard) (Worcester, Mass., 1908), 35–37; Preston, History of the 10th Regiment, 14, 27.

72. Henry Norton, Deeds of Daring, or, History of the 8th New York Volunteer Cavalry (Norwich, N.Y., 1889), 17–18.

73. Samuel C. Farrar, The Twenty-Second Pennsylvania Cavalry and the Ringgold Battalion (Pittsburg, 1911), 213–14. The 4th and 5th Independent Battalions (Ohio) and the 13th Ohio, raised at the beginning of 1864, "received its first headache by being required to take Springfield rifles and infantry equipments, when the expectancy was horses and cavalry arms . . . but the exigencies of the service required infantry. . . . Lots of grumbling and swearing. . . . Some of the boys say they won't take muskets. . . . but if given cavalry equipments they are ready to do their duty as such, according to their enlistment." Howard Aston, History and Roster of

Such were the officers and men who made up the volunteer cavalry of the Union army, this was the manner in which the regiments were formed, and these were the problems and vicissitudes that beset the oganization of a regiment of cavalry. In the perspective of a hundred-plus years and the sophistication engendered by two world wars, some of the vicissitudes seem comic and many of the problems avoidable. To a considerable extent they were the result of bureaucratic incompetence and bungling, but viewed in their contemporary setting, they appear, in the main, as the inevitable consequence of the government operating without adequate administrative machinery and largely without precedents, trying desperately to find solutions for problems of an unparalleled magnitude and urgency. Everything had to be improvised and improvised in a hurry. But, despite all the fumbling, the errors, confusion, and clutching at expedients, despite the absence of a carefully considered, authoritative program directed by a central government possessing unquestioned power to impose its will, eighty-two regiments of cavalry had been enrolled by the end of 1861 and were preparing to do battle with rebellion.

---

the Fourth and Fifth Independent Battalions and Thirteenth Regiment Ohio Cavalry Volunteers (Columbus, Ohio, 1902), 8, 18.

IV

Arms and the Man

THE CAVALRY RECRUIT OF THE EARLY SUMMER OF 1861 needed an above average fund of patriotic enthusiasm and physical stamina to survive his first few weeks or months in the service of his country. The "camp" to which he reported with his company or regiment was as often as not bare farmland, a camp in name only. The 1st and 4th Iowa were by no means alone in reporting to camps that were only open meadows. Given piles of lumber and a supply of saws, hammers, and nails, they were directed to build their own barracks. The inauspicious combination of green lumber and amateur carpentry usually produced structures whose walls "were like sieves, through which the cold air circulated freely," and the men of the 7th Michigan, who occupied such barracks in the bitter cold of a northern winter, ate their meals standing, because it was too cold to sit.[1] Still, they were probably better off than the troopers of the 9th New York, in the northwestern corner of their state; encamped in tents, they would have been in sorry straits if the people of Westfield had not taken

1. Asa B. Isham, *An Historical Sketch of the Seventh Regiment Michigan Volunteer Cavalry* (New York, 1893), 10.

pity and invited the soldiers into their homes on cold and stormy nights.[2]

The men of the 3rd Ohio slept on the bare ground in unheated tents until the end of January, 1862, in a typical northern Ohio winter of rain, sleet, snow, and cold.[3] The 1st Maine, encamped in the state fair grounds at Augusta, were housed in tents in "weather [that] was extremely cold, even for Maine, and were not supplied with stoves until the end of November."[4] With an initial strength of 1,160, this regiment lost 200 men by death and disability during the winter and, on January 28, reported that 261 were hospitalized. The regimental historian relates:

The condition of the troops in camp attracted the attention of . . . the members of the Legislature, and a bill was introduced to give each man an extra blanket, at the expense of the state; but, after some discussion, it was so amended as to authorize the governor to give one to such as he thought deserved it; and with this amendment the bill passed. [But the 1st Maine] . . . got no extra blankets, the knowledge that every man had a horse blanket, and that many had quilts, comforters and blankets furnished from home, being generally understood to be the reason why.[5]

More fortunate regiments had adequate but not necessarily conventional shelter. The 8th Illinois was quartered in vacant homes in St. Charles. The 10th New York was ordered to a camp in Gettysburg, Pennsylvania, a town none of the men had ever heard of, where they were housed in a "Lecture room, Coach-shop, Court house, warehouse, ten-pin alley, etc." until a delegation of officers was sent to Washington "to lay before the Secretary of War the advisability of providing barracks for the Regiment"; the necessary authority having been obtained and the supplies assembled, eight men were detailed from each company to build the barracks.[6]

2. Newel Cheney, *History of the Ninth Regiment, New York Volunteer Cavalry* (Poland Center, N.Y., 1901), 17.

3. Crofts, *Third Ohio Veteran Volunteer Cavalry*, 10.

4. Tobie, *First Maine Cavalry*, 13. "The mercury repeatedly fell to more than twenty degrees below zero, whilst the snow was from five to six feet in depth." Samuel H. Merrill, *Campaigns of the First Maine and First District of Columbia Cavalry* (Portland, Maine, 1866), 24.

5. Tobie, *First Maine Cavalry*, 7.

6. Preston, *History of the 10th Regiment*, 20.

Auxiliary facilities in camps such as these were as primitive and inadequate as the housing. The 19th New York had an old barn for its first hospital; the troopers who had the misfortune to require hospitalization were provided with heaps of cornstalks for bedding.[7] The 1st Maine had for its hospital the judge's stand on the Augusta fair grounds; its amenities and even its sanitary facilities were hopelessly inadequate.[8] The 8th Illinois housed its sick in a large tent; when the weather turned cold and a requisition for stoves was turned down, the regiment built its own ingenious heating system. A "hole about two feet square and one foot deep, was dug . . . in the center of the hospital from which a trench about one foot broad and six inches deep was dug to the outside of the tent, where a barrel with both heads knocked out, was placed for a chimney. The trench was covered with boards and dirt, and near the centre-hole with a stone. A fire was now built in the centre-hole, and smoke made its way through the trench and out of the barrel, and this was found sufficient to make the hospital quite comfortable, when the wind did not blow in the wrong direction."[9]

To supply a thousand-man regiment with three adequate meals a day requires much more than goodwill. Food must be bought, large-scale cooking equipment assembled, kitchens and dining facilities built and equipped, cooks assigned and trained. These essentials were lacking, to a considerable extent, in nearly every cavalry camp in the fall and winter of 1861. None of the deprivations and hardships the men had to endure was so strongly resented, or caused so much trouble, as did the shortcomings of the culinary services. The 6th New York, encamped on Staten Island, had to eat its meals, which were "very plain but sufficient," standing at long board trestles in a rough shed, open on one side to all the wintry winds that blow in New York Harbor in Novem-

7. Bowen, *Regimental History of the First New York*, 20. This regiment liked to be known by the distinctive name of 1st New York Dragoons, but its official designation was the 19th New York Cavalry; the official designation will be used in the text, to avoid confusion with the 1st New York (Lincoln) Cavalry.
8. Tobie, *First Maine Cavalry*, 7.
9. Hard, *History of the Eighth Cavalry*, 34.

ber and December.[10] In August, 1861, the 1st Iowa was fed on musty bread and maggoty bacon; not until the men staged a full-scale riot was their diet improved. In the same month the 3rd Ohio manifested "considerable dissatisfaction . . . in regard to the manner of cooking and serving the meals. . . . The beans and soup were frequently scorched; the pork was fat, the beef was tough. . . . But what the men grumbled about was the dirty, slovenly manner in which the cooking and serving was done. The dissatisfaction of the men finally culminated in a riot. . . . the tables were turned over and wrecked and dishes and food trampled under the feet of the angry men."[11] When the regiment moved to another camp in October, the "cooking was all done over open fires built outside the tents. There was no shelter whatever for . . . [the] cooking arrangements. Each mess was provided with two camp kettles, one for making coffee and the other for meat and vegetables. They also had a skillet for frying meat. Each mess made arrangements for its own cooking, either by changing off or by hiring one of their number to cook all the time."[12] The 19th New York enjoyed the luxury, if it may be called that, of a regular issue of freshly baked bread, "usually drawn loose in dirty wagons and dumped upon the ground by indifferent teamsters. We, however, usually skinned our loaves, that is, cut off the outside before using."[13]

Some regiments, the 1st New York for one, avoided such problems by arranging with a local restaurateur to provide the meals. The 8th Illinois contracted for its rations at what was even then the low price of sixteen cents per man per day; nevertheless, the food supplied met with the "entire satisfaction" of the regiment.[14] All these early camps were of course in "friendly" territory, many of them located near the men's homes. Families sent packages or brought hampers of food to camp; nearby farmers donated wagonloads of vegetables, poultry, fruit, and milk, and the women

10. E. P. McKinney, *Life in Tent and Field* (Boston, 1922), 29.
11. Crofts, *Third Ohio Veteran Volunteer Cavalry*, 8.
12. *Ibid.*, 10.
13. Bowen, *Regimental History of the First New York*, 37.
14. Hard, *History of the Eighth Cavalry*, 34.

from the adjacent towns contributed delicacies for the sick. There were no actual shortages of food, but the abrupt change from the variety and amenities of their meals at home to the Spartan monotony of army fare, the absence of vegetables, fruit, pies, and butter, the poor, amateurish, and sometimes slovenly preparation of the food, and even the change to tin plates and cups from the tableware to which they were accustomed, came as a disagreeable surprise.

The impact of these inadequacies in shelter and rations on the men's physical well-being and sensibilities would have been far worse if many of them had not arrived in camp with immense quantities of baggage containing a generous assortment of everything that fond parents, wives, and sweethearts thought might be useful in protecting their loved ones from the hardships of life in the army and the hazards of war. The contrast between the lavish supplies they had brought from home—the "amount of personal baggage . . . [which] would have made a corps of newly-arrived Italian immigrants envious"—and the bare minimum which the seasoned trooper learned after a year or two to get along with, is one of the entertaining staples of memoirs and regimental histories.[15] The historian of the 7th Pennsylvania thus describes the progress of his regiment to its first camp: "With a huge bundle on each shoulder, and an occasional umbrella raised to break the rays of the warm October sun, we footed it . . . to [camp]. . . . Of course our bundles included only the loose baggage—the trunks and extra bedding were sent out by wagon."[16] And as Isaac Gause of the 2nd Ohio noted in 1865, "We could now move better with an hour's notice than we could have moved with ten days' notice in 1861."[17]

15. Preston, *History of the 10th Regiment*, 15. Stanton P. Allen, whose sprightly tales are not entirely free from the taint of exaggeration, writes that a heartless inspector made him discard the following articles, all of which he had brought from home: two boiled shirts, one pair of calfskin shoes, two boxes of paper collars, one vest, one scarf, one quilt, one pillow, one soft felt hat, one tin basin, one folding camp stove, two jars of preserves, a pair of slippers, a pair of mittens, three neckties, a bottle of hair oil, a mirror, a hammer, a checker board, an extra haversack filled with food, and a peck sack of walnuts. Allen, *Down in Dixie*, 94–95.
16. Dornblaser, *Sabre Strokes of the Pennsylvania Dragoons*, 15.
17. Isaac Gause, *Four Years with Five Armies* (New York, 1908),

The shortage of nearly everything needed to clothe and equip the great numbers of troops raised by an unprepared national government has been described too often to require retelling in detail. These shortages, however, affected the cavalry to a greater degree than they did the infantry, simply because a cavalryman needed a much greater amount and variety of gear than did a footsoldier. The regulation equipment of a trooper consisted of his uniform, made up of a dark blue, canvas-lined jacket, a blouse, heavily reinforced trousers, a change of underclothing, shirt and stockings, shoes, a stiff, heavy "Puritan" hat ornamented with a black plume, crossed sabers insignia and company letter in brass, an overcoat, rubber poncho or "talma," and stable frock. Next came a blanket, saddle blanket, a pair of spurs, canteen, haversack, saddle, saddle bags, surcingle, nose bag, picket pin and lariat, curb bit and bridle, halter, watering bridle, curry comb and brush. Finally, the weapons: a saber, carbine, revolver, and gun tools, together with a saber belt, carbine sling, holsters for revolver and carbine, and two cartridge boxes. Nor did the equipment of the individual trooper exhaust the list. As late as January, 1862, Colonel Lewis Zahm of the 3rd Ohio was begging for guidons, colors, sashes for the noncommissioned staff and the orderly sergeant, and even bugles, "very much [needed] to learn the different calls."[18]

These lengthy lists, however, represented a counsel of perfection; hardly a cavalryman or regiment marched to war before perhaps 1863 with everything the regulations required them to have, and when perchance they did, a part of the process whereby the individual cavalryman became a veteran was the discarding of a major portion of his lavish outfit.[19] The overcoat and hat were

352. When the 8th Illinois moved its camp from Washington to near Alexandria in early December, 1861, it needed eighty-one heavy army wagons to transport its belongings. Hard, *History of the Eighth Cavalry*, 53. "It took twenty-five wagons to move the . . . [7th Michigan] to Fairfax Court House and then everyone complained that everything had to be left behind. In the course of time the regiment possessed but one wagon, and this one would not be seen by us for weeks." Isham, *An Historical Sketch*, 15.

18. Lewis Zahm to Thomas Swords, January 22, 1862, in 3rd Ohio O&L Books, RG 94, NA.

19. McClellan could have warned the War Department that it was a

generally the first to go, and many a cavalryman remembered after the war that when his regiment was first sent to the front, the road behind it was strewn for miles with overcoats and "that d——d old hat."[20] The evidence of hundreds of daguerrotypes demonstrates that for a couple of years after the demise of the regulation hat, there was "no sort of regularity in head coverings. . . . Every sort of battered old tile was used."[21] Not until Sheridan was given the command of the cavalry of the Army of the Potomac and compelled the adoption of the familiar forage cap—which he did not himself wear—was cavalry headgear again standardized. And soldiers being creatures of habit, notwithstanding the universal dislike of the original hat, the compulsory change to the forage cap was greatly resented.[22]

The classic description of the fully equipped cavalryman is to be found in the history of the 4th Iowa:

Fully equipped for the field, the green cavalryman was a fearful and wonderful object. Mounted upon his charger, in the midst of all the paraphernalia and adornments of war, a moving arsenal and military depot, he must have struck surprise, if not terror, into the minds of his enemies. Strapped and strung over his clothes, he carried a big sabre and metal scabbard four feet long, an Austrian rifle or a

---

great waste to burden cavalrymen with excessive gear. In his report on the admirable Austrian cavalry, which he had studied in 1855, he had written, "The number of things carried by the men, and the excessive weight of the equipment, seem pernicious and absurd in the extreme. I was informed by cavalry officers that the men usually manage to throw away the greater part of their load before many days passed in the field." McClellan, *European Cavalry*, 64.

20. [Whittaker], *Volunteer Cavalry*, 46. Early in the war, General Meigs "learned with horror that as many as 800 overcoats were picked up behind a regiment on the march." Weigley, *Quartermaster General of the Union Army*, 254. "As we moved forward [beyond Yorktown] the day being warm, we found hundreds of infantry had thrown away their overcoats and some other clothing, which literally strewed their camp ground." Hard, *History of the Eighth Cavalry*, 108. Needless to say, the cavalry was no less wasteful than the infantry.

21. [Whittaker], *Volunteer Cavalry*, 46. "In the way of hats—we see them in every known and conceivable variety—the regulation hat, the same minus feather and cord, then the burlesque on the inverted coffee pot, fatigue cap, then the kepi, then comes the Kossuth, Monitor, Straw, Wide Awake, and in variety ad infinitum, all represented in the same squadron." Quoted in Thiele, "The Evolution of Cavalry," 72n.

22. Tenney, *War Diary*, 134.

heavy revolver, a box of cartridges, a box of percussion caps, a tin canteen for water, a haversack containing rations, a tin coffee-cup, and such other devices and traps as were recommended to his fancy as useful or beautiful. . . . This mass of furniture, with the saddle, would weigh in most cases seventy pounds. . . . When the rider was in the saddle, begirt with all his magazine, it was easy to imagine him, protected from any ordinary assault. His properties rose before and behind him like fortifications, and those strung over his shoulders covered well his flanks. To the uninitiated it was a mystery how the rider got into the saddle.[23]

The troopers of the 4th Iowa, and their fellows in many another cavalry unit raised in the first months of the war, would not have been hampered in mounting by any excess of gear issued by the army. The 4th Iowa, assembled in camp in October, 1861, received its blankets and the first installments of its uniforms when the winter was half over and was not fully uniformed until March. In its first camp in Iowa, the sentries had to be called in on extremely cold days to save them from freezing, "because many of the men had not greatcoats or sufficient other clothing."[24] The 1st Iowa, by contrast, had no such problem. Raised in September, 1861, by the twentieth of the month its men had received "one heavy pair of Pantaloons and the promise of another soon, a very heavy overcoat with cape[,] a *Fighting Jacket* . . . a blue sack coat for a fatigue dress[,] a pair of Boots, pair of shoes . . . three Blankets . . . Shirts[,] two pair drawers, two pair Socks, a canteen, and all the little necessaries."[25] The 3rd Iowa, raised in the same month, had to fend for itself. Its colonel, Cyrus Bussey, "in order to have his command ready for the field without delay, went to Chicago and contracted for clothing, blankets, tents and horse equipments," which, the chronicle adds, "turned out to be the best the regiment ever received."[26]

23. Scott, *Story of a Cavalry Regiment*, 26–27; see also Curry, *Four Years in the Saddle*, 25, and Crowninshield, *A History of the First Regiment*, 11.
24. Scott, *Story of a Cavalry Regiment*, 22–23.
25. Max Hendricks Guyer (ed.), "The Journal and Letters of Corporal William O. Gulick," *Iowa Journal of History and Politics*, XXVIII (1930), 205.
26. Lurton D. Ingersoll, *Iowa and the Rebellion* (Philadelphia, 1866), 397.

The 3rd Ohio, assembled in early September, 1861, was still without uniforms in November.[27] The 10th New York also waited two months for its uniforms. The 2nd New York arrived in Washington at the end of August, 1861, with the men clad in the tattered remnants of the civilian clothing they had worn when the regiment was organized a month earlier.[28] The 1st Kentucky received uniforms in installments; trousers and shirts came first, followed by overcoats two months later; after the lapse of another two months, the rest of the uniform was issued.[29] The 4th Illinois was more fortunate; it received its uniforms one month to the day after it was mustered in. In Iowa, "loyal women responded nobly to the task of outfitting the first Iowa regiments. They formed 'Soldiers Aid Societies' and undertook to cut the cloth purchased [by the State] and make it up into uniforms. . . . No wonder . . . that the product was 'somewhat lacking in the trim, artistic finish of the "Tailor Shop."'"[30] A major problem in Iowa and elsewhere was the shortage of blankets. In Iowa, the state being unable to find enough of them to buy, the adjutant general published an order requesting officers who were bringing in recruits to have each of them bring along at least one good blanket, comfort, or quilt. Shoes too were generally a problem, the available supply being insufficient in quantity and poor in quality as well.

Many a volume of reminiscences and many a regimental history relate the time-honored and doubtless exaggerated stories of

27. Crofts, *Third Ohio Veteran Volunteer Cavalry*, 12. The 2nd Ohio, on the other hand, raised at practically the same time as the 3rd, was fully uniformed and armed well before the end of November. Tenney, *War Diary*, x.

28. Willard Glazier, *Three Years in the Federal Cavalry* (New York, 1873), 28. The 2nd New York was not the only regiment to arrive in Washington with the men wearing the civilian clothing in which they had been mustered in. See deTrobriand, *Four Years with the Army of the Potomac*, 89.

29. Tarrant, *Wild Riders of the First Kentucky*, 27. Not that the lack of the regulation uniform made much difference to the troopers of this regiment. In the summer of 1862, by which time uniforms were plentiful, one of them was seen wearing "a slouch hat, hickory shirt, two linen breeches, home made galluses, and two immense Texas spurs on his naked heels." *Ibid.*, 109.

30. Upham, "Arms and Equipment for the Iowa Troops," uniforms, 31; blankets, 36; shoes, 40–41.

ill-fitting uniforms, of a "No. 2 man in a No. 4 jacket, with the collar chafing his ears and a loose overloaded belt dragging it awry; in trousers a world too large, a slouching cap and enormous boots." Such stories have been told of every army in every war since uniforms first came to be worn. No doubt a process of judicious swapping corrected most mismatches.

The shortages of wearing apparel were but one facet of the pervasive scarcity of everything needed to equip an army. The 1st New York received its horses promptly, but could not ride them because it had neither saddles nor bridles.[31] The 3rd Indiana was unusually fortunate in receiving promptly its full quota of uniforms and blankets, and the men brought their own horses into the service, but the army issued them only halters. When six companies of the regiment were ordered East, they traveled by boat up the Ohio to Wheeling; then "the command took to the mountains. . . . As they traveled across the country the farm houses along the way were besieged by the men for wheat sacks or anything else out of which they could improvise some sort of saddle, by stuffing the same with straw, while clotheslines procured in the same manner were used for stirrups."[32] Not until they arrived in Washington were the Hoosiers issued saddles, bridles, haversacks, and canteens.

The 4th Iowa had its full complement of mounts when it was mustered in, but did not receive saddles and bridles until three months later.[33] Lacking these essentials, this regiment and many others in the same situation could not begin mounted drill, or even the elementary riding instruction the troopers badly needed. Since even the most fortunate of these early regiments had far less time for training than they should have had before taking the field, the drill and training time lost due to a lack of equipment had lamentable results. Not the least of these was the loss of enthusiasm and the damage to morale. For the 3rd Ohio, which had horses but lacked saddles and bridles, "camp life was getting to be very irksome and monotonous. Our drilling was simply the dismounted drill. Until we got our saddles we could make no head-

31. Adams, *The Story of a Trooper*, 148.
32. Pickerill, *History of the Third Indiana*, 11–12.
33. Scott, *Story of a Cavalry Regiment*, 22.

way with mounted drill. . . . many of the men became impatient, saying we did not enlist to do this; we enlisted to put down the rebellion. . . . they wanted to get at it, to get it done and get home again."[34]

When saddles were issued at last, they were likely to be covered with rawhide instead of leather. The result was highly unsatisfactory; the alternate wetting and drying to which the saddle was frequently subjected caused the rawhide cover to crack and split. It was said that rawhide was used in the interests of economy, but its substitution for tanned leather as the saddletree covering was one of the 1858 modifications made in McClellan's original design, and it may well be that the modification was retained because of the shortage of tanned leather in the war years, caused by the huge increase in demand.[35]

The worst and most damaging of these shortages was that of weapons. Believers in the traditional cavalry doctrine considered that "a swift horse, a good pair of spurs, and a sharp sabre, are the chief weapons of a trooper. Pistols and carbines are but incidentals."[36] But the supply of cavalry weapons in the hands of the government at the outbreak of war was utterly inadequate to meet even that undemanding standard. To make a desperate situation nearly hopeless, the Ordnance Bureau, aware of General Scott's aversion to the raising of volunteer cavalry regiments, placed practically no orders for cavalry arms in the first few months

34. Crofts, *Third Ohio Veteran Volunteer Cavalry*, 13. The 7th Pennsylvania was similarly unhappy after two months of dismounted drill, varied only by the saber exercise. Dornblaser, *Sabre Strokes of the Pennsylvania Dragoons*, 19, 17. In a rather unusual move, the War Department had authorized Colonel Zahm of the 3rd Ohio to contract in northwestern Ohio for saddles for his regiment. He reported to Colonel James W. Ripley on October 10, 1861, that he had done so at a price of $27.50 each, the saddles to be delivered thirty days from that date. Zahm to James Ripley, October 10, 1861, in 3rd Ohio O&L Books, RG 94, NA. In the same letter, Zahm also reported that he had been unable to buy "spurs, curry combs, blankets, etc." at the prices specified by the War Department and asked Colonel Ripley to furnish these items as soon as possible. Needless to say, the saddles were not delivered in thirty days, but the regiment did have them all by December 6.
35. Harris, "The Union Cavalry," 354. The decision to substitute rawhide for tanned leather was made by the Ordnance Bureau in November, 1858. Hutchins, "The United States Cavalry Saddle," 155.
36. Stevenson, *"Boots and Saddles,"* 44.

after Fort Sumter. When, after Bull Run and the replacement of Scott by McClellan in November, orders were at last placed in quantity, it was too late. By then the demand already so greatly exceeded the supply that it was not until 1863 that, generally speaking, the cavalry was fully equipped with reliable modern weapons, and there were occasional local exceptions even then. Ten days after Bull Run, the War Department sent Colonel George L. Schuyler to Europe to purchase rifles and bayonets for the infantry, and sabers, carbines, and revolvers for the cavalry. He found ten thousand carbines and ten thousand revolvers in France and Belgium which he bought for $6.00 and $12.50 each, respectively, and twenty-one thousand sabers in Germany, which he bought at an average cost of $3.96.[37] There were no weapons to be had in England, whose armorers were busy with orders for Indiana, New York, Massachusetts, Connecticut, Pennsylvania, and the Confederacy, all of whom, more foresighted than the War Department, had sent agents to buy up and place orders for arms long before Schuyler arrived on the scene.[38]

Thus it came about that General-to-be John Pope, then a mustering officer, reported from Chicago in July, 1861, that there were neither sabers nor revolvers for any of the regiments of cavalry then being mustered in that area, and three months later McClellan reported that he had in the Army of the Potomac 3,163 partially armed and 4,268 totally unarmed cavalry.[39] On November 21, General Grant wrote his department commander, General Henry W. Halleck, from Cairo, Illinois, "My cavalry force are none of them properly armed—the best being deficient in sword belts and having the old pattern carbines. Eight companies are entirely without arms of any description."[40] General Don Carlos Buell reported from Louisville in February, 1862, that he had in his command only two companies of cavalry properly armed, and nine full regiments without any firearms whatever.[41]

37. Meneely, *The War Department, 1861*, p. 285 ff.
38. Not surprisingly, Colonel Schuyler found that the competition of the state agents with each other and with the Confederate agents had caused prices to double. Nevins, *The Improvised War*, 353.
39. Thiele, "The Evolution of Cavalry," 64.
40. Catton, *Grant Moves South*, 93.
41. Thiele, "The Evolution of Cavalry," 64.

The inability of either the national or the state governments to supply the cavalry with weapons inevitably produced every kind of well intentioned and sometimes ludicrous improvisation. The 1st Maine, lacking sabers, procured laths which the men whittled into swords "of the most grotesque shape" so that they could learn and practice the saber drill; the results were so farcical that the experiment was discontinued after a brief trial. No doubt the "swords" ended their army career as kindling.[42] This regiment, mustered in on October 31, 1861, did not receive revolvers and real sabers until March, 1862, and not until January, 1863, was it fully armed with sabers, revolvers, and carbines.[43] The 4th Illinois was another regiment that tried to learn the saber drill with homemade wooden swords. The sentries of the 1st Vermont patrolled their beats armed with clubs, and the 9th New York used its total stock of firearms, twenty muskets, to arm its sentries.[44] The sentinels of the 1st New York were armed with axes, the nearest approximation to a weapon the regiment was able to obtain. Early in the evening of the day when the axes were first issued, "the sergeant of the guard appeared and reported that one of the sentinels had been arrested by the police and carried off to the station-house for cutting down a pear tree."[45]

The regiments that did receive firearms were hardly better off than those just mentioned. Four hundred men of the 4th Iowa were armed with Austrian rifles, the 7th Pennsylvania received Belgian rifles ("a short, heavy barreled, old-style, cap-lock gun. When one was discharged, it was about as dangerous to stand at one end as on the other. ... After a number of men had their ears marked by these old arquebuses, they were condemned and returned to the ordnance department."), and all but three companies of the 1st Kentucky were given old infantry muskets.[46]

42. Tobie, *First Maine Cavalry*, 17.
43. Merrill, *Campaigns of the First Maine*, 24, 85.
44. Avery, *History of the Fourth Illinois*, 47; Benedict, *Vermont in the Civil War*, II, 138; Cheney, *History of the Ninth Regiment*, 17. The 2nd Illinois was another regiment with wooden swords. Samuel F. Fletcher, *The History of Company A, Second Illinois Cavalry* (Chicago, 1912), 13.
45. Stevenson, *"Boots and Saddles,"* 29.
46. Scott, *Story of a Cavalry Regiment*, 25; Dornblaser, *Sabre Strokes*

All these were heavy, unwieldy weapons, eminently unsuitable for use by cavalry. Yet the historian of the 4th Iowa relates that as late as March, 1863, "The clumsy Austrian rifles, issued when the regiment was first equipped, were still in the hands of those men who had not the hardihood or ingenuity to lose them."[47]

Six companies of the 3rd Indiana and all of the 4th Iowa were given "horse pistols . . . the smooth-bore, single-barreled muzzle-loader used in the Mexican war"; this pistol was about a foot long, "and when fired kicked about as hard as it would shoot, and the man behind it was in more danger than the man in front. . . . In practicing marksmanship it was never wise to choose for a mark anything smaller than a good sized barn."[48] When the 1st New York was at last armed, after its arrival in Washington, many of the arms issued to it were old and out of order, and the sabers received by the 6th Pennsylvania were "defective in temper and . . . of objectionable pattern."[49] The 4th Ohio, as well as the 1st and 2nd Iowa, received no carbines, only sabers and unreliable revolvers; the totally unarmed 2nd Ohio had to borrow muskets and revolvers from another regiment to make its first scout.[50]

The rare regiment that was "fully armed" from the start usually had a miscellany of weapons. The 3rd Ohio received three different makes of carbines; three companies of the 7th Kansas were given Sharps carbines, but the other seven "had at first to content themselves with nondescript weapons that ranged from obsolete horse-pistols mounted on temporary stocks to Belgian infantry muskets."[51] Such arrangements not only complicated the job of keeping the regiment supplied with ammunition, especially in combat, but also made it difficult, if not impossible, to use the entire regiment as a single tactical unit in a fight, placing an undue

of the Pennsylvania Dragoons, 32; Tarrant, *Wild Riders of the First Kentucky*, 26.

47. Scott, *Story of a Cavalry Regiment*, 63.

48. Pickerill, *History of the Third Indiana*, 12.

49. Beach, *First New York (Lincoln) Cavalry*, 48; Gracey, *Annals of the 6th*, 34.

50. Wulsin, *The Story of the Fourth*, 28; Upham, "Arms and Equipment for the Iowa Troops," 25; Curry, *Four Years in the Saddle*, 34.

51. Crofts, *Third Ohio Veteran Volunteer Cavalry*, 19; Fox, "The Story of the Seventh Kansas," 29.

burden on the modest tactical skills of inexperienced commanding officers. The same untoward effect was produced by another
common solution to the problem of weapons shortages, namely
the practice of arming only ten or a dozen men in each company
with carbines; examples of regiments armed in this manner are
the 1st Vermont, and the 1st, 3rd, and 6th Pennsylvania. A more
practical and not uncommon version of the same expedient was
to issue carbines to one or two entire battalions in a given regiment; thus, the 2nd Michigan had a "saber battalion" and two
"dragoon battalions," the latter armed with carbines.[52]

Among the eternal verities is the tendency of the official mind
to ignore inconvenient realities; the higher the post of the official
and the farther removed he is from the point at which the facts
can be determined by direct observation, the greater that tendency
becomes. Thus, Secretary Cameron reported on July 1, 1861, that
the "embarrassment" in the early days of the war over the shortage of weapons had "been in a great measure overcome."[53] Actually, at least as far as the cavalry was concerned, the "embarrassment" was just on the verge of becoming serious when the
secretary penned his report.

When George B. McClellan, one of the officers sent by Secretary of War Davis in 1855 to study the latest developments in the
art of war in Europe, visited Russia, he was greatly impressed by
the Cossacks of the Russian army, and by their traditional weapon, the lance.[54] As general-in-chief after November, 1861, he

52. Thatcher, *A Hundred Battles in the West*, 55.
53. *Official Records*, Series III, Vol. 1, pp. 308–309.
54. McClellan had also seen lancers while serving in the Mexican
War; "The Mexican lancers . . . made a most splendid appearance, with
their flashing lances, bright pennons and green uniforms. They also performed good service at the battles of Buena Vista and San Pascual." Brackett, *History of the United States Cavalry*, 83. He may also have known that
two companies of the 2nd United States Dragoons were trained as lancers
before the Mexican War, but the experiment was a failure, "for the American trooper did not take naturally to that weapon." Herr and Wallace,
The Story of the U.S. Cavalry, 31. A lancer regiment made up mostly of
Canadians was raised in 1862 by Colonel Arthur Rankin of Windsor, On-
tario, and was mustered into the U.S. service as a Michigan unit, but was
ordered disbanded by the secretary of war with no reason given and under
the protests of Governor Austin Blair. John Robertson, *Michigan in the
War* (Lansing, Mich., 1882), 744. Part of a company of the 9th New York

had the authority to give practical effect to his interest in the exotic weapon, and he ordered the 6th Pennsylvania to be armed with it. The order created consternation in the regiment, and three months later Colonel Richard Rush reported:

The lance being a new weapon in our service, and the Department having none to issue, a careful study of the weapon, as used in foreign service, was necessary, and great attention was paid to their manufacture. Valuable advice and assistance in this matter was received from the Duc de Chartres, Compte [sic] de Paris, and Major von Hammerstein, all then on Gen. McClellan's staff, and resulted in the adoption of the Austrian pattern. It is about nine feet long, with an eleven inch three-edged blade; the staff is of Norway fir, about one and a quarter inches in diameter, with ferrule and counterpoise at the heel; the whole weighing four pounds thirteen ounces, with a scarlet swallow-tailed pennon. . . . The regiment places all confidence in this weapon, if applied to its legitimate use, and only regrets that an opportunity has not offered which would enable them to show that this confidence is not misplaced.[55]

The 6th Pennsylvania was certainly pleased with its distinctive name of Rush's Lancers, but it never got the opportunity to demonstrate its confidence in the novel weapon; no Confederate was ever skewered by the lance. Eventually the lances were discarded, to the general relief of the men, one of whom wrote, "The officers like it, but the men do not, and the officers wouldn't if they had to use [it]."[56]

Uniforms were important, equipment and weapons essential, but the cavalryman's true glory was his horse. Sooner or later in the early days of every cavalry regiment came the proud moment, alloyed with a degree of apprehension, when the steeds made their first appearance in camp. In this, too, there was little con-

---

had been raised by Captain James Smolenski under an authorization to enlist a regiment of lancers for the Union army. Cheney, *History of the Ninth Regiment*, 19–20. The South too had its lancers, "Slayback's Regiment" of Missourians, armed with "lances tipped with steel and decorated with gay flags made by fair hands. This was one of General [John] Magruder's ideas. . . . the clumsy and unwieldy lances [were] more dangerous to the horses and the rear ranks . . . than they could ever be to the enemy." John N. Edwards, *Shelby and His Men, or, The War in the West* (Cincinnati, 1867), 496.
55. Gracey, *Annals of the 6th*, 34–35.
56. Thiele, "The Evolution of Cavalry," 76.

sistency of practice from one regiment to another. As in all else, variety was the rule.

The War Department rules in force when the first of the volunteer regiments were being raised required the men to furnish their own horses and tack. The inability of the Philadelphia Light Cavalry Troop to attract recruits was due to the disinclination of the cautious sons of Pennsylvania farmers to risk a valuable mount in an uncertain service. The government paid the owner forty cents a day for the use of his horse, supplied the feed, and paid the appraised value of the animal if it was killed in battle— but not if it died of disease, starvation, or overwork. It will be noted that by War Department standards, the services of a cavalry private, whose wage was thirteen dollars per month, were worth a mere one dollar per month more than those of his horse. Before the regulations were changed on August 31, 1861, and the states and the national government assumed the responsibility of furnishing horses for the cavalry, a number of regiments whose troopers owned their horses entered the service; among these were the 1st Iowa, 3rd Indiana, 9th New York, 2nd Illinois, 1st Kentucky, and the Ringgold Battalion.[57] The 1st Kentucky was furloughed for ten days after the regiment was organized, to allow the men to "furnish themselves with horses. Those unable to furnish themselves, their Captains endorsed their obligations with the permission to retain a certain portion of the men's pay until the obligations of each were liquidated."[58]

The quality of the horses owned by the men in all these units was uniformly high. The same can be said of a few of the regiments that were mounted by the government under the new system. The 3rd Iowa had the best of both worlds; volunteers for that regiment were requested to bring to the rendezvous "good cavalry horse[s] to sell to the government."[59] The 1st Rhode Island received Morgans and Canadians ("Canucks"), hardy animals, some of which survived all the hazards of four years of war and

57. All cavalry officers were required to furnish their own horses.
58. Tarrant, *Wild Riders of the First Kentucky*, 11. Some troopers of the 1st New York also owned their horses. Beach, *First New York (Lincoln) Cavalry*, 47.
59. Ingersoll, *Iowa and the Rebellion*, 396.

were still being ridden in the spring of 1865. Colonel Albert G. Brackett of the 9th Illinois put to good use the knowledge of horseflesh he had acquired as an officer in the 2nd United States; every horse sent to his regiment had to pass his scrutiny before it was accepted. Most of the horses for the 1st Pennsylvania were selected and purchased for the government by the officers of the regiment, and the rest were picked out in the government corrals by its colonel, George D. Bayard, a former Regular.[60] The War Department authorization under which the 4th Iowa was raised specified at the request of Senator James Harlan of that state that the horses for the regiment were to be purchased in Iowa. This was clearly a pork barrel order, but it had good results; the horses purchased in Iowa under the personal superintendence of the colonel of the regiment were of uniformly good quality.[61] The 1st Maine and the 1st Ohio, similarly mounted in their home states, also received excellent horses.

The great majority of cavalry regiments whose horses were supplied by the government did not fare as well as those just mentioned, for their horses were purchased under an inexcusably lax system, riddled with gross corruption. The historian of the 6th Pennsylvania did not exaggerate unduly when he remarked that "he who had a horse that had the glanders, or the heaves, or was spavined, or was going blind, brought him to the government, and the government purchased him."[62] The horses supplied to the 1st New York "were of the very worst description, and not one of six of them fit for the cavalry service. They were of bad stock, many of them blemished beyond cure, and of an age that showed that they should have long since been sent to die in a different and less hazardous service. . . . Many of these horses had evidently been nursed into tolerably good condition externally, but they would show their defects, and break down under the least hardship or exposure."[63] The 1st Massachusetts received what the

60. Denison, *Sabres and Spurs*, 31; Davenport, *History of the Ninth Regiment*, 19; Lloyd, *History of the First Reg't.*, 11.
61. Scott, *Story of a Cavalry Regiment*, 3.
62. Gracey, *Annals of the 6th*, 358.
63. Adams, *The Story of a Trooper*, 149. A historian of the same regiment, however, writes that the horses furnished "were good, serviceable

men thought were all the vicious and unmanageable horses in the
state, "a motley lot, few ever having been ridden."[64]

The following letter, written by Colonel Zahm of the 3rd Ohio
to Quartermaster General Montgomery C. Meigs, indicates the
quandary in which a conscientious commanding officer found
herself when horses supplied by the government began to arrive
in his camp:

[Horses] are coming in on an average of 25 per day. Among them, in
near every lot, I discover more or less unfit for Cavalry service. What
is my duty in regard to them? Shall I have them accepted and re-
ceipted irregardless of their fitness for service[?] The horses are
branded before they are ever brought into camp. I have demurred
with the Quartermaster, told him I did not feel like receiving horses
that were not fit for service. He told me that I was obliged to receive
everything in the shape of a horse which he sent in, whether he was
good for anything or not. Please to instruct me in regard to it.[65]

The hierarchical system was observed in most regiments in
matching up men and horses. The noncommissioned officers
chose first in order of rank, and the enlisted men drew lots for the
horses the sergeants and corporals did not take. A few regiments
—the 3rd Ohio was one—tried to follow the Regulars' peacetime
practice of giving each company horses of the same color; this,
however, was a showy luxury that did not survive the first few
weeks or months of campaigning.[66]

The regiment was now in camp. The troopers had all or some
part of their uniforms, some or all of their equipment, an incom-
plete or inadequate armament, and either had their horses, or
were about to receive them. The time had come to turn raw recruits into cavalrymen. That, first of all, meant drill, and more
drill.

Drill began on foot, with the "School of the Trooper, dismounted," the prescribed positions of the soldier, facings right

---

animals. Some of them well cared for were kept in the service till near the
close of the war." Beach, *First New York (Lincoln) Cavalry*, 47.
    64. Crowninshield, *A History of the First Regiment*, 35–36.
    65. Zahm to Montgomery C. Meigs, October 11, 1861, in 3rd Ohio
O&L Books, RG 94, NA. The reply to this letter, if any, is not in the records.
    66. Zahm to Meigs, November 16, 1861, *ibid*.

and left, followed by endless marching up and down the parade ground, performing the evolutions from column into line and from line into column. There were squad drill, and company drill, and battalion drill, usually climaxed by a dress parade of the entire regiment at sundown. Guard mount, sentry duty, and the innumerable formalities of the army day had to be learned and practiced. Since each regiment was a law unto itself, the amount of drill it had depended entirely upon the vigor and enterprise of the colonel or the lieutenant colonel. There were regiments that did not drill when the colonel decided the day was too hot, and others that drilled in every kind of weather for six to eight hours a day, six days a week. The 19th New York, with Alfred Gibbs, a veteran of twenty years' service in the Regular Army, as its colonel, had as much as eight hours of drill daily, with company drill in the morning and battalion drill in the afternoon, "so that," the regimental historian writes, "after our evening dress parade the men were as weary as after a hard day's work in the harvest field or shop. . . . While we were sweltering in the heat . . . some of the other regiments were quietly resting in the shade or gathering on the borders of our drill ground to chaff us."[67]

The officers who had to conduct these exercises were for the most part as ignorant of the drill, or "tactics," as it was called, as the enlisted men. General McClellan's *Regulations and Instructions* prescribed, "The colonel is responsible for the instruction of the regiment. . . . He shall be present, as often as his other duties permit, at the theoretical and practical instructions, and especially at that of the officers assembled together. . . . the colonel assembles the officers twice a week for the theory of the different parts of their instruction. The major and adjutant assemble, in a like manner, the sergeants and corporals."[68] This precept was followed in many regiments; in many others, it was not. Fully as important to the budding officer as the knowledge of the tactics was an intimate knowledge of the holy writ of army administration, the *Revised United States Army Regulations of 1861*, which in good bureaucratic fashion set forth rules, which officers were

67. Bowen, *Regimental History of the First New York*, 96, 26.
68. McClellan, *Regulations and Instructions*, 136–37.

expected to know by heart, for all conceivable (and many inconceivable) situations, events, and problems that could occur in the army. In some instances, however, instruction in the tactics and regulations was hampered by a shortage of books.[69]

Colonel Duffié of the 1st Rhode Island, who assembled his officers in his tent for lessons in the tactics and regulations, was doing precisely what he was required to do. Colonel Josiah H. Kellogg of the 17th Pennsylvania established a "school of instruction," and any officer who failed to master the tactics "had but a short stay with the regiment."[70] Lieutenant Colonel Ingerton of the 13th Tennessee "had the frame of an old building covered with tarpaulins, and called it West Point. He had the . . . Tactics placed in the hands of the officers, and they were required to make a study of them and make daily recitations."[71] Similarly, Colonel O. P. Ransom of the 1st Ohio organized an officers' school, "and every officer was required to get a set of cavalry tactics and devote his time to study and drill, and the company officers were required to organize a school for the non-commissioned officers and give them instruction every night."[72] Colonel James B. Swain of the 11th New York compiled and distributed to his officers a ninety-six-page book entitled "Rules, Regulations, Forms and Suggestions for the Instruction and Guidance of the First United States Volunteer Cavalry," made up of "suggestions or instructions relative to every duty of a cavalryman."[73]

Colonel Bayard of the 1st Pennsylvania assembled his officers once or twice daily to study the tactics, and company, squadron,

69. Zahm to E. P. Buckingham, January 28, 1862, in 3rd Ohio O&L Books, RG 94, NA. It is to be noted that this letter was written more than three months after the regiment was organized.

70. Moyer, History of the 17th Regiment, 28.

71. Scott and Angel, History of the Thirteenth Regiment, 143.

72. Curry, Four Years in the Saddle, 21.

73. Smith, "Scott's 900," Eleventh New York, 50–51. When Colonel Swain, formerly a lieutenant in the Regular Army, organized the regiment in October, 1861, it was with the intention of having it (like the 1st New York [Lincoln] Cavalry) directly in the United States service without a state affiliation. Hence the name "First United States Volunteer Cavalry." However, on October 25, 1862, the War Department turned the regiment over to the state of New York, where it had been raised, and it thereby became the 11th New York.

and regimental drill, held every morning and afternoon with the field-grade officers in attendance, was conducted under his eye. Colonel Gordon Granger of the 2nd Michigan was a believer in the value of practical instruction; he devoted a part of each day to drilling the officers and thereby also provided entertainment for the enlisted men; "as there was a good sized company of [officers], more or less amusement was caused by the awkwardness of some who were not as well drilled as most of their men."[74]

Notwithstanding such instruction, or in the absence of it, many an officer drilled his company with the book of tactics open in his hand. One unnamed lieutenant of the 7th Michigan added a special emphasis to his commands at drill by arriving on the drill ground each morning "with a pocket full of rocks, that, with a volley of blood-curdling oaths, he was wont to discharge at any luckless wight that might miss a step or fall out of line."[75] In some regiments the officers tried to make up for their own shortcomings by hiring a drill instructor. The officers of the 1st Ohio employed one "Major Flanagan," a former "U.S. officer," to drill the regiment; the 10th New York hired a former Prussian officer named Bernstein, but the result in their case was unsatisfactory, for Bernstein "was a vain old fellow, displaying a profusion of gold lace and temper—vanity and profanity. He had a large, subterranean voice, of considerable compass . . . but as a drillmaster he was a dismal failure."[76]

The deadly monotony of close order drill tries the spirit of even the most dedicated soldier. For a man who had enlisted in the cavalry in preference to the infantry to have to spend most of his waking hours on the hay foot-straw foot routine, long after those evolutions had become purely mechanical, was anything but inspiring. No regimental history has a good word to say for these early drills on foot. The 6th Michigan was the only regiment whose records indicate the addition of a much-needed element of spice to the dismal proceedings. Soon after the regiment

74. Lloyd, *History of the First Reg't.*, 13; Thatcher, *A Hundred Battles in the West*, 30.
75. Isham, *An Historical Sketch*, 10.
76. Gillespie, *A History of Company A*, 12; Preston, *History of the 10th Regiment*, 12.

was assembled in camp, the colonel announced that the companies would be lettered, and the seniority of line officers in their respective grades determined, by the relative proficiency of each company in drill by a certain date. The introduction of competition and of a meaningful reward for excellence made the drill routine acceptable for everyone concerned.[77] The colonel of the 6th New York, wishing to relieve the monotony of dismounted drill with "mounted" evolutions before horses had been issued to the regiment, had the bizarre inspiration of handing out ropes for the men to hold on to, to form squads, companies, and even squadrons, and then had them trot through the mounted evolutions on foot.[78]

In most regiments, drill did not begin to interest the men until the sabers were issued. Every movement of the cavalry saber drill was as precisely regulated as was the manual of arms for the infantry. But the saber was the cavalry arm par excellence, and to add to its glamor, it even had a French name, the *arme blanche*, which looked well in letters sent home. The use of the saber in combat proved to be relatively infrequent, and the heavy, clanking steel scabbard, impossible to keep free of rust, was an unmitigated nuisance, but all that was still in the future when the weapon was issued and saber drill began. "Our first saber drill," says the historian of the 1st Ohio, "was something to be remembered. . . . could the hosts of rebeldom have seen the way in which we cut great gashes in the atmosphere they would have realized that their cause was hopeless and would at once have given up the conflict."[79] The sabers were heavy, the drill was difficult to master, and there was considerable awkwardness at first—the historians of the 13th Tennessee expressed the opinion that most of their fellow troopers "could have handled pitchforks more gracefully and to better advantage"—but the men liked the saber drill and actually professed to be delighted with it.[80] The enlisted men

77. Kidd, *Personal Recollections*, 47.
78. Committee on Regimental History, *History of the 6th New York*, 31.
79. Crofts, *Third Ohio Veteran Volunteer Cavalry*, 18.
80. Scott and Angel, *History of the Thirteenth Regiment*, 38. William Gulick of the 1st Iowa wrote his parents, "I am quite tired to night as we have been . . . handling a saber of 3½ lbs[.] my arm is very tired. . . . We

of the 9th Illinois had as a bonus Colonel Brackett's custom of assembling the officers for saber practice at eight o'clock every morning; many of the troopers were in attendance on the side-lines and doubtless commented freely on the performance.

The 2nd Iowa acquired its skill with the saber "under the tutelage of a German gladiator by the name of Graupner. Officers paid him $5.00 each; enlisted men $2.50 for his instruction. He was a master of the science and under his instruction the majority of the regiment acquired a good degree of efficiency in the use of the saber."[81]

In the light of the pride taken by the American army in later years in the marksmanship of its men, it is surprising how little attention was paid in 1861 to that important aspect of the trooper's skills. Not more than a handful of cavalry regiments are definitely known to have had target practice, and it can be deduced from incidental comments that the great majority had none. The 3rd Pennsylvania is one of those that did; the best shots in each company competed for a regimental prize, each contestant firing ten rounds at a target two hundred yards distant.[82] The 4th Illinois had a similar competition, the target being a board with a life-size figure of "Jeff Davis" painted on it. Company I, which won the competition, gained an unfair advantage over the other companies. Some of its men had found "some powder and lead pipe in an old magazine and with this made up a lot of extra cartridges . . . [and] spent many hours shooting at snags in the Mississippi river"; the regimental historian, himself a member of the winning company, adds, "We had thus got a little handy with our carbines while some of the other companies had never fired a shot."[83] Colonel John Kennett of the 4th Ohio had his men prac-

have to drill with the saber making the cuts . . . on a dead run. It is fun." Guyer, "Corporal William O. Gulick," 222.

81. Pierce, History of the Second Iowa, 11.

82. Regimental History Committee, History of the 3d Pennsylvania, 34. "Considerable ammunition was wasted by the Seventh Pennsylvania in Target practice." Dornblaser, Sabre Strokes of the Pennsylvania Dragoons, 32.

83. Avery, History of the Fourth Illinois, 47–48. Getting the jump on the rest of the regiment in marksmanship did not exhaust the resourcefulness of the captain of Company I. His next exploit was a "weeding out." "There is a fleet of gunboats just completed [at Cairo, Ill.]. Men were

tice target shooting with their revolvers, while their horses were going at a full gallop.[84]

Why this neglect of training in marksmanship? Did commanding officers simply fail to recognize its importance, or did the widely held belief in the preeminence of the saber result in a corresponding downgrading of firearms? Some colonels may have thought that American volunteers, heirs of the Minuteman and frontier tradition and half of them farm-bred, did not have to be taught to shoot straight; if so, they were badly mistaken. The notion did not hold true even for most of the country boys, and certainly not for the artisans and clerks from the cities. General Charles H. Smith, formerly colonel of the 1st Maine, said in a speech in 1880, "The average Maine volunteer was less familiar with the use of fire-arms than with the uses of theodolites or telescopes. With revolver in hand, the trooper was more likely to shoot off his horse's ears, or kill his next comrade, than hit an enemy, however near."[85] Perhaps the principal reasons for the neglect of target practice were the delayed distribution of firearms, the inferior quality of many of those issued, and the lack of ammunition. Colonel Zahm of the 3rd Ohio begged no less an authority than Colonel Ripley, head of the Ordnance Bureau, for some "Ball cartridges for Target practice." He also asked for a supply of "Blank Cartridges to accustom the horses to firing," an important phase of training, especially in the light of the inferior horsemanship of most Federal troopers.[86] Lastly, given the lim-

---

wanted to man them . . . and . . . there was a call for volunteers . . . to be transferred to the gun boats. But the Captain took it upon himself to detail such men that we would rather spare and told them they had to go. . . . They were mostly Norwegians and Germans that could hardly speak English." *Ibid.*, 51.

84. Wulsin, *The Story of the Fourth*, 118.

85. Tobie, *First Maine Cavalry*, 124. "In the North, particularly in the East, the population of farmers and mechanics devoted to peaceful pursuits was unaccustomed to all manner of arms . . . and as a rule strange to any horse but a work horse . . . while a very large proportion had never fired a gun." Benjamin W. Crowninshield, "Cavalry in Virginia During the War of the Rebellion," *Papers of the Military Historical Society of Massachusetts*, XIII (1913), 3.

86. Zahm to Ripley, October 25, 1861, in 3rd Ohio O&L Books, RG 94, NA. The records do not indicate the outcome of Colonel Zahm's request.

ited and usually inadequate amount of time most regiments had between organization and active service, a colonel of volunteers may be forgiven for passing up training in marksmanship even when his men had adequate arms, in favor of the more difficult and more immediately urgent task of teaching them to ride and to control their horses.

The magnitude of the task of turning the average volunteer into a horseman is illustrated by the sad experience of the 7th Indiana. It had been in camp for some weeks when Governor Oliver P. Morton announced his desire to review the regiment. Colonel John P. C. Shanks was "naturally ambitious that his men should present as fine an appearance as possible . . . [and] therefore issued orders for the regiment to appear mounted, on the field for review." What happened then could have been told of nearly any regiment of volunteer cavalry on the Union side in the autumn of 1861:

The horses having been but recently drawn, had never been exercised in drill. Some of them had never been backed. . . . The men were as green as the horses. Some of them never having been on a horse's back, did not know how to mount. Those who had wild steeds, had great difficulty in maintaining their positions in the saddle, and some in attempting to mount suddenly found themselves on the ground. However, after great effort, the horses were sufficiently quieted, so as to stand in reasonable proximity to each other. The hour having arrived for the review, the companies were marched to the parade ground, and the regiment, after long and patient effort, formed in a reasonably straight line. Governor Morton and his Staff, accompanied by Colonel Shanks, took their positions in front of the regiment. Colonel Shanks, in genuine military style, gave the command "Draw Sabres." The men obeyed the order. The sabres in being drawn made a great rattling and clatter, and waved over the horse's heads, the sight and sound of which greatly frightened them. This was more than they could bear. Some of them reared and plunged, depositing their riders on the ground; some wheeled and dashed madly for the company quarters; others darted over the commons, their riders hatless, holding on with both hands to the horses' manes, or the pommels of their saddles, presenting pictures not in keeping with accomplished equestrianism. . . . So ended the first *grand review* of the regiment.[87]

87. Cogley, *History of the Seventh Indiana*, 64–65.

This humiliating episode points up a fact that was generally overlooked, namely that the cavalry mount needed training as much as its rider. Assuming that it had been broken to the saddle, then, in the words of an officer with long experience in the cavalry,

When a horse has been suppled and trained until the rider is enabled to devote his own attention to the performance of his duties without constantly thinking of what the animal may do; when the trooper feels entire confidence that at the proper indication the horse will move out and promptly take any gait desired; that he will proceed in any direction without resistance; that the breaking of a strap, firing of a gun or any unforeseen occurrence or accident will not disconcert the animal . . . then both man and horse have acquired a degree of efficiency which should increase the chances of success in a campaign.[88]

The records show that at least two regiments (there may of course have been others) trained their horses to stand gunfire. The 5th Iowa engaged in "training of horses to run up on the muskets and the mouths of the cannons, while firing, and also being drawn up in line when the foot would charge on them with muskets & fixed bayonets."[89] The 1st Iowa also trained its horses, and the men as well, by staging sham battles, the charging infantry firing blank cartridges.[90]

In European armies, horses, carefully selected to begin with, were put through a lengthy course of training by experienced horsemen before being issued to troopers who had had equally thorough training in horsemanship. In the Union army, by necessity, completely untrained horses, many of them not even broken to the saddle, were issued to soldiers who, like their colleagues of the 7th Indiana, were in far too many cases as untrained as their

88. Carter, *Horses, Saddles and Bridles*, 126. Charles Francis Adams of the 1st Massachusetts wrote in January, 1862, "As for active service . . . You couldn't get our horses within a mile of firearms. . . . We are all green, officers, men and horses, and long practice is absolutely necessary." W. C. Ford (ed.), *A Cycle of Adams Letters, 1861–1865* (2 vols.; Boston, 1920), I, 98.

89. John S. Ezell (ed.), "Excerpts from the Civil War Diary of Lieutenant Charles Alley, Company 'C,' Fifth Iowa Cavalry," *Iowa Journal of History*, XLIX (1951), 246.

90. Guyer, "Corporal William O. Gulick," 222.

mounts. Nearly every regimental historian could have echoed Frederick Denison of the 1st Rhode Island (and most of them did) in a rueful description of the "laughable mishaps connected with the breaking and training of green and vicious horses by some green and unphilosophical men. A beast sharply touched by the spurs, would dash from the ranks, with his rider holding by both hands to the reins, or mane, or neck, and clasping more tightly with his limbs, till his spurs added new jump and speed to his military departure."[91]

There were mishaps of every conceivable kind. Men were thrown, kicked, and dragged. They collected broken bones, aches, pains, and bruises along with experience in controlling a powerful, refractory, and unpredictable animal. A favorite technique of sweating the devilment out of intractable horses was to run them repeatedly up the steepest nearby hill, with a liberal application of sharp spurs. Unfortunately for horses and riders alike, the army had seen fit to issue curb bits to the cavalry, on the theory that a severe bit was needed to control an untrained animal; however, the effect on a jittery, panic-stricken horse of having an equally jittery, panic-stricken trooper tugging and jerking at the reins was just the opposite of what was intended. The cruel bit drove the horse into a frenzy and made it uncontrollable.

In spite of everything, however, progress was made. It was evident to knowledgeable observers that "the greater portion of [cavalrymen] were not horsemen," but by dint of much yelling and swearing they were taught to retain their seats in the saddle, at least at the walk and the trot, and to guide their horses through the mounted drill with only the left hand on the reins.[92] They learned also to go through the mounted drill without the "crowding in the ranks . . . getting out of place and striving to get back into place, and pushing forward and hanging back, and going backwards and sideways . . . and all sorts of haps and mishaps" that distinguished the initial essays in equestrianism.[93] But it can safely be said that not a single regiment of volunteer cavalry in the Union army ever approached as a unit the proficiency in

91. Denison, *Sabres and Spurs*, 55.
92. deTrobriand, *Four Years with the Army of the Potomac*, 89.
93. Tobie, *First Maine Cavalry*, 15.

horsemanship that would have been considered acceptable by a European cavalry officer. Charles Russell Lowell wrote of being ordered at a review of his 2nd Massachusetts to "take them around at a gallop. I knew I was well mounted and could keep ahead of my command. I knew I could take round most of my horses and perhaps a few of my men."[94] In December, 1861, the British war correspondent, William Howard Russell, attended the presentation of colors to the 2nd New York. President and Mrs. Lincoln, and a large assemblage of civilian and military dignitaries were in attendance. After the flag had been presented and accepted in speeches appropriate to the occasion, "the regiment went through some evolutions, which were brought to an untimely end by a feu de joie from the infantry in the rear, which instantly broke up the squadrons, and sent them kicking, plunging and falling over the field, to the great amusement of the crowd."[95]

It came to be recognized, especially in the first two years of the war when mounted combat was more common than it was afterward, that inferior horsemanship was a major contributing factor in the poor performance of the Federal cavalry. Cavalrymen on the Union side never developed into a race of centaurs. One trooper wrote after the war, "Our regiment was one of the best drilled and most efficient bodies of mounted men in the service; but for all that, at our best, to have turned us off the road (taking the going as it came) and set us across country at any such gait as is understood by a cavalry charge, and out of our whole ten troops there would not have been so much as a corporal's guard left at the end of six hundred yards."[96]

Some regiments did receive courses in horsemanship that in severity, if not in length, approximated the prewar training of recruits in the Regular cavalry. The great majority of the troopers of the 15th New York lacked the ability to ride a horse when they entered the service. But they learned. As a beginning, for several days they were made to ride bareback. Then for a few days they were permitted to ride on folded blankets "which afforded . . .

94. Edward W. Emerson, *The Life and Letters of Charles Russell Lowell* (Boston, 1907), 241.

95. Russell, *My Diary North and South*, II, 414–15.

96. C. E. Lewis, *War Sketches: With the First Dragoons in Virginia* (London, 1897), 63–64.

some relief." Next, they were allowed to use their saddles, but without stirrups, "and the agony increased tenfold." At last the stirrups were added, and the regiment's miseries "were over, but some of the men were nearly used up with the hardships endured."[97]

The troopers of the 3rd Pennsylvania were completely stumped by the task of assembling the tack issued to them, until the officers and men of the 5th United States, which happened to be camped nearby, took pity on them and not only helped them fit the parts together, but also explained what each item was for. The regiment had already had several weeks of active service when William W. Averell became its colonel and saw to it that the men learned to ride properly. Drills became "incessant." "We could not then understand why we should be compelled to jump our horses over ditches and fences, especially so if we were awkward and both riders and horses . . . fell into the ditches instead of jumping over them. Nor could we see the necessity of our being required to mount with stirrups crossed. . . . These exercises were irksome and were not relished by the officers any more than by the men."[98] Lieutenant Colonel Ingerton of the 13th Tennessee had ditches dug "and officers and men were required to train their horses to jump ditches, logs and fences, charge up and down steep hills, and handle their horses skillfully. It was now considered a disgrace for an officer to get 'unhorsed' and it required a basket of champaigne to remove the stigma."[99] The troopers of the 1st Iowa had "a fine old time"; they "went out in the woods to run and jump [their] horses over logs and Ditches."[100]

In the long run much of this effort turned out to be a waste of time and energy. Horses were destroyed faster than they could be trained. As for the men, long before the end of the war the functions and tactics (in the modern sense of the word) of cavalry evolved in directions that seldom called for anything more than a modest degree of equestrian skill.

97. Norton, "The Red Neck Ties," 17.
98. Regimental History Committee, History of the 3rd Pennsylvania, 23.
99. Scott and Angel, History of the Thirteenth Regiment, 150.
100. Guyer, "Corporal William O. Gulick," 222.

V

Officers and Gentlemen

"I AM A MAN UNDER AUTHORITY," SAID THE CENTURION of Capernaum in the New Testament, "having soldiers under me; and I say to this man, Go, and he goeth; and to another, Come, and he cometh." Many a cavalry officer who knew his Bible, and in 1861 most of them did, must have thought of the Centurion with admiration and envy. His confident assertion breathes the self-assurance of a man who has the habit of command and knows its language and technique. These accomplishments were not common among the recently commissioned volunteer cavalry officers as they faced their men in camp and on the drill ground in the first few months of an experience that was novel and strange for all alike. The men, for all their fractious individualism, expected and wanted to be led, but most of those certified as leaders by their commissions and shoulder straps lacked the skill and knowledge needed to lead. There were many to be taught but few to teach, and those who had to do the teaching had themselves to learn the mechanics of soldiering so that they could transmit their knowledge, however uncertain and undigested it may have been, to their men. They also had to acquire the far more difficult arts of looking after the welfare of their pupils and of inspiring them with confidence. They had to develop the assumption—perhaps the arrogant assumption—that their commands would be obeyed, without which the mere issuance of orders is ineffective. They were already officers; they had to become leaders.

With commissions earned for recruiting ability followed by election, from the standpoint of military knowledge there was little to choose among lieutenants, captains, majors, and colonels. With few exceptions, all were equally ignorant. Hence the lieutenants could not learn from the captains, the captains from the majors, or the majors from the colonels. The tactics and the army regulations could be—and had to be—learned by heart from books, but the essence of what a good officer had to know was not to be found in any book. It had to come partly from instinct, partly from character, and partly, as Charles Francis Adams wrote of himself, from "rough experience and as an outcome of [his] own blunders."[1]

The eighty-two cavalry regiments enrolled by the end of 1861 had nearly thirty-three hundred officers of the line, staff, and field. Perhaps one out of every seven or eight was a transfer from the Regular Army, a former officer of a European army, or had served as an officer in the Mexican War or in the militia. The rest, nearly three thousand, had had no command experience whatever. Moreover, as Governor David Tod of Ohio was to write a few months later, and as every other governor could have written, "In my efforts to popularize volunteering I have been compelled to appoint many officers who I fear are unfit for their positions."[2] The astonishing thing, however, is not the number of such men who failed as officers, but the far greater number who met the searching tests of command and became competent and even excellent officers.

Those who could not meet the test failed for a variety of reasons. Some merely lacked physical stamina. Some were incurably stupid or lazy. Some were irresponsible or shiftless, or, in the words of Regis deTrobriand, were "unfitted from their education,

1. Charles F. Adams, *Charles Francis Adams, 1835–1915: An Autobiography* (Boston, 1916), 132.
2. *Official Records*, Series III, Vol. II, p. 538.

moral character, or mental deficiencies, for ever acquiring the requisite efficiency."[3]

The most common "moral" failing among officers was addiction to the bottle. In the 1st New York "there was intemperance among some of the officers, and they neglected their duties. The percentage of intemperance among the enlisted men was less than among the officers."[4] One of the 7th Pennsylvania historians has written, "Our regimental officers were distinguished more for their bravery than for their sobriety, and their example was not calculated to promote habits of temperance among those under their command."[5] A dozen or more regimental histories and numerous entries in regimental order and letter books are sufficiently outspoken to make it evident that the bottle was the cause of many "resignations" and dismissals from the service. The major commanding Charles Francis Adams' battalion of the 1st Massachusetts "got drunk before [the regiment] left [the state] and has remained so ever since, and the battalion has taken care of itself. That officer has now disappeared, we hope forever."[6] When he wrote about the major Adams did not know that his colonel, Robert Williams, a good organizer and a ruthless disciplinarian, was an excellent commanding officer so long as the regiment was in camp, "but in the field he got speedily demoralized, and in moments of emergency, invariably drunk"; in the midst of the Antietam Campaign Williams disappeared altogether for two days and then, mercifully, resigned.[7] Adams also mentions the "drunken insanity" of his captain which, together with the "insane vanity" of this captain's older brother, who succeeded Williams as colonel, "utterly ruined the finest regiment that ever left Massachusetts."[8] The lieutenant colonel of the 2nd Michigan was compelled to resign "for the all-too common offense of intoxication," and scores of other officers of every rank were lost to the service for the same reason.[9]

3. deTrobriand, *Four Years with the Army of the Potomac.*
4. Beach, *First New York (Lincoln) Calvary,* 74.
5. Dornblaser, *Sabre Strokes of the Pennsylvania Dragoons,* 36.
6. Ford, *A Cycle of Adams Letters,* I, 97.
7. Adams, *An Autobiography,* 138.
8. *Ibid.,* 146.
9. Thatcher, *A Hundred Battles in the West,* 276. The colonel of the

Considering the heterogeneous origins of the officer corps, it is not surprising that cases of dishonesty among them were not unknown. Lieutenant E. B. Edwards, Company A, 1st Vermont, was ordered to "report immediately in writing . . . whether he sold to Sutler E. Walker, on or about the 6th day of June last, for the sum of $50, a large bay gelding horse, and if so, state whether the horse so sold was the private property of him, the said Edwards, and if so, how, when and where he got his title to said horse, and of whom he purchased it, and the price paid therefor."[10] With cavalry horses being bought by the government for $110 and up, this order clearly implies that Lieutenant Edwards' title to a horse he was willing to sell for $50 was questionable. Lieutenant A. J. Grover of the same regiment was requested to submit "an immediate report in writing of the authority . . . [he] had for taking from Company E . . . one saddle, and equipments complete, one girth, one nose bag, one shirt, two pairs drawers, and one pair stockings."[11]

Then there were the officers who on one excuse or another— or on none—absented themselves from their regiments. Captain George E. Conger, 1st Vermont, was requested by the regimental adjutant to "reply to the following interrogatory: By what authority are you absent from the regiment?"[12] Lieutenant F. S. Dunham, Company L, 2nd Iowa, was ordered to "return to his company for duty within one hour from the receipt of this order, and there remain, and will not be permitted to leave camp."[13] Officers

17th Pennsylvania was another high-ranking officer who was forced to resign because of drunkenness. Why did so many men, presumably temperate in civil life, become drunkards in the army? Was it the removal of the restraints of an accustomed family and social structure, or was it the stress induced by the effort to cope with a set of strange and complex responsibilities? This is a problem the present writer is content to leave to the psychohistorians.

10. Special Orders No. 48, March 13, 1863, in 1st Vermont Volunteer Cavalry, Regimental and Company Order and Letter Books, Record Group 94, National Archives. Hereinafter cited as 1st Vermont O&L Books.

11. Edgar Pitkin to A. J. Grover, June 26, 1862, *ibid.*

12. Letter from Pitkin to George E. Conger, June 26, 1862, *ibid.*

13. Special Orders No. 110, October 5, 1863, in 2nd Iowa Volunteer Cavalry, Regimental and Company Order and Letter Books, Record Group 94, National Archives. Hereinafter cited as 2nd Iowa O&L Books.

who sought to escape the hardships of life under canvas—and coincidentally, the performance of their duties—by quartering themselves in farmhouses in the vicinity of camp, were ordered by Philip Sheridan, then colonel of the 2nd Michigan, to "rejoin their proper companies" forthwith, on pain of "immediate arrest for violation of orders and shirking duty in face of the enemy."[14] Such absences could be arranged with the help of an accommodating regimental surgeon, as shown by a 2nd Iowa order:

Hereafter, no officer upon the sick report of the surgeon will be allowed to leave camp under any pretext except by written order of the surgeon. . . . [The] surgeon will be held responsible for all officers whose names appear upon the sick report, and will give no permits for officers to leave camp except it be approved by the commanding officer of the regiment. Officers will do well to remember that they have no right whatever to put themselves upon the sick report, and the person so reported not being able to show good cause, he will be immediately recommended to be mustered out of the service.[15]

An apparently unique case was that of Lieutenant Jed P. Clark, Company B, 1st Vermont, as reported by Colonel Charles H. Tompkins to the Secretary of War:

On the morning of the __ day of __, 1862 . . . Lieutenant Clark came into camp and stated that he had been taken prisoner by some of the enemy while absent from camp on the previous evening (and while within our own lines) and by them released upon his parole. . . . He is now absent with leave in accordance with orders received to that effect. Since he has left the regiment on leave, I have come to the deliberate conclusion that the whole affair was a "*canard*" upon his part to rid himself of active duty while he retains his rank and pay. Many of the officers of the regiment agree with me in this opinion. Adding to this the fact that his trunk was packed and sent home several days before the affair happened, that the horse which he claims was shot under him . . . was a horse belonging to the government, and that he stole a horse when he left the regiment . . . and I think the evidence is conclusive against him, and I most respectfully recommend that the said . . . Clark . . . be discharged from the military service of the U. S.[16]

14. General Orders No. 29, July 15, 1862, in 2nd Michigan O&L Books, RG 94, NA.
15. General Orders No. 152, October 4, 1863, in 2nd Iowa O&L Books, RG 94, NA.
16. Charles H. Tompkins to Secretary of War Stanton, in 1st Vermont O&L Books, RG 94, NA. The date of Clark's "capture" is blank in

What was a colonel to do with subordinate officers who in his opinion failed to measure up? If he was tough enough, personally and politically, he could persuade or compel them to offer their resignations, or in extreme cases he could dismiss them. Williams of the 1st Massachusetts was one colonel who dismissed "many officers." After his appointment as colonel of the 3rd Pennsylvania, William Averell performed a wholesale slaughter of his officers; between October 31, 1861, and April 4, 1862, he got rid of one major, seven captains, six first and seven second lieutenants, and, for good measure, the surgeon and the assistant surgeon.[17] The men too had ways of seeing to the departure of officers who failed to meet with their approval. "Some of . . . [the] acts" of Lieutenant Colonel M. T. Patrick of the 5th Iowa "not being palatable to the men," they "agreed to report him to the general."[18] The troopers of Company I, 3rd Ohio, petitioned Colonel Zahm to "remove" Lieutenant William Goodnow, who, they declared, had "lost all their confidence and respect"; inasmuch as the lieutenant's failings included drunkenness, absence without leave, and neglect of duty, the men's disapproval would seem to have been well justified.[19] The 1st Vermont may have been unique in having a "regimental town meeting . . . always in session," but every cavalry regiment had its court of public opinion, with its own crude but effective machinery, unknown to the regulations, for enforcing its sentences.[20]

Another method for hastening the departure of unwanted of-

---

the O&L Books copy of the letter. By Special Orders No. 353, War Department, Adjutant General's Office, November 19, 1862, in *ibid.*, Clark was dismissed from the army "for feigning capture by the enemy to escape active service."

17. Regimental History Committee, *History of the 3rd Pennsylvania,* 23, 27. Between the beginning of April, 1862, and the end of November, when Averell was promoted and left the regiment, another thirteen officers (the lieutenant colonel, a major, six captains, and five lieutenants) "resigned," and three lieutenants were dismissed. *Ibid.*, 101, 112, 152.

18. Ezell, "Civil War Diary of Charles Alley," 249.

19. Zahm to Dennison, December 18, 1861, in 3rd Ohio O&L Books, RG 94, NA.

20. Benedict, *Vermont in the Civil War*, II, 535. The night before Captain Menken, Company C, 1st Ohio, "resigned and left for parts unknown," his tent was stoned and "his departure hailed with cheers and groans. He was bitterly hated by his men." Gillespie, *A History of Company A*, 126.

ficers was for their colonel to order them to appear before one of the examining boards authorized by Congress "to inquire into the capacity, qualifications, efficiency and propriety of conduct" of volunteer officers.[21] The minatory effect of the existence of these boards was far greater than their actual accomplishments. The number of officers dismissed for failure to pass the scrutiny of an examining board was small, but the threat of having to appear before one stimulated the energies of the lazy and the devotion to duty of the shiftless. Moreover, many of those ordered to undergo an examination resigned rather than face the ordeal and the disgrace of a possible dismissal from the service.[22] Lieutenant Samuel Harris of the 5th Michigan, ordered by his colonel to go before an examining board, passed the examination easily, but, he wrote, "The strain I had been under . . . unnerved me more than any engagement I had ever been in, and [I] was laid up for the next ten days unfit for even camp duty."[23]

At least one case on record suggests that on occasion a hearing before an examining board seemed more like a trial than an examination. Gordon Granger, having become commander of the Second Cavalry Division, Department of the Mississippi, ordered that regimental commanders "presenting the names of officers for examination . . . will specify particularly in what such officers are deficient, and also the names of witnesses to prove and verify the same."[24] In March, 1862, some of the officers of that exceedingly informal body of men, the 1st Kentucky, were ordered to appear before an examining board. Most of those examined were ordered

21. "Act to authorize the employment of volunteers" of July 22, 1861, Section 10. The congressional enactment was given effect by War Department, Adjutant General's Office, General Orders No. 49, August 3, 1861. General Jacob D. Cox, commanding the District of West Virginia, ordered that the examining boards in his district consider as disqualifications for continued service as officers, "gross immorality, habitual drunkenness, keeping low company, shirking duty, undue familiarity with subordinates, or incapacity to govern men." Special Orders No. 69, December 16, 1862, quoted in Stanley L. Swart, "The Military Examination Board in the Civil War: A Case Study," *Civil War History*, XVI (1970), 231.
22. Preston, *History of the 10th Regiment*, 63. See also Pyne, *First New Jersey Cavalry*, 23; Swart, "The Military Examination Board," 227 ff.
23. Harris, *Personal Reminiscences*, 67–70.
24. General Orders No. 39, June 23, 1862, in 2nd Michigan O&L Books, RG 94, NA.

to be mustered out of the service, but "fortunately for most of [the] officers [the regiment] was not permitted to remain idle long enough for the examination to be completed."[25]

However useful the examining board system may have been, directly or indirectly, in weeding out misfits in the first years of the war, it was misused in typically blind bureaucratic fashion. Officers of the 22nd Pennsylvania had to appear before one of the boards as late as March, 1865, to be examined "as to their knowledge of military tactics . . . military laws and usages, etc. Some of . . . [the] officers who had three years of splendid fighting record in the field, were unable to get on paper to the satisfaction of the . . . board and were consequently discharged. This was done but a few weeks before the final muster-out of the volunteer troops, and was certainly a most unjust proceeding."[26]

Serious cases of misconduct were dealt with by bringing charges against the offender, who was then tried by court martial. If convicted he could, depending on the gravity of the charges and the inclinations of the court, be sentenced to dismissal from the service. Thus, Captain William W. Eaton, 2nd Iowa, was dishonorably dismissed for "neglect of duty, disobedience of orders, cowardice, misbehavior in the face of the enemy, conduct unbecoming an officer and gentleman, and general inefficiency."[27]

These weeding-out processes were neither sufficiently systematic nor sufficiently searching to rid the service of every commissioned ignoramus, coward, drunkard, loafer, and misfit. Far too often those weeded out, or who resigned to avoid being weeded out, could get themselves reinstated if they had the right political connections. In December, 1861, Colonel Zahm of the 3rd Ohio persuaded Lieutenant Goodnow, who had lost the confidence and respect of his men, to resign rather than face a court martial on charges of ungentlemanly and unsoldierlike conduct. The next day, Zahm thought it well to report the circumstances of the case to Governor William Dennison of Ohio. A month passed, and then Zahm sent orders to Goodnow to return to duty. The governor's

25. Tarrant, *Wild Riders of the First Kentucky*, 72.
26. Farrar, *The Twenty-Second Pennsylvania*, 458.
27. Special Orders No. 49, War Department, Adjutant General's Office, February 1, 1864, in 2nd Iowa O&L Books, RG 94, NA.

hand is apparent in Goodnow's restoration to a post he was not qualified to fill.[28] Politics is even more obvious in the case of Major E. B. Sawyer, 1st Vermont, who took advantage of an ankle sprain sustained in April, 1862, to remain away from his post for six months, enjoying the cool comfort of his home in Vermont while his men sweltered and fought in Virginia. Dismissed from the service for "neglect of the welfare of his regiment," Sawyer's dismissal was revoked and he was restored to his rank and command, following a plea on his behalf by the governor of Vermont to the secretary of war.[29] Similarly, Captain E. H. Bean of the same regiment, dishonorably dismissed in October, 1862, was promptly reinstated, only to be dismissed a second time a few months later, this time for "cowardly conduct in the presence of the enemy."[30]

There was yet another injurious facet of the weeding-out problem: no law or regulation existed to prevent an officer, after dismissal or forced resignation from one regiment, from turning up in the same or an even higher rank in another. To obtain a new commission he needed only the right political connections, or the ability to recruit men for a new regiment.[31] Thus, Captain Lorenzo H. Whitney, whose resignation from the 8th Illinois was accepted with alacrity by Lieutenant Colonel William Gamble on the grounds that the regiment "would be better" without him, was a short time later appointed colonel of the 140th Illinois Infantry.[32]

28. Zahm to Dennison, December 18, 1861, and Zahm to William Goodnow, January 28, 1862, in 3rd Ohio O&L Books, RG 94, NA.

29. Special Orders No. 314, War Department, Adjutant General's Office, October 27, 1862, and Special Orders No. 405, December 20, 1862, in 1st Vermont O&L Books, RG 94, NA. In fairness to Sawyer, it should be added that he was eventually promoted to colonel and commanded the regiment with credit. It is reported also, but with no indication of the source of the statement, that Sawyer was "on crutches for months" while in Vermont. Benedict, *Vermont in the Civil War*, II, 564.

30. Special Orders No. 289, War Department, Adjutant General's Office, October 11, 1862, and Special Orders No. 193, April 28, 1863, in 1st Vermont O&L Books, RG 94, NA.

31. Upton, *The Military Policy of the United States*, 438.

32. William Gamble to George Stoneman and J. F. Farnsworth, July 18, 1862, in 8th Illinois Volunteer Cavalry, Regimental and Company Or-

Two examples—if any are needed to prove a point so obvious —illustrate the results produced by the incompetence of officers who escaped through the wide meshes of a haphazard elimination system and remained in the service. When the 5th Michigan made its first scout in Virginia, the captain who had the advance reached the brow of a hill and saw twenty-five or thirty Confederate cavalry a short distance ahead. He then halted his company and sent a message back to the main body, reporting rebels ahead and asking, what should he do? [33] And there was Lieutenant William C. Garrett of the 7th Pennsylvania, who was sent with thirty of his men to escort a forage train to a camp a short distance from Nashville. Garrett did not bother to see if his men were properly armed. More than a third of them had left their carbines behind, and some had neglected to take their sabers and revolvers. After the train started Garrett made no effort to keep the wagons closed up. He left his men to shift for themselves, and while he enjoyed his dinner in a farmhouse along the way, with "the wagons . . . scattered along for half a mile [and] the men still farther to the rear, driving some beef cattle," the train was pounced upon by Confederate cavalry and captured. Only four troopers and a few teamsters managed to escape.[34]

The shortcomings of volunteer officers showed up most glaringly in the area of discipline. It would have been exceedingly difficult at best to establish discipline in regiments composed of men who, with the exception of a small number of Europeans and former Regulars, could see neither the purpose nor the sense in the diminution of their right to do as they pleased. The manner in which regiments had been raised and officers selected made it unlikely that anything approaching the European standard of military discipline could take root in the Union cavalry. Companies generally, and frequently entire regiments, raised in a

---

der and Letter Books, Record Group 94, National Archives. Hereinafter cited as 8th Illinois O&L Books.

33. Harris, *Personal Reminiscences,* 14–15. The captain in question had the grace—or the good judgment—to turn in his resignation when the regiment got back to Washington.

34. Dornblaser, *Sabre Strokes of the Pennsylvania Dragoons,* 82–86.

small geographic area, were made up of men who in many cases had known each other since childhood. Officers elected by school-mates, neighbors, and friends were not likely to receive, or even to expect, the unquestioning obedience of their constituents. The men had no reason to be in awe of officers who had been their equals in civil life and knew no more of the trade of soldiering than they did. On the other hand, the officers lacked the self-assurance that is an essential ingredient of command. Thus, the fundamental elements of discipline were lacking. To add to the problem, there was an apparently sincere and well-intentioned reluctance on the part of many officers to keep the distance between themselves and their men which is also needed for maintaining discipline.

The problem of this relationship is summarized by Thomas Wentworth Higginson, himself a former officer:

The weak point in our volunteer service . . . [is] that the soldier, in nine cases out of ten, utterly detests being commanded, while the officer, in his turn, equally shrinks from commanding. . . . In many cases there is really no . . . difference between officers and men, in education or in breeding. . . . all are from the same neighborhood, all will return to the same civil pursuits side by side; every officer knows that in a little while each soldier will again become his client or his customer, his constituent or his rival. Shall he offend him for life in order to carry out . . . stricter discipline?[35]

John Tewksbury, who had begun his career in the 1st Massachusetts as an enlisted man and rose to be its commanding officer, thought it necessary to issue an order ("to be promulgated only to the officers of the command") in which he noted with "regret . . . the familiarity as allowed by the officers from the enlisted men . . . which is not only improper, but highly prejudicial to good order and military discipline"; he went on to direct that "in future, officers will be particular in this respect, and at no time will they allow an enlisted man to approach them for any purpose unless they do so in a respectful and soldierly manner."[36]

35. Thomas Wentworth Higginson, "Regular and Volunteer Officers," *Atlantic Monthly* (XIV), 1864, 348–57, quoted in Commager, *The Blue and the Gray*, II, 483–84.
36. Special Orders No. 3, January 9, 1865, in 1st Massachusetts Volunteer Cavalry, Regimental and Company Order and Letter Books, Record

The historian of the 17th Pennsylvania noted, how accurately can no longer be determined, that after the regiment received "many new recruits" in the winter of 1864, "it soon developed that the very friendly and cordial feeling that originally existed between the enlisted men and the officers was no longer a distinguishing feature. The lines drawn between the new recruits and the officers became more marked."[37] This comment gains significance from the fact that by the winter of 1864 most of the officers of the 17th Pennsylvania, as of every cavalry regiment that had been in service for two or three years, were former enlisted men.

An order issued by Colonel E. B. Sawyer of the 1st Vermont dealt with two aspects of the officer-enlisted man relationship problem. "Soldiers will not," he wrote, "visit officers' tents except in cases of necessity, and when a soldier visits an officer's tent from such necessity, he will rap at the tent entrance, and not enter until bidden to come in, and when he enters the tent, he will uncover, salute, and remain standing until his business is accomplished, unless ordered to sit, and when his business is done, he will salute and immediately retire. Officers are enjoined to enforce this rule, and to improve every occasion to give their soldiers the proper instructions on all matters of military courtesy." He went on to call the officers' attention to "the gross impropriety of allowing themselves to be addressed by soldiers by familiar titles or by their christian names, or of so addressing their men. . . . Every officer should be addressed by his proper military title, and men by their surname."[38] And to make sure these admonitions sank in, he directed that the order be read "at retreat for three consecutive days." This order, be it noted, was issued when the regiment had been in existence for nearly one and a half years.

The enlisted men's reaction to such orders is illustrated by an entry in the diary of a trooper of the 5th Iowa: "Today," wrote Charles Alley on January 6, 1862, "among the orders read on inspection was one to the effect that no officer should hold any

Group 94, National Archives. Hereinafter cited as 1st Massachusetts O&L Books.
37. Moyer, *History of the 17th Regiment,* 287.
38. Special Orders No. 39, January 23, 1863, in 1st Vermont O&L Books, RG 94, NA.

communication with his men except on duty. How pleasant for the sovereigns to be reminded that they were no longer fit company for 'gentlemen'!" Then, two weeks later, came the following: "Last week the Colonel complained that the men of Co. C did not take off their hats when business brought them to his office. On Tattoo the men were told of it by the second Lt. and enjoined to take off their caps. . . . there was a storm of hisses for the Col. and an outspoken declaration to refuse compliance. They said they were willing to take off their caps in any man's *house*, but not to any *man* when they went to an office for business."[39]

A "limited element" among the officers of the 19th New York wanted to introduce the Regular Army custom of having enlisted men communicate with officers only through a sergeant. At a meeting to consider the matter, one of the officers declared, "I'm opposed to this whole thing on the ground that these men are in every respect our equals in civil life. When the war is over, I expect to live among them, and will be ashamed to meet them if I should sanction this project." And, the regimental historian adds, "To the honor of our officers the scheme was quickly squelched."[40]

Any strict or perhaps only conscientious officer who tried to establish discipline was at once dubbed a martinet or tyrant and was disliked and sabotaged accordingly. When Lieutenant Colonel Thomas Drummond set about disciplining the 4th Iowa and gave its troopers "for the first time the idea that a soldier is a man who obeys another man's orders," his efforts "had little support or encouragement from either officers or men, and he met constantly as much difficulty and obstruction as could be put in his way"; for, as the regimental historian remarks, "with such men as composed the average volunteer regiment at the beginning of the war it would be hardly possible for such an officer to succeed."[41]

In contrast to the 4th Iowa, the 1st Ohio, which had a "great contempt" for its Colonel O. P. Ransom "in the beginning, as he

39. Ezell, "Civil War Diary of Charles Alley," 244.
40. Bowen, *Regimental History of the First New York*, 119. Charles Russell Lowell of the 2nd Massachusetts commented in one of his letters that it was "hard to get new officers to keep the proper line between the men and themselves." Emerson, *Charles Russell Lowell*, 252.
41. Scott, *Story of a Cavalry Regiment*, 13–14.

was a regular martinet," as soon as the regiment got into the field began to see the reasons for what the colonel had tried to do and ended by developing "very high regard" for him. The junior officers paid Colonel Ransom the supreme compliment of using his "good round oaths."[42]

The greatest failing of volunteer officers, and the most damaging in its effect on the efficiency and welfare of their commands, was their own lack of discipline. The great majority of officers of volunteer regiments were themselves volunteers, the products of a society that placed a premium on individualism and was just beginning to discover the uses and the need of organization and discipline. Once in the army, commissions in hand, uniforms, shoulder straps, sashes, side arms, and chargers purchased, the novices read about discipline in the army regulations and heard about it from the former Regulars and foreign officers in their regiments, but it is open to question how much meaning they attached to the word, and to what extent they understood it to apply not only to the enlisted men under them but to themselves as well. In an exhortation to the officers of the 8th Illinois, Lieutenant Colonel William Gamble called attention to a "want of improvement in discipline and obedience to orders on the part of *a few* of the officers of the Regiment" and reminded them that "the first duty of a soldier is a prompt and cheerful obedience to all lawful orders, and no one is fit to command, in any capacity, that is not himself willing to obey."[43]

Every regimental commander who understood the nature of his command problems realized that the establishment of a sense of discipline among his officers was the key to a solution. Here as an example is a May, 1862, order issued by Colonel Tompkins of the 1st Vermont:

The attention of officers . . . is called to the loose and very unmilitary manner of performing duty in the regiment, and the commanding officer is obliged to exact an immediate reform, or bring the delin-

42. Curry, *Four Years in the Saddle*, 16, 18. With all of his strictness, Colonel Ransom also "looked after the smallest details of clothing, rations and all things that pertained to the comfort of the men . . . and whatever was poor in quality or short in quantity he rejected . . . with a savage threat of arrest to the quartermaster or commissary." *Ibid.*, 16.

43. Orders No. 14, November 11, 1861, in 8th Illinois O&L Books, RG 94, NA.

quents before a court martial. Orders are issued ... to be obeyed, and in future no excuse will be received for non-compliance with regimental orders. The presence of *all* officers is required at the stated roll calls, reveille, retreat and tattoo. ... The commissioned officers will give more of their attention to their companies in an endeavor to promote the soldierly bearing and efficiency of the regment.[44]

This was the state of affairs in an eastern regiment. The situation was no better in western regiments, as evidenced by an order issued by Philip Sheridan to the 2nd Michigan, also in May, 1862, after he had studied the state of his new command for three weeks:

Battalion commanders will hereafter be held strictly accountable for the discipline of the men, the cleanliness and good order of the camps, and the grooming and feeding of horses. They will be required to attend all roll calls and stable duty, and see that every officer and soldier is present promptly, reporting every delinquent to these headquarters. They will be expected by close and unremitting personal attention to bring their respective commands to a state of the greatest possible efficiency. They will also be held responsible for the enforcement and faithful performance of all orders coming from these headquarters. Lieutenant-Colonel Gorham is ... charged with the condition of the horses. He will make daily inspection during stable duty and see that the horses are properly cared for.[45]

The crucial importance of the problem of discipline among the officers is illustrated further by orders the commanders of two other cavalry regiments issued, the first being an order of Colonel William B. Sipes of the 7th Pennsylvania:

The commanding officer regrets that he finds it necessary to call attention of Company officers to the fact that on the part of many of them, a manifest and causeless neglect of the most simple and plain duties exists. Notwithstanding [that] imperative orders have been issued and reiterated, requiring company officers to attend stable calls, and see that the horses are properly groomed and watered, these duties are systematically neglected. ... Officers are reminded that such conduct is deemed sufficient cause for their dismissal from the service, and a sense of duty will require that the Regimental Com-

44. Special Orders No. 1, May 28, 1862, in 1st Vermont O&L Books, RG 94, NA.
45. Regimental Orders No. 8, June 17, 1862, in 2nd Michigan O&L Books, RG 94, NA.

mander *without further warning* report delinquents to Headquarters.[46]

The order then proceeds to list straggling, unauthorized absence from camp, the wearing of nonregulation clothing, and negligent performance of guard duty as types of misconduct on the part of the enlisted men that officers took no pains to correct.

The second order was issued by Major, later Colonel, Datus E. Coon to the 2nd Iowa: "The major commanding desires to call the attention of company commanders, that many officers are fast coming to a lax state of discipline. Many officers take but little pride in the appearance of their men when at roll call. . . . Some men are allowed to appear without hats, blouses or shoes. This morning, several in one company were barefooted. These occurrences of gross neglect will be punished by reprimand in general orders from headquarters, read at the head of the regiment."[47] As with many another such order, the effect of Major Coon's admonition was not lasting, for eleven months later he announced:

The Colonel Commanding has observed with regret the careless manner of many soldiers in many companies of the Second Iowa Cavalry. This arises for the most part from the careless manner and indifference of several company commanders and noncommissioned officers. . . . Notwithstanding [that] order after order has been issued it is the most uncommon thing [to] witness a company commander's report of any violation of orders. They seem to think themselves merely ornamental, and all punishment and enforcement of orders rests with the Regimental commander. . . . Good discipline cannot be obtained without the hearty cooperation of every commissioned officer in the regiment.[48]

How did officers fail in their duties? The question can be answered by simply listing the duties they were required to perform. The records of every cavalry regiment are filled with orders, repeated time after time, directing officers to be present at roll calls, to attend stable calls and see to it that horses were properly groomed, fed, and watered, to inspect regularly the persons, cloth-

46. Circular, April 17, 1863, in 7th Pennsylvania O&L Books, RG 94, NA.
47. Circular, July 11, 1863, in 2nd Iowa O&L Books, RG 94, NA.
48. Circular, June 14, 1864, *ibid.*

ing, arms, accoutrements, quarters, and cooking arrangements of their men, to turn out at reveille and for drill, plus all the rest of the most elementary duties of a cavalry officer. The colonels of the 1st Massachusetts, 3rd Ohio, 2nd Iowa, 5th New York, and many other regiments deemed necessary a frequent repetition of such orders, a special emphasis being placed on the importance of the officers' presence at stable calls and at reveille, retreat, and tattoo roll calls.[49] On a more serious level are the many orders directing officers to suppress straggling, pillaging, and marauding and to report for punishment troopers guilty of these offenses, to guard the health and comfort of their men, to report for disciplinary action noncommissioned officers who neglected their duties, to set an example of punctuality, to keep their commands on the alert and ready to move at short notice, to become familiar with the topography of the area in which their commands were stationed, and to be assiduous in collecting reliable information about the enemy.[50]

The cavalry was by no means unique in having the problems that made necessary the issuance of such orders. It may have pleaded in extenuation of its own sins that they were no worse than those of the infantry and the artillery and cited as proof the following General Orders No. 167, issued to the entire Army of the Potomac on October 24, 1862: "The reports of recent inspections exhibit shameful neglect of duty on the part of many officers, of the higher as well as the lower grades . . . in those lesser details of discipline, failure to attend diligently to which will pro-

49. Orders No. 4, November 11, 1861, and Orders No. 22, February 20, 1862, in 3rd Ohio O&L Books, RG 94, NA; General Orders No. 152, October 4, 1863, in 2nd Iowa O&L Books, RG 94, NA; General Orders No. 121, March 5, 1863, and Special Orders No. 16, April 19, 1864, in 5th New York Volunteer Cavalry, Regimental and Company Order and Letter Books, Record Group 94, National Archives, hereinafter cited as 5th New York O&L Books; General Orders No. 3, undated, General Orders No. 6, October 27, 1861, and General Orders No. 16, February 10, 1862, in 1st Massachusetts O&L Books, RG 94, NA.

50. A few examples: General Orders No. 3, undated but clearly issued in August, 1863, in 1st Vermont O&L Books, RG 94, NA; Regimental Order No. 8, June 17, 1862, in 2nd Michigan O&L Books, RG 94, NA; Circular, July 13, 1862, in 2nd Iowa O&L Books, RG 94, NA; General Orders No. 6, February 17, 1865, in Pennsylvania O&L Books, RG 94, NA.

duce the demoralization of any body of troops. Inspections in many organizations are rarely made; drills poorly attended and infrequent; cleanliness disregarded; the care of arms and ammunition but little attended to; and the instruction of officers in tactics and regulations entirely neglected."[51]

Several of the orders that have been cited were issued in 1861 and 1862. The charitable inference is that they were needed merely to remind novice officers of certain of their duties. But as Charles Francis Adams wrote his family, "Perpetual roll calls . . . become tiresome, and the daily superintendence of the grooming of eighty-five horses is not a pleasant phase of existence."[52] Unfortunately, many of an officer's responsibilities were as unglamorous and tiresome as these, and frequent orders were needed to coax or badger officers to perform duties they considered disagreeable and evaded as much as possible. Moreover, orders essentially like those cited were being issued in 1863 and 1864 and were therefore directed to officers who had lost the status of novices and were fully aware of what was expected of them.

As the war went on and the majority of the original lot of officers left the service in one way or another, their places were taken by enlisted men promoted to commissioned rank on merit, nearly always after serving as corporals or sergeants.[53] Many of those who had left were good or potentially good officers, but in the main it was the summer patriots, the politicians, lawyers, and orators who departed, together with the elderly, the misfits, weaklings, cowards, drunkards, and incompetents. The turnover in the officers' corps was extensive. Typically, in the 1st Ohio, only four of the original forty-six officers were left at muster-out; in the 4th Kentucky, two of forty-six; in the 112th Illinois Mounted Infantry, eight of forty-six; and in the 7th Kansas, five of forty. Similarly, nearly all the officers of the 4th Iowa, 15th Pennsylvania, 1st Massachusetts, 2nd New York, and the cavalry battalion of

51. *Official Records*, Vol. XIX, Pt. 2, p. 476.
52. Ford, *A Cycle of Adams Letters*, I, 124–25.
53. There is at least one case, that of Mason A. Stone of the 1st Vermont, of a trooper who was promoted from private to first lieutenant in one breathtaking leap. Special Orders No. 90, September 9, 1863, in 1st Vermont O&L Books, RG 94, NA.

the Sherman Brigade were, at the end of the war, former enlisted men.

A few of the replacements were political appointments from civil life, whose arrival was resented by fellow officers and enlisted men alike. In the 72nd Indiana Mounted Infantry, and perhaps in other regiments as well, men sent home to enlist recruits to replenish the ranks were rewarded with commissions for above-average success.[54] A strange case was that of musician Charles Waltz, 4th United States; the commanding officer of the 7th Pennsylvania asked for his release from the Regular service, to enable him to accept a second lieutenant's commission in the Pennsylvania regiment.[55] These, however, were exceptional situations; by 1863, the norm was promotion from within on merit.

The practice of granting commissions to enlisted men began surprisingly early—in November, 1861, in the 1st Massachusetts, in January, 1862, in the 8th Illinois, in February and March, 1862, in the 5th New York and the 2nd Michigan. Sometimes the promotions were made singly and sometimes in batches of a half-dozen or more. The 2nd Michigan was unique in requiring men slated for promotion to commissioned rank to go before an examination board and obtain its favorable verdict as a condition of receiving their commissions.[56] Generally, however, the decision of the commanding officer of the regiment was final, and his appointees received their commissions in due course from the governors of their states.[57] In theory, all such promotions were made on merit, but given the politicized atmosphere of the time—and of the armies—and the close ties of volunteer regiments to their home states and localities, promotions were neither always made on merit alone, nor were they expected to be. Colonel Tompkins of the 1st Vermont thought it well to announce: "It is the inten-

54. McGee, *History of the 72nd Indiana*, 229.
55. Benjamin E. Dartt to E. B. Beaumont, January 27, 1865, in 7th Pennsylvania O&L Books, RG 94, NA.
56. General Orders No. 11, March 27, 1862, in 2nd Michigan O&L Books, RG 94, NA. There is no evidence to show whether this practice continued, and if so, for how long.
57. In the 1st Massachusetts, men appointed to commissioned rank and awaiting issuance of their commissions by the governor, held rank as acting second (or first) lieutenant.

tion of the colonel commanding to recommend for promotion, only such officers and privates as display zeal in the performance of their duties and are possessed of sufficient military capacity for the performance of their duty, and as he disapproves of the practice of political influence influencing promotions, he wishes it understood that all have an equal chance."[58]

It is impossible to generalize on the quality as officers of the many enlisted men promoted to that rank. Some of them lived up to their new responsibilities with conspicuous success. Hartwell B. Compson had run away from home in September, 1861, to enlist at age seventeen as a private in the 8th New York. After holding in succession every noncommissioned and commissioned rank he became colonel of the regiment in March, 1865, two months short of his twenty-first birthday, and was awarded the Congressional Medal of Honor for heroism in the battle of Waynesboro. Eli H. Kelly of the 3rd Kentucky advanced from enlisted man to major, and as senior officer present commanded a cavalry brigade at the ripe age of twenty-one. John Tewksbury of the 1st Massachusetts, whose order prohibiting undue familiarity between officers and men has been cited, had himself risen from the ranks and attained the rank of lieutenant colonel.

Still, not every promotion of an enlisted man to officer was a success. Acting Second Lieutenant Robert J. Warren of the 1st Massachusetts was reduced to the ranks for "having since his appointment . . . been known to be grossly intoxicated, and to use language highly impertinent and disrespectful to his superior officer, and in other ways abusing the confidence and trust reposed in him."[59] Second Lieutenant Daniel Hall and First Lieutenant Frank B. Diffenbacher of the 2nd Iowa, both promoted from the ranks in 1862, were dismissed from the service sixteen months later, Hall for "drunkenness and general inefficiency," and Diffenbacher for "gross neglect of duty."[60] Then there is the odd case of

58. Orders (not numbered), August 6, 1862, in 1st Vermont O&L Books, RG 94, NA.
59. Special Orders No. 28, December 21, 1864, in 1st Massachusetts O&L Books, RG 94, NA.
60. General Orders No. 58, September 28, 1862, and Special Orders No. 49, War Department, Adjutant General's Office, February 1, 1864, in 2nd Iowa O&L Books, RG 94, NA.

Acting Second Lieutenant Charles V. Holt of the 1st Massachusetts, who was "returned to his company as a private," because he had "shown himself unworthy of the position of a commissioned officer by having listened to and repeated the stories of enlisted men derogatory to the character of his colonel, which were untrue, and professing not to have believed them himself."[61]

Unquestionably, the replacement of most of the initial cadre of officers who had made an overnight transition from civilian to cavalry officer via the election process, by men who had had several months or years of cavalry experience in the ranks, produced a marked improvement in the level of professional knowledge in the officer corps. The men promoted were veterans, with all that the word implies in the way of expertise. Their skill as fighting men is a major factor in explaining the dramatic improvement in the efficiency and effectiveness of the Federal cavalry from mid-1863 on. On the other hand, in the many noncombat duties cavalry officers were required and expected to perform—the maintenance of discipline in the broadest sense, and the manifold facets of promoting the efficiency of a cavalry regiment by a ceaseless and minute attention to the well-being of men and animals—the officers commissioned from the ranks were as lax and unreliable as their elected, inexperienced predecessors had been.

Innumerable orders issued in 1863, 1864, and even in the spring of 1865, repeat the same admonitions, complaints, and exhortations that commanding officers had been forced to issue in 1861 and 1862. Thus, Colonel Sipes of the 7th Pennsylvania wrote on May 21, 1864, that he regretted "to notice a gradual but sure neglect of horses . . . in almost every Company. Less care is day after day paid to grooming and feeding; but above all, the want of proper attention to saddling . . . is rapidly ruining many animals. For this, company officers are to blame, and he assures all that they will be held to a strict accountability . . . and any officer failing to perform his duty as a Cavalry Officer will be reported to the Department Commander."[62] Major Tewksbury's order complaining of the familiarity between officers and their men was

61. General Orders No. 22, March 5, 1862, in 1st Massachusetts O&L Books, RG 94, NA.
62. Circular, May 21, 1864, in 7th Pennsylvania O&L Books, RG 94, NA.

issued in January, 1865. Another 1st Massachusetts order admonishing officers to "see that their orders are promptly obeyed and without murmurs" was issued in July, 1864.[63] A January 25, 1865, order from General James H. Wilson states, "On account of continued neglect of duty on the part of many officers it has been found necessary to call for weekly reports of officers absent from reveille and roll calls."[64] The "Circular" in which Colonel Coon of the 2nd Iowa complains of the "careless manner and indifference" of his officers and finds fault with their attitude of considering "themselves merely ornamental," thus saddling the regimental commander with the task of enforcing orders and punishing delinquents, is dated June 14, 1864.[65] It was on December 6, 1864, that Colonel R. H. G. Minty issued orders to his brigade requiring "all company officers . . . [to] attend reveille, retreat and tattoo roll calls and all drill and stable calls, and one officer from each Company . . . [to] take charge and accompany the horses of his company to and from water."[66]

Many more orders, dealing ostensibly with the soldierly failings and misdeeds of enlisted men—straggling, marauding, want of cleanliness, wearing of nonregulation clothing, failure to turn out for drill and parades, firing of guns in camp, and the like—were in fact a criticism, express or implied, of the officers who permitted such misconduct to occur and to go unpunished. As Colonel Gamble of the 8th Illinois had pointed out, "No one is fit to command . . . that is not himself willing to obey." The orders and comments cited make it abundantly clear that the typical officer of a regiment of volunteer cavalry in the Civil War, whether he received his shoulder straps via the votes of his men in the early days of the war, or via promotion from the ranks later on, was generally anything but a model of soldierly discipline in the performance of his duties. His men inevitably followed his example.

63. General Orders No. 2, July 5, 1864, in 1st Massachusetts O&L Books, RG 94, NA.
64. General Orders No. 6, January 25, 1865, in 2nd Michigan O&L Books, RG 94, NA.
65. Circular, June 14, 1864, in 2nd Iowa O&L Books, RG 94, NA.
66. General Orders No. 8, December 6, 1864, in 3rd Ohio O&L Books, RG 94, NA.

VI

Gone for a Soldier

GENERALLY SPEAKING, OFFICERS' ATTEMPTS TO ESTAB-
lish discipline were resented, evaded, quietly sabotaged, or at best
acquiesced in with a minimum of grace by their men.[1] What the
historian of the 51st Indiana Mounted Infantry writes on the subject reflects what could have been heard around any cavalry
campfire: "We had enlisted to put down the Rebellion, and had
no patience with the red-tape tomfoolery of the regular service.
Furthermore, our boys recognized no superiors, except in the line
of legitimate duty. Shoulder straps waived, a private was ready at
the 'drop of a hat' to trash his commander, a feat that occurred

---

1. Roger Hannaford, 2nd Ohio, tells the following story: "[Col. A.
Bayard Nettleton] would sneak all over camp at hours the most unreasonable to catch a Company neglecting an order; the hardest was the currying
on [sic] hour before breakfast, when the thermometer was below zero &
the wind just howling. . . . Nettleton would be sure on such a morning to
pass up & down before every row of "quarters"; a woe to the Company
whose picket line was thin of men or whose Sergeant was not overlooking.
It was not long however before we came up to him; the moment he was
seen to mount his horse . . . to make his spying tour, signals would be flying
all over the camp . . . to look out & be ready to recieve [sic] him. . . . So it
went & his inspections were a perfect farce." Hannaford, "Reminiscences,"
249(b).

more than once."[2] Clearly implicit in this uncompromising statement is the fact that cavalrymen in the ranks considered themselves not only qualified but also entitled to judge for themselves
what was and what was not "in the line of legitimate duty."

In the face of a vast amount of evidence to the contrary, the
historian of the 3rd Ohio must have seen the past through a haze
of romantic piety when he wrote nearly fifty years after the end
of the war that the "efficiency of a regiment hinges on its drill
and discipline. The great majority of the men realized this, and
submitted gracefully and cheerfully to the officers placed over
them, and the rules governing camp life." The order and letter
books of his regiment tell a very different tale, and even the historian adds the revealing sentence, "And yet it was not always
easy to get along without friction."[3] The troopers of the 8th New
York firmly believed that neither their colonel, Benjamin F. Davis,
nor anyone else could bring a volunteer regiment under "regular
army style with success," and they no doubt made it their business to prove their own thesis.[4]

The 4th Ohio took the step, unusual even in that self-
consciously rhetorical age, of affirming its virtue in a series of resolutions that the regiment adopted and for maximum effect sent
to their hometown newspapers to be published. The first of these
resolutions declared "That we will entirely submit to strict and
impartial discipline and obey our superiors in its exercise."[5]

One of the basics of the "regular army style" that Colonel
Davis and other commanding officers did their best to inculcate
was that of saluting. Colonel Zahm of the 3rd Ohio announced in

2. Hartpence, *History of the 51st Indiana*, 36.
3. Crofts, *Third Ohio Veteran Volunteer Cavalry*, 11.
4. Norton, *Deeds of Daring*, 24.
5. The other resolutions were: "2. *Resolved*, That we will show all
due respect and subordination to those in office over us, as well as kindness
and consideration to those who may be our subordinates. 3. *Resolved*, That
we will carefully abstain from all those disparaging vices so common and
ruinous among inconsiderate men in military life. 4. *Resolved*, That like
a band of brothers, we will cherish for each other a fraternal regard, striving at all times to promote each other in interest and honor . . . and being
assured of the righteousness of our country's cause, we will trust in the
God of Battles for victory and reward." Wulsin, *The Story of the Fourth*,
111.

orders, "Courtesy being essential in the army, the commanding officer directs that the enlisted men of the regiment shall observe without fail what is laid down in the Army Regulations which is that they shall salute all officers. Officers saluted must invariably return the salute in a most respectful manner."[6] Colonel Zahm's order was issued in the infant days of his regiment. In November, 1862, when the 1st Vermont had been in existence for just over a year, Major William D. Collins, then in command of the regiment, called the officers' and troopers' attention "to the general and increasing negligence on their part of an important point in 'military etiquette,' namely the saluting of officers. Military salutes is [sic] universally acknowledged as a mark of soldierly instruction and discipline, and no soldier, especially when on duty or under arms, can neglect it without insulting the officer or confessing to an inexcusable ignorance on his part."[7]

The striking thing about the comments on the lack of discipline in regimental histories is that they are either quite general (for example, "the standard of our discipline was quite as low as our drill"), or, when more specific, they most frequently concern relatively venial sins, such as "running the guards" to enjoy the fleshpots of the nearest metropolis or the amenities, culinary and social, of a nearby farmhouse.[8] The chronicle of the 1st Maine may be taken as representative in that respect: "The discipline of the camp was strict," their historian writes, "the men considered it unnecessarily so. . . . they could hardly see the need of being obliged to remain so closely in [an] uncomfortable camp after the day's duty was done. . . . The consequence was, running the guard was largely . . . practiced. Punishment was severe . . . and several wore the ball and chain for absenting themselves from camp, only to repeat the operation as soon as possible after the fetters were removed."[9]

6. General Orders No. 4, November 11, 1861, in 3rd Ohio O&L Books, RG 94, NA.

7. General Orders No. 13, November 13, 1862, in 1st Vermont O&L Books, RG 94, NA. It will be recalled that Major Collins had been an artillery sergeant in the British army.

8. Adams, *The Story of a Trooper*, 193; Hinman, *Story of the Sherman Brigade*, 49; Moyer, *History of the 7th Regiment*, 28.

9. Tobie, *First Maine Cavalry*, 22; see also Norton, *Deeds of Daring*,

Closely allied to the running of the guards was the totally unstoppable practice of straggling. The attitude of the 1st Kentucky toward discipline in any of its manifestations was of the most casual variety, but its greatest and most persistent vice was straggling. B. F. Thompson of the 112th Illinois Mounted Infantry reports, perhaps with a touch of envy, that the 1st Kentucky "seemed to be everywhere at the same time. They . . . seemed to have carte blanche to go when and where they pleased, and to return when they got ready. They knew but little about drill, and discipline was a stranger to them. . . . Every man was a brigadier on his own hook, and the majority of them believed themselves superior to the average brigadier."[10] The Kentuckians' own historian does not deny the charge, but blames the wandering propensities and indiscipline of his comrades on the fact that "about eight companies—enough to give type to the regiment—came from the outlying spurs and valleys of the Cumberland Mountains. The habitual freedom of their former lives rendered them more restive under too much restrictions than those reared in the more populous . . . sections of the State. . . . it is not strange that they should have a distaste against military martinets."[11]

The cavalry, whose overworked and underfed horses gave them a mobility the infantry and artillery lacked, were particularly prone to wander away from camp or to straggle on the march. Generally, the wandering and straggling had as their purpose nothing more sinister than a search for a home-cooked meal as relief from the monotonous horrors of army rations and camp

---

15–16. In the 8th Indiana, passes to leave camp were an article of commerce. Jacob W. Bartmess of that regiment reported to his wife that "there is from 30 to 49 in the guard house here all the time for breaking guard and other things"; then, after lamenting, "Here I am Pent up in this camp, O. how tired I get," he wrote her a few days later, "I got a pass to go out of camp yesterday and Sold it for 25 cents." Jacob W. Bartmess, "Civil War Letters," *Indiana Magazine of History*, LII (1956), 52–53. The 15th Pennsylvania had no "running the guard" problem, because, "if a soldier wanted to go to Philadelphia for a few days, he wrote his own pass, which was usually honored by the guard." Kirk, *History of the Fifteenth Pennsylvania*, 63.

10. B. F. Thompson, *History of the 112th Regiment of Illinois Volunteer Infantry in the Great War of the Rebellion* (Toulon, Ill., 1885), 30.

11. Tarrant, *Wild Riders of the First Kentucky*, 34.

170 THE UNION CAVALRY IN THE CIVIL WAR

cooking, or a raid on the hen roosts, pigpens, beehives, orchards, smokehouses, and corncribs of any farm within reach and not previously plundered. As Private William O. Gulick of the 1st Iowa explained to his family, cavalrymen were healthier than footsoldiers because "when tired of *camp* we can mount horse and ride out in the country & get some fruit[,] perchance a good dinner[,] and take the fresh cool air[.] This we do when ere we choose."[12] There were times, however, when foraging was the only means the men had of keeping themselves and their horses alive. Nevertheless, in far too many cases, the thin line separating legitimate foraging and undisguised marauding was overstepped. Whether a regiment was in enemy or friendly territory seemed to make little difference, and the troopers did not always stop with the taking of a few chickens, pigs, or sacks of corn. The historian of the 2nd Iowa reports, "This system of foraging was made the means of many great wrongs inflicted on the citizens. . . . many stopped not when their necessities were supplied, but . . . they carried on a wholesale robbery business. Money, watches, jewelry and valuables of any kind were stolen by them, calling themselves foragers; they were literally thieves, and robbing banditti."[13]

Straggling from the column on the march or wandering away from camp frequently entailed serious risk. The historian of the 1st Massachusetts noted that while his regiment was campaigning near Waterloo and Orleans, Virginia, "if a soldier in search of food or adventure went to a house two hundred yards away from the road, he was pretty sure of trouble . . . for the whole country around about was swarming with partisan rangers."[14] This state of affairs was not peculiar to Virginia. In February, 1865, while General Wilson's Cavalry Corps was encamped at Gravelly Springs and Waterloo preparing for the Selma Campaign, Colonel Minty called the attention of the regimental commanders of his brigade "to the loose manner in which their camp guards perform their duty. Soldiers from every regiment in the Brigade are strag-

12. Guyer, "Corporal William O. Gulick," 454.
13. Pierce, *History of the Second Iowa*, 11.
14. Crowninshield, *A History of the First Regiment*, 169.

gling over the country with their horses. On the 12th Inst. two soldiers of the 3d Ohio Cavalry were captured by a party of eight guerillas only a few miles from camp, and their horses, arms and equipments were taken from them."[15] Straggling presented commanding officers with major problems over and above the marauding it sometimes led to, or the occasional loss of a trooper and all his gear. It caused a further deterioration of horses that were in poor condition to begin with. Then, commanding officers, the ranks of their regiments already depleted by a host of legitimate and unavoidable causes, had their ability to deal with a sudden emergency further sapped by the absence of dozens of their men wandering about the countryside. An extreme example is again provided by the incorrigible 1st Kentucky. The regiment was reequipped and reorganized at Nicholasville, Kentucky, in April, 1864. Ordered to Georgia to take part in the forthcoming Atlanta Campaign, it began its march, eight hundred strong, via Burnside, Kentucky, and Kingston, Tennessee. Before the march began, General George Stoneman, commanding the Cavalry Corps, Army of the Ohio, issued the usual strict orders forbidding straggling. When the 1st Kentucky arrived in Kingston, two officers and seventy-one men were present with the colors. The rest, more than seven hundred of them, came in eventually, singly and in groups; not until the regiment reached Varnell's Station, Georgia, nearly two weeks later, had "nearly all" the stragglers turned up.[16]

Regimental records, and the records of all larger organizations, are filled with prohibitions of marauding and pillage, and threats of dire punishment to offenders, as well as to officers who failed to stop them from doing so. General Wilson was one of the many commanding officers who tried. In a January, 1865, order to his Cavalry Corps, he directed, "Strong camp guards will be established by brigade and division commanders in order to prevent men from leaving camp for improper purposes. Marauding and pillaging must be stopped, and for this purpose all officers of

15. General Orders No. 30, February 14, 1865, in 7th Pennsylvania O&L Books, RG 94, NA.
16. Tarrant, *Wild Riders of the First Kentucky*, 314–19.

the command are authorized to shoot at once all those caught in the act of stealing and destroying wantonly the property of unoffending citizens."[17]

If anyone was shot pursuant to this order, which is highly unlikely, the records fail to show it. As to its effectiveness in halting the wandering habits of cavalrymen, it is to be noted that Colonel Minty's order concerning the capture of two of his men by guerillas was issued a month following General Wilson's tough order. Indeed, even after the capture of Selma on April 2, nearly three months later, Minty, who had succeeded to the command of the Second Division after General Eli Long was wounded, issued a circular in which he said that "the men of this Division are hourly seen moving about the country outside our lines, which must be stopped at once."[18]

Another serious problem for commanding officers to cope with was that of drink, for intemperance was as troublesome and caused as much damage among the enlisted men as among the officers. Dozens of troopers who had negotiated the first rung or two of the promotion ladder were stripped of their corporal's or sergeant's chevrons for "repeated instances of drunkenness," for being "found . . . in a beastly state of intoxication," for being "grossly intoxicated" or "drunk repeatedly and unfit for duty," and for "repeated drunkenness."[19] It may be assumed that in many cases the effects of drink were nothing worse than a return to camp in a "condition of hilarity" of boys who had run the guards for an evening in town, and who paid for their misconduct by twenty-four hours in the guardhouse. There were, however, too many cases far more serious. In December, 1861, Colonel John Kennett of the 4th Ohio was moved to express his "regret and astonishment at the number of men composing his regiment who brutalized their manhood by becoming intoxicated after reaching

17. Special Field Order No. 6, January 14, 1865, in 2nd Michigan O&L Books, RG 94, NA.
18. Circular, April 4, 1865, in 7th Pennsylvania O&L Books, RG 94, NA.
19. General Orders No. 56, March 21, 1862, and Regimental Order No. 5, February 9, 1862, in 5th New York O&L Books, RG 94, NA; Order No. 5, January 28, 1862, and Order No. 28, May 16, 1862, in 8th Illinois O&L Books, RG 94, NA.

Cincinnati from Camp Dennison."[20] The 11th New York, about to leave its first camp on Staten Island for Washington, had to cross by ship to the mainland to start its journey. The regimental historian relates:

On the day of leaving, the steamer did not come . . . until late in the evening. Of course there was a great deal of drinking that day and the lieutenant-colonel [Louis Palma di Cesnola] got the regiment together and began, as he said, to drill the liquor out of the boys. . . . While in line at parade rest, a big fellow of H Company, named Quirk . . . walked off. Cesnola watched the man for a few moments, and then, calling the orderly sergeant of H Company, said, "Sergeant French, go and bring that man back." French at once started after his man; when he got close to Quirk, he ordered him to halt. Quirk replied by drawing his sabre and making a vicious cut at the orderly, but French . . . neatly parried the blow and giving a right cut laid open the fellow's head. . . . Quirk was hauled off for repairs and the drill was resumed.

When at last the steamer arrived and the men went on board, the regimental historian was ordered to make a detail from each company for guard duty: "after a great deal of trouble we finally got a sufficient number to post a few sentries. . . . the sentry placed near the quartermaster's stores . . . was Bloody Murray of A Company; he was drunk, and having been a man-of-war's man, he had stripped himself down to his waist, and thus equipped for action he marched up and down his beat, flourishing his sabre and daring any man to touch the stores."[21] Perhaps because he was writing a history to be read by former comrades and their families, the historian thought it well to add, "These drunken men were not representative . . . of the regiment, but there were enough of them . . . to create the impression that the regiment had been recruited in hades. Fortunately for the good of the service, these fellows deserted or were imprisoned soon after reaching Washington."[22]

20. Wulsin, *The Story of the Fourth*, 116.
21. Smith, "*Scott's 900*," *Eleventh New York*, 11.
22. *Ibid.*, 11. The regiment arrived in Washington on May 7, 1862. By August 1, less than three months later, and before hearing the first shot fired by the enemy, two hundred of its original roster had deserted,

Demon Rum caused trouble enough even when there were no saloons or grog shops within easy reach. An order of the 2nd Iowa prohibited the "introduction into the quarters and camps of the regiment of liquor, including lager beer"; later, Private Justice Canfield—presumably a trustworthy and incorruptible teetotaler —was appointed "to receive and examine all packages . . . received by enlisted men . . . through the express office."[23] The 11th New York, in camp outside Washington and happily purged of its Quirks and Murrays, attracted large numbers of peddlers "with numerous and various wares to sell." The officers discovered that the men were managing to get drunk without ever leaving camp. A quiet investigation revealed that liquor was being smuggled into camp by the peddlers, including a "nice, pleasant motherly old woman," who sold her whiskey under cover of a tempting display of "fine looking pies and ten cents apiece." When that source of supply was cut off, the existence of another came to light; the colonel had made it a rule that all boxes from home had to be opened in his presence, so that he could confiscate any liquor they might contain; even his eagle eye, however, failed to detect the bottles of whiskey that replaced more conventional kinds of stuffing inside the roast geese and roast turkeys.[24]

Lack of discipline was also conspicuous in the personal appearance and grooming of the men. William Howard Russell watched General McClellan's arrival at a review with "an escort of the very dirtiest and most unsoldierly dragoons, with filthy accoutrements and ungroomed horses, I ever saw."[25] This was while the Army of the Potomac was still in its camps about Wash-

---

"and the regiment was greatly improved thereby, the loss being quickly replaced by the enlistment of better men." *Ibid.*, 24.

23. General Orders No. 10, January 17, 1862, and Special Orders No. 116, December 13, 1863, in 2nd Iowa O&L Books, RG 94, NA. Colonel Zahm, 3rd Ohio, regretted "to notice that intemperance . . . [was] so prevalent in the regiment" and announced that "in order to put a stop to so debasing a crime in the future, any person bringing liquor into camp will be severely punished." Order No. 14, November 28, 1861, in 3rd Ohio O&L Books, RG 94, NA.

24. Smith, "Scott's 900," *Eleventh New York*, 15; see also Stevenson, "*Boots and Saddles*," 51: "It was evident that the boys obtained liquor somehow, notwithstanding the stringent orders of prohibition."

25. Russell, *My Diary North and South*, II, 306.

ington, and the men had both the time and the facilities to keep themselves and their gear reasonably clean. Two years later, Theodore Lyman noted that no two of General Meade's cavalry escort had caps alike, that "none had their jackets buttoned; all were covered with half an inch of dust, and all eschewed straps to their pantaloons."[26]

The records of every cavalry regiment include numerous orders on the subject of personal cleanliness and grooming. Company commanders of the 1st Massachusetts, for example, were notified in January, 1863, that they were to be "held to a strict responsibility for the cleanliness of their men. Today is warm enough for an improvement in this respect. The necks, faces and hands of the men are very dirty."[27] But such general reminders had only a temporary effect. An inspection three months later "showed the clothing, arms and equipment" of the men "to be in a very dirty state."[28] A year passed, and another order directed, "The men's hair will be closely cut and where the beard is worn, it will be neatly trimmed. No side whiskers will be permitted. The men will bathe as often as possible in the cool of the day."[29] The men from the Bay State were not, however, exceptional in their seeming repugnance to water, as the records of the 2nd Iowa indicate. After the surgeon of that regiment had reported "a want of cleanliness on the part of some of the men," Colonel Washington L. Elliott ordered that each company should "provide itself with buckets or tubs for washing the persons of their men."[30] A

26. George R. Agassiz (ed.), *Meade's Headquarters 1863–1865: Letters of Colonel Theodore Lyman* (Boston, 1922), 8.

27. General Orders No. 8, February 8, 1863, in 1st Massachusetts O&L Books, RG 94, NA.

28. General Orders No. 23, May 17, 1863, *ibid.*

29. General Orders No. 2, July 5, 1864, *ibid.* There appeared to be a great fear of bathing in the midday sun in the nineteenth century. The 1st Vermont was forbidden to bathe between the hours of eight A.M. and five P.M. The 2nd Michigan was not only forbidden to bathe between nine A.M. and five P.M., but in addition, orders laid it down that "a commissioned officer will accompany bathing parties, and the medical officers . . . will prescribe the length of time to remain in the water." Circular, July 12, 1864, in 1st Vermont O&L Books, RG 94, NA; General Orders No. 90, July 15, 1862, in 2nd Michigan O&L Books, RG 94, NA.

30. General Orders No. 13, October 26, 1861, in 2nd Iowa O&L Books, RG 94, NA.

few months later, the attention of officers was "called to the want of cleanliness in the men. They should bathe not less than twice a week, keep the hair short, and the head clean."[31] Two years later, the troopers of the 2nd Iowa were again, or probably still, found to be "dirty and ragged."[32]

Charles Russell Lowell of the 2nd Massachusetts was one of many officers who tried to make his men improve their grooming, but he found it a thankless task. "It is . . . so hard," he wrote in June, 1863, "to make men understand that the only way to keep tolerably clean is to keep perfectly clean."[33] Colonel Charles G. Harker of the Sherman Brigade had his own perhaps excessively forceful method for inculcating cleanliness. Near his headquarters ran a small stream in which his men were encouraged to bathe. Those who did not avail themselves of the opportunity with sufficient regularity were marched into the stream at the point of a bayonet.[34]

Some commanding officers used the carrot and stick approach to solve the grooming problem. Lieutenant Colonel Ingerton had his adjutant pick out at guard mount each morning the two cleanest and neatest troopers of the 13th Tennessee; one was rewarded with a twenty-four-hour pass and the other appointed to the coveted post of orderly for the day. The adjutant was also to select the two most slovenly soldiers with the dirtiest arms; their job for the day was to clean the regimental horse lines.[35] The fatigue duties in the 5th New York were assigned daily to the six men of each company who paid "the least regard to their . . . neatness, cleanliness and soldierly appearance. . . . this duty will be considered as punishment for uncleanliness and disregard of duties."[36] A short time later, a second 5th New York order improved

31. Circular, May 11, 1862, *ibid.*
32. Circular, June 14, 1864, *ibid.*
33. Emerson, *Charles Russell Lowell*, 252.
34. Hinman, *Story of the Sherman Brigade*, 232.
35. Scott and Angel, *History of the Thirteenth Regiment*, 143. In the 9th New York, the usual punishment given to delinquents was the job of policing the camp.
36. Special Orders No. 7, undated but probably issued in late March or early April, 1864, in 5th New York O&L Books, RG 94, NA.

on the first; it declared that "All men of this command who do not comply with the orders given as to keeping their hair closely cut and their persons cleanly will be daily detailed for police and fatigue duty . . . and will be designated the dirty squad."[37] Private Michael Henessey, Company G., 2nd Iowa, on the other hand, was excused from police and fatigue duty and from all picket and camp guard assignments for ten days, "as a reward for cleanliness of arms and clothing, and military appearance at inspection."[38]

A special facet of the general problem of grooming was the men's seemingly ineradicable penchant for wearing a mixture of the uniform and civilian clothing. There were extenuating circumstances for this nearly universal practice. The army regulations provided an annual clothing allowance of forty-two dollars per man, against which was charged the cost—regulated in minute detail by orders from the adjutant general's office in Washington and periodically revised—of each item of clothing he drew from his company quartermaster, from brass company letters to boots, and from socks to overcoats. If the trooper managed to end the year with less than forty-two dollars charged against his account, he was entitled to the difference in cash; if he overdrew his account, the excess was deducted from his pay.[39] If the clothing issued had been of uniformly good quality, and if the men had taken reasonably good care of it, the allotment would ordinarily have been sufficient, but neither of these conditions was always met. General W. B. Hazen wrote after the war that the

37. Special Orders No. 16, April 19, 1864, *ibid.*
38. General Orders No. 102, February 28, 1863, in 2nd Iowa O&L Books, RG 94, NA.
39. War Department, Adjutant General's Office, General Orders No. 202, December 9, 1862, and General Orders No. 176, July 1, 1864; these orders were copied into nearly all the Regimental and Company Order and Letter Books here cited. Prices of a number of common items ran as follows: jacket, $5.55 in 1862, $6.25 in 1864; trousers, $4.60 in 1862, $4.15 in 1864; boots (sewed), $3.25 in 1862, $3.85 in 1864; flannel drawers, $.95 in 1862, $.90 in 1864; sergeant's chevrons, $.24 in 1862, $.20 in 1864; blankets, $3.60 in 1862, $3.55 in 1864. On at least one occasion, the War Department furnished a complete new outfit free of charge to a number of cavalry regiments, after an exceptionally arduous campaign; see Chapter VI (Vol. II) of the present study.

"quality of nearly everything which the centralized departments
. . . furnish[ed] . . . was several grades below the standard, and
lower than what was paid for, the blankets being detestable
cheats, and the clothing the vilest quality of swindling 'shoddy'."[40]
Hazen's strictures may have been somewhat exaggerated, but
there is ample evidence to show that neither the material nor the
workmanship of the clothing and footwear issued were what they
should have been. The familiar forage cap, adopted as the regulation headgear for the cavalry, will serve as an example. We are
told that "the regulation . . . cap, as issued, was even more worthless than the hat. . . . But the sutlers sold very nice little caps of
similar pattern, and nine-tenths of the men preferred paying two
dollars for a decent and serviceable cap, to drawing one at sixty
cents, literally worthless."[41]

The men's care for their clothing was certainly no better than
its quality, if as good. The records mention repeated instances of
overcoats, the price of which varied from a low of $8.75 to a high
of $14.50, being thrown away by the hundreds when the weather
turned warm, and of cavalrymen whose horses gave out on a raid
or a long march throwing away their spare clothing, and often
enough their saddles and weapons as well, rather than carry
them.[42] There were occasions also, as in and immediately after
the Antietam Campaign, when logistics broke down and replacements for worn-out uniforms and footwear were unobtainable.

40. W. B. Hazen, *The School of the Army in Germany and France*
(New York, 1872), 232. Allan Nevins, on the other hand, states that
"there were hardly any complaints of defective material or workmanship
[of clothing] and but few cases of infidelity or fraud by inspectors." Allan
Nevins, *The War for the Union: The Organized War, 1863–1864* (New
York, 1971), 294. In late December, 1864, Roger Hannaford, who had
been promoted to quartermaster sergeant of his company of the 2nd Ohio
and is an unimpeachable witness, wrote, "The boys grumbled considerably at their blankets, in truth there was cause the regulation blanket
ought to weigh 7 lbs & to be of close texture; it took a good one to reach
3 lbs now & when hung on a line a load of buckshot could be fired
through [it] without much detriment." Hannaford, "Reminiscences," 234
(d).
41. [Whittaker], *Volunteer Cavalry*, 46. Whittaker's memory was at
fault. The forage cap was charged to the men at $.56 in 1862 and $.65 in
1864.
42. Hard, *History of the Eighth Cavalry*, 108.

Many a letter written then and later to "loved ones" at home complains of the ragged state of the writer's uniform.

The 1st Massachusetts spent the spring and summer of 1862 in and near Beaufort, South Carolina. It was transferred to Maryland in August, 1862, with the men "in the lightest clothing." There was no heavy clothing, or even socks or boots, to be had from the Quartermaster's Department until late in November, by which time the entire regiment was in rags and freezing.[43]

The effect on the men of the conditions that have been described was precisely what might have been expected; they did their best to minimize charges against their clothing accounts (or, in the case of the 1st Massachusetts and other regiments with similar problems, to keep from freezing) by having civilian clothing sent to them from home, or, as an alternative, begging for such clothing or acquiring it by less legitimate means from houses along the line of march. There are even cases on record of clothing being taken from equally ill-clad Confederate prisoners.[44]

Judging from their frequent repetition, orders forbidding the wearing of articles of civilian clothing were utterly without effect, even when they went as far as the following, of the 2nd Iowa: "The regiment having been supplied with clothing, no article of citizens' apparel whatever will be allowed to be worn. All such clothing in possession of the men must be disposed of to-day. Company officers will make a minute inspection of Company quarters and men's knapsacks to-morrow morning, and all hats, coats and pants other than the prescribed uniform will be taken possession of and burned."[45] Because of its high visibility, civilian headgear was a special sore spot with commanding officers. The wearing of civilian hats, including straw hats, was repeatedly forbidden, and sutlers were prohibited from selling them to the soldiers. The wearing of wide-brimmed civilian hats became a major problem after the forage cap replaced the cavalry hat. The colonel of the 1st Massachusetts eventually gave up the hopeless struggle and granted his men permission to wear civilian hats—

43. Crowninshield, *A History of the First Regiment*, 70, 84.
44. Circular, January 22, 1865, and General Orders No. 17, March 20, 1863, in 2nd Michigan O&L Books, RG 94, NA.
45. Circular, July 24, 1864, in 2nd Iowa O&L Books, RG 94, NA.

as they were evidently doing already—but he forbade them to dress up the hats with officers' gold hat cords and crossed sabers insignia.[46]

An odd manifestation of the desire to evade uniformity in clothing was the well-nigh universal reluctance of noncommissioned officers to sew on their coat sleeves the chevrons of their ranks. Colonel A. H. White of the 5th New York was one of many commanding officers who ordered—or entreated—noncommissioned officers "to wear their chevrons at all times, that they may procure the respect and obedience of those under their charge, as well as to be themselves examples of neatness and Soldierly bearing for their men to imitate."[47] In at least one regiment, even officers had to be told that "Hereafter no officer will appear upon duty without the clothing and insignia of his rank."[48] Nothing in the records explains this strange unwillingness to wear badges of rank. It may have been an expression of democratic principles, or of laziness, or perhaps it was nothing more than a measure of salutary self-preservation in the face of the marksmanship of Confederate sharpshooters.

There was a host of annoying but relatively harmless disciplinary problems to darken the days and gray the hair of commanding officers, forms of misbehavior that testify to the ingenious deviltry of Civil War soldiers. Using nearby fences for firewood despite repeated prohibitions was a universal habit, unstoppable even by the assessment of substantial damages against the offending regiment, as happened twice to the 2nd Iowa.[49] But why should it have been necessary to direct soldiers "not to interfere in any manner with the Poles or Wires of the Military Tele-

46. General Orders No. 2, July 5, 1864, and Special Orders No. 33, March 15, 1864, in 1st Massachusetts O&L Books, RG 94, NA.

47. General Orders No. 3, January 5, 1865, in 5th New York O&L Books, RG 94, NA; see also Special Orders No. 3, January 9, 1865, in 1st Massachusetts O&L Books, RG 94, NA; and Circular, February 9, 1865. in 7th Pennsylvania O&L Books, RG 94, NA.

48. General Orders No. 17, March 20, 1863, in 2nd Michigan O&L Books, RG 94, NA.

49. General Orders No. 147, September 12, 1863, Special Orders No. 106, September 14, 1863, and General Orders No. 216, September 4, 1864, in 2nd Iowa O&L Books, RG 94, NA. See also General Orders No. 12, March 13, 1863, in 2nd Michigan O&L Books, RG 94, NA.

graph" and to remind them that "Serious inconvenience to the service may result from the injury of this important auxiliary of the army"? [50] Why too was it necessary to prohibit time after time the causeless firing of guns in camp and on the march, and the throwing of cartridges on campfires? [51] Colonel Sipes had to remind the 7th Pennsylvania that the "promiscuous discharge of firearms" led to false alarms and endangered the safety of the army, and that "cartridges must not be scattered over the ground to be swept into fires, as such negligence not only wastes ammunition but endangers life." [52] In July, 1864, the 2nd Iowa was told, "The habit of discharging fire arms in camp and throwing cartridges in the fire has become so prevalent that means must be taken to prevent and if possible discover the guilty parties. After noon roll call this day To Arms will be sounded and the entire regiment not actually on duty will fall in . . . and drill for half an hour at the manual of arms . . . for every shot or cartridge fired, unless the guilty one is produced." [53] Seven months later, the threat of an even stiffer penalty was needed. "The habit of firing off arms and throwing cartridges on the fire is getting so frequent that it has become necessary to issue the following order: If the man who wilfully fires off his gun or who throws cartridges in the fire cannot be found, the Company in daytime will drill one hour, at night stand under arms half an hour. If the Company cannot be found, the Battalion will be punished, then if the Battalion cannot be ascertained, the Regiment." [54]

The totally ineffective prohibition of swearing—"this wicked and vulgar habit," which all commissioned and noncommissioned officers were "directed to prevent as much as possible"—may be ascribed to the misplaced zeal of a commanding officer who

50. General Orders No. 6, May 16, 1863, in 7th Pennsylvania O&L Books, RG 94, NA.
51. General Orders No. 2, March 5, 1862, General Orders No. 12, March 13, 1863, and Regimental Orders No. 52, April 16, 1863, in 2nd Michigan O&L Books, RG 94, NA; see also Circular, July 18, 1862, and Circular, February 9, 1864, in 1st Vermont O&L Books, RG 94, NA; and Orders No. 26, March 9, 1862, in 3rd Ohio O&L Books, RG 94, NA.
52. General Orders No. 8, May 25, 1863, in 7th Pennsylvania O&L Books, RG 94, NA.
53. Circular, July 24, 1864, in 2nd Iowa O&L Books, RG 94, NA.
54. Special Orders No. 14, February 25, 1865, *ibid.*

should have known better.[55] But it should not have been necessary to order men not "to injure the property of the sutler," or to
inform a regiment that anonymous "letters . . . will not be noticed,
that channel of correspondence being neither military nor manly," or even to tell the men that the letters they habitually sent
directly, instead of through channels, to the War Department and
the adjutant general's office would be "returned without answer."[56]

Putting up with minor irritants like these—and the list of
them is endless—was part of the price regimental commanders
had to pay for their rank and perquisites. There was, however,
another group of problems, far more serious, that caused tens of
thousands of preventable deaths, the result of the utter impossibility of making the men observe the most elementary hygienic
precautions. Despite the relatively primitive state of the medical
knowledge of the day and the modest skills of many regimental
surgeons, there was a reasonably clear understanding of the cause
and effect relationship between some of the men's practices and
habits that repeated orders were powerless to correct, and the
waves of disease and death that swept through every regiment at
one time or another. The knowledge existed, but taking advantage of it was usually difficult and sometimes impossible.

Nearly every regiment, cavalry, infantry, and artillery alike,
experienced epidemics that riddled its ranks during the first few
months after its organization. The 2nd Iowa, "crowded into small,
poorly ventilated" quarters in Benton Barracks, St. Louis, buried
sixty of its men in as many days. "So reduced were we by sickness," the regimental historian reports, "that it was . . . common
for our strongest companies to appear on dress parade with not to
exceed ten men in ranks."[57] The 7th Pennsylvania, encamped at
Louisville, had 70 percent of its men on the sick list in February,
1862. Most of the sick had camp diarrhea, "traced to the impure,
and as some claimed poisoned water used by the soldiers."[58] The

55. General Orders No. 1, January 1, 1862, in 1st Vermont O&L
Books, RG 94, NA.
56. General Orders No. 38, December 2, 1861, General Orders No. 18,
January 29, 1862, and General Orders No. 204, June 18, 1864, in 2nd
Iowa O&L Books, RG 94, NA.
57. Pierce, History of the Second Iowa, 11.
58. Vale, Minty and the Cavalry, 45; see also Dornblaser, Sabre
Strokes of the Pennsylvania Dragoons, 45–46.

1st, 6th, and 19th New York, the 1st Maine, the 2nd and 7th Michigan, and the 17th Pennsylvania, are only a few of the many regiments whose historians tell much the same grim story of disease and death.

Poor camp sanitation, tolerated by some field and line officers because they knew no better and by many more out of carelessness, was a major source of disease. Contaminated water, exposure, improper diet, filthy utensils, kitchens, and camps, ignorance, and in the case of regiments raised mainly in rural areas, the crowding together of hundreds of men who had not previously been exposed to such childhood diseases as measles, decimated regiment after regiment. But the problem underlying all these immediate causes was the ignorance of the men, and the great difficulty of teaching them to abide by a few relatively simple rules of hygiene and sanitation. The sixty deaths in sixty days in the 2nd Iowa are to a large extent explainable by orders like the following:

The colonel commanding cannot but express his mortification upon inspecting this morning . . . the quarters of the regiment. With such an intelligent body of men, so prompt in learning the drill, that the police should be so bad shows neglect of duty and comfort on the part of the men and want of supervision on the part of the company officers. The want of uniformity in the arrangement of the bunks, dirty shoes and boots in and about the bunks, scraped sweepings from the floor under the bunks, tables and underneath same, rear of quarters and messrooms not properly policed . . . all goes to show that officers . . . do not give their personal attention to their companies.[59]

The 2nd Michigan, commanded by Gordon Granger, whose orders were not to be disregarded with impunity, was at Benton Barracks at the same time as the 2nd Iowa, but it did not experience the Iowa regiment's shocking toll of deaths. Perhaps the following order accounts for the difference: "Captains of companies . . . will see that the ground in front and rear of their quarters is cleaned immediately, and that they are kept clean hereafter. They will also see that the barracks in which their companies are quartered are properly ventilated night and day. They will also see that conveniences for bathing are provided and require the men under

59. General Orders No. 9, January 12, 1862, in 2nd Iowa O&L Books, RG 94, NA.

their command to bathe at least once a week."[60] Another order Granger issued two weeks later added, "In order to secure the health of the soldiers, the straw tics and blankets must be aired every five days by exposing them to the sun and wind from 9 am to 3 pm. The quarters must be scrubbed out at least once in four days."[61]

Measles was probably the greatest single scourge of green regiments. Fully a third of the 4th Iowa caught the disease and, owing to inadequate hospital facilities and lack of proper care and diet, the percentage of fatalities was high. The members of the 1st Kentucky from the mountain regions of the state were particularly susceptible to the disease, and few of its troopers who were sent to the hospitals recovered. General George H. Thomas took the drastic step of furloughing measles victims whose homes were not too far from camp. "The results," the regimental historian relates, "showed the wisdom and humanity of this course; for having the comforts of home and the skillful nursing of their families and friends, most of these recovered."[62] The historian, perhaps wisely, fails to relate what effect the return home of men carrying the infection had on their "families and friends."

The historian of the 8th Illinois, Abner Hard, was the regimental surgeon, and his history contains by far the best and most detailed account of the health problems that beset a cavalry regiment in its early days. While Hard's unit was encamped first in Washington and then across the river in Alexandria, he not only had to cope with an epidemic of colds and fever brought on by "exposure and imprudence," but also had seven cases of typhoid fever on his hands. Then, with "small pox . . . making its ravages among the troops about Washington," Hard decided to vaccinate the entire regiment, from the colonel on down. "A few objected and even determined to resist. . . . one man, in particular, declared he 'would die first,' but the presence of a rope with which he was about to be tied brought him to his senses."[63] In January, 1862, Hard relates,

60. Battalion Order No. 7, November 27, 1861, in 2nd Michigan O&L Books, RG 94, NA.
61. Regimental Order No. 35, December 12, 1861, *ibid.*
62. Tarrant, *Wild Riders of the First Kentucky*, 34.
63. Hard, *History of the Eighth Cavalry*, 46.

More than five hundred were on the sick list. The diseases were mostly typho-malarial fever, while a large number of cases were genuine typhoid fever. . . . We had but two hospital tents, and consequently were obliged to send a large number to the general hospital in Alexandria, where many of them died. . . . to obtain a permit to send patients to the general hospital . . . we were obliged to send a messenger through the mud to Washington, eleven miles distant, who could not return until night, and then the permit was good for that day only. Aroused by a sense of our suffering, the Medical Director sent four large ambulances from Washington to convey our sick to the hospital, but . . . they did not arrive until nearly dark, and the drivers were so intoxicated that they could not be trusted.[64]

Hard's grim recital continues, "In the camps around us there was even more sickness than in ours, and most of them adopted the plan of issuing whisky. The Fifty-Third Pennsylvania had thrice the number of deaths that we had, simply, as I believe, because they resorted to the use of spirits. . . . the measles soon broke out among us, and we soon had twenty to thirty beds filled with that disease alone."[65]

As disease struck the cavalry, an interesting discovery was made. City boys generally stood up better under physical hardship and illness than did boys from the rural areas, and "the more cultured, refined and delicately nurtured the soldiers had been at home, the better they seemed to endure . . . hardships."[66] The large, robust six-footers, the lumbermen and bear hunters filled the hospitals and the cemeteries, or were discharged for physical disability, whereas the striplings thrived and the "waspy . . . little daredevils grew strong and athletic."[67]

64. *Ibid.*, 59. After his difficulties with the general hospital in Washington, Hard took possession of a vacant house in Alexandria and set up his own regimental hospital.

65. *Ibid.*, 69, 72. A bitter mixture of quinine and whiskey was a widely used febrifuge and, in some regiments, was issued to the men daily. Regimental History Committee, *History of the 3d Pennsylvania*, 76. General Jefferson C. Davis was his own pharmacist: "I put a handful of quinine in a bottle of whiskey [and] placed the bottle into the saddle bag. . . . My horse was a hard trotter, and when I took the bottle out for a drink, and I did so frequently, the whiskey and quinine were churned as white as milk. . . . So there's your remedy: whiskey, quinine, and a hard-trotting horse." Sipes, *The Seventh Pennsylvania*, 71–72.

66. Aldace F. Walker, *The Vermont Brigade in the Shenandoah Valley, 1864* (Burlington, Vt., 1869), 21.

67. Clark, "Making of a Volunteer Cavalryman," 10; see also Petten-

The men's care of their own health did not improve when their regiments took the field. If anything, it grew worse. Lieutenant Colonel Johnson of the 5th New York announced,

The condition of the company tents is like a whited sepulchre, clean without and foul within. . . . Sickness seems to run in tents. The cause is obvious. When a soldier is sick the door of the tent he is in is strapped shut, the cap of the tent is fastened down, and all the air being excluded, his comrades breathe a foul atmosphere. Officers commanding Companies will see at once that there is free ventilation. . . . Such a day as this all blankets and bedding should be aired, and tents kept open and the cap of tents removed.[68]

Officers of the 7th Pennsylvania had their attention called "to the dirty condition of the camp generally. The Colonel Commanding on inspection this morning found but two company streets that had been properly policed. Several of the kitchens are in a filthy condition, and only one in good condition."[69] Lieutenant Colonel Horace N. Howland of the 3rd Ohio found the camp of his regiment "very poorly cleaned and parts of which was in a very filthy condition and with little or no policing done."[70] The 2nd Michigan had to be ordered "to take immediate steps to have all carcasses and offensive matter of every description . . . buried and the rubbish burned. A sufficient number of sinks . . . will be dug and properly secured, and every precaution taken to guard against disease by attention to cleanliness of person and quarters."[71]

In anticipation of an inspection the next day, the 1st Vermont was ordered to bury all dead horses lying in the vicinity of its camp and to police thoroughly the camp itself. On another occasion, the regiment had its attention "called to the shameful practice, now so common, of defiling the outlines of the camp by daily

gill, *College Cavaliers*, 11; Beach, *First New York (Lincoln) Cavalry*, 79–80; Copp, *Reminiscences of the War*, 26; and Hinman, *Story of the Sherman Brigade*, 317.

68. Regimental Orders, unnumbered, March 9, 1863, in 5th New York O&L Books, RG 94, NA.

69. Circular, February 26, 1865, in 7th Pennsylvania O&L Books, RG 94, NA.

70. Letter from Horace Howland, February 19, 1865, in 3rd Ohio O&L Books, RG 94, NA.

71. General Orders No. 12, March 13, 1863, in 2nd Michigan O&L Books, RG 94, NA.

public deposits of filth. Hereafter, any person neglecting the proper use of the sinks will be arrested and punished. This matter has been made the subject of complaint at brigade headquarters, and all such embarrassing nuisances must be avoided in the future."[72] The Vermonters even needed a reminder to draw their drinking water from running streams instead of the doubtless contaminated dug wells in and about their camp.[73]

Winter camp, with the men living in small log huts covered by their shelter halves, two to four troopers to a hut, presented its own hygienic problems. "Upon the recommendation of the surgeon," company commanders of the 1st Vermont were ordered to "have the men of their respective companies immediately remove the roofs of their huts and replace them at 1 o'clock p. m."[74] The following winter, a brigade order laid it down that

Medical officers in charge of regiments will make daily inspections of the quarters of their commands, accompanying the officer of the day when he performs that duty, and take a memoranda at the time, specifying the degree of cleanliness, order and general condition of the quarters, keeping a separate record for each company, and every week make a report to the commanding officer of the regiment, embodying the results of these inspections. Any plan may be adopted in making these reports which will indicate clearly the relative excellency of each company during the week. It is suggested for consideration of regimental commanders, in order to excite a wholesome rivalry among the different companies in a matter of such sanitary importance, that the company most deserving be favored in regard to detail for fatigue, police and other laborious duties, or by any other means they may deem proper.[75]

It would be a gross misreading of the evidence to infer that the camp of a volunteer cavalry regiment was never anything but a sink of disorder, drunkenness, and filth, and that cavalrymen

72. General Orders No. 13, November 13, 1862, in 1st Vermont O&L Books, RG 94, NA.

73. General Orders No. 16, August 4, 1862, ibid.

74. Circular, April 1, 1864, ibid. When the "bell" (or Sibley) and large wall tents used in the early part of the war were replaced by the well-known pup tent, each of the two tentmates had one wall of the tent (commonly placed under the saddle, above the saddle blanket, on the march) and the two halves were attached to each other by buttons to make a tent; hence "shelter halves."

75. Circular, February 18, 1865, ibid.

were a collection of delinquents officered by heedless incompetents. Conditions were sufficiently disorderly, to be sure, and at times shockingly and unnecessarily squalid. It is evident nonetheless that for all the men's complaints, justified or otherwise, and the scoldings and faultfindings of commanding officers, more than mere patriotism kept the average trooper in the army. By and large, beneath the obligatory grousing and complaining, and despite hardships utterly beyond the comprehension of more pampered generations, there ran an undercurrent of satisfaction and even of pleasure. Taking the good times with the bad, the men more often than not enjoyed their life in the service.

The 6th Pennsylvania Cavalry (Rush's Lancers) in bivouac

George W. Bayard

John Buford

Philip St. George Cooke

Alfred N. Duffié

Judson Kilpatrick

VII

To the Tented Field

THERE WAS AN ORDERLY PROGRESSION OF THE DAY'S routine in a cavalry camp, each step signaled by a bugle call. It began well before daybreak, with the chief bugler of the regiment blowing the call for the "Assembly of Buglers," in response to which the twenty-four company buglers (or twenty, if it was a ten-company regiment) assembled at headquarters and blew "Reveille," more or less in unison. As soon as the men were dressed, each company formed in two ranks on its company street and the orderly sergeants called the roll.[1] Then came the "Stables" call, to signal the grooming and feeding of the horses, the feed being issued by the quartermaster sergeants. After a short interval to allow the men to wash up came the call for breakfast. The morning meal was followed by the water call, when the men rode

---

1. The orderly sergeants of the 3rd Pennsylvania were required to learn the rosters of their companies by heart, so that they could call the roll in the dark. Regimental History Committee, *History of the 3rd Pennsylvania*, 20. A 1st Massachusetts order declared, "Hereafter the orderly sergeants will not use their roll books in calling the roll. Any orderly sergeant who is unable to learn the rolls, so as to be able to call it without the book will be replaced." General Orders No. 15, March 13, 1864, in 1st Massachusetts O&L Books, RG 94, NA.

their horses bareback and supposedly at a walk to the nearest stream or pond, each company under command of a lieutenant or sergeant to prevent running of the horses. Then, in succession, came the "Sick Call," the "Fatigue Call" for policing the company streets, the horse lines, and the camp, and then the "First Call for Guard Mount," in response to which five or six men from each company, whose turn it was to stand guard that day, rode to the color line under command of a sergeant, were inspected by the officer of the guard, counted off into watches, and the members of the first watch were conducted to their assigned positions by the corporal of the guard. Then came the "Drill Call," whereupon the first sergeant of each company gave the orders "Saddle Up" and "Lead Out" and, after forming the company, turned it over to the captain with the ritual words "Sir, the company is formed." The captain then gave the commands "Prepare to Mount," "Mount," and "Form Ranks" and led the company to the drill ground. Drill was ended by the "Recall from Drill," which was followed by the "Dinner Call." The afternoon drill came after the noon meal and was in turn followed by the second water call of the day. Then came the dress parade of the entire regiment, the evening "Stables" call, supper, "Retreat," and the evening roll call. Finally, at about nine P.M., came "Taps," and the long day, which had begun at about five A.M., was ended.[2] These routines were extensively altered when the regiment was in the field, particularly when it was in the midst of a campaign, but the standard routine was resumed as completely as circumstances allowed whenever the regiment settled down in camp.

Sunday was customarily a day of rest; there was no "Fatigue Call" and no drill, but otherwise the day's routine was much the same as on other days. The horses had to be fed, watered, and groomed, and guard had to be mounted. Following breakfast and

2. The sequence of bugle calls and activities in the text is based on Allen, *Down in Dixie*, 172, and Cheney, *History of the Ninth Regiment*, 47–48. There were variations in the number and exact sequence of calls from one regiment to another, and even in the same regiment circumstances, the weather, location, and the needs of the service at any given moment dictated changes in the routine; much of the routine was eliminated entirely when the regiment was on a scout or in a campaign. It was said that the horses learned the bugle calls as quickly as the men.

in place of the weekday drill, it was customary to have an inspection of more or less thoroughness and severity. If the regiment had a chaplain, as most of them did, and he was present in camp, divine services were held on Sunday. As with the officers and the men themselves, the quality of chaplains varied. The chaplain of the 5th West Virginia held "preaching services . . . whenever practicable, and with . . . [him] that meant when it was not impossible."[3] On the other hand, when the chaplain of the Sherman Brigade preached a sermon after a long absence, it had to last the brigade three or four months.[4] Conscientious chaplains, when not engaged in their religious functions, acted as postmasters, wrote letters for the illiterate, looked after the remittances the men sent home, and comforted the sick. Chaplain Charles H. Lovejoy of the 7th Kansas, in addition to the zealous performance of his religious duties, organized a school for the contrabands who had "adopted" the regiment and taught eighty of them, men, women, and children, to read and write.[5] But there was also another kind of chaplain, who, "finding no pulpit open to him at home . . . would, through political influence, secure a Chaplain's commission with its rank and pay of Captain of Cavalry, and be foisted upon a devoted regiment. . . . He was often in the surgeon's quarters, to take a social glass with the officers . . . and most of his time was spent in the Colonel's tent, where he smoked the good cigars to be found there, played whist with the officers, told stories, and sang songs."[6]

3. Frank S. Reader, *History of the Fifth West Virginia Cavalry, Formerly the Second Virginia Infantry, and Battery G, First West Virginia Light Artillery* (New Brighton, W.Va., 1890), 127. Private George W. Gorham, 1st West Virginia, was "detailed to act as chaplain and regimental postmaster" by means of a regimental order. Special Orders No. 2, September 5, 1864, in 1st Massachusetts O&L Books, RG 94, NA.
4. Hinman, *Story of the Sherman Brigade*, 242.
5. Stephen Z. Starr, *Jennison's Jayhawkers* (Baton Rouge, La., 1973), 269.
6. Edward Anderson, *Camp Fire Stories* (Chicago, 1900), 251–52. Some chaplains were "Soldiers of the Lord" in a literal sense. In a fight with Turner Ashby's Confederate cavalry, Chaplain John H. Woodward of the 1st Vermont brought up the reinforcements; "his eagerness to take a hand in any fighting had brought him considerably in advance of the position commonly occupied by army chaplains." Benedict, *Vermont in the Civil War*, II, 549.

Among the more pleasant aspects of army life in the early days of the war for the newly enlisted trooper was the visit of relatives and friends, male and female, who came to camp in large numbers daily, especially on Sundays and holidays, bearing hampers of gifts. Indeed, if the new regiment was within easy reach of the locality where the men had been recruited, the crowds of kinfolk and sightseers who came to watch the novel spectacle of the cavalry drill became a nuisance. The 6th Pennsylvania "found [it] necessary to establish a guard around the camp, to keep off the great crowds that gathered there daily, interfering with order and discipline, and rendering mounted drill almost impossible."[7]

Flag presentations and national holidays were signalized with ceremony and speechmaking. The presentation of a flag, usually the handiwork of the mothers, wives, sisters, and sweethearts of the troopers, provided the local member of Congress or other prominent politico an opportunity to unfurl his patriotic oratory and the colonel of the regiment to make the eagle scream in reply. The celebration of Washington's Birthday in 1862 by the 10th New York "made a further draft on the large stock of patriotism always kept on hand by the regiment. The memory of the Father of his Country was duly polished up by parade and serenade, promenade and lemonade, firing of cannon and speechmaking."[8] On July 4, 1863, at Corinth, Mississippi, the band of the 7th Kansas, ensconced on one of the regimental wagons fitted up for the purpose "and with the Old Flag floating to the breeze . . . visited each regiment in Corinth and gave them a sample of 7th Kansas music."[9]

When the day's work was done, the men amused themselves in their barracks or tents or around their campfires by writing letters, singing songs, and telling stories. The serious-minded organized temperance societies, Bible-reading groups, and literary societies which presented lectures and staged debates. The

7. Gracey, *Annals of the 6th*, 20. The College Cavaliers entertained their visitors by holding a reception after dress parade, and they "sang their college songs and the patriotic airs which were familiar at the time throughout the North." Pettengill, *College Cavaliers*, 16.
8. Preston, *History of the 10th Regiment*, 22.
9. Starr, *Jennison's Jayhawkers*, 275.

frivolous formed minstrel troupes and theatrical companies. Reading, especially the reading of newspapers, was a favorite pastime; for the men of the 1st Maine the newspapers "filled up pleasantly and profitably many an otherwise lonely hour, and . . . [were] borrowed, and lent, and read, by this one and that one, till literally read to pieces."[10] Enterprising news dealers followed the armies and kept them supplied with the latest metropolitan papers, but with results that were not always satisfactory. The historian of the 8th Illinois reports that in the spring of 1862 on the Peninsula "northern newspapers among which the New York Herald was most conspicuous, were brought daily to camp . . . and sold at prices from ten to twenty-five cents each; the monopoly of this trade being given to certain individuals who, it was said, supplied the headquarters free of charge, but made thousands of dollars out of the soldiers."[11] On the other hand, and proving once again that hardly a statement can be made about army life in the Civil War whose opposite was not also true, William O. Gulick of the 1st Iowa wrote his family from Arkansas in the spring of 1863, "We get the news almost as quick as you do for we take the St. Louis Democrat & have it brought to our tent By a Brigade news dealer[.] He furnishes us with any kind of reading matter at reasonable prices."[12]

The day's activities were supposed to close with the blowing of "Taps," but the colonel of the 1st Massachusetts, for one, found "it necessary, notwithstanding that an order has already been issued on the subject, to call the attention of the officers and men of the regiment to the fact that too much noise is still made in camp after Taps. He trusts that this mention of it will be sufficient to prevent its occurrence in the future."[13] Colonel Williams' confidence in the efficacy of his order was misplaced, for

10. Tobie, *First Maine Cavalry*, 24. While the 1st New York was in camp in Washington, the New York *Tribune* sent the regiment a number of free copies of its semiweekly edition. The copies "were passed along from tent to tent and closely read." Beach, *First New York (Lincoln) Cavalry*, 49.
11. Hard, *History of the Eighth Cavalry*, 73.
12. Guyer, "Corporal William O. Gulick," 589.
13. General Orders No. 3, undated, but clearly issued in October, 1861, in 1st Massachusetts O&L Books, RG 94, NA.

nearly three years later it was still necessary to announce to the 1st Massachusetts that "no shouting or noisy demonstrations will be allowed in camp . . . and at taps all lights will be put out and all noise cease."[14]

Card playing, checkers, and chess flourished. But even such innocent pastimes were frowned upon by the more straitlaced troopers, of whom there were many in every regiment, and of course there were other forms of recreation that deserved their censure. Jacob Bartmess of the 8th Indiana wrote his wife, "Well Amanda there is every thing going on here at the same time play cards, pitching horse Shoes[,] Swearing of the most blasphemous nature," and a month later, "While I am writing there is fiddling, card playing, Swearing and all kinds of wickedness going on all around me but it has no influence over me Why. I am perfectly disgusted at it."[15] William Glazier of the 2nd New York reported to his family:

Our regiment is made up principally of young men from highly re-spectable families, reared under the influence of a pure morality, who find that the highest standard of morality presented here is much lower than they were wont to have at home, and they soon begin to waver. Thus, having lost their first moorings of character, they start downward, and in many instances are precipitated to hor-rible depths. . . . Only a very few have sufficient force in themselves to effectually resist these evils. . . . Consequently our camp is infested more or less with gambling, drunkenness and profanity, and all their train of attendant evils, and at times we long for campaigning in the field, where it seems to us we may rid ourselves of this de-moralization.[16]

As is always the case in wartime—and the reticences of the postwar literature to the contrary notwithstanding, the Civil War was not the Quest of the Holy Grail—conditions in the neighbor-hood of many of the camps were such as to justify the righteous horror of the Bartmesses and Glaziers. The majority of regimen-

14. General Orders No. 2, July 5, 1862, *ibid.*
15. Bartmess, "Civil War Letters," 51, 53. According to William R. Hartpence, "at least 90 per cent of the Union soldiers knew nothing of card playing before entering the service. It came to all as a positive neces-sity and was as generous and edifying to the moral and mental manhood as coffee was to the physical." Hartpence, *History of the 51st Indiana*, 17.
16. Glazier, *Three Years in the Federal Cavalry*, 30–31.

tal historians and diarists preserve a discreet silence on a subject so delicate, but the more outspoken make it abundantly clear that those who wanted more lively forms of entertainment than a game of checkers or the singing of hymns did not have far to seek. The "open saloons" near the camp of the 7th Pennsylvania in Louisville "were an absolute curse. Several companies were recruited from the coal-mining regions of Pennsylvania. When removed from temptation they were among the bravest and most faithful of soldiers, but when whiskey was within their reach, they became riotous, and at times it seemed as if one-half of the regiment was required to guard the other half."[17] Lieutenant Charles Alley of the 5th Iowa reported to his family from St. Louis that he found the city worse than he had expected: "Oh! what wickedness, evil in every shape, moral degradation everywhere showing itself."[18] The 2nd Iowa reached Memphis in 1863 and found that the city more than lived up to its reputation as a sink of iniquity. "The city afforded far greater temptations to vice," the regimental historian has written, "than any other place in which we had been quartered. Gambling hells, drinking saloons, and houses of ill fame were to be met on every corner, and were the weapons used by Satan to rob the soldier of his money and drag his soul down to the black gulf of despair."[19]

The historian of the 8th Illinois notes that in Alexandria, Virginia, where the regiment had its camp in the winter of 1861–1862, "numerous places where liquor is sold and . . . houses of ill-fame . . . were found on almost every street." He adds that "compared with those recruited in the eastern cities, the morals of the Eighth were such as to make us proud of belonging to it," a statement which may, perhaps, be taken with a grain of salt.[20]

The state of sexual morality among the men, a subject hinted at in gingerly fashion by a small minority of regimental historians and referred to not at all by most of them, is impossible to pin down with any degree of certainty. It is evident, however, that "houses of ill-fame" were not confined to Memphis or Alex-

17. Dornblaser, *Sabre Strokes of the Pennsylvania Dragoons*, 36.
18. Ezell, "Civil War Diary of Charles Alley," 246.
19. Pierce, *History of the Second Iowa Cavalry*, 67.
20. Hard, *History of the Eighth Cavalry*, 73.

andria. Lieutenant Colonel Davies of the 2nd Michigan discovered, while his regiment was at Benton Barracks, St. Louis, in the early months of the war, that there were "several women connected with . . . [the] regiment who are not married and [are] consequently bringing down disgrace upon the regiment. Be it therefore understood that all such characters must leave the camp forthwith."[21] Four months later when the regiment was about to leave New Madrid, Colonel Gordon Granger, having learned that "laundresses connected with the regiment have made preparations to embark with this command and are now embarking," let it be known that "this is positively forbidden."[22] Orders issued to the 2nd Iowa in December 1864, announced, "Every woman white or black in the command will be required to leave the camp."[23] An order to the same regiment, directing the establishment of a regimental laundry, leaves nothing to the imagination:

A regimental laundry is hereby established, and will consist of not more than two washerwomen to each company, who will have separate quarters outside the regimental lines. Each company wishing to avail itself of this offer will furnish the washerwoman it employs with one small tent in which they will sleep and be quartered, and furnish them with rations which will be cooked and eaten at the regimental laundry. None but those of the best character will be admitted to these quarters. A sentinel will be posted at these quarters each day, charged with the responsibility of keeping good order, and also responsible for the safekeeping of the clothing taken to the laundry. Any negro woman conducting herself improperly will be peremptorily driven from the camp.[24]

Immorality could and did take many forms besides the sexual. Private Nathan B. Lincoln, 1st Massachusetts, was sentenced "to wear a thief's badge for thirty days . . . to have his head shaved, to be called Thief Lincoln at roll call for six months, and to forfeit one month's pay" for "a scandalous theft while on post as a sentinel, and causing the punishment of two innocent

21. Regimental Orders No. 26, November 27, 1861, in 2nd Michigan O&L Books, RG 94, NA.
22. General Orders, unnumbered, April 13, 1862, *ibid.*
23. Special Orders No. 170, December 16, 1864, in 2nd Iowa O&L Books, RG 94, NA.
24. General Orders No. 123, May 21, 1863, *ibid.*

men."[25] William Comer of the 5th New York was sentenced to the loss of one month's pay, "to be confined in the Guard Tent one month during the nights, for fourteen days of the said month to be fed on bread and water, and during all the month to report each morning to the Surgeon, for police and fatigue duty at the hospital," for stealing a watch and chain from a comrade.[26] While campaigning in Kentucky—technically friendly country —troopers of the 2nd Michigan were informed, "Complaints have been entered at these headquarters by citizens of the passing of counterfeit and broken bank money by persons belonging to this regiment. Hereafter any person passing the same, on its being proven against him, shall be severely punished, and any commissioned officer doing the same or giving countenance to it shall be court-martialed for disobedience of orders."[27] Two months later Corporal Edward Knapp of the same regiment received the light punishment of reduction to the ranks "for conduct unbecoming a soldier and disgraceful to a non-commissioned officer. . . . It must be a source of mortification to every man in the regiment to find himself connected with one so base and depraved as to be found guilty of the penitentiary crime of counterfeiting."[28]

Raising cash by selling one's weapons was not unknown.[29]

25. Special Orders No. 1, January 8, 1863, in 1st Massachusetts O&L Books, RG 94, NA.
26. Regimental Order No. 24, December 5, 1861, in 5th New York O&L Books, RG 94, NA.
27. Regimental Order No. 13, November 23, 1862, in 2nd Michigan O&L Books, RG 94, NA.
28. Regimental Order No. 8, January 9, 1862, *ibid.*
29. A member of the 2nd Illinois relates with much complacency that some members of his regiment escaped in small groups when General Earl Van Dorn captured Holly Springs in December, 1862; "having lost their camp equipage . . . [they] fixed upon a ruse whereby they might recoup in part from the rebel citizens. Good arms at high prices were in active demand throughout the south. A standard revolver was valued at from $50 to $75 in greenbacks. Southern citizens were always ready to buy arms from any of our men who were willing to sell. Knowing this, one of the officers sent out several men to sell their arms and with each was sent a guard to watch. Upon the completion of the sale the guard would arrest the citizen and confiscate his purchase. In this way they collected about $1,000, which was credited against losses at Holly Springs." Fletcher, *The History of Company A*, 73. No doubt there were such sales by

Colonel Gordon Granger informed the 2nd Michigan that "any noncommissioned officer who shall lose, sell or otherwise lose [*sic*] his arms will have double its value deducted from his pay."[30] And it is impossible to categorize the following 2nd Iowa order:

> The colonel commanding has been notified that the practice of trading horses with parties outside of the regiment and getting old, worn-out horses for good ones and receiving return money as difference to defray their expenses. It is therefore ordered that all company officers of this regiment shall recommend such persons as are suspicioned for such transactions for transfer to the infantry. . . . Company commanders will immediately report to these Headquarters all enlisted men . . . who have been engaged or suspicioned to have been engaged in horse stealing or trading to the detriment of the Government, that they may be transferred to some Infantry Regiment in the Army of the Potomac, or wherever the War Department may direct for a term of not less than three years from the time of such alleged transaction.[31]

The order is noteworthy partly because of the kind of transaction it sought to halt and partly because of the nature of the threatened punishment. It rests on the assumption that a transfer to the infantry was the most effective deterrent to a cavalryman. The threat of a transfer to an infantry unit in the Army of the Potomac, whose footsoldiers had sustained appalling casualties in May, 1864, added a special menace to the order.

In the case of noncommissioned officers the most common form of punishment was reduction to the ranks. The humiliating loss of authority, coupled with the reduction of pay to that of a private, was deemed punishment enough for nearly any misconduct of a corporal or sergeant. Corporal Erlon G. Elder of the 8th Illinois, however, was reduced to the ranks for resisting arrest and using mutinous language and was also sentenced to forfeiture of a month's pay, to be "confined at hard labor for 30 days

---

members of this and other regiments that did not, and were not intended to end with the confiscation of the weapons sold.

30. Regimental Order No. 6, January 6, 1862, in 2nd Michigan O&L Books, RG 94, NA.

31. General Orders No. 187, May 29, 1864, in 2nd Iowa O&L Books, RG 94, NA.

. . . [and to be] handcuffed when not at hard labor."[32] Drunkenness was the most common cause of a corporal or sergeant being stripped of his chevrons, but there were numerous other causes. Sergeant Major Goodwin and Sergeants Edward J. Russell and Thomas Preston of the 1st Massachusetts were demoted for "having shown themselves unworthy of their positions" by circulating untruths about their colonel's character.[33] Sergeant James H. Emery of the 8th Illinois was broken for disrespectful and contemptuous conduct toward his superior officer, in that, having refused to obey his lieutenant's order to have his trouser legs outside his boots and upon the lieutenant "insisting that he should do so, came from his room with the bottom of his pantaloons torn off about two thirds of the way from his feet to his knees."[34] Another sergeant of the same regiment was demoted for having "permitted himself to be detailed in a menial capacity in a northern hospital for more than four months after being fit for duty."[35] Noncommissioned officers of the 1st Vermont "neglecting the proper courtesies to their superiors in rank," or "who do not command the respect of the men under their charge, and who do not enforce obedience to their orders" were threatened with reduction to the ranks.[36] Sergeant Major H. D. Smith of the same ruggedly individualistic regiment *was* reduced to the ranks "for insolent conduct toward his superior officer, and for writing letters to the press, reflecting upon his colonel."[37] In August, 1864, seventeen sergeants and nineteen corporals of the 1st Massachusetts were broken in one fell swoop, "for continued absence from their regi-

32. Orders No. 18, February 27, 1862, in 8th Illinois O&L Books, RG 94, NA.
33. General Orders No. 22, March 5, 1862, in 1st Massachusetts O&L Books, RG 94, NA.
34. Orders No. 18, February 27, 1862, in 8th Illinois O&L Books, RG 94, NA.
35. Order No. 24, December 1, 1863, *ibid.*
36. Special Orders No. 39, January 23, 1863, in 1st Vermont O&L Books, RG 94, NA.
37. Special Orders No. 21, December 23, 1862, *ibid.* Commissary Sergeant Rufus G. Barber of the same regiment was reduced to the ranks "for contracting a disease of his own seeking, thereby rendering him unfit for military duty." Special Orders No. 26, April 16, 1865, *ibid.*

ment," there being no indication whether the absences were without leave, or were due to details and hence beyond the men's control.[38] One poor fellow, Sergeant John Ryan of the 8th Illinois, was reduced to the ranks in mid-October, 1862, "having been incapacitated by a wound rec'd at Gaines' Mills June 27, 1862."[39] Corporal George Hibbard of the 7th Pennsylvania, "having confessed himself guilty of the disgraceful and unsoldierly crime of Theft," was not only reduced to the ranks, but it was also ordered that "his emblems of rank will be stripped from him by the Orderly Sergeant in presence of his Company mustered for the purpose immediately after dress parade."[40]

Misdeeds like these were out of the common run. In most cases reduction to the ranks was the punishment for such offenses as "repeated disobedience of orders and total incapacity for the duties" of a corporal or sergeant, for "inefficiency and neglect of duty," "disobedience of orders," "disrespectful language to officers," and "disobedience of orders and neglect of duty."[41] There are also instances on record of noncommissioned officers resigning, whether voluntarily, under pressure, or to save themselves from punishment, the records do not disclose.[42]

Enlisted men's sins were dealt with in more drastic fashion. In the early months of the war, following the practice of the Regular Army in peacetime, even the minor transgressions of enlisted men required a court martial, with the presence of three

38. General Orders No. 5, August 30, 1864, in 1st Massachusetts O&L Books, RG 94, NA.

39. Orders No. 62, October 16, 1862, in 8th Illinois O&L Books, RG 94, NA.

40. Special Orders No. 21, May 13, 1863, in 7th Pennsylvania O&L Books, RG 94, NA. Corporal Frederick Deiner of the same regiment pleaded guilty to "the larceny of one bridle" and was sentenced "to be reduced to the ranks and pay the sum of ten dollars . . . into the Regimental fund." Special Order No. 34, June 4, 1863, ibid.

41. For example, General Orders No. 18, February 14, 1862, and Special Orders No. 26, June 24, 1863, in 1st Massachusetts O&L Books, RG 94, NA; Orders No. 49, August 14, 1862, in 8th Illinois O&L Books, RG 94, NA; Special Order, unnumbered, September 13, 1864, in 3rd Ohio O&L Books, RG 94, NA.

42. General Orders No. 29, April 6, 1862, in 1st Massachusetts O&L Books, RG 94, NA; Special Orders No. 24, April 15, 1864, in 7th Pennsylvania O&L Books, RG 94, NA.

or more officers and the observance of all the formalities of a trial, including the preparation of an elaborate record of the proceedings for review by higher authority. The colonel of the regiment, in addition to his many other duties and responsibilities, was obliged to review and comment on a dozen or more cases that had been disposed of in a single session of his regimental court martial. In one such review, Colonel Washington L. Elliott of the 2nd Iowa disapproved the proceedings in three of thirteen cases and pointed out that "if the prisoner does not plead guilty, testimony should be taken as though the plea was not guilty. The court erred in not examining the witnesses named on the charges. The delay in making up the record, as well as the want of neatness in the same, and irregularities of the proceedings, shows a want of care on the part of the court, particularly inasmuch as the member who recorded its proceedings was carefully shown how to make the record, and a form for the same was pointed out to him."[43] On a subsequent occasion, after reviewing the record of six cases, Colonel Elliott informed the court that in his opinion, it had been "too lenient in awarding sentences. If discipline is to be maintained, courts martial must award sentences without partiality, favor or affection."[44]

In the latter part of 1862, the cumbersome court martial system for the trial of enlisted men was done away with, and the commanding officer of the regiment or a deputy designated by him was empowered to dispose of routine cases involving relatively minor breaches of discipline. The sentences imposed were commonly one or another of the often-described methods of physical punishment, including standing on a barrel, carrying a log or saddle for a specified number of hours, bucking, and bucking and gagging. Extra guard or fatigue duty was another frequently imposed punishment. In more serious cases, men were sentenced to confinement in the guardhouse, with or without "hard labor," sometimes coupled with forfeiture of all or part of the culprit's pay for a month or longer. Forfeiture of pay was a particularly serious blow to men whose families depended on

43. General Orders, unnumbered, November 18, 1861, in 2nd Iowa O&L Books, RG 94, NA.
44. General Orders No. 14, January 24, 1862, *ibid.*

their pay, which at best was from two to as many as eight months in arrears.

Depending on circumstances and the nature of the offense, punishment could be even more severe. Two troopers of the 3rd New Jersey were executed on January 6, 1864, for trying to desert to the enemy.[45] In May of the same year, in Memphis, three troopers of the 2nd New Jersey were executed by firing squad in the presence of ten thousand soldiers and many thousands of civilians for the crimes of rape and robbery.[46] But sentences could be severe enough even in far less heinous cases. Private John H. Williard of the 1st Vermont, convicted of "mutinous conduct," was sentenced "to forfeit $10 per month of his pay for one year, to wear for one month on his left ankle a chain six feet long with a ball weighing twelve pounds attached thereto, and have his head and beard shaved." General George Stoneman confirmed and approved the sentence "with the exception of the words 'and beard,' this not being among the punishments prescribed by Army Regulations."[47] Private William Godfrey of the 3rd Ohio, who pleaded guilty to the charge of deserting his post while on vedette duty, "leaving his horse and arms on Post and going to a house about 4 rods distant," was sentenced to be "confined with ball and chain attached to hard labor for . . . three months, to forfeit all pay and allowances during that time and then to be dishonorably discharged from the United States service."[48]

The rigors of army discipline failed utterly to make volunteers forget that they were citizen soldiers. The army—more correctly, their regiment—had their loyalty, but it was a temporary and sometimes insecure allegiance, second in importance to their permanent status of free and independent citizens of the Republic. Being citizen soldiers, troopers took a keen interest in the questions of the day and had strong opinions on them, which they were not at all loath to voice. What Augustus Buell wrote

45. Hannaford, "Reminiscences," 252(d)–253(a).
46. Pierce, *History of the Second Iowa*, 96–97.
47. General Orders No. 64, October 20, 1862, in 1st Vermont O&L Books, RG 94, NA.
48. Orders No. 83, January 14, 1863, in 3rd Ohio O&L Books, RG 94, NA.

of the Army of the Potomac in winter quarters in 1862–1863 could have been said of any cavalry regiment, East or West, from the beginning of the war to its end: "Probably the ideal army is one in which no such thing as public opinion exists. But the Army of the Potomac was not made up of that sort of soldiery. On the contrary, every . . . camp was a community of American citizens, and every log hut . . . was an improvised 'debating society' of bright, smart young men . . . retaining, despite military discipline, the habits of free thought and free speech. . . . Hence the army was full of public opinion, which was neither slow nor diffident in finding expression."[49]

The most readily available subject (or target) for this "public opinion" was army leadership, from sergeants and regimental officers to the commanding general of whatever army a particular regiment happened to be a part of. But there was also public opinion and to spare on all the political and social issues of the moment. On occasion, this public opinion found expression in strange or excessively direct ways.

Company K of the 7th Kansas was recruited in Ashtabula County, Ohio, a hotbed of abolitionist sentiment—it was the home of Senator Benjamin F. Wade—by John Brown, Jr., eldest son of the martyr. A member of the regiment wrote after the war:

Co. K was made up of abolitionists of the intense sort. . . . For a while after the company joined the regiment the men would assemble near the captain's tent in the dark after "retreat" and listen to the deep utterances of some impassioned orator; the voice was always low and did not reach far beyond the immediate circle of the company, who stood with head bent, drinking in every word. The speaker always closed with "Do you swear to avenge John Brown?" and the answer always came back low and deep, "We will, we will"; then would follow the John Brown hymn, sung in the same repressed manner. . . . At first, the whole regiment used to gather just outside of the sacred precincts to listen, but it soon ceased to attract, and the company itself became too busy avenging to hold their regular meetings.[50]

49. Augustus C. Buell, *"The Cannoneer": Recollections of Service in the Army of the Potomac* (Washington, D.C., 1890), 49.
50. Fox, "The Story of the Seventh Kansas," 26.

A "rebel sheet" called the *Citizen* was published in Alexandria while the 8th Illinois had its camp there. The paper aroused "the contempt and indignation of all loyal hearts by its vituperous and abusive articles." One day its building caught fire—no one knew how. And none of the hundreds of soldiers who rushed to the scene "seemed disposed to assist in extinguishing the flames. . . . the hose was cut in some very mysterious manner, so that it was useless, and the soldiers would not work, consequently the building with the entire contents was a total loss."[51] In the spring of 1862, the 2nd Ohio decided that the *Crisis*, published by Samuel Medary in Columbus, Ohio, was "the most bitter and disloyal 'Copperhead' sheet published. . . . Its utterances distinctly encouraged the Rebellion [and] instigated desertions of Union soldiers." And so, on the night of March 5, "a considerable number of Second Ohio boys mysteriously got through the guard line of . . . Camp Chase . . . went quietly down town, threw out pickets for protection from police, entered the Crisis office and thoroughly gutted it, throwing the type, presses, etc. out of the back window into the Scioto River. . . . it proved impracticable to identify any of the participants."[52]

When a regiment of cavalry was thought to be needed at the front, it was ordered to report at the "seat of war," regardless of the state of its training or even its preparedness with respect to arms and equipment. Generally, eastern regiments were ordered to Washington, western regiments to Louisville or St. Louis. But the mysterious ways of army administration dispatched the 2nd New Jersey and the 7th and 9th Pennsylvania to the West, and the 8th Illinois, several Michigan regiments, most of the 3rd Indiana, and a part of the 2nd Ohio to the East.

More than one regiment, in the early months of the war, fearful that the rebellion would be put down before it had a go at the rebels, pulled strings to get sent to the front. Thus, after the 9th Illinois had been three months in camp there was "considerable discontent among both officers and men at what seemed to be unnecessary delay" in moving the regiment to the front. The men

51. Hard, *History of the Eighth Cavalry*, 77.
52. Tenney, *War Diary*, 58–60; see also Gause, *Four Years with Five Armies*, 115.

had not as yet received their arms, but that did not prevent Colonel Albert G. Brackett from writing Governor Yates of Illinois, "Sir, the Ninth Regiment Illinois Cavalry, which I have the honor to command, is now full and ready to take the field. I am most anxious to get into active service, and this feeling is shared by every officer and man in the regiment. I would, therefore, most respectfully ask of you to telegraph to General Halleck, to move my regiment at once to St. Louis or Cairo, or to such other point as you and the General may think best."[53]

Travel accommodations to get the cavalry to the front were seldom adequate and never luxurious. The 1st New York rode to Washington in boxcars fitted with plain board benches so arranged as to get the largest possible number of men into each car; holes were cut into the sides and ends of the cars to provide ventilation that was plentifully seasoned with soot and dust.[54] The 19th New York rode from Elmira to Harrisburg "crowded into offensive-smelling cattle cars"; for seats they had "rough hemlock boards, without backs." For the second stage of their journey they were "hustled aboard a train of dirty coal cars" at Harrisburg and arrived in Baltimore "a begrimed and disconsolate set."[55] When the men of the 9th New York discovered that they were to travel to Washington in freight and cattle cars with boards placed on blocks of wood for seats, whereas a coach had been attached to the back of the train for the officers, the inevitable happened: before the train started, the coach became uncoupled by some mysterious means, and the train departed without the officers.[56]

The train carrying the 3rd Wisconsin from its camp of rendezvous to St. Louis was wrecked outside Chicago. Twelve troopers were killed and twenty-eight injured. But it was the 6th New

53. Davenport, *History of the Ninth Regiment*, 20–21.
54. Beach, *First New York (Lincoln) Cavalry*, 42.
55. Bowen, *Regimental History of the First New York*, 10–11. Bribery of officers by the railroad companies was not unknown. "So lucrative was the railroad business . . . that regimental officers were often able to play off the companies against each other, troops being sent over the line that paid the officers the biggest bonus." Meneely, *The War Department, 1861*, 244.
56. Cheney, *History of the Ninth Regiment*, 22.

York that had probably the grimmest introduction to the perils of war. They were ordered to be ready on the morning of December 23, 1861, to leave their Staten Island camp of rendezvous on board a ship to Elizabethport, New Jersey, whence they were to take a train to York, Pennsylvania. With tents taken down and all the baggage packed, the regiment stood in a cold drizzle all day, waiting for the ship. When it arrived at nightfall, the "ship" turned out to be a pair of decked barges towed by a tug. Their clothes already soaked from the day's rain, the men had to remain on the open decks of the barges until three A.M. in the piercing cold December wind, exposed to the waves dashing over the decks. A member of the regiment relates that "this engagement with the elements was more fatal than any battle in which the Regiment was engaged during the war. Thirty men are reported to have died from exposure that night."[57]

Eventually, all the regiments mentioned in this account of their organization and tribulations in infancy were physically ready to take the field. The men and officers were present. The regiment had its horses, uniforms, and arms of some sort. But what nearly all of them lacked was anything approaching adequate training. In World War I the average American *infantry-man* had six months' training in the United States, two more months of training in France, and then a month in a quiet sector of the trenches, before exposure to battle.[58] Contrasted with this was the experience of Captain W. H. Boyd's Philadelphia companies of the 1st New York. Mustered in on July 19, 1861, Boyd and his men arrived in Washington on July 22, received their uniforms, arms, and horses on July 24, spent the next few days in "horse-breaking, which at times looked like neck-breaking," crossed the Potomac into Virginia on August 7, and had their first brush with the enemy and sustained their first casualty on August 18, one day short of a month from their muster-in.[59] The 6th New York was not fully mounted and did not have its first

57. McKinney, *Life in Tent and Field*, 31–32; see also Committee on Regimental History, *History of the Sixth New York*, 33–34.

58. William K. Naylor, *The Principles of Strategy as Illustrated by the Civil War* (Fort Leavenworth, Kan., 1917), 81.

59. Stevenson, "Boots and Saddles," 35–43.

regimental mounted drill until July 11, 1862. Twelve days later it was ordered to report to General Irvin McDowell at Warrenton, Virginia, for active service.[60] Some of the companies of the Ringgold Battalion were mounted, armed, equipped, and doing picket duty and going on scouts all within ten days after they were organized; the arms supplied to them were "old horse pistols, which had been changed from flintlocks to percussion cap locks; and it was almost as dangerous to be behind them as in front when they were fired." The historian of the battalion adds that "most of the drill the men received was on the march."[61] The 7th Kansas, organized in Leavenworth in early September, 1861, was on active duty in guerilla-infested western Missouri from September 26 on, a month before the regiment went through the formality of muster-in.

These were admittedly extreme cases, but it is a fact that hardly any regiment of volunteer cavalry, whenever or wherever it was raised, had had adequate training, either of its men or its horses, when it was called upon to face the enemy. Unquestionably correct is B. W. Crowninshield's observation that "whole regiments of exquisite greenness were shoved into the Virginia mud . . . there to learn, practically without a teacher, from books and hard knocks in a few weeks, or months at best, what in Europe in the best of schools, under chosen instructors, and on trained horses, only years can accomplish."[62] The mud of Kentucky, or Tennessee, or Missouri, may be substituted for Crowninshield's Virginia mud, but otherwise, as far as the extent of training is concerned, the situation was everywhere the same.

Generally speaking, none of these regiments became "cavalry" in the traditional, European sense of the word. General Scott's melancholy prophecy that the war would be over before any volunteer cavalry could be adequately trained proved accurate, notwithstanding that the war lasted longer than the general may have anticipated. But he was thinking of textbook cavalry on the European model. This lack of adequate *cavalry* training, the

60. Committee on Regimental History, *History of the Sixth New York*, 43.
61. Farrar, *The Twenty-Second Pennsylvania*, 25.
62. Crowninshield, "Cavalry in Virginia," 4.

techniques these regiments had no chance to learn properly, was an important element in the evolution of a new kind of cavalry in the Civil War, the kind that won the battles of Nashville and Five Forks and stormed the fortifications of Selma. Other factors were of course involved, but with officers and men who had learned little out of the manuals and hence had little to unlearn, experience and their own pragmatic good sense were allowed free play. Gaining that experience, learning what worked and what did not, was a long, bitter, humiliating, and unnecessarily costly process, but the end result was spectacular. As General Sheridan, who was not given to issuing congratulatory addresses or to bestowing praise not abundantly earned, was to say after completing his tour of duty as an observer in the Franco-Prussian War, his Cavalry Corps of the Army of the Potomac as he left it in 1865 could whip any equal number of cavalry on the face of the earth.[63] And the Cavalry Corps with which Wilson captured Selma was, if anything, superior to Sheridan's.

63. Clark "Making of a Volunteer Cavalryman," 3.

VIII

Jine the Cavalry

THE NATURAL ANTAGONIST OF CAVALRY IS CAVALRY. The Union cavalry was now taking the field. What manner of men were their southern counterparts, how did they come to be in the cavalry, and how were they organized and equipped for the war?

The war these men were about to fight was a *civil* war. Until the breakup came at the end of 1860, the North and the South shared the same political and military institutions and, more importantly, many of the same attitudes, prejudices, habits, and customs. In a military sense there were few virtues and few vices that the North and South did not have in common. There were important differences between the sections, to be sure, but to a student of the military side of the Civil War, they appear less significant than the similarities.

Despite the superficially languid pace of southern life, the slow, measured drawl, the casual lawlessness of the people, there was a capacity for intensity and violent energy in southerners that magnified the virtues and vices of its soldiers and caused both to stand out larger than life. First of all, there was more of a taste for peacetime soldiering in the South than in the North, as mentioned earlier, and this was expressed in the greater vitality and better repute of its militia organizations. Companies of militia were common. Whatever their real military value, and it was generally modest, they were a firmly established and popular social institution. To belong to a militia company, especially one that had something of a tradition, bespoke social acceptance and was an important part of a southern gentleman's way of life.[1] The drills, held weekly, or monthly, or on "court days," were casual affairs, but the John Brown Raid gave them a new seriousness.[2] The raid also resulted in the formation of militia companies where there had been none before. The bitterness of the presidential campaign of 1860 and the election of a "Black Republican" president further heightened the tension between North and South and sharpened the truculently defensive attitude of the latter, well expressed in the toast, popular in Charleston as early as 1851, "The sword! The arbiter of national dispute. The sooner it is unsheathed in maintaining Southern rights, the better."[3] The result was the filling up of the ranks of many of the existing militia companies and the formation of many new ones.[4]

1. The "annals . . . [of the Charleston Light Dragoons] consist perhaps chiefly of recollections of dinners and suppers"; the fine for being unhorsed was a dozen bottles of Madeira or a basket of champagne. Even after Fort Sumter, "No new members were admitted contrary to the wishes of the old ones. . . . The reputation of the 'Drags' as a crack corps, and the pleasant companionship to be found there, were very attractive, and resulted in a social composition probably unique even in the Confederate service." Edward L. Wells, *A Sketch of the Charleston Light Dragoons from the Earliest Formation of the Corps* (Charleston, S.C., 1888), 7–8; see also Thomas A. Ashby, *Life of Turner Ashby* (New York, 1914), 41.

2. Hackley, *The Little Fork Rangers*, 21; Frank M. Myers, *The Comanches: A History of White's Battalion, Virginia Cavalry* (Baltimore, 1871), 8; Luther W. Hopkins, *From Bull Run to Appomattox: A Boy's View* (Baltimore, 1908), 13. In Mississippi alone, as a result of the John Brown raid, sixty-five volunteer companies were organized between January, 1860, and January 1861; eight of these were cavalry units. Thiele, "The Evolution of Cavalry," 121.

3. Manly Wade Wellman, *Giant in Gray: A Biography of Wade Hampton of South Carolina* (New York, 1949), 46. See also J. G. Deupree, "The Noxubee Squadron of the First Mississippi Cavalry, C.S.A., 1861–1865," *Publications of the Mississippi Historical Society*, III, 1918), 13.

4. F. A. Montgomery, *Reminiscences of a Mississippian in Peace and War* (Cincinnati, 1901), 38; see also Wellman, *Giant in Gray*, 46; and Deupree, "The Noxubee Squadron," 13.

Upper-class white southerners held firmly to the belief that they had been taught from boyhood to ride, shoot, and tell the truth.[5] In the upper South fox hunting was a popular sport, and tournaments, somewhat on the medieval model and inspired by the Waverly novels, brought out the beauty and the chivalry of the countryside. No self-respecting southerner walked when he could ride, and a good seat in the saddle was a well-nigh universal accomplishment. George Cary Eggleston's comment that the men of the 1st Virginia "if not actually 'born in the saddle,' had climbed into it so early and lived in it so constantly that it had become the only home they knew" applied with equal justice to thousands more who hastened to organize or join mounted companies at the outbreak of war.[6] It was said that "the best blood of the South rode in the cavalry." Excellent horsemen to a man, they had at their fingertips the art of training, managing, and caring for horses, accomplishments that in 1861 were a mystery to most of their contemporaries in the North.

It was only natural that large numbers of southerners, so conditioned, should have enlisted in the cavalry.[7] They were aided in their choice, if any aid was needed, by the same and even more gaudy romantic notions about the wild raider, the plumed knight, the ambuscade, the whirlwind attack on the cowering foe, that operated so powerfully in the North. Sir Walter Scott and Charles O'Malley, the Irish Dragoon, were potent recruiting agents for the southern cavalry. What, indeed, could be more pleasant in the midst of the warlike enthusiasm sweeping the country than to join one's kinfolk, friends, and neighbors in a mounted unit, to fight a war that would be over in six months? The belief was widely held that "Yankee trash won't fight," and that if they did, the "vulgar, fanatical, cheating

5. Edward L. Wells, *Hampton and His Cavalry in '64* (Richmond, Va., 1899), 24; Clarence Thomas, *General Turner Ashby* (Winchester, Va., 1907), 3–4.

6. Eggleston, *A Rebel's Recollections*, 77; see also Duke, *A History of Morgan's Cavalry*, 175.

7. Officially, the Confederacy mustered a total of 127 regiments plus 47 unattached battalions of cavalry, and 8 regiments and 1 unattached battalion of Partisan Rangers. Livermore, *Numbers and Losses in the Civil War*, 26.

counter-jumpers" could be "whipped with cornstalks" by the chivalrous Southrons. Any young man who showed an inclination to hang back was reminded of his patriotic duty by receiving anonymous gifts of knitting needles and petticoats from the bellicose young ladies of his acquaintance.[8]

Governor Henry T. Clark of North Carolina informed the Confederate War Department, "So great is the preference for cavalry that infantry cannot be raised where cavalry can be received."[9] And General Gideon Pillow wrote Adjutant General Samuel Cooper that "the fact of existence of . . . cavalry organizations (that service being universally preferred) keeps alive the aversion to infantry service. . . . desertion of the infantry to join the cavalry service is an evil of such magnitude as to demoralize the infantry and endanger its existence."[10]

A Confederate regiment of cavalry, even at full strength, was usually smaller than a Federal cavalry regiment. A Confederate War Department circular of November, 1861, directed that cavalry regiments should consist of ten companies and that the minimum strength of a company was to be 60; most Federal regiments had twelve companies, and a Federal cavalry company at full strength had 104 officers and men, increased to 112 in July, 1862. An Act of the Confederate Congress of October 11, 1862, increased the minimum strength of a company of cavalry to 80 rank and file, but by that date most Confederate cavalry regiments had already been formed.[11]

The decision of the Confederate government to have cavalrymen furnish their own horses, for the use of which they were paid the same forty cents per day that was paid to northern troopers, remained in effect nearly to the end of the war and, as time went on, was to have a disastrous effect on the efficiency of the Confederate cavalry.[12] At the beginning, however, the results of

8. Hackley, *The Little Fork Rangers*, 19; see also Eggleston, *A Rebel's Recollections*, 70; and John N. Opie, *A Rebel Cavalryman with Lee, Stuart and Jackson* (Dayton, Ohio, 1972), 15.

9. Thiele, "The Evolution of Cavalry," 119.

10. *Ibid.*, 119–20.

11. Livermore, *Numbers and Losses in the Civil War*, 30–31.

12. Act of March 6, 1861. C. W. Ramsdell, "General Robert E. Lee's Horse Supply, 1862–1865," *American Historical Review*, XXXV (1930),

the system were wholly favorable. The upper South, particularly Virginia, Kentucky, and Tennessee, was horse-breeding country, and in the first year of the war, splendid animals, the product of generations of careful breeding, were plentiful. It was a point of pride with families to have the son of the house go off to war with the best horse in the stable, or the best that money could buy. The horses of a typical unit, Company D, 4th Virginia, raised in and about Culpeper, were valued at from $125 to $150, and some as high as $190, all of them sound and trained to the saddle, unlike the inferior, untrained animals the Federal government was buying for its cavalry at $110 each from cheating contractors.[13]

The southerners who enlisted in the cavalry in the first flush of war enthusiasm were mostly young. Captain John Castleman was under twenty-one when he raised Company D of the 2nd Kentucky; the average age of his forty-one troopers, all from the environs of Lexington, was under twenty.[14] Of the initial fifty-seven men of Company D, 4th Virginia, thirty-two were under

758. Major E. W. Ewing, inspector of field transportation, reported to Richmond on September 1, 1864, "The policy adopted at the beginning of the war by the Government of making cavalrymen mount themselves is, in my opinion, the most extravagant to the government, and has done more to demoralize the troops of this branch of the service than any other cause. When a soldier is dismounted . . . he is entitled to a furlough of thirty days to go home and remount himself. This makes every cavalry soldier, or at least all that desire to be, mere horse traders, selling their animals whenever they desire to go home. . . . I respectfully suggest that all private animals now ridden by cavalrymen be taken possession of by the Government and paid for. This mode of mounting the troops will . . . do away with much of the odium now attached to the cavalry arm." Quoted in Lloyd Lewis, *Sherman: Fighting Prophet* (New York, 1932), 341.

13. Hackley, *The Little Fork Rangers*, 31–32. As in the case of the few early Federal volunteer regiments whose men owned their horses, the Confederate trooper was to be paid the value of his horse if it was killed or disabled in battle. Hence when a unit was mustered in, all the horses were appraised and their value entered in the regimental records. Troopers were not paid for horses disabled or dead of natural causes, or captured by the enemy. A trooper who lost his horse and could not replace it promptly was in theory subject to be transferred to the infantry or the artillery. Henry B. McClellan, *I Rode with Jeb Stuart: Life and Campaigns of Major-General J. E. B. Stuart* (Bloomington, Ind., 1958), 256.

14. John B. Castleman, *Active Service* (Louisville, Ky., 1917).

twenty-five years old.[15] Data are lacking for a wholly accurate comparison, but it would seem that on the average southern cavalrymen were younger and closer to Union General Sheridan's ideal age range of eighteen to twenty-two for cavalrymen than those of the North. In one respect, vitally important in a service requiring dash and initiative verging on recklessness, the South had an advantage it retained until the Custers, Merritts, Wilsons, and Uptons came to the fore in the northern army: nearly without exception, the commanding officers of the Confederate cavalry were young men. At the start of the war Jeb Stuart was twenty-eight, Fitzhugh Lee twenty-five, W. H. F. Lee twenty-four, Matthew C. Butler twenty-four, Lunsford Lomax twenty-six, Thomas Rosser twenty-four, William Wirt Adams twenty-six, P. M. B. Young twenty-one, and Robert Ransom, twenty-four.

As one would expect in an area that was even less urbanized than the contemporary North, the great majority of southern cavalrymen were farmers and planters, or the sons of farmers and planters.[16]

The use of the word "enlisted" to refer to Confederate cavalrymen is subject to qualification, in view of a practice that was peculiar to the South. Under Confederate law in effect in the first year of the war, state militia companies whose members had enlisted to serve for one year could be mustered into the Confederate States Army. The period of service was increased to three years in 1862. Apparently, however, thousands of cavalrymen did not bother to enlist in any formal way or, if they did, did not look upon their enlistment as a binding contract between themselves and their government in the sense of tying them to a given company or regiment. Seven troopers of R. R. Hancock's company of the 2nd Tennessee were "with the . . . Company from time to time during the war, and did more or less service, though they were not really members of the company."[17] While the 1st

15. Hackley, *The Little Fork Rangers*, 31–32.
16. Company D, 4th Virginia, had in it thirty-seven farmers, eight artisans, six merchants and clerks, four teachers, one physician, and one "unknown." Hackley, *The Little Fork Rangers*, 31–32.
17. R. R. Hancock, *Hancock's Diary, or, A History of the Second Tennessee Cavalry* (Nashville, Tenn., 1887), 27.

Louisiana was in camp in Decatur, Alabama, in March, 1862, "many recruits from Louisiana and elsewhere joined. . . . Some regularly enlisted and some joined as independents ('peacocks,' the boys called them), that is, they were willing to fight with us and do guard duty, but would not be sworn in; they wanted to reserve the right to leave when they felt so disposed."[18] J. N. Opie was a "visitor" with two cavalry regiments while he was deciding which of them he should join; eventually he chose the 6th Virginia, but not until he had obtained the advice of no less an authority than Jeb Stuart himself.[19]

But even formal enlistment made little difference to the footloose southern trooper. George Naylor started in April, 1861, as a member of Turner Ashby's cavalry company, transferred himself to the infantry in May, and rejoined the cavalry ten months later.[20] Thomas Henry Hines's independent company of Kentuckians voted to disband in early 1862 on the curious ground that they had enlisted to fight in Kentucky and did not propose to do so in Tennessee; the men then joined other commands more to their liking, or went home.[21] When it was proposed to attach White's Battalion of Virginia Cavalry, raised as an independent unit for service on the Virginia-Maryland border, to General W. E. ("Grumble") Jones's brigade, the Marylanders in the battalion objected to the point of "almost open mutiny"; they contended that "as Marylanders, they owed no allegiance to the Confederacy. They had come over voluntarily because their sympathies were with the South, but being foreigners, they had the right to select for themselves the manner in which they would serve her . . . and that now, the contract being broken . . . [by] the Government, they were no longer bound to remain in the battalion."[22]

There will be occasion later to comment on the greatest fail-

18. Howell Carter, *A Cavalryman's Reminiscences of the Civil War* (New Orleans, n.d.), 24–25.
19. Opie, *A Rebel Cavalryman*, 83.
20. George Baylor, *Bull Run to Bull Run, or, Four Years in the Army of Northern Virginia* (Richmond, Va., 1900), 18, 33.
21. Stephen Z. Starr, *Colonel Grenfell's Wars* (Baton Rouge, La., 1971), 94.
22. Myers, *The Comanches*, 148–49.

ing of the Confederate cavalry, namely, absence from the ranks, with or without a legitimate reason. Whether or not these absences amounted to desertion in the technical sense, they were in many cases nothing more than an expression of a dislike of restraint, and of a rootless, wandering disposition on the part of many Confederate cavalrymen. If they did not like the way they were treated in one unit, or if it did not provide the amount or kind of activity they liked, or if they simply grew tired of it and wanted a change, they moved on, with or without an interval at home to recruit their strength and refurbish their wardrobe, or simply to have a visit with the folks.[23]

When militia companies entered the Confederate army, they came clad either in their ornate militia uniforms, in hastily sewn uniforms of Confederate gray, or, as often as not, in their civilian clothes.[24] Much to the surprise of some of the men, the government assumed the responsibility for providing their uniforms. The supply was wholly inadequate and, on one recorded occasion, not to the taste of the troopers. When Captain (later General) Grumble Jones made requisition on the quartermaster for gray uniforms for his company, he was furnished "suits of a very rough quality of goods manufactured in the Virginia penitentiary." The result was a near mutiny; the indignant troopers, accustomed to clothing of a better quality, piled up the offending uniforms in front of Captain Jones's tent and left them there.[25] On the other hand, the First Battalion of Tennessee Cavalry, later grown into the 2nd Tennessee, had its boots made to measure by

23. After the battle of Mill Springs, the captains of the 1st Battalion of Tennessee Cavalry held a meeting in the absence of their colonel, "and after taking all things into consideration—no rations, camp equipage, etc. —they decided to disband, allow the men to go home for a few days, get a better supply of clothing and return to . . . [the] command." One of the captains and fifteen of his men had second thoughts and remained in camp. The rest departed. Hancock, *Hancock's Diary*, 127–28.
24. Hackley, *The Little Fork Rangers*, 27–28. The Rangers' gray uniforms were cut by a tailor in Warrenton and sewn by the ladies of the neighborhood. See also R. L. T. Beale, *History of the Ninth Virginia Cavalry in the War Between the States* (Richmond, Va., 1899), 9; and Ashby, *Life of Turner Ashby*, 75.
25. John S. Mosby, *Mosby's War Reminiscences: Stuart's Cavalry Campaigns* (New York, 1958), 10.

the inmates of the state penitentiary at Nashville, with no recorded protests on either side.[26]

Whatever the young gentlemen of the Confederate cavalry may have lacked in the way of regulation uniforms, they more than made up for in nonregulation gear. Like their northern opponents, they came to camp with mountains of duffle. When the Natchez Troop joined the 1st Virginia, it brought along two wagonloads of trunks, having "left most of [its] baggage behind in Richmond."[27] The Virginia companies of the same regiment were equipped on an equally lavish scale; each company had two wagons for the men's baggage and four more for the officers', for a total of six per company or sixty per regiment for that purpose alone. Long before the end of the war, the six wagons would have been ample for as many brigades.[28] And such conditions were not peculiar to the effete East. Braxton Bragg, in the West, complained to his wife after the battle of Shiloh that "many Lieutenants and Captains have baggage enough for a trip to Saratoga."[29] Some of the large trunks brought to camp by the officers and men of Wade Hampton's Legion contained private libraries to provide diversion in camp when there were no parties in Charleston for their owners to attend.[30]

A young man of family, as many cavalrymen were, would have thought it unbecoming to arrive in camp without a body servant to look after his clothes, groom his horse, polish his weapons, and generally relieve him of the chores gentlemen did not perform at home and saw no reason to perform in the army. George Cary Eggleston of the 1st Virginia explains that "whenever a detail was made for the purpose of cleaning the campground, the men detailed regarded themselves as responsible for the proper performance of the task by their servants, and uncomplainingly took upon themselves the duty of sitting on the

26. Hancock, *Hancock's Diary*, 33, 54.
27. William W. Blackford, *War Years with Jeb Stuart* (New York, 1945), 50.
28. Susan Leigh Blackford (comp.), *Letters from Lee's Army* (New York, 1947), 7.
29. Don C. Seitz, *Braxton Bragg: General of the Confederacy* (Columbia, S.C., 1924), 113.
30. Wellman, *Giant in Gray*, 58.

fence and superintending the work."[31] Lieutenant Colonel (later General) Richard S. Ewell, in command of the post at Ashland, Virginia, made himself vastly unpopular with his young cavaliers by insisting that they stand guard themselves instead of delegating that duty also to their Negro servants. But the 1st Virginia found a way to foil Colonel Ewell; the "two or three men of the overseer class who were to be found in nearly every company turned some nimble quarters by standing other men's turn of guard duty at twenty-five cents an hour."[32]

The Confederate cavalry had the same weapons and equipment shortages that plagued the Federal cavalry. Generally, and particularly with respect to weapons, the situation in the South was worse than it was in the North, for the South lacked the industrial base that could be rapidly expanded or converted to manufacture arms, and state governors promptly claimed for their own militia the mostly obsolete weapons in the government armories and arsenals taken over from the Union.[33] The mounted militia companies came to camp with whatever firearms the men themselves owned or could get from patriotic friends and relatives, and the government had no better arms to give them. Hence most cavalrymen had to make do with single- and double-barreled shotguns, squirrel rifles, fowling pieces, pistols of every make, caliber, and degree of reliability, and a miscellany of heirlooms, relics of the Mexican and earlier wars, obsolete United States cavalry carbines, infantry rifles, and muzzle-loading flintlock muskets; indeed, many cavalrymen had no firearms of any kind.[34]

31. Eggleston, *A Rebel's Recollections*, 73.

32. Percy G. Hamlin, *"Old Bald Head" (General R. S. Ewell): The Portrait of a Soldier* (Strasburg, Va., 1940), 60; Eggleston, *A Rebel's Recollections*, 73.

33. Thiele, "The Evolution of Cavalry," 144.

34. Ashby, *Life of Turner Ashby*, 75; Hackley, *The Little Fork Rangers*, 27; Morton, *Artillery of Forrest's Cavalry*, 47; Thiele, "The Evolution of Cavalry," 145–46. Some units did, however, receive useful weapons. The Bolivar Troop of the 1st Mississippi received from the state sabers, Colt pistols, and Maynard rifles, the last a breechloader firing metal cartridges. Montgomery, *Reminiscences of a Mississippian*, 44. More typically, Virginia had few arms of any kind, and no "cavalry weapons of any value." Jubal A. Early, *Autobiographical Sketch and Narrative of the War Between the States* (Philadelphia, 1912), 3.

A shotgun loaded with "buck and ball" (a bullet and three large buckshot) was not a weapon to be despised. The gun was fragile and its range short, but at close quarters it was capable of "terrible execution."[35] To eke out their armament of about twenty-five double-barreled shotguns without straps and fewer than a dozen percussion pistols, the Little Fork Rangers of the 4th Virginia had "Uncle" Wash Fitzhugh, the Culpeper blacksmith, make dirks for them out of files and rasps. Many of the troopers of Ross's 3rd Texas, made up of companies bearing such warlike names as the Texas Hunters and the Dead Shot Rangers, equipped themselves with huge bowie knives, some as long as three feet "and heavy enough to cleave the skull of a mailed knight through helmet and all"; within a year, however, these grotesque weapons had been discarded.[36]

Sabers were the one weapon most Confederate cavalrymen had from the beginning, but notwithstanding Ivanhoe and Charles O'Malley and the partiality for the weapon shown by former cavalry officers of the "Old Army" like Jeb Stuart, the majority of Confederate cavalrymen, especially those of the western regiments, had little use for them. John Mosby, who started his brilliant wartime career as an utterly unspectacular trooper in the 1st Virginia ("he was rather a slouchy rider, and did not seem to take any interest in military duties"), expressed the opinion that probably most of his fellow troopers had of the saber; he wrote, "We had been furnished with sabres before we left Abingdon, but the only real use I ever heard of their being put to was to hold a piece of meat over the fire for frying. I dragged one through the first year of the war, but when I became commander, I discarded it. . . . certainly the sabre is of no use against gunpowder."[37] The 4th Kentucky was given heavy English sabers, "splendid weapons," which it, however, "despised" and, convinced that it was extremely unlikely that there would

35. William Witherspoon, "Reminiscences of a Scout, Spy and Soldier of Forrest's Cavalry," in R. S. Henry (ed.), *As They Saw Forrest* (Jackson, Miss., 1956), 88.

36. V. M. Rose, *Ross' Texas Brigade* (Louisville, Ky., 1881), 18.

37. Blackford, *War Years with Jeb Stuart*, 12; Mosby, *Mosby's War Reminiscences*, 30; see also Myers, *The Comanches*, 154.

ever be any use for them, managed to "lose" as quickly as possible.[38]

It would be difficult to fault the cavalrymen of Wade Hampton's Legion if they too had deliberately lost their sabers, for the ones Hampton had a Columbia, South Carolina, manufacturer make for them were ponderous weapons, straight, two-edged, forty inches long, each weighing nearly six pounds.[39] Any member of John Hunt Morgan's 2nd Kentucky who "attempted to carry . . . [a saber] would be forever after a laughing stock for the entire command."[40] The 7th Tennessee had sabers at the beginning, "but discarded them as fighting weapons, useless, only good on dress parade in the hands of officers, making them . . . feel they might be a little better or different from the men."[41]

The equipment and weapons shortages of Confederate cavalry were made good not by its own government but by the government from which it had seceded, and the supply problems of the Union cavalry were compounded by the unhappy fact that the War Department in Washington, in addition to providing for the wants of its own mounted troops, also had to serve as the unwilling source of horses, weapons, tack, ammunition, clothing, and gear of all kinds for the Confederate cavalry as well. The historian of the 9th Virginia expatiates on the "greatly improved military appearance" of his comrades at the conclusion of the Antietam Campaign, in the course of which they acquired, mainly by means of an attack on the camp of Colonel Duffié's 1st Rhode Island, an ample stock of excellent pistols, sabers, bridles, blankets, and good McClellan saddles, the latter greatly superior to those supplied by the Confederate government.[42] When a trooper of the 2nd South Carolina lost his horse, he either had to get a remount at once or go into the infantry. "That was one rea-

38. George D. Mosgrove, *Kentucky Cavaliers in Dixie: Reminiscences of a Confederate Cavalryman* (Jackson, Tenn., 1957), 183.

39. Wellman, *Giant in Gray*, 52. It is not clear whether the forty-inch, six-pound saber was issued to all the cavalrymen in the Hampton Legion or was made for Hampton alone.

40. India W. P. Logan, *Kelion Franklin Pedicord of Quirk's Scouts, Morgan's Kentucky Cavalry, C.S.A.* (New York, 1908), 114.

41. Witherspoon, *Reminiscences of a Scout*, 99.

42. Beale, *History of the Ninth Virginia*, 47, 54.

son," the regimental historian writes, "why the Yankees lost so many horses at their picket posts. We had to have horses, and the United States government furnished us with at least one-third of our horses, saddles, bridles and carbines and Colts [sic] army pistols and, last but not least, blankets and haversacks."[43]

A member of the 12th Virginia records that "Uncle Sam very kindly and very soon provided us the very best pistols, sabres, saddles and bridles. . . . Everything but ourselves was branded U.S."[44] The historian of White's Battalion gleefully reports that after the battle of Winchester in May, 1862, "nearly every man" in his unit "was completely armed and equipped with everything necessary to fit them for service, including Yankee bridles and halters, and many saddles bearing the letters U.S., which letters also embellished the shoulders of many of their horses and all their blankets." A few days earlier, at Front Royal, they had acquired, also from the Yankees, all the "gum cloths, canteens and other articles of great value to soldiers" that they needed.[45]

On the evening of September 14, 1862, when Harper's Ferry was about to be surrendered to Stonewall Jackson, the 8th New York and 12th Illinois, about thirteen hundred cavalrymen in all, escaped through the lines of the besiegers. This was a spectacular feat, to be described in its proper place, but the reaction of the Confederate cavalry present was one of "infinite disgust." "To think," wrote Lieutenant Colonel William W. Blackford of Stuart's staff, "of all the fine horses they carried off, the saddles, revolvers and carbines of the best kind, and the spurs, all of which would have fallen to our share, and the very things we so much needed, was enough to vex a saint."[46]

However pleasant and rewarding it may have been for Confederate troopers to spoil the Egyptians and equip themselves at

43. U. R. Brooks (ed.), *Butler and His Cavalry in the War of Secession, 1861–1865* (Columbia, S.C., 1909), 39.

44. Baylor, *Bull Run to Bull Run*, 38.

45. Myers, *The Comanches*, 53–54, 50. While these and earlier quotations concerning the capture of arms and equipment from the Yankees are taken from the writings of men who served in the East, it is to be understood that the situation in the West was precisely the same; see, for example, Duke, *A History of Morgan's Cavalry*, 178–79.

46. Blackford, *War Years with Jeb Stuart*, 146.

the expense of the Union, the need to rely on the enemy as a major source of supply had its drawbacks. In the course of Stonewall Jackson's Valley Campaign, Ashby's cavalry, equivalent to nearly three full regiments, would have been far more effective "had not many of the men—who being recent volunteers, had not acquired the habit of strict obedience—been carried away by their captures and spoils. . . . these raw men were so busy picking up the plunder that they forgot the duties of a soldier. It was impossible for their officers to keep up an effective organization and the fruits of victory were often lost because of demoralization and for want of men to press the retreating enemy."[47] After the battle of Winchester in the same campaign, Jackson could well have bagged most of General N. P. Banks's beaten and retreating army if much of Ashby's cavalry had not vanished with the loot it had taken at Front Royal a few days before.[48]

The best known characteristic, indeed, the hallmark, of Confederate cavalry was its lack of discipline. There was indiscipline and to spare in the Federal cavalry, but nowhere in the Union army was it carried to such outlandish extremes as among the Confederate mounted troops. Every Confederate unit history, every volume of reminiscences of Confederate cavalrymen, speaks of the grotesque manifestations of the lack of discipline in the writer's regiment or company. Usually these stories are told, or the comments made, in a tone of unctuous disapproval, which, however, seldom succeeds in hiding the writer's relish in the memory of the deviltries perpetrated by himself and his friends in the days of their youth. The belief that "high-born freemen and gentlemen . . . [did] not require the rigid discipline of regulars to make them soldiers" was part of the southern credo.[49] Southern folkways, and especially the way of life of the well-to-do land- and slave-owning and professional classes whose members en-

47. Ashby, *Life of Turner Ashby*, 174–75.
48. Lenoir Chambers, *Stonewall Jackson* (2 vols.; New York, 1959), I, 543; see also Henry Kyd Douglas, *I Rode with Stonewall* (Chapel Hill, N.C., 1940), 74.
49. Thomas F. Berry, *Four Years with Morgan and Forrest* (Oklahoma City, 1914), 16.

listed in the cavalry in great numbers and set its tone, did not make for a ready acceptance of discipline, or of restraints of any kind.

The number of men qualified by some degree of training and knowledge to become officers was probably greater, proportionately, in the South than in the North. Not only were militia officers available, and officers of the Regular Army who resigned their commissions to go with their states, but there were also hundreds of graduates and students of the nine military schools in the South; the North had only one such school.[50] But, as in the Federal cavalry, Confederate troopers elected their officers, and in the South the election system was universal. There were no exceptions. This meant that in too many cases it was not the best qualified but the most popular who were commissioned. The southern cavalry elected their noncommissioned officers as well, and it was the accepted custom that officers whose conduct was for any reason displeasing to their constituents should resign if they were petitioned by the enlisted men to do so.

A lieutenant's, or captain's, or even a colonel's commission did not in and of itself confer command authority. In the Virginia regiments, and to a lesser extent in regiments from other states as well, prewar social position counted for as much or more than army rank. George Cary Eggleston, himself one of the socially elect, has pointed out that the "man of good family felt himself superior, as in most cases he undoubtedly was, to his fellow-soldier of less excellent birth, and this distinction was sufficient, during the early years of the war, to override everything like military rank." And he added, "I have known numberless cases in which privates have declined dinner and other invitations from officers who had presumed upon their shoulder-straps in seeking the company of their social superiors."[51]

A few examples will illustrate the atmosphere in which officers of all ranks had to operate and the trials of those who endeavored to inculcate some degree of discipline in their units. A

50. John Bigelow, Jr., *The Campaign of Chancellorsville: A Strategic and Tactical Study* (New Haven, Conn., 1910), 16.
51. Eggleston, *A Rebel's Recollections*, 72.

member of Company E, 7th Tennessee, noted that his fellow troopers "knew little of restraint and less of discipline."[52] When Colonel Ben Hardin Helm of the 1st Kentucky was promoted to brigadier general, Colonel John Adams, a West Pointer from Mississippi, was appointed to his place. The regiment, of course, resented the appointment of an "outsider." Colonel Adams sent for J. W. Dyer of his new regiment, handed him a dispatch announcing his intention to assume command the next day, and ordered him to take it to the regimental camp. Dyer, who tells the story, "politely but firmly informed him that I would see him in hell first. He ordered his orderly to arrest me. I demanded his authority and held the door with two good pistols . . . and the whole thing resulted in the colonel delivering his own dispatch." Three years later, when Dyer's regiment was in a brigade commanded by Colonel J. Warren Grigsby, whom the boys "didn't like," they obeyed his orders only when it suited them to do so; "The captain and the orderly sergeant were about all the company who mustered for morning drill and an aggregate of these officers composed the battalion muster in the afternoon. The rest of the command was absent without leave enjoying the luxuries of roast pig, stuffed turkey and the like. . . . A very military set of orders were issued, which no one took any pains to obey. Tiring of this, the colonel resigned." And Dyer adds, not surprisingly, that the rule in his regiment was "for every man to be his own captain and manoeuver his own forces."[53]

Captain French, having been promoted to the command of Company F of White's Battalion, "found it an extremely difficult task to bring any of the men into any sort of subjection to discipline."

[He] had given positive orders that no man should leave camp without permission. . . . the order . . . was hardly spoken before some of his men were gone and remained out all night. In the morning . . . French met one of them and inquired where he had been, to which the soldier replied, "Out in the country to stay all night." "Did you not hear my order last night?" asked the Captain. "Yes, but I don't

52. J. M. Hubbard, *Notes of a Private* (Memphis, Tenn., 1909), 1.
53. J. W. Dyer, *Reminiscences, or, Four Years in the Confederate Army* (Evansville, Ind., 1898), 23–24, 157–58, 164.

mind orders when I want to go anywhere" was the answer, but it was scarcely given before the Captain's sabre came down on his head, and the man fell, badly hurt. This created great excitement in the company, and while most of them joined in a petition to the Captain to resign, some of them threatened him with personal violence; but when he heard of it, he came out among the men alone, and proposed to give any or all of them the satisfaction they required, and awed by his fearless manner, all of them to a man submitted . . . and ever afterwards Capt. French's orders were law in Co. F.[54]

It is doubtful if more than a handful of Confederate officers would have adopted Captain French's drastic methods—Nathan Bedford Forrest would certainly have been one if in his judgment the occasion called for it. In some units, in Company B of the 12th Virginia, for example, in which all the troopers "bore the relation of brother, cousin, schoolmate, neighbor and friend to each other," a semblance of discipline was maintained "by affection and example" and by the officers' treatment of the men as equals.[55] In the 2nd Kentucky, officers established their authority by outdoing their men in reckless bravery; George St. Leger Grenfell, a British soldier of fortune who served for a time as Morgan's assistant adjutant general, told Colonel A. J. L. Fremantle that in that regiment, "every atom of authority had to be purchased by a drop of blood."[56]

To a great degree, the disciplinary problems of the Confederate cavalry are traceable to the fact that the officers who should have set a good example by their own conduct were just as unruly and insubordinate as their men, and many of them seemed to glory in a cavalier disregard of, and lack of respect for, authority. One cannot think harshly of an eighteen-year-old trooper who ran the guard against orders for the sake of a decent meal, when Lieutenant General Joseph E. Johnston, an army commander, permitted himself the luxury of returning instructions he

54. Myers, *The Comanches*, 255.
55. Baylor, *Bull Run to Bull Run*, 38–39. There were eight troopers named Timberlake in the company. There were six Deuprees in Company G, 1st Mississippi. J. G. Deupree, "The Capture of Holly Springs, Mississippi, Dec. 20, 1862," *Publications of the Mississippi Historical Society*, IV (1901), 51.
56. Arthur J. L. Fremantle, *The Fremantle Diary* (Boston, 1960), 127.

had received from the Secretary of War with the endorsement, "Sir, I had the honor to receive your 'letter of instructions' yesterday. Having perused it more than once, I respectfully inclose it herewith, that you may do me the favor to affix your signature and return it."[57] Nor would one readily condemn the misconduct of an enlisted man in the 1st Louisiana whose colonel, John S. Scott, commanding a brigade, had to be placed under arrest by General Bragg for "contemplating an independent trip with his brigade without permission."[58]

In the final stages of Bragg's invasion of Kentucky in 1862, General Edmund Kirby Smith sent John Hunt Morgan orders to march his regiment to Saltville, Virginia, to guard the salt works there which, in an age without refrigeration, were of vital importance to the Confederacy. Smith's courier delivered the order to one of Morgan's staff officers, who "pocketed it and dismissed the courier. The officer reasoned that the salt works were in no danger . . . [and] that it was more important to operate upon the railroads, in front of Nashville, than to look after salt works." Morgan eventually learned of the order, but he too decided to ignore it and went ahead with his own plans. The staff officer,

57. Joseph E. Johnston, *Narrative of Military Operations During the Late War Between the States* (Bloomington, Ind., 1959), 264. General Lee wrote in August, 1864, "What our officers lack is the pains and labor of inculcating discipline. It is a painful tedious process & is not apt to win popular favour. Many officers have too many selfish views to promote to induce them to undertake the task of instrucing & disciplining their commands. To succeed it is necessary to set the example & this necessarily confines them to their duties, their camp & mess, which is disagreeable and deprives them of pleasant visits, dinners, etc." Douglas S. Freeman and Grady McWhiney (eds.), *Lee's Dispatches to Jefferson Davis* (New York, 1957), 369.

58. Carter, *A Cavalryman's Reminiscences*, 50. In the fall of 1863, Colonel Scott sent the following dispatch to Major General Frank Cheatham: "If you have no especial use for my two companies that you picked up this morning please send them to me as I think they will be of more use to me than you." Having had Scott as their commanding officer, it is understandable that when, after his departure, "Col. Ogden, whom the boys had never seen or even heard of, was sent to take command—no one in the regiment liked it—they thought one of their own officers should be in command . . . and they were so worked up over this matter that the first time Col. Ogden called them to make a charge nobody moved." *Ibid.*, 93, 107–108.

who in any other army would have been cashiered if not shot, was not punished in any way, and neither was Morgan.[59]

In the course of his Valley Campaign, Jackson sent orders to the 6th Virginia, which had the advance, to camp at Kernstown. This did not suit the regiment:

Being entirely without those things which can make a soldier comfortable, both officers and men were highly incensed. . . . our colonel . . . ordered Asher W. Harman, captain of the first company, to countermarch his men, they having refused to obey the order when given by the Colonel. This the Captain refused to do. Whereupon the Colonel told him to consider himself under arrest and then ordered the next in command, Lieut. Simms, to countermarch his company. Simms also refused and was placed under arrest. Then the Colonel commanded the orderly sergeant, George Bunch, to countermarch the company. This Bunch refused to do, whereupon the Colonel drawing his sword, rode at Bunch, swearing by the eternal he would run him through if he did not obey; but Captain Harman, drawing his sword, rushed between the enraged Colonel and Bunch, declaring that if the Colonel attacked Bunch, he would attack the Colonel.[60]

Like officers, like men. When everyone cooled off and Captain Harman at last consented to countermarch the company, the trooper who describes the incident "stepped out and loudly proclaimed that if anyone wanted to go to Winchester, he should follow me."[61] Edmund Kirby Smith, a West Pointer, was undoubtedly guilty of a degree of bias, but the surviving records make it amply clear that he was not far off the mark in commenting that the volunteers, "though the best blood of the country is found in the ranks . . . will not submit to the necessary

59. Duke, *A History of Morgan's Cavalry*, 294.

60. Opie, *A Rebel Cavalryman*, 49. When Colonel E. W. Rucker was given command of a brigade of four regiments of Tennessee cavalry, the four colonels, who thought that the senior among them should have been given the post, refused to obey Rucker's orders, whereupon Forrest suspended all four and placed them under arrest. J. P. Young, *The Seventh Tennessee Cavalry, A History* (Nashville, 1890), 100–101. Colonel Henry L. Giltner of the 4th Kentucky "became restive and inclined to rebel against the iron rule of General Ransom. . . . On the morning of November 4, the general, desiring a conference with Giltner, had to send for him two or three times before the dauntless colonel condescended to honor the summons." Mosgrove, *Kentucky Cavaliers in Dixie*, 88.

61. Opie, *A Rebel Cavalryman*, 50.

discipline . . . [and are] not far removed from an irregular, undisciplined mob."[62]

From the standpoint of efficiency, probably the most damaging manifestation of the lack of discipline in the Confederate cavalry was the men's uncontrollable urge to absent themselves from their commands. Wandering away from one's unit for extended periods and without permission was in the Union army the specialty of a handful of regiments like the 1st Kentucky; in the Confederate cavalry it seemed to be a way of life. The nominal strength of a company, regiment, or brigade was a mere fiction, and no commanding officer could tell from one day to the next how many men he would have available to picket, scout, march, or fight.

The Confederate system of depending on cavalrymen to furnish their own mounts was a major factor, but not by any means the only one, in keeping the ranks of the cavalry undermanned. When a trooper lost his horse and could not get one from the Yankees to replace it, he was entitled to a thirty-day furlough to go home for another. Even Virginia troopers were gone from thirty to sixty days on these remount errands, and those from the Carolinas and the Deep South commonly stayed away much longer. But at least these absences were authorized, however much troopers may have stretched them either because of a genuine difficulty in getting a horse or simply because they were loath to leave the comforts of home. Apparently, however, totally unauthorized absences had an even greater impact on numerical strength. In the spring of 1862, long before the procurement of remounts became truly difficult, Turner Ashby's twenty-six companies were reduced to half or less their proper strength, because the men were "constantly leaving their commands. The real work of the cavalry was done by less than half the men in the com-

---

62. A. H. Noll, *General Kirby-Smith* (Sewanee, Tenn., 1907), 174. More than one thoughtful southern cavalryman realized—when it was much too late—as did D. Howard Smith of the 5th Kentucky, that lack of discipline greatly handicapped the Confederate cavalry; "At no time was . . . [discipline] what it ought to have been. This, indeed, was the great trouble throughout the Confederate army. . . . This was one thing that gave the Federals the decided advantage." S. K. Smith, *Life, Army Record, and Public Services of D. Howard Smith* (Louisville, Ky., 1890), 54.

mand."[63] Some men simply wandered away from their regiments and returned when it suited their convenience. One group, given leave to attend church in Winchester on a Sunday morning, did not return for a week and were not punished. Another group, bored with camp, asked W. E. Jones's permission to "make a scout in the lower [Shenandoah] Valley, but the request was refused on grounds ... [the men] esteemed unreasonable and insufficient," so they went anyway, led by a lieutenant. Some of them were captured by the Yankees and did not rejoin their units until they were exchanged, several months later.[64]

Troopers left their units to go adventuring with one of the several Partisan Ranger groups, the raising of which was authorized by the Confederate Congress on April 21, 1862. Membership in these units, whose personnel came and went as they pleased and were subject to none of the drudgery and discipline, such as they were, of the "regular" cavalry, had an irresistible appeal to the younger, more adventurous men and also to those who were more attracted by looting than by fighting. The former, at least, were usually the very men who would have been most useful in the cavalry if they could have been kept with their units.[65] Lastly, there was outright desertion, an increasingly serious problem in both armies as the war went on, but especially so in the Confederacy, whose manpower resources were severely limited.

Records are too sparse and unreliable to permit an accurate

63. Ashby, *Life of Turner Ashby*, 148.
64. Baylor, *Bull Run to Bull Run*, 82–83, 125.
65. For the Partisan Rangers in general, see E. C. Barksdale, "Semi-Regular and Irregular Warfare in the Civil War" (Ph.D. dissertation, University of Texas, 1941), esp. 61–73; also Lonn, *Desertion During the Civil War*, 15, and Andrew Brown, "The First Mississippi Partisan Rangers, C.S.A.," *Civil War History*, I (1955), 371–72. The Confederate Congress repealed the Partisan Ranger Law on February 17, 1864. Two months later, General Lee wrote Adjutant General Samuel Cooper, "Experience has convinced me that it is almost impossible [for] the best officers even to have discipline in these bands of partisan rangers, or to prevent them from becoming an injury instead of a benefit to the service, and even where this is accomplished the system gives license to many deserters and marauders, who assume to belong to these authorized companies and commit depredations on friend and foe alike." Quoted in Barksdale, "Semi-Regular and Irregular Warfare," 374–75.

assessment of the effect of these factors, individually or in the aggregate, on the numerical strength of the Confederate cavalry, though there is no question but that it was crippling. For example, Fitzhugh Lee's brigade, with a nominal strength of twenty-five hundred, had only eight hundred present at the battle of Kelly's Ford on March 17, 1863, and fewer than fifteen hundred at Chancellorsville, two and a half months later, by which time many of its absentees had returned.[66] Even after allowance is made for those legitimately absent, the great discrepancy between nominal and actual strength had an increasingly serious impact, both in the East and in the West, on the ability of Confederate cavalry to fulfill its proper role. It may well be that this factor was as important as the increasing skill and self-confidence of the Federal cavalry, the improvement of its organization, its more effective leadership and better weapons, in establishing the superiority of Federal mounted troops in the last year and a half of the war.

Disease was as serious a problem in the Confederate cavalry as it was on the other side, and the means of dealing with it were just as primitive and inadequate. Careless and unconcerned officers and shiftless men tolerated filthy camps, the breeding ground of disease. In one such camp, in the winter of 1861–1862, "Typhus (jail or camp fever) and pneumonia made the prevalent coughing . . . at night a desolation. . . . Sanitation was horrible, drinking water bad."[67] The improvised hospitals were understaffed, crowded beyond capacity, and from the standpoint of sanitation, little better than the camps. And as in the North, it was discovered that the "soldiers who . . . best sustained privations and hardships were not those whose previous habits would be expected to fit them for a rough mode of life."[68]

There was little to choose between the blue and the gray cavalry from the standpoint of drill and training in the early months of the war. In both armies, the amount of drill a unit had depended on the commitment and energy of the commanding officer. At

66. McClellan, *I Rode with Jeb Stuart*, 259.
67. Hamlin, *"Old Bald Head,"* 68; see also George M. Neese, *Three Years in the Confederate Horse Artillery* (New York, 1911), 248.
68. Wellman, *Giant in Gray*, 5.

best, the amount of time available for drill was limited by the urgent need for troops at the front. Turner Ashby, admittedly an extreme case, had all of his twenty-six companies under his direct command; his only field-grade subordinate was Major O. R. Funsten. The twenty-six companies, with a nominal strength of a good-sized brigade, were not grouped into battalions and regiments but were "like a tribal band held together by the authority of a single chief."[69] Ashby's men had no regimental drill and little drill of any kind, nor did they act in regimental units, either in camp or in the field. The companies with a prewar militia nucleus had had some drill before they joined Ashby, but the majority were, and remained, innocent of the tactics.

Nathan Bedford Forrest, in the West, "regarded . . . exhaustive cavalry drill an unnecessary tax upon men and horses. He cared nothing for tactics further than the movement by twos and fours in column, and from column right or left into line, dismounting, charging and fighting."[70] On the other hand, Jeb Stuart's first command, the 1st Virginia, had plenty of drill. The 2nd Virginia, known originally as the 30th Regiment, Virginia Volunteers (Mounted), had as its colonel R. C. W. Radford, formerly of the 2nd United States Dragoons, and had three sessions of drill every day, for a total of six hours, in the thirty days that elapsed between its organization and its departure for the front.[71] The 1st Mississippi, Debray's (26th) Regiment of Texas Cavalry, the 1st Kentucky (C.S.A.), and the 4th Virginia were regiments that had a fair amount of drill, and the Hampton Legion cavalry had so much of it that one of its troopers wrote to the newspapers to complain about it.[72]

69. William N. McDonald, *A History of the Laurel Brigade* (Baltimore, 1907), 51.

70. Morton, *Artillery of Forrest's Cavalry*, 12.

71. T. T. Munford, "A Confederate Cavalry Officer's Reminiscences," *Journal of the United States Cavalry Association*, IV (1891), 279. The regiment was not organized as such until after the battle of Bull Run and was made up of companies that had operated independently until they were grouped into a regiment. The 2nd Tennessee did not begin serious drill until December, 1861, by which time it had been in the field for six months. Hancock, *Hancock's Diary*, 188.

72. Wellman, *Giant in Gray*, 58; Deupree, "The Noxubee Squadron," 15; Xavier B. Debray, *A Sketch of the History of Debray's (26th) Regiment*

Southern troopers did not have to be taught horsemanship and, in that respect, had a tremendous initial advantage over their northern brethren. A cavalryman whose "heart is in his boots" because he is unable to control his excited mount and suspects that he is in imminent danger of parting company with it is of little use in a mounted action, offensively or defensively. This was one problem the South did not have and the North had in abundance.

Here, then, was the Confederate cavalryman, even more of an individualist and more restive under discipline than his colleague of the North, but fighting in his own country and hence confident that he could count on help, if he needed it, in every village and farmhouse; he was beautifully mounted, though indifferently equipped, and he possessed an unshakeable conviction of his own superiority over the "mongrel hordes" and "Lincoln's hirelings" with whom he was about to do battle. He was daring to the point of recklessness, improvident, a fine horseman, delighted when a raid or an advance against the enemy was afoot and he was in the thick of it, but irresponsible, undisciplined, and footloose in camp. Typically, he had a McClellan or a Mexican saddle on his horse and a pair of large spurs on the heels of his (usually worn) boots. He was armed eventually with a light, long-range gun and a brace of Colt's revolvers, the latter taken from the enemy, the usual source also of much of his clothing, his blanket, rubber poncho, and most of the rest of his equipment and gear. In good times he had a haversack full of food and a canteen well filled, but not necessarily with water or buttermilk. He was an inveterate raider of hen roosts, pigpens, smokehouses, and cellars. He was fond of gay attire when he could get it, especially large cavalry boots, a sash, and a black felt hat of the slouch variety with a wide brim turned up on one side and pinned to the crown with a silver crescent or star, the whole confection adorned by a black ostrich plume, the larger the better. He was, too, part of an army whose leadership from the start appeared to have a greater appreciation of the potential of cavalry and

---

of *Texas Cavalry* (Austin, Tex., 1884), 3; Dyer, *Reminiscences*, 17; Hackley, *The Little Fork Rangers*, 37.

handled it more confidently than did their northern counterparts. He never had any reason to feel that his branch of the service was an encumbrance, best kept out of the way; its acceptance as a valuable adjunct of the armies was reflected in his high morale. The gaudy trappings and adornments of the Confederate cavalry did not last, but the physical and moral qualities that made the southern cavalryman, so long as he chose to remain with his unit, both a formidable fighting man and a poor soldier remained to the end.

IX

Prepare to Mount

GEORGE B. McCLELLAN WAS THE ONLY GENERAL TO WIN victories for the Union in the summer of 1861. The victories were minor, won in the mountains of western Virginia, but being the only victories the Union could boast of, they and the general's grandiloquent proclamations filled the newspapers and, after the loss of the battle of Bull Run, made him the inevitable choice to replace the unfortunate Irvin McDowell. McClellan was summoned to Washington on July 22, while the footsore stragglers of McDowell's army were still arriving in the city. The first task of the "Young Napoleon," as he was dubbed, somewhat prematurely, by the newspapers, was to organize into an army McDowell's demoralized troops and the dozens of volunteer regiments of horse and foot that the War Department called to Washington in the aftermath of the lost battle.

Described as a "brilliant administrator and a fine trainer of troops . . . at his best in getting an army ready to fight," McClellan did in fact create the Army of the Potomac, but he showed evidence of a blind spot that was to prove costly to himself as well as to what he got into the habit of calling "his" army.[1] His

1. The quoted phrase is from T. Harry Williams, *Lincoln and His Generals* (New York, 1952), 29.

blind spot was the cavalry. He seemed not to know what to do with it, a curious lack of vision in a former captain of cavalry, an officer of superior intelligence who had quite recently spent a year abroad studying the military establishments of Great Britain, Austria, Prussia, France, and Russia, and had not only written an able report on their cavalry forces, but had also incorporated the results of his investigations in a volume of *Regulations and Instructions for the Field Service of the United States Cavalry in Time of War*. He had even designed the McClellan saddle, which the United States Cavalry continued to use until it became mechanized.

From the point of view of administration and command, McClellan did what was clearly necessary and proper: as fast as regiments of infantry arrived in Washington, he grouped them into brigades and divisions. But only the footsoldiers benefited from this obviously appropriate form of organization; the artillery and the cavalry did not. As McClellan had seen, the regiment was the basic building block of army administration in Europe, but there the regiments of cavalry were grouped to form brigades, and brigades grouped into divisions. Nevertheless, instead of forming divisions, or even brigades, of cavalry, McClellan saw fit to attach his mounted regiments singly to divisions of infantry. McClellan did in fact form one cavalry brigade, made up of the 1st Vermont and the 5th New York, under Brigadier General John P. Hatch, but this was simply a training organization, and when the campaigning season opened in the spring of 1862 the two regiments were sent into the field separately.

The first and easily predictable result of McClellan's system, or excuse for the lack of a system, was to "place the cavalry at the disposal of generals without experience, who still further divided it, so that each brigade, almost, was provided with its troop or squadron whose duty it was to add to the importance of the general by following him about, to provide orderlies for dashing young staff officers and strikers for headquarters."[2] On October 15, some eleven or twelve regiments of cavalry were attached in this way to as many divisions of infantry. In the following March, after the organization of the infantry divisions into corps

2. Harris, "The Union Cavalry," 351.

had been forced on McClellan by the president, two to five regiments of cavalry were assigned as individual units, without being formed into one or two brigades, to each of the five corps of infantry.[3] The fundamental flaw of this arrangement was not cured by forming the mounted regiments left over into a "Cavalry Reserve" under General Philip St. George Cooke, Jeb Stuart's father-in-law.

In August, 1861, McClellan created the post of chief of cavalry of the Army of the Potomac and appointed as its first incumbent his West Point classmate, George Stoneman. Appointed to the academy from New York, Stoneman graduated thirty-third in the fifty-nine-man class of 1846, which also included Stonewall Jackson and George E. Pickett. He was sent to the 1st Dragoons in time to see service in the Mexican War as acting assistant quartermaster of the Mormon Battalion on its march to San Diego. After several years of frontier service, Stoneman was promoted to captain in the 2nd United States Cavalry in 1855. In May, 1861, he commanded the cavalry in the capture of Alexandria, Virginia, and from June to mid-August was with McClellan in West Virginia. Promoted to brigadier general on August 13, 1861, he became chief of cavalry of the Army of the Potomac the next day.[4] In March, 1862, when most of the cavalry was parceled out among the corps of infantry, each corps was also given a chief of cavalry. Notwithstanding their grandiose titles, Stoneman himself and the five corps chiefs of cavalry were "ornamental staff officers" with duties that were exclusively administrative, their job being to inspect cavalry regiments, handle the paper work, and pass on McClellan's and the corps com-

3. Thiele, "The Evolution of Cavalry," 86. On November 12, 1861, the Army of the Potomac had 8,125 cavalry, with 4,735 of them "present for duty equipped"; by January, 1862, the total had risen to 22,497, about half of that number being "present for duty equipped." Rhodes, *Cavalry of the Army of the Potomac*, 9; Thiele, "The Evolution of Cavalry," 264. The "Cavalry Reserve" in March consisted of five regiments grouped into two brigades.
4. George W. Cullum, *Biographical Register of the Officers and Graduates of the U.S. Military Academy* (2 vols.; New York, 1868), II, 160–62. McClellan's General Order No. 10 of March 26, 1862, stating that "the duties of the chiefs of . . . cavalry are exclusively administrative" is quoted in Thiele, "The Evolution of Cavalry," 87.

manders' orders to the cavalry. They had no command authority whatever.[5] The commanders of corps and divisions were to decide when, where, and how the cavalry regiments attached to their units were to function.

McClellan's lack of vision created a pattern of organization for the cavalry of the Army of the Potomac that was to hamstring not only the cavalry, but the army as a whole, for the best part of three years. He may have thought that his cavalry had neither the leadership nor the training to be capable of large-scale, independent operations separated from the infantry; if so, he had on his side European wisdom regarding the length of time needed to train cavalry. An army commander who, at a review in October, 1861, had to order the 1st New York, his best-trained regiment of cavalry, off the field and back to its camp, because "there was so much confusion and the officers were so wanting in the ability to quietly restore order," might be held free of blame for mistrusting the capability of his volunteer mounted troops to operate in large masses against a tough enemy.[6] On the other hand, the lack of officers of proven ability to command brigades, divisions, and corps of mounted troops cannot be cited in justification of McClellan's organizational scheme, because there was precisely the same lack in the infantry. Despite this, infantry brigades, divisions, and later corps were organized and placed under the command of completely inexperienced and untried brigadier and major generals who, only a few months earlier, had been civilians, or captains and majors in the Regular Army, and whose difficulties were compounded by being given cavalry as well as infantry to command.

McClellan was not alone in scattering his cavalry broadcast. In the West, Generals Fremont and Buell did the same. So did Grant, who at a later stage of his illustrious career remarked that the height of his ambition in 1861 had been to command a brigade of cavalry in the Army of the Potomac. "I suppose," he said, "it was my fondness for horses that made me feel that I should be more at home in the command of cavalry, and I thought that

5. Thiele, "The Evolution of Cavalry," 87.
6. Beach, *First New York (Lincoln) Cavalry*, 51.

the Army of the Potomac would present the best field of operations for a brigade commander in that arm of the service."[7] On the last point, General Grant was in error. Organized as it was, the cavalry of the Army of the Potomac would have given him little opportunity to serve with any credit to himself. The only exception before 1863 to the cavalry-scattering system was John Pope in the West, who consolidated his mounted troops into brigades with results that were beneficial both to his cavalry and to his army.

It was on the other side of the line that the proper foundation was laid for an effective cavalry force. Urged on by Joseph E. Johnston, the Confederate War Department ordered in October, 1861, the formation into a brigade of the regiments of cavalry then in Virginia. Command of the brigade was given to Jeb Stuart, newly promoted to brigadier general on Johnston's enthusiastic recommendation: "He is a rare man, wonderfully endowed by nature with the qualities necessary for an officer of light cavalry. Calm, firm, acute, active and enterprising."[8] Two months later, Stuart's brigade had one North Carolina and four Virginia regiments and the Jeff. Davis Legion; by the following autumn, promoted meanwhile to major general, Stuart had a cavalry division of four brigades, commanded by Wade Hampton, Beverly Robertson, Fitzhugh Lee, and Grumble Jones. Attached to the division were five batteries of horse artillery. The gospel of cavalry consolidation spread promptly to the western armies of the Confederacy. At the start, Albert Sidney Johnston had parceled out most of his cavalry, attaching from one to seven companies of it to each of his infantry brigades, but he also organized a separate cavalry brigade, and when Braxton Bragg took over command in the West, he grouped all his cavalry into two brigades, one commanded by Forrest and the other by Joseph Wheeler.[9]

Meanwhile, the 4th United States had two companies in Fort Leavenworth, Kansas, one in Paducah, Kentucky, three in Sedalia,

7. Horace Porter, *Campaigning with Grant* (New York, 1897), 25.
8. Kenneth P. Williams, *Lincoln Finds a General* (5 vols.; New York, 1949–59), I, 123.
9. Thiele, "The Evolution of Cavalry," 167.

Missouri, two in Fort Kearny, Nebraska, and two in Washington, D.C.[10] This was an extreme case, and it involved a regiment of Regulars accustomed to serving in small, widely separated packets. But the 1st Iowa, within a few months of its organization, had four companies at Booneville, Mississippi, four at Benton Barracks, two at Jefferson City, Missouri, and two at Otterville, Missouri.[11] The 1st Maine, in Virginia, did not see service as a complete, united regiment until just before Second Bull Run and had been broken up so often, serving "a little here, and a little there," that a common remark among the men was, "Whose kite are we going to be tail to next?"[12] The historians of the 6th New York thought it necessary to excuse their deviation from the normal chronological arrangement of a regimental history with the comment that "the regiment being . . . [in the Antietam Campaign in 1862] attached to Gen. Burnside's Corps, as escort and advance guard, and broken up in squadrons, companies and squads on special duties, was seldom anywhere as a regiment, but in that detached shape was practically all over the field, thus making . . . [a] short but general account necessary."[13]

Some of the fragmenting of cavalry regiments was the fault of the War Department. Six companies of the 3rd Indiana were ordered East to join the Army of the Potomac; the other four companies did their soldiering in the West, being assigned individually to different divisions of infantry. Not until the war had ended, when they began to meet at reunions, did the men of the two parts of the same regiment become acquainted with each other.[14]

10. Vale, *Minty and the Cavalry*, 13.

11. Lothrop, *A History of the First Regiment*, 46.

12. Merrill, *Campaigns of the First Maine*, 55; Tobie, *First Maine Cavalry*, 123. The regimental returns for September, 1862, showed that three entire companies *plus* 210 individual officers and men were away from the regiment on detached duties, 105 of the latter serving as orderlies.

13. Committee on Regimental History, *History of the Sixth New York*, 63.

14. Pickerill, *History of the Third Indiana*, 9, 40–41. Despite the splitting up of the regiment, "officers were commissioned and promoted as though the two . . . [sections] were operating together." *Ibid.*, 182. One would think that the unit could have been reunited with much less ingenuity than was needed to accomplish this feat.

Before the 1st Ohio was fully organized, two of its companies were ordered to West Virginia and campaigned with the Army of the Potomac for three years, whereas the rest of the regiment did its campaigning in Kentucky, Tennessee, and Georgia.[15]

Such dispersals, however they came about, had a crippling effect on the discipline and training of units that had not been together long enough to acquire much of either, or to develop the *esprit de corps* that is an essential ingredient in the success of any military organization. But even this was not the worst effect of the scattering system; its greatest vice lay in the work that the detached companies, squads, and individuals were given to do. "Those who served in the Army of the Potomac will remember that from the Fall of 1861 to the Summer of 1862 the cavalry were for the most part scattered about and used as escorts, strikers, dog-robbers and orderlies for all the generals and their numerous staff officers from the highest in rank down to the second lieutenants," writes one victim of the system.[16] The 3rd Pennsylvania had no sooner arrived in Washington in July, 1861, and received its equipment and horses, when "there was an immediate demand upon it from infantry generals to furnish them with escorts and orderlies, and the companies soon became scattered in many directions. . . . the regiment never assembled as a unit until . . . October."[17] The 11th New York was "so broken up by detachments and details of from three to ten men at different points, on courier, orderly, picket, vidette and guard duties, that it was difficult to keep track of them. . . . indeed, some were reported as deserters that reported to their companies three or four months after we arrived in Louisiana, but who had been employed on special details."[18] One of the duties for which this regiment had to provide details was "to break up the gambling dens" in Washington;

15. Curry, *Four Years in the Saddle*, 21.
16. Hampton S. Thomas, *Some Personal Reminiscences of Service in the Cavalry of the Army of the Potomac* (Philadelphia, 1889), 2.
17. Regimental History Committee, *History of the 3rd Pennsylvania*, 10–11.
18. Smith, *"Scott's 900," Eleventh New York*, 53. Company A of the 4th Pennsylvania was also on provost duty in Washington for a time. William Hyndman, *History of a Cavalry Company* (Philadelphia, 1870), 40.

"as a usual thing," the regimental historian writes, "the night patrol was a monotonous affair, a tramp from house to house, examining the passes of officers and soldiers; but sometimes something out of the common would happen to enliven the boys and drive away for a time, 'that tired feeling'."[19] Troopers of this regiment served as orderlies at the headquarters of Generals Henry W. Halleck, Nathaniel P. Banks, Christopher C. Augur, Silas Casey, and Samuel P. Heintzelman, "at various departments in the city, also at the brigade headquarters at the forts in the defenses of Washington," and a part of one company was on call to escort the president on his journeys about the city.[20]

General Wesley Merritt wrote after the war that "the smallest infantry organization had its company or more of mounted men, whose duty consisted in supplying details as orderlies for mounted staff officers, following them mounted on their rapid rides for pleasure or for duty, or in camp acting as grooms and bootblacks. . . . It is not wonderful that this treatment demoralized the cavalry."[21] Even more revealing is a letter sent by Colonel William Gamble of the 8th Illinois to General Alfred Pleasonton, then chief of cavalry of the Army of the Potomac, in late 1862: "I am informed that a considerable number of the enlisted men of this Regiment who were sick and sent during last summer to the several Hospitals at New York, Philadelphia, Baltimore, Washington, Georgetown, Alexandria, and Point Lookout, have recovered and are detained as Hospital Cooks and attendants, officers' cooks and waiters, Guards at Hospitals and Rail Road Stations, &c., thus impairing their discipline and efficiency as cavalry soldiers . . . to the manifest injury of the Regiment to which they properly belong."[22]

19. Smith, "Scott's 900," Eleventh New York, 58. Smith adds, "The night patrol . . . gained for the regiment an unenviable notoriety among the men of the army whose habits while in Washington brought them under the surveillance of the patrol. . . . there were many exciting experiences, and every line officer of the regiment could give interesting reminiscences, many of which might, perhaps, better remain untold." Ibid., 52.

20. Ibid., 13.

21. Rodenbough, From Everglade to Canon, 284.

22. William Gamble to Alfred Pleasonton, December 2, 1862, in 8th Illinois O&L Books, RG 94, NA.

General W. B. Hazen, who was sent as an observer to the Austro-Prussian War of 1866, remarked, "The King [of Prussia] drives with a less guard than escorted the commanders of our small armies. I never see here the spectacle, so common in the first two years of our war, of a general thundering along the street with a whole cavalcade at his heels, making the dust fly and every body run for life."[23]

Some regiments, fortunately, were given more serious work to do. Poorly planned for the most part, and often enough not planned at all, these assignments were nevertheless a better preparation for cavalry duties than riding about Washington as uniformed errand boys or even as policemen. Dennis Hart Mahan had laid it down that the principal duty of cavalry was "to secure the front and flanks of the position occupied by the main body, from any attempt to reconnoitre or attack it." To perform this function, "the detachments which form the advanced-posts must be so distributed as to embrace all the avenues by which the enemy can approach the position," and were to be deployed in two or sometimes three concentric lines of posts, the "Out-Posts" nearest the enemy and an inner line of "Grand-Guards" an appropriate distance behind.[24] In addition, patrols were to be sent out to find the enemy, "gain a good idea of his position and strength, and to bring in an accurate account of his distance from the outposts of their own force; and the character of the ground between the positions occupied by the respective forces."[25]

General McClellan's *Regulations* also assigned outpost duty to the cavalry; only "in cases of absolute necessity" was that task to be entrusted to the infantry. He prescribed that a chain of mounted vedettes was to be placed not more than three miles in advance of the main body, with the vedettes so stationed that "in the daytime they can see each other, and in the night hear every thing that happens between them."[26] A second line of pickets was to be posted not more than three-quarters of a mile behind the vedettes, and a third line, the main guard, about the same dis-

23. Hazen, *The School of the Army*, 27–28.
24. Mahan, *Advanced Guard*, 87.
25. *Ibid.*, 114.
26. McClellan, *Regulations and Instructions*, 57–58.

tance behind the pickets. Cavalry patrols had as their principal duty "to discover the enemy betimes, and thus to secure the detachment to which they belong, as well as the rest of the army, against sudden attacks." Patrols, if attacked by surprise, were to defend themselves "to the utmost, and fire a few shots . . . to warn the detachment of its danger." McClellan also laid down the principle that "there are few circumstances which can justify the surrender of cavalry; proper precautions on the march render a surprise next to impossible; and when a party of cavalry is attacked, no matter how suddenly, or by what superiority of force, a determined and instantaneous charge will always enable the greater part to escape."[27]

With the rebel army encamped at Manassas, less than twenty-five miles from Washington, and its ever-active cavalry scouting all the roads and lanes between the armies, there was ample opportunity for the Union cavalry to gain practical experience in the outpost duty and scouting prescribed by Professor Mahan and General McClellan. However, with the conspicuous exception of the 3rd Pennsylvania, the schooling of the men in these essential cavalry functions was not too well conducted.[28]

Cavalry officers who had studied their manuals were familiar enough with the theory of the duties of cavalry in the field. They knew all the accepted maxims and might well have performed creditably if in the crucially important first few weeks of active campaigning they could have had at their elbows an experienced lieutenant or sergeant of the Regular cavalry to inspire confidence and to teach those tricks of the trade—and there were many— that were not to be learned from books. Even in the absence of such coaching, the relatively passive and undemanding outpost work went well enough. Posting the lines of vedettes and pickets

27. *Ibid.*, 45, 49.
28. After William Averell took command of the 3rd Pennsylvania, he taught officers and men the duties of pickets, patrols, advance guards, rear guards, scouting parties, flanking parties, and convoys, and since the camp of the regiment was "not far from those of the enemy, facilities were on hand for the practical illustration of some of these lessons, and many minor skirmishes occurred, in which men learned more in a day than could otherwise have been taught in months." Hess, "The First Cavalry Battle," 6.

was not beyond the capabilities of even an inexperienced officer. This involved stationing the line of vedettes nearest the enemy, the main reserve, commanded by a captain, in a sheltered spot a mile or so to the rear and midway between the two reliefs, commanded by a lieutenant or sergeant and able within minutes to come to the aid of any part of the line of vedettes upon the sounding of an alarm; all the horses of the reliefs and the reserve had to be saddled and bridled, ready for any emergency.

As to the vedettes themselves, "We go out upon our shivering horses," a trooper has written, "to sit in the saddle for two hours or more, facing the biting wind, and peering through the storm of sleet, snow or rain, which unmercifully pelts us in its fury. But it were well for us if this was our worst enemy, and we consider ourselves happy if the guerilla does not creep through the bushes impenetrable to the sight, to inflict his mortal blows. The two hours expire, relief comes, and the vedette returns to spend his four, six or eight hours off post, as best he may."[29] Not all regiments followed the practice of relieving the pickets every two hours; in the 7th Pennsylvania, "for several weeks the able-bodied men were required to go on . . . duty every night. . . . from sunset to sunrise they were required to sit in the saddle with carbine advanced. . . . No respite was permitted by way of relief. . . . The nights were damp and chilly; with shivering limbs and longing eyes we welcomed with exultant joy the increasing light of the morning star. It was quite a relief from the dreadful monotony to have the enemy's scouts advance upon the outposts and exchange a few random shots with our pickets."[30]

29. Glazier, *Three Years in the Federal Cavalry*, 54–55.

30. Dornblaser, *Sabre Strokes of the Pennsylvania Dragoons*, 58. The 1st Rhode Island "were put out to picket duty in rain and snow and severe cold; compelled to stand on outpost duty, in our turns, for three succesive days at a time—men and horses suffering what pen may not describe. . . . The pickets were divided into small bodies for reliefs and reserves, and have the reserve head quarters in deep wooded hollows or other concealed places, where fires are allowed, the men remaining dismounted, with the privilege of keeping themselves as comfortable as possible, but always keeping themselves girded for attack. The horses are kept saddled and bridled, hitched to the nearest trees. . . . The men on post always remain in their saddles, their horses' heads in the direction of the enemy." Denison, *Sabres and Spurs*, 182, 199.

As time went on, a degree of sophistication crept into this dreary activity. The 1st New York hit upon the sensible practice of changing the position of the vedettes after dark, to foil any lurking "bushwhacker" (often only a Confederate cavalryman on the hunt for a remount from the Yankees, but deadly enough for all that) who might have marked their location in the daytime. At the suggestion of General Philip Kearny, the 3rd Pennsylvania adopted the following stratagem:

It was usual, very late at night, for a party of rebel cavalry to charge upon our outposts, fire off their carbines, and get away in the ensuing excitement. These frequent alarms at night made . . . picket duty uncomfortable and dangerous. . . . a detail was sent out one evening beyond our lines . . . with instructions to stretch telegraph wires across the road and quietly await developments. About midnight the rebel cavalrymen made their appearance. They came down the road at a lively trot. . . . the wire caught the advance and tangled up the column, the horses falling over one another, a confused mass of men and beasts. Our men, who were hidden in the woods close by, opened a brisk fire upon the crowded road. . . . Scarcely any of the enemy got away, for those who were not killed or wounded were captured. That put an end to the night surprises of our pickets.[31]

The 17th Pennsylvania developed a picketing system of its own. Its companies were assigned to picket duty in rotation, for ten days at a time, but instead of posting a line of stationary pickets, the outpost companies went on night patrols along the picket line, "right and left, at agreed upon hours . . . made afresh each day in advance of the night, for if the patrols were regular as to routes and hours, the prowlers who were always alert would know when and where to strike."[32] The system worked just as well as the conventional arrangement of stationary pickets and was not only much less wearing on men and horses, but also served to develop the troopers' keenness and initiative.

The scouts and patrols into "no man's land" required far more skill than did vedette duty, especially on the part of the line officers; at the beginning, the outcome of such expeditions was frequently grim or embarrassing. Many a scout ended with the Fed-

31. Regimental History Committee, *History of the 3rd Pennsylvania*, 14.
32. Clark, "Making of a Volunteer Cavalryman," 18.

erals in "a state of rapid ambulation from the enemy," as one
trooper described it.[33] Before Averell's arrival on the scene, a
small patrol of the 3rd Pennsylvania was caught near Vienna,
Virginia, and chased back to camp by a detachment of the 1st
North Carolina; many of the Pennsylvanians fell off their horses
in the chase and were captured.[34] The Ringgold Battalion, out on
a scout, had its first "fight" with the Confederate cavalry at Hanging Rocks; "the Lieutenant-Colonel in command . . . gave no orders whatsoever; we were afraid to go forward, and could not get
back. . . . Fortunately for us, the enemy did not know we were so
demoralized, and after a few volleys, retreated. . . . This was a
ludicrous performance, each belligerent retreating in haste from
the other."[35] There were occasional Union successes, probably
embellished in the telling for the benefit of posterity, as is the
account of an attack by a detachment of the 5th New York on
"the redoubtable Ashby": "Our men all eager for the fight fell like
a whirlwind upon the enemy, and using their sabers with terrible
effect, soon scattered and turned them back in confusion. And
now commenced a scrambling race. Clouds of dust arose from
the road, which almost entirely enveloped both the pursued and
the pursuers. Occasionally the Rebels rallied, but were swept
away again, badly defeated."[36]

More common in the early days than this small triumph were
incidents of the kind described by the historian of the 8th Illinois:

A party of the Fourth New York . . . was sent out after forage but
soon came in with the report that they had encountered a brigade of
rebel cavalry, who were coming down upon us. All hands were soon
under arms, and a part of the Eighth Illinois at once started in pursuit of the enemy, prepared for a desperate encounter . . . when about
two or three miles from camp they met a foraging party of about
twenty of our Eighth Illinois men with bundles of hay on their horses
. . . and these were all the "rebels" that had been seen. Such frights
were very common and disgusting.[37]

33. William Hyndman, *History of a Cavalry Company* (Philadelphia,
Pa., 1870), 96.
34. Thiele, "The Evolution of Cavalry," 250.
35. Farrar, *The Twenty-Second Pennsylvania*, 17.
36. Louis N. Boudrye, *Historic Records of the Fifth New York Cavalry, First Ira Harris Guard* (Albany, N.Y., 1868), 25.
37. Hard, *History of the Eighth Cavalry*, 95.

Even more "disgusting" was the fate of the first scouting party of thirty men under Captain Charles E. Pratt sent out by the 10th New York; the detachment was captured to a man, without firing a shot.[38]

Scouting details were variously organized, depending on the purpose of the expedition or the idiosyncracies of the regimental commander. Seldom did an entire regiment go on a scout; normally small parties of from a half dozen to a dozen men were sent out under the command of a lieutenant or a sergeant, or a company or two under a captain. In some units it was customary to make up a scouting detail by having each company furnish a proportionate share of the total number needed.

Depending on the outcome, or even on the weather, a scout could be a thoroughly miserable experience or a delightful excursion into the country to be savored and long remembered. Three companies of the 1st Maine were ordered to scout toward Warrenton, Virginia, ten miles away, in April, 1862, "it having been reported that the famous Black Horse Cavalry had visited the village the previous night." The expedition left camp at nightfall:

The orders were to keep as quiet as possible, and no loud talking. We soon struck into the woods, and then commenced the finest ride ever known. There we were, on a bright moonlight night, in a fine stretch of woods, riding ... now through mud to the horses' knees, now through water to their bellies ... now getting a switch in the face from overhanging limbs, now losing a cap by the same means, now taking a good smart gallop over a smooth place, now over a stump and round trees, now in a ditch and now over a fence ... frogs singing, sabres clashing, stars shining—pleasant scenery all the way— with just excitement enough. ... I let myself out to the full enjoyment of it, and drank to the full the wild scene; for one, I did not wish to talk. I was happy enough—talk would have destroyed the spell. Then I ... blessed the day that I chose cavalry instead of infantry. ... That ride was worth a great deal to me, and I have heard many of the boys say that they were never so happy as on that ride. There's where one *lives*.[39]

A contrasting picture of utter exhaustion was recorded after the 2nd New York's return from a scout to the Virginia Central

38. Preston, *History of the 10th Regiment*, 41.
39. Tobie, *First Maine Cavalry*, 57. No rebels were found at Warrenton, which undoubtedly added to the bucolic charm of the expedition.

Railroad at Gordonsville, an expedition that involved a march of eighty miles in thirty hours:

Others slept in their saddles, either leaning forward on the pommel of the saddle, or on the roll of coat and blanket, or sitting quite erect, with an occasional bow forward or to the right or left, like the swaying of a flag on a signal station, or like the careerings of a drunken man. The horse of such a sleeping man will seldom leave his place in the column, though this will sometimes occur, and the man awakes at last to find himself alone with his horse which is grazing along some unknown field or woods. . . . Sometimes a fast-walking horse in one of the rear companies will bear his sleeping lord quietly along, forcing his way through the ranks ahead of him, until the poor fellow is awakened, and finds himself just passing by the colonel and his staff at the head of the column.[40]

And the 1st Maine, once again, on its initial foray into Virginia experienced similar discomforts:

Next morning . . . the boys waked up in good spirits and . . . [were] soon on the move. Shortly after starting, a mixed storm commenced— drizzle and rain, then rain and drizzle, drizzle and snow, and then snow; and the marching was made more uncomfortable by the condition of the roads, which fast grew muddy and rough. . . . A few miles farther on . . . [we were] ordered to dismount and go into camp. But "go into camp" was a mere form of words. The horses were hitched up, and that is about all that was done. . . . the wagons were five miles away, stuck in the mud and unable to cross the stream; consequently, the regiment was without rations, forage, tents, axes, cooking utensils, dishes, or anything else needed for comfort. The morning brought no change for the better, except daylight; the storm of rain and drizzle still continued in all its force and lasted all day, and there was no prospect of the wagons coming up. . . . The next day it still stormed, the air was colder, the mud was deeper.[41]

The cavalry had other duties besides picketing and scouting. One battalion of the 3rd Indiana was ordered to patrol the Potomac and picket the mouths of the numerous creeks flowing into it from the Maryland side, to stop the contraband traffic in both directions that was carried on by small sailboats and rowboats. Gunboats on the river had not been able to stop the traffic, but the

40. Glazier, *Three Years in the Federal Cavalry*, 74–75.
41. Tobie, *First Maine Cavalry*, 52–54.

3rd Indiana did and captured many of the blockade runners.[42] The 1st Vermont was given the job of guarding the telegraph lines behind Banks's advance up the Shenandoah Valley; finding its twenty-three army wagons insufficient to carry its baggage, the Vermonters pressed farm wagons into service to carry the excess and lost everything, baggage and wagons, to the Confederates at Winchester.[43] Five companies of the 1st Maine were sent to guard the line of the B & O Railroad west of Washington; each company, out of touch with the others, was stationed at a point on the road thought to be vulnerable to attack. The men found little "to relieve the tedium of the duty after the first novelty of camp life in active service wore off."[44]

The Vermonters were not by any means unique in marching off on their first campaign encumbered with what by later standards was an immense wagon train. Their twenty-three army wagons were more than matched by the twenty-five wagons of the 7th Michigan, the thirty-four wagons of the 9th Illinois, the sixty wagons plus "a number of ambulances" of the 1st Rhode Island, and the unbelievable eighty-one wagons of the 8th Illinois.[45] With six mules needed to pull an army wagon, such figures make apparent the magnitude of the problem of keeping even a single cavalry regiment, to say nothing of an entire army, supplied with forage alone.

The most onerous duty cavalry was asked to perform was to escort a wagon train. It was a job cavalrymen thoroughly detested, "for the movement is altogether too slow, especially when bad

42. Pickerill, History of the Third Indiana, 14.
43. Benedict, Vermont in the Civil War, II, 546, 552, 563.
44. Tobie, First Maine Cavalry, 28–29.
45. Isham, An Historical Sketch, 15; Davenport, History of the Ninth Regiment, 23; Denison, Sabres and Spurs, 57; Hard, History of the Eighth Cavalry, 81. It is reported that "the [wagon] drivers were a happy-go-lucky set of men. They were better provided for than the soldiers. They usually slept in their great canvas covered wagons, and were thus assured of good shelter. They had abundant facilities for the transportation of blankets, foraged provisions, and cooking utensils, and many of them lived in sumptuous style. Their chief weakness was 'trading off' their crippled or unruly mules. . . . They said it wasn't stealing, because the brutes all belonged to Uncle Sam anyway." Hinman, Story of the Sherman Brigade, 72–73.

roads are encountered. And in case a team becomes balky or gives out, or a wagon breaks down (incidents which occur frequently) the whole column is in statu quo until the difficulty or disability is removed. And so we are halting, advancing, halting and advancing again, with the monotonous variety repeated ad libitum, while the halts are often longer than the advances."[46] On the same subject, the historian of the 3rd Ohio concluded:

If you knew where you were going you never knew when you would get there, and when . . . [the train] moved you didn't know how soon it would stop. And if it stopped you didn't know how long it would be before it would start again. And if at a halt you sat on your horse awhile expecting it to move, until both you and your horse were tired and you dismounted for a rest, it would at once move forward, and you could mount and move along at a snail's pace. And so it was, halt and move forward, interspersed with helping wagons over the mountains, across the streams, over bad places in the road, from morning until night, and sometimes all night, before you reached camp and could get your cup of coffee and lie down to rest.[47]

Whether on a scout or escorting a wagon train, the Yankees made the acquaintance of Virginia mud. Kentucky mud was said to have a special adhesive quality of its own—a trooper of the Sherman Brigade cavalry remarked after his comrades had pried him out of the mud that as long as the rain lasted, "Kentucky would 'stick to the Union'"—and Tennessee mud, "from four to six inches in depth and in some places half-knee deep, and of the consistency of cream or very thick paint ready for use" had its champions, but by universal consent Virginia mud was in a class apart.[48] Indeed, some of the stories about it strain the reader's credulity. On one of the marches of the 9th New York, the sets of

46. Glazier, *Three Years in the Federal Cavalry*, 65. "When night came on," wrote the historian of the 5th New York, "we were ordered to be rearguard of a large train. And Oh! deliver cavalry from such a job as this, especially when the roads are almost impassable. . . . Our progress was exceedingly slow, and had it been steady, it would have been more tolerable. But it was halt, advance, halt, advance . . . at every five or ten rods, and the halts were frequently much longer than the advances." Boudrye, *Historic Records of the Fifth*, 140.
47. Crofts, *Third Ohio Veteran Volunteer Cavalry*, 47.
48. Hinman, *Story of the Sherman Brigade*, 66; Henry H. Eby, *Observations of an Illinois Boy in Battle, Camp and Prisons, 1861 to 1865* (Mendota, Ill., 1910), 66.

four threw up ridges of mud as much as two feet high on both sides of the road, and the wagons following behind the column of horsemen would have had to be abandoned if the contrabands who had attached themselves to the regiment had not literally and repeatedly heaved them out of the mire; "frequently a horse was abandoned through inability to extricate him."[49] On its way to Dumfries, Virginia, the 1st New Jersey used a road on which supplies had been hauled during the winter of 1861–1862 for the Confederates at Manassas and found "a depth and consistency of mud for which even the experiences of a Washington winter had been unable to prepare the mind. . . . in the middle of April . . . when the ground had been settling for six weeks, and the road had been untraveled for the greater part of the time, the troopers did not dare to venture into the middle of the track."[50] But at least the Virginia mud played no favorites. In the same spring of 1862, near Winchester, Confederate cavalryman George H. Neese twice in one day "helped to pry out with fence rails a horse that was in the mud up to its shoulders."[51]

As the Union regiments in the East crossed the Potomac into Virginia—commonly referred to by their historians as "the sacred soil"—and the western regiments entered Kentucky, Tennessee, and Missouri, they came, most of them for the first time, face to face with slavery. As soon as a Union regiment came within reach, Negroes flocked to its camp. When the 1st New Jersey advanced to Fredericksburg, "hour after hour long trains of negroes, men, women and children, came trooping into camp. With shouts and exulting laughter they swarmed into the lines. . . . as many of them as could obtain places took service in the regiment, so that for a day or two every private rejoiced in the possession of a groom. Then, in self-defense, the camp was cleared of all . . . except those retained by the officers. . . . Night after night, in canoes, on rafts, by swimming, the slaves beyond the [Rappahannock] river made their way to us."[52] Not long after the arrival of

49. Cheney, *History of the Ninth Regiment*, 248, 252; Committee on Regimental History, *History of the Sixth New York*, 254.
50. Pyne, *First New Jersey Cavalry*, 27.
51. Neese, *Three Years in the Confederate Horse Artillery*, 51.
52. Pyne, *First New Jersey Cavalry*, 31.

the 7th Pennsylvania in Tennessee, most of its officers acquired Negro servants, the quartermaster had Negro teamsters, and when orders came from the War Department authorizing the employment of two Negro cooks for each company, the 7th already had all the cooks it was entitled to hire. But, the regimental historian adds, the "appearance of the regiment, when on the march, was not improved by the addition of this dark contingent. Mounted as they all were on mysteriously acquired steeds, with pans and cans dangling in rhythmic profusion, the array would have given odds to Falstaff's army."[53]

On occasion, there was a grim sequel to the arrival in camp of a crowd of jubilant former slaves. While the national government groped for a policy to deal with slavery and the Negro in the midst of the war, a slaveowner whose chattels had fled to the nearest Federal regiment could get an order from headquarters, especially if the commanding officer was of the conservative persuasion, to allow him to search the camp and recover his slaves if he could find them. Every such search in the camp of a northern regiment, especially if it resulted in the finding and carrying off of an escaped slave, helped prepare the way for the final abolition of slavery. A typical incident of this sort occurred in the camp of the 3rd Ohio in Tennessee. Lieutenant Oliver M. Brown, "an ardent abolitionist," hid an escaped slave in his tent. In defiance of an order from headquarters authorizing the slave's owner to search the camp, Brown refused to allow the man to enter his tent. During the ensuing argument, the slave escaped, and "as far as most of the men were concerned, the fugitive had their sympathy and they hoped he never would be caught."[54]

Even more of an omen of the future was a similar incident in the camp of the 7th Pennsylvania, also in Tennessee:

Early one morning, a party of eight armed men presented themselves at the entrance of the camp, with an order from General Rousseau, commanding in Nashville, authorizing them to search for, and if found, seize a certain colored man, claimed as the property of one of the party. The officer of the day . . . escorted them . . . through the regiment, offering every possible facility to assist them in the search. The political complexion of all the companies, except one, was that

53. Sipes, *The Seventh Pennsylvania*, 15.
54. Crofts, *Third Ohio Veteran Volunteer Cavalry*, 47.

of decided Democrats, and but little anti-slavery sentiment was heard in the regiment. . . . The search commenced at K company, and progressed without incident . . . until they came to the rear of C company, when a colored man ran out of the cook-tent, and darting through the company streets, sought to gain the woods. The visitors called excitedy to him to stop: "Stop, you d——d nigger!" . . . "Stop, or I'll shoot," &c.: at the same time dashing after him at a gallop, and firing their guns indiscriminately in the direction in which he was running. The officer of the day commanded them to halt and cease firing in camp, but they paid no attention to him. . . . Almost instantly, however, after they opened fire, the soldiers, as one man, flew to arms, surrounded the citizens, dismounted and disarmed them . . . and marched them, as prisoners, to the colonel's quarters. . . . The entire political sentiment of the regiment was changed by the incident, and henceforth, it was one of the strongest anti-slavery regiments in the service.[55]

It was "one of the strongest," perhaps, but not *the* strongest. That distinction unquestionably belongs to the 7th Kansas. Its Company K was raised and commanded by Captain John Brown, Jr., and after his resignation because of ill health, by George H. Hoyt, who had been one of the elder Brown's defense lawyers at his trial for treason at Charles Town, Virginia. Hoyt, appointed provost marshal of Humboldt, Tennessee, posted the following notice on the door of his headquarters: "Slave hunting at this post or within the jurisdiction of the undersigned is strictly prohibited. Persons from whom bondsmen have escaped are hereby notified that all men are regarded as 'Free' and 'Equal' at this office and will therefore desist from invoking the military power in aid of their efforts at rendition."[56] Lieutenant Colonel Daniel Read Anthony of the same regiment, brother of Susan B. Anthony and member of a fervently abolitionist family, was in command of General R. B. Mitchell's cavalry brigade in the general's absence and took advantage of the opportunity by issuing the following general orders to the brigade:

1. The impudence and impertinence of the open and armed Rebels,

55. Vale, *Minty and the Cavalry*, 52–53. William B. Sipes, who commanded the regiment, wrote, "The regiment, without being at all tainted by politics, was very far from entertaining abolition ideas when it entered the slave holding states, but contact with the institution, as exhibited by owners and slaves, soon revolutionized its views." Sipes, *The Seventh Pennsylvania*, 14.

56. Leavenworth, Kansas *Conservative*, July 11, 1862.

Traitors, Secessionists and Southern-Rights men of this section of Tennessee in arrogantly demanding the right to search our camp for their fugitive slaves has become a nuisance, and will no longer be tolerated. Officers will see to it that this class of men who visit our camp for this purpose are excluded from our lines.

2. Should any such parties be found within the lines, they will be arrested. . . .

3. Any officer or soldier of this command who shall arrest and deliver to his master a fugitive slave shall be summarily and severely punished.[57]

The first close look at the South that eastern cavalrymen had was in northern Virginia in the winter of 1861–1862 and the spring of 1862. This was before the repeated marches and countermarches of the armies had turned the region into a wilderness, but the impress of war was already plainly visible. The initial impression the 1st Maine gained of Virginia as it marched south from Washington was anything but favorable:

The roads were muddy and in bad order, and houses were few and far between, not particularly good, even before the war, and now presenting a dilapidated, tumble-down appearance. The whole country wore a deserted, unhealthy look, to which the earth-works, abandoned camp-grounds, and the waste and destruction that accompany an army . . . added an extra gloom. There was an indescribable feeling of sadness on the part of the boys, as they were introduced to and began to learn what the devastation of the war meant, which the exhilaration of being at last on the way to the front . . . could hardly overcome.[58]

A few months later, but still in 1862, Charles Francis Adams described what he and his regiment saw on their way to Stratford Heights:

Our road lay . . . in sight of Mount Vernon and was a picture of desolation—the inhabitants few, primitive and ignorant, houses deserted and going to ruin, fences down, plantations overgrown, and everything indicating a decaying country finally ruined by war. On our second day we passed through Dumfries . . . now the most god-forsaken village I ever saw. There were large houses with tumbled down

57. Manuscript copy of order in Kansas State Historical Society, Topeka; the order is also quoted in John A. Logan, *The Great Conspiracy: Its Origin and History* (New York, 1886), 397–98.
58. Tobie, *First Maine Cavalry*, 50.

stairways, public buildings completely in ruins, more than half the houses deserted and tumbling to pieces, not one in repair, and even the inhabitants, as, dirty, lazy and rough they stared at us with a sort of apathetic hate, seemed relapsing into barbarism.[59]

The troopers of the 1st Ohio were "surprised" at the neglected appearance even of Mount Vernon. The local citizens' "little interest" in the historic building was sufficient proof, as far as the Ohioans were concerned, of "the loss of all true patriotism by the people of the South."[60]

And it was much the same in Tennessee. Near Nashville, "beautiful, rolling land stretched away on every side. . . . But it was mournfully desolate. Houses along the road were, for the most part, deserted; and where they were not, only a few women and children appeared, staring in wondering silence at the passing Yankees. One village through which we passed was entirely uninhabited; houses and stores were open but empty; not a living thing was to be seen in the place. The fences along the road were stripped away, leaving only scattered heaps of black ashes and charred rails, along which had gathered in turn the Federals and the Confederates."[61]

Some of the desolation that shocked Adams and saddened the orderly and thrifty troopers from Maine was the result of the aimless, haphazard destruction caused by armies on the march; much of it, however, was the consequence of deliberate and wanton destruction. Houses abandoned by their owners were invariably ransacked and their contents destroyed or carried away; books were taken by officers and men alike and thrown away after they had been read or when they merely became a burden to carry. Dr. Hard of the 8th Illinois, "when passing the house of a Dr. Randolph . . . saw books strewn over the fields for a distance of half a mile."[62] Pohick Church, in the woods near Mount Ver-

59. Ford, *A Cycle of Adams Letters*, I, 200.
60. Gillespie, *A History of Company A*, 97. Gillespie adds, on an "It has been said" basis, that "if a man traveling through Virginia would feed his horse only when he came to a school house his horse would starve." *Ibid.*, 133.
61. John A. B. Williams, *Leaves from a Trooper's Diary* (Philadelphia, 1869), 67.
62. Hard, *History of the Eighth Cavalry*, 98; see also Beach, *First New York (Lincoln) Cavalry*, 67.

non, was historic because of its age and its association with George Washington. The historian of the 11th New York visited the church while his regiment was camped nearby, and he found the "interior a scene of . . . vandalism; cavalry had evidently used it as a picket station; one pew only was left, the others having probably been used for firewood. The one remaining pew was said to have been spared because of its having been occupied by the Father of his Country."[63]

In their march up the Shenandoah Valley in the summer of 1862 in pursuit of the elusive Stonewall Jackson, the men of the 1st New Jersey saw "in every direction . . . a frightful scene of devastation. Furniture, valuable in itself and utterly useless to . . . [the soldiers] was mutilated and defaced; beds were defiled and cut to pieces; pictures and mirrors were slashed with sabres or perforated by bullets; windows were broken, doors torn from their hinges, houses and barns burned down. . . . articles of crockery, the covering of . . . beds, the change of clothing necessary for comfort and decency, were rent in pieces or borne away to serve a few hours' use in camp."[64]

Fairfax Court House, prominent in the history of Virginia and of the nation, was, in 1860, the thriving seat of Fairfax County, in which Arlington and Mount Vernon were located. It began to change its appearance within hours after the 3rd Pennsylvania entered it. An eyewitness, an officer of another cavalry regiment, reports that a "spirit of mischief and plunder for a time seized upon the men, who lost all discipline and began an indiscriminate pilfering."[65] Fairfax Seminary was plundered of its valuable library, works of art, musical and scientific instruments, furniture, and everything valuable it contained. And the same officer remarks, "I regret to say that some of the worst cases of plundering . . . were committed either by . . . officers, or by those who would share with them the ill-gotten gains."[66]

63. Smith, "Scott's 900," Eleventh New York, 64.
64. Pyne, First New Jersey Cavalry, 70–71. Pyne reports that the troopers of his own regiment "had once or twice attempted wanton destruction and unlicensed pillage, but the practice had been at once and sternly checked." Ibid., 70.
65. Adams, The Story of a Trooper, 289.
66. Ibid., 200.

When the 1st Maine reached Fairfax Court House a few days later, it found the venerable old courthouse already "sadly desecrated. From top to bottom the walls were defaced, while record books, deeds, bonds, wills, inventories, mortgages and papers of all kinds were scattered about the floors with every appearance of having been overhauled time and again."[67] One of the sergeants of the 1st New York found in the heap of papers a document dated "in the fifth year of the reign of our sovereign lord King George the Third" and signed by George Washington; an officer of the regiment tried to buy the paper from him, but the sergeant, who evidently had a shrewd idea of its value, wanted more for it than the officer was willing to pay.[68]

Certainly, the cavalry did not have a monopoly of plundering and vandalism. Charles Francis Adams commented in one of his letters that "[The Virginians] say they don't fear the cavalry, but they dread the infantry and the Germans [of the XI Corps]. . . . I can only say if they don't fear the cavalry, I don't want to see those they do fear, as I see only the Cavalry, and I daily see from them acts of pillage and outrage on the poor and defenceless which make my hair stand on end and cause me to loathe all war."[69] And, too, the plundering and destruction were not the work of a few exceptionally vicious regiments, nor were they confined to Virginia. Adams' own regiment, the 1st Massachusetts, did more than its share while stationed on Beaufort Island, South Carolina, in February, 1862: "Here was a new house on a beautiful island . . . built evidently by a gentleman of refinement . . . and there was the garden before it filled with rubbish, and with broken furniture, scraps of books and letters. . . . Scattered over the floors, piled in the corners were the remains of a fine library . . . and panels and glasses were broken whenever so doing was thought an easier course than to unlock or open. . . . I thought how I should feel to see such sights at Quincy."[70]

67. Tobie, *First Maine Cavalry*, 50.
68. Stevenson, *"Boots and Saddles,"* 83.
69. Ford, *A Cycle of Adams Letters*, II, 73.
70. *Ibid.*, I, 111–12. It is important to add that the "depredations," as they were called, in northern Virginia, were by no means entirely the work of undisciplined and unprincipled Federals. The Confederates encamped at Manassas were equally guilty, and without the excuse of being

Samuel Gillespie of the 1st Ohio visited the house of a "distinguished rebel named Colonel Conn" near Woodstock, in the Shenandoah Valley. "The house was deserted and the furniture destroyed. A fine piano had been chopped to pieces with an axe and the keys carried away. Fine mirrors were broken, chairs, tables and every portable thing had been carried away or wantonly destroyed."[71] In the West, on the Kansas-Missouri border, "jayhawking"—a fancy word for unmitigated robbery and plundering, with murder and arson added—was developed into a fine art by the 7th Kansas, under its first colonel, Charles Rainsford Jennison.

The Army of the Potomac was to experience more than one winter of discontent, but none so trying to the spirits and morale of its men as its first, the winter of 1861–1862. The long period of inactivity, while General McClellan built and organized his huge army and tried to decide when, where, and how to use it, was a sore trial to President Lincoln and no less so to cavalrymen, who were condemned to spend the winter in squalid, unhealthy camps deep in mud, drilling when the weather and the footing allowed, doing bootless errands around Washington, going on picket and on an occasional scout, and having the fine edge of their eagerness and enthusiasm blunted by the evident lack of progress in putting down the rebellion.[72] No doubt many of them realized that time was needed to organize, equip, and train the army if the disgrace of Bull Run was not to be repeated, and in a curious way McClellan even became the object of their admiration and hero worship. And yet, being young, impatient by nature, and heirs of a national tradition desiring quick results, of the "let's get on with it" spirit, they were heartily sick of the lack of activity long before the winter was over. There were Grand Reviews, in which they caught glimpses of the president and of

in enemy country. General R. S. Ewell wrote in March, 1862, "The depredations and outrages committed by this army . . . are as bad as though they had been in the enemy's country. Every bad soldier is trying to get off from his company to pillage and maraud." Hamlin, "Old Bald Head," 76.

71. Gillespie, A History of Company A, 68.
72. Hard, History of the Eighth Cavalry, 46; see also Beach, First New York (Lincoln) Cavalry, 92.

the general-in-chief. And there were snowball fights in which the contending armies "went through all the manoeuvers of battle; throwing out skirmishers, executing flank movements, and charging in fine style," with the losers "driven into their tents amid the shouts and cheers of the victors." Such things were all to the good, and pleasant entertainment, but it was not to trot past reviewing stands, or to win snowball fights, that they had joined the cavalry.[73] They wanted to get at the job, win the war, and go home.

73. Stevenson, *"Boots and Saddles,"* 76.

X

Who Ever Saw
a Dead Cavalryman?

GENERAL WINFIELD SCOTT, AGED AND ILL, RETIRED ON
November 1, 1861. On the same day, George B. McClellan, still
short of his thirty-sixth birthday, was appointed general-in-chief,
at the same time retaining direct command of the Army of the
Potomac. What he proposed to do with that army, and when, was
what the president, the entire administration, the press, and indeed his own soldiers and the whole country were wondering
about.

Three months later, still without an answer, the president issued his Special War Order No. 1. It directed that on or before
February 22, the Army of the Potomac was to break up its camps
and engage Joseph E. Johnston's army, which, free from Federal
molestation, was peacefully wintering at Manassas, practically
within sight of Washington. Thus spurred to action, McClellan
unveiled his plan on February 3. Starting from the premise that
"it was by no means certain" that the Confederates, whose numbers he greatly overestimated, could be beaten at Manassas, Mc-
Clellan offered an alternative whose success he "regard[ed] as
certain by all the chances of war."[1] Rather than fight the Confed-

1. Quoted in Williams, *Lincoln Finds a General*, I, 141.

erates at Manassas and then follow the long, hazardous, and logistically difficult overland route to Richmond, he proposed moving his army by water down Chesapeake Bay to Urbanna, at the mouth of the Rappahannock, and with a secure and easy line of communications from that point back to his base in Washington, the army would march to Richmond, less than fifty miles away. Should Urbanna prove impracticable as a forward base for any reason, then, said McClellan, he would land his army at Fort Monroe instead and, with the Potomac-Chesapeake Bay-York River as his line of communications, would get at Richmond by marching up the Peninsula.

McClellan's plan was eventually approved, subject to the proviso that he was to leave sufficient troops behind so that "Washington shall be . . . entirely secure." Before he could put his plan into execution, however, two events occurred: word reached Washington on March 9 that the Confederate army had disappeared from Manassas, and four days later a council of war of McClellan's corps commanders decided against Urbanna and in favor of Fort Monroe as the forward base.[2] The campaign against Richmond was thus to be an advance up the Peninsula.

By mid-March the shipping needed to move the Army of the Potomac, its impedimenta, and supplies to Fort Monroe was assembled, a huge armada of 113 steamers, 188 schooners, and 88 barges, and on March 17 the troops began to embark. McClellan was to have under his command four corps of infantry, but the government held back one of these for the defense of Washington, and McClellan regrouped the remaining three, plus the reinforcements sent to him, into five army corps under Generals Edwin V. Sumner, Erasmus D. Keyes, S. P. Heintzelman, FitzJohn Porter, and William B. Franklin. He began the campaign with an army made up of 150 regiments of infantry, 59 batteries of field artillery, a siege train of heavy artillery, 2⅓ regiments of engineers, and a miscellany of sharpshooter companies, medical and quartermaster units, and headquarters troops.[3]

McClellan was to write in his report on the campaign that "The country [*i.e.*, the Peninsula], notwithstanding its early settlement, was *terra incognita*. We knew the York River and the

2. *Ibid.*, 156.
3. *Official Records*, Vol. XI, Pt. 2, pp. 24–37.

James River, and we had heard of the Chickahominy, and this was about the extent of our knowledge. Our maps were so incorrect that they were found to be worthless."[4] Even in the absence of other military uses for it, a strong, well organized and well led cavalry would have been of great benefit to McClellan, merely to explore and map the twisted, meandering country roads and obscure plantation paths over which he had to move his troops, and to locate the many natural obstacles—dense woods, streams, and swamps—that made movement on the Peninsula a military nightmare.[5] However, the manner in which McClellan had seen fit to organize his cavalry made it impossible for him to take a powerful mounted force to Fort Monroe, even if he had wanted to, or to use it properly after it got there. The II Army Corps had attached to it four companies of the 6th New York; the III, the 3rd Pennsylvania; the IV, Colonel David McM. Gregg's 8th Pennsylvania; Porter's V Army Corps, the largest, with three divisions of infantry instead of the others' two each, had a mere two companies of the 5th Pennsylvania. As a separate unit, commanded by General Philip St. George Cooke, there was the "Cavalry Reserve," made up of the 6th Pennsylvania, the 6th United States, and four companies each of the 1st and 5th United States. The functions and mission of the Cavalry Reserve were of the vaguest description, and it is difficult not to conclude that it was merely a grouping for administrative convenience of all the cavalry left over after each of the corps of infantry had received its packet.

In addition to the cavalry already mentioned, McClellan had

4. *Ibid.*, Pt. 1, p. 126.
5. W. W. Averell noted that the "topography and soil of the peninsula presented a most difficult field for cavalry operations. From Fort Monroe to Hanover Court House there was hardly a field with sufficient scope for the manoeuvers of a single regiment of cavalry. After a rain the deep alluvium became, under the tread of horses, a bed of mortar knee deep. The forests were filled with tangled thickets and unapproachable morasses. These conditions made cavalry operations in this region affairs of squadrons." R. V. Johnson and C. C. Buel (eds.), *Battles and Leaders of the Civil War* (4 vols.; New York, 1887–1888), II, 429, hereinafter cited as *Battles and Leaders*. In his report on a reconnaissance from Hanover Court House toward Richmond, Colonel Jesse A. Gove of the 22nd Massachusetts Infantry wrote, "There is no point along the road . . . where cavalry or artillery could be used outside of the road. . . . The character of the whole country is low and swampy."*Official Records*, Vol. XI, Pt. 1, p. 712.

at his headquarters the 2nd United States, two companies of the 4th United States, and two unattached companies of volunteer cavalry, the McClellan Dragoons from Illinois and the Oneida Cavalry from New York. Finally, floating in a vague state of independence, there was the 1st New York, which was not, so far as can be determined, attached to anything or anyone. Thus, for a huge army of 210 infantry regiments and artillery batteries, McClellan had 8 complete regiments of cavalry, plus enough odd companies (16, representing 5 different regiments) to make up the equivalent of another 1½ regiments.[6]

Years later, McClellan declared that he had been "sadly deficient in that important arm [*i.e.*, the cavalry] as many of the regiments belonging to the Army of the Potomac were among those which had been retained near Washington."[7] There is nothing to suggest that McClellan did not have a free hand to take with him as large a force of cavalry as he thought he needed, but he misused even the cavalry he did have. Had he organized his nine and a half regiments of cavalry into a three-brigade division, properly led at the brigade and division level and properly used, the cavalry could conceivably have had a decisive effect on the course of the campaign. The volunteer portion of his cavalry was inexperienced—though no more so than the cavalry on the other side—and there were no cavalry officers with proven ability to command brigades or a division, but given McClellan's overcautious, hesitant direction of the entire campaign, it is doubtful if a larger, better organized cavalry could have had a significant effect on the outcome. It is at any rate certain that split up as it was and hampered by inexperience at all levels, not much could have been expected of the cavalry; in general, its performance

6. These data are a summary of *Official Records*, Vol. XI, Pt. 2, pp. 24–37, and represent the organization in the period from June 25 to July 2. As initially organized into three corps, the army included one hundred regiments of infantry, fifty-one batteries of artillery, and eight regiments plus three odd companies of cavalry. *Ibid.*, Pt. 1, pp. 279–84, covering the period from April 5 to May 4. Averell's statement, "In the Peninsular campaign there were employed 14 regiments of cavalry, entire or in parts, and two independent squadrons," (*Battles and Leaders*, II, 429) is not substantiated by the organizational lists in the *Official Records*.

7. *Battles and Leaders*, II, 173.

was of a piece with the lackluster character of the entire campaign.

The Peninsular Campaign began on April 4 with a Federal advance northwestward from Fort Monroe and came to a halt two days later before the Confederate fortifications at Yorktown. It then took McClellan a month to collect and emplace a massive concentration of heavy artillery for a textbook siege, which the Confederates forestalled by evacuating the defenses on May 4, just as McClellan's preparations were completed. The Federal advance now resumed, interrupted briefly by a fight at Williamsburg. By the end of May the Confederates had retreated to the outer defenses of Richmond. The Union army faced them with the corps of Keyes and Heintzelman to the south of the Chickahominy, a swampy, treacherous stream. Keyes and Heintzelman became isolated from the three corps still on the north bank by a violent storm on May 30 that washed away several of the bridges and flooded a wide area on both sides of the stream. The next day, the Confederates attacked Keyes and Heintzelman at Fair Oaks-Seven Pines, the important result of the drawn battle being the replacement of the wounded General Johnston by Robert E. Lee as commander of the Army of Northern Virginia. A month later, on June 25 at Oak Grove, began the battles of the Seven Days—Mechanicsville, Gaines's Mill, Savage Station, Frayser's Farm, and Malvern Hill—at the conclusion of which the Army of the Potomac, minus sixteen thousand casualties, lay under the protection of Federal gunboats at Harrison's Landing on the James River. The army had given a good account of itself, but with the campaign in ruins McClellan was the Young Napoleon no longer.

In early March, when preparations began for the movement of the Army of the Potomac to Fort Monroe, the cavalry units scheduled to go received orders to leave behind all their dismounted men and all their sick; the latter were to be sent to the general hospital or given their discharges.[8] Only fully sound horses were to be taken and no nonregulation baggage.[9] The col-

8. Beach, *First New York (Lincoln) Cavalry*, 97; Hard, *History of the Eighth Cavalry*, 105.
9. Each company of the 3rd Pennsylvania was provided with a large packing case into which the men had to deposit their nonregulation cloth-

onel of the 1st New York was ordered to make requisition for a supply of entrenching tools—spades, picks, shovels, and axes; the men must have wondered what purpose such gear would serve in the hands of a regiment whose anticipated role was to deliver thundering charges against the enemy.[10] The journey to Fort Monroe was anything but pleasant, but it was mercifully short. The horses were carried on the open decks of transports, in two long rows facing inwards, with no room for the animals to lie down and no protection from the elements. The men slept where and when they could find space to lie or sit; there were of course no bunks. Nonetheless, the change from the increasingly irksome routine of the camps around Washington was universally welcomed, and when the march up the Peninsula actually began, the men greeted the commanding general with enthusiastic cheers whenever they caught sight of him.[11]

The role played by the cavalry from the beginning to the end of the campaign was of such minor importance that a detailed recital of its marches and skirmishes would contribute little of value to a history of Civil War cavalry operations, other than to establish a baseline of mediocrity and to point up the low estate from which the Federal cavalry was eventually and painfully to rise. Nevertheless, a number of incidents deserve to be described. They do not involve corps or divisions of veteran cavalrymen schooled in all the ramifications of a difficult trade, but mainly novices, most of whom, at any rate in the volunteer units, had never been exposed to enemy fire. They were now operating in small groups, on an unfavorable terrain, in an enervating climate. When the operations against the enemy began, not even the eight regiments that were on the Peninsula as complete regiments were ordinarily used as integral units; generally, it was a company here, or two or three companies there. The 1st New York was broken up into detachments as soon as it landed and did not again assemble as a regiment until, four months later, it got ready

---

ing and gear, to be stored until they got back to Washington. They never saw the boxes again. Regimental History Committee, *History of the 3d Pennsylvania*, 40.

10. Beach, *First New York (Lincoln) Cavalry*, 97.
11. *Ibid.*, 112.

to embark for the return trip North. Meanwhile, its squadrons, companies, and smaller groups did picket and outpost duty for the infantry and went on scouts, but their principal occupation was to serve as escorts and orderlies for corps and divisional commanders.[12] The work was arduous enough; when, at the end of the Seven Days, several detachments of the regiment reached Harrison's Landing, the men were "entirely played out" and their horses had not been unsaddled for six days.[13]

Toward the end of the campaign, General George Stoneman reported to McClellan, "Commanding officers of scouting parties and brigade commanders complain that the men of their commands are taken away by generals, colonels and other officers to act as orderlies, &c. I have the honor to request that the general commanding give orders that this be stopped in future."[14] The fact that such a request had to be made in the midst of a campaign goes at least part way to explain the undistinguished performance of the cavalry. Stoneman at any rate had ill health as an excuse; he went through the campaign "with infirmities that would have kept a man of less fortitude in the hospital."[15] Moreover, under circumstances that the records fail to explain, he was at times in direct command of what appear to have been hastily collected groups of cavalrymen, and at other times he performed only the administrative duties McClellan had relegated to his chief of cavalry. The future was to show that Stoneman was not in the first rank, or even in the second, as a dynamic, aggressive leader of cavalry, but the impossible command structure McClellan had established for his cavalry is certainly responsible to a major degree for Stoneman's weak performance in this his first campaign.

Leadership of questionable competence, indistinct lines of command, and poor organization were problems for the upper echelons to deal with, or to ignore. The men in the ranks had

---

12. *Ibid.*, 121, 123, 130–31, 161.
13. Stevenson, *"Boots and Saddles,"* 119.
14. Dispatch dated July 10, 1862, in *Official Records*, Vol. XI, Pt. 2, p. 930; Regimental History Committee, *History of the 3d Pennsylvania*, 96.
15. *Battles and Leaders*, II, 430. In fact, Stoneman went on sick leave when the cavalry reached Harrison's Landing.

their own problems, which they could not easily dismiss. There was, to begin with, the matter of health. The drinking water from the wells and springs, mostly brackish, caused an epidemic of diarrhea.[16] As a not too successful prophylactic against the prevalent fevers, the men were issued a daily ration of quinine and whiskey.[17] When, after the Seven Days, the army encamped at Harrison's Landing, the crowding together of a hundred thousand men and thousands of animals in a constricted, low-lying, marshy area, coupled with the midsummer heat and poor camp sanitation, brought on a veritable plague of flies. The men were eager for picket duty as an escape from the stench and flies of the camp, and the horses were "so worried, and wore themselves out so completely, stamping their feet and whisking their heads and tails, that many of them became unable to stand up, and actually died of exhaustion and the sting of the flies"; the 3rd Pennsylvania alone lost seventy horses in three weeks in this way.[18] On the other hand, on the favorable side, there were the novel excitements of a first full-fledged campaign. Sabers were sharpened, and the troopers had the pleasure of watching the ascensions of Professor T. S. Lowe's observation balloons. Encamped within reach of the York or the James, the men fished for crabs, which, with biscuits bought from the ubiquitous Negroes, made a wel-

16. Hard, *History of the Eighth Cavalry*, 106.
17. Regimental History Committee, *History of the 3d Pennsylvania*, 76.
18. *Ibid.*, 98, 101; Gracey, *Annals of the 6th*, 80–81. As to camp sanitation, W. W. Averell, commanding a brigade under Stoneman, reported on July 23, "I regret exceedingly that there should have been any grounds for complaints of the condition of the police, &c., of the 1st New York. Now that Lieutenant-Colonel von Schickfuss has assumed command of that regiment there is hope for a better state of things. I have now a hundred spades at work, and will soon present the brigade in an improved condition." *Official Records*, Vol. XI, Pt. 2, p. 932. The reference to von Schickfuss was a backhanded compliment to Colonel Andrew McReynolds, who left the army and went to Washington to protest, after Averell, junior to him in rank, has been appointed brigade commander. Beach, *First New York (Lincoln) Cavalry*, 158–59. On an earlier occasion, the historian of the 8th Illinois noted, "The First New York . . . encamped by the side of our hospital . . . were very noisy; besides which they left their dead horses lay in close proximity to us, until we were obliged to complain to their colonel to abate the nuisance." Hard, *History of the Eighth Cavalry*, 135–36.

come and salutary change from army salt pork and hardtack. Northern newspapers arrived regularly, were peddled through the camps, and were eagerly read.

One of the cavalrymen present on the Peninsula was recently promoted Captain George A. Custer of the 5th United States, a year out of West Point, having graduated last in the thirty-four-man Class of 1861. Young Captain Custer was beginning to make a name for himself as much for his bravery as for his sartorial idiosyncracies, the latter of which, however, were not to come to full flower until the following year, when he was described by a more conservatively minded colleague as having the appearance of a circus rider gone mad. John W. Lea of Mississippi, a classmate of Custer's at West Point, had gone with his state and became an officer in the Confederate army. While recovering from a wound and on parole at Williamsburg, he became engaged to marry a local belle. On the day of the wedding, shortly after the end of the Seven Days' battles, Lea wore a brand-new full-dress uniform of a Confederate officer, made of the finest gray cloth and plentifully decorated with gold braid. His best man, dressed for the role in the full uniform of a Union cavalry officer, was none other than his classmate, good friend, and official enemy, Captain George A. Custer.[19]

Captain E. J. Farnsworth, Company K, 8th Illinois, on picket with his company, sent an invitation to the officers at regimental headquarters to visit him and view at first hand the hardships of life on a picket post. On arrival, "they found the Captain's headquarters in an elegant mansion, which had been deserted by the owners—the colored people preferring to remain."

The guests were ushered into the splendidly furnished parlors, and after a short time, were invited into the dining hall, where the table was groaning under its weight of luxuries. Colored waiters were in attendance. . . . The china was of the most exquisite pattern, and silver spoons, forks, etc., in abundance. After the substantials were disposed of . . . the dishes were removed, and the waiters brought from the cellars some of the rich old wine, such as Virginia planters usually keep. After dinner, an elegant carriage, with silver mounted harness, was brought to the door to escort the guests to the picket posts.[20]

19. Frederick Whittaker, *A Complete Life of General George A. Custer* (New York, 1876), 127.
20. Hard, *History of the Eighth Cavalry*, 131.

But life for the 8th Illinois was not ease and luxury unalloyed. On the night of June 29, after the fight at Savage Station, the regiment escorted the army's huge wagon train to the James River. The seventy ambulances in the train were loaded to capacity, "yet thousands of sick and wounded were on foot, begging earnestly that they might be permitted to ride."

The night became very dark; vivid lightning flashed . . . peals of thunder rent the air, which, mingled with the roar of cannon in our rear, made the night hideous. . . . Squads of rebel cavalry were in front . . . and although the road could not be seen save when a flash of lightning broke in through the inky darkness, we were ordered not to light a lantern for fear the enemy's cavalry, which hung about our flank, would send the deadly minie ball in our midst. Many times did we dismount and pull the weary and wounded footmen out of the road and under the horses' hoofs, where they had sunk down, too exhausted to go farther or even crawl from beneath the wheels of the train.[21]

The historian of the 1st New York has recorded to the credit of the men from Illinois that they "would dismount and help the wounded to the saddle, while they themselves would walk."[22]

The 6th Pennsylvania also received an initiation into the harsher side of war. Their vaunted lances turned out to be an unmitigated failure as an offensive weapon in the tangle of underbrush and woods in which much of their fighting on the Peninsula had to be done. But even when the terrain was suitable, their

21. *Ibid.*, 151. At an earlier stage of the campaign, the advance of the army was held up at Black Creek, a deep stream with high, muddy banks. The bridges over the stream had been destroyed by the retreating Confederates. Colonel Farnsworth of the 8th Illinois learned that "West Point engineers had taken a survey of the spot . . . [and] had made a profile view of the structure to be erected . . . which had consumed much valuable time and was likely to occupy many days more. . . . 'I can take a few of my men and construct a bridge in half a day'" said Farnsworth, and he was told to go ahead; "a small squad of the Eighth went to work and in two hours and a half constructed a substantial bridge of logs." *Ibid.*, 120–21. On July 2, when the army moved from Malvern Hill to Harrison's Landing, General Keyes wanted Turkey Bridge broken up to block the Confederate pursuit. The 8th Illinois demonstrated that it was as capable of destroying a bridge as it was of building one. Keyes called for twenty-five axmen "on whom [he] could rely"; in fifteen minutes after the last of the Federals had crossed, the 8th Illinois had the bridge down. *Official Records*, Vol. XI, Pt. 2, p. 194.
22. Beach, *First New York (Lincoln) Cavalry*, 134.

lack of experience with the exotic weapon placed the "Lancers" at a serious disadvantage. General Lee's plan to drive McClellan away from the outskirts of Richmond required Stonewall Jackson to descend from the northwest upon the unprotected right and rear of the Union army. Stuart, marching with his cavalry along Jackson's outer (left) flank, met the 6th Pennsylvania on June 27. "I felt," wrote W. W. Blackford, a member of Stuart's staff, "a little creeping of the flesh when I saw this splendid looking body of men, about seven hundred strong, drawn up in line of battle in a large open field two or three hundred yards off, armed with long poles with glittering steel points. . . . The appearance they presented was certainly very fine, with a tall forest of lances held erect, and at the end of each, just below the head, a red pennant fluttering in the breeze." If Blackford and Heros von Borcke, Stuart's volunteer aide, late of the Prussian army, are to be believed, the Pennsylvanians here learned that the lance is a fine weapon for an attack, but useless for defense. Stuart was not at all frightened by the forest of lances; he "quickly threw a regiment into line and ordered the charge . . . and down upon them we swept with a yell, at full speed. They lowered their lances to a level and started in fine style to meet us midway, but long before we reached them the gay lancers' hearts failed them and they turned to fly. For miles the exciting chase was kept up, the road was strewn with lances thrown away in their flight, and nothing but the fleetness of their horses saved them all from capture."[23]

General Lee's plan of campaign was based on information Stuart had brought back from the most glamorous of his exploits, his ride around McClellan's army. Directed to locate the end of McClellan's lines north of the Chickahominy and also the Union lines of communication back to their supply base on the York,

23. Blackford, *War Years with Jeb Stuart*, 72–73; Heros von Borcke, *Memoirs of the Confederate War for Independence* (2 vols.; New York, 1938), I, 54, has the same story. Indeed, the two accounts are sufficiently alike to suggest that Blackford based the quoted passage on von Borcke's previously published book. Both accounts appear to be greatly exaggerated. Stuart, never one to play down his triumphs, reported merely that "all day we were skirmishing with, killing and capturing small detachments of the enemy's cavalry, mostly the Lancers." *Official Records*, Vol. XI, Pt. 2, p. 514. There is no mention of an incident even faintly resembling the Blackford and von Borcke stories in the 6th Pennsylvania regimental history.

Stuart started out on the morning of June 12 with four regiments of cavalry and a section of horse artillery. After riding north from Richmond that day as far as the South Anna River, he turned east and then southeast toward Hanover Court House and Old Church. This brought him to the rear of FitzJohn Porter's corps, which formed the right wing of the Federal line. About noon of the second day—Friday, June 13—at Gibson's Mill, Stuart had his first brush with the Federals, a hundred-man picket of the 5th United States, subsequently reinforced to about two hundred men and commanded by Captain William B. Royall.[24] Charged in a column of fours by a squadron of the 9th Virginia, the Federals were driven back and eventually scattered, after a sharp tussle, saber to saber.[25]

General Cooke's Cavalry Reserve, for whom this turned out to be the worst possible Friday the thirteenth, was stationed near Porter's corps. At about three P.M. Cooke learned of Stuart's advance, which was accurately reported as consisting of "from 1,000 to 2,000 cavalry, some artillery."[26] But then, disastrously for Cooke, Lieutenant Richard Byrnes of the 5th United States, who had escaped after the fight with Stuart at Gibson's Mill, came in with the report that he had seen three to five regiments of infantry following the Confederate horse.[27] Cooke had a mere 240 men of the 5th and 6th Regulars immediately available, but General William H. Emory was nearby with the 6th Pennsylvania and a part of the 1st United States. Now came a series of hesita-

24. *Official Records*, Vol. XI, Pt. 1, pp. 1021, 1022. Lieutenant Edward H. Lieb, in command of the hundred-man picket which was initially attacked and forced to retreat by Stuart's advance guard, said in his report, "I felt most seriously the superiority of the enemy, who were armed with rifles and shotguns, and had my command been furnished with carbines, I would have been able to do him more injury and hold him longer in check. After I had emptied all my pistols, I drew sabres and endeavored to charge." *Ibid.*, 1022.
25. *Battles and Leaders*, II, 271–72. Colonel Fitzhugh Lee of the 1st Virginia had been a lieutenant in the 5th United States. "It was interesting and impressive to see," wrote an eyewitness, "a number of [5th United States troopers] held as prisoners, crowd around [Lee], shake hands with him, and hear them greet him in a familiar manner as 'Lieutenant'." Beale, *History of the Ninth Virginia*, 27.
26. *Official Records*, Vol. XI, Pt. 1, p. 1072.
27. *Ibid.*, 1008, 1025.

tions and inept moves on Cooke's part that caused General Porter to report, in garbled English, that he had "seen no energy or spirit in the pursuit by General Cooke of the enemy, or exhibited the characteristics of a skillful and active guardian of our flanks" and to order an investigation.[28] Intimidated by the specter of the non-existent three to five regiments of infantry, uncertain of where the raiders had gone from Gibson's Mill, and unable to decide whether he should try to protect the Federal depots at White House Landing, go after the raiders, or stay where he was and pitch into them when (as he thought possible) they retraced their route to get back to their own lines, Cooke waited for a force of infantry and artillery to join him and did not move out until the late dusk of a mid-June day.[29] Not until eight o'clock the next morning did Major Robert Morris, Jr., at the head of a squadron of the 6th Pennsylvania, strike Stuart's trail, but by that time it was too late for even cavalry to catch him; encumbered as Cooke was with infantry, it was manifestly impossible for him to do so. In midafternoon, Major Morris' squadron reached the Chicka-hominy, just as Stuart's rear guard on the far bank was setting fire to the makeshift bridge on which the Confederates had crossed the stream.[30] Stuart was now safe, with an unfordable, unbridged stream between him and his pursuers; and on the fif-teenth he arrived back in Richmond with 165 prisoners, 260 captured horses and mules, and glory enough to satisfy even his well-developed ego.[31]

In a narrowly military sense, Stuart's ride had limited value, for it merely confirmed what General Lee already suspected,

28. *Ibid.*, 1006.

29. Major Henry B. Clitz, 12th United States Infantry, was ordered by General Porter to investigate the circumstances of Stuart's escape. He reported that seven officers of the 5th United States agreed that if Cooke had moved promptly with the cavalry he had "and pursued with vigor, leaving the infantry supports to guard the road between Old Church and New Castle Ferry over the Pamunkey, as he was urged to do by Colonel [G. K.] Warren [of the 1st United States], the enemy must have been over-taken." *Ibid.*, 1007–1008.

30. Gracey, *Annals of the 6th*, 50–54.

31. It is to be regretted that Cooke failed to catch Stuart, who, as has been noted, was his son-in-law. A direct encounter between father-in-law and son-in-law would have added a memorable page to Civil War legend.

namely that McClellan's right wing was "in the air." It was this confirmation, however, that set the pattern for the combined Lee-Jackson attack on the Army of the Potomac ten days later. The dramatic impact of the ride and its moral effect far exceeded its strictly military utility. McClellan might well minimize its importance by declaring in his report, "The burning of two schooners laden with forage and 14 government wagons, destruction of some sutlers' stores, the killing of several of the guard and teamsters at Garlick's Landing, some little damage done [the Richmond & York River Railroad] at Tunstall's Station and a little *eclat* were the precise results of this expedition."[32] General Lee came much closer to the truth in calling it a "brilliant exploit."[33] Its psychological effect was enormous. Thenceforth, Stuart himself, other commanders of Confederate cavalry, and, eventually, commanders of the Federal cavalry as well, entertained a wholly unrealistic notion of the value of such hit-and-run raids. It led them to undertake harebrained, militarily useless, self-destructive enterprises like Stuart's ride around the Federal army in June, 1863, and John Hunt Morgan's Indiana-Ohio raid a month later. Such adventures made a splash in the newspapers, and a few of them, particularly the Van Dorn-Forrest raids on Grant's line of communications in December, 1862, had a significant strategic effect. Generally, however, as Federal General Jacob Dolson Cox, viewing cavalry raids with the more realistic, or perhaps jaundiced eye of an infantryman, noted, "as to the raids on both sides, the game was not worth the candle. Men and horses were used up, wholesale, without doing any permanent damage to the enemy, and never reached that training of horse and man which might have been secured by steady and systematic attention to their proper duties."[34]

The more immediate effect of Stuart's exploit was to make him the cavalryman *par excellence* of the Confederacy, in the eyes of the public and his own men as well. He was not far off the mark when he wrote in his report, in his characteristically high-flown language, "There was something of the sublime in the

32. *Official Records*, Vol. XI, Pt. 1, p. 47.
33. *Ibid.*, 1042.
34. Cox, *Military Reminiscences*, II, 290.

implicit confidence and unquestioning trust of the rank and file
in a leader [*i.e.*, himself] guiding them straight, apparently, into
the very jaws of the enemy, every step appearing to them to di-
minish the faintest hope of extrication."[35] The men not only
gained "implicit confidence" in Stuart's leadership, but what was
equally important, they gained confidence in themselves. And for
the Federal troopers involved in the mismanaged, unimaginative,
futile chase, there was a well advertised, humiliating failure to
digest. It is tempting, but perhaps risky, to read into the minds
of the rank and file of the Federal cavalry a sense of failure or
of inferiority; it may well be a distortion of history to accept without question the unanimous postwar comments to that effect
made by regimental historians and writers of reminiscences. Still,
the blue cavalrymen would have had to be less perceptive and
less intelligent than they were if, after an event like Stuart's un-
hindered ride around the army they had the responsibility of protecting, they had not felt that something was radically wrong
with the way they were used and led.

Ten days after Stuart's exploit, another failure of the Federal
cavalry had to be entered in the records. Jackson's army had left
the Shenandoah Valley and was on its way to Richmond via Ashland. Pursuant to General Lee's plans, on June 26 the divisions
of D. H. Hill, A. P. Hill, and James Longstreet were to cross to the
north bank of the Chickahominy, wheel to their right, drive the
Federals out of Mechanicsville, and attack their main position,
manned by Porter's corps, on the ridge above the east bank of
Beaver Dam Creek.[36] At the same time Jackson, coming down
from the northwest with 18,500 of his own men and four regiments of Stuart's cavalry, was to turn the headwaters of the creek
and attack the unprotected Federal right (or northern) flank.

McClellan had had word two days before from Stoneman,
commanding what Federal cavalry there was out beyond his right

35. *Official Records*, Vol. XI, Pt. 1, p. 1038.
36. The historian of the 8th Illinois professed to believe that Mechanicsville got its name by virtue "of its great superiority in mechanic
arts," having *two* blacksmith shops, whereas the general run of Virginia
settlements made do with only one. Hard, *History of the Eighth Cavalry*,
123.

flank, that Jackson had reached Frederick's Hall.[37] This was an effective piece of scouting and a good mark for Stoneman and his horsemen. It was in response to this obvious threat to his flank that McClellan had Porter occupy the Beaver Dam position. Due to poor staff work and Jackson's delayed arrival, the Confederate attack on the twenty-sixth miscarried and was beaten off with loss. Nevertheless, McClellan decided to pull Porter back nearer the main body of his army and had him occupy a naturally strong position above and to the east of Boatswain "Swamp," actually a small, sluggish stream that flowed southward a half mile to the east of Gaines's Mill, toward the Chickahominy.

Behind the left, or southern, flank of Porter's line there was a level area running down to the Chickahominy. It was here that Porter posted General Cooke, who had under his command five companies of the 5th United States, four "skeleton" companies of the 1st United States, and six companies of the 6th Pennsylvania, which, Colonel Rush complained, were in poor condition, "men and horses worn down . . . with previous picket and outpost duty. Some of the companies had not been unsaddled for a week."[38] Cooke's orders, according to General Porter, were "to watch [the] left flank, and should an opportunity occur, to strike the enemy on the plain. He was told that he would have nothing to do on the hill"; indeed, "under no circumstances [was he] to appear upon the crest."[39]

The attack on Porter's position, manned by George Sykes's division on the right and G. W. Morell's on the left, got under way at 2:30 in the afternoon and, in the five hours that it lasted, produced some of the grimmest, most costly fighting of the entire war.[40] Every Confederate assault was beaten off until, just at sunset, John B. Hood's Texas brigade advanced through the dusk and the dense battle smoke, crossed the swamp at a lope, and broke into Morrell's position. Cooke was on the ridge where three of Morell's reserve batteries were posted. He saw the Federal front

37. *Official Records*, Vol. XI, Pt. 2, p. 19.
38. *Ibid.*, 45.
39. *Ibid.*, 224–25.
40. A superb description of the battle is to be found in Douglas S. Freeman, *R. E. Lee: A Biography* (4 vols.; New York, 1941), II, 136–57.

line beginning to give way, whereupon "Without orders . . . [he] instantly conducted the Fifth and First Cavalry to the front, and deployed them in two lines . . . just filling the interval of the two right batteries." He then ordered Captain Charles J. Whiting, in command of the five companies of the 5th United States, "to charge when the support or safety of the batteries required it."[41] As one of Whiting's men remembered it, however, what Cooke actually said was, "Captain, as soon as you see the advancing line of the enemy rising the crest of the hill, charge at once, without any further orders, to enable the artillery to bring off their guns" —a very different thing.[42] Cooke then directed Colonel George A. H. Blake of the 1st United States to support Whiting with his four under-strength companies and placed the 6th Pennsylvania, with similar orders, to the left of the southernmost battery.[43] Whatever Cooke's exact language to Whiting may have been, or however Whiting may have interpreted it, he turned at once to his men, ordered them to draw sabers, and charged in two lines down the hill against the oncoming Confederates, 250–275 yards away, far enough to give the latter ample time to draw a bead on the cavalrymen galloping toward them. The charge was sheer suicide. Of Whiting's 250 men, 150 were killed, wounded, or captured; of the seven officers in the charge, only one escaped unhurt.[44]

Whiting's charge had not the slightest effect on the Confederate advance; in fact, the accounts of the charge either state outright, or imply, that the survivors of the sheet of fire into which they rode veered off well before they reached the Confederate infantry. As the troopers and the riderless, maddened horses came galloping back, they first blanketed the fire of their own artillery and then threw both the gunners and the infantry into confusion.

41. *Official Records*, Vol. XI, Pt. 2, p. 41.
42. *Battles and Leaders*, II, 346.
43. *Official Records*, Vol. XI, Pt. 2, p. 41.
44. Colonel Blake interpreted Cooke's order as discretionary and did not join in the charge. The historian of the 6th Pennsylvania states that "ten or twelve" of his regiment participated in the charge. Gracey, *Annals of the 6th*. There is no mention of that fact in any official report, including that of Colonel Rush.

Inevitably, the charge gave rise to one of the numberless acrid controversies that survived the war and caused the shedding of untold gallons of ink well seasoned with bile. General Cooke and his friends contended, then and later, that Whiting's charge "prevented the entire destruction of the Union army"; they spoke of the "devoted and successful effort of a few squadrons of cavalry ... to save some of the artillery and some of the honor of the army after it had suddenly retreated in disorder."[45] FitzJohn Porter, on the other hand, claimed, "All appeared to be doing well, our troops withdrawing in order to the cover of the guns, the enemy retiring, and victory, so far as possession of the field was concerned, had already settled upon our banners, when ... the artillery on the left were thrown into confusion by a charge of cavalry coming from the front. . . . the bewildered horses, regardless of the efforts of their riders, wheeled about, and dashing through the batteries, convinced the gunners that they were charged by the enemy."[46] Porter had not changed his mind when he wrote "Hanover Court House and Gaines's Mill" for Century Magazine nearly twenty-five years later, and neither had Cooke, who hastened to call attention to the "singular errors" and "injurious statements and insinuations" in Porter's account.[47]

It was absurd for Porter to claim that the enemy was retiring and to speak of victory settling upon his banners; General Morell reported correctly that his division was attacked in "irresistible force" and that his men were "swept from the ground," but he also suggests that what had been an orderly retreat was turned into a rout when the cavalry, returning from its disastrous charge, galloped obliquely through the ranks of the infantry and artillery.[48] The only proper verdict on Cooke's order is that it was both

45. *Official Records*, Vol. XI, Pt. 2, pp. 43–44; *Battles and Leaders*, II, 344–45.
46. *Official Records*, Vol. XI, Pt. 2, pp. 225–26.
47. For Porter, *Battles and Leaders*, II, 340–41; for Cooke, *ibid.*, 344–45.
48. *Official Records*, Vol. XI, Pt. 2, p. 273. An eyewitness wrote, "It is a thrilling sight to see these gallant men draw their sabres, and dash into those lines of steel. But it is like sending men to certain death. The officers are nearly all killed; the men are cut down by the score . . . and the shattered remnant that returns to us only tramples down our own men,

murderous and senseless. Indeed, it led to his being relieved, and justly so.[49]

The only Federal cavalryman to come out of the campaign with some degree of credit was William Averell. On June 29 on the Willis Church Road, by means of a cleverly laid trap, he administered a "bloody repulse" of two regiments of overconfident cavalry General Lee had sent out to locate the position of the Union army.[50] After this small but heartening success, Averell galloped to McClellan's headquarters and "ventured to suggest that the roads were tolerably clear toward Richmond, and that he might go there."[51] It is interesting to speculate on what might have happened had McClellan acted on the suggestion. The likelihood is that he would have been trapped between the James, the defenses of Richmond, and the Confederate army, and destroyed. In command of a rear guard of his own 3rd Pennsylvania and five regiments of infantry, Averell covered the retreat of the Union army from Malvern Hill to Harrison's Landing in a manner that led FitzJohn Porter to write that he had held "the enemy in check by the boldest demonstrations," and that his "dispositions were in every respect brilliant in conception and satisfactory in result."[52]

---

and increases the disorder already begun." Adams, *The Story of a Trooper*, 565.

49. General Morell urged Colonel Blake to "make a demonstration" on the left with his troopers, to help rally the infantry. Blake was willing, but received a "peremptory order" from Cooke to leave the field, whereupon the cavalry "rode at a brisk pace to the rear." *Official Records*, Vol. XI, Pt. 2, p. 273.

50. Freeman, *R. E. Lee*, II, 176; *Battles and Leaders*, II, 431. The two Confederate regiments were the 1st North Carolina and the 3rd Virginia.

51. *Battles and Leaders*, II, 431. On August 11, another cavalryman, Alfred Pleasonton, also urged an attack on Richmond. In a note to General R. B. Marcy, McClellan's chief of staff (and father-in-law), Pleasonton wrote, "There are moments when most decided action is necessary to save us from great disasters. I think such a moment has arrived. The enemy before us is weak. A crushing blow by this army at this time would be invaluable. . . . That blow can be made in forty-eight hours. Two corps would do it. . . . I have guides ready and know the roads sufficiently well to accomplish anything the General wants. . . . I think he has an opportunity at this time few men ever attain." Quoted in Frank A. Flower, *Edwin McMasters Stanton* (Akron, Ohio, 1905), 173.

52. *Official Records*, Vol. XI, Pt. 2, p. 230. There is a tantalizing pas-

When McClellan and the Army of the Potomac departed for the Peninsula, they left behind them, guarding the exit from the northern end of the Shenandoah Valley, General Nathaniel P. Banks and a small army of nine thousand men of all arms, made up of a division of infantry and some "unattached" troops. For cavalry, Banks had the 1st Vermont and the 5th New York, plus five companies each of the 1st Michigan and the 1st Maryland.[53] For administrative purposes, the Vermonters, the New Yorkers, and the detachment of Marylanders were grouped into a brigade, commanded by General John P. Hatch.

Banks was a "political" general, a former governor of Massachusetts and speaker of the national House of Representatives, who had tendered his services to the government immediately after the fall of Fort Sumter and was commissioned a major general. After a short stint in charge of the Department of Annapolis, he was given the Shenandoah Valley command. Aside from a commendable degree of pugnacity, Banks's qualifications for a major independent military command were modest, and he also had the misfortune to be pitted against Stonewall Jackson, who commanded the Valley District of the Department of Northern Virginia for the Confederacy.

In late March, 1862, the division of James Shields, brought to the Valley from the Upper Potomac, defeated Jackson at Kernstown. Jackson retreated southward, whereupon Shields and Banks advanced up the Valley and took post at Harrisonburg, sixty-five miles south of Winchester, near the southern end of Massanutten

---

sage in one of General Emory's reports, to the effect that "during the day [April 4] two squadrons of General Averell's cavalry were sent to the rear to repress disorders of a serious character. This was done thoroughly and with good effect." *Ibid.*, Pt. 1, p. 434. Emory does not say what the "serious disorders" were; Averell nowhere mentions the incident, and the regimental historian merely records that four (not two) squadrons "took possession of Shipping Point in the evening." Regimental History Committee, *History of the 3d Pennsylvania*, 43.

53. Banks also had as part of his "cavalry" five companies of the 8th New York, for whom, as late as May, 1862, the government had not supplied horses. Indeed, only a month earlier, General William S. Rosecrans had suggested getting some use out of the regiment by putting the men to work repairing the "nearly broken down" Winchester & Potomac Railroad. *Official Records*, Vol. XII, Pt. 3, p. 71.

Mountain, which, from Harrisonburg on the south to Front Royal on the north, divides the Valley into two unequal halves.

To reach Harrisonburg on their march south, the Federals had to cross the North Fork of the Shenandoah River, which was in flood and unfordable. The only available bridge was set on fire by the retreating Confederates. A charge by two companies of the 1st Ohio and a detachment of the 1st Michigan, drove the Confederate infantry away from the burning bridge; the troopers then dismounted and, using their despised cavalry hats as fire buckets, put out the fire and saved the bridge.[54]

While Banks and Shields were following Jackson up the Valley, another political general, John Charles Fremont, whose military career as a commander in Missouri in the early months of the war had been considerably less than distinguished, but for whom a command had to be found to appease the radical Republicans and the abolitionists, was assembling his troops for a march into the upper Valley from western Virginia. Fremont commanded Lewis Blenker's division of predominantly German regiments, plus three separate brigades of infantry, and, for cavalry, the 4th New York, 6th Ohio, and a detachment of the 3rd West Virginia. At a later stage, General George D. Bayard's cavalry brigade, consisting of the 1st New Jersey and the 1st Pennsylvania, was transferred from east of the Blue Ridge to reinforce Fremont.[55]

On May 12, Shields left the Valley to join General McDowell and his corps in a march from Fredericksburg to reinforce McClellan on the Peninsula. With Shields gone, Banks thought it

54. The two companies of the 1st Ohio were attached to General Shields's division; the rest of the regiment was serving in the West. The detachment of the 1st Michigan was led in this action by Corporal George R. Maxwell, who was later commissioned, rose to the colonelcy of the regiment, and eventually commanded a cavalry brigade under Sheridan. *Battles and Leaders*, II, 308.

55. Indicative of the command confusion of the moment is the plaintive dispatch Bayard sent off from Harrisonburg on June 7: "I write for instructions. Am I to stay here? Am I to regard myself as belonging to General Fremont's army? If not, what am I to do?" *Official Records*, Vol. XII, Pt. 1, p. 676. Bayard's command of a brigade will be explained in the next chapter, in connection with General John Pope's reorganization of the cavalry.

best to retreat to Strasburg, at the north end of Massanutten Mountain, separated by the North Fork of the Shenandoah from Front Royal, where he had a small garrison guarding the northern exit of the Luray Valley, a narrow trough between Massanutten Mountain on the west and the Blue Ridge on the east. Jackson lost no time taking advantage of the opportunity that Shields's departure and Banks's retreat handed him. He had been reinforced by Richard Ewell's division of infantry, and for cavalry he had the twenty-six companies of poorly armed and undisciplined but eager horsemen under the aggressive leadership of Turner Ashby. The fact that Jackson outnumbered Banks two to one— seventeen thousand against nine thousand—does not detract in the least from the brilliance of the campaign he now conducted. Taking maximum advantage of the terrain, of secrecy and speed, Jackson overwhelmed the small Federal garrison at Front Royal, flanked Banks's army as it retreated in great haste and considerable disorder from Strasburg to Winchester, gave Banks no time to organize a proper defense there, defeated him, and drove his disorganized and scattered troops out of the Valley. When the campaign was over, Banks insisted that he had not been routed, as in fact he had been, and claimed that he had conducted a "premeditated march of near 60 miles in the face of the enemy."[56] Actually, when he at last succeeded in crossing the Potomac to safety, he had lost nearly a third of his men and most of his equipment and supplies; had all of Ashby's cavalry been in its proper place at the battle of Winchester on May 25, Banks's defeat would have been more decisive and his losses greater than they were.

The day after the battle of Winchester, when word of Banks's defeat reached Washington, McDowell's orders to join McClellan were canceled and he was directed to send twenty thousand of his men to the Valley by forced marches. At the same time, Fremont was ordered to march east to Harrisonburg.[57] These moves were intended to trap Jackson, by interposing two Federal armies between him and his base at the upper end of the Valley. Speed,

56. *Ibid.*, 551; but to the contrary see *Ibid.*, 564, 585, 597.
57. *Ibid.*, 643.

however, was essential. McDowell was reminded by the president himself that it was "a question of legs," and the marches his men made on the waterlogged, rough roads from Fredericksburg to the Valley are nearly unbelievable.[58] Nonetheless, Jackson escaped the trap laid for him and was eventually able to leave the Valley and join General Lee on the Peninsula.

Unlike the countryside to the south of Richmond, the rolling terrain of the Valley was good cavalry country. Much of the area was still wooded, but since a great deal of the land was under cultivation, there were plenty of clearings and open fields on which cavalry could manoeuver. This, however, merely added to the burdens of the Federal horsemen. At the start of the campaign, Banks, with about sixteen hundred horsemen in his nine thousand-man army, had enough cavalry as far as numbers went, and he praised Hatch, his chief of cavalry, "for the spirit infused into his troops during the brief period of his command, which, by confession of friend and foe, had been made equal, if not superior, to the best of the enemy's long-trained mounted troops."[59]

The latter part of Banks's statement is pure hyperbole. Most certainly, Ashby's troopers would not have joined in any such "confession." Still, the Federal cavalrymen did enjoy an occasional small triumph. Banks made a special point of reporting that the 5th New York had "made a succession of most spirited charges against superior numbers [of Ashby's cavalry], killing 10, wounding many, and capturing 6. . . . Their chief weapon was the saber."[60] But his and his subordinates' reports and observations on the cavalry were generally far less flattering; they were, in fact, for the most part a litany of disappointments and complaints. Banks himself described his cavalry as made up of "mostly inexperienced men and untrained horses" and spoke of them as "weak in numbers and spirit—much exhausted with night and day work."[61]

For the Federals, the Valley was enemy country. There were

58. The Lincoln remark is quoted in Williams, *Lincoln Finds a General*, I, 211.
59. *Official Records*, Vol. XII, Pt. 1, p. 456.
60. *Ibid.*, 456. This is the engagement described in winged words by the regimental historian, quoted on page 246.
61. *Ibid.*, 50. 51.

Unionists in the Valley, to be sure, but generally speaking, Federal commanders could not count on a friendly population for information about the movements of the enemy. The Negroes, so far as their knowledge went, were uniformly helpful; many Federal reports on enemy positions, strengths, and movements were based on information brought in by the ever-present "intelligent contraband." In the main, however, Banks, Fremont, and their colleagues had to rely on their cavalry scouts for intelligence of what was happening on the other side of the hill. Banks was correct in reporting that he had "so many mountain valleys to scout and such an extended line to protect that, independent of strong cavalry in action [he needed] a large and efficient cavalry force."[62]

As was the case always and everywhere, the shortage of horses and the poor condition of those the cavalry did have presented a major problem. Fremont reported that his cavalry horses were "so nearly starved and broken down as to be nearly useless," and further, that the 6th Ohio, potentially the best of his regiments of cavalry, "was kept unmounted . . . and inactive, for the sole reason that animals could not be obtained to supply it"; when horses were at length supplied, they arrived in installments, only enough at a time to mount one company, and the last company to be mounted did not receive its horses until May 27, when the campaign to trap Jackson was about to get under way.[63] General Bayard, rushed to the Valley after Banks's defeat at Winchester, arrived with the horses of his two regiments "staggering with exhaustion" and many of them "unserviceable" for want of horseshoes.[64] General Rufus Saxton, sent hurriedly to Harper's Ferry to organize its defenses after Banks's expulsion from the Valley, reported that the 1st Maryland, stationed at that post, was in "shocking condition—horses not shod and no saddles."[65]

Quartermaster General Montgomery Meigs, acting on a report

62. *Ibid.*, Pt. 3, p. 50.
63. *Ibid.*, Pt. 1, pp. 8, 6. Fremont was denied authority to arrange for the purchase of horses for the 6th Ohio, despite his "earnest and repeated requests." *Ibid.*, 6. Doubtless the War Department wanted to avoid a repetition of the scandals that had surrounded Fremont's procurement of weapons and supplies in Missouri in the summer of 1861.
64. *Ibid.*, 25, 19.
65. *Ibid.*, Pt. 3, p. 627.

that there were plenty of horses owned by disloyal people in the Valley, pronounced that a "horse fit for military service is as much a military supply as a barrel of gunpowder" and recommended that the cavalry be authorized to "levy a contribution upon that territory of not less than 1,500 horses."[66] His recommendation was approved, but this was still early in the war when rebels not actually in arms were to be treated—and expected to be treated—with tenderness and a due regard for the Bill of Rights; horses "absolutely needed" for agriculture were not to be seized.[67]

Weapons were a problem just as intractable as that of horses. Lieutenant Colonel Charles R. Babbitt, in command of a detachment of the 8th New York in its retreat from Winchester to the Potomac, reported, "The men were armed with Hall's carbines (unserviceable) and but few were brought in. All that had Sharps brought them in."[68] But there were few Sharps or any other carbines of a good pattern in the Valley regiments. Fremont's cavalry had only sabers and revolvers.[69] Major Charles H. Town, who led a number of companies of his own 1st Michigan and of the 1st Maine in a skirmish with the Confederates, reported that "inasmuch as I had but 20 carbines in the entire command, and as our pistols were altogether too short range to cope with our adversaries with long rifles, with which all of them were armed. . . . I deemed it prudent to retire. . . . I would respectfully represent that, owing to the topography of the country, and the character of the force with which we [have] to contend, armed as our regiment is with only pistol and saber, barring the few carbines already mentioned, it is next to impossible to encounter our foes successfully, as he is never in a position where saber and pistol

---

66. *Ibid.*, 60.
67. *Ibid.*, 62. The owner of every horse taken was to be given a receipt, which he could present for payment "upon the suppression of the rebellion"; he would then be reimbursed if he could offer proof that he had been a loyal citizen and had not given aid and comfort to rebels. Three months later, shortly before Second Bull Run, Pope also was authorized to seize horses for his cavalry, "giving receipts." *Ibid.*, 589.
68. *Ibid.*, Pt. 1, p. 585. Babbitt's five companies, "under fire for the first time," were broken up and scattered in the retreat. Of the 250–300 making up the detachment, only 129 escaped.
69. *Ibid.*, 9.

can be used."[70] Major Town's complaint was echoed, generally with less restraint, by other commanders.[71]

Given these difficulties, it is not surprising that General Shields complained that the 1st West Virginia was "good for nothing"; the 1st Rhode Island, Colonel Duffié's pride and joy, Shields described as "an encumbrance. I have to take care of them instead of them taking care of me," and he begged General Banks's chief of staff to send him "cavalry that can work, forage, &c., . . . cavalry that can march and know how to take care of themselves."[72] Shields's dispatches have a uniformly shrill, overwrought tone, and may therefore be at least partially discounted, but their evidentiary value is supported by more sober accounts of poor cavalry performance. Colonel Gustave P. Cluseret, leading a reconnaissance unit of a battalion of cavalry, artillery, and two regiments of infantry (the use of infantry to make a reconnaissance is itself significant) came up against Ashby's cavalry near Strasburg on the night of June 1. "Disobeying the order to charge, after a scattering fire, [the] cavalry broke in a shameful panic to the rear, passing over and carrying with them the artillery."[73] Four companies of Bayard's own regiment, the 1st Pennsylvania, rode into an ambush, and the general had the humiliation of having to report that two of the companies "fled back to camp without having either horse or man injured."[74] Colonel Wyndham's 1st New Jersey, following on the heels of Jackson's army in its retreat up the Valley, rode into a belt of woods held by the Confederate rear guard near Harrisonburg on June 6. The men panicked. Lieutenant Colonel Joseph Kargé reported (Wyndham having been captured by the enemy), "All the officers . . . behaved brave-

70. *Ibid.*, 816.
71. Bayard: *Ibid.*, Pt. 3, p. 617; Burnside: *Ibid.*, 556; Pleasonton: *Ibid.*, 803. Only seventy-two men of the 1st Maine were armed with carbines; the rest had only revolvers and sabers. Merrill, *Campaigns of the First Maine*, 58.
72. *Official Records*, Vol. XII, Pt. 3, pp. 208, 321, 361. For good measure, Shields also referred to the 1st Rhode Island as "rubbish cavalry," which "one good regiment . . . [could] cut up . . . . on all sides," and he claimed that with "good cavalry I could stampede [Jackson] to Richmond," which might have taken considerable doing. *Ibid.*, 321.
73. *Ibid.*, Pt. 1, p. 14.
74. *Ibid.*, 430.

ly in trying to rally their men, but to no avail. They retreated without order and in the greatest confusion—for the most part panic stricken. . . . Our retreat lasted 1½ miles, when the men again came to their senses and rallied."[75]

The literature of the Civil War is replete with descriptions of the blood-stirring intoxication of the cavalry charge—the thundering hooves of the horses, the shouting of the troopers, the flashing sabers, the clouds of dust. One may ride in spirit with the 4th Missouri, in Pontotoc, Mississippi: "At the command 'Forward' excitement ran down the line, and there was a disposition for an immediate rush. But 'Steady—right dress—trot!' in a measured tone, taken up in turn by the company officers, brought back all the effect of our three years' discipline of the drill ground. Later, 'Steady—gallop—right dress!' accelerated the speed without disturbing the alignment, and then at last, 'Charge!' and with a universal yelling and brandishing of sabres we went forward like the wind."[76]

As an antithesis of the cavalry charge, there was the cavalry rout:

If a cavalry charge is glorious, a cavalry rout is dreadful. Pressing upon one another, straining to the utmost of their speed, the horses catch an infection of fear which rouses them to a frenzy. The men, losing their places in the ranks, and all power of formation or hope of combined resistance, rush madly for some point of safety upon which it may be possible to rally. Each check in front makes the mass behind more dense and desperate, until horses and men are overthrown and ridden over, trampled on by others as helpless as themselves. . . . The speed grows momentarily greater. Splashing through the pools of mire, breaking down fences, darting under trees, with a clang of sabres and din of hoofs, officers wild with shame and rage, shouting themselves hoarse with unavailing curses, and the bullets of the ene-

75. *Ibid.*, 680. See also Pyne, *First New Jersey Cavalry*, 53–55. It is difficult to reconcile the various accounts of this fight, but they seem to agree in at least one respect: namely, that the First New Jersey was "ambuscaded," as General Bayard called it. One Confederate account describes the capture of Wyndham as follows: "The Yankee officer in command dismounted and came leading his horse to meet us. He handed his sword to Holmes Conrad, saying he could not command such cowards." Edward H. McDonald, "Fighting Under Ashby in the Shenandoah," *Civil War Times Illustrated*, V (1966), 33.

76. Waring, *Whip and Spur*, 120–21.

my whistling shrilly overhead, the mingled mass sweeps on, until utter exhaustion stops them, or their commanders, struggling to the front, can indicate the place to form.[77]

This is what the 1st New Jersey experienced on June 6. They escaped from "the field of their defeat, leaving their colonel, three captains, one-twelfth of their troopers, and the regimental colors in the hands of the enemy."[78]

Jackson succeeded in escaping the Federal pincers. His own superb leadership was the major factor but not the only one in making his escape possible. Of the many handicaps that made the Federal concentration against him ineffectual and destroyed any possibility of success, only one needs to be mentioned. Within a few days after arriving in the Valley, General Bayard reported his two regiments as "utterly used up" and estimated that he would "certainly require at least a week" to get the men and horses in condition for an active campaign.[79] Five days later, not having been allowed any part of the time he believed his regiments needed for recuperation, Bayard reported that his "horses and men have been broken down. . . . I have not two serviceable horses in either regiment. . . . To attempt to go to Luray [where he had been ordered to march] as I am, would utterly destroy the horses . . . I think I shall need at least 400 horses to fill up the regiments as they are."[80]

77. Pyne, *First New Jersey Cavalry*, 55–56.
78. *Ibid.*, 56.
79. *Official Records*, Vol. XII, Pt. 1, pp. 676, 677. "Day and night we marched through heavy rain-storms, over the mountains and swimming swollen streams. The last ten miles was made in one hour and twenty minutes." Hampton S. Thomas, *Some Personal Reminiscences of Service in the Cavalry of the Army of the Potomac* (Philadelphia, 1889), 3.
80. *Official Records*, Vol. XII, Pt. 3, pp. 376–77. The phrase "not two serviceable horses" is suspect. Bayard may have been exaggerating, but more likely the word "hundred" (or the words "per company") following "horses" was omitted, either from the dispatch or from the transcription of it into the *Official Records*.

XI

A Noise of Horses

THE PRESIDENT HIMSELF AND THE SECRETARY OF WAR, aided for a time by General McDowell, attempted to direct from Washington the movement of the forces trying to intercept Jackson by issuing orders and directives to the three independent commands of Banks, Fremont, and Shields. This was a hopelessly bad system of command, and on June 25, when the battles of the Seven Days were about to begin, General John Pope, called to Washington from the West, was given command of a new "Army of Virginia," to which were assigned the armies of Banks, Mc-Dowell (of which Shields's command was a part), and General Franz Sigel, the latter a replacement for Fremont, who resigned in a huff upon the appointment of Pope, junior to him in rank, to the command. Two weeks later, on July 11, General Henry Wager Halleck, also called to Washington from the West, was given command of the whole of the Federal armies, as general-in-chief.

Pope, a West Point graduate of the Class of 1842, had made his reputation with a well-planned campaign which resulted in the capture of Island Number 10 in March, 1862. He has been described as "pugnacious and confident and conceited," all of which he was, in addition to being impressionable, easily rattled, impulsive, not unduly bright, and given to issuing bombastic, excessively fussy, and too frequent orders.[1] He was to lose the battle of Second Bull Run and to be the cause of the phrase "as great a liar as John Pope" being added to the vernacular, but he was also the author of what may be termed the emancipation proclamation of the northern cavalry.

While still in the West, as the historian of one of his cavalry regiments has recorded, Pope, "being himself an old cavalry officer, showed the world that he could make this branch of the service very effective."

Instead of mixing them with infantry in the same regiments and brigades, he organized cavalry brigades and divisions, placing them under cavalry officers, and when thus organized, he assigned to them their appropriate duty. When advancing we were required to reconnoiter every foot of the country before the infantry occupied it. We were kept constantly on duty, either as pickets ourselves, or feeling the pickets of the enemy, and gaining information relative to the whereabouts of the foe, or raiding to their rear, and cutting their base of supplies.[2]

In August, 1862, in the midst of the Second Bull Run Campaign, Pope used his authority as commanding general, Army of Virginia, to issue Special Orders No. 45, which must be quoted in full:

Hereafter the cavalry of each army corps will be massed and placed under the command of the chief of cavalry of that corps.
Commanders of army corps will be allowed to detach for duty at their own headquarters such cavalry as may be necessary for their personal escorts.
Companies or detachments of cavalry now on duty at division or brigade headquarters will be sent at once to report to the chief of cavalry of their respective corps.
Ten mounted men will be allowed to each division headquarters, and five only to each brigade headquarters as orderlies.[3]

The order did not go far enough toward the consolidation of the cavalry—it left it still divided, with each army corps having its

1. The quoted phrase is from Williams, *Lincoln and His Generals*, 120.
2. Pierce, *History of the Second Iowa*. Pierce was mistaken on one point. Pope served with the topographical engineers before the war; he was not an "old cavalry officer."
3. *Official Records*, Vol. XII, Pt. 3, p. 581.

own cavalry organization—but it was a notable first step in the right direction. A few weeks earlier, Stuart, trying to deal with Federal raids on the Central of Virginia Railroad, had been "beset by numerous interested gentlemen to station the cavalry at various points along the railroad." Stuart's reaction was firmly to the point: "This policy of frittering away the command into little detachments, on any one of which the enemy could concentrate and overpower it, I steadfastly opposed, with the approval of the commanding general."[4] Stuart and General Lee saw clearly and from the start what the North saw imperfectly and did not effectively act on until 1863, that in the case of the cavalry, the whole was considerably greater than the sum of its parts, that the effectiveness of a division far exceeded that of its individual brigades added together, and that the potency of a cavalry corps was greater by an even larger factor than the sum total of the effectiveness of the individual divisions composing it.

Pope's plans for his army went beyond his primary missions of protecting Washington and guarding the Valley. He assumed that McClellan would maintain pressure on Richmond, forcing Lee and Jackson to remain there. This, Pope reasoned, would open up the area north and west of Richmond to a Federal invasion. To take advantage of this opportunity, the Army of Virginia would advance along the Orange & Alexandria Railroad, block Richmond's access to its granary in the Shenandoah Valley, capture Charlottesville, and destroy the rail communications between the Confederate capital and the West. Having done this, the army would march east to Richmond to become the upper half of a trap (McClellan and the Army of the Potomac being the lower half), in which General Lee's army would be caught and destroyed. This was strategy on a grand scale. The concept was eminently sound, but by the time Pope got his scattered forces assembled, organized, and reequipped, McClellan was already bottled up at Harrison's Landing and the lower half of the trap was gone. Moreover, General Lee, with the advantage of interior lines, could now deal with the threat to his rear.

As the crucial phase of the campaign began, Pope's troops were on or near the Rapidan and his cavalry was picketing the

4. *Ibid.*, Pt. 2, p. 119.

fords across the river. Pope admonished General Banks to "dismiss any idea that there is any purpose whatever to retreat . . . or that there is any design whatever to await any attack of the enemy" and ordered him to send his chief of cavalry, General Hatch, reinforced by Bayard's brigade, on a raid to the south. Hatch was to break up the Virginia Central Railroad on both sides of Gordonsville, go on to Charlottesville and destroy as much as he could of the railroad from there to Lynchburg, and to finish the expedition by destroying the James River Canal, twenty miles farther south.[5] Banks was to tell Hatch first that "promptness and vigor, quick and bold marches, boldness and skill" were the essential ingredients of success, and second, that the president had promised a step up in rank for him as a reward for success.[6] Two days later Pope learned to his dismay, which he expressed in far more temperate terms than the situation justified, that Hatch had taken along on what should have been a fast-moving cavalry raid a force of infantry and artillery, and even a wagon train.[7] Thus hampered, the raid could not have been anything but a failure, and a failure it was. Hatch was still ten miles short of Gordonsville when he learned that Jackson and Ewell were there, whereupon he prudently turned around and marched back to his base at Culpeper.[8] Hatch was ordered to submit an explanation of his failure, but before he could do so he was ordered to try again. This time, Pope wrote, he was to take "four regiments of cavalry with two days' cooked rations and nothing else"; he was to live on the country, impress guides as he went along, "with the understanding that they were to be shot if they misled him," and he was to bear in mind that "it [did] not matter what force of infantry the enemy [had]. . . . Infantry cannot pursue cavalry." Above all, he was "to move at once and with the utmost rapidity."[9]

On July 18, Pope felt it necessary, and with good reason, to issue General Orders No. 6, in which he declared:

Hereafter in any operation of the cavalry forces in this command no

5. *Ibid.*, 472. The Virginia Central, which had a junction with the Orange & Alexandria at Gordonsville, was the only direct rail connection between Richmond and the Shenandoah Valley.
6. *Ibid.*, 23–24; *ibid.*, Pt. 3, pp. 475, 476.
7. *Ibid.*, Pt. 3, p. 484.
8. *Ibid.*, 488.
9. *Ibid.*, 490–91.

supply or baggage trains of any description will be used. . . . Two days' cooked rations will be carried on the persons of the men, and all villages and neighborhoods through which they pass will be laid under contribution . . . for the subsistence of men and horses. Movements of the cavalry must always be made with celerity, and no delay in such movements will be excused hereafter on any pretext. Whenever the order for the movement of any portion of this army emanates from these headquarters, the time of marching and that to be consumed in the execution of the duty will be specifically designated, and no departure therefrom will be permitted to pass unnoticed without the gravest and most conclusive reasons.[10]

Pope's dispatch to Banks directing Hatch's second raid and his General Orders No. 6 contained language that it should not have been necessary to use in directing the operations of any competent cavalry commander. It is instructive to compare Pope's language with that of General Lee's orders to Stuart, which merely indicated the geographic objective and purpose of an operation, outlined in broad terms the role the cavalry was to play, and left the mechanics and details up to Stuart. It is most unlikely that General Lee would have ordered Stuart "to move at once and with the utmost rapidity."

Hatch's second effort was as great a failure as the first. Within thirty hours after starting he was back in Culpeper, having gotten no nearer Gordonsville than on the first occasion. His lack of success this time was too much for Pope. Hatch blamed his failure on "the utter breaking up of his horses, the state of the roads and the storms."[11] Nevertheless, Pope ordered Hatch relieved and replaced him with John Buford, then serving on his own staff as a major in the inspector general's department.[12]

John Buford was a native of Kentucky (he was a younger half-brother of Union General Napoleon B. Buford and a kin of Confederate General Abraham Buford) and a graduate of West Point, Class of 1848. Commissioned a second lieutenant in the 2nd Dragoons, his prewar service had been on the plains. Colonel Theodore Lyman, who met him when Buford visited General Meade's headquarters in 1863, gave the following description of him:

10. *Ibid.*, Pt. 2, p. 50.
11. *Ibid.*, 512.
12. *Ibid.*, Pt. 3, pp. 514, 525.

Yesterday came General Buford, commander of the Second Cavalry Division, and held a pow-wow. He is one of the best officers of that arm and is a singular-looking party, figurez-vous . . . a compactly built man of middle height, with a tawny moustache and a little, tri-angular gray eye, whose expression is determined, not to say sinister. His ancient corduroys are tucked into a pair of ordinary cowhide boots and his blue blouse is ornamented with holes; from one pocket thereof peeps a huge pipe, while the other is fat with a tobacco pouch. Notwithstanding this get-up, he is a very soldierly-looking man. He is of a good natured disposition but not to be trifled with. Caught a notorious spy last winter and hung him to the next tree, with this inscription: "This man is to hang three days; he who cuts him down before shall hang the remaining time."[13]

Over and above this, Buford was also an outstandingly able cav-alry commander. One of his former troopers wrote of him after the war that "General Buford . . . many of us claim, was the best cavalry officer ever produced on this continent"; another called him a "model commander."[14] Whether or not he was fully deserv-ing of such high praise, the crucial fact is that his men thought him deserving of it. Unlike several of his colleagues—Averell, Kil-patrick, and Pleasonton, for example—he never permitted news-papermen to accompany his command. His performance as a commander of a brigade under Pope, and later of a division, is deserving of the praise he has received: "Few bolder or more en-terprising soldiers ever rode at the head of a column of horse . . . [He was] tireless in the search for information and always eager to fight . . . the perfect cavalryman."[15] Indeed, had he lived—he died of illness at the age of thirty-seven on December 13, 1863, the very day he learned of his promotion to major general—it is not impossible that he, not Sheridan, would have had command of the cavalry of the Army of the Potomac in the last year of the war.

When it became apparent that McClellan was content to re-main at Harrison's Landing and at least for the time being was no longer a menace to Richmond, General Lee recovered his free-dom of movement. He received word on July 12 that the Federals had occupied Culpeper, only twenty-seven miles north of the Vir-

13. Agassiz, *Meade's Headquarters*, 21.
14. [Whittaker], *Volunteer Cavalry*, 60–61; Clark, "Making of a Vol-unteer Cavalryman," 26.
15. Williams, *Lincoln Finds a General*, I, 264, 326.

ginia Central at Gordonsville. Considering the protection of the railroad a matter of vital importance, Lee ordered Jackson to proceed to Gordonsville with his own and Ewell's divisions, and later sent him A. P. Hill's division as well. Lee's orders gave Jackson full discretion either to remain on the defensive or to "suppress Pope," as he thought best.[16] Information Jackson received on August 7 suggested the possibility that by a swift advance he could fall on the leading units of Pope's army at Culpeper before the rest of it could reach the scene, and he moved forward the same day with his three divisions of upwards of twenty-four thousand men.[17]

As Jackson began his march, Pope's cavalry pickets lined the north bank of the Rapidan; Bayard, with four regiments, covered the stretch from Raccoon Ford to the Orange & Alexandria Railroad; Buford's five regiments picketed the stretch between the railroad and the Blue Ridge.[18] From August 8 on, Pope, at Culpeper, was receiving reports of Jackson's advance from Bayard, Buford, and his signal station atop Thoroughfare Mountain. Early on the morning of the ninth Buford reported that the Confederate infantry "was in heavy force on his right, his left, and partly on his rear" and that he was slowly retreating.[19] Pope thereupon ordered Banks to move forward from Culpeper with two divisions, and on the blistering hot afternoon of the same day, at Cedar (or Slaughter) Mountain south of Culpeper, the two forces met and fought what can fairly be called a drawn battle.[20]

Jackson's and Banks's infantry and artillery had been engaged for several hours when, toward the end of the day, Jackson repelled an attack by the Federal right wing which for a time had him in serious trouble. He then launched an attack of his own against the exhausted Federal infantry. Seeing the attack com-

16. Freeman, *R. E. Lee*, II, 256–71.
17. Douglas S. Freeman, *Lee's Lieutenants: A Study in Command* (3 vols.; New York, 1942–44), II, 1–24.
18. *Official Records*, Vol. XII, Pt. 2, pp. 24–25.
19. *Ibid.*, 26; *ibid.*, Pt. 3, pp. 541–49.
20. There was considerable postwar dispute about the terms of the orders under which Banks acted. He understood that he was to attack Jackson. Pope insisted that Banks was to engage only with his skirmishers and was to await the arrival of Sigel's corps before launching a full-scale

ing, Bayard ordered Major Richard I. Falls to charge the advancing gray infantry with his four companies of the 1st Pennsylvania. "I immediately formed squadron [column]," Major Falls
reported, "[and] moved forward at rapid gait until within 50 yards
of the enemy's lines, which I found in great force and three in
number, when I gave the command 'charge,' when with loud and
terrific cheering, my command charged through the enemy's lines,
cutting and running down and scattering them in every direction,
causing sad havoc and discomfiture in their ranks."[21] Thus said
Major Falls; but he had been given an impossible assignment. He
was expected to stop, or at least disrupt, the advance of General
L. O'Brien Branch's brigade of five regiments of North Carolina
infantry.[22] Major Falls's chest-thumping report to the contrary
notwithstanding, the gallant charge of his 164-man detachment
did not, and could not, accomplish a task that might have been
too much for Bayard's entire brigade. Nonetheless, the charge
was made, and of the 164 rank and file who made it, 71 returned,
"the remainder having been killed, wounded or otherwise placed
hors du combat by their horses falling over other killed or wounded."[23] Like Captain Whiting's charge at Gaines's Mill, it was magnificent, but it was not war.

Cedar Mountain did nothing to enhance Jackson's reputation,
notwithstanding his claim of having beaten the Federals. Two

---

attack. Banks's casualties of 2,381 were far greater than Jackson's 1,365.
Battles and Leaders, II, 496.

21. *Official Records*, Vol. XII, Pt. 3, p. 40.

22. *Ibid.*, 40.

23. The regimental historian claims that the charge broke "three successive lines of [Confederate] infantry." Lloyd, *History of the First Reg't.*,
22. But Confederate General Jubal Early, an eyewitness, wrote, "Finding
himself being driven from the field . . . the enemy made a desperate effort
to retrieve the fortunes of the day by a charge of cavalry. We had no regular lines formed at this time, and our men were much scattered in advancing, when a considerable body of cavalry came charging along the
road. . . . Without being at all disconcerted . . . small regiments nearby . . .
poured a volley into the head of the cavalry, when it had gotten within a
few yards, causing it to turn suddenly to its right . . . followed by the
whole body." Early, *Autobiographical Sketch*, 100. The likelihood that
Early's account is closer to the truth is suggested by the fact that the
losses of Branch's brigade in the entire battle were twelve killed and
eighty-eight wounded. *Battles and Leaders*, II, 496.

days after the battle, in a move more indicative of a defeat than a victory, Jackson had "campfires lighted all along his front, and, while they burned, he led his troops back along the Rapidan," "pursued" (Pope's word) by Buford's and Bayard's cavalry and leaving behind him as part of the detritus of battle nearly 1,500 Federal wounded "packed in miserably ventilated buildings [in Culpeper] during the burning August weather, with insufficient medical and hospital attendance, and with very limited supplies."[24] A praiseworthy exception to these dreadful conditions was the situation of the more than one hundred wounded of the 1st New Jersey, under the ministrations of Assistant Surgeon Ferdinand V. Dayton. Only one of his patients died, "and that from a hopelessly mortal hurt; while injuries which had elsewhere cost many a limb and not a few lives were . . . treated without the necessity of a single amputation. Sufficient food, wholesomely cooked, was provided almost from the first; beds of dry and clean hay or straw were made up . . . and the building kept in a perfect condition of purity and ventilation."[25]

On August 3, six days before Cedar Mountain, a decision had been made in Washington that was to change the complexion of Pope's campaign. General Halleck notified McClellan that day that the Army of the Potomac was to leave the Peninsula, to be carried by water to Aquia Creek, and then to join Pope. By August 14, General Lee had sufficient information to satisfy him that McClellan was evacuating Harrison's Landing. The threat to Richmond being ended, Lee was presented with a great opportunity. Following Jackson's retreat from Cedar Mountain to Gordonsville, Pope had advanced to the Rapidan and occupied the north bank of that stream, from Raccoon Ford on the east to the Blue Ridge on the west, and was thus in an exposed position, eighty miles or more from Washington. The Confederate troops at Richmond, no longer needed to protect the city, were free to join Jackson and provide him with the strength to smash Pope before he was reinforced by McClellan's troops, which would be forced to move around the circumference of a large circle to reach him.

24. Freeman, *Lee's Lieutenants*, II, 43; *Official Records*, Vol. XII, Pt. 2, p. 28; Pyne, *First New Jersey Cavalry*, 90.
25. Pyne, *First New Jersey Cavalry*, 90.

The ensuing manoeuvers, spanning the period from July 13 to August 30, the day of Second Bull Run, were to show Lee, Jackson, and their men at their absolute best.[26]

On August 17, the 1st Michigan of Buford's command captured Major Norman R. Fitzhugh, who was carrying an order that spelled out in detail General Lee's plans to "suppress" Pope before he was reinforced by the Army of the Potomac. Pope thus learned that Lee was moving his troops west from Richmond to join Jackson, and he therefore moved back from his exposed position on the Rapidan to the Rappahannock, where he posted his army on the north bank of the stream, from Kelly's Ford on the south to Rappahannock Station on the north, and made ready to hold that position until the arrival of McClellan's army.

Longstreet's infantry, Stuart's cavalry, and General Lee himself joined Jackson and followed Pope to the Rappahannock.[27] Unsuccessful in his efforts to force a crossing of the river—as the Confederate army sidestepped to the north, Pope conformed, and had each of the many fords over the river blockaded before the Confederates could cross—General Lee eventually broke the stalemate by sending Jackson with three divisions, twenty-five thousand men, on the classic march of the war. Jackson swung northwest along the south bank of the Rappahannock, through Amissville, Orleans, and Salem, around the western side of the Bull Run Mountains, and then east through Thoroughfare Gap to Gainesville and Manassas Junction, which he reached on the evening of August 26. He was now squarely between Pope and Washington, and in possession of the huge supply base of the Army of Virginia, with its endless rows of warehouses, hundreds of loaded freight cars, and fields covered with mountains of boxes, bales,

26. Lee ordered Longstreet to follow Jackson to Gordonsville on July 13, the day before he had definite word that the Army of the Potomac was starting to leave the Peninsula. Most military historians consider Chancellorsville the greatest of the Lee-Jackson collaborations, but in terms of geographic range, of the risks taken, of the quality of the performance of their duties by the entire army, from Jackson's foot cavalry up to and including Jackson and Longstreet themselves, Second Bull Run, in this writer's opinion, is a matchless and flawless masterpiece.

27. Lee now had about fifty-five thousand effectives. Freeman, *R. E. Lee*, II, 289.

and barrels. Jackson's men ate and carried away what they could, then set fire to the rest.[28]

In the meantime, five divisions, twenty-five thousand men, of the Army of the Potomac had arrived to reinforce Pope, who now had to turn his army 180 degrees, front to back, to deal with Jackson in his rear. Knowing that the rest of Lee's army was following Jackson, Pope's first impulse was to try to block their route through Thoroughfare Gap, but then he changed his mind. He decided that he had time to concentrate on Jackson and defeat him before the arrival of the rest of the Confederate army. For Pope's infantry this meant several changes of direction and much retracing of steps in the torrid August heat. On the afternoon of August 28, when the concentration of Pope's divisions on Manassas was at length completed, Jackson had vanished. Knowing that the Federals were massing against him, he found as a hiding place an excellent defensive position stretching from Groveton to the Bull Run stream, on the Bull Run battlefield of two years before, within easy reach of Thoroughfare Gap, which he knew Longstreet would use on his march to join him.

The Federals found Jackson when John Gibbon's brigade stumbled across his position—2,100 men against 25,000—at sundown on the twenty-eighth. In an encounter-battle lasting only two hours, Gibbon sustained casualties of 33 percent; one of his regiments, the 2nd Wisconsin Infantry, lost 298 of the approximately 500 men it took into the fight.[29]

There was severe fighting on the twenty-ninth, while, unknown to Pope, Longstreet joined Jackson. On the afternoon of the thirtieth, Pope, ignorant of Longstreet's presence on the field, attacked Jackson head on. The attack was beaten off by the fire of Jackson's infantry and artillery, and the deadly enfilading fire of Longstreet's massed artillery on the Federal left flank.

28. Four days earlier, Stuart had ridden around the right wing of Pope's army, crossed the Bull Run Mountains, and on the night of August 22, raided Pope's headquarters at Catlett's Station; W. H. F. ("Rooney") Lee's 9th Virginia captured three hundred prisoners, Pope's personal baggage, horses and camp furniture, and most importantly, Pope's dispatch books and files of correspondence, which gave General Lee a great deal of valuable information about Pope's situation and intentions.

29. Alan T. Nolan, *The Iron Brigade* (New York, 1961), 95.

Then the Confederates went over to the attack, and by nightfall the Union army, beaten back and badly battered but still retaining its cohesion, was in full retreat across Bull Run to Centreville. On September 5, with his army safe in the defenses of Washington, Pope was relieved of command. He was replaced by McClellan, and the Army of Virginia ceased to exist, its formations being absorbed into the Army of the Potomac.

An examination of the role of the Federal cavalry in these events leads to the repetition in a new context of much that has already been noted in connection with the Valley Campaign. To begin with, the Federal cavalry was badly undermanned for the role Pope expected it to fulfill. At the start, Bayard's and Buford's nine regiments, with a total effective strength of no more than about four thousand of all ranks, less the hundreds of troopers detached to serve as escorts, orderlies, and dispatch riders, were required to picket a line of more than forty miles along the Rapidan, and to scout and patrol in all directions as the corps and divisions of Pope's army moved about the country.[30] The men had had little time to recover from the wear and tear of the Valley Campaign, in which, typically, the 1st Pennsylvania had "thirty days of incessant marching, skirmishing and fighting, having in that time, marched nearly four hundred miles, skirmishing the greater part of the way . . . and having been engaged in two battles, and ten or twelve considerable skirmishes."[31] As early as August 7, Bayard complained that "the enemy are driving in my pickets. . . . It is needless again to report that it is impossible to hold the line I am ordered with my present effective force. I have picket men on duty who have been on post for four days."[32]

30. The seriousness of the detachment problem is pointed up by the experience of the 1st Maine. In August, 1862, 104 of its men were absent from the regiment on detached duties; in September, 210 were absent, serving as escorts, dispatch riders, etc. Tobie, *First Maine Cavalry*, 123. It must be remembered that after a year in the service, few cavalry regiments numbered at full strength more than four to five hundred men.

31. Lloyd, *History of the First Reg't.*, 21.

32. *Official Records*, Vol. XII, Pt. 3, p. 541. Bayard managed to introduce a humorous note into the same dispatch. He had been ordered to establish a line of "estafettes" (dispatch riders). Bayard queried, "That means couriers, does it not? Excuse my ignorance, but I have no dictionary to see what it is."

In an effort to build up the strength of Pope's mounted troops, a long series of urgent dispatches was sent to Fort Monroe and Yorktown to hurry the embarkation of McClellan's cavalry. The quartermasters on the Peninsula were given such admonitions as, "Every minute is important"; "everything must give way to this."[33] But there was confusion at both ends. After three companies of the 8th Illinois and two of the 8th Pennsylvania were disembarked at Aquia Creek, they vanished and could not be located.[34] There was insubordination; the colonel of a Massachusetts infantry regiment had to be ordered in arrest for refusing to give up a vessel needed to transport cavalry.[35] There was also red-tape stupidity, requiring the personal intervention of the general-in-chief to persuade Quartermaster Captain James J. Dana to issue fifteen hundred horses to McClellan's cavalry as it disembarked on its way to reinforce Pope, because Dana had been told to issue the horses to Pope's cavalry.[36] And finally, much of the cavalry transferred north was of no immediate value. McClellan's chief of staff was told that four companies of the 1st Massachusetts had arrived at Alexandria from South Carolina, but "the officer in charge reports them unfit for duty for at least ten days."[37] In any event, the transfers were too late. By August 30 and 31 and the first few days of September, when most of the transferred units arrived, the campaign had already been lost.

The frequent changes of direction, the marches and countermarches, following Pope's decision to retreat from the Rapidan, created impossible supply problems for his entire army, and particularly the cavalry. After Jackson's destruction of the Union supply base at Manassas the already bad situation became desperate. The prescribed daily ration for a cavalry mount was fourteen pounds of hay and twelve pounds of corn, oats, or barley. This meant that for a regiment down to half strength—five hundred horses—six and a half tons of feed were needed every day to keep the animals properly fed. The task of supplying forage on that scale to nine regiments of cavalry in a highly mobile,

33. *Ibid.*, 693, 736–37, 760. See also *ibid.*, 761, 778–79, 799.
34. *Ibid.*, 791.
35. *Ibid.*, 760.
36. *Ibid.*, 773.
37. *Ibid.*, 800.

chaotic situation was utterly beyond the ability of the quarter-masters. The men too were in bad straits. For ten days following August 26, the 1st Pennsylvania "was forced to subsist . . . on the scanty fare this desolate and wasted region afforded, which consisted principally of green corn, savored by an occasional emaci-ated sheep or pig. All who experienced the hardships of these . . . trying days . . . will remember the sleepless nights, after days of exhausting toil, and the commencement of another day's duty, without the preface of a breakfast or the prospect of a dinner."[38] And the rest of the cavalry fared no better than did the 1st Penn-sylvania.

As always, the condition of the horses was disastrous. There was a great deal of truth in General Meigs's observation that "the men are inexperienced . . . and they destroy their horses by hard and unnecessary riding"; he urged that "the strictest rules should be adopted to prevent all riding faster than a walk, except when actual service makes it necessary. In this hot season a cavalry regiment may be broken down by a few days' improper use of their horses."[39] Carelessness, neglect, ignorance, and abuse were all factors, but so were starvation and hard, continuous service in torrid heat, and whether the reasons were good or bad, and they were assuredly a mixture of both, the fact is that there was a huge wastage of horses throughout the campaign, with a corre-sponding decrease in the numbers and effectiveness of the cav-alry. Colonel William R. Lloyd reported that his 6th Ohio lost from one to ten horses every day "from sheer exhaustion," the result of "excessive work and want of forage"; at the end of the campaign he needed 448 replacement horses for his 596 men.[40] The historian of the 1st Rhode Island writes of the "shoeless, jaded, wounded, starving horses" of his regiment, which, at one point in the campaign, "were not unsaddled for one hundred and four hours; were without food for sixty-four hours; without water for thirty-seven hours."[41] The chronicler of the 1st Pennsylvania noted that its horses "with their backs actually putrid from the

38. Lloyd, *History of the First Reg't.*, 31.
39. *Official Records*, Vol. XII, Pt. 3, p. 596.
40. *Ibid.*, Pt. 2, p. 278.
41. Denison, *Sabres and Spurs*, 150, 152. See also *Official Records*, Vol. XII, Pt. 3, p. 644.

constant pressure and wear of the saddles, which had not been permitted to be removed for weeks, fell down in the ranks from exhaustion and starvation, and were abandoned by the wayside," leaving half the regiment dismounted at the end of the campaign.[42]

Colonel John Beardsley, commanding the cavalry brigade of Franz Sigel's corps, reported that "the horses of the command have been taxed to the utmost of their strength. . . . They had been almost constantly under saddle since the battle of Cedar Mountain, having been irregularly and scantily fed upon what the barrenness of the country afforded. . . . [By August 29] My horses were completely worn out and almost in a starving condition. All along our route . . . they were dropping down with their riders and dying, so that . . . most of my horses were unable to carry the rider and had to be led."[43] Near the end of the campaign, both Bayard and Buford told Pope that in their respective brigades "there was not 5 horses to the company that could be forced into a trot," and on August 31, and again the next day, Pope, in despair, wired Halleck, "I need cavalry horses terribly. Send me 2,000 . . . I need them badly—worse than I can tell you."[44]

And yet, despite these handicaps, Bayard, and particularly Buford, managed to give good accounts of themselves. In his report on the campaign, Pope made generous acknowledgment of their performance. "Their duties," he wrote, "were particularly arduous and hazardous, and it is not too much to say that throughout the operations . . . scarcely a day passed that these officers did not render service which entitles them to the gratitude of the government."[45]

On August 26, Buford spotted and reported Jackson's swing around Pope's right, and on the morning of the twenty-ninth he reported the approach from the direction of Thoroughfare Gap of what proved to be Longstreet's corps. This second report was a

42. Lloyd, *History of the First Reg't.*, 31–32.
43. *Official Records*, Vol. XIII, Pt. 2, pp. 271–72.
44. *Ibid.*, 45, 81, 80, 82.
45. *Ibid.*, 49.

model of careful observation and precise reporting, in that it identified the presence in the Confederate advance of seventeen regiments of infantry, a battery, and five hundred cavalry.[46]

The Federal cavalry was showing definite signs of improvement and of increased self-confidence after its five or six months of service in the field. "The men had now become 'old campaigners,'" wrote the historian of the 1st Maine, "They had learned, by that best of all schools, experience, how to take care of themselves, under any and all circumstances. . . . the men were ready to go into camp at any time, in any place . . . and with any weather, and to make themselves comparatively comfortable. They had learned to carry their own rations, and to cook their own coffee and pork and beef, instead of having them carried in their wagons. . . . In short, each one had learned, or was fast learning, to depend on himself and his own resources."[47]

And further, the cavalry had learned "to campaign, with all that term implies."

It learned, by experience, to cast off all unnecessary impediments . . . and when forage is lacking, to stand by its horses, even at midnight, while they grazed. It learned to bivouac, and make itself comfortable too, in bivouac. On the march, it learned during a halt of five minutes to cook coffee in tin cups over a blaze of burning faggots. It learned to make three days' rations last six days. . . . It learned to forage liberally and discriminately. It learned how to kill a pig within hearing of the provost marshal without letting it squeal. It learned also that wonderful art of kindling fires in drenching rains, in the wettest of places, with the wettest of materials.[48]

Such accomplishments were necessary for physical survival and were hence an important phase of the process of civilians becoming soldiers. What was even more important, the Federal cavalry had begun to learn how to hold its own in a skirmish with the Confederate cavalry, not always, by any means, but with increasing frequency. Competent leadership was beginning to emerge, and the unfortunate Pope, whatever may be thought of his quali-

46. *Ibid.*, 69; Williams, *Lincoln Finds a General*, I, 325.
47. Tobie, *First Maine Cavalry*, 76–77.
48. *Ibid.*, 125.

ties as an army commander, had at least established a much-needed precedent by grouping his cavalry. The grouping was carried out imperfectly in the full stress of a campaign and had no chance to develop the organic cohesion that was needed for the effective operations of brigades and divisions, but it was a vital ingredient of a better future for the mounted arm. At the beginning of September, 1862, the exhausted and nearly unhorsed Federal cavalry was back in the defenses of Washington, which it had left with high ambitions and high hopes in March and April, but it was not the same cavalry it had been. A little of the amateurishness, a little of the ineptness, had worn off, and a modest degree of professional skill was beginning to show itself.

The Confederate pursuit of the beaten Union army ended with the battle of Chantilly, in a storm of thunder and rain on the night of September 1. Four days later, General Lee began crossing the Potomac to carry the war into Union territory. Maryland, a slave state with a tenuous allegiance to the Union, was expected to welcome the invaders with open arms. General Lee believed, and President Davis agreed with him, that carrying the war to the enemy and occupying western Maryland, aside from its specifically military advantages—removing the Union army from Virginia, threatening Washington, Baltimore, and even Philadelphia, drawing the Union army out of the powerful defenses of Washington and into the open, and cutting the communications of the Federal capital with the West—would have a decided effect on both northern and southern morale and might even bring about the fervently hoped-for recognition of the Confederacy by England and France.

After occuping Frederick and Hagerstown, Lee found it necessary to secure his line of communications back to Richmond via the Shenandoah Valley. To that end, he had to have possession of Harper's Ferry, held by twelve thousand Federals commanded by ill and elderly Colonel Dixon S. Miles. General Lee now made the most daring—or, depending on the point of view, most foolhardy—move of his entire career. He knew that the Army of the Potomac and the Army of Virginia had been consolidated, that Pope had been dismissed, and that McClellan was back in command of what was once again the Army of the Potomac.[49] Counting on McClellan's "slows," and on the demoralization of an army that had sustained sixteen thousand casualties at Second Bull Run, Lee divided his army on September 10. He sent nearly half of it, twenty-five thousand men, under Stonewall Jackson, to capture Harper's Ferry. With the remainder he moved north to Hagerstown, to draw McClellan farther away from Washington and create a situation in which he could accept battle on favorable terms. By September 13, Jackson had Harper's Ferry surrounded. Miles and his men were trapped, and on the morning of the fifteenth, Miles surrendered the town and everything it contained. There was, however, an important gap in the ranks of the troops captured by Jackson. The cavalry was not among them.

It was already obvious on Sunday afternoon, September 14, that in a matter of hours Miles would have to surrender. Among the trapped Federals were "nearly 2,500" cavalry: the College Cavaliers, Cole's Battalion, the 12th Illinois, 8th New York, a battalion of the 1st Maryland, one squadron of the 1st Rhode Island, and an unattached company of Maryland cavalry.[50] In command of the 8th New York was Colonel Benjamin F. ("Grimes") Davis, an Alabama-born Mississippian, graduate of West Point, Class of 1854, a captain in the 1st United States when secession came, who chose to throw in his lot with the Union. Davis' regiment had been raised in the Rochester area and was mustered in on No-

49. To be strictly accurate, McClellan was not formally reinstated in command of the Army of the Potomac. He exercised that command pursuant to an order of September 2, which announced that he was to "have command of the fortifications of Washington and of all the troops for the defense of the capital."

50. "Nearly 2,500" is based on the testimony of Lieutenant Henry M. Binney, aide of Colonel Miles, before a military commission appointed to investigate the circumstances of the Harper's Ferry surrender. *Official Records*, Vol. XIX, Pt. 1, p. 583. "About 1,500 officers and men" is found in a paper written thirty years later by former Lieutenant William M. Luff of the 12th Illinois: "March of the Cavalry from Harper's Ferry, September 14, 1862," in MOLLUS, Commandery of Illinois, *Military Essays and Recollections* (4 vols.; Chicago, 1891–94), II, 40. John W. Mies gives a figure of "about 1,300" in "Breakout at Harper's Ferry," *Civil War History*, II (1956), 15. The "unattached company" from Maryland was commanded by a "renegade" Virginian, S. C. Means, who was particularly anxious to escape because he was convinced that he would be hanged if he was captured. *Official Records*, Vol. XIX, Pt. 1, p. 752.

vember 28, 1861. It spent the first seven months of its existence fighting as infantry as part of Banks's command in the Shenandoah Valley.[51] Not until July, 1862, was the regiment mounted; barely a month later, on August 29, it was ordered to Harper's Ferry, and now, after two weeks at that post, it faced seemingly certain capture. But Davis did not propose to allow himself and his regiment to fall into Jackson's hands. In midafternoon on the fourteenth, he told Miles that the cavalry could be of no further use or help at Harper's Ferry and should be allowed to try to escape before the inevitable surrender. Miles agreed and held a meeting of the commanding officers of all the cavalry units present to discuss ways and means. After considerable debate, it was agreed that the troopers should be assembled at nightfall in the lightest marching order, cross the pontoon bridge to the Maryland side of the Potomac, and guided by an "old settler" named Noakes, try to escape via the "John Brown Road" running at the foot of Maryland Heights, and then by mountain paths leading northward toward Sharpsburg and beyond. Colonel Miles stipulated that the cavalry leave quietly, without bugle calls, because "he did not want the infantry to be aware of it until they were gone."[52]

As soon as it was dark, the troopers ate supper, fed their horses, and by eight o'clock they were in line, ready to move off.[53] Led by Colonel Davis himself, they crossed the pontoon bridge in pairs and at a walk and broke into a run as soon as they reached *terra firma*. To avoid the rebel pickets and camps, the column followed a "circuitous path, through lanes and byroads, woods and fields."[54] Davis set a killing pace, the moonless night was "intensely dark," and the column stretched out to a length of several miles. Despite this, only 178 of those who had started were missing when the escapees reached Greencastle, Pennsylvania, at be-

---

51. Being forced to serve as infantry had led "some" members of the regiment to take "French leave." Norton, *Deeds of Daring*, 18.

52. *Official Records*, Vol. XIX, Pt. 1, p. 584.

53. The College Cavaliers, as they were tightening their saddle girths preparatory to moving out, were encouraged by their major, Augustus W. Corliss, with the remark that by morning "they would either be in Pennsylvania, or in hell, or on the way to Richmond." Pettengill, *College Cavaliers*, 78.

54. Luff, "March of the Cavalry," 42.

tween nine and ten o'clock the next morning, and most of the missing turned up later.[55]

The worst of the danger was past, and the pace moderated after the column got beyond Sharpsburg and struck the Hagerstown turnpike about two miles north of Williamsport. At this crossroads, Davis had the good fortune to run into the reserve ammunition train of Longstreet's corps. Taking advantage of the darkness and without firing a shot, he captured some ninety-seven wagons, each drawn by six mules, the escort of between two and three hundred infantry, and, for good measure, a large herd of beef cattle.[56] As the sun rose on the morning of the sixteenth, "bright and warm, the scene upon the pike was very enlivening."

> The long train of heavily loaded wagons rumbling over the hard smooth road as rapidly as they could be urged forward, enveloped by clouds of cavalrymen with a solid column in their rear, the clouds of dust, the cracking of whips, the cries of the drivers, and the shouts of the officers and men, formed a striking contrast to the long march in the silence and darkness of the previous night. The command . . . was welcomed by the citizens of Pennsylvania with the utmost enthusiasm. . . . Long before reaching Greencastle, the people thronged the road, handing up fruit, cakes and pies to the soldiers.[57]

It was estimated that the zigzag, roundabout route covered by the column in about fourteen hours measured between fifty and sixty miles. It is no wonder, therefore, that "the command arrived in Greencastle in an exhausted condition, especially the horses, which were unfit to move for several days."[58]

A week later, McClellan wrote the general-in-chief that the "conspicuous conduct" of Benjamin Davis merited the "special notice of the Government" and recommended that he be given the brevet rank of major in the Regular Army. The promotion was

55. Mies, "Breakout at Harper's Ferry," 27.
56. *Ibid.*, 24. Norton, in *Deeds of Daring*, 32, gives seventy-five as the number of wagons captured.
57. Luff, "March of the Cavalry," 45–46.
58. *Ibid.*, 46. Other accounts of the breakout are in *Official Records*, Vol. XIX, Pt. 1, pp. 629, 770–71, and 753–54, and in C. Armour Newcomer, *Cole's Cavalry, or, Three Years in the Saddle in the Shenandoah Valley* (Baltimore, 1895), 43–44.

duly made.[59] Davis received another promotion that may have meant more to him that his new rank. In the early days of his regiment, his men had thought him too much of a Regular Army spit-and-polish disciplinarian. They changed their minds after the Harper's Ferry escape and, thereafter, "would follow [Davis], for they thought the Colonel could go anywhere and take them through all right."[60] The escape of some number between fifteen hundred and twenty-five hundred Union cavalrymen was not likely to affect the outcome of the war, but it was not without significance as a demonstration of what even relatively inexperienced troops were capable of doing under resolute and competent leadership.

Two days before the Harper's Ferry escape, on September 13, Corporal Barton W. Mitchell of the 27th Indiana Infantry found the famous "Lost Order." Delivered to McClellan on the evening of the same day, it revealed the whereabouts of Lee's army, division by division. McClellan had an army of six corps, about ninety thousand men and, as usual, greatly overestimated the enemy's numbers. Nevertheless, the Lost Order told him that the Confederate army was divided, and a glance at the map showed that he was nearer to each of its two segments than they were to each other. He had the advantage of good roads and fine weather for marching; by moving fast and crossing South Mountain westward, his army would be squarely between the two halves of Lee's army, each of which it outnumbered three to one or better, and it could destroy the halves one at a time. But General Lee learned that McClellan had the Lost Order. He immediately sent D. H. Hill to block Turner's Gap, over which the National Road crossed South Mountain, and ordered Longstreet's corps to Boonsboro, where it could support Hill and at the same time be twelve miles nearer Jackson. For two days, the fourteenth and fifteenth, McClellan had Lee at his mercy, but his advance lacked the drive that the situation required, and Lee was given time to concentrate his army in front of Sharpsburg, in the tongue of land between Antietam Creek and the Potomac.

59. *Official Records*, Vol. XIX, Pt. 1, pp. 802, 796n.
60. Norton, *Deeds of Daring*, 24, 35. The Confederate reaction to the escape of the cavalry, quoted previously, is in Blackford, *War Years with Jeb Stuart*, 146.

There, on the seventeenth, after another lost day, McClellan attacked. The ensuing battle produced some of the deadliest fighting of the entire war. Losses were about even, twelve thousand to a side, but the result for the Army of the Potomac was at best a draw. When firing died down on the night of the seventeenth, the badly mauled Confederates were still in position behind Antietam Creek. General Lee waited all day on the eighteenth to see what McClellan would do. McClellan did him the favor of doing nothing, and that night the Confederates recrossed the Potomac without molestation. For six weeks following the battle the Union army remained on its side of the river. These six weeks were filled with increasingly acrimonious correspondence between McClellan and the War Department, and eventually the president himself, mainly on the subject of horses.

Except for Stuart's Chambersburg Raid, cavalry played a minor role in the Maryland Campaign. The Federal cavalry began the campaign practically unhorsed, and the provision of remounts was beset by confusion and recrimination. McClellan contended, correctly, that when the Army of the Potomac marched away from Washington into Maryland on September 8, it was "greatly deficient in cavalry horses, the hard service to which they had been subjected . . . having rendered about half of them unserviceable."[61] Then, within a few days after the campaign began, an epidemic of "greased heel" struck the weakened animals.[62] From the second of September until the twentieth, no forage was issued to the cavalry, and the horses "fed . . . on green corn-stalks almost entirely, a very poor food . . . and supposed to have much to do with producing the epidemic of 'grease heel'."[63] Colonel Rufus Ingalls, the able and energetic chief quartermaster of the Army of the Potomac, reported after the campaign was over,

The artillery and cavalry required large numbers [of horses] to cover losses sustained in battle, on the march, and by disease. Both of these

61. *Official Records*, Vol. XIX, Pt. 1, p. 17.
62. Greased heel (also called grease heel, greasy heel, or simply grease) is a chronic inflammation of the skin of the horse's fetlocks and pasterns, marked by the oozing of an oily secretion, ulcerations, and in severe cases, a general swelling of the legs, nodular excrescences, and a foul-smelling discharge. It usually attacks horses kept or worked under unsanitary conditions.
63. Crowninshield, "Cavalry in Virginia," 26.

arms were deficient when they left Washington. A most violent and destructive disease made its appearance at this time, which put nearly 4,000 animals out of service. Horses reported perfectly well one day would be dead or lame the next, and it was difficult to foresee where it would end or what number would cover the loss. They were attacked in the hoof and tongue. No one seemed to be able to account satisfactorily for the appearance of the disease. Animals kept at rest would recover in time, but could not be worked.[64]

There was the usual amount of bureaucratic bumbling and bungling in the replacement of dead and broken-down horses, and it led to the exchange of innumerable letters between McClellan, Halleck, Stanton, Meigs, and the president. The stream of messages on this wearisome topic continued in spate until McClellan's removal from command. He complained to Halleck on October 12 that his entire army, including the portion of it assigned to the defenses of Washington, was receiving a total of only 1,050 cavalry and artillery horses per week, and that it was "absolutely necessary that some energetic measures be taken to supply the cavalry . . . with remount horses."[65] Halleck countered with the claim that in the six weeks following the beginning of September, a weekly average of 1,459, not 1,050, horses had been issued to McClellan, and he added the not particularly helpful remark that McClellan's "present proportion of cavalry and of animals is much larger than that of any other of our armies."[66] McClellan's rejoinder contended that "this army," by which he doubtless meant the portion of his command still at the Antietam, had received only 1,964 horses since September 8, and, opening a new line of attack, he wrote that "of those delivered very many were totally unfit for the service and should never have been re-

64. *Official Records*, Vol. XIX, Pt. 1, p. 95. B. W. Crowninshield of the 1st Massachusetts states that "the result [of the epidemic] was disastrous. Nearly half of the horses of the Army of the Potomac were rendered unserviceable, and vast numbers died. . . . Those of the 1st Massachusetts Cavalry were easy prey for the disease, and the regiment within two weeks from the battle of Antietam was practically unhorsed." Crowninshield, *A History of the First Regiment*, 77.

65. McClellan's telegram of October 12 to Halleck, as printed in the *Official Records*, Vol. XIX, Pt. 1, p. 13, shows 150 as the number of horses received per week. The same wire, as quoted in McClellan's report of the campaign, has the doubtless correct figure of 1,050. *Ibid.*, 77.

66. *Ibid.*, 79.

ceived," which was probably true. He closed by quoting General Alfred Pleasonton, then in command of a so-called "Cavalry Division," who had reported that "the horses now purchased for the cavalry are much inferior to those first obtained, and are not suitable for the hard service of cavalry horses."[67]

Then General Meigs, who, if there had been a special award in the Civil War for patience and restraint under extreme provocation, would have won it hands down, pointed out that when McClellan resumed command, he directed that horses were to be issued only on his own or his designated staff officers' orders, and that the remounts had been divided between the field army and the defenses of Washington on the basis of these officers' orders. All of the 11,000 actually issued could have been sent to the Antietam if McClellan and his officers had so directed. "If General McClellan," Meigs went on, "will instruct the officers authorized to approve requisitions in his name to confine this approval to issues to be made on the Upper Potomac, all the horses will be sent there till his wants are fully supplied; but if by his authority . . . they approve requisitions for the troops in front of Washington, the horses will be issued to these troops."[68]

As to the quality of the horses supplied, General Meigs explained,

The horses lately provided have been procured . . . on specifications and inspection identical with those formerly used, excepting that, finding five year-old horses liable to distemper and disease, officers . . . have generally been instructed to buy no horses under six years of age. The demand for horses has been so great lately that they have been carried off and put to use in many cases before they recovered from the fatigue and exhaustion of transportation. . . . A case is reported in which horses remained fifty hours on the cars without food or water, were taken out, issued and put to immediate service. The horses were good when shipped, and a few days' rest and food would have recruited them, but the exigencies of the service, or perhaps carelessness and ignorance, put them to a test which no horses could bear.

67. *Ibid.*, 17.
68. This and the following quotation are from *ibid.*, 19. See also *ibid.*, Pt. 2, pp. 416 and 422–24. General Meigs was not the man to be satisfied with scoring a debating victory over McClellan. He also authorized Colonel Ingalls to purchase 2,500 horses locally, as fast as he could get them.

It is of interest to note that at the same time McClellan was begging for more cavalry and for remounts for the cavalry he already had, General Banks, in immediate command of the Washington defenses, was also clamoring for more cavalry and more horses.[69]

The return of McClellan to command had produced a nearly miraculous resurgence of morale and spirit in the Army of the Potomac. The same formations that were badly beaten and sustained heavy casualties at Second Bull Run, only three weeks later drove D. H. Hill out of Turner's Gap, and at Antietam charged through the Cornfield and East Wood and over the Bloody Lane. The postwar reminiscences of a relatively small number of literate individuals are not always a safe guide to the emotional state of their fellow soldiers at any given moment, and contemporary orders and reports of the Civil War era hardly ever dealt in such abstractions as morale. Nevertheless, what evidence there is suggests that McClellan's cavalry did not share in the revival of morale experienced by the rest of the army.

This is not surprising. The experience of two of McClellan's cavalry regiments was sufficiently typical to account for a disheartened, dispirited cavalry. The 1st Massachusetts, seven hundred strong at the end of August when it arrived from South Carolina, received no rations for eighteen days, from September 2 to September 20 ("The troopers fed upon green corn, apples, and past recollections, with an occasional feast at some farmhouse"), and lost horses daily until by the end of October, the dismounted men having been sent to the rear, fewer than three hundred men were left with the colors, their uniforms in rags, many without boots or even stockings, and not a tent in the entire regiment.[70] The 3rd Pennsylvania began the Maryland Campaign as a "skele-

69. *Ibid.*, 8–9, 349.

70. Crowninshield, "Cavalry in Virginia," 26; Crowninshield, *A History of the First Regiment*, 77–84. In an October 25 dispatch, McClellan quotes a report of Colonel Williams of the 1st Massachusetts, to the effect that he had only 267 horses, 128 of which "are positively and absolutely unable to leave the camp, for the following causes, viz., sore-tongue, grease and consequent lameness, and sore backs." McClellan added that of the 5th United States' 70 horses, 53 "are worthless from the above causes. . . . The horses that are still sound are absolutely broken down from fatigue and want of flesh." *Official Records*, Vol. XIX, Pt. 2, pp. 484–85.

ton of a regiment," most of its men having been sent to dismounted camp; those remaining were in a state "almost of destitution as
regards clothing."[71]

On September 20, McClellan appointed John Buford chief of
cavalry of the Army of the Potomac, a thoroughly worthy appointment, but the post remained what it had been, a staff assignment
without command authority.[72] That authority, insofar as it existed
at all independently of the infantry commands, was—or seemed
to be—vested in Alfred Pleasonton, who was placed in charge of
a cavalry division made up of five small brigades.[73]

Pleasonton, a graduate of West Point, Class of 1844, a captain in the 2nd United States when the war broke out, was to have
his moment of glory at Hazel Grove in the battle of Chancellorsville, but his effectiveness was greatly hampered by the distrust
and dislike he inspired among the officers serving under him. He
suffered from serious personality faults which were to show up
most conspicuously in 1864, when, exiled to the West, he commanded the cavalry in the operations against Sterling Price's last
invasion of Missouri.[74] Charles Russell Lowell, colonel of the 2nd

71. Regimental History Committee, *History of the 3d Pennsylvania*,
117, 130.
72. By Special Orders No. 242, in *Official Records*, Vol. XIX, Pt. 2,
p. 242.
73. For the table of organization of the division, see *ibid.*, Pt. 1, p.
180. Pleasonton's brigade commanders were Major C. J. Whiting (First
Brigade), and Colonels J. F. Farnsworth (Second), R. H. Rush (Third),
A. T. McReynolds (Fourth), and B. F. Davis (Fifth). The Second Brigade
had four regiments; the others had two each. Parts of every one of the
twelve regiments in the division were serving on escort and provost duty
with the various corps and divisions of army infantry, a total of twenty-
five companies—17 percent of the whole—being assigned to such duties
and hence absent from their regiments. In addition to the regiments making up the division, eight companies of the 6th New York were attached
to General Burnside's IX Corps "as escort and advance guard . . . being
broken up in squadrons, companies and squads . . . [and] practically all
over the field." *Ibid.*, 169–79; Committee on Regimental History, *History
of the Sixth New York*, 63.
74. Pleasonton served with the Dragoons on the frontier, in the Mexican and Seminole wars, and on the Missouri border at the time of the
Kansas-Missouri troubles in the 1850s. He transferred as a captain to the
2nd United States. He was promoted to brigadier general of volunteers in
July, 1862, and major general in June, 1863, and was brevetted brigadier
general and major general in the Regular Army.

Massachusetts, wrote of him, "I can't call any cavalry officer good who can't see the truth and tell the truth. With an infantry officer this is not so essential, but cavalry are the eyes and ears of the army and ought to see and hear and tell truly; and yet it is the universal opinion that P[leasonton]'s own reputation and P[leasonton]'s late promotions are bolstered up by systematic lying."[75] However truthful or untruthful Pleasonton may have been, he clearly lacked the dynamism that was needed at the top to bring the cavalry of the Army of the Potomac up to its full potential.

It must, however, be said in Pleasonton's behalf that at this moment at least, he had to work within the confines of a cavalry command structure that was a triumph of inept confusion. On September 19, the Confederate army having the night before crossed the Potomac unmolested, McClellan announced to Halleck that "Pleasonton is driving the enemy across the river. Our victory is complete. The enemy is driven back into Virginia."[76] Deception, or self-deception, could go no further. The next day, the selfsame Pleasonton sent the following dispatch to General Randolph B. Marcy, McClellan's chief of staff and father-in-law: "The order of Major-General FitzJohn Porter of yesterday [i.e., of the 19th] sending my command to the rear, by order of General McClellan, and which was transmitted by General Buford, has interfered most materially with a proper pursuit of the enemy. . . . I trust, after the past experience of yesterday, the general commanding will not permit corps commanders to interfere with the cavalry under my command, for it breaks up all my system and plans."[77]

75. Emerson, *Charles Russell Lowell*, 279. Charles Francis Adams, Jr., was equally scathing. He wrote, "Pleasonton is the bete noire of all cavalry officers. . . . He is pure and simple a newspaper humbug. You always see his name in the papers, but to us who have served under him he is notorious as a bully and a toady. . . . Yet mean and contemptible as Pleasonton is, he is always *in* at Head Quarters." Adams to his mother, May 12, 1863, in Ford, *A Cycle of Adams Letters*, II, 8.

76. A more accurate account of what happened is, "The morning after Lee with perfect success crossed the Potomac, the cavalry rode down to the high river banks, looked across . . . and collected the very meager leavings of Lee's army, a few abandoned wagons, a caisson or two, and other worthless trash. This was heralded in McClellan's dispatches as 'the cavalry pursuing Lee's routed columns across the Potomac'." Crowninshield, "Cavalry in Virginia," 10.

77. *Official Records*, Vol. XIX, Pt. 2, p. 334. General Marcy had in-

The strength reports for October 10 show Pleasonton still in command of the cavalry division, but Special Orders No. 290 of October 21 announce the formation of a five-regiment cavalry *brigade*, with Pleasonton in command.[78] All five of the regiments in the new brigade had been in the cavalry *division*, about which nothing more is heard thereafter. The reasons, if any, for the change do not appear in the records.

Early in the Maryland Campaign, the Confederates occupied Frederick—thus providing the basis for the Barbara Frietschie legend—and held it for a few days, until General Lee divided his army and marched north with part of it to Hagerstown, while Jackson led the rest south to Harper's Ferry. Last to leave Frederick was Wade Hampton's cavalry. Just as its rear guard marched out of the town, Captain Charles Francis Adams, Jr., of the 1st Massachusetts wrote:

[The 8th Illinois,] commanded by Colonel Farnsworth . . . hurried into the town [and] were cracking away with their carbines, and giving to me, at least, the idea of a sharp engagement in progress . . . but, as I rode through the single street of the pretty little town, a little excited and pistol in hand, I was . . . surprised . . . at the number of women who were waving their handkerchiefs and hailing us with delight as liberators. . . . It certainly didn't look to me much like a battle. . . . In vain I looked for the rebels, nary one could I see and at last it dawned on my mind that I was in the midst of a newspaper battle . . . lots of glory but n'ary reb.[79]

On September 13, Pleasonton had led the march of the army across Catoctin Mountain to Middletown and reconnoitered the Confederate position at Turner's Gap. At daylight on the fifteenth, after D. H. Hill's division had been driven out of the gap, Pleasonton with the 8th Illinois "started in pursuit of the enemy"; it is puzzling why, with several regiments of cavalry at his disposal, he "pursued" with one regiment only, and that far below full strength. This small detachment came up with the Confederate rear guard, the 9th Virginia, at Boonsboro, near the western foot

formed Porter, presumably during the night of September 18/19, that "Pleasonton had been directed to have his cavalry and artillery at the river by daylight." *Ibid.*, 331. Since the dispatch is dated September 19, it must have been written sometime after midnight.

78. *Ibid.*, 460.
79. Ford, *A Cycle of Adams Letters*, I, 186–87.

of Turner's Gap. Here there was no repetition of the Frederick "newspaper battle," and there were plenty of "rebs." By means of repeated charges, the 8th Illinois drove them out of the town and two miles beyond it, where the Virginians scattered in all directions. It was a soul-satisfying success for the men from Illinois, who captured two pieces of artillery and "a very large number of prisoners, among whom were several hundred stragglers." Pleasonton claimed that the Confederates also left thirty killed and "some 50 wounded" on the field; his own losses were one killed and fifteen wounded.[80]

One southern trooper recorded at this time the opinion that "the Yankee cavalry . . . is getting bold, adventurous, mighty and numerous." Another, perhaps in a better position to judge, wrote that on the retreat of Lee's army from Boonsboro to the Antietam position, "the [Confederate] cavalry covered the rear and engaged in constant and fierce conflicts with the advanced guard of the foe. Their cavalry never, at this time, ventured within our reach without heavy infantry support, so that all we could do was to drive them back a short distance behind their reserves."[81]

The 4,320 Union cavalry present at the Antietam had only a passive role in the battle.[82] Much of it was assigned to the job of "supporting the artillery," the major portion of which (including the five batteries of Regulars belonging to the cavalry division) shelled the Confederate infantry and artillery from the high ground east of Antietam Creek.[83] Supporting a battery was a job

80. *Official Records*, Vol. XIX, Pt. 1, pp. 210, 26–27. See also Ford, *A Cycle of Adams Letters*, I, 189, and Hard, *History of the Eighth Cavalry*, 178. The fight at Boonsboro is a rarity in that the Federal and Confederate accounts agree on the fact that the latter were driven from the field. See Beale, *History of the Ninth Virginia*, 39. The 9th Virginia was part of a brigade commanded by Colonel Fitzhugh Lee, who was unhorsed early in the action, but managed to escape.

81. The favorable comment is from Neese, *Three Years in the Confederate Horse Artillery*, 118; the unfavorable comment is in Blackford, *War Years with Jeb Stuart*, 142.

82. *Official Records*, Vol. XIX, Pt. 1, p. 67.

83. Pickerill, *History of the Third Indiana*, 30; Ford, *A Cycle of Adams Letters*, I, 189; Hyndman, *History of a Cavalry Company*, 66. The 4th Pennsylvania lost its colonel and had three troopers killed and five wounded by enemy counter-battery fire in this totally senseless assignment. Parts of the cavalry were also assigned to the job of "driving up

frequently assigned to the Federal cavalry, especially in the first years of the war, by general officers who were not inspired to use horsemen in any effective way.[84] The Federal batteries at the Antietam were in no danger whatever of being attacked by Confederate infantry, and the cavalry's pistols and relatively few carbines could not have stopped a determined infantry attack if there had been one. Nevertheless, the cavalry was present, something had to be done with it, and hence it was ordered to support the batteries. It occurred to no one, as perhaps it should have, to order the cavalry to patrol or block the road up to Sharpsburg from Harper's Ferry (the road on which Colonel Davis and his men had made their escape) on the chance that more Confederate troops might be coming from that direction to join in the battle. As it happened, A. P. Hill's division actually took that road from Harper's Ferry and arrived just in time to overwhelm the outer flank of Ambrose Burnside's greatly delayed but successful attack on the Confederate right. Had Hill been held up for an hour or two by a fighting retreat of the Federal cavalry, the outcome of the battle might well have been a disaster for Lee and a clear-cut victory for the Union.[85] The Federal losses at Antietam were 12,469 killed, wounded, and missing. The cavalry's share of the total was 5 killed and 23 wounded.

Encouraged by McClellan's boastful "Our victory is complete" telegram, the entire North, and the administration most of all, expected that he would press his advantage by following the Confederates across the Potomac. The days went by, however, and there was no such move, nor any indication of it being in prospect. The president himself paid McClellan a visit of several days to try to find out what his intentions were. On his return to Washington, he had Halleck wire McClellan on October 6 an order "to

stragglers while awaiting opportunity for other service." *Official Records,* Vol. XIX, Pt. 1, p. 31.

84. In contrast, Stuart and his cavalry were posted on the Confederate left wing. When Hooker's attack smashed through Jackson's left, Stuart's horse artillery, and his horsemen fighting dismounted, delivered an effective flank fire on the Federal advance.

85. See the interesting critique of McClellan's use of his cavalry at Antietam in Edward P. Alexander, *Military Memoirs of a Confederate* (New York, 1907), 270–71.

cross the Potomac and give battle to the enemy or drive him south. You must move now while the roads are good."[86] It was at this point that the vast correspondence began concerning the lack of transportation, clothing, supplies, and especially horses and cavalry, shortages which, McClellan contended, made it impossible for his army to advance.

The Confederate army also had shortages at least as serious as those that filled McClellan's messages, but a lack of willingness to make maximum use of the resources it did have was not one of them. On October 4, Confederate cavalry under John D. Imboden rode north toward Cumberland, Maryland, and burned the Little Cacapon bridge. W. W. Averell, who had just been given command of a cavalry brigade, was directed to "set out with all . . . [his] disposable force . . . and endeavor to intercept this cavalry, and show them that these raids cannot be made with impunity."[87] Imboden was not intercepted, but with Averell's brigade drawn off to the west in a futile chase, the field was cleared for Stuart. With eighteen hundred picked men and two sections (four pieces) of artillery, on the morning of October 10 he crossed the Potomac at McCoy's Ferry, headed north to Chambersburg, and then east and southeast, skirting a small Pennsylvania town named Gettysburg. He rode through Emmitsburg, Liberty, Hyattstown, and Barnesville and on the morning of October 12 recrossed the Potomac to Leesburg at White's Ford, about twenty-five miles southeast of Harper's Ferry. On the ride from Chambersburg to Leesburg, Stuart covered eighty miles in twenty-seven hours, with only one half-hour break on the evening of the eleventh to feed the horses. With one man wounded as his only casualty, Stuart had once again ridden around the Federal army. Aside from the twelve hundred horses he picked up in the villages and farms along the way and took back to Virginia, the only loss suffered by the North was a loss of face, but that was serious enough, and to no one more so than to the army commander who had now for the second time suffered this indignity.[88] Stuart was squarely on

86. *Official Records*, Vol. XIX, Pt. 1, p. 72.
87. *Ibid.*, Pt. 2, p. 389.
88. In his report of the raid, Stuart made a point of complimenting his men on their "behavior toward the inhabitants," which, he wrote, was

the mark in claiming in his report that "the result of [the] expedition, in a moral and political point of view, can hardly be
exaggerated."[89]

In one important respect, the Union army met the challenge
of this raid in creditable fashion. With his army posted along the
Potomac between the mouth of Antietam Creek and Harper's
Ferry, McClellan had prompt notice of the raid and remarkably
accurate reports of Stuart's strength.[90] Every commanding officer
upstream and downstream of army headquarters was alerted in
ample time, and had it not been for bumbling performances by
some of them, and just plain bad luck, Stuart would have had to
fight his way back to Virginia. Pleasonton, with the eight hundred
mounted men he had available, was sent north to the neighborhood of Hagerstown to "cut off the retreat of the enemy should
he make for any of the fords below the position of the main army
. . . to pursue them with the utmost rapidity, and not to spare his
men or horses, and to destroy them or capture them if possible."[91]
Stoneman, at Poolesville, ten miles below White's Ford, was ordered "to keep his cavalry well out on all the different approaches
from the direction of Frederick . . . to give him [Stoneman] time
to mass his forces so as to resist . . . [the enemy's] crossing into
Virginia."[92] No fault can be found with Pleasonton's performance
of his assignment. His scouts located the raiders and determined
that they were headed for the mouth of the Monocacy. Pleasonton followed at the best speed of his horses, but he was not fast

"worthy of the highest praise; a few individual cases only were exceptions
in this particular." *Ibid.*, 53. For an interesting description of the Confederates' order of march on this raid, see Blackford, *War Years with Jeb
Stuart*, 170–71.

89. *Official Records*, Vol. XIX, Pt. 2, p. 53.

90. General Marcy telegraphed General George Crook on October 10,
"It is said that the force of the rebels consists of four regiments of cavalry
and four pieces of artillery." *Ibid.*, 63.

91. *Ibid.*, Pt. 1, p. 72. Pleasonton's eight hundred was made up of
portions of the 8th Illinois and the 3rd Indiana, and a section (two pieces)
of artillery under Lieutenant A. C. M. Pennington, Jr. The 3rd Indiana was
one of the regiments whose men owned their horses; there was a lesson in
the fact that throughout the troubles of September to October, 1862, it was
the one cavalry regiment with McClellan whose horses remained in reasonably good condition.

92. *Ibid.*, Pt. 2, p. 30.

enough. By the time he reached White's Ford with the four hundred men who had been able to keep up after a grueling seventy-eight-mile march, Stuart had already crossed into Virginia "without . . . molestation."[93] Stoneman had scattered most of his forces (mainly infantry) up and down the river to guard every possible crossing: The few pickets he had at White's Ford were brushed aside, and by the time he got there from Poolesville with his main body, Stuart was already across the river.

The general reaction of the army to Stuart's exploit was voiced by Colonel Charles S. Wainwright of the artillery, who wrote in his journal, "It is a burning disgrace that with 2,000 cavalry . . . [Stuart] should have been permitted to ride rough-shod through so well settled a country, and not a shot fired at him, as it is that our cavalry should have allowed it. It is said that what little cavalry we have is so badly off for horses that they can do nothing. But with the exception of the few regulars and two or three other regiments, I fear our cavalry is an awful botch."[94] And there was scant comfort for the unfortunate McClellan in the remark of the usually considerate president that Halleck was at pains to pass on to him. "The President," Halleck wrote, "directs me to suggest that, if the enemy had more occupation south of the river, his cavalry would not be so likely to make raids north of it."[95]

The dispute about McClellan's lack of sufficient cavalry was given fresh impetus by Stuart's raid, and he now used that as the principal reason for his inability to advance. The responses to his constantly reiterated pleas and complaints became steadily more impatient and frosty in tone, as the administration saw the campaigning season drawing to a close with no apparent prospect of a forward move by its showcase army, and as it reached the conclusion that the general's clamor for more cavalry and more horses was a mere excuse for continued inaction. Even after October 26, when at long last he began crossing the river, and almost up to November 7, when he was relieved of his command and replaced by Burnside, he continued to complain that he was

93. Ibid., 39–40.
94. Allan Nevins (ed.), A Diary of Battle: The Personal Journals of Colonel Charles S. Wainwright, 1861–1865 (New York, 1962), 115.
95. Official Records, Vol. XIX, Pt. 2, p. 421.

"still very deficient [in horses]," and "still too weak in cavalry."[96] Nevertheless, for all his clamor and despite the example of Stuart that he could have followed, McClellan failed to take the one step that might have enhanced the effectiveness of the cavalry he did have. He left it scattered in regiments and detachments among the infantry; brigades existed mainly for administrative purposes; Pleasonton's cavalry division quietly disappeared as an organization; and John Buford, who, given the chance, might have been able to turn McClellan's cavalry into a truly useful force, remained a staff officer.[97]

And yet the potential for better things was there and was demonstrated just two days before McClellan was replaced. On October 26, Pleasonton with his brigade and a battery of horse artillery crossed the Potomac at Berlin to scout the country in the direction of Leesburg, Aldie, Middleburg, and Philomont. On November 3, he was joined by Averell and his brigade. The ranks were thin; nevertheless, here was cavalry actually operating in brigade strength, and here were two brigades engaged in a joint operation. On November 5, Stuart, with three thousand of his troopers and a battery of horse artillery, met the Federals at Barbee's Cross Roads. Pleasonton sent David McM. Gregg with the 8th Pennsylvania and the 6th United States to attack Stuart's right flank, Benjamin F. Davis and his 8th New York to attack his left, and John F. Farnsworth and the 8th Illinois to move against the center. Davis, moving forward, saw that the Confederates, in numbers much larger than his, were preparing to charge him. He dismounted two of his companies, lined them up behind a stone wall, allowed the Confederates to advance, and,

96. *Ibid.*, 517 (October 31) and 532 (November 2). It is amusing to learn that at the very time McClellan was wearing out the patience of his superiors with his contention that his cavalry, "even when well supplied with horses, is much inferior in numbers to that of the enemy," General Lee wrote Secretary of War George W. Randolph that his cavalry was "greatly outnumbered by that of the Federals." *Ibid.*, Pt. 1, p. 81; Pt. 2, p. 701.
97. "During the Maryland campaign the cavalry, although brigaded, did not act by brigades." Crowninshield, *A History of the First Regiment,* 81. There is no indication of it in the records, but the reduction of Pleasonton's command from a division to a brigade may well have been caused by his failure to catch Stuart.

as soon as he saw that the flank and frontal fire of his dismounted men had thrown the enemy column into confusion, charged
it with the mounted portion of his regiment. His charge "routed
the enemy and sent them flying in all directions. Thirty-seven of
the rebel dead were left on this field, and more than that number
of arms, horses and prisoners were captured," at a cost of five
killed and eight wounded.[98]

Just as a thousand men need training and experience to operate effectively as a regiment, so regiments need training and
experience to operate as a brigade, and brigades as a division.
Neither the regiments nor the two brigades present at Barbee's
Cross Roads had had that kind of training or experience. Nevertheless, this engagement showed once again, if still only in a
small way, that the much maligned Federal cavalry had in it the
makings of an effective and valuable branch of the service. But
the three magic keys to success: better leadership, sounder organization, and more experience, were not yet in its possession.

98. *Official Records*, Vol. XIX, Pt. 2, p. 126; see also Rhodes, *Cavalry
of the Army of the Potomac*, 27.

Alfred Pleasonton

George Stoneman

James Harrison Wilson

Percy Wyndham

XII

The Edge of the Sword

THE BULK OF THE ARMY OF THE POTOMAC WAS AT WAR-
renton, Virginia, on the night of November 7, 1862, when Mc-
Clellan was relieved of his command and replaced by his good
friend, Ambrose Burnside.[1] A West Pointer, Class of 1847, Burnside had resigned from the army in 1853 to engage in the manufacture of firearms in Rhode Island. That enterprise failed, and
McClellan, then a vice-president of the Illinois Central Railroad,
gave Burnside a job. Offered the command of a brigade of Rhode
Island troops when the Civil War broke out, Burnside led it in the
battle of Bull Run. In the spring of 1862, he commanded the successful Federal expedition to capture Roanoke Island. Promoted
to major general, he was given command of the IX Corps in the
Army of the Potomac and was twice offered, and he twice refused, command of that army, first after McClellan's "change of
base" on the Peninsula, and then after Pope's defeat at Second
Bull Run. The third "offer" was an order which, in an evil moment for himself and for the army, Burnside felt obliged to obey.[2]

1. Order dated November 5, 1862, in *Official Records*, Vol. XIX, Pt. 2,
p. 545.
2. On taking over command, Burnside wrote General Halleck's chief

When Burnside assumed command of the army, it had James Longstreet's corps facing it near Warrenton. Jackson with his corps was still in the Valley, separated from Longstreet by the Blue Ridge. McClellan had intended to attack and defeat Longstreet before Jackson could come to his assistance. On the day he took over the command, Burnside proposed a different plan. He intended to "concentrate all the forces near . . . [Warrenton] and impress upon the enemy the belief that . . . [he was going] to attack Culpeper and Gordonsville, and . . . then . . . make a rapid move of the whole force to Fredericksburg with a view to a movement to Richmond from that point."[3]

To make Burnside's plan succeed, speed was essential. To establish itself in Fredericksburg, on the south bank of the Rappahannock, the army had to cross the river. The pontoons Burnside needed to make the crossing were delayed as a result of poor staff work, and by the time they arrived and the bridges were laid, the entire Confederate Army of Northern Virginia, 80,000 strong, was in position and well dug in on the high ground along the south bank of the stream. The Federals made good their crossing on December 11. On the thirteenth, they attacked the positions the Confederates had had two weeks to prepare and strengthen. The attacks were made with the utmost gallantry, particularly those against Longstreet's impregnable position on Marye's Heights, but the heroism of the Union infantry served only to increase the toll of casualties, which reached the ghastly total of 12,653 killed, wounded, and missing—15 percent of the troops actually engaged.[4]

One of Burnside's organizational changes prior to the battle was to group the six corps of his army into three "grand divisions."[5] Each of the grand divisions was made up of two corps of infantry and had assigned to it a cavalry component: a division

of staff, "The General-in-Chief will readily comprehend the embarrassments which surround me in taking command of this army. . . . Had I been asked to take it, I should have declined; but being ordered, I cheerfully obey." *Ibid.*, 554.

3. *Ibid.*, 552; see also a more detailed statement in *ibid.*, Vol. XXI, 99–101.

4. *Ibid.*, 142.

5. *Ibid.*, Vol. XIX, Pt. 2, p. 579. See also *ibid.*, XXI, 48–61.

of two brigades (six regiments) under Pleasonton was attached to the Right Grand Division, a brigade of four regiments under Averell to the Center Grand Division, and a five-regiment brigade under Bayard to the Left Grand Division.[6] The returns for November 10 showed 6,312 cavalry (including its horse artillery) then with the army, and although the orders assigning the cavalry to the grand divisions directed that "all detachments of cavalry serving with corps, divisions, brigades, &c., will at once rejoin their respective commands," Burnside himself, as well as General Edwin V. Sumner commanding the Right Grand Division, had cavalry escorts, and the provost guard contained, besides infantry, two unattached companies and an entire regiment —the 2nd United States—of cavalry. Hence the fifteen regiments under Pleasonton, Averell, and Bayard had an average strength of fewer than 400 men each.

Because of the nature of the battle of Fredericksburg, the weakness of the cavalry did not matter. Some of the horsemen served as dispatch riders and orderlies, but most of them were mere spectators, remaining in rear of the ridge on the north bank of the Rappahannock, whence 150 pieces of artillery, many of them large-caliber guns, bombarded the Confederate lines. They continued to occupy that position until the infantry retreated across the river two days after the battle.[7] Chaplain Henry R. Pyne, whose regiment, the 1st New Jersey, formed a part of Bayard's brigade, was posted behind the left of the Union artillery and observed,

[The] advance of the whole line of battle was a spectacle of such extended grandeur as almost to be called sublime. As the shrouding mist cleared away, and the bright rays of the sun glanced back from their glittering muskets, over half a mile of disciplined men moved forward with one accord, without a waver in their alignment. In

6. *Ibid.*, XXI, 785–86. See also *ibid.*, 48–61. One writer has suggested that this organizational scheme was the brainchild of General Bayard. Moore, *Kilpatrick and Our Cavalry*, 40. The change was a major step in the right direction, for Pleasonton's division and Averell's and Bayard's brigades were tactical as well as administrative units; it did not, however, go far enough.

7. Hyndman, *History of a Cavalry Company*, 76; see also *Official Records*, XXI, 220.

their appointed intervals the batteries of artillery rumbled across the plain, while before all the lightly equipped skirmishers darted forward from cover to cover toward the enemy.[8]

The spectator's role played by the cavalry throughout the battle is evidenced by its minuscule casualty roll of two killed and six wounded. One of the two killed, however, was one of the most promising officers of the mounted arm, Brigadier General George D. Bayard, struck by a piece of shell while at the headquarters of the Left Grand Division at General William B. Franklin's request, "to receive such orders as might be necessary for the cavalry."[9] The only portion of the cavalry to play anything more than a passive role was a part of Averell's brigade, sent upstream to guard against a possible Confederate crossing of the river—which did not occur—beyond the right flank of the Union position.[10]

In the days before the battle, the cavalry had been strung out along the north bank of the Rappahannock, guarding the many fords (the names of which were to become household words a few months later—United States Ford, Ellis' Ford, Kelly's Ford, and others) upstream from Fredericksburg.[11] On November 21, Pleasonton reported from Deep Run Creek (a small tributary of the Rappahannock) that the forage to be found in the neighborhood was exhausted, that the roads back to Hartwood, whence additional supplies could be had, were "almost impassable for wagons," and that the picketing duty assigned to his cavalry could be done much better by infantry, for, Pleasonton wrote, "the country is wooded and the river is very rocky, rendering it difficult for horsemen to navigate in its vicinity, and with no forage, they will soon be reduced to infantry."[12]

Be it said to Pleasonton's credit that in addition to dealing with the immediate problems of picketing, obtaining forage for his starving animals, and collecting infantry stragglers, he also gave thought to what he considered the fundamental problems

8. Pyne, *First New Jersey Cavalry*, 134.
9. *Official Records*, XXI, 451.
10. *Ibid.*, 113.
11. *Ibid.*, 102.
12. *Ibid.*, 781–82.

plaguing the Federal cavalry. He expressed his concerns and views in a "Memorandum" of December 1:

To obviate some of the defects existing at present in our cavalry organization, the following suggestions are . . . submitted:

1st. That portion of the army whose duties are to cover the front and flanks of the army[,] form advanced guards, and . . . perform all the functions of cavalry as a corps, should be organized as such into brigades and divisions, with a common commander, under the direct orders of the commander of the army. The cavalry is a distinct arm of the service, having specific duties to perform, that can only be properly discharged under an organization conformable to those duties. It is, therefore, recommended that such legislation be obtained as will give the cavalry a corps organization.

2nd. [Recommends that for the "orderly(,) escort and detached service" with corps, divisions, and grand divisions of infantry, "cavalry regiments just entering the service" be used.]

3d. To insure accuracy and uniformity in the reports to the commanding general of the army, the cavalry used in obtaining the information must be under the orders of the same person. . . . under different independent commanders, each gets mistrustful of the other in the field, is soon confounded . . . and eventually becomes timid. Such has been the experience of this war up to this time. Our cavalry can be made superior to any now in the field by organization. The rebel cavalry owe their success to their organization, which permits great freedom and responsibility to its commanders, subject to the commanding general.

4th. The horse artillery should invariably belong and serve with the cavalry. Eight batteries would be a proper allowance to a corps of two divisions of cavalry.[13]

When Joseph Hooker reorganized the cavalry two months later, the pattern he adopted followed the recommendations of Pleasonton's first and third paragraphs, although nothing indicates that he was guided specifically by the cavalryman's suggestions. It is more likely that these ideas were common talk around cavalry campfires—ideas whose time had come. Hooker, like his predecessors, also had the example of the Confederate army to follow, as Pleasonton pointed out. However, to create the corps organization for the cavalry, action by Congress was needed; his-

13. *Ibid.*, 815.

torians, accustomed as they now are to legislation that lays down broad guidelines and delegates to the executive the implementation of the policy enunciated, tend to forget that in the Civil War era, the army's tables of organization, down to the number of buglers per regiment, were regulated in minute detail by Congress.

The records fail to indicate to whom Pleasonton submitted his memorandum. If it was seen by Burnside, he failed to act on it; considering his problems (of which the Confederate army was only the most apparent) it is not surprising that he did not do so. Near the end of December, however, he had a conversation with Averell, who proposed (and confirmed in a dispatch later the same day) forming a body of a thousand picked men by taking fifty to two hundred men from each of nine different regiments (the 1st, 2nd, 4th, and 5th United States, 3rd and 4th Pennsylvania, 8th New York, 1st Rhode Island, and 1st Massachusetts) plus Alexander C. M. Pennington Jr.'s battery. With this force, he said, he would cross the Rappahannock at Kelly's Ford, then the Rapidan at Raccoon Ford, approximately half-way between Culpeper and Orange Court House, and march thence southeastward, across the James to the south of Petersburg, and on to the Federal lines at Suffolk, Virginia. Averell may have explained to Burnside what he expected the military benefits of this ambitious expedition to be; in his confirmation he says merely that "a topographical engineer . . . with 20 well-mounted men, provided with means of destroying bridges, culverts, telegraph wires, &c., would be very essential" and that he also intended to take along twenty axes.[14] If the object of the march was to raise the morale of the Federal cavalry by demonstrating that it too could mount a long-distance raid, with, as a bonus, some incidental destruction of bridges and culverts miles from the area of active operations, it may be questioned whether it was worth the risks involved. Even if fully successful, it would have removed for an indefinite period from the army, already short of cavalry, a thousand of its best

14. *Ibid.*, 895–96. There is a suggestion in Burnside's report that he intended to have a cavalry raid precede or coincide with a move by the entire army. *Ibid.*, 95–96. If that was actually the case, the idea of the raid may well have been Burnside's, with only the details being Averell's.

cavalrymen and their horses, and considering the probable state of Virginia roads in early January, the odds against success were high indeed. Nevertheless, Burnside approved the proposal within twenty-four hours, and Averell, who wasted no time, had apparently already started when "owing to information received from Washington," he was ordered to suspend the operation and to try instead to intercept a Confederate cavalry raid on the Orange & Alexandria Railroad.[15]

With the Union and Confederate armies facing each other across the Rappahannock and winter closing in, the Federals began to build their winter camps. In the dismal aftermath of the defeat at Fredericksburg, the morale of the Army of the Potomac was at its lowest point of the entire war. The lack of a systematic program of furloughs, lack of confidence in the leadership that prevaded all ranks and was particularly and viciously vocal in the highest ranks, and the lack of pay, several months in arrears, created an atmosphere of "gloom and despondency" and "increased the number of desertions to a fearful extent."[16]

Nonetheless, the men busied themselves with the building of their little log huts and went about the job of making themselves

15. *Ibid.*, 902. The order to Averell to proceed is not in the *Offiicial Records*, but it was probably dated December 19, for the order to Hooker, spelling out the manner in which the infantry was to assist Averell, bears that date; *ibid.*, 897. The reference in the countermanding order to "information . . . from Washington" is to a telegram of December 30 from the president to Burnside, reading, "I have good reason for saying you must not make a general movement of the army, without letting me know." The "good reason" was the stories that had reached the president of the poor morale of the Army of the Potomac.

16. *Ibid.*, 96. Testimony is unanimous on the poor morale of the army in the weeks following Fredericksburg. Charles Francis Adams, Jr., wrote, "The Army of the Potomac is thoroughly demoralized. They will fight yet, but they will fight for defeat. . . . There is a great deal of croaking, no confidence, plenty of sickness, and desertion is the order of the day." Ford, *A Cycle of Adams Letters*, I, 241. Augustus Buell wrote that "even the capability of enthusiasm seemed to have died out of the army at this time. It was ready to fight again as it had fought before. . . . But the rank and file . . . had begun to consider themselves better soldiers than their commanders. Buell, *"The Cannoneer,"* 49. As to the openly insubordinate talk of grand division and corps commanders, see Nevins, *A Diary of Battle*, 157–58. "Desertions ran from 43 to 136 in the different corps. . . . about one man in every ten was in desertion or absent without leave." Bigelow, *The Campaign of Chancellorsville*, 36.

as comfortable as possible for the winter. The troopers of the 1st Maine missed the "clear, steady cold, and clean snow" of their native state and learned that the "hardest work [in camp] was to keep comfortable." Their historian relates,

What wood was originally in the vicinity of the camp-ground was soon used up, and before the winter was over the boys had to go a long distance for fuel. The camp-ground was always covered with from four to twenty inches of mud, or from two to twelve inches of snow, and wet feet were the rule. . . . there were drills, company, regimental and brigade, at every opportunity, and frequent reviews and inspections, without much regard for the weather. . . . Fatigue duty was plenty. The horses could not be allowed to stand in the soft mud, so the stables were corduroyed, as were many of the company streets, most of which work was done on Sundays. . . . the men were kept busy all the time. . . . The rations issued were excellent. The regular rations, bread, hard and soft, pork, beef, coffee, etc., were good, and besides these, potatoes and other vegetables were issued frequently. . . . Many men received boxes from home. Clothing was drawn at will, and every man could have an extra blanket, if he wished, or two, for that matter. The mail facilities were also excellent, and writing and receiving letters and reading the home papers and other reading matter sent by kind friends formed a standard of enjoyment.[17]

The opportunities of the 1st Maine, in common with every other regiment of cavalry, to enjoy the comforts of winter camp were, however, severely limited. The historians of ten regiments all speak at length and with much feeling of the unrelieved misery of picket duty in the winter of 1862–1863, of "men and horses suffering what pen may not describe."[18] The length of the line to be picketed was so long that with most regiments down to 300–350 men, it was necessary for half of each regiment to take its turn of picket duty on a three days on, three days off basis. And since the section of line assigned to a given regiment might be as much as eight or ten miles from its camp, the "three days on" common-

17. Tobie, *First Maine Cavalry*, 18–19. The 1st Maine was at this time part of D. McM. Gregg's (formerly Bayard's) brigade, attached to the Left Grand Division. William Glazier of the 2nd New York also noted in December, 1862, "It is wonderful to witness how the forests are disappearing in and around our camps. From morning till night the woodman's axe resounds." Glazier, *Three Years in the Federal Cavalry*, 114.
18. Denison, *Sabres and Spurs*, 198–99.

ly meant four days, and the "three days off" was correspondingly reduced to two days, with a half-day's march or more through twelve to twenty inches of Virginia mud or slush at both ends of its turn of picket duty.[19] General Hooker, after he replaced Burnside, remarked to an officer of the 1st Massachusetts that to have the outpost duty for his army performed properly, he should have had 30,000 cavalry in good condition, whereas it was doubtful if he had more than about 5,000.[20] As a result, the 1st Pennsylvania, for example, with 300 men available for duty, had to try to picket a twenty-five-mile stretch of the river, from Falmouth down to Port Conway, a manifestly impossible assignment.[21]

The technique of picketing had become fairly well standardized. Headquarters of the picket detail (the "picket reserve") was located out of sight of the enemy, in a hollow or in the woods a half mile or more behind the outpost line. The men at the picket reserve were allowed to have a fire, but they had to be armed and their horses had to be saddled and bridled at all times, ready for immediate service. The pickets on post were relieved every two hours; while on duty they were required to remain in the saddle, carbine on thigh, and facing the enemy. Not surprisingly, how-

19. Merrill, *Campaigns of the First Maine*, 84; Hyndman, *History of a Cavalry Company*, 79.
20. Crowninshield, *A History of the First Regiment*, 101.
21. Lloyd, *History of the First Reg't.*, 47. At the end of February, 1863, General Stoneman reported that the 11,995 men in the Cavalry Corps (which Hooker had established earlier in the month) had to guard a line just under one hundred miles long; "one third on duty at one time gives 40 men to the mile on post at one time, and one third of these [*i.e.*, the pickets operating on a three-reliefs schedule] gives 13 to the mile. . . . I consider it my duty to call these facts to the attention of the general commanding . . . which I should have done before, perhaps, but for the thought that I might possibly be considered as complaining." *Official Records*, Vol. XXV, Pt. 2, p. 111. Stoneman's figure of thirteen pickets to the mile meant that if evenly spaced, which of course was never the case, the pickets were 135 yards apart, much too far to be able to assist each other in a sudden emergency. See also an earlier Stoneman dispatch, in which he urged that the stretch of the river between United States Ford and Corbyn's Neck be picketed by infantry. "This line," he wrote, "can be much better guarded by foot than by horse, and the arrangement will save the services of two regiments of cavalry . . . which, considering the terrible roads over which cavalry with its supplies of forage has to pass, is an important item." *Ibid.*, 97.

ever, "Although there were spasmodic efforts on the part of the commanding officers to be very strict concerning the pickets, the men soon got over each new stringent order, and performed their duty in their own way. Not that the duty was not well performed, but it certainly was not always done according to the strict letter of Army Regulations or General Orders. It was the almost universal practice to enjoy the quiet solace of the pipe while on post, especially in the night time, of which no complaint was ever made."[22] On bitter cold nights, pickets did the sensible thing; ignoring orders, they dismounted and tramped up and down to keep their feet from freezing.[23] There was, however, no protection for their horses. Benjamin Crowninshield of the 1st Massachusetts wrote after the war that "the picket duty was something horrible. . . . Sometimes, on relieving the vedettes, horses were found dead from exposure and hunger."[24]

Depending on the number of troopers available for duty and the number of posts to be manned, the picket detail was divided into three, four, or five "reliefs"; three reliefs—which meant that each trooper was on post for two hours, followed by four hours back at the reserve, to eat, sleep, and make himself as comfortable as he could in the snow, slush, and mud—were usual; four, and especially five, reliefs were quite exceptional.

Exposure to the wintry weather was not the worst of the pickets' tribulations. Particularly at night, guerillas and bushwhackers were an ever-present menace, but both at night and in daytime, a picket was ever in danger of being shot. The 8th New York was one of many regiments that lost "quite a number" of men, killed or wounded while on picket.[25] The troopers were justifiably bitter that they were nearly always attacked from ambush; "such conduct," one of them wrote, "cannot be regarded in any other light than midnight murder."[26] When Trooper John Schenk of the 10th New York managed to catch a guerilla who was creeping up on him in the underbrush and brought him into camp, he

22. Tobie, *First Maine Cavalry*, 116–17.
23. Norton, *Deeds of Daring*, 56–57.
24. Crowninshield, "Cavalry in Virginia," 24–25.
25. Norton, *Deeds of Daring*, 57.
26. Moyer, *History of the 17th Regiment*, 35.

received "not the plaudits of his comrades, but their execrations, for bringing the would-be murderer in alive."[27]

In addition to the lone bushwhacker or guerilla, or a Confederate cavalryman in quest of a remount and willing to kill to get one, the pickets also had to cope with the sudden rush out of the night of a dozen or two Confederate cavalrymen, a scouting party, or a band of Partisan Rangers, the latter being merely guerillas under another and more respectable name. Such groups took advantage of their knowledge of the countryside, or the help of the local citizenry, to work their way through gaps in the picket line, or around it, in order to swoop down on a supposedly safe picket reserve, kill or wound a few troopers, and let the rest go after taking their horses, weapons, and in many cases, their personal valuables as well. John Mosby made himself famous by his successes in such patriotic, exciting, and profitable exercises, but there were many lesser practitioners who made the lives of Union cavalrymen miserable with such raids. Captain George Johnson of the 3rd Pennsylvania was dismissed from the service for "disgraceful and unofficerlike conduct" in that, "while in charge of a cavalry picket (near Hartwood) . . . by his negligence, continued after repeated warnings from his commanding officer, [he] permitted his party to be surprised by the enemy and himself and a number of his officers and men to be captured."[28] Lieutenant Jacob H. Hoffman of the 1st New Jersey allowed his fourteen-man picket reserve to be surprised, with the loss of sixteen horses, fifteen sabers, thirteen carbines, fourteen pistols and seven men taken prisoner and was recommended for a dishonorable discharge.[29] In March, near Dranesville, a picket reserve of the 1st

27. Preston, *History of the 10th Regiment*, 80.
28. *Official Records*, XXI, 14. The regimental historian comments that Johnson's dismissal from the service "cannot be said to have been unjustified." Regimental History Committee, *History of the 3d Pennsylvania*, 173.
29. *Official Records*, XXI, 28–29. Lieutenant Colonel Joseph Kargé, Hoffman's commanding officer, reported that the lieutenant, "after having placed badly his vedettes, and allowed his men to lay aside their arms, went . . . to provide for his belly, in a neighboring house, leaving his command to the care of Providence. . . . the inmate of this house is a young and attractive female, whose husband is a captain in the rebel army." *Ibid.*, 29.

Vermont was surprised in broad daylight, with the loss of twenty-five officers and men and all their gear; "The surprise was so complete that the men made little or no resistance. The [enemy was] . . . led on by citizens, and entered on foot by a bridlepath in rear of the post, capturing the vedette stationed on the road before he was able to give the alarm."[30]

Johnson and Hoffman were doubtless culpable, but in many of these "surprises" the Federal officers were not at fault. They and their men were the victims of the enterprise, skill, and local knowledge of the Confederate horsemen, both regulars and irregulars, and, as often as not, of the enthusiastic help they could always count on receiving from the local inhabitants. General Stoneman's anger was understable when he commented on one of these incidents, "These annoyances will continue until some stringent measures are taken to clear that section of country of every male inhabitant, either by shooting, hanging, banishment or incarceration. I had a party organized some time ago to do this, but the commanding general did not at that time think it advisable to send it out. . . . The country is infested with a set of bushwhacking thieves . . . who should be eradicated, root and branch."[31]

Occasionally, picket duty had its compensations. Surgeon Hard, whose regiment, the 8th Illinois, did its picketing southeast of Fredericksburg, remarked that despite the abominable weather ("Snow, six or eight inches deep, was followed by rain and mud —a few cold days then rain again. The roads were indescribable.") the men of his unit "preferred to stand picket in King George County, where they could forage freely, to remaining in camp and living on hard-tack and pork."[32] And the historian of the 1st Pennsylvania, which picketed twenty-five miles of the Rappahannock, also in King George County, has recorded that he and his comrades "lived in a 'land flowing with milk and honey' and good cheer. . . . This beautiful and fertile country [was] plentifully supplied with poultry, milk and eggs, which were readily obtained in exchange for sugar, coffee and salt. . . . And

30. *Official Records*, Vol. XXV, Pt. 1, p. 65.
31. *Ibid.*, 46.
32. Hard, *History of the Eighth Cavalry*, 222–23, 220.

as the spring advanced, the river swarmed with shad, herring and other choice fish, of which the Yankees soon invented means of catching more than they could use."[33]

Some lines of pickets also faced the outposts of the official enemy. The pickets of the 1st Maine, shivering on horseback on the north bank of the Rappahannock, could only envy "the enemy's pickets, just across the river and in plain sight. . . . [They] were infantry, had their tents close to their posts, relieving each other regularly, had picket fires burning brightly all night long, and in wet weather could do duty under shelter of the tents."[34] It is not surprising that after seeing the Confederates' method of performing picket duty, the Federal cavalrymen wondered if their own commanding officers, in their handling of their mounted troops, were not in the position of the farmer who won an elephant in a raffle and then did not know what to do with it. On a more serious note, Captain Frederick C. Newhall of the 3rd Pennsylvania spoke for the thoughtful members of the mounted service when he wrote in January, 1863, "Goodness knows, we hope to do *something* to bring the cavalry out of the sort of disgrace into which it has fallen. . . . The fact is, we are worked to death and nobody knows it, because they never let us do anything for which the cavalry was intended."[35]

With only the width of the Rappahannock between the two lines of pickets and no language barrier to separate them, fraternization was inevitable. The 2nd New York did its picketing along a stretch where the river was easily crossed; and there "The Federal and Rebel pickets . . . mutually arranged that there shall be no firing on either side, unless an advance is undertaken. . . . Squads of soldiers from both armies may be observed seated together on either side of the Rappahannock, earnestly discussing the great questions of the day. . . . During all these interviews, trading was the order of the day, and a heavy business was carried on in the tobacco, coffee and hardtack line. There was also a special demand on the part of the Rebels for pocket knives and

33. Lloyd, *History of the First Reg't.*, 47.
34. Tobie, *First Maine Cavalry*, 116.
35. Regimental History Committee, *History of the 3d Pennsylvania*, 185.

canteens."[36] On the sector occupied by the 1st Maine, where the river was too deep to wade, business—Virginia tobacco for Yankee coffee—was equally brisk, but required what may perhaps be described as Yankee ingenuity: "One method of sustaining commercial relations was to build a raft a foot or so square, generally of corn stalks, fix a mast with a late newspaper for a sail, load the raft with tobacco, and so set the sail that the wind would carry the raft across the river. The recipient would reciprocate in coffee . . . and it was quite common, on asking a man where he got his tobacco, to receive the reply, 'I had a ship come in.' Of course this was without the knowledge of the officers."[37]

Ambrose Burnside had a most attractive personality. Everyone who knew him liked him. It was his misfortune to have thrust upon him the command of an army, a position for which he was totally unfitted. Having made up his mind that he wanted to cross the Rappahannock, he held on to the idea with bulldog tenacity and was incapable of thinking of an alternative. Despite the bloody repulse of December 13 and the unanimous opposition to another such attempt of the commanders of his three grand divisions and of several of their principal subordinates, Burnside meant to try again. After a pause of five weeks, on January 20, he put his army in motion westward, with the intention of crossing the river at Banks's Ford, which was six miles from the Federal camps at Falmouth and, Burnside hoped, well beyond the left flank of the Confederate army. Early that evening, a furious northeaster struck the area and lasted without a letup for thirty hours, turning the roads and fields into bottomless quagmires. The wagons carrying the pontoons, the supply wagons, and the artillery, bogged down beyond hope of movement. By noon on the twenty-third, Burnside had no choice but to give up the hopeless struggle with the mud and ordered the troopers back to their camps. This was known forever after as the "Mud March."

The troopers of the 6th Pennsylvania, who took part in the Mud March as General Franklin's escort, witnessed "An inde-

36. Glazier, *Three Years in the Federal Cavalry*, 118, 121.
37. Tobie, *First Maine Cavalry*, 110.

scribable chaos of pontoons, wagons and artillery . . . supply wagons upset by the roadside, artillery stalled in the mud, ammunition trains mired by the way. Horses and mules dropped down dead, exhausted with the effort to move their loads. . . . A hundred and fifty dead animals, many of them buried in the liquid muck, were counted in the course of a morning's ride."[38] With the wagons carrying rations unable to move, even with doubled teams, several cavalry regiments were given the job of carrying boxes of hardtack on the pommels of their saddles, to distribute to the infantry along the line of march. This work of mercy was performed none too well; the "horses as well as their riders showed their distaste for this type of work, and often stumbled and fell. It was almost impossible to manage the horses and hold the boxes at the same time, and in many cases the hard-tack was dumped in the mud."[39] Within two days after the return of the rain-soaked, mud-smeared, dejected regiments to Falmouth, Burnside was relieved of the command of the Army of the Potomac and Joseph Hooker was appointed in his place.[40]

Hooker owns the unenviable distinction of being the favorite whipping boy of the historians of the Civil War, hardly any of whom have a good word to say for him. This he owes partly to the way in which he lost the battle of Chancellorsville, partly to his conduct toward Burnside, partly to his relations with the administration in the weeks preceding Gettysburg, and partly to his conduct as a corps commander in the West under Grant and Sherman. The general verdict on Hooker is that his conduct was frequently discreditable or worse and was the expression of a seriously flawed personality. But this assessment of Hooker, for which there is certainly ample justification, fails to give him due credit for the administrative miracle he brought about with the aid of his gifted chief of staff, General Daniel Butterfield, in the three short months between his appointment to the command of the Army of the Potomac and the start of the Chancellorsville Campaign.

38. Gracey, *Annals of the 6th*, 127–28.
39. Regimental History Committee, *History of the 3d Pennsylvania*, 186; see also Hyndman, *History of a Cavalry Company*, 85.
40. *Official Records*, XXI, 1004–1005.

McClellan has received great and perhaps excessive credit as an able administrator for creating the Army of the Potomac in the fall and winter of 1861–1862. But McClellan did his work when everything was new, when morale was high, when the volunteers streaming into Washington were filled with enthusiasm, eager to learn and to be led. Hooker, on the other hand, came to the head of what was little better than a disheartened mob of 100,000 men, demoralized by defeat, riddled with desertion, its self-confidence gone, its capacity for enthusiasm destroyed, distrustful of its leaders, its top ranks seething with mutual jealousies and hostilities. In ninety days, by means of a series of wise, timely, and effective administrative measures, Hooker made of it the army that stood up to some of the toughest fighting of the war at Chancellorsville, shrugged off its defeat there, fought and won the battle of Gettysburg only two months later, and eventually fought the campaign of 1864 under Grant. Allowing for the difference in scale, what Hooker accomplished in the early months of 1863 stands comparison with Philippe Petain's revitalization of the French armies after the mutinies of 1917.

Many of Hooker's measures affected the entire army; these included the issuance of ample rations, including fresh bread and vegetables, and of all the clothing the men needed; a rational system of furloughs; a strong effort to recruit up the depleted ranks of old regiments; abolishment of the grand divisions; institution of the corps badge system (suggested by Butterfield); improved hospital facilities for the sick; frequent inspections and reviews and a lot of drill to keep the men occupied. After the furlough system was instituted, it was amended, with highly beneficial results, by a proviso that increased the number of furloughs in regiments that showed up exceptionally well on inspection; it was ordered, on the other hand, that "The commandant of the Cavalry Corps will discontinue the leaves and furloughs . . . to regiments of his command neglectful of discipline, care of arms, equipments, animals, &c."[41] Regiments were directed to reactivate schools of instruction for commissioned and noncommissioned officers, examining boards were appointed to weed out incompe-

41. *Ibid.*, Vol. XXV, Pt. 2, p. 120.

tent officers, and younger and better men were promoted to take their places.

Special hosannas are due Hooker in any history of the Union cavalry for taking the long-overdue step of liberating it from the control of commanders of brigades, divisions, and corps of infantry and giving it a corps organization of its own. The emancipation of the cavalry—for it was nothing less—was effected by Hooker's General Orders No. 6 of February 5, 1863: "III. The cavalry of the army will be consolidated into one corps, under the command of Brigadier-General Stoneman, who will make the necessary assignments for detached duty."[42] Two days later, Stoneman formally assumed command of the corps, which then numbered 8,943 cavalrymen and 450 gunners "Present for duty equipped."[43] On February 12, Stoneman announced in orders the organization of the corps into three divisions, made up entirely of volunteer regiments; the First, under Pleasonton, contained seven regiments and an independent squadron; the Second, under Averell, had seven regiments; and the Third, under Gregg, had six regiments and an independent company. In addition, there was to be a "Reserve Brigade" under Buford of five badly under-strength regiments of Regulars. A quirk of the sacred seniority system, or perhaps political and personal influence, gave Buford, by all odds an abler cavalryman than any of his three colleagues, command of a mere brigade, whereas they had command of divisions. For no known reason, the 6th Pennsylvania remained outside the divisional/brigade scheme, to "act under special instructions from [corps] and superior headquarters." It was ordered

42. *Ibid.*, 51. Paragraph I of the same order did away with the grand divisions. General-in-Chief Halleck's comment on the consolidation of the cavalry into a corps was that it was a step in the right direction. If so, one wonders why so scientific a soldier as Halleck had not ordered the consolidation in the seven months that he had been the professional head of the Union armies. On March 31, the cavalry of the newly created Department of Washington (formerly the "Defenses of Washington") was also consolidated into a nine-regiment, three-brigade cavalry division under Major General Julius Stahel. Thiele, "The Evolution of Cavalry," 104.

43. The figures are as of February 10, 1863. *Official Records*, Vol. XXV, Pt. 2, pp. 65–66. On the same date, Stoneman had 11,110 officers and men "Present for Duty," 13,452 "Aggregate Present," and 17,166 "Present and Absent."

further that each of the division commanders was to divide his regiments into two brigades "as nearly equal in effective strength as possible . . . regard for efficiency superseding all other considerations." All regiments, squadrons, and troops of cavalry scattered about the army were called in and ordered to report to the division or brigade to which they had been assigned. Each of the seven corps of infantry into which the army was now divided was to have assigned to it one, and only one, squadron of cavalry "to act as orderlies, messengers, &c."[44]

The reaction of cavalrymen to these changes ranged from favorable to enthusiastic. Willard Glazier recorded that he and his fellow troopers of the 2nd New York had speculated "that while the efficiency of infantry is known to depend largely upon its organization into brigades, divisions and corps . . . the same may not be true of the cavalry."[45] Now that the high command had agreed that the cavalry would benefit from the same type of organization, words like "emancipation" and "a new life" recur in cavalrymen's comments on the change. There was, however, a vastly important ingredient still missing in the production of a fully effective cavalry; however, here too the new corps organization worked to advantage, for it became glaringly and quickly apparent that to reach its full potential, the cavalry needed better leadership than two, perhaps three of the five brigadier generals now at the head of it had the capacity to supply.

Another of Hooker's innovations, instituted with the best of intentions, was nevertheless anything but a success. Hooker wanted his cavalry to be fully mobile; hence it could not be allowed to continue to operate, as it had been in the habit of doing under commanders like John Hatch, encumbered with a lengthy tail of supply wagons. Hooker therefore had Stoneman announce, "The general commanding the corps is desirous that every legitimate means within the reach of the officers and men under his command may be made use of to fit and perfect themselves for the most vigorous and rapid movements. Requisitions have been made for pack-saddles sufficient to supply the wants of the whole

44. *Ibid.*, 71–72.
45. Glazier, *Three Years in the Federal Cavalry*, 125.

command, and the general gives this timely notice to all that it is his intention to dispense with the use of wagons in all active field service of cavalry."[46]

In the cavalry there was "but one opinion as to [Hooker's] management of [the] army in winter quarters. Finding the Army of the Potomac a disorderly, dissatisfied, ill-provided, uncomfortable crowd of men . . . he transformed [them] into a well-disciplined, contented, enthusiastic body of soldiers. . . . Troops soon learn to appreciate this kind of administrative ability . . . and during the winter of sixty-two—sixty-three, 'Joe Hooker' held a place in their esteem only second to the man who first organized them into an army."[47] But to turn cavalrymen into mule skinners and unbroken mules into beasts of burden was a different thing altogether. The veterans in the ranks knew at once that the experiment, like many others introduced by the "wise and knowing ones," would be a failure, and a failure it was. It was found that when the mules were loaded and ready to move out, "some of the poor, overloaded creatures would lie down, refusing to carry such burdens; while others would run frantically about, scattering the cooking utensils with which they were loaded, in every direction."[48] This noble experiment was given its *coup de grace* by an able report turned in by Lieutenant Colonel C. G. Sawtelle, chief quartermaster of the Cavalry Corps, who pointed out:

1. It is impossible to find a sufficient number of men in the ranks who have had any experience in packing mules, and packing is an art which can only be learned by . . . long experience.
2. The pack-mule system takes away largely from the effective . . . strength of the command. To manage properly the pack-mule train, it [is] necessary to detail at least 1 man for every 2 mules; in many regiments 1 man to each mule has been detailed to pack, take care of the mules, and keep them closed up on the road. To carry subsistence for 400 mounted men and [10 pounds of grain each for 400 horses at] 200 pounds to the mule . . . requires 25 mules. This amount could be transported by two army wagons drawn by 12 good mules, and requiring the attention of only two teamsters. . . . Nearly two-thirds of all the pack-mules in this corps are now more or less broken down . . . on account of sore backs . . . in part owing to the inferior

46. *Official Records*, Vol. XXV, Pt. 2, 71–72.
47. Pyne, *First New Jersey Cavalry*, 137–38.
48. Hard, *History of the Eighth Cavalry*, 215.

quality of the pack-saddles used . . . and the unsuitable kind of saddle blankets which are little better than cotton rags.[49]

In due time the troopers themselves solved the problem of excess baggage. The pack mules disappeared, but so did the long lines of supply wagons that had clogged the movements of the cavalry in the first two years of the war. Only a minimum that would have been considered unthinkable earlier was left—no more than one or two wagons to a brigade, in many cases, to haul the indispensable reserve ammunition, medical supplies, and the like.

In his final report on his stewardship as commanding general of the Army of the Potomac, Hooker wrote, "The cavalry was consolidated in a separate corps and put in the best condition ever known in our service. Whenever the state of the roads and of the [Rappahannock] river permitted, expeditions were started out to attack the pickets and advance posts of the enemy, and to forage in the country he occupied. My object was to encourage the men, to incite in their hearts, by successes, however unimportant they might be, a sentiment of superiority over their adversaries."[50] There is no question but that the rank and file of the cavalry were badly in need of encouragement. They had come to believe that the army command had no faith in volunteer cavalry and thought of it is as no better than a "mounted mob."[51] Men who had gotten into the habit of thinking that in their encounters with the enemy their only choices were to "surrender, die, or run," and who "often felt heartily ashamed of belonging to a branch of the service which it was costing the government so much to maintain, and which was of so little real service," most certainly needed a spiritual rebirth, to learn to have faith in themselves, before they

49. *Official Records*, Vol. XXV, Pt. 2, pp. 561–62. Sawtelle neglects to mention that the five thousand pounds of subsistence which it required 25 mules to carry was made up of minimum rations for four hundred men *for one day*, and in the case of feed for the horses, only a little more than one third of the prescribed ration of twenty-six pounds of grain and hay per horse for one day. Thus, to carry rations for four hundred troopers for a five-day scout would have required 125 mules, plus the mules needed to carry feed for five days for the mules themselves.

50. Quoted in deTrobriand, *Four Years with the Army of the Potomac*, 415–16.

51. Tobie, *First Maine Cavalry*, 122.

could become a worthwhile military organization.[52] Consolidation into a corps of their own gave the troopers an essential focus of identity and the expectation that at long last their "duties would be of that dashing nature peculiar to their own arm of the service."[53] More, however, was needed; the ability of the corps commander and of the division and brigade commanders to inspire their men, to restore or build their morale, and to lead them successfully in combat, had to be tested.

The first of the divisional commanders to be tested were Averell and Pleasonton, and the results were equivocal. On February 24, Fitzhugh Lee crossed the Rappahannock at Kelly's Ford on a reconnaissance with a 400-man cavalry detachment, variously estimated in Federal reports as "five regiments," "from 500 to 1,000," "about 2,000," and "three brigades."[54] The next day, Lee drove in the Federal cavalry pickets near Hartwood Church, "attacked [the] reserve and main body," and subsequently claimed to have "routed them and pursued them within 5 miles of Falmouth to their infantry lines," killing and wounding "many," and taking 150 prisoners "with all their horses, arms and equipments."[55] Lee's advance was reported promptly to army headquarters, and Butterfield at once ordered Averell to attack the raiders head on; at the same time Pleasonton was ordered to march upstream with all speed, so as to cut Lee off from the fords.[56] Averell was told that he was not to return until he had captured the enemy "or found it utterly impossible to do so," and as an added but highly questionable incentive, he, as well as Pleasonton, were told that "a major-general's commission is staring somebody in the face in this affair, and . . . the enemy should

52. The "surrender, die or run" sentiment was expressed in Asa B. Isham, "The Cavalry of the Army of the Potomac," in *MOLLUS*, Commandery of Ohio, *Sketches of War History, 1861–1865* (7 vols.; Cincinnati, 1888–1910), V, 303; the "heartily ashamed" statement is in Tobie, *First Maine Cavalry*, 123. For examples of actions that damaged the self-confidence of the Federal cavalry, see *Official Records*, XXI, 19, 694.
53. Denison, *Sabres and Spurs*, 206.
54. *Official Records*, Vol. XXV, Pt. 1, p. 21; Pt. 2, pp. 107, 103.
55. *Ibid.*, Pt. 1, p. 25.
56. *Ibid.*, 21. Other dispatches and orders relating to this affair will be found in *ibid.*, Pt. 2, pp. 101–108.

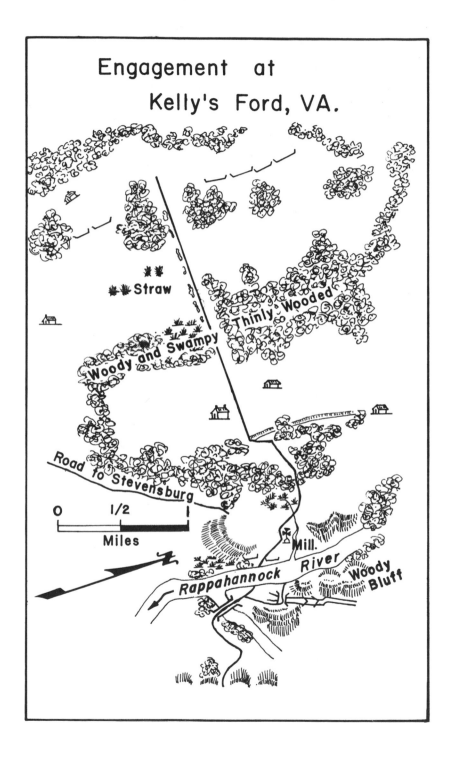

Engagement at
Kelly's Ford, VA.

Straw

Thinly Wooded

Woody and Swampy

Road to Stevensburg

0   1/2

Miles

Rappahannock River

Mill.

Woody Bluff

never be allowed to get away from us."[57] The orders sent by Butterfield and later by Stoneman, who was called to headquarters to help direct the operation, were appropriate and helpful enough, but Lee, whose horses were correctly reported to be very tired, was able to recross the river the way he had come and made a clean getaway with his prisoners and booty. Pleasonton, who had been ordered by Stoneman to "get off at once, and if you can find out where the enemy is, push him to the utmost of your ability wherever he may go. Be sure to get between the enemy and the river," unaccountably stopped short at Aquia Church.[58] The numerous dispatches and reports related to this minor affair fail to disclose such essential facts as the state of the roads, the condition of Averell's and Pleasonton's horses, or the start Lee had when he began his retreat. Hence it cannot be said flatly that the two Federal commanders so mishandled their assignments that the small enemy force they should have been able to capture made good its escape. It is clear, however, that Pleasonton's decision to halt at Aquia Church angered both Hooker and Butterfield, and their anger appears to have been fully justified.[59]

Three weeks later, Averell was given an opportunity to show what he could do when he, rather than the enemy, had the initiative. It is said that Hooker remarked to him, or it may have been to Pleasonton or Stoneman, "We *ought* to be invincible, and by God, sir, we *shall* be! You have got to stop these disgraceful cavalry 'surprises.' I'll have no more of them. I give you full power over your officers, to arrest, cashier, shoot—whatever you will— only you must stop these surprises. And by God, sir, if you don't do it, I give you fair notice, I will relieve the whole of you and

57. *Ibid.*, Pt. 2, pp. 102, 101, 103.
58. *Ibid.*, 104.
59. After receiving Pleasonton's dispatch in which he announced that he was "in position" at Aquia Church, Butterfield countered with "I don't know what you are doing there. Orders were sent to you . . . to push for the enemy without delay." *Ibid.*, 108. The tone of Hooker's order to Stoneman, requesting "an exact report" of the affair, including "the movements in full of each portion of your command, and the delay of any portion to execute promptly and completely the part assigned to it, together with the reasons therefor," indicates clearly enough the commanding general's dissatisfaction with the outcome. *Ibid.*, Pt. 1, p. 22.

take command of the cavalry myself."[60] Whoever the actual target of Hooker's vehemence may have been, it was Averell who was assigned the task of squaring accounts with his West Point classmate and good friend Fitzhugh Lee. It had been learned from prisoners that Lee's brigade was encamped at Culpeper, eleven miles from Kelly's Ford. With the Hartford Church fiasco fresh in his mind, Hooker ordered Averell to cross the Rappahannock at Kelly's Ford with three thousand cavalrymen and a six-gun battery of horse artillery, attack Lee, and "rout and destroy him."[61]

The movement began on March 16. Averell assembled his troopers at Morrisville, about six miles from the ford. There had been reports of a few hundred Confederate cavalry to the north, on his side of the river, which caused him for reasons no one has been able to fathom from that day to this, to detach two regiments, nearly a third of his force, "to guard the fords" north of Kelly's and "look out" for the enemy.[62]

Averell's artillery did not reach Morrisville until eleven o'clock on the night of the sixteenth, with its horses "in poor condition" after a thirty-two-mile march. Nevertheless, at four A.M. on the seventeenth, the command moved out for Kelly's Ford, which it reached four hours later. Fitz Lee had word of the Federal advance in midmorning of the sixteenth, and again in the early evening, when his scouts reported the Federals at Morrisville.[63] The ford was blocked with felled trees, and the south bank of the stream was lined with rifle pits manned by sixty sharpshooters. Two of Averell's squadrons were dismounted to force a crossing. They tried three times but were beaten back each time by the rebel marksmen. Then a party of twenty men on horseback, led by Lieutenant Simeon A. Brown of the 1st Rhode Island, forced

60. Quoted in Walter M. Hebert, *Fighting Joe Hooker* (Indianapolis, 1944), 186. The source is not given.

61. *Official Records*, Vol. XXV, Pt. 1, p. 47.

62. *Ibid.*, 47. Bigelow comments, "It is hard to justify this weakening of his force. He had no train or depot between himself and the Army of the Potomac. There was nothing to be guarded in his rear except his line of retreat, and that he should have been able to open, if any force which the enemy could spare from his front had presumed to close it." Bigelow, *The Campaign of Chancellorsville*, 89–90.

63. *Ibid.*, 60–61.

its way across.[64] Brown's forlorn hope was followed by the 4th New York, 6th Ohio, and 1st Rhode Island of Colonel Alfred Duffié's brigade, then Colonel John B. McIntosh's brigade of the 3rd, 4th, and 16th Pennsylvania. Captain Marcus A. Reno, leading the 1st and 5th United States, brought up the rear.

It was noon before the horses had been watered, everyone was across, and Averell was able to deploy his command on the south bank, with Duffié on the left, McIntosh in the center, and the Regulars on the right. Lee had marched forward from Culpeper with his brigade of five regiments of Virginia cavalry—the 1st, 2nd, 3rd, 4th, and 5th—a total of "less than 800" against Averell's 2,100, and encountered the Federals a half mile south of the Ford, advancing toward him.[65] Lee attacked at once. His route was such that two of his regiments, the 2nd and 4th Virginia, were able to attack the left flank of Duffié's brigade. Duffié waited until the Virginians were within a hundred yards of his line, and then, on his own responsibility, ordered a countercharge.[66] It was a fight of Federal sabers against Confederate pistols, and the Virginians were driven back. There is a story, which may or may not be true, that in the melee Lee's men shouted, "Draw your pistols, you Yanks, and fight like gentlemen."[67]

64. In his transmittal of Averell's report of the operation to Halleck, Hooker wrote that Brown's "clothes were pierced with five bullets, and his horse with three, and yet he bravely pushed on at the head of his party." Hooker recommended that Brown be promoted one grade, as of the date of his "distinguished service." *Official Records*, Vol. XXV, Pt. 1, p. 1074. A passage through the felled trees was chopped by twenty axmen from the 16th Pennsylvania.

65. The figure of "less than 800" is given in Stuart's report of the action; he was present on the field as a mere spectator. *Official Records*, Vol. XXV, Pt. 1, p. 59. Lee himself does not give the strength of his force in his report. Stuart's figure is difficult to believe; it would mean that Lee's five regiments averaged a mere 160 officers and men each—an incredibly low figure.

66. Bigelow, *The Campaign of Chancellorsville*, 98. Averell criticized Duffié's decision to order a charge "without prearranged support." *Ibid.*, 49. Averell, says Bigelow, "then and there issued a very emphatic order that troops once assigned a position in line should under no circumstances leave it without orders. . . . Such an order is prohibitive of effective cavalry action." *Ibid.*, 98.

67. Regimental History Committee, *History of the 3d Pennsylvania*, 210.

While Duffié was having his fight on the left, McIntosh also advanced and drove back the Confederate left. With both of Lee's wings pushed back, the Federals paused long enough to straighten out their alignment, then resumed their advance, which took them through a belt of woods three-quarters of a mile deep. As they emerged from the trees, they were attacked again by Lee's troopers, but they held their own and forced back both of Lee's wings. The Federals now came within range of a number of heavy guns Lee had in position some distance behind his right, and at this time also Averell was told that "infantry had been seen at a distance to [his] right, moving toward [his] rear, and the cars could be heard running on the road in rear of the enemy, probably bringing re-enforcements."[68] It was now half past five. Averell reasoned that "it was necessary to advance my cavalry upon their intrenched positions, to make a direct and desperate attack, or to withdraw across the river. Either operation would be attended with imminent hazard. My horses were very much exhausted. We had been successful thus far. I deemed it proper to withdraw . . . and the regiments retired in succession until the ford was reached and crossed without the loss of a man."[69] The most notable features of this engagement were that it was an all-cavalry fight, and, with the exception of a small number of Federal carbineers dismounted and fighting behind the protection of a stone wall, the entire action from beginning to end was fought on horseback.[70]

Not surprisingly, Fitzhugh Lee issued a grandiloquent general order to his command, claiming a victory over the "insolent enemy."[71] In more restrained language, Averell did the same. "The principal result achieved by this expedition," he wrote, "has been that our cavalry has been brought to feel their superiority in bat-

68. *Official Records*, Vol. XXV, Pt. 1, p. 50.
69. *Ibid.*, 50.
70. Casualties as reported by the two commanders were amazingly light for a close action lasting more than nine hours. Lee reported eleven killed, eighty-eight wounded, and thirty-four taken prisoner; Averell, six killed, fifty wounded, and twenty-two taken prisoner. *Ibid.*, 63, 53.
71. *Ibid.*, 64. The order contains the following interesting sentence: "You have taught certain sneerers in our army that placing a Southern soldier on horseback does not convert him into a coward."

tle."[72] Lee's claim of a victory was absurd. The Federal horse had gained the upper hand in an engagement that their commander lacked the nerve or the killer instinct to fight to a finish; he was like a boxer content to win on points when he might have scored a knockout. Averell must nevertheless be given credit for a competent conduct of the fight—leaving aside the unaccountable weakening of his command by the detachment of two regiments —up to the moment when his imagination got the better of him and he ordered a retreat. It was this last point that caused Hooker to decide that essentially, Averell had failed to measure up. In Hooker's opinion,

After . . . [Averell] had permitted one-third of his force to remain on the north bank of the Rappahannock, his passage of the river with the residue of his force appears to have been eminently soldierlike, and his dispositions for engaging and following the enemy, up to the time of his recrossing the river, were made with skill and judgment; and had he followed his instructions and persevered in his success, he could easily have routed, fallen upon his camp, and inflicted a severe blow upon him. The enemy was inferior to the command he had in all respects. The reason assigned—that he heard cars arriving at Culpeper, and not knowing but that they might be bringing reenforcements to the enemy—is very unsatisfactory, and should have had no influence in determining the line of . . . [his] conduct. He was sent to perform a certain duty, and failed to accomplish it from imaginary apprehensions.[73]

In fairness to Averell, it should be said that this damaging assessment of his performance at Kelly's Ford was written by Hooker on May 13, after he had removed Averell from his command and after he himself had lost the battle of Chancellorsville. It is proper to set against it the opinion of Captain Alexander Moore, one of Hooker's staff officers, who accompanied the expedition and reported when he returned that Kelly's Ford had been "a brilliant and splendid fight—the best cavalry fight of the war—lasting five hours, charging and recharging on both sides, our men using their sabers handsomely and with effect, driving the enemy 3 miles into the cover of earthworks and heavy guns."[74] It was, in-

72. *Ibid.*, 50.
73. *Ibid.*, 1073.
74. *Ibid.*, Pt. 2, p. 147.

deed, a "splendid fight," but not the victory it might and should have been.

The view that Kelly's Ford brought about a miraculous transformation of the Federal cavalry is advanced in numerous regimental histories and cavalrymen's reminiscences, all written after the war, and has become conventional wisdom in the writings of military historians of the Civil War. It rests on the thesis that the confidence engendered by a fight at brigade strength in which the Federals had more than held their own against the Confederate cavalry inspired not only the regiments actually engaged, but the rest of the Federal cavalry as well. The thesis is certainly attractive, but it rests on questionable logic. The idea of a sudden transformation, of a spiritual rebirth, is pleasing, and it has good biblical precedent besides, but it would be difficult to demonstrate convincingly that the entire Federal cavalry experienced a Journey to Damascus. Assuredly Kelly's Ford was a helpful and inspiriting step in the right direction, but much more than Averell's imperfect, partial success on March 17 was needed to make the Federal cavalry what it eventually became.

XIII

The Divide

GEORGE STONEMAN WAS THE SECOND OF HOOKER'S CAV-
alry commanders to be tested. It was getting on toward mid-April,
1863. The spring rains were due to end, good campaigning weather was ahead, and after a winter of reequipment, reorganization,
and morale building, the Army of the Potomac, nearly 125,000
strong, was ready to move against the enemy. Once again the objective was to be Richmond, as it had been for Generals McDowell, McClellan, Pope, and Burnside, and for the many thousands
of their men who had been killed or crippled in what was already
a lengthy series of efforts to get there.

Facing the Union army was General Lee with an army of
62,000 manning a carefully sited, heavily fortified line along the
south bank of the Rappahannock, running for twenty-five miles
upstream from below Fredericksburg and effectively blocking all
the river crossings. After Burnside's bloody fiasco in December,
there were to be no more head-on Union attacks uphill against
well-fortified, well-manned positions. Manoeuver was the word;
Hooker planned to pry Lee out of his lines and into the open,
where the two-to-one manpower superiority of the Union army
could be brought to bear and the Confederate army destroyed.

The instrument Hooker chose to cause Lee to evacuate the Fredericksburg position was Stoneman's corps of 9,895 cavalrymen plus 427 gunners serving the three-inch rifled guns of the six batteries of horse artillery.[1]

On April 12, Stoneman was ordered to march upstream with his entire corps less one brigade. He was to cross to the south bank of the Rappahannock west of the Orange & Alexandria Railroad—twenty miles as the crow flies from the western end of Lee's fortified line—and was then to proceed south and southeast by way of Culpeper, Gordonsville, and the line of the Virginia Central Railroad ("destroying along . . . [the] whole route the railroad bridges, trains, cars, depots of provisions, lines of telegraphic communication, etc.") to its junction with the Richmond, Fredericksburg & Potomac Railroad about twenty-seven miles south of Fredericksburg.[2] At that point, Stoneman would be squarely astride Lee's only direct line of communication back to his base at Richmond, and within less than twenty miles of the Confederate capital. Hooker reasoned that the cutting of his main supply line and the threat to Richmond would force Lee to leave the Fredericksburg area and retreat southward. He would then be followed by the Army of the Potomac and attacked at the first good opportunity.

1. *Official Records*, Vol. XXV, Pt. 1, p. 1067. The organization of the Cavalry Corps on May 1, 1863, was as follows: First Division (Pleasonton), First Brigade (B. F. Davis): 8th Illinois, 3rd Indiana, 8th and 9th New York; Second Brigade (Devin): 6th New York, 8th and 17th Pennsylvania, Company L, 1st Michigan; 6th Battery, New York Light Artillery. Second Division (Averell), First Brigade (Sargent): 1st Massachusetts, 4th New York, 6th Ohio, 1st Rhode Island; Second Brigade (McIntosh): 3rd, 4th, and 16th Pennsylvania; Battery A, 2nd United States Artillery. Third Division (Gregg), First Brigade (Kilpatrick): 1st Maine, 2nd and 10th New York; Second Brigade (Wyndham): 1st New Jersey, 1st Maryland, 1st Pennsylvania, 12th Illinois. Reserve Brigade (Buford): 6th Pennsylvania, 1st, 2nd, 5th, and 6th United States; Batteries B, L, and M, 2nd United States Artillery and Battery E, 4th United States Artillery. Additionally, a total of ten companies belonging to the above regiments were detached and serving as escorts and orderlies at army and corps headquarters. *Ibid.*, 156–70.

2. *Ibid.*, 1066–67. See also Hooker's explanation to the president: "I hope that when the cavalry have established themselves on the line between . . . [Lee] and Richmond, they will be able to hold him and check his retreat until I can fall on his rear." *Ibid.*, Pt. 2, p. 199. In most of the orders cited, the Richmond, Fredericksburg & Potomac Railroad is called the "Aquia and Richmond," and Saxton's Junction, "Sexton's."

At Saxton's Junction, where the Virginia Central and the Richmond, Fredericksburg & Potomac tracks crossed, Stoneman was directed to "select the strongest positions" on Lee's probable line of retreat, and "fall upon his flanks, attack his artillery and trains, and harass and delay him until he is exhausted and out of supplies." To make certain that Stoneman understood precisely what was expected of him, the orders went on, "If you cannot cut off from . . . [Lee's] columns large slices . . . you will not fail to take small ones. Let your watchword be fight, and let all your orders be fight, fight, fight, bearing in mind that time is as valuable . . . as rebel carcasses. . . . It devolves upon you . . . to take the initiative in the forward movement of this grand army. . . . Bear in mind that celerity, audacity and resolution are everything in war, and especially is it the case with the command you have and the enterprise upon which you are about to embark."[3]

Stoneman led his cavalry out of its camps on the morning of the thirteenth and reached the fords in the vicinity of the Orange & Alexandria Railroad the next day. He had the benefit of two days of fine weather for his march upstream.

Fitzhugh Lee had been reported to be in or near Culpeper with his cavalry brigade, which Hooker's orders told Stoneman he was expected to be able to "disperse and destroy without delay to . . . [the] advance." Stoneman's own orders to his command for crossing the river—which he later justified as "being merely to make a feint and hide my intentions from the enemy"—were of an excessively elaborate character and difficult to square with the "celerity, audacity and resolution" that Hooker's orders to him called for.[4] However, on the evening of the fourteenth, before the orders for the crossing could be executed, it began to rain. It was a heavy downpour, particularly so in the mountains to the west, at the headwaters of the Rappahannock. At once the river began to rise—at Rappahannock Bridge, a few hundred yards upsteam from the fords Stoneman intended to use, the river rose an unbelievable seven feet in a few hours—and crossing became out of the question.[5] Even Buford, who was not to be stopped by any-

3. *Ibid.*, Pt. 1, pp. 1066–67.
4. Hooker's orders are in *Ibid.*, Pt. 2, p. 220; Stoneman's in *ibid.*, 204.
5. Nevins, *A Diary of Battle*, 182. Wainwright noted in his diary on

thing short of a total impossibility, reported that "such rains and roads I had never seen."[6] Benjamin Davis' brigade, which had gotten across ahead of the high water, was ordered to recross, and the entire command settled down in acute discomfort to wait for the flood to subside.

Hooker had reported to the president on the fifteenth that Stoneman expected to be across the river before daylight that morning. As soon as he learned that Stoneman had not crossed, he reminded him that the entire army was awaiting his movement and directed that if he was held back by the difficulty of getting his artillery across, he was to leave it behind.[7] The president, informed in a second dispatch on the evening of the fifteenth that Stoneman had been unable to cross, responded with a message to Hooker that speaks eloquently of his trials and frustrations. "It is now 10:15 p.m.," Lincoln wrote,

An hour ago I received your letter of this morning, and a few moments later your dispatch of this evening. The latter gives me considerable uneasiness. The rain and mud . . . were to be calculated upon. General S[toneman] is not moving rapidly enough to make the expedition come to anything. He has now been out three days, two of which were unusually fair weather, and all three without hinderance [sic] from the enemy, and yet he is not 25 miles from where he started. To reach his point he still has 60 to go, another river (the Rapidan) to cross, and will be hindered by the enemy. By arithmetic, how many days will it take him to do it? I do not know that any better can be done, but I greatly fear it is another failure already. . . . I am very anxious.[8]

Hooker either decided that Stoneman was not to blame for his failure to cross or at least was willing to make excuses for him; he wrote the president, "[Stoneman's] failure to accomplish speed-

---

April 19 that "[Stoneman's] part of the move is by this time fully known to Lee as a matter of course. Even the privates seem well informed about it . . . [and rebel] pickets call across the river to ours, asking what is the matter with our cavalry that it does not get across." *Ibid.*, 182.

6. *Official Records*, Vol. XXV, Pt. 1, p. 1089.

7. Hooker to Lincoln, in *ibid.*, Pt. 2, p. 213; Hooker to Stoneman, *ibid.*, 214.

8. *Ibid.*, 214.

ily the objects of his expedition is a source of deep regret to me, but I can find nothing in his conduct . . . requiring my animadversion or censure."[9] In the aftermath of Chancellorsville, Hooker's attitude toward Stoneman was to change drastically. At the moment, however, with the torrential rains continuing and the river and all its tributaries unfordable, his most urgent problem was to recast his entire plan of campaign. The idea that Stoneman's presence on his lifeline would force General Lee to leave Fredericksburg was cast aside; on the twenty-second, Hooker instructed Stoneman that after crossing the Rappahannock and then the Rapidan, he was to divide his command into detachments and have "them take different routes. . . . These detachments can dash off to the right and left, and inflict a vast deal of mischief, and at the same time bewilder the enemy as to the course and intentions of the main body."[10]

Six days later, on April 28—two weeks past the date when Stoneman was to have crossed the Rappahannock—the floods having subsided sufficiently to make the fords practicable, he was directed to cross the following morning without fail and to send a portion of his force toward Louisa Court House to mask the march of the main body, which was "to move by forced marches to strike and destroy the line of the [Richmond, Fredericksburg & Potomac Railroad]."[11] Stoneman was thus faced with the problem of deciding whether to follow this modification of his original orders, or whether, proceeding on the basis of Hooker's directions of the twenty-second, to scatter his command after crossing the two rivers and cause as much destruction in as wide an area as possible. He chose the latter course. He had been told on the eighteenth that the only opposition he was likely to encounter was "two small brigades of cavalry . . . numbering between 4,000 and 5,000 sabers . . . wretchedly mounted, as we know they must be."[12] Nevertheless, after crossing the Rappahannock at Kelly's Ford on April 29, he detached Averell's entire division, plus another brigade and a battery of artillery—more than a third of his

9. *Ibid.*, 220.
10. *Ibid.*, 244.
11. *Ibid.*, Pt. 1, p. 1065.
12. *Ibid.*, Pt. 2, p. 229.

entire force—with orders to march by way of Brandy Station and Culpeper toward Rapidan Station and deal with this Confederate cavalry force, which was thought to be lurking in that area, while he himself with the rest of the command marched away southeastward.[13]

A strange sidelight is cast on the expedition by an order Stoneman issued on April 17 to David McM. Gregg, in command of his Third Division. Stoneman had his assistant adjutant general say to Gregg that "too much leniency has been shown to bushwhackers, and . . . the command is becoming encumbered with prisoners. [Stoneman] desires you to give such instructions to the officers in charge of your scouting and picket parties as in your opinion will tend to obviate these difficulties."[14] What Gregg did about this order, and its effects, if any, do not appear in the records.

At long last, on the twenty-ninth, Stoneman was across the river, and for ten days, until he returned to the Rappahannock on May 8, his command, less the large detachment with Averell, went rampaging about the Virginia countryside. Gregg's troopers "seemed to have but the single desire of inflicting the greatest amount of injury upon the enemy without violating any of the recognized rules of civilized warfare."[15] Colonel Percy Wyndham, with two regiments, rode south to Columbia, where he destroyed four bridges over the James River Canal; following the canal for some distance eastward, he destroyed canal boats loaded with commissary stores and forage, as well as locks and gates, which he hoped would render "the canal irreparable and impracticable for a long time."[16] He also captured 140 horses and mules. Lieu-

13. *Ibid.*, Pt. 1, p. 1068; see also *ibid.*, 1074–75.
14. *Ibid.*, Pt. 2, p. 223.
15. *Ibid.*, Pt. 1, p. 1083.
16. *Ibid.*, 1085. The historian of the 6th Pennsylvania recorded that upon reaching Columbia, "Parties were . . . detailed to cut the canal, destroy the locks, burn the bridges, tow-boats, canal boats, etc. In ten minutes from the time we entered the town, flames were issuing from five bridges and several canal-boats loaded with forage and commissary stores; while two parties . . . were engaged in cutting down the bank of the canal, and destroying the locks, and another party . . . were in town, destroying an immense storehouse filled with supplies of every description for the rebel army." Gracey, *Annals of the 6th*, 143, and 145–46.

tenant Colonel Hasbrouck Davis, with the 12th Illinois, burned depot buildings, storage sheds, trestles, and culverts on the Richmond, Fredericksburg & Potomac at Ashland Station, and on the Virginia Central at Hanover Station within seven miles of Richmond, causing damage that he estimated, no doubt generously, at one million dollars. With 175 captured mules and horses added to his command, and with only "a common map of the State of Virginia" to guide him on his way, he escaped to safety at Gloucester Point, across the York River from Yorktown.[17] Among the items destroyed by Davis' men were two locomotives and tenders at Ashland, which were "rendered useless by a mechanic from the ranks."[18]

Judson Kilpatrick, with the First Brigade of Gregg's division, appears to have caused the greatest amount of damage. At Hungary Station on the Richmond, Fredericksburg & Potomac, he "destroyed the depot, telegraph wires, and railroad for several miles"; then, passing within two miles of Richmond, he burned Meadow Bridge on the Chickahominy, ran a train of cars into the river, burned a train of thirty wagons loaded with bacon, another train of fifty-six wagons, and a depot containing sixty thousand barrels of corn, wheat, and other stores, and, after capturing and paroling three hundred prisoners, reached safety at Gloucester Point also, having marched nearly two hundred miles in five days and having sustained a loss of one officer and thirty-seven men.[19] Buford's brigade burned the Virginia Central bridge over the North Anna at Frederick's Hall Station, and pumps, water tanks, and miscellaneous stores at Trevilian Station.

On the night of May 7, the bone-weary Federal troopers recrossed the Rapidan and reached the Rappahannock the next day. In a circular letter to Generals Grant, Rosecrans, Dix, Pope, and Curtis, and to the governors of all the loyal states, Secretary Stanton described Stoneman's expedition as a "brilliant success."[20] But was it?

17. *Official Records*, Vol. XXV, Pt. 1, pp. 1085–87.
18. *Ibid.*, 1087.
19. *Ibid.*, 1083–84. The destruction of "several miles" of the railroad, or at least the thoroughness of that destruction, may well be questioned. It was reported later that the line was out of operation for only one day.
20. *Ibid.*, Pt. 2, p. 438.

Having been forced to recast his plans by Stoneman's inability to cross the Rappahannock on schedule, Hooker effected his own crossing with three corps of infantry during the night of April 25 at Kelly's Ford, and after crossing the Rapidan, marched southeast toward Chancellorsville, in the midst of an area known as the Wilderness. The advance of the Federal infantry was led by Pleasonton's small brigade of three regiments of cavalry, which had remained with the army when Stoneman went off on his expedition. On the Confederate side, Stuart, with Fitzhugh Lee's brigade, took post beyond and behind Lee's left flank. After an initial and quickly corrected miscalculation of Hooker's intentions, Stuart's reports enabled General Lee to deduce that the crossing of the Rappahannock below Fredericksburg by two corps of Federal infantry was a feint and that the real attack was coming in on his left; and Lee deployed his troops accordingly.

The basic concept of Hooker's plan was faultless, and the execution up to the early evening of April 30 was nearly so. Then, however, Hooker lost all chance of success by halting his advance four miles short of Banks's Ford, possession of which would have given the rest of his army, still on the north bank, a short and easy route to join the troops on the south bank. By the late forenoon of May 1, when Hooker ordered the advance resumed, it was too late. General Lee had had ample time to shift his troops to meet the threat from the west, and they had had twelve hours or more to strengthen their lines with crude but effective breastworks. The Federal advance, blinded and disorganized by having to force its way through the dense thickets of scrub and second-growth timber, was stopped in its tracks. By sundown, four corps of the Federal army were posted in a rough semicircle in front of Chancellorsville, with George G. Meade's corps on the left, touching the Rappahannock, and on the right, General O. O. Howard's XI Corps. Near the center, and in rear of General Daniel E. Sickles' III Corps, Pleasonton's cavalry occupied a patch of relatively clear high ground called Hazel Grove.

By nightfall on May 1, it was evident to both commanding generals that neither could make a frontal attack on the other with any hope of a decisive success. The terrain was nearly impassable, and both sides had had time to dig in. During the night, however, Stuart had his men out scouting the Federal position, and they came back with the information that Howard's outer flank was in the air and that there were roads of sorts, running beyond the range of Federal observation, over which that flank could be reached. The result was a triumph of the Lee-Jackson partnership, inferior in glory only to Second Bull Run. Jackson, with twenty-six thousand men—nearly half the Confederate army—went on a wide sweep through the woods toward Howard's flank. Jackson's march was detected in the early morning, and at 9:30 A.M. Hooker warned Howard to guard against a possible attack on his right flank; Howard did nothing, and when Jackson's attack came in at 6:00 P.M., the XI Corps—its arms stacked, the men cooking supper, playing cards, and otherwise amusing themselves—was simply overrun.

A mile to the east of where Howard's right flank had been was the Hazel Grove clearing. Pleasonton, who had been out most of the day probing for Jackson's advance, was ordered back to Hazel Grove with the 8th and 17th Pennsylvania and Lieutenant Joseph W. Martin's 6th Battery, New York Light Artillery.[21] As Pleasonton tells the story, before he reached the grove he was met by an aide-de-camp from Hooker's staff "in a state of great excitement," with the message that the XI Corps "was falling back rapidly and a regiment of cavalry was needed to check the movement." Thereupon Pleasonton ordered the 8th Pennsylvania, under Major Pennock Huey, to charge the advancing Confederate infantry. Huey charged in the only manner permitted by the nature of the terrain, with his four hundred-man regiment in a column of twos along the Plank Road. Major Peter Keenan, Captain Charles Arrowsmith, and Adjutant J. Haseltine Haddock were killed, three of the total of thirty killed, wounded, or missing in the charge. The Confederates were checked by the charge for the few moments Pleasonton needed to line up a grand battery of twenty-three guns on the Hazel Grove clearing. He ordered the guns loaded with double canister, and when Jackson's infantry

21. The third regiment of Pleasonton's Second Brigade, the 6th New York (down to 254 rank and file), remained with the III Corps and fought as dismounted skirmishers. Committee on Regimental History, *History of the Sixth New York*, 101.

emerged from the thickets two hundred yards away, he met them with a volley that "fairly swept them from the earth."[22] Without question the charge of the 8th Pennsylvania and Pleasonton's resourcefulness in organizing and commanding his *ad hoc* artillery concentration were instrumental in preventing a serious defeat from becoming a major disaster.[23]

It has been generally accepted for many years that Hooker's defeat at Chancellorsville was due at least in part to the absence of his cavalry, which, it is claimed, could have protected his right flank and could either have stopped Jackson's outflanking move, or at least have given timely warning of it.[24] This view assumes that if Stoneman had been present, he would have been positioned on the outer flank of the Union line, which might or might not have been the case; and it ignores three important facts: first, the characteristics of the terrain which, except for a few widely scattered clearings and narrow roads and paths through the woods, was impassable for cavalry; second, Jackson's flank march was in fact detected; and third, Pleasonton's brigade was actually present, and when the 8th Pennsylvania made its charge, it and the 17th Pennsylvania were on their way to Hazel Grove because the terrain over which they might have attacked Jackson's column was totally unsuitable for cavalry operations, and May, 1863, was not yet the day for the dismounted operations that became second nature to the Federal cavalry a year later. It was not Stoneman's absence, but the superb generalship of Lee and Jack-

22. Pleasonton's report of the action is in *Official Records*, Vol. XXV, Pt. 1, pp. 772–76; Lieutenant Joseph W. Martin's (commanding the 6th New York Battery), in *ibid.*, 785–89; and Major Huey's, in *ibid.*, 783–84. Pleasonton also wrote an account of his role in the battle, entitled "The Successes and Failures of Chancellorsville," for *Battles and Leaders*, III, 172–82. His account of the charge of the 8th Pennsylvania led to controversy; a number of officers of the regiment contended that Pleasonton did not order the charge, but that it came about spontaneously after the regiment had found itself between the skirmish line and the main body of the Confederate infantry and had to cut its way out. It was contended also that Major Keenan, not Major Huey, led the charge. *Battles and Leaders*, III, 183.

23. When the bodies were recovered after the battle, thirteen bullet holes were found in Major Keenan's body and nine in Adjutant Haddock's. *Battles and Leaders*, III, 183.

24. For example, Alexander, *Military Memoirs*, 374.

son, and Hooker's loss of nerve and loss of grip on the battle, that produced the great Confederate victory.

Secretary Stanton had called the Stoneman raid a "brilliant success," and the Richmond papers that reached Washington, as well as the reports of General Edwin H. Stoughton, who had just returned from Richmond as an exchanged prisoner of war, gave considerable justification to that view.[25] They spoke of widespread destruction and "great panic."[26] For the men who made the raid, it was more than anything else a test of endurance, but it was also a morale-boosting demonstration of the value of the corps organization, and of their ability to match the accomplishments of the Confederate cavalry as raiders. Some of the participants, however, assessed the raid differently, called it a failure, "not well managed," and an enterprise that "only exasperated, without terrifying the enemy, and gave color to the accusations that the Federal cavalry were merely mounted robbers." Another participant severely criticized the "absurd plan by which the force was scattered and dispersed, instead of being concentrated to fight the enemy."[27] If the actual accomplishments of the raid are measured against Hooker's original hopes and intentions for the expedition, these strictures are fully justified, but they leave out of account the fact that Hooker himself modified its objectives by his orders of April 22 and 28, after the flooded Rappahannock made execution of the original scheme impossible. The raid did in fact fulfill the objective spelled out in the April 22 directive, which, however, deprived it of any strategic value. In its short-term tactical results, the raid was no less and no more successful than all but two or three of the much written about (and much written-up) cavalry raids of the war.

Hooker was, or claimed to be, dissatisfied with Stoneman's

25. *Official Records*, Vol. XXV, Pt. 2, p. 439.
26. The contemporary orders of Confederate Secretary of War James A. Seddon, of General Wade Hampton, and others, do not convey an impression of panic.
27. Thiele, in "The Evolution of Cavalry," 409, called the raid a "failure"; Cheney, in *History of the Ninth Regiment*, 92, labeled it "not well managed"; Whittaker, in *George A. Custer*, 144, said it merely "exasperated . . . the enemy"; and Harris, in "The Union Cavalry," 362, called it an "absurd plan."

performance. He was to write in a postwar letter, speaking clearly of Stoneman, "One word more, in regard to the cavalry. I had to have, under the seniority rule of the service, a wooden man for its commander."[28] In the bitter aftermath of the battle of Chancellorsville, which by all odds he should have won, Hooker looked for scapegoats, and Stoneman was an obvious choice. Hooker wrote Stanton on May 10, "From the most reliable information I have been able to gather, railroad communication between Fredericksburg and Richmond, by the direct route, was interrupted but for one day. The bridges of importance appeared to have remained untouched. With the exception of Kilpatrick's operations, the raid does not appear to have amounted to much. . . . My instructions appear to have been entirely disregarded by General Stoneman."[29] Later, in a letter to Stanton about a concentration of Confederate cavalry at Culpeper and Jefferson, Hooker wrote that he would pitch into them if "Stoneman had not almost destroyed one-half of my serviceable cavalry force."[30] And, intentionally or otherwise, his chief of staff's dispatch to Stoneman on May 12, requesting a "full report" on the raid, was distinctly abrupt in language and hostile in tone.[31]

Despite all this, and for whatever reason, Stoneman remained in command until May 22; not so, however, the unfortunate Averell. He had been ordered by Stoneman to march to Rapidan Station and defeat any Confederate cavalry he found there or encountered en route. Hooker learned on May 1 that Averell was at Rapidan Station and had an aide-de-camp send him a dispatch to tell him that "the major-general commanding . . . does not understand what you are doing . . . [there]. If this finds you at that place, you will immediately return to United States Ford, and remain there until further orders, and report in person."[32] Averell's reply took the form of a copy of Stoneman's order, which had directed him to "push the enemy as vigorously as possible, keep-

28. Owens, *Sword and Pen*, 145–46.
29. *Official Records*, Vol. XXV, Pt. 2, p. 463.
30. Samuel L. French, *The Army of the Potomac from 1861 to 1863* (New York, 1906), 351.
31. *Official Records*, Vol. XXV, Pt. 2, p. 468.
32. *Ibid.*, Pt. 1, p. 1080.

ing him fully occupied, and if possible, drive him in the direction of Rapidan Station."[33] Averell was doubtless in Hooker's black books already because of his failure to accomplish all that had been expected of him at Kelly's Ford in March, and on May 3, immediately upon receiving Averell's explanation and before seeing his formal report of his operations, Hooker ordered Averell to depart to Washington for reassignment and had Pleasonton take over command of Averell's division.[34] In a letter to the adjutant general of the army, Hooker justified his abrupt dismissal of Averell by citing his April 12 and 28 orders to Stoneman and went on to say, "It is no excuse or justification of [Averell's] course that he received instructions from General Stoneman in conflict with my own. . . . If he disregarded all instructions, it was his duty to do something. If the enemy did not come to him, he should have gone to the enemy."[35] Hooker's reasoning, insofar as it implied that Averell should have disregarded the orders of his immediate superior, was certainly at fault; in a more fundamental sense, however, he had full justification for relieving Averell. In a six-day "campaign," with four thousand sabers under his command, Averell managed to capture thirty-one prisoners and a few barrels of flour, salt, and pork, with the loss of one of his men killed and four wounded. That is not the way wars are won, and Hooker, whatever his own shortcomings may have been, was himself a fighter and expected his subordinate commanders to

33. *Ibid.*, Pt. 2, pp. 352–53.
34. *Ibid.*, Pt. 1, p. 1080.
35. This and the quotation which follows are from *Ibid.*, 1073. It should be noted that Stoneman reported that he had sent Averell copies of all of Hooker's orders to himself. *Ibid.*, Pt. 2, p. 474. In a report of his own to the adjutant general, Averell spoke of the "extraordinary" form and tenor of Hooker's order relieving him and, with some justice, ascribed its motive to a desire "to place upon . . . [him] by implication, an indefinite share in the responsibility for whatever may have been of failure in the operations of the Army of the Potomac in the recent attack upon the enemy's forces." *Ibid.*, Pt. 1, p. 1077. Averell was not by any means alone in holding this view. Frederick C. Newhall, for one, wrote, "After Chancellorsville there was a good deal of bad blood in military quarters; great promise was followed by small fulfillment, and scape-goats were needed on whom to fasten blunders. . . . Stoneman and Averell figured in that capacity." Frederick C. Newhall, *With General Sheridan in Lee's Last Campaign* (Philadelphia, 1866), 43.

fight. He was on solid ground in pointing out that "this army will never be able to accomplish its mission under commanders who . . . display so little zeal and devotion to the performance of their duties. I could excuse General Averell . . . if I could anywhere discover in his operations a desire to find and engage the enemy. I have no disposition to prefer charges against him [for disobedience of orders] and in detaching him from this army my object has been to prevent an active and powerful column from being paralyzed in its future operations by his presence."

The troopers who made the raid endowed it with a moral effect that may have been more apparent in the postwar years than it was at the time. The historian of Wyndham's regiment, the 1st New Jersey, wrote:

Though this raid called general attention to the cavalry, and was indeed the first grand appearance in its distinctive character of that corps . . . among the cavalry themselves there was not the same feeling of satisfaction as was expressed over the country. But that a great moral effect was produced by this independent manoeuver of the mounted troops is undeniable. . . . For the first time the cavalry found themselves made useful . . . and treated as something better than military watchmen for the army. They saw that the long desired time had come when they would be permitted to gain honor and reputation, and when they would cease to be tied to the slow moving divisions of infantry, without liberty to strike a blow for the cause of the nation and the credit of their commanders. It gave our troopers self-respect, and obliged the enemy to respect them; and was thus a fitting inauguration of that campaign which included in it the cavalry combats of Brandy Station, Upperville, Gettysburg, Shepherdstown and Sulphur Springs.[36]

The historian of the 1st Maine, writing of the raid after the war, remembered, "Arguments, orders, curses loud and frequent, and even blows, could not keep the men awake, or the horses in their places, or scarcely any place, some of them stopping in the road sound asleep . . . with horses so tired and worn that not one of them would go faster than a walk." He then went on, as his colleague of the 1st New Jersey had done, to call the raid "the first great achievement of the Union cavalry of the Army of the Potomac, and from which dated the rise of that branch of the service in the estimation of soldier and citizen. . . . the First Maine

36. Pyne, *First New Jersey Cavalry*, 146–47.

Cavalry was a part of this expedition . . . and . . . it was ever after a matter of pride with the boys that they were on 'Stoneman's Raid'."[37]

In a fundamental sense, these regimental historians, reflecting the views of their fellow troopers, were correct in their assessment of the Stoneman raid; in its strategic, and even short-term tactical results, its accomplishments were insignificant. But the raid had an unintended, indirect, and in the long run important effect. A large body of Federal cavalry, having gone through the dress-rehearsal stage at Kelly's Ford six weeks earlier, was given an independent mission and had an opportunity to work as a self-contained unit. The raid was bedeviled by the elements, by changes in purpose, and by something less than hard-driving, firm leadership. Those handicaps, however, were incidentals. The key fact was the demonstration that, figuratively speaking, the cavalry could stand on its own feet. That demonstration was to have an enduring effect. From the all-important standpoint of building self-confidence, self-respect, and morale, the Stoneman raid, nearly barren as it was of strategic or tactical results, and not Kelly's Ford, was the major step forward for the Federal cavalry.

---

37. Tobie, *First Maine Cavalry*, 140, 143–44. An incidental feature of the raid, namely the work of Chief Quartermaster Rufus Ingalls and Chief-of-Staff Daniel Butterfield, deserves honorable mention. On May 7, Ingalls informed Captain C. B. Ferguson, quartermaster at Alexandria, that Stoneman was expected to reach Rappahannock Station the next day, destitute of subsistence for his four thousand men and animals. Ferguson was to have trains run out on the Orange & Alexandria immediately, with ample supplies of food and forage plus rafts to get it across the river ("as it is not fordable") to Stoneman. Ingalls also requested General Herman Haupt, superintendent of military railroads, to make "extraordinary exertions" to have trains available and "in motion early." Butterfield notified Stoneman the next day that a train had already left Alexandria with two days' supplies of foodstuffs for him, and "with floats to be used in the case of necessity for floating them across the Rappahannock, with guards and everything that could be done to make it certain that they will reach you." He then proceeded to give Stoneman a well-deserved rap across the knuckles. In his dispatch asking that these supplies be sent, Stoneman had written that if they failed to arrive he "would not be responsible for the consequences." To this, Butterfield responded with the tart question, "who[m] . . . would [you then] consider responsible?" *Official Records*, Vol. XXV, Pt. 2, pp. 439, 440, 450.

XIV

Their Arms Flash
in the Sun

ON MAY 5, THE ARMY OF THE POTOMAC BEGAN TO CROSS
back to the north bank of the Rappahannock, the Chancellorsville Campaign a depressing failure.[1] A Confederate army of sixty
thousand had fought a Federal army twice its size to a standstill
and, at one point, the evening of May 2, had it on the ragged edge
of disaster. By the evening of May 6, the baffled Union army, its
numbers reduced by seventeen thousand casualties, was back in
the camps it had left in hope and confidence a few days earlier.

On the evening of the same day, after receiving the report
that Hooker was recrossing the Rappahannock, the sorely tried
president's first words were, "My God! My God! What will the
country say!" But despite disappointments and failures, the war
had to go on, and in two years of thwarted hopes the president
had learned that whatever the shortcomings of his army commanders might be, the past was irretrievable, and he, more than
anyone else, had to look ahead. And so, on May 7, he queried
Hooker on his plans for the future.

1. Crowninshield, *A History of the First Regiment*, 121: "A terrible
feeling of depression and disappointment settled down upon all these
troops, who two weeks before had marched out with confident anticipation
of success."

The recent movement of your army is ended without effecting its object, except, perhaps, some important breakings of the enemy's communications. What next? If possible, I would be very glad of another movement early enough to give us some benefit from the fact of the enemy's communications being broken; but neither for this reason or for any other do I wish anything done in desperation or rashness. An early movement would also help to supersede the bad moral effect of the recent one, which is said to be considerably injurious. Have you already in your mind a plan wholly or partially formed?[2]

By the evening of May 8, the cavalry under Stoneman, less the regiments that Kilpatrick and Hasbrouck Davis had led to Gloucester Point, were back on their own side of the Rappahannock, ready to join Averell's division, which Hooker had recalled from Rapidan Station earlier, and the brigade under Pleasonton, which had remained with the army. The horses that had made the raid had been "much exhausted and weakened by the march," and "a very large proportion" of them returned with sore backs.[3] About a thousand of the animals were abandoned on the march, most of them shot so that they would not fall into the hands of the enemy. Those losses, however, had been more than made good by captures.[4] The men whose horses had given out came back on captured mounts, but most of the replacements were brood mares and work horses, not suitable for cavalry service.[5] In addition, many of the horses, both old and new, were suffering from "mud fever." Hence Hooker had on his hands the chronic problem of a largely immobilized cavalry.

On May 20, Stoneman was granted leave of absence on the ground of ill health, and two days later, Pleasonton, who two weeks before had taken command of Averell's division in addition

2. *Official Records*, Vol. XXV, Pt. 2, p. 438. This letter was sent under the same impression of Stoneman's accomplishments, not yet corrected by his and his subordinates' reports, that caused Stanton to call the raid "a brilliant success."

3. *Ibid.*, Pt. 1, p. 1069.

4. "The air of Virginia is literally burdened today with the stench of dead horses. . . . You pass them on every road and find them in every field. . . . On this last raid dying horses lined the road on which Stoneman's divisions had passed, and we marched over a road made pestilential by the dead horses of the vanished rebels." Ford, *A Cycle of Adams Letters*, II, 5.

5. *Official Records*, Vol. XXV, Pt. 1, p. 1069.

to his own, was given command of the Cavalry Corps.[6] He took four days to inspect his new command and then reported to Hooker on its condition, which, as always, revolved around the sad state of its horses. His own former division, the First, Pleasonton wrote, had 2,784 serviceable and 735 unserviceable horses, a remarkably good showing. Of the approximately 6,000 horses of the Second (now commanded by Alfred Duffié as senior colonel) and Third Divisions, only half were fit for service. Buford's Reserve Brigade, with 2,226 troopers present, had only 830 serviceable horses. In just under two months, the effective mounted strength of the corps had been cut nearly in half, from 12,000 to 6,677, and Kilpatrick's and Hasbrouck Davis' commands, approximately 2,000 of the 6,677, had either not as yet returned from the Peninsula, or were absent on detached duty.[7]

So far, Pleasonton's report was a factual and sober (and sobering) statement, but it ended with a self-serving declaration

6. There was apparently adequate justification for Stoneman's request for leave on medical grounds; it is said that he suffered from a severe case of hemorrhoids all through the raid. But he may also have seen the handwriting on the wall as far as his retention of his command was concerned. Charles Francis Adams, Jr., wrote on May 12, "They . . . say that Hooker wishes to depose Stoneman and hand the command over to Pleasonton." Ford, *A Cycle of Adams Letters*, II, 8. Stoneman's separation from the Cavalry Corps was made permanent by Special Orders No. 153 of June 5, in *Official Records*, Vol. XXV, Pt. 3, p. 11. Officially, Pleasonton's assignment to the command of the Cavalry Corps was temporary, during Stoneman's absence. *Ibid.*, Pt. 2, p. 513. It is said that Hooker would have preferred to appoint Buford, but felt obliged to appoint Pleasonton, whose brigadier general's commission antedated Buford's by eleven days. Edwin B. Coddington, *The Gettysburg Campaign: A Study in Command* (New York, 1968), 44.

7. *Official Records*, Vol. XXV, Pt. 2, p. 538. Two weeks earlier, Stoneman had reported that "the horses were pretty well used up. . . . A large number . . . want shoeing, and the majority of them are afflicted with what is termed the mud fever. . . . As to force . . . which is fit for immediate duty in the field . . . the general can count upon 2,000 horses, provided but little marching is required." *Ibid.*, 474. An immediately helpful effect of Pleasonton's report was to cause Hooker to order General James Barnes's division of Meade's corps to take over from the cavalry the picketing of the fords from Banks's on the south to Kelly's on the north. *Ibid.*, 535. B. F. Crowninshield reports that Pleasonton personally took in hand the establishment of an effective system for getting his dismounted men remounted and back to their regiments. Crowninshield, *A History of the First Regiment*, 121.

that did its author little credit. "In taking this command," he wrote, "I cannot do myself such an injustice as to remain silent as to the unsatisfactory condition in which I find this corps. I shall use every exertion to bring it to a state of efficiency at the earliest possible moment, but the responsibility of its present state, it is proper the major-general commanding should know, does not belong to me." An attitude such as this was doubtless part of the total impression that led to the generally unfavorable verdict on Pleasonton by his subordinates. Charles Francis Adams had written a few days earlier, "Stoneman we believe in. We believe in his judgment, his courage and determination. We know he is ready to shoulder responsibility, that he will take good care of us and won't get us into places from which he can't get us out. Pleasonton we have also served under. He is pure and simple a newspaper humbug. . . . He does nothing save with a view to a newspaper paragraph."[8]

Hooker's response to Pleasonton's report took a form that the latter probably did not find particularly comforting. He was told,

The general desires that you will spare no labor to place the cavalry . . . in a high state of efficiency at the earliest practicable moment. He cannot but feel that the force of this arm has been greatly impaired from want of system, organization, and judicious employment. He enjoins upon you to require company officers to look after, and regimental officers to exact, the proper care and treatment of animals, and that their employment be confined to the demands of service. Every day bands of cavalry are to be seen all through the camps, and oftentimes abusing their animals by fast riding and neglect. This must be checked at once, or we will never have more than one-half of our cavalry in a serviceable condition.[9]

8. Ford, *A Cycle of Adams Letters*, II, 8.
9. *Official Records*, Vol. XXV, Pt. 2, p. 517. Hooker wrote Stanton that Stoneman had destroyed nearly half the "serviceable" cavalry force, whereupon General Meigs wrote Hooker that Stanton had spoken to him about his (Hooker's) need for horses. "I am using every exertion to procure them," Meigs went on, "and . . . they are beginning to come in rapidly. . . . I had fortunately ordered contracts and purchases in expectation of your movements, and the result . . . is now being felt. . . . No horses of any kind should be left in possession of residents in the rebel country. A horse is as much a contraband of war as a barrel of gunpowder, and, being used by a guerilla, a spy, or a messenger, more injurious to us. Even in the plow they relieve the men from the necessity of digging for a living, and leave

Hooker's admonition to Pleasonton is anything but unique. From the beginning to the end of the war, every army commander felt impelled, not once but many times, to counter complaints like Pleasonton's with countercomplaints about the mistreatment of their animals by the free spirits of the cavalry. The order and letter books of cavalry regiments are filled with such admonitions and orders, cascading down the ladder of command. As long as nearly all cavalry mounts were government (*i.e.*, no one's) property, and so long as a trooper whose horse had given out could get a replacement from the government or by capture without too much trouble, or find a snug haven in dismounted camp, the neglect and abuse of the miserable animals remained a fact of cavalry life that no orders ever succeeded in stopping.

When for better or for worse Pleasonton received command of the Cavalry Corps, he had under him three under-strength divisions plus Buford's Reserve Brigade. The Union and Confederate armies were in position on either bank of the Rappahannock, facing each other in the lines they had occupied since December, and the two commanding generals were thinking out their plans for the summer.

From the beginning, General Lee had in mind an invasion of the North, for a series of reasons, but primarily to draw the Union army out of Virginia. Hooker, faced with the loss of about 20 percent of his manpower due to the expiration of the terms of enlistment of two-year and ninety-day regiments, had not settled on a firm plan of his own when rumors and reports began to reach him and Washington of an imminent major move by the Confederate army.[10] The most remarkable of these reports, worthy to rank in quality with intelligence assessments in World Wars I and II, was compiled by Colonel George H. Sharpe, head of the "Bureau of Information," the establishment of which was one of Hooker's innovations, to replace the haphazard and ineffectual intelligence-gathering methods on which his predecessors

---

them free to plot mischief. I hope within ten days to bring in 2,500 horses, and shortly afterward to supply your wants entirely." *Ibid.*, 543.

　　10. The 20 percent of his manpower Hooker lost due to the departure of a large number of time-expired regiments was in addition to the nearly 15 percent (seventeen thousand) he lost at Chancellorsville.

had been content to rely. Sharpe's report listed in detail the positions of the six Confederate divisions manning the line along the river; he noted the near approach of the divisions of Pickett and Hood; he stated that the "Confederate army . . . [was] under marching orders, and an order from General Lee was very lately read to the troops, announcing a campaign of long marches and hard fighting." Of special interest is the fifth paragraph of the report, which recorded the presence between Culpeper and Kelly's Ford of the cavalry of the brigades of Hampton, Fitzhugh Lee, and W. H. F. Lee, forty-seven hundred men for duty, plus many dismounted men.[11]

A few days later, a report of General Erasmus D. Keyes to Hooker, sent from Yorktown, reinforced Colonel Sharpe's findings. "It seems apparent," General Keyes wrote, "from the reports that reach me that a movement of rebel troops is going on from south to north, and that the idea prevails over the lines that an invasion of Maryland and Pennsylvania is soon to be made. I have heard nothing definite, but all the rumors concur to produce the impression stated."[12]

The most urgent problem, as Hooker saw it, was the presence of the three brigades of Confederate cavalry near Culpeper, well placed either to make a raid or "to cover and conceal the movement of other troops," and he ordered Buford "to aid in fixing the locality and numbers of the enemy's cavalry . . . with a view to our future movements."[13] Three days later, on June 5, Buford reported, correctly, that "all the available cavalry of the Confederacy is in Culpeper County. Stuart, the two Lees, Robertson, Jenkins, and Jones are all there." Buford was also correct in reporting that "since the Chancellorsville fight, their cavalry has been very much increased," but the twenty thousand figure he gave as Stuart's numbers, on the strength of information given him by "a refugee from Madison County," was nearly double the actual figure.[14] In a second report the next day, Buford wrote that he was "certain there is a very heavy cavalry force on the grazing

11. *Ibid.*, 528.
12. *Ibid.*, 595.
13. *Ibid.*, 595.
14. *Ibid.*, Vol. XXVII, Pt. 3, p. 8.

grounds in Culpeper County"; he was even able to add the information that Stuart was to have had an inspection of his entire command the previous day.[15]

Based on these reports, Hooker concluded that Stuart was poised for a raid north in heavy force. To anticipate him, he decided on an aggressive move of his own. Orders went to Pleasonton that two days later, he was "to cross the Rappahannock at Beverly and Kelly's Fords, and march directly on Culpeper. For this you will divide your cavalry force as you think proper, to carry into execution the object in view, which is to disperse and destroy the rebel force assembled in the vicinity of Culpeper, and to destroy his trains and supplies of all descriptions to the utmost of your ability. . . . If you should succeed in routing the enemy, the general desires that you will follow him vigorously as far as it may be to our advantage to do so."[16] Hooker thought the report crediting Stuart with a strength of twenty thousand was greatly exaggerated, as it was.[17] Nevertheless, he decided to strengthen Pleasonton's thrust across the river by reinforcing him with the excellent infantry brigades of Generals Adelbert Ames and David A. Russell, a total of three thousand men. The footsoldiers brought Pleasonton's strength up to eleven thousand, and Hooker suggested that he "keep . . . [the] infantry force together, as in that condition it will afford . . . a moving *point d'appui* to rally on at all times, which no cavalry force can be able to shake."[18] Hooker also recommended that Pleasonton "make use of the forest and the cavalry to mask the movements of the infantry . . . and to keep the enemy ignorant of their presence as long as pos-

15. *Ibid.*, 12.

16. *Ibid.*, 27–28; see also *ibid.*, Pt. 1, p. 33. The orders were hand-delivered to Pleasonton by Captain Ulric Dahlgren, because Hooker "fear[ed] to telegraph the instructions." *Ibid.*, Pt. 3, p. 30.

17. Butterfield wired Pleasonton, "The general thinks 10,000 a very liberal calculation to cover all the cavalry within your reach . . . this from all data obtained here so far." *Ibid.*, Pt. 3, p. 39. In a dispatch from Brandy Station, Pleasonton reported that prisoners had told him that Stuart had thirty thousand cavalry on the field. *Ibid.*, Pt. 1, p. 903. To this Butterfield replied, "General says, if the enemy say they have 30,000, you give out you have 60,000." *Ibid.*, Pt. 3, p. 40.

18. This and the following quotation are from *ibid.*, 28.

sible, in order that at the proper time you may be able to cut off and destroy great numbers of them."

Pleasonton's dispatches make it evident that the projected movement had been discussed with him in detail before these excessively elaborate orders for it were issued, for on June 6 he divided his corps into two "commands," one, under Buford, consisting of the First Division and the Reserve Brigade, and the other, to be led by Gregg, of the Second and Third Divisions.[19] Ames's infantry brigade was assigned to Buford, Russell's to Gregg. On the morning of the seventh, before receiving Hooker's written orders, Pleasonton wired him, "let us act soon and please telegraph my instructions. My people are all ready to pitch in."[20]

Except that Jenkins' brigade was not with Stuart, and the exaggeration of the size of the Confederate Cavalry Corps—Stuart's cavalry and six batteries of horse artillery numbered just over ten thousand troopers and gunners—the information Buford sent Hooker was remarkably accurate.[21] To reinforce Stuart for the forthcoming invasion of the North, the brigade of Beverly H. Robertson had been brought to Culpeper from North Carolina, and that of William E. ("Grumble") Jones from the Shenandoah Valley. With these accessions added to the commands of Hampton and the two Lees Stuart now had a corps of five brigades. During May, "hundreds of men" rejoined "daily," bringing fresh horses with them, as did many of the men of Hampton's brigade, who had taken their horses to winter in South Carolina and Mississippi.[22] The troopers were "in the highest spirits, and were kept in constant and salutary activity by incessant drilling and other preparations for the impending campaign."[23] None were in higher spirits than Major General Stuart himself, and having under him "a more numerous and better equipped force than ever before," he

19. *Ibid.*, Pt. 1, pp. 23–24. Including the infantry, Buford's command numbered 5,418, Gregg's, 5,563. *Ibid.*, 906.

20. *Ibid.*, 27.

21. Alexander, *Military Memoirs*, 370; Alexander's exact figure is 10,292.

22. von Borcke, *Confederate War of Independence*, II, 263.

23. This and the following quotation are from *ibid.*, II, 263.

decided to mark the occasion by holding a grand review of his corps on June 5, on the open fields east of Culpeper.

The review was to be more than a military display. It was also to be a gala social event of the kind dear to the heart of the commanding general. Stuart's inspector general, Major Heros von Borcke, has told the story with evident relish.

Invitations having been sent out to the whole circle of our acquaintance far and near, the hotels of the town (Culpeper) and as many private houses as had any accommodation to spare, were got ready for the reception of our guests, many of whom, after all, we had to put up under tents. . . . Every train brought in fresh crowds of our guests, and we all assembled at the station to receive them, and forward them to their destination by the ambulances and wagons we had got prepared for that purpose. In the evening there was a ball at the Town Hall, which went off pleasantly enough, although . . . our supply of light was limited to a few tallow candles; and when the moon rose, we were glad to avail ourselves of her services by adjoining to the spacious verandah.[24]

The following morning, the day of the review, dawned "bright and beautiful," Major von Borcke continued, and at "about eight o'clock General Stuart and his Staff mounted their horses and made for the plains of Brandy Station. . . . Our little band presented a gay and gallant appearance as we rode forth to the sound of our bugles . . . our plumes nodding and our battle-flags waving in the breeze. . . . As our approach was heralded by the flourish of trumpets, many of the ladies of the village came forth to greet us . . . and showered down flowers upon our path." This was indeed the Civil War of legend, a war of moonlight and flowers, of the scents of a Virginia springtime, of the sunlight and warmth of June, of lovely women and gay cavaliers whom the hand of age would never touch, a war without wounds and without death.

The review itself, a magnificent pageant, was the spiritual zenith of Stuart's proud cavalry. With the artillery in the van, the entire corps passed in review at a fast walk, with three bands playing and a flag fluttering at the head of each regiment. Then the column divided into brigades and regiments that performed drill evolutions and, in the climactic finale, charged with yells

24. This and the following quotation are from *ibid.*, II, 264–65.

and the flourishing of sabers upon the artillery, which, posted at intervals around the perimeter of the field, delivered a rapid, properly noisy, but harmless fire with blank cartridges against the onrushing horsemen.[25]

Inevitably, the great day ended with another ball "on a piece of turf near headquarters, and by the light of enormous wood fires, the ruddy glare of which upon the animated groups . . . gave to the whole scene a wild and romantic effect."[26] Regrettably, however, some of the troopers, presumably other than those who attended the festivities described so glowingly by Major von Borcke, did not approve of the review and "grumbled at the useless waste of energy, especially that of the horses"; there were even comments to the effect that the command was being "worried out by the military foppery and display."[27]

General Lee had been invited as a matter of course to honor the review with his presence, but he was unable to accept the invitation, and for his benefit a second review was held on the eighth.[28] The cavalry passed before him first at a walk and then at a trot, and this time there was no grumbling, since the review was staged for the beloved and revered commanding general. As soon as the review was over, the baggage was packed, Stuart issued his orders for a forward move to begin the following day, and the brigades were moved down nearer the Rappahannock in preparation for an early start the next morning.[29]

25. Neese, *Three Years in the Confederate Horse Artillery*, 168.

26. von Borcke, *Confederate War for Independence*, II, 266–67.

27. McDonald, *A History of the Laurel Brigade*, 132; Myers, *The Comanches*, 181.

28. The second review gave rise to one of the classic stories of the war. John B. Hood and his division of Longstreet's corps had reached Culpeper, and Fitzhugh Lee invited his friend Hood to attend the review, adding, hospitably, "Bring any of your people." Hood arrived at the review with his "people"—his entire division.

29. Stuart's posting of his brigades for the night is sufficient evidence in itself that the Federal attack the next morning was totally unexpected. Fitzhugh Lee's brigade (commanded temporarily by Colonel T. T. Munford) was at Oak Shade Church, seven and a half miles northwest of Fleetwood. Jones's brigade was camped at St. James Church, two miles west of Beverly Ford. All but one battery of the artillery was in park in front of Jones, between him and the ford. Hampton's camps were well to the south, near Stevensburg. W. H. F. Lee was at Welford, a short distance behind

Early on the morning of June 8, as the Confederates were making ready for the review for General Lee, the quartermaster sergeants of the Union cavalry regiments at Warrenton Junction
were busy issuing rations, forage, and ammunition to the men of
their companies.[30] The troopers of the 10th New York spent the
morning sharpening their sabers on an old grindstone that one of
them had brought into camp. Then "some wag started the story
that, by the rules of war, any soldier found with a sharp saber
. . . was liable to be shot. Some of the susceptible youths proceeded to put an edge on their blades as dull as their comprehen-
sions."[31] Judson Kilpatrick had returned from Gloucester Point
with his brigade, and Captain George A. Custer of the 5th United
States, eager for advancement, turned up to serve as volunteer
aide-de-camp to General Pleasonton.

At two in the afternoon the "General" was sounded and the
blue cavalrymen fell in for their march to the Rappahannock. In
keeping with Hooker's instructions, Pleasonton directed Gregg to
cross the river at Kelly's Ford at dawn with the Second and Third
Divisions of cavalry and Russell's brigade of infantry. After crossing, Gregg's own Third Division and the infantry were to march
northwest about seven miles to Brandy Station, while Colonel
Duffié and his Second Division marched due west to Stevensburg,
six miles from the ford and about four miles south of Brandy
Station. Buford, with the First Division, the Reserve Brigade, and
Ames's footsoldiers, was also to cross the river at dawn, at Beverly
Ford seven miles upriver from Kelly's, and with the cavalry in the
lead was to march to Brandy Station, four miles to the southwest
of the ford, where he would meet Gregg. The united body was
then to go on toward Culpeper. It was expected that the Confederate horse would be met somewhere between the station and the

---

Jones, and Robertson was at the John Minor Botts farm, a short distance
southwest of Brandy Station.

30. Gracey, *Annals of the 6th*, 156; Preston, *History of the 10th Regiment*, 82.

31. Preston, *History of the 10th Regiment*, 82. Lieutenant B. B. Porter
of the 10th New York recalled, "The Regiment . . . never counted so many
men in any other engagement, nor was the *esprit de corps* ever better. In
my connection with the Regiment I never witnessed more enthusiasm and
confidence by the men than on this occasion." *Ibid.*, 85.

town. Duffié, at Stevensburg, was to provide flank protection for the main body as it marched toward Culpeper.

On the evening of the eighth, the two infantry brigades and all the cavalry except Duffié's division were in position in the woods, within a short distance of their respective fords. The approach march had been timed so that the troops would reach their destination after nightfall. Fires were forbidden; the men were deprived of their beloved hot coffee and had to make do with a supper of cold pork and hardtack, washed down with water.[32] Two hours past midnight, they were awakened in whispers, and after eating a cold breakfast and feeding their horses, they saddled, mounted, and started for the river in the darkness. There were no bugle calls, all orders were given in whispers, and by four o'clock the lead regiments had reached the fords and were ready to cross.

For reasons never explained, Duffié's division was late for the rendezvous.[33] The division did not leave its camps at Warrenton Junction until five o'clock on the afternoon of the eighth. "What with various delays," Charles Francis Adams wrote, it was eleven o'clock before the division reached Morrisville, six miles from Kelly's Ford. "It was well past twelve before we got down to sleep. . . . at two o'clock we were on the road. Heaven only knows where they marched us, but . . . after five hours hard marching we had only made as many miles and reached Kelly's Ford."[34]

32. Gracey, *Annals of the 6th*, 156; Preston, *History of the 10th Regiment*, 83.

33. Gregg called it an "unnecessary delay" which "seriously interfered with the movement." David McM. Gregg, "The Second Cavalry Division, Army of the Potomac, in the Gettysburg Campaign," *Journal of the United States Cavalry Association*, XVIII (1907), 216. Pleasonton's orders, given to Duffié on the 8th, read: "It is much desired that your command should reach Morrisville as early as possible in the afternoon, not after sunset, if it can be avoided." However, the same orders directed that Duffié's "entire wagon train" was to accompany the command, and although the roads were dry, that may have caused the delay. To encumber the march even more, it was also ordered that "each trooper must have 15 pounds of forage on his horse." *Official Records*, Vol. XXVII, Pt. 3, p. 37.

34. Ford, *A Cycle of Adams Letters*, II, 31. Duffié, in his report, says that he reached Morrisville at seven P.M. *Official Records*, Vol. XXVII, Pt. 1, p. 961. If he did, it made his late arrival at the ford the next morning even less excusable.

Beverly Ford, where Buford's command, with Benjamin F. Davis and the 8th New York in the van, was to cross, was picketed by Company A of the 6th Virginia. The rest of that regiment was somewhat less than two miles back, near St. James Church, behind a mile-wide belt of woods. Most of Stuart's artillery was in park between the 6th Virginia and the ford. It was the rule in the Confederate cavalry, as in the Union cavalry, that the horses of the picket reserve were to be kept saddled, ready for immediate use; on this occasion, however, in the absence of any apprehension of an attack, the horses of Jones's brigade, including those of the 6th Virginia, had been unsaddled and turned out for the night to graze some distance from camp.[35]

Davis, to whom Custer had attached himself, moved out at half past four—"at earliest dawn"—and got across the river without difficulty. Once on the south bank, his advance, restricted to movement in column of fours by the narrowness of the road flanked by woods and drainage ditches on both sides, was slowed down somewhat by the resistance put up by the 6th Virginia pickets, firing as they retreated, dodging from cover to cover. Then Davis was brought to a halt by a charge of about a hundred men of the same regiment—all the troopers whose horses happened to be within reach—led by Major C. E. Flournoy.[36] The check was momentary, but it gave the Confederate artillery time to limber up and gallop to the rear and General Jones was able to bring up the 7th Virginia, many of them half-dressed, including Jones himself, some on foot and some riding bareback.[37] While the two

35. Opie, A Rebel Cavalryman, 147.
36. John Opie of the 6th Virginia, who was himself in the charge, has it that Major Flournoy's charge "broke" the 8th New York. He then reports that Flournoy's scratch group, having lost "more than half" of its men, (actually thirty out of about a hundred) was "driven out of the woods back to . . . [its] camp." Obviously, to do this the 8th New York could not have been "broke[n]" as Opie claims. Ibid., 149–50.
37. Here Colonel Davis, directing the advance, was shot and killed by Lieutenant R. V. Allen of the 6th Virginia. McClellan, I Rode with Jeb Stuart, 265. Elias Beck of the 3rd Indiana of Davis' brigade, who served as a regimental surgeon "for money and experience," wrote his wife the next day, "our Brigade Commander Col. Davis was killed. . . . [He] was . . . a proud tyrannical devil—& had the ill will of his whole Command—& Il bet was killed by our own men." Elias W. H. Beck, "Letters of a Civil War Surgeon," Indiana Magazine of History, XXVII (1931), 154.

Virginia regiments made a fighting retreat, Thomas T. Munford, temporarily in command of Fitzhugh Lee's brigade, and W. H. F. Lee moved down from the north, Hampton with four of his regiments came on from the south, and they and Jones's brigade, as well as the artillery, formed a strong battle line behind the protection of a stone wall at St. James Church, with a half-mile belt of open ground before them. Their line curved outward at both ends and hence threatened both of Buford's flanks. The fighting before the stone wall swayed forward and back, each side charging the other repeatedly. Eventually, however, the threat to his flanks forced Buford to draw back to the protection of the woods, but before he did so he sent the 6th United States, with the 6th Pennsylvania in support, on a charge against the Confederate gun line. Major James F. Hart of Stuart's horse artillery thus describes the charge: "[The charge] was made over a plateau fully eight hundred yards wide, and the objective point was the artillery at the church. Never rode troopers more gallantly than did those steady Regulars, as under a fire of shell and shrapnel, and finally of canister, they dashed up to the very muzzles, then through and beyond our guns, passing between Hampton's left and Jones' right. Here they were simultaneously attacked from both flanks and the survivors driven back."[38]

Jeb Stuart's camp equipage was packed after the review on the eighth, in anticipation of the next day's move, and he spent the night under a tent fly on Fleetwood Hill. He was awakened at dawn by the firing at Beverly Ford. Suspecting the possibility of a second Federal crossing at Kelly's Ford, he sent Robertson's brigade to block the road thence to Brandy Station. He sent the 2nd South Carolina and the 4th Virginia to the station itself, to guard the rear of the regiments fighting at St. James Church, and, after ordering the corps' wagon train to move out of harm's way back to Culpeper and posting his adjutant general, Major H. B. McClellan, on Fleetwood Hill to receive and transmit messages, rode off to direct the fighting against Buford.

It was now past ten o'clock. Buford's advance, facing the bulk

38. McClellan, *I Rode with Jeb Stuart*, 168; see also Gracey, *Annals of the 6th*, 159–60.

of Stuart's forces, was stalled. The advance of W. H. F. Lee's brigade from the north, joined by three regiments of Munford's, had posed a serious threat to Buford's right and rear and made it necessary for him to realign his forces. He decided to move the Reserve Brigade from the church around to his right rear and to replace it with Ames's infantry. There was a lull in the fighting while these moves were taking place. In the midst of the lull, a courier sent by McClellan came galloping up to Stuart with the shocking message that Federal cavalry in strength was at Fleetwood Hill.

Duffié's late arrival at Kelly's Ford had seriously delayed Gregg's crossing of the river.[39] Gregg intended to have Duffié lead the crossing and ordered him to be at the ford at 3:30 A.M., but he did not arrive until past seven o'clock, and Gregg's crossing, instead of being made at "earliest dawn," was not completed until past eight o'clock, by which time Buford's command had been fighting for nearly four hours.

The crossing completed at long last—there had been practically no opposition—Gregg sent Duffié forward on his way to Stevensburg and with the rest of his command set out for Brandy Station.[40] Except for a narrow belt of woods along the river and patches of woodland on and around the slopes of "Mount Dum-

39. *Official Records*, Vol. XXVII, Pt. 1, p. 950. In Duffié's report there is no mention of the late arrival of the division at the ford. *Ibid.*, 961.

40. There is considerable doubt about Gregg's orders to Russell. Gregg himself says that he "directed General Russell . . . to proceed directly . . . to Brandy Station." *Ibid.*, 950. On the other hand, his orders to Duffié read, "At the point at which the Third Division will turn north for Brandy Station, there will be posted 500 infantry, which will remain there . . . as a support for both columns." *Ibid.*, Pt. 3, p. 42. H. B. McClellan, whose account is based on a careful postwar investigation, says that Gregg "left Russell's infantry brigade in the vicinity of Kelly's Ford." McClellan, *I Rode with Jeb Stuart*, 286. The historian of the 10th New York writes that Company L of his regiment was detached for duty with General Russell, who ordered it to "post pickets to give warning of any movement down the road in his front," which certainly does not suggest that he was moving forward or was planning to do so. Preston, *History of the 10th Regiment*, 89. Russell's two reports on the Gettysburg Campaign make no mention of the role of his brigade at Brandy Station. *Official Records*, Vol. XXVII, Pt. 1, pp. 673, 674.

pling" a short distance south of the station, the march led through open country; "the waste of war had removed the obstacles to cavalry manoeuvers . . . fences and forests; and the ground was open, level and firm."[41]

And now Gregg violated a fundamental precept of war. Even before his crossing of the river had begun, the gunfire of Buford's battle upriver could be heard, but instead of marching to the sound of the guns by the most direct road, Gregg followed Duffié on the Stevensburg road, which ran southwest—*away* from Buford—for four and a half miles before it crossed the byroad that ran northwest to Brandy Station. By taking this roundabout route, he added four miles—an hour's march—to the distance to be covered; he did, however, avoid a head-on clash with Robertson's 1,500-man brigade, deployed two miles from Kelly's Ford across the direct road to Brandy Station.

Robertson played a strangely inert role in this day's events.[42] In a battle that accounted for 1,287 total casualties, the losses of his brigade came to "4 horses mortally wounded or totally disabled."[43] His pickets brought him timely word that the Federal cavalry and infantry were crossing the ford in great strength, and he in turn sent couriers with the information to Stuart, but beyond that, the only action he took was to dismount a portion of his command "to oppose the enemy's infantry in the woods."[44] He also received word later from his scouts that the enemy were marching toward Brandy Station on a road beyond his right flank,

41. Blackford, *War Years with Jeb Stuart*, 215. Gregg wrote in his report, "The country about Brandy Station is open, and on the south side extensive level fields [are] particularly suitable for a cavalry engagement." *Official Records*, Vol. XXVII, Pt. 1, p. 950. But see note 74, in this chapter.

42. Readers will recognize the author's debt in the present account of the battle to the splendid description of it in H. B. McClellan's *I Rode with Jeb Stuart*, 262–95. McClellan was a participant in the battle—indeed, his quick thinking was largely instrumental in saving Stuart from defeat—and much of his account is based on his own observations. D. S. Freeman wrote, "The Battle of Brandy Station is not described in full detail here because, from the Confederate side, nothing of importance is to be added to the clear, trustworthy account in *H. B. McClellan*." Freeman, *Lee's Lieutenants*, III, 8, 31n.

43. *Official Records*, Vol. XXVII, Pt. 2, p. 736.

44. *Ibid.*, 733.

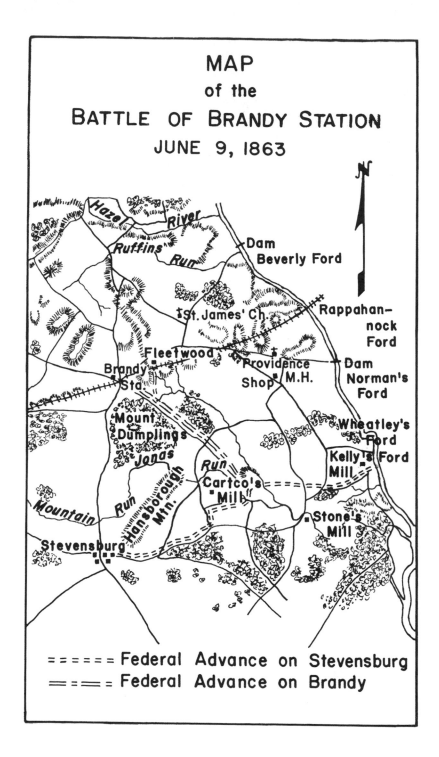

MAP
of the
BATTLE OF BRANDY STATION
JUNE 9, 1863

===== Federal Advance on Stevensburg
===== Federal Advance on Brandy

but he did not consider it his duty to shift some or all of his brigade westward to intercept them. Stuart came as near as he ever did to outright criticism of a subordinate, writing in his report that "Robertson kept the enemy in check on the Kelly's Ford road, but did not conform to the movement of the enemy to the right, of which he was cognizant, so as to hold him in check or thwart him by a corresponding move of a portion of his command in the same direction. . . . His detailed report will, I hope, account for this."[45]

Robertson's two reports, the second of which is clearly a response to a request for an explanation of his inaction, were those of a subordinate who lacks the initiative to do anything more than to follow the strict letter of his orders, regardless of any subsequent change of circumstances.[46] He had been ordered to block the direct road from Kelly's Ford to Brandy Station, and he did so. He had not been told to block the enemy's march on another road a short distance away. Hence he did not do it, and Gregg was therefore able to march to the station unopposed and undisturbed. Stuart, his conscience not entirely clear on the subject of the battle, forwarded Robertson's "explanation" that did not explain anything, to General Lee, with the unenthusiastic endorsement, "It is very clear that General Robertson intended to do what was right."[47]

It was some time near eleven o'clock, or perhaps between eleven and twelve, when, after a rapid march in choking dust, Gregg's brigades, Wyndham on the left and leading, and Kilpatrick on the right, crossed the railroad a little to the west of the station and headed for Fleetwood Hill, a few hundred yards beyond. The "Hill," actually a low, narrow ridge two miles long running north and south and dominating the terrain around it, was the key to the position. With Fleetwood in the hands of the Federals, Stuart's line of battle at St. James Church would have been between two fires and thus untenable; even his escape route to Culpeper would have been blocked.

45. *Ibid.*, 683.
46. *Ibid.*, 733–34, 734–35.
47. *Ibid.*, 735.

When the Federals arrived in sight of Fleetwood, the ridge was bare of troops. The 2nd South Carolina and the 4th Virginia had ridden off to the southwest to block Duffié's route to Stevensburg, and the hill was "occupied" by Major McClellan, a few orderlies, and, by good fortune, a single 6-pounder howitzer, commanded by Lieutenant John W. Carter. The gun happened to be there because, having fired off all but a few imperfect shells and round shot in the fighting at St. James Church, Carter was on his way to refill his limber with ammunition.[48] In less than five minutes after one of Robertson's orderlies brought McClellan word that the Yankee cavalry was approaching—information McClellan treated with total disbelief—there, within cannon shot, came a long column of the enemy. McClellan sent off his orderlies, one after the other, with urgent messages to Stuart asking for immediate help, and he then had Carter run his gun up to the crest of the hill and open a slow fire on the Federals. This was a mere charade, but McClellan's initiative and resourcefulness had the success they deserved. Wyndham, or Gregg, were led to believe that the Confederates held the hill in force. Instead of going ahead full tilt as a more daring and aggressive cavalryman might have done, one or the other of them halted the column to bring up J. W. Martin's battery and to organize a textbook attack.[49] The brief time it took to do this is what saved Stuart from a humiliating and quite possibly crippling defeat. He refused to believe the first of McClellan's reports of the approach of the Federals—had he not posted Robertson to prevent it?—but a second report convinced him, and he ordered the 6th and 12th Virginia and White's 35th Virginia Battalion back to Fleetwood Hill to deal with them. The Virginians rode the one and a half miles at a hard gallop and, when they reached the hill, charged the oncoming Federals without pausing to form up. Their horses were blown

48. Stuart changes Lieutenant Carter's accidental presence on Fleetwood Hill with a single gun and practically no ammunition to, "To this point I also ordered a section of artillery in reserve." *Ibid.*, 681.

49. The order to form "line of battle" and to bring up Martin's battery was apparently given by Wyndham. *Ibid.*, Pt. 1, pp. 965, 1024; see also William V. Kennedy, "The Cavalry Battle at Brandy Station," *Armor* (January-February, 1956), 30.

and their ranks "completely disordered" by their hard ride. They had sufficient momentum to drive back the 1st New Jersey, Wyndham's lead regiment, but were then charged in turn by Kilpatrick's brigade and "broke . . . all to pieces . . . lost all organization and sought safety in flight."[50]

Now Stuart, who had himself ridden to Fleetwood, ordered up Hampton's and Jones's brigades. Hampton too came up at a gallop; with two of his regiments, the 1st South Carolina and the Cobb Legion, he charged head on into the Federals who had reached the crest of the hill, while his other two regiments, the 1st North Carolina and the Jeff. Davis Legion, charged their right flank, south of the railroad.

It was here and at this time that the fighting took the form that made Brandy Station the classic cavalry battle of the war.[51] Charges were followed by countercharges, in regimental, battalion, and squadron strength. With organization partially or totally lost on both sides, and the absence of anything resembling a battle line, squadrons, small groups of all sizes, and lone individuals engaged in a general melee. Their uniforms undistinguishable in the thick cloud of dust and powder smoke that overhung the field, men rode in every direction, sabering or shooting down anything that crossed their path, and being sabered or shot themselves.[52]

The three guns of Martin's battery that had been run forward

50. Opie, A Rebel Cavalryman, 153.
51. The fighting on and below Fleetwood Hill is described in General Hampton's report (critical of Stuart's handling of the battle) and in the reports of Confederate regimental commanders, in Official Records, Vol. XXVII, Pt. 2, pp. 721–22, 726, 727–28, 732–33. The more important Federal reports are in Ibid., Pt. 1, pp. 985–86 (Kilpatrick), 965–66 (Wyndham), 949–52 (Gregg), and 1044–46 (Pleasonton). Unfortunately, there is no report of Buford's on his part in the battle.
52. A member of the 1st Pennsylvania wrote, "At one time the dust was so thick we could not tell friend from foe." Thomas, Some Personal Reminiscences, 9. A member of the 10th New York stated, "The rebel line that swept down upon us came in splendid order, and when the two lines were about to close in, they opened a rapid fire upon us. Then followed an indescribable clashing and slashing, banging and yelling. . . . We were now so mixed up with the rebels that every man was fighting desperately to maintain the position until assistance could be brought forward." Preston, History of the 10th Regiment, 85.

to the foot of Fleetwood Hill were overrun by White's Battalion; the guns changed hands three times before they finally remained in the hands of the Confederates.[53] Of the thirty-six men Martin took into the fight, thirty were killed, wounded, or taken prisoner.[54] The Confederate artillery, sections and individual pieces belonging to a number of different batteries, which had been assembled in hot haste on the crest of the hill, was attacked by a portion of the 1st New Jersey and saved only after a desperate fight with sabers, pistols, carbines, and even sponge-staffs.

Both sides were now exhausted, and many of the men, Federals as well as Confederates, had been unhorsed. The second squadron of the 1st New Jersey, for example, had lost twenty-seven horses out of thirty-nine, and the regimental historian comments that "men and horses had been fighting for over three hours and were now utterly exhausted. . . . there were not a dozen horses that could charge—not a man who could shout above a whisper."[55]

The result of the wildly confused fighting on and below Fleetwood was that Gregg was gradually forced back to the south, beyond the railroad. As soon as he was out of range of the Confederate artillery on the hill he stopped, to sort and reform his regiments and brigades. Here he was joined by Duffié's division, which he had ordered up from Stevensburg. The two divisions then marched off to the northeast along the river and, after making contact with Buford's left, made an unhurried and undisturbed crossing of the Rappahannock over a ford near the railroad.

Duffié's somewhat half-hearted advance on Stevensburg during the morning was made by troopers who were already exhausted before they were called upon to do any fighting, by lack of sleep and the long marches they had made that day and far into the night of the day before. They were held in check at Stevensburg by a single regiment, the 2nd South Carolina, handled with

53. Blackford, *War Years with Jeb Stuart*, 215.
54. *Official Records*, Vol. XXVII, Pt. 1, p. 1025.
55. Pyne, *First New Jersey Cavalry*, 152. This regiment went into the fight 280 strong. It lost 56 officers and men killed, wounded, and missing. Among the killed was Lieutenant Colonel Virgil Brodrick, commanding the regiment. *Ibid.*, 154.

great skill and determination by its colonel, Matthew Calbraith Butler.[56] Recalled urgently by Gregg, Duffié arrived at Fleetwood too late to be a factor in the fight there.[57]

It will be recalled that Buford was realigning his forces when Gregg launched his attack on Fleetwood Hill. Before Buford was ready to go back to the attack, Gregg had been repulsed, and with the threat to his rear eliminated, Stuart was able to establish a new battle line facing Buford and running the full length of Fleetwood Hill.

Having moved the Reserve Brigade around to extend his right flank northward, Buford ordered the 2nd United States, with the 6th Pennsylvania in support, to charge the 9th Virginia, which held the left flank of Stuart's new position. This led to a repetition on a smaller scale and in a more orderly form, of Gregg's battle. If the account of Colonel R. L. T. Beale of the Virginia regiment is to be believed, his men met and drove back the charge of the two Union regiments.[58] Then, however, the 9th Virginia was struck in flank by a charge of a "fresh regiment," not otherwise identified, and driven back in turn. Reinforced by the 10th and 13th Virginia, the 9th charged again, and for the second time the Federals were driven back. Colonel Beale then reformed his regiment in preparation for following up the advantage he had gained, but before he could order another charge, he discovered that Buford had begun to retreat to Beverly Ford, and here, too, the fighting ceased.

56. Butler, struck by a shell, lost a foot in the fight. Colonel W. C. Wickham's 4th Virginia, sent forward by Stuart to reinforce Butler, was charged and routed by the 1st Massachusetts, 1st Rhode Island, and a squadron of the 6th Ohio. McClellan, *I Rode with Jeb Stuart*, 289; see also *Official Records*, Vol. XXVII, Pt. 1, p. 961.

57. Pleasonton's dissatisfaction with Duffié's performance is shown by the fact that he recommended Buford and Gregg, but not Duffié, for promotion; further, he requested permission to have Martin's battery, the regiments of Gregg's and Buford's divisions and of the Reserve Brigade, but not those of Duffié's division, inscribe "the name of Beverly Ford" on their flags. *Official Records*, Vol. XXVII, Pt. 1, p. 1045.

58. There is a hint in McClellan's restrained language that he was somewhat skeptical of Colonel Beale's claim of having "met and driven back" the charge of the 2nd United States and the 6th Pennsylvania. *I Rode with Jeb Stuart*, 282.

Buford broke off the action and moved off to recross the river in compliance with an order from Pleasonton. Gregg and Duffié had come up from below the railroad, and Pleasonton had word of the arrival at Fleetwood of Confederate infantry. He ordered the retreat in the conviction that he had fulfilled the mission that had been assigned to him.[59]

The arrival of Confederate infantry came about as a result of Stuart ordering Captain W. W. Blackford of his staff, who owned a pair of powerful field glasses, to look for the presence of Federal infantry with their cavalry. Blackford was able to spot Federal footsoldiers in the distance, and so reported to Stuart, who ordered him to ride to Culpeper in haste and inform General Lee. "After a hot ride of six miles," Blackford reached General Longstreet's headquarters, gave him Stuart's message, whereupon, as Blackford recalled, "General Lee . . . came down himself with some infantry."[60] But Blackford's recital is suspect on several counts. It is unclear when and where—at St. James Church in the morning, or at Fleetwood Hill at noon—Blackford "discovered" the presence of Federal infantry. Why he should have been asked to look for Federal infantry is a puzzle in itself. Stuart himself supervised the fight at St. James Church, and to a soldier of his experience, it would have been evident from the sound of the small arms fire alone that Buford had infantry with him. On the other hand, Russell's infantrymen were several miles away from Gregg's battle at Fleetwood, and it is nearly impossible that Blackford could have seen them, even with "powerful" field glasses. Finally, it was not in response to the message brought by Blackford that Confederate infantry joined Stuart. Actually, the message Blackford carried—however it had come about—had been anticipated by General R. E. Rodes; alerted perhaps by the arrival of Stuart's wagon train at Culpeper, he marched his division to the sound of the guns and halted at the Botts farm, two miles from Fleetwood, to await orders.[61] Presumably it was in response to Captain Blackford's message that he was ordered to go on to

59. *Official Records*, Vol. XXVII, Pt. 1, pp. 903, 904.
60. Blackford, *War Years with Jeb Stuart*, 216.
61. *Official Records*, Vol. XXVII, Pt. 2, p. 546; see also Freeman, *Lee's Lieutenants*, III, 12.

Fleetwood to help Stuart, but by the time he arrived at the Barbour house, still a half mile short of the hill, the fight at Fleetwood was already over, and Gregg had begun his retreat.

Contrary to Pleasonton's report to Hooker, in which he repeated a dispatch from Gregg to himself, there were no "cars loaded with infantry" brought by rail from Culpeper to Brandy Station.[62] Pleasonton was correct in reporting the presence of Confederate infantry behind Stuart, but there is no evidence in the records that he identified the organization to which the infantry belonged. That identification was the crux of his assignment and the elementary object of any cavalry reconnaissance.[63]

D. Howard Smith of the 5th Kentucky, C.S.A., wrote in the bitterness of his soul, twenty-five years after the war, "The Federal army was composed very largely of the foreign element—paid hirelings, like the Hessians of the war of the Revolution—the scum of Europe and the great northern cities, who went into the war solely from motives of gain and pillage. It could not be expected that such men would evince that degree of courage, had they possessed it, shown by the native-born American soldier, fighting for his country, moved by the loftiest motives of patriotism."[64] This was the language of postwar southern reunion oratory. It is doubtful if Stuart's troopers would have endorsed it on the evening of June 9 at Brandy Station. Not only had their own casualties been high—at least 51 killed, 250 wounded, and 132 missing—but the even higher Federal casualties—484 killed and

62. *Official Records*, Vol. XXVI, Pt. 1, pp. 951, 903.
63. McClellan's verdict on the battle, so far as supplying information Hooker wanted was concerned, was: "The information which General Pleasonton obtained was positive, but after all, was meagre. He developed the presence of the Confederate cavalry, and a portion of the Confederate infantry at Brandy Station. Beyond this he learned nothing." McClellan, *I Rode with Jeb Stuart*, 294.
64. Smith, *Services of D. Howard Smith*, 55. It should be said to Smith's credit that he also recognized lack of discipline as the major problem of Confederate armies: "This was one thing that gave the Federals the decided advantage towards the close of the war." *Ibid.*, 54. He was also capable of facing up to the fact that the Federals were not alone in being guilty of "pillage." See his comments on Morgan's last raid into Kentucky. *Ibid.*, 116 ff.

wounded and 372 taken prisoner—gave evidence of a hard-fought battle, with plenty of courage and determination on both sides.[65]

The 6th Pennsylvania made "a dash of conspicuous gallantry" (the phrase is that of a Confederate trooper) across an open field a half-mile wide on Major R. F. Beckham's horse artillery; the day's casualties of this regiment alone were 146 officers and men killed, wounded, and taken prisoner.[66] The 2nd United States, which, as a regiment of Regulars might with some justice be described as made up of "paid hirelings," "fought so tenaciously" that it lost 68 officers and men killed or wounded, nearly a third of the 225 present.[67] But it is not the casualty figures alone that tell the story; there is the testimony of another Confederate troopere, J. N. Opie of the 6th Virginia, who recorded, "In this battle the Federal cavalry fought with great gallantry, and . . . they exhibited marked and wonderful improvement in skill, confidence and tenacity."[68]

Pleasonton had crossed the river at dawn with Buford's command and remained with it throughout the fight. Hence he could neither see nor picture what Gregg was doing, apart from what he could deduce from the sounds of artillery and small arms fire two or three miles away. The only messages Gregg received from Pleasonton were two in the morning, to let him know that Buford

65. The Federal losses, as reported by Pleasonton, were 81 killed, 403 wounded, and 382 missing, for a total of 866; this was 70 fewer than the 936 arrived at by McClellan in his postwar analysis. *Official Records*, Vol. XXVII, Pt. 1, pp. 168–70; McClellan, *I Rode with Jeb Stuart*, 293. Of the Federals taken prisoner, 60 were wounded. *Official Records*, Vol. XXVII, Pt. 2, p. 719. Confederate casualties are tabulated in *ibid.*, 719, but with the footnote, "No report from White's Battalion. . . . Loss heavy." McClellan's postwar conclusion was that Confederate losses totaled 523. *I Rode with Jeb Stuart*, 292–93.

66. Beale, *History of the Ninth Virginia*, 85; Gracey, *Annals of the 6th*, 167. Two weeks before Brandy Station, the 6th Pennsylvania ceased to be "Rush's Lancers"; the regiment gave up its lances on May 24 and was rearmed with carbines. Gracey, *Annals of the 6th*, 154.

67. J. I. Lambert, *One Hundred Years with the Second Cavalry* (Topeka, Kan., 1939), 70.

68. Opie, *A Rebel Cavalryman*, 137. Thomason, in his fine biography of Stuart, writes, "Brandy Station was an ominous fight. . . . The gray troopers would no longer have it all their own way. Those Yankees, they conceded, could always fight; now they were learning to ride and fight at the same time." John W. Thomason, Jr., *Jeb Stuart* (New York, 1941), 409.

was contending with a superior force of the enemy, and a third early in the afternoon, ordering him to recross the river over Rappahannock Ford, near the railroad.[69]

Pleasonton's handling of the battle has been severely criticized. One student, himself a cavalryman, has commented that if Pleasonton had "used his opportunities with the vigor and skill that Stuart displayed in the conduct of an obstinate and desperate defense, the Confederate cavalry would have been dealt a blow from which it would hardly have recovered."[70] Another, viewing Brandy Station from the standpoint of the Federal cavalry, calls it a "classic battle of lost opportunities."[71] Still another is of the opinion that Stuart was saved by Pleasonton's failure to coordinate his pincers movement.[72] Charles Francis Adams, habitually critical of Pleasonton, wrote five days after the battle, "I am sure a good cavalry officer would have whipped Stuart out of his boots; but Pleasonton is not and never will be that."[73] Adams' verdict may well reflect the "public opinion" in the corps in the days following the battle.

The Brandy Station fight did not come about as or where Hooker and Pleasonton had expected. Stuart's camps were not in the eastern outskirts of Culpeper, but in the vicinity of Brandy Station. If Stuart had been where he was thought to be, Pleasonton might have met him with his own command united, in the open country near the village. The fact that Stuart led the bulk of his forces to oppose Buford, coupled with Robertson's inertia, gave the Federals a heaven-sent opportunity of catching him squarely between two fires, Buford on the north and Gregg on the south, and in this respect alone, Gregg's long delay in crossing at

69. *Official Records*, Vol. XXVII, Pt. 1, 950–51.
70. J. G. Harbord, "The History of the Cavalry of the Army of Northern Virginia," *Journal of the United States Cavalry Association*, XIV (1904), 448.
71. Russell F. Weigley, "John Buford," *Civil War Times Illustrated*, V (1966), 20.
72. Thiele, "The Evolution of Cavalry," 419.
73. Ford, *A Cycle of Adams Letters*, II, 32. Nevertheless, nine days after the battle, Hooker sent General Halleck a request that Pleasonton be promoted to major general and that his assignment to the command of the Cavalry Corps be made permanent. *Official Records*, Vol. XXVII, Pt. 1, p. 56.

Kelly's Ford worked to Pleasonton's advantage. There is, however, no indication that Pleasonton was aware of the opportunity. In any event, Gregg's delay in crossing threw the timing of the operation as planned badly out of kilter, and the presence of a numerous, fast-moving and tough enemy squarely between the two widely separated portions of his own command, with communication between the two wings slow and difficult, added greatly to Pleasonton's problems.

Nevertheless, after every allowance is made for Pleasonton's difficulties—terrain, communications, synchronization—a residue of doubt still remains about the quality of his leadership at Brandy Station.[74] His own formal report, as well as those of his subordinates, creates the impression of an absence on the Federal side, in striking contrast to the Confederate, of a strong directing hand at the top, and the absence, too, of the fortunate accidents that commonly reward resolute and aggressive leadership.[75] The message Pleasonton sent General Julius Stahel at 2:40 P.M., with more than five hours of daylight still ahead—"I will recross this p. m."—was not that of a commander determined to force the pace and see the fight through to a finish.[76] Gregg, for his part, must share whatever blame attaches to Pleasonton for a lack of decisive leadership; he should not have allowed himself to be intimidated at a crucial moment by Lieutenant Carter's single gun.

The success of Stuart's countermoves cannot disguise the fact—not apparent in his report of the battle—that the Federal attack had taken him completely by surprise. His own men were fully aware that it had. Charles M. Blackford of the 2nd Virginia wrote home that "Stuart was certainly surprised and but for the supreme gallantry of his subordinate officers and men . . . it

74. As to the terrain, Colonel G. F. R. Henderson, biographer of Stonewall Jackson, whose assessment of Brandy Station was that "there is no finer . . . cavalry battle," wrote, "I have carefully measured the scene of the battle . . . and I can find no open ground, free from wood or stream, more than a mile square." G. F. R. Henderson, *The Science of War* (London, 1913), 246.
75. *Official Records*, Vol. XXVII, Pt. 1, pp. 1044–46; see also his dispatches, *ibid.*, 903–904.
76. *Ibid.*, Pt. 3, p. 39.

would have been a day of disaster and disgrace."[77] General Lee's
dismay can be read between the lines of his less than enthusiastic
endorsement of Stuart's report of the action.[78] Back in Richmond,
J. B. Jones, the "Rebel War Clerk," noted in his diary, "The surprise of Stuart on the Rappahannock has chilled every heart."[79]
But most damaging of all to Stuart's self-esteem was the comment
of the Richmond *Examiner*:

The more the circumstances of the late affair at Brandy Station are
considered, the less pleasant do they appear. If this was an isolated
case it might be excused under the convenient head of an accident
or chance; but this much puffed cavalry of Northern Virginia has
been twice, if not three times, surprised since the battles of last December and such repeated accidents can be regarded as nothing but
the necessary consequences of negligence and bad management. If
the war was a tournament invented and supported for the pleasure
and profit of a few vain and weak-headed officers, these disasters
might be dismissed with compassion. But the country pays dearly for
the blunders which encourage the enemy to overrun and devastate
the land with a cavalry which is daily learning to despise the mounted troops of the Confederacy. It is high time that this branch of the
service be reformed.[80]

Stuart's congratulatory order to his men, typical of its kind, spoke
in glowing terms of the "saber blows, inflicted on that glorious
day."[81] Nonetheless, the humiliation of an undoubted surprise,
and the evident disapproval of his own men and of the country at
large, rankled and were to have a material effect on his actions in
the days ahead.[82]

The Federal horsemen's assessment of the battle and of their
own role in it ranged from favorable to enthusiastic. Contrary to

77. Blackford, *Letters from Lee's Army*, 175.
78. *Official Records*, Vol. XXVII, Pt. 2, p. 687.
79. Quoted in Thiele, "The Evolution of Cavalry," 420. General Lafayette McLaws wrote his wife, "Our cavalry were surprised by the enemy
yesterday and had to do some desperate fighting to retrieve the day."
Quoted in Coddington, *The Gettysburg Campaign*, 59. Coddington also
quotes diary entries and letters of Stuart's men that speak of the surprise.
Ibid., 617.
80. Quoted in Freeman, *Lee's Lieutenants*, III, 19.
81. General Orders No. 24, June 15, 1863, in *Official Records*, Vol.
XXVII, Pt. 2, p. 719.
82. Coddington, *The Gettysburg Campaign*, 60.

Pleasonton's claim in his dispatch to Hooker on the evening following the battle, they had not succeeded in "crippling the enemy," but they had certainly given Stuart's corps all it could handle.[83] Willard Glazier of the 2nd New York viewed Brandy Station as "a glorious fight, in which the men of the North had proved themselves more than a match for the boasted Southern chivalry."[84] Noble D. Preston, whose 10th New York had fought as a unit for the first time, recorded that in the first place, the battle provided him and his fellow troopers a chance to show what they could do when acting as a regiment, and second, that it "forever settled the question of superiority as between the gray and the blue cavalry in favor of the latter."[85] For Edward P. Tobie's 1st Maine, Brandy Station stood for the glory of the regiment's first saber charge: "As soon as the regiment debouched through the woods, it formed squadrons at a gallop, drew saber, and in a moment more was charging across the field. . . . On they go, faster and faster . . . over fences and ditches, driving the enemy a mile or more. Oh, it was grand!" And he continues, "But a higher value attaches to Brandy Station as affecting the regiment. . . . It was . . . the first time it had ever tasted . . . the fruit of victory. The battle aroused its latent powers, and awoke it . . . to a new career. It became self-reliant, and began to comprehend its own possibilities. It became inspired with an invincible spirit that never again forsook it. These remarks might be extended . . . to our cavalry generally."[86]

The 3rd Pennsylvania formed the rear guard when Gregg's and Duffié's divisions recrossed the river. Their historians asserted flatly that "Confederate authorities" to the contrary notwithstanding, the Union cavalry was not "driven back," that, in fact, the "crossing was made without a single Confederate in view." Their verdict on the battle was that "the occurrences of that memorable day established for the first time the equality of our cavalry with, if not its superiority over, that of our adversaries."[87] To the troop-

83. *Official Records*, Vol. XXVII, Pt. 1, p. 903.
84. Glazier, *Three Years in the Federal Cavalry*, 223.
85. Preston, *History of the 10th Regiment*, 85, 77.
86. Tobie, *First Maine Cavalry*, 155.
87. Regimental History Committee, *History of the 3d Pennsylvania*, 274, 245.

ers of the 8th New York, "it was a mystery" why Pleasonton decided to retreat across the river.[88] The recollections of Lieutenant Frederick Whittaker of the 6th New York were more personal, and nothing less than ecstatic. Whittaker was a devotee of the saber, and the melee around Fleetwood Hill was greatly to his taste; it was, to him, fighting "of the most inspiriting, romantic and thoroughly delightful kind," the "wild intoxication" of which he savored in retrospect; "Glorious days were those," he wrote, "and green to the memory of those who shared in them."[89]

With considerably more restraint, Benjamin W. Crowninshield of the 1st Massachusetts, one of the most thoughtful of regimental historians, recorded that there had been "more fighting than generalship" in the battle, but that the Federal horse had proved themselves "fully a match for Stuart's cavalry." In his judgment, Brandy Station was "the turning point of the war" for the Federal cavalry.[90] On the Confederate side, H. B. McClellan shared this view; in his opinion, "One result of incalculable importance certainly did follow this battle—it *made* the Federal cavalry. Up to that time confessedly inferior to the Southern horsemen, they gained on this day the confidence in themselves and their commanders which enabled them to contest so fiercely the subsequent battle-fields of June, July and October."[91]

88. Norton, *Deeds of Daring*, 67.

89. [Whittaker], *Volunteer Cavalry*, 18–19. W. W. Blackford of Stuart's staff was equally rhapsodic. "There now followed," he wrote, "a passage of arms filled with romantic interest and splendor to a degree unequaled by anything our war produced. . . . Not a man fought dismounted, and there was heard but an occasional pistol shot. . . . It was what we read of in the days of chivalry, acres and acres of horsemen sparkling with sabres, and dotted with brilliant bits of color where their flags danced above them. . . . The next morning we rode over the field and most of the dead bore wounds from the sabre, either by cut or thrust. I mean the fields around Fleetwood; in other places this was not the case to so great an extent." Blackford, *War Years with Jeb Stuart*, 215–17.

90. Crowninshield, *A History of the First Regiment*, 18.

91. McClellan, *I Rode with Jeb Stuart*, 294.

XV

Cold Steel

WHEN THE BATTLE OF BRANDY STATION WAS FOUGHT, the Confederate infantry was already in motion to the northwest. On June 10, General Richard Ewell's corps left Culpeper and, after crossing the Blue Ridge, marched toward Winchester, held by Federal General Robert H. Milroy and his "weary boys," a sobriquet they were to acquire in this campaign. On June 14, as soon as the Federal infantry began to leave the lines opposite Fredericksburg to conform to the westward shift of the Confederates, General A. P. Hill's corps was also ordered to march, following Ewell's route to the Valley and then north. Longstreet, last to leave Culpeper, was to march north along the eastern face of the Blue Ridge, which he was to cross via Ashby's and Snicker's gaps; until he crossed over into the Shenandoah Valley, his right was to be screened by Stuart's cavalry, operating in the Bull Run Mountains and in the Loudoun Valley between those and the Blue Ridge.

Hooker suspected as early as June 5 that the departure of the Confederate infantry from Fredericksburg portended an invasion of the North via the Upper Potomac.[1] The numerous dispatches

1. *Official Records*, Vol. XXVII, Pt. 1, p. 30.

he sent the president and General Halleck during the succeeding two weeks look superficially like those of an army commander in the midst of a more than ordinarily impenetrable fog of war, but perhaps they can more accurately be interpreted as those of a man who has a reasonably clear idea of what the enemy is doing, but wants to shift to someone else the responsibility for the necessary countermoves. On June 13, at any rate, Hooker reported that pursuant to the president's and Halleck's suggestions, he had ordered four of his corps to march northwest to Manassas Junction and three others to Dumfries.[2]

The effect of these moves, Confederate and Federal, was that by June 16, Ewell's corps was north of Winchester in the Shenandoah Valley, Hill's corps was west of Culpeper on its way to the Valley, and Longstreet's corps was somewhere between them. The Federal army was echeloned along the Orange & Alexandria Railroad, as far north as Manassas Junction. On that day, Halleck wired Hooker to advise (*not* to order) "the movement of a force, sufficiently strong to meet Longstreet, on Leesburg, to ascertain where the enemy is. . . . With the remainder of your force in proper position to support this, I want you to push out your cavalry to ascertain something definite about the enemy."[3] In compliance with this suggestion, Pleasonton was directed on the seventeenth to "put the main body of . . . [his] command in the vicinity of Aldie, and push out reconnaissances toward Winchester, Berryville, and Harper's Ferry."[4] He was told further that the "commanding general relies upon you with your cavalry force to give him information of where the enemy is, his force and his movements. You have a sufficient cavalry force to do this. Drive in . . . [his] pickets, if necessary, and get us information. It is better that we should lose men than to be without knowledge of the enemy, as we now seem to be. . . . the general directs that you leave nothing undone to give him the fullest information."[5] Such detailed and fussy directions and exhortations to a cavalry commander should have been entirely unnecessary in the third sum-

2. *Ibid.*, 38.
3. *Ibid.*, 47.
4. *Ibid.*, Pt. 3, p. 172.
5. *Ibid.* These orders, dated June 17, are clearly a confirmation of verbal orders given to Pleasonton the previous day or evening. His own movement orders to Gregg, cited below, are datelined three A.M., June 17.

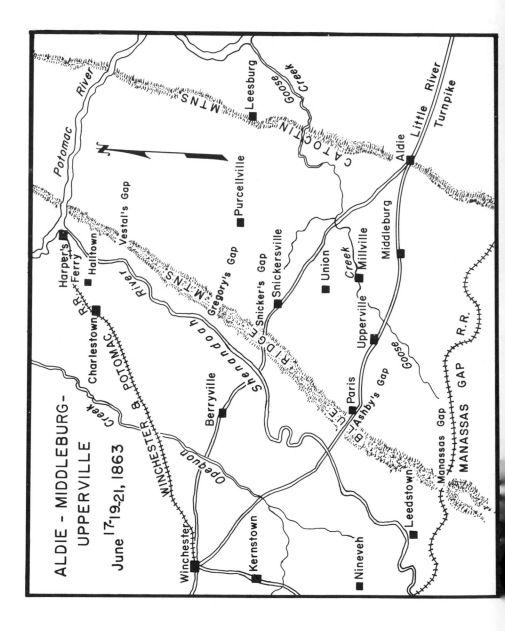

ALDIE - MIDDLEBURG-
UPPERVILLE
June 17-19-21, 1863

Potomac River

Harper's Ferry

Halltown

Charlestown R.R.

Berryville

Winchester

Kernstown

Nineveh

POTOMAC &

WINCHESTER

Opequon Creek

Shenandoah River

Vestal's Gap

Gregory's Gap

Snicker's Gap

Snickersville

BLUE RIDGE MTNS

Purcellville

CATOCTIN MTNS

Leesburg

Goose Creek

Aldie

Little River Turnpike

Middleburg

Millville

Union

Goose Creek

Upperville

Paris

Ashby's Gap

Leedstown

Manassas Gap

MANASSAS GAP R.R.

N

mer of the war. They imply a lack of confidence in Pleasonton's grasp of the most elementary duties of his post, which he would have had every right to resent. Whether he did so does not appear in the records; he did, at any rate, act promptly. At three A.M. on the seventeenth, orders were given to Gregg to have his division march within two hours, from his camp at Manassas Junction to Aldie, which he was to reach the same evening. He was also ordered to send one of his regiments via Thoroughfare Gap to Middleburg, "scouting the country well in that vicinity."[6]

Hooker's orders to Pleasonton for this movement found the Cavalry Corps in reasonably good condition. Most of its regiments were down to three hundred to four hundred officers and men, but a good start had been made to replace the horses and weapons lost in the Brandy Station fight.[7] Pleasonton himself concluded, after reviewing the corps on June 11, that the men were "in fine spirits and good condition for another fight."[8] On the same day, with Hooker's approval, Pleasonton made a major contribution to the efficiency of his command by a sensible reorganization.[9] The manpower of the corps, reduced to under seven thousand by his losses at Brandy Station, was too small for three divisions plus a separate Reserve Brigade. Pleasonton proceeded to divide the corps into two divisions, the First, under Buford, to be made up of the regiments of Pleasonton's own former division and of the Reserve Brigade; and the Second, to be commanded by Gregg, of the former Second and Third Divisions. Each of the two new divisions was to be divided into three brigades, and Buford and Gregg were given the authority to work out the brigade organization for their divisions.

Aldie was a village at the eastern foot of the gap of that name through the Bull Run Mountains. The Little River Turnpike from

6. *Ibid.*, 171.
7. *Ibid.*, 93.
8. *Ibid.*, 58.
9. General Orders No. 18, *ibid.*, 64. Pleasonton had previously submitted the plan for Hooker's approval. The commanding general's response, sent by General Butterfield, was: "If you consider it essential for the efficiency of your corps and the good of the service, make the change." *Ibid.*, 57. There is no indication in the records that either General Halleck or the War Department were consulted.

Alexandria had its western terminus at Aldie; it was continued northwestward by the Snicker's Gap Turnpike, running fifteen miles across the Loudoun Valley to Snicker's Gap, across the Blue Ridge into the Shenandoah Valley. Aldie was the eastern end also of the Ashby's Gap Turnpike, running eighteen miles nearly due west through Middleburg and Upperville to Ashby's Gap, nine miles southwest of Snicker's Gap. Aldie was thus an excellent base for scouts into the Shenandoah Valley in two directions, with good roads leading to the gaps and into the Valley beyond.

Kilpatrick, a brigadier general since June 14, led the advance of Gregg's division to Aldie. His brigade reached the village shortly after noon on the seventeenth and found Fitzhugh Lee's brigade, still commanded by Colonel Thomas T. Munford, in possession.[10] Characteristically, Kilpatrick did not hesitate; he charged at once and drove Munford's pickets out of the town and into the fields beyond. Then, as frequently happened to him, he found himself in serious trouble. His four regiments—the 2nd New York, 1st Massachusetts, 6th Ohio, and the 4th New York—were not only outnumbered by Munford's five regiments—the 1st, 2nd, 3rd, 4th, and 5th Virginia—but were also confined to narrow roads and lanes and had to run the gauntlet of dismounted Confederate sharpshooters who lined the stone walls, some of which lined the roads, others being perpendicular to them.[11]

10. There is some doubt about the exact time of day when the fighting at Aldie began. One historian has Kilpatrick arriving at Aldie at "around 4:00 p.m.," on the basis of a dispatch of Pleasonton's datelined "Near Aldie, June 17, 1863—4.15 p.m.," in which Pleasonton uses the phrase, "Upon arriving at this place a short time since." Coddington, *The Gettysburg Campaign*, 77, citing *Official Records*, Vol. XXVII, Pt. 3, p. 173. It would appear, however, that the 1st Massachusetts, leading Kilpatrick's brigade, reached Aldie considerably earlier, probably between noon and one P.M. Roy R. Stonesifer, Jr., "The Union Cavalry Comes of Age," *Civil War History*, XI (1965), 277. The 1st Maine, the lead regiment of J. Irvin Gregg's brigade, reached Aldie "about two o'clock P.M.," when Kilpatrick's brigade had already been fighting for some considerable time. Tobie, *First Maine Cavalry*, 159.
11. William P. Lloyd of the 1st Pennsylvania wrote of the fighting at Aldie, "Stone fences, with which this country is covered, rocks, ravines, woods, ditches, buildings and everything available for defense was held by the enemy." *History of the First Reg't.*, 57–58. In terms of naval warfare, the Confederates had crossed Gregg's "T," which gave them a great advantage.

After a brief skirmish, Munford deployed his brigade of about two thousand men on a ridge some distance west of Aldie, in a position that covered both turnpikes and, before Kilpatrick had time to bring up all his men for an attack in full force, took the offensive himself. The 4th and 5th Virginia, led by Colonel Thomas L. Rosser of the latter regiment, drove back the 1st Massachusetts on Kilpatrick's right flank; the 4th New York, ordered to countercharge, broke and ran, leaving their colors and their badly wounded Colonel Louis Palma di Cesnola in the hands of the enemy.[12]

Charles Francis Adams' squadron was in the van of the 1st Massachusetts and received the full shock of Rosser's charge. Adams wrote two days later:

I went into action with ninety-four men in my squadron and came out with between thirty and forty. . . . My poor men were just slaughtered and all we could do was to stand still and be shot down, while the other squadrons rallied behind us. The men fell right and left, and the horses were shot through and through, and no man turned his back, but they only called on me to charge. I couldn't charge, except across a ditch, up a hill and over two high stone walls, from behind which the enemy were slaying us. . . . then I fell slowly back to some woods. Here I was ordered to dismount my men to fight on foot. . . . I gave the order and the men were just off their horses and all in confusion, when the 4th N. Y. on our right gave way . . . and in a second the rebs were riding yelling and slashing among us.[13]

The emergency created by Rosser's charge was made to order for Kilpatrick. The 1st Maine, the lead regiment of J. Irvin Gregg's brigade, now reached the scene. Kilpatrick placed himself at the head of the regiment, led them in a charge (in which his horse was killed under him) against the Confederate regiments, and drove them back to their starting point. He then decided that the time had come to sweep the Confederates from the field with a full-blooded attack and sent the 1st Massachusetts and the 1st

12. The Confederate reports of the fight are in *Official Records*, Vol. XXVII, Pt. 2, pp. 739–41, 742, 742–43, 745, 746, 747–48. The more sketchy Federal reports are in *ibid.*, Pt. 1, pp. 952–53, 975–76, 906–907, 907–908.

13. Ford, *A Cycle of Adams Letters*, II, 36–37. The total of Union casualties at Aldie was 50 killed, 131 wounded, and 124 captured or missing. *Official Records*, Vol. XXVII, Pt. 1, p. 171.

Maine on a charge along the Snicker's Gap Turnpike against Munford's left.

When Colonel Rosser made his attack on the 1st Massachusetts, he prepared for the possibility of being driven back by laying an ambush. He posted Captain R. B. Boston with about fifty sharpshooters in a deep ditch running perpendicular to the turnpike and hidden from view from the east by a row of haystacks. When, leading Kilpatrick's final attack, the 1st Massachusetts galloped down the turnpike in column of fours, Boston waited for the leading squadrons of the regiment to get beyond the ditch and then raked them flank and rear with the fire of his sharpshooters. Only the rear squadron of the regiment escaped. The 1st Massachusetts, with but 300 rank and file present at Aldie, sustained 167 casualties in the fight—20 killed, 57 wounded, and 90 missing or captured—55 percent of the total loss suffered by the five Union regiments engaged, and most of its loss occurred in this ambush.[14]

The 1st Maine, with Kilpatrick again at its head, was far enough behind the 1st Massachusetts to escape Captain Boston's ambush and, in fact, captured Boston and his entire detachment. Then, with the 2nd New York in support, the men from Maine advanced a half mile and came upon the Confederate reserves waiting for them, dismounted and behind the protection of a stone wall. The two regiments charged the wall, and at the cost of heavy casualties, drove the Confederates from it.[15]

It was now growing dark and the action gradually ceased. Honors for the day were about even. At the cost of casualties that were high for an all-cavalry fight, and particularly so for the numbers engaged, the Federals had driven Munford some distance back from Aldie, but at nightfall, his command was undamaged and still firmly astride the shortest route to the Shenandoah Valley.[16]

14. Crowninshield, "Cavalry in Virginia," 24; see also *Official Records*, Vol. XXVII, Pt. 1, p. 171.

15. Colonel Calvin S. Douty of the 1st Maine was one of those killed in the charge on the stone wall. He is mistakenly identified as "Lieutenant" Douty in the list of officers killed, in *Official Records*, Vol. XXVII, Pt. 1, p. 171.

16. The story of the fight in the text differs in some respects from

The regiment Pleasonton had sent to Middleburg to scout "the country well in that vicinity" was the 1st Rhode Island, with 275 rank and file present, and commanded once again by Alfred Duffié, who had been passed over when the new divisional and brigade commands were given out. After a march of twenty-five miles, Duffié reached Middleburg a little after four P.M., surprised and captured a Confederate picket in the outskirts, and then ordered Captain Frank Allen's squadron to charge into the village. Confederate cavalry, which the townspeople reported to be 2,000 strong, had marched away from Middleburg a half hour before Duffié arrived, leaving behind Stuart and his staff, whom the Rhode Islanders nearly captured, and a rear guard, which Captain Allen's charge drove out of town. Duffié realized that the Confederates would be back in much greater force than his own. Perhaps he should have done the sensible thing, and left Middleburg while he could do so in safety, to join Gregg at Aldie. Instead, most unwisely, he chose to stay and fight. He had his men barricade the roads leading into town and sent Captain Allen to Kilpatrick at Aldie, to report his arrival at Middleburg and to ask for help. After a courageous cross-country ride of more than seven miles through an area swarming with enemy cavalry, Allen reached Aldie at nine P.M. and delivered his dispatches to Kilpatrick, who told him that "his brigade was so worn out that he could not send any re-enforcements to Middleburg."[17]

Meanwhile, at about seven o'clock, the Confederate cavalry returned to Middleburg, just as Duffié had expected, and did so in overwhelming strength. Duffié dismounted his men to provide a defense for his crude barricades and the stone fences nearby, but, attacked by Robertson's brigade from the west and a part of W. H. F. Lee's brigade from the south, the weak Federal regiment

---

that in McClellan, *I Rode with Jeb Stuart*, 297–303. The partial, differing, or conflicting accounts of these fast-moving, confused cavalry fights in the reports and reminiscences of participants make nearly impossible an accurate reconstruction of the exact sequence of events. It does not appear that McClellan conducted the careful postwar investigation of this fight that makes his account of Brandy Station so trustworthy.

17. *Official Records*, Vol. XXVII, Pt. 1, 964–65. Stonesifer is in error in stating that the messenger was captured; a minor flaw in an excellent account. Stonesifer, "The Union Cavalry Comes of Age," 279.

was overrun. Duffié with four officers and twenty-seven troopers
—what he called "the debris of . . . [his] much-loved regiment"—
reached Aldie and safety on the afternoon of the next day, after
fighting his way through Confederate cavalry "in front, rear and
both flanks."[18] It says much for the French colonel's stamina that
he was able to write the official report of his misfortunes that very
day.

After sending Hooker a series of dispatches while the fighting
at Aldie was still going on, Pleasonton wrote a more detailed report at five A.M. the next day. He spoke of the "dash and ease"
with which his men had driven the enemy "from a strong position" (the survivors of the 1st Massachusetts and the 1st Maine
might well have taken issue with the word "ease"), and went on
to say that he was about to send a brigade to Snicker's Gap "to
scout the valley, and send parties toward Winchester, Harper's
Ferry, and Sperryville," which was, of course, precisely what he
had been sent to Aldie to do.[19] The only crumb of valuable information he was able to send Hooker was that there was "no force
of consequence of the enemy's infantry this side of the Blue
Ridge."[20] This was negative information, but worth having. Hooker's response nevertheless drew a pointed distinction between
negative and positive information; he had General Butterfield tell
Pleasonton, "The general says your orders are to find out where
the enemy is, if you have to lose men to do it."[21]

Nothing of consequence occurred on the eighteenth. Kilpatrick led his brigade on a scout to see if the Confederates were still
at Middleburg and, having ascertained that they were, returned
to Aldie.

The next day, at Middleburg, Pleasonton mounted a full-scale

18. *Official Records*, Vol. XXVII, Pt. 1, pp. 962–64. Robertson charged
Duffié's barricades twice and was driven back both times. His third charge,
however, broke through. Chambliss and Robertson reported capturing a
total of 130 of Duffié's men. Stonesifer, "The Union Cavalry Comes of
Age," 279. By June 10, 6 more officers and upwards of 25 troopers reached
Aldie (and more were "gradually coming in") after escaping from Middleburg. *Ibid.*, Pt. 3, p. 223.
19. *Ibid.*, Pt. 1, p. 907.
20. *Ibid.*
21. *Ibid.*, Pt. 3, p. 195.

attack by Gregg's division, with J. Irvin Gregg's brigade in the lead.[22] In a severe fight, the Confederates were driven out of the town to their main defensive position a mile to the west. There, in a belt of woods running across the turnpike, and behind the inevitable stone wall, with open fields to their front providing a clear field of fire for their carbineers, the Confederates made their stand. Gregg ordered the 10th New York of Kilpatrick's brigade and the 1st Maine to storm the position. The two regiments attacked on horseback. They were driven back, but Gregg ordered up reinforcements, the charge was repeated, and this time it was successful. The Confederates were driven through the woods and into the open country beyond, where Stuart himself, with the brigades of W. H. F. Lee and Robertson, was waiting. The Federals charged these two brigades, but were repulsed. Stuart's men then went over to the attack and tried to drive the Federals out of the woods, but they were driven back, and as Stuart withdrew "to a more commanding position a half mile to the rear," the firing died out.[23]

Lieutenant G. W. Beale of the 9th Virginia describes an incident that occurred when his regiment tried to drive Gregg's troopers back through the woods:

We were able to pursue these Maine men but a short distance before their heavy skirmish line, on both the right and left, checked us with their fire, and very quickly the 10th Pennsylvania Regiment, hastening to support the one we had met, came bearing down on us. . . . The hand-to-hand encounter that ensued between us and these men of Maine and Pennsylvania was sharp and bloody. One of them, I observed, who had been unhorsed, and had backed up against an oak tree in the grove, and having fired his last cartridge, was defending himself with rocks, which he furiously hurled at his assailants until he fell from their pistol shots dead at the roots of the tree.[24]

22. J. Irvin Gregg's brigade was made up of two regiments, the 1st Maine and the 4th Pennsylvania, plus Battery C, 3rd United States Artillery.
23. *Official Records*, Vol. XXVII, Pt. 2, pp. 689–90. Major von Borcke was severely wounded in this retreat, while riding at Stuart's side.
24. Beale, *History of the Ninth Virginia*, 102. Beale was in error, however, in suggesting that the unfortunate Federal trooper might have belonged to the "10th Pennsylvania Regiment." That regiment was not at

During the night of the eighteenth the irrepressible John Mosby made his way into the Federal lines outside Aldie and captured one of Hooker's staff officers carrying dispatches to Pleasonton. He sent these on to Stuart immediately, and from them the latter learned that he was opposed by Hooker's entire Cavalry Corps. This information caused Stuart to decide "in no event to attack with cavalry alone the enemy at Aldie. As long as he kept within supporting distance of his infantry at that point, my operations became necessarily defensive, but masking thereby the movement of our main body by checking the enemy's reconnaissance and by continually threatening attack."[25] This has all the earmarks of wisdom after the event; nevertheless, it was an entirely correct appreciation of Stuart's role, which was to shield from Federal observation the march of the Confederate infantry down the Shenandoah Valley. On the other hand, Stuart was in error in reporting that at that moment there was infantry "within supporting distance" of Pleasonton's cavalry.[26]

On Saturday, the twentieth, serious fighting was prevented by a heavy all-day rain, but on that day Pleasonton was able to send Hooker the kind of information he had been ordered to get. He reported having captured the previous day infantrymen belonging to "Garnett's and Pickett's divisions," that Longstreet covered the gaps through the Blue Ridge and was "moving up his forces as the rebel army advances toward the Potomac." So far, so good, but Pleasonton was unable to resist the temptation to add, "I have been attacking Stuart to make him keep his people together, so that they cannot scout and find out anything about our forces. . . . Lee is playing his old game of covering the gaps and moving his forces . . . [down] the Shenandoah Valley. . . . The infantry on this side is simply to assist Stuart."[27]

Aldie. The rock-throwing trooper, if he did not belong to the 1st Maine, was a member either of the 4th Pennsylvania or the 10th New York. It may be added that the 1st Maine lost in this fight 37 killed or wounded out of the 257 rank and file present. Tobie, *First Maine Cavalry*, 168.

25. *Official Records*, Vol. XXVII, Pt. 2, p. 689.

26. The nearest Federal infantry, Meade's V Corps, was four or five hours' march from Aldie, which by any standard is not within "supporting distance."

27. *Official Records*, Vol. XXVII, Part 3, p. 223. General R. B. Garnett

Encouraged by the fighting on the seventeenth and nineteenth
—Pleasonton wrote that his men had "behaved splendidly and are
in the highest spirits and confidence"—he proposed that, "the general commanding permit me to take my whole corps to-morrow
morning, and throw it at once upon Stuart's whole force, and
cripple it up. . . . to do this effectually, I should like to have a
couple of large brigades, or a division of infantry, to . . . get in
position without being seen by the enemy, and engage the dismounted sharpshooters with Stuart while the cavalry attacks and
puts to flight their horses."[28] The proposal was at once approved,
but it was coupled with some helpful but gratuitous advice. "The
commanding general thinks," Pleasonton was told, "you cannot
have more than 4,000 of the enemy's cavalry in your vicinity, and
he suggests that you make your attack in front with a very small
force, and turn the enemy's position with your main body."[29] At
the same time, however, orders were sent to General Meade to
have General James Barnes's division of his corps march at two
A.M. the same night to join Pleasonton.

Stuart, who in the meantime had been reinforced by Hampton's and Jones's brigades, remained in the position he occupied
when the fighting ended on the nineteenth. Despite the fact that
he had decided only a few hours earlier "in no event" to attack the
Federals, he reported that upon Hampton's arrival he became "extremely anxious . . . to attack the enemy as early as possible."
The twenty-first, however, was a Sunday, and the attack on the
enemy had to wait, for Stuart "recognized . . . [his] obligation to
do no duty other than what was absolutely necessary."[30]

Pleasonton recognized no such obligation. General Barnes's

(killed at Gettysburg) did not have a division; his brigade was part of
Pickett's division of Longstreet's corps. In a dispatch sent a few hours
later, Pleasonton was able to supply more specific and more accurate information. He reported, "A rebel infantry soldier, brought in to General
Gregg this morning, states that the infantry force which was on this side
of the Blue Ridge, and was of Longstreet's corps, passed through Ashby's
Gap yesterday . . . and that only Stuart's force is this side of the Blue
Ridge." *Ibid.*, Pt. 1, p. 911.
28. *Ibid.*, Pt. 1, p. 911.
29. *Ibid.*, Pt. 3, p. 227.
30. *Ibid.*, Pt. 2, p. 690.

division arrived at Middleburg, and Pleasonton launched his attack shortly after seven A.M. on the Sabbath. He had been given a full division of three brigades in response to his request for "a couple of large brigades or a division," but, unaccountably, he left Barnes himself and two of the three brigades of footsoldiers at Middleburg and used in his attack only the brigade of Colonel Strong Vincent, made up of the 83rd Pennsylvania (Vincent's own regiment), the 16th Michigan, 44th New York, and 20th Maine.[31] Vincent, who was to be mortally wounded two weeks later, and his entire brigade covered themselves with glory in the defense of Little Round Top on the second day of the battle of Gettysburg. They gave a foretaste of their quality on this twenty-first of June; led by Vincent, they were an army by themselves.

Pleasonton's tactics in this Sunday battle followed Hooker's suggestion; they were simple but effective. He was to advance toward Upperville, eight miles west of Middleburg, along the Ashby's Gap Turnpike over terrain that gave the defense every advantage, with ridges, stone fences, belts of timber, and small streams running athwart the pike, making the advance of mounted troops against any kind of opposition extremely difficult and costly, and the opposition here was the battle-hardened troopers of Stuart's corps. Accordingly, Pleasonton posted Vincent's infantry to the left (south) of the pike. Hampton's and Robertson's brigades manned what Stuart described as "a position previously chosen, of great force against a force of ordinary size, or against cavalry alone"; viewed from the Federal side, "the dismounted men of the enemy were in position on the south side of . . . [the] road, behind a series of stone walls running at right angles with it, the cavalry in the fields, and a battery of six guns placed near the road on the left. A belt of woods some 200 yards [sic] marked their position."[32] Pursuant to Pleasonton's instructions, Vincent

31. Vincent, an Erie, Pennsylvania, lawyer, had his twenty-sixth birthday a few days after this fight. On the second day of the battle of Gettysburg, acting on his own responsibility, he led his brigade to Little Round Top. His initiative, coupled with his own and his men's heroism, "saved Little Round Top and the Federal army." Vincent, mortally wounded in this fight, was most fittingly given posthumous promotion to brigadier general. Glenn Tucker, *High Tide at Gettysburg* (Indianapolis, 1958), 257–68.
32. *Official Records*, Vol. XXVII, Pt. 2, p. 690, and Pt. 1, p. 614.

sent three of his regiments straight forward to dislodge Stuart's sharpshooters from the shelter of their stone walls and to pick off the gunners manning the battery; at the same time he sent Captain Orpheus S. Woodward with the 83rd Pennsylvania on a wide swing to the left, with orders to keep "his force concealed, and the instant he had passed the stone walls, to emerge and take the enemy in flank and rear."[33] Pleasonton, meanwhile, had Kilpatrick's troopers ready to charge mounted, at the first sign of disorder or a retreat among the Confederates.

One senses in Stuart's account of this action a feeling that the Federal tactics were somehow unfair. Forgetting his own use of dismounted men sheltering behind the protection of stone walls to pick off the Federal mounted troops, he implies that Pleasonton's use of infantrymen to assist the mounted troops was unworthy of a cavalry commander.[34] Nonetheless, Pleasonton's tactics worked to perfection. Stuart's two brigades were driven four miles to Upperville and beyond. Each time they attempted to make a stand behind another series of stone walls, or beyond the bottoms of Crummer's Run and later at the crossing of Goose Creek, the same tactics were repeated and with equal success: a flank attack by Vincent's infantry, followed by a saber charge by the mounted troops. In Stuart's version of the fight, he is seen directing Hampton to "withdraw to the next height whenever his position was hard pressed"; in Vincent's, "the enemy fled in confusion, followed by our cavalry, who drove them repeatedly from one position to another . . . into and beyond Upperville."[35]

Vincent, in his report, paid tribute to the gallantry and stamina of his own footsoldiers, but he also had an admiring word for the horsemen. "The charges of the cavalry," he wrote, "a sight I had never before witnessed, were truly inspiring, and the triumphant strains of the bands, as squadron after squadron hurled the enemy in his flight up the hills and toward the gap, gave us

33. *Ibid.*, Pt. 1, p. 614.
34. William Hyndman of the 4th Pennsylvania reports that his "regiment suffered considerably, having made a severe charge, in column of fours, up the road into Upperville, with stone fences on both sides, behind which the enemy awaited us." Hyndman, *History of a Cavalry Company*, 101.
35. *Official Records*, Vol. XXVII, Pt. 2, p. 690, and Pt. 1, p. 614.

a feeling of regret that we, too, were not mounted and could not join in the chase."[36]

One of Stuart's troopers recorded in his reminiscences that the defense was not wholly passive, but that, when the opportunity offered, his side too charged the enemy.

Our cavalry made a bold and gallant charge on their position, but the Yanks received the charge stubbornly and did not give way in the least nor budge from their position, but in turn made a desperate charge on our cavalry, and soon after the fight became general all over the field. Sabres flashed all around us and the fire of small arms was raging all over the field. . . . It looked to me as if the mixed-up men on both sides were charging in every direction. . . . The enemy drove us back slowly all day. Several times . . . I saw our shell plunge right in their advancing line, break their ranks, and check for a moment the advancing host, but they quickly closed up and came at us again. They were certainly the bravest and boldest Yankees that ever fought us on any field.[37]

And W. W. Blackford noted that although the Federals' horsemanship had not yet advanced to the point where they could hold their own against the Confederates in a mounted melee, yet the "improvement in the . . . [Union] cavalry . . . became painfully apparent in the fights around Upperville."[38]

While Kilpatrick and J. Irvin Gregg, joined later by the Reserve Brigade, attacked along the turnpike, John Buford, with the First Division, moved forward from Middleburg on their right flank and had a much easier time of it than did David Gregg's brigades, being opposed mostly by skirmishers.[39] When within a mile of Upperville, seeing that Gregg's division appeared to be outnumbered, Buford led his men at a brisk trot to the left to join the fight, but his way was blocked by ditches and stone walls, which threw his column into confusion. He then saw a train of enemy wagons going toward Ashby's Gap on a side road and de-

36. *Ibid.*, pt. 1, p. 615.
37. Neese, *Three Years in the Confederate Horse Artillery*, 182–83.
38. Blackford, *War Years with Jeb Stuart*, 221.
39. The total casualties of Buford's division at Upperville were 4 killed, 43 wounded, and 5 captured or missing; the total Federal casualties in the action, including those of Vincent's brigade, were 12 killed, 130 wounded, and 67 captured or missing. *Official Records*, Vol. XXVII, Pt. 1, pp. 171–72.

cided to go after it. But before he could reach the wagons, which eventually escaped, he was himself attacked by Jones's and W. H. F. Lee's brigades, coming from the direction of Snickersville to join Hampton and Robertson; he was able to beat them off with the carbine fire of two of his regiments, the 8th Illinois and the 3rd Indiana.[40]

Pleasonton's two divisions, now joined, and the Reserve Brigade pressed forward five miles from Upperville to Ashby's Gap. Although Stuart speaks in his report of a "leisurely" retreat to the gap, it is significant that he sent four of his batteries of horse artillery on ahead to find good firing positions in the gap itself; he also names two high-ranking officers, a colonel and a lieutenant colonel, as severely wounded and left behind to be captured by the Federals, which was neither typical of Stuart's men, nor characteristic of a leisurely retreat.[41]

The Upperville fight ended with Stuart driven back to the gap, which was occupied that evening by General Lafayette McLaws' division of Longstreet's corps, the cavalry retreating to a position behind them "for rest and refreshment, of which it was sorely in need."[42] Pleasonton, no doubt feeling that he had done enough, returned to Aldie, leaving a brigade behind to hold Middleburg and sending another to picket the Snicker's Gap road. Based on information brought in by Buford's scouts and supplied by deserters from one of Longstreet's regiments, Pleasonton reported to Hooker that General Lee himself, and the corps of Longstreet and A. P. Hill, were in the Shenandoah Valley, on their way north.[43] He had not "crippled up" Stuart's command, but he had

40. *Ibid.*, 920–21. The stone fences of Upperville played no favorites. When Buford intercepted Jones's brigade on its way to join Stuart, "Never was a brigade taken at a greater disadvantage than in this engagement. Buford had arrived first at a point intersecting Jones' line of march, and assailed him on the left of his marching column. . . . The road . . . was between stone fences, which made it impossible for Jones to get his regiments into any sort of formation, and the stone fences beyond in the fields occupied by the enemy furnished protection for his sharpshooters who fired with decidedly deadly effect upon the almost helpless Confederate masses." McDonald, *A History of the Laurel Brigade*, 151.
41. *Official Records*, Vol. XXVII, Pt. 2, p. 691. The two officers were Colonel P. G. Evans and Lieutenant Colonel M. Lewis.
42. *Ibid.*
43. *Ibid.*, Pt. 1, pp. 912–13.

beaten it back in a head-on fight in which he had been the aggressor throughout, and in conditions that gravely handicapped the attacker.

Pleasonton's dispatches are far from being models of clarity and precision—Stuart could have given him lessons in that respect—but he did obtain for Hooker valuable information on the whereabouts of the Confederate army. In all essential respects he had accomplished the mission assigned to him. The fight at Aldie on the seventeenth was to all appearances managed by Kilpatrick and the two Greggs without the benefit of any direction from Pleasonton (he did not reach Aldie until about three hours after the engagement began) but he did direct the fighting at Upperville on the twenty-first and deserves full credit for the clever use of infantry and cavalry in combination, whereby he overcame the natural and man-made obstacles favoring the defense. It is worthy of note also that Pleasonton used the reverse of the usual tactic: he had the infantry attack in flank and the cavalry head on, instead of the reverse.

The historian Roy P. Stonesifer, Jr., has written that the Union cavalry came of age in these fights; indeed, for the first time— it had not had a fair chance at Brandy Station—it displayed a combination of aggressiveness and competence that had thitherto been a monopoly of Stuart's men.[44] Nearly as important as a foretaste of the future was Pleasonton's demonstration at Upperville of what an intelligently conceived combined operation of infantry and cavalry could accomplish.

An important sequel of the Aldie-Middleburg-Upperville chain of fights deserves emphasis. In the final stages of Second Bull Run and throughout the Antietam Campaign and its aftermath, Pope's and later McClellan's cavalry was practically immobilized by lack of horses. Much had changed for the better in the succeeding seven or eight months. Amateurishness, fumbling, and frenzied improvisation were a hallmark of the Quartermaster's Corps no longer. Like the cavalry, they too were becoming professionals and veterans. On June 22, Pleasonton wrote to General Seth Williams, "In the various engagements in which my com-

44. Stonesifer, "The Union Cavalry Comes of Age," 283.

mand has been since the 8th instant, it has lost very heavily in . . . horses, some 800 . . . being killed or wounded, besides those that have been rendered unfit for service by the very hard labor to which they have been necessarily subjected, so that it will take at least 1,500 horses to supply the losses of the last 14 days."[45] But Colonel Rufus Ingalls, chief quartermaster of the Army of the Potomac, had not waited for Pleasonton's letter to start the wheels rolling to provide remounts for him. Two days before, on June 20, Ingalls wrote General Meigs, "Pleasonton will probably engage Stuart's entire cavalry force to-morrow. . . . The loss in horses will doubtless be great. He has been fighting every day with splendid effect, but, of course, with a daily loss of horses. Please do all you can to have as many good horses ready as possible. It is most important."[46] Nor were General Meigs and his organization wanting; they made it possible for General Williams to inform Pleasonton on June 24 that "every effort is being made to keep . . . you supplied with horses. . . . 750 horses were forwarded to you yesterday."[47] The absence of any further mention of a lack of horses in Pleasonton's dispatches makes it evident that the rest of the horses needed by his command were supplied also, and with none of the acrimony that had marked the exchanges between McClellan and the War Department in October, 1862.[48]

45. *Official Records*, Vol. XXVII, Pt. 3, p. 258.
46. *Ibid.*, 230.
47. *Ibid.*, 287.
48. In his dispatch asking for 1,500 horses, Pleasonton also asked that his corps "be augmented by some regiments drawn from other commands, until I shall have been able to scatter or destroy the enemy's cavalry, which now so largely outnumbers me." Hooker had General Seth Williams tell Pleasonton that he (Hooker) was of the opinion "that you very much overestimate the strength of the rebel cavalry. . . . He [Stuart] had at the beginning but 12,000, and his losses certainly cannot have been less than your own. Of this, a heavy force is in Maryland, Hampton's brigade is on the Rappahannock, and lesser forces scouting everywhere." Although basically correct, Hooker was mistaken in his belief that Stuart's losses had exceeded Pleasonton's, and Hampton was actually with Stuart and not on the Rappahannock; nevertheless, Pleasonton's plea had the result he hoped for. On June 28, the two-brigade cavalry division of General Julius Stahel was transferred from the defenses of Washington to the Cavalry Corps; this led to a major reorganization of the command structure of the corps, which will be noted hereafter. *Ibid.*, 230, 287, 373.

XVI

Solstice

WHILE PLEASONTON WAS REMOUNTING AND REEQUIP-
ping his men following the fights at Aldie, Middleburg, and Upperville, the three corps of General Lee's army continued their
northward march. General Ewell had begun crossing the Potomac
on June 15, and by the twenty-seventh the entire Army of Northern Virginia, except its rear guard of two brigades of cavalry, was
across the river and was fanning out in a wide swathe across
Maryland and southeastern Pennsylvania, collecting supplies and
spreading waves of alarm throughout the North. As the main
body of the Confederate army marched up the Cumberland Valley
toward Chambersburg, Hooker's army was also moving north,
two days' march behind the Confederates but keeping between
them and Washington and Baltimore by following a line that led
it from Leesburg, Virginia, across the Potomac at Edwards Ferry,
and on through Frederick toward Mechanicsville, Emmitsburg,
and Gettysburg. In the van of the Union advance, in the heat and
dust of midsummer, were the I, III, and XI Corps, commanded,
in a revival of the grand division organization without the name,
by General John Reynolds, a "first-class fighting man, universally
respected and admired," who, after Chancellorsville, was offered

command of the Army of the Potomac, but declined the appointment.[1]

There was a conspicuous absence from the ranks of the Confederate army as it marched north through the lush and prosperous Pennsylvania countryside. The divisions of Ewell's corps were preceded by detachments of General A. G. Jenkins' cavalry brigade, and the Confederate rear was brought up by the cavalry brigades of Grumble Jones and Beverly Robertson. But where was Stuart? He left on the night of June 25 on a march around the rear of the Federal army, taking with him the brigades of Fitzhugh Lee, Wade Hampton, and W. H. F. Lee, the last commanded by Colonel John R. Chambliss, Jr., in the absence of "Rooney" Lee, who had been gravely wounded and taken prisoner at Brandy Station. The controversy, unsettled after more than a hundred years, of the intent and meaning of General Lee's orders to Stuart and of the validity of Stuart's interpretation of them is not within the scope of the present study.[2] But whether Stuart's course was within the letter or spirit of Lee's orders, or a piece of flamboyant egoism, its effect was the same. It took Stuart himself, and his best brigades, out of the campaign for a critically important week and left General Lee deep in enemy territory without the help of the man on whose eyes and judgment he had learned to rely. Stuart was not there to supply the information about the Union army Lee needed to guide his own movements; hence the unintended, "accidental" battle of Gettysburg.[3]

Pleasonton, who had had a second pair of stars on his shoulder straps since June 22, promoted on Hooker's recommendation

1. Coddington, *The Gettysburg Campaign*, 37.
2. Those interested in what became one of the bitterest of postwar debates may wish to consult Freeman, *R. E. Lee*, III, 40–48; Freeman, *Lee's Lieutenants*, III, 54–60; Coddington, *The Gettysburg Campaign*, 107–12; Williams, *Lincoln Finds a General*, II, 662–65; McClellan, *I Rode with Jeb Stuart*, 315–18; and *Battles and Leaders*, III, 251–53. Stuart's own labored explanation (or apologia) is in *Official Records*, Vol. XXVII, Pt. 2, pp. 707–709.
3. *Official Records*, Vol. XXVII, Pt. 2, p. 318. General Lee was to say in his second report on the campaign, written after he had had ample time to consider Stuart's report, that "the movements of the army preceding the battle of Gettysburg had been much embarrassed by the absence of the cavalry." *Ibid.*, 321.

"for his surprise of Stuart's force . . . on the Rappahannock, June 9," covered the crossing of the Potomac by the Union army.[4] By the twenty-seventh, the cavalry too was across the river, Gregg heading for Frederick "with the utmost expedition consistent with the condition of . . . [his] horses," and Buford marching toward Middletown, Maryland, west of Frederick.[5] On the same day, Hooker directed that the cavalry be moved well in advance of the infantry toward Emmitsburg and Gettysburg, to "see what they can of the movements of the enemy."[6] Also on the twenty-seventh, Hooker, in one of his last orders as commander of the Army of the Potomac—he was replaced by George Meade the following day—assigned to Pleasonton's command General Julius Stahel's two-brigade, thirty-five hundred-man cavalry division, previously a part of the forces defending Washington.[7] Stahel, a moderately competent but unexciting officer, had latterly commanded the division "in fine soldierly style in a covered spring wagon drawn by four white mules," hardly the most appropriate means of conveyance for a dashing leader of cavalry.[8]

Hooker ended his command of the Army of the Potomac with an order relating to the cavalry; Meade began his the same way. The records fail to reveal the whole story, but within hours after taking over from Hooker, he wired General Halleck to request the promotion of both Elon J. Farnsworth of the 8th Illinois and George Custer of the 5th United States in one jump from captains to brigadier generals.[9] Then, without waiting for approval from Washington, Meade and Pleasonton proceeded to reorganize the cavalry command. Buford and David Gregg retained command of the First and Second Divisions, respectively. Judson Kilpatrick was given command of Stahel's division, reconstituted as the Third Division of the Cavalry Corps. Farnsworth received com-

4. *Ibid.*, Pt. 1, p. 51. Hooker got prompt action on his recommendation, Pleasonton's promotion being dated June 22. But Hooker's request that Pleasonton be given command of the Cavalry Corps in his own right, instead of as a temporary substitute for Stoneman, was ignored. *Ibid.*, 51, and Pt. 3, p. 333.
5. *Ibid.*, Pt. 3, pp. 337, 338, 348, 349.
6. *Ibid.*, 349.
7. *Ibid.*, 373, and Pt. 1, p. 991.
8. Isham, *An Historical Sketch*, 20.
9. Coddington, *The Gettysburg Campaign*, 220. Alfred Duffié was promoted to brigadier general at the same time.

mand of the First Brigade of this division, consisting of the 1st Vermont, 5th New York, and 1st West Virginia; Custer was given command of the Second, "Michigan" Brigade, made up of the 1st, 5th, 6th, and 7th regiments from that state.[10]

Judson Kilpatrick, now about to be tested in divisional command, was a New Yorker, born in 1836. A member of the West Point Class of 1861, he was married on the day of graduation and three days later was commissioned captain in the 5th New York Infantry (Duryée's Zouaves). Severely wounded in the battle of Big Bethel, he arranged in June, 1861, to be transferred to the 2nd New York with an advance in rank to lieutenant colonel. Four days after the battle of Brandy Station he was made a brigadier general. He was a "wiry, restless, undersized man," with black eyes, a lantern jaw, and a scraggly beard, given to high-flown oratory on every occasion, appropriate or inappropriate. Had he never risen above command of a regiment of cavalry, his reputation, both contemporary and posthumous, would have been considerably higher. His chief talents were a reckless bravery and a gift for leadership in combat, unmatched by sound judgment or the intellect needed for high command. Colonel Theodore Lyman of Meade's staff judged him a "frothy braggart without brains . . . [who] gets all his reputation by newspapers and political influence"; Custer's biographer, himself a cavalryman in the war, wrote, "with the possession of plenty of physical courage, Kilpatrick mingled so much besotted rashness and vanity . . . that his greatest successes were always marred by unnecessary slaughter, while he suffered more than one mortifying and humiliating defeat"; Charles Francis Adams, more succinctly, put him down as "a brave, injudicious boy, much given to blowing."[11] His own men's name for him was "Kill Cavalry," and when, in the spring of 1864, he left the Army of the Potomac to serve in the West, his

10. *Official Records*, Vol. XXVII, Pt. 3, p. 376. Wesley Merritt, 2nd United States, was also promoted from captain to brigadier general on Pleasonton's recommendation and was assigned to the command of the Reserve Brigade, made up of the 6th Pennsylvania, and the 1st, 2nd, 5th, and 6th United States and operating under Buford's general direction. *Ibid.*, Pt. 1, pp. 913, 166–67.

11. Agassiz, *Meade's Headquarters*, 79; Whittaker, *George A. Custer*, 192; Ford, *A Cycle of Adams Letters*, II, 44–45. It should be added, in fairness to Kilpatrick, that he had the approval of some of his men. When

successor in command of the Third Division, James H. Wilson, recorded that he had left it "badly run down. Its camps were badly placed and badly policed; its equipment and clothing nearly used up, and its heterogeneous collection of carbines dirty and out of order." But Wilson also credited Kilpatrick with being "as brave, enterprising, and energetic as any officer on either side of the Great Conflict."[12]

On June 28, when these command assignments were made, Buford was at Middletown guarding the left of the Union army as it marched northward at the best speed of its footsoldiers. The right of the army was covered by Gregg, from Frederick toward Ridgeville on the Baltimore-Hagerstown Turnpike. The Third Division, in the center, was at Frederick, awaiting with apprehension the arrival of its newly appointed commanding officers.[13]

The march into Pennsylvania tested the endurance of the Army of the Potomac. The marches were long, the heat intense. In addition to the physical hardships, there was also, prior to June 28, a spiritual unease, a legacy of Chancellorsville, a distrust of Hooker's capacity to command the army. As Charles Francis Adams put it, in his usual blunt fashion, "lack of confidence has steadily grown upon us. In Hooker not one soul in the army that I meet puts the slightest. . . . All whom I do see seem only to sadly enquire of themselves how much disaster and slaughter this poor army must go through before the Government will consider the public mind ripe for another change . . . [from] the drunk-murdering-arson dynasty now prevailing."[14]

---

he left the Army of the Potomac in April, 1864, the historian of one of his regiments wrote, "Kilpatrick had many traits that commended him to soldiers, and it was not without regret that we saw him go away." Isham, *An Historical Sketch*, 40. A trooper of the 1st Ohio wrote, "Kilpatrick is the most daring and skillful officer we have yet met. He fights the rebels as we expected to fight them when we enlisted. His ability to get his men out of tight places has won the confidence of all his men. . . . Whatever may be said of General Kilpatrick, he certainly has wonderful skill in managing his men in the excitement of battle." Gillespie, *A History of Company A*, 163, 175.

12. Wilson, *Under the Old Flag*, I, 372.
13. *Official Records*, Vol. XXVII, Pt. 1, p. 913.
14. Ford, *A Cycle of Adams Letters*, II, 38. The quoted passage is in a letter Adams wrote on June 25.

The cavalry had its own special hardships to bear, as illustrated by the ordeal of a typical regiment, the 3rd Pennsylvania.

[The men] had previously been in the saddle on an average for twenty hours out of the twenty-four for three days, without sleep and with scarcely anything to eat for man or horse. The intense heat at times was almost unbearable, the dust almost impenetrable. Horses by scores fell from exhaustion along the road. . . . Officers and men, begrimed past recognition, trampled along on foot, leading their worn-out horses to save their strength. . . . Dismounted cavalrymen, whose horses had fallen dead or dying, struggled along, some carrying their saddles and bridles in hopes of being able to beg, borrow, buy or help themselves to fresh mounts, others without anything but their arms.[15]

And here, from the pen of the historian of the 17th Pennsylvania of Buford's division, is a genre painting of a cavalry regiment in the midst of this campaign:

The division had been marching and picketing for almost a week with no rest for man or beast. They had marched all night to reach this point. . . . The column halted before the light of day with orders to "dismount and stand to horse." . . . an hour passed, and the gray dawn . . . lighted up a picture I can never forget. The men, who were completely exhausted, had slipped the bridle rein over their arms and lay down in front of their horses in a bed of dust (8 inches deep) that almost obscured them from sight. Their jaded steeds seemed to know they should not move, and propping themselves with extended necks and lowering heads, stood like mute sentinels over their riders dead in sleep.[16]

But the march north also had its compensations. "The change of scene from the war-worn, barren, inhospitable plains and hills of Virginia was most enjoyable," the historians of the 3rd Pennsylvania have written; "here all felt at home. No longer did we

15. Regimental History Committee, *History of the 3d Pennsylvania*, 266. See also William Brooke-Rawle, "Gregg's Cavalry Fight at Gettysburg, July 3, 1863," *Journal of the United States Cavalry Association*, IV (1891), 259–60. The ever-active Rufus Ingalls took steps to make up for the loss of horses. He wired Pleasonton on June 26, "There are 700 horses at Alexandria which I have ordered shod before being issued to you. . . . what number of horses do you stand in need of now?" *Official Records*, Vol. XXVII, Pt. 3, p. 338. As soon as the army crossed the Potomac, he ordered his subordinates "to procure all artillery and cavalry horses in the country fit for service," but they found that "the number that can be thus obtained is small." *Ibid.*, 543.
16. Moyer, *History of the 17th Regiment*, 57–58.

watch for the crack of the bushwhacker's rifle from behind each clump of underbrush. . . . The rich farms, the fields of clover and of waving grain . . . the commodious barns, the comfortable dwellings and the general prosperity, all stood out in strong contrast with the region we had just left."[17] And, the historians continue,

Our reception through central Maryland was all that could be wished for. There was nothing that the inhabitants could do for us that was not willingly offered. Along the route of the march men, women and children stood by the roadsides with pails of fresh milk and cold water and basketfuls of bread, cakes and pies, dispensing with free hands to all. . . . This enthusiastic welcome continued after we had crossed the line into Pennsylvania, though in some few localities our reception was not calculated to arouse in our minds very kindly feelings. . . . some of the inhabitants whose lives and property we had come to save were to be seen standing along the roads with bread and water *for sale* at the best prices they could induce us to pay.

On June 29, George Custer arrived to take command of his new brigade. The troopers from Michigan beheld with astonishment,

An officer superbly mounted. . . . He was clad in a suit of black velvet, elaborately trimmed with gold lace, which ran down the outer seams of his trousers, and almost covered the sleeves of his cavalry jacket. The wide collar of a blue navy shirt was turned down over the collar of his velvet jacket, and a necktie of brilliant crimson was tied in a graceful knot at the throat. . . . A soft, black hat with wide brim adorned with a gilt cord, and rosette encircling a silver star, was worn turned down on one side, giving him a rakish air. His golden

17. This and the subsequent quotation are from Regimental History Committee, *History of the 3d Pennsylvania*, 264–65. As the 17th Pennsylvania crossed the Maryland-Pennsylvania border, one of the guidon carriers was "stationed at the line, making the announcement to each company . . . that they were at that point entering upon Pennsylvania soil. The boys raised their caps and lustily cheered." Moyer, *History of the 17th Regiment*, 48. It is interesting to note, in connection with the comment about "the crack of the bushwhacker's rifle," that after the Confederates crossed into Maryland, Cole's battalion of Maryland (Union) Cavalry gave them a taste of the same medicine; acting as "partisans," they were "constantly annoying the enemy, capturing their pickets and picking up stragglers." Newcomer, *Cole's Cavalry*, 51. A foraging party of the 10th New York collected "some corn, oats and German anathemas" near Littlestown; the regimental historian adds, "the women at once began to transform flour into greenbacks. Every morsel of food was sold to the boys, at exorbitant prices." Preston, *History of the 10th Regiment*, 122.

hair fell in graceful luxuriance nearly or quite to his shoulders, and his upper lip was garnished with a blond moustache. A sword and belt, gilt spurs, and top boots completed this unique outfit.[18]

The first of Custer's many biographers thought he detected the rationale of this bizarre and highly irregular costume, which "surprised and captivated everyone," as well it might, and made its wearer look "as if he had just stepped out of one of Vandyck's pictures, the image of the seventeenth century." It was, this writer thought, "a challenge to all the world to notice him."[19] The idiosyncratic costume was a natural expression of Custer's exuberantly exhibitionistic personality, and it must not be forgotten that he was a mere twenty-three when he received his brigadier general's stars. His own officers' reaction—which, for all his bravery and magnificent leadership qualities he never succeeded in overcoming—was one of suspicion, distrust, and dislike.[20] Making his officers turn out for reveille roll call and compelling them to oversee the grooming of the horses at each stable call, both of which Custer made the "rigid rule," were not calculated to elicit the admiration and affection of lieutenants and captains of cavalry.

On June 29, the two opposing armies drew closer together. Pleasonton did not receive detailed orders from Meade; he was merely told "to protect well the front and flanks of this army with your Cavalry."[21] To this was added the next day the admonition that it was of the utmost importance that Meade receive "reliable information"; "your cavalry force," Pleasonton was told, "is large and must be vigilant and active. The reports must be those gained by the cavalry themselves, and the information sent in should be reliable. . . . Cavalry battles must be secondary to this object."[22]

18. Kidd, *Personal Recollections*, 128–29.
19. Whittaker, *George A. Custer*, 168–69. "West Point has had many a character to deal with; but it may be a question whether it ever had a cadet so exuberant, one who cared so little for its serious attempts to elevate and burnish, or one on whom its tactical officers kept their eyes so constantly and so unsympathetically searching as upon Custer. And yet how we all loved him." Morris Schaff, *The Spirit of Old West Point* (New York, 1907), 194.
20. Whittaker, *George A. Custer*, 170.
21. John Gibbon, *Personal Recollections of the Civil War* (New York, 1928), 129.
22. *Official Records*, Vol. XXVII, Pt. 3, p. 421.

Pleasonton's orders for the twenty-ninth directed Buford to advance via Emmitsburg to Gettysburg and to be there by the evening of the next day. Kilpatrick's division was to move to Littlestown, ten miles southeast of Gettysburg. Gregg and two of his brigades were to ride to Westminster, Maryland, and his third brigade to New Windsor, Maryland, a hamlet six miles from Westminster just south of Pipe Creek, a stream which was to acquire a notoriety of its own in the controversies swirling in the aftermath of the battle of Gettysburg.[23] The orders taking Gregg so far to the east and south of the infantry's route were the result of information telegraphed to Meade by Halleck on the twenty-eighth that Confederate cavalry had captured "150 wagons" near Rockville, Maryland. Halleck warned that "unless cavalry is sent to guard your communications with Washington, they will be cut off."[24] Then, later on the twenty-ninth, presumably on the receipt of information that the Confederate cavalry, identified as Fitzhugh Lee's brigade, had headed north after capturing the wagons, Gregg was ordered to take his division north also, to Hanover, Pennsylvania, to keep communications open with Baltimore.[25]

While Buford and his division were marching north, his men caught a spy near Frederick. A drumhead court-martial condemned the man to death, and the sentence was carried out at once. "A committee of indignant citizens called on . . . Buford and wanted to know why he was hanged. . . . Buford informed them that the man was a spy and he was afraid to send him to Washington because he knew the authorities would make him a brigadier-general."[26]

It is no reflection on solid, dependable, but unspectacular David Gregg, "a rare combination of modesty, geniality and ability . . . universally liked and respected," or on Kilpatrick, new to

23. *Ibid.*, 400.
24. *Ibid.*, Pt. 1, p. 63.
25. *Ibid.*, Pt. 3, p. 399.
26. Moyer, *History of the 17th Regiment*, 58. Chaplain Gracey has a similar story, but in his account the spy is caught and hanged on July 5. Gracey, *Annals of the 6th*, 183. It is possible that two spies were caught on two separate occasions. Was Buford's reference to Washington his wry commentary on the promotion of three captains of cavalry to be his equals in rank, just a few days before?

divisional command, to say that it was no less than just, as well as providential for the Army of the Potomac, that it was Buford whom fortune and Pleasonton's orders placed nearest the Confederate army.[27] It was shortly before noon on the thirtieth when Buford entered Gettysburg. He found the town buzzing like an overturned beehive, "in a terrible state of excitement," as he reported to Pleasonton.[28] Jubal Early's division had passed through four days before, on its way to York, and moments before Buford's arrival J. J. Pettigrew's brigade had come nearly to the town on an expedition for shoes.[29] His report continued, "I have sent parties . . . [to Chambersburg and Mummasburg] . . . toward Cashtown, and . . . Littlestown . . . My men and horses are fagged out. I have not been able to get any grain yet. It is all in the country, and the people talk instead of working. Facilities for shoeing are nothing. Early's people seized every shoe and nail they could find."[30] At 10:40 P.M., after the return of the scouting parties he had sent out in every direction from which the enemy might be approaching, Buford was able to send Pleasonton, at Meade's headquarters at Taneytown, information about the Confederate army: "A. P. Hill's corps, composed of Anderson, Heth and Pender, is massed back of Cashtown, 9 miles from this place. His pickets, composed of infantry and artillery, are in sight of mine. . . . Rumor says Ewell is coming over the mountains from Carlisle."[31] This was cavalry scouting and reporting at their best, a model of precision and accuracy, with fact carefully separated from rumor.

Hooker's assignment to General Reynolds of the responsibility of directing the Federal vanguard, composed of Reynolds' own I Corps and the III and XI Corps, was an arrangement General Meade left undisturbed. Buford saw to it that Reynolds had the same information that he was sending to Pleasonton, and wrote him the same evening, "I am satisfied that A. P. Hill's corps is

27. *Dictionary of American Biography*, VII, 596.
28. *Official Records*, Vol. XXVII, Pt. 1, p. 923.
29. Coddington, *The Gettysburg Campaign*, 167–68, 262–64.
30. *Official Records*, Vol. XXVII, Pt. 1, p. 923. Colonel Devin had scouting parties out "to observe the approaches from Carlisle, Harrisburg and York." *Ibid.*, 938.
31. *Ibid.*, 924.

massed just back of Cashtown. . . . The enemy's pickets are within 4 miles of this place. . . . I have many rumors and reports of the enemy advancing upon me from towards York. I have to pay attention to some of them, which causes me to overwork my horses and men. I can get no forage nor rations. . . . The people give or sell the men something to eat, but I can't stand that way of subsisting; it causes dreadful straggling."[32]

Quite properly, Pleasonton remained at General Meade's headquarters. With his three divisions disposed in a wide arc from Gettysburg on the west to Hanover on the east, he was, as he should have been, in a central position, in close touch with the commander of the army and hence able to direct the movements of his command in conformity with those of the army as a whole. Pleasonton had no new directives for his divisional commanders on June 30, nor, generally speaking, were such directives needed. Based on the information about the enemy available that morning, the cavalry was where it should have been, out ahead of the infantry. Buford on the left, Kilpatrick on the right, and Gregg in the center were well placed; in addition, Gregg was in a position to reinforce either Buford or Kilpatrick, as the situation might require. With no major strategic problem to occupy his mind, Pleasonton issued an exhortation to his command. Considerably less than Napoleonic in spirit, it called "the attention of all commanders, as well as the troops . . . to the immense issues involved in the issue of the engagement that may soon be expected with the enemy" and ended on a note that might have terrified the innocent recruits of 1861, but must have caused grins of derision among the veterans of 1863. "Corps and other commanders," Pleasonton announced, "are authorized to order the instant death of any soldier who fails in his duty at this hour."[33]

While Buford, on the same day, was writing his late evening dispatches to Pleasonton and Reynolds, his men settled down for the night. Colonel William Gamble's First Brigade, consisting of

32. *Ibid.*, 923–24. See also his earlier dispatches to Reynolds, datelined 5:30 A.M. and 12:20 P.M., June 30. *Ibid.*, 922.
33. *Ibid.*, Pt. 3, pp. 425–26. It should be said in Pleasonton's defense that his singularly inept language merely repeated the wording of General Meade's order. *Ibid.*, 415.

the 8th Illinois, 8th New York, four companies of the 12th Illinois, and six companies of the 3rd Indiana, sixteen hundred rank and file, camped on Seminary Ridge, a mile west of Gettysburg, with pickets well out toward Cashtown on the Chambersburg Pike.[34] Colonel Thomas C. Devin's Second Brigade, made up of the 6th and 9th New York, 17th Pennsylvania, and 3rd West Virginia, bivouacked on the far side of town, guarding the approaches from the north and east.

At five A.M. on July 1, Confederate General Henry Heth's division moved out from Cashtown toward Gettysburg "to get those shoes"—the shoes for the men that Pettigrew's brigade had failed to get the previous day. A short distance east of Cashtown, Heth's vanguard came up against Colonel Gamble's vedettes, who retreated slowly under fire toward Gettysburg.

Alerted at eight o'clock to Heth's approach by a message from his pickets, Gamble deployed a line of battle on Herr's Ridge, a mile west of Seminary Ridge, with his right touching the cut of an unfinished railroad about four hundred yards north of the pike, and his left near the Fairfield road, about a mile to the south. Soon thereafter, Devin moved his men to the same line, connecting with Gamble's right and extending the line northward to where the Gettysburg-Mummasburg road passed the foot of another elevation, called Oak Ridge. Lieutenant John F. Calef's six three-inch guns of Battery A, 2nd United States Artillery, were placed in three two-gun sections, one on each side of the Chambersburg Pike and the third some distance to the south.

Within a short time after Heth's leading brigades came within range of Herr's Ridge, Gamble was forced back across the wooded bottoms of Willoughby Run to McPherson's Ridge. There, although greatly outnumbered and their carbines outranged by the rifles of Heth's footsoldiers, Gamble's troopers managed to hold the Confederates in check for nearly two hours.[35] Then, at about ten o'clock, General James S. Wadsworth's division of the I

34. *Ibid.*, Pt. 1, pp. 166–67, 934.
35. It is claimed that Corporal Alpheus Hodges, Company F, 9th New York, fired the first shot in the battle of Gettysburg, and that Corporal Cyrus W. James, Company G, of the same regiment, was the first man killed. Cheney, *History of the Ninth Regiment*, 106, 108.

Corps arrived, led cross-country at the "double-quick" by General Reynolds himself, and took the place of the hard-pressed cavalry. There was little rest for Gamble's men, even after they were relieved by Wadsworth's infantry, the black-hatted Iron Brigade conspicuous among them. Commanded by Abner Doubleday after Reynolds was killed by a sharpshooter's bullet, the I Corps was being pressed back by Heth, joined now by Dorsey Pender's division. As the I Corps retreated step by step, Buford rushed his First Brigade to its assistance. At the same time he sent an orderly to Pleasonton with an urgent dispatch: "A tremendous battle has been raging since 9:30 a.m., with varying success. At the present moment the battle is raging on the road to Cashtown, and within short cannon range of . . . [Gettysburg]. . . . General Reynolds was killed early this morning. In my opinion, there is no directing person. . . . P. S.—We need help now."[36] As they ran forward to help the infantry, Gamble's men found a low stone wall; sheltering behind it, their carbine fire at short range checked and broke the Confederate advance.[37] With O. O. Howard's XI Corps now arriving on the field, Buford was able to withdraw his command from the fighting line and lead them to a flank position to the south, near the Gettysburg-Fairfield road.

Buford's stand on the Chambersburg road has been extravagantly praised. "For two of the most vital hours in our nation's history, Buford's cavalry . . . held the field until Reynolds and the Union infantry came up," one writer tells us; another calls Buford's stand "the most valuable day's work done by the cavalry in the Civil War."[38] Such judgments are necessarily subjective and need not be accepted as the literal truth. In this instance, they are probably inspired more by the glamor that attaches to the most dramatic battle in American military history, than by the facts. Buford himself, his entire command, and Gamble's regiments in particular, are entitled to great credit for holding at bay for two hours a force of Confederate infantry outnumbering them three to one. Yet the result of their stubborn defense—in which the

36. *Official Records*, Vol. XXVII, Pt. 1, pp. 924–25.
37. *Ibid.*, 927.
38. Buckeridge, *Lincoln's Choice*, 55; M. F. Steele, *American Campaigns* (Washington, D.C., 1922), 392.

role of Lieutenant Calef and his gunners must not be forgotten—
was only that the climactic battle of the invasion was fought at
Gettysburg, where neither of the two army commanders expected,
or perhaps wanted, to fight, instead of elsewhere; its effect on the
outcome of the battle itself was minimal.[39] For that effect, insofar
as the Federal cavalry was concerned, one must look first to a
relatively obscure fight on June 30 at Hanover, involving Stuart's
three brigades and the division of Judson Kilpatrick.

Stuart and his troopers departed on their eccentric ride
around the Federal army at one A.M. on June 25, from Salem Depot. After being held up momentarily by Winfield Scott Hancock's
II Corps at Hay Market and having a brush at Fairfax with
"Scott's 900"—actually, with an eighty-two-man detachment of
that regiment—Stuart crossed the Potomac at Rowser's Ford on
the night of June 27.[40] At Rockville, eight miles north of the river
and only thirteen miles from Washington, Fitzhugh Lee's brigade
happened across a wagon train—eight miles long, in Stuart's report—carrying supplies to what was just then becoming Meade's
army. "Not one escaped," Stuart reported, "though many were upset and broken, so as to require their being burned. More than one
hundred and twenty-five best United States model wagons were
secured and driven off. The mules and harness of the broken
wagons were also secured."[41] Heading north and now encumbered
by a lengthy and balky wagon train, Stuart marched all night,

39. On July 1, Pleasonton issued orders to his three divisional commanders and to Wesley Merritt to retreat to Taneytown, Manchester, Westminster, and Emmitsburg, respectively; "in case the enemy should advance
in force upon you and press you hard . . . dispute every inch of the ground,
and fall back very slowly to the point designated." *Official Records*, Vol.
XXVII, Pt. 3, p. 471. These orders, which were never acted on, were doubtless issued pursuant to Meade's "Pipe Creek Circular."

40. *Ibid.*, Pt. 2, p. 693. "Of the 82 men who rode out of camp . . . 4
were killed, 1 officer and 20 men were seriously wounded and captured;
57 men, including 3 officers, were captured, all of these 57 having had
their horses fall or killed, and many of them badly injured by being trampled upon by the charging horsemen." Smith, "*Scott's 900*," *Eleventh New
York*, 86.

41. H. B. McClellan calls the capture of the wagons "a misfortune";
had the wagons not slowed down the subsequent march, McClellan be-
lieves, Stuart could have reached General Lee before nightfall on June 28,
instead of four days later. *I Rode with Jeb Stuart*, 325.

crossed the Baltimore & Ohio Railroad on the morning of the twenty-ninth, tore up a stretch of track and the telegraph wires, and encamped for the night at Union Mills, midway between Westminster and Hanover.

Resuming the march on the thirtieth, Stuart and his troopers reached Hanover in midmorning. Kilpatrick had also marched for Hanover that morning, coming from the west. Custer's brigade had already marched through the town and Farnsworth's was in the process of doing so when J. R. Chambliss' brigade of Stuart's command arrived from the south. There are, as usual, two versions of the ensuing events, and the truth is hidden in the fog of war created by the conflicting accounts of the principal protagonists. Both sides were apparently surprised by an unexpected encounter. Chambliss, the first to recover, was also the first to attack. Charging from a side street, he caught the rear of Farnsworth's column in flank and drove the 18th Pennsylvania, which was in its first fight as a complete unit, into the other regiments in the column, thereby throwing the entire brigade into confusion; or, in another version, he "drove . . . [the enemy] pell mell through the town . . . capturing his ambulances and a large number of prisoners. . . . [Chambliss] cut the enemy's column in twain. . . . Fitz. Lee in the meantime fell upon the rear portion, driving it handsomely."[42] Farnsworth, however, rose to the occasion, quickly restored order, went over to the attack, and drove Chambliss and Lee back through the town in the opposite direction.[43] Farnsworth's success in retrieving a potentially dangerous situation was partly due to a factor not usually present in a cavalry engagement, but one that Judson Kilpatrick did not fail to notice. "The [Confederate] attack was determined and fierce," he wrote in language habitual with him, "The main and side streets swarmed with rebel cavalry. . . . For a moment, and a moment only, victory hung uncertain. For the first time our troops had met the enemy in close contact; but they were on their own free soil; fair hands, regardless of the dangerous strife, waved them on, and bright, tearful eyes looked pleadingly out from every window. The brave Farns-

42. *Official Records*, Vol. XXVII, Pt. 2, pp. 695–96. The 18th Pennsylvania was added to Farnsworth's brigade subsequent to June 28.
43. *Ibid.*, Pt. 1, pp. 992, 1005, 1008–1009.

worth made one great effort, and the day was won. The foe turned and fled. He had for the first and last time polluted with his presence the fair town of Hanover."[44]

Kilpatrick's turgid prose was correct in at least one respect, which, however, was to be the most important result of this brief scuffle: when the fight was over, the Federals were in possession of Hanover and blocked Stuart's direct road to Gettysburg, a mere twelve miles to the west.[45] There is, of course, no way of knowing whether Stuart would have turned toward Gettysburg that day if his men had retained possession of the town; it was, however, clearly an after-the-fact rationalization for him to contend in his report that Hanover was "by no means desirable for us to hold."[46] It is more likely that those 125 wagons clogged his thinking even more than they clogged his movements, and to save them he decided on a long detour, which took him first ten miles east, to Jefferson, then thirty-five miles northwest to Carlisle, where, on the afternoon of the next day he bombarded the town and burned the Cavalry School barracks. This was a fitting climax of futility to a harebrained expedition that even some of Stuart's own men condemned as motivated by his desire to "do some great thing."[47]

The utter exhaustion of the entire command on the afternoon of July 1, after more than thirty-six hours in the saddle, broken only by the fight at Hanover on June 30 and a brief halt, after an all-night march, on the morning of the next day, is difficult to picture. Stuart himself was made of iron, but here is a description of his men:

It is impossible for me to give you a correct idea of the fatigue and exhaustion of our men and beasts at this time. From our great exertion, constant mental excitement, want of sleep and food, the men

44. Ibid., 992. Surgeon Lyman W. Bliss, 10th New York, in charge of the field hospital at Hanover, noticed "a regiment . . . give way, and then he saw that they appeared to be without an officer to lead them . . . [so he] obtained a saber and sailed in, urging the men forward to renew the action, but they appeared somewhat demoralized . . . and broke, leaving the gallant quinine-dispenser in the hands of the enemy." Preston, *History of the 10th Regiment*, 104.

45. Kilpatrick's casualties in this affair were 19 killed, 41 wounded, and 123 missing. *Official Records*, Vol. XXVII, Pt. 1, p. 992.

46. *Ibid.*, Pt. 2, p. 696.

47. Blackford, *Letters from Lee's Army*, 195.

were overcome and so tired and stupid as almost to be ignorant of what was taking place around them. Couriers in attempting to deliver orders to officers would be compelled to give them a shake and call before they could make them understand. . . . As for [the] men, though in line and in momentary expectation of being made to charge, they would throw themselves over on their horses' necks and some even down on the ground and fall asleep.[48]

Stuart was still at Carlisle when he learned that General Lee and his army were at Gettysburg, and he started at once on the thirty-mile march to join them.[49] Kilpatrick, who had gone north from Hanover to Berlin, where he hoped to intercept Stuart, was ordered on July 2 to move to Gettysburg and take up a position astride the York Turnpike, to block any attempt to turn the eastern flank of the Union position on Culp's Hill facing Ewell's corps.[50] Stuart's horsemen reached the same area late on the afternoon of the second, and at sundown, near the hamlet of Hunterstown, found Kilpatrick in their path. The result was a "spirited affair of two hours," wherein, in Kilpatrick's version, "the enemy was driven from this point with great loss," and in Stuart's, his arrival at Hunterstown was "just in time to thwart a move of the enemy's cavalry upon our rear . . . [in] a fierce engagement in which Hampton's brigade performed gallant service, a series of charges compelling the enemy to leave the field and abandon his purpose."[51] The actual outcome was that both sides—less the casualties—retained their original positions and settled down for the night, in ignorance of the bitter and far more costly fighting that

48. G. W. Beale, *A Lieutenant of Cavalry in Lee's Army* (Boston, 1918), 114.
49. The order to turn southward to Gettysburg found Hampton's brigade at Dillsburg, ten miles south of Stuart's other two brigades at Carlisle, the ten-mile gap being the result of the slow pace of the captured wagons behind which Hampton marched. McClellan, *I Rode with Jeb Stuart*, 330–31.
50. *Official Records*, Vol. XXVII, Pt. 1, p. 992.
51. *Ibid.*, 992. Kilpatrick singles out the 6th Michigan, Custer's entire brigade (which had 32 casualties in the action), and Lieutenant A. C. M. Pennington, Jr.'s, battery as "deserving of the highest praise" for their performance. For Custer's report, which has the Confederates "precipitately . . . surrender the field," see *ibid.*, 999; for Stuart's version see *ibid.*, Pt. 2, p. 697.

had taken place a few miles to the west, at the Round Tops, at the same time they were fighting their "spirited affair" or "fierce engagement."

Stuart had ridden south from Carlisle in advance of his men, and, in the early afternoon of the second, reported to General Lee on Seminary Ridge. The orders he received from the commanding general are not on record, but they evidently directed him to position his troopers to the east of Ewell's left flank, whether to protect it from a Federal attack or himself to attack the Federal right and rear is not known. On the morning of the third, after his men had had a welcome and much-needed night's sleep, Stuart moved forward to what he decided was an ideal position, three miles east of Gettysburg, "where a commanding ridge completely controlled a wide plain of cultivated fields," a position which not only "render[ed] Ewell's left entirely secure . . . but commanded a view of the routes leading to the enemy's rear. Had the enemy's main body been dislodged . . . I was in precisely the right position to discover it and improve the opportunity."[52]

The position described by Stuart was at the northern end of Cress's Ridge, another of the many parallel ridges running generally north and south in the Gettysburg area. The sector chosen by Stuart not only overlooked the open plain, nearly a mile wide, to the east, but had the further advantage of being heavily wooded to the north and west, between the Stallsmith and Rummel farm buildings, enabling Stuart to approach it from the York Turnpike unseen by the Union cavalry, which was posted in a north-south line on the far side of the plain along the Old Dutch Road.

Stuart now had four brigades under his immediate command. In addition to the brigades of Hampton, Fitzhugh Lee, and Chambliss (W. H. F. Lee) that had ridden around the Federal army with him, the brigade of Albert G. Jenkins had been ordered to report to him.[53]

The Federal cavalry was also on the move on July 2 and 3. On

52. *Ibid.*, Pt. 2, pp. 697, 699.
53. Stuart reported his casualties from the start of his march on June 25 to the evening of July 2 at the amazingly low total of 117: 9 killed, 50 wounded, and 58 missing. *Ibid.*, 713–14.

the second, Buford was moved from the left flank at Gettysburg back to Westminster, to guard the trains of the army.⁵⁴ The First (John B. McIntosh) and Third (J. Irvin Gregg) Brigades of David Gregg's division—his Second Brigade was at Westminster —after acting on a series of conflicting orders were moved forward to the east of the Federal lines on Culp's Hill, to block access to the Union flank via the Gettysburg-Hanover Turnpike. On the morning of the third, Kilpatrick was sent to that position and Gregg was sidestepped to the south, extending Kilpatrick's line to the neighborhood of the Gettysburg-Baltimore Turnpike.⁵⁵

Stuart's command was not alone in showing the effects of a hard campaign. As an officer of the 3rd Pennsylvania of McIntosh's brigade recalled, "By this time we had become a sorry-looking body of men, having been in the saddle day and night almost continuously for over three weeks, without a change of clothing or an opportunity for a general wash; moreover, we were much reduced by short rations and exhaustion, and mounted on horses whose bones were plainly visible."⁵⁶ The same officer adds:

[As] evidence of how the division was reduced by hard marching and hard fighting . . . the morning report of the 3d Pennsylvania on the 30th of June—one of the strongest regiments in the division—showed present for duty 29 officers . . . 365 enlisted men, and 322 serviceable horses. . . . we had seventy-two men whose horses had dropped from the ranks. Many of these men were traveling along on foot and carrying their saddles in the hope of procuring remounts. The above report was made out at Westminster. Our march from there through the broiling sun and clouds of dust entailed a still larger loss of men and horses from exhaustion, so that by the time we reached Gettysburg the 3d Pennsylvania did not number three hundred men all told.

Gregg received word at noon from General O. O. Howard, commanding the XI Corps, that "large columns of the enemy cavalry were moving toward the right" of his line.⁵⁷ This was Stuart's column, visible from Cemetery Hill, as it moved from the York Pike toward the woods above Cress's Ridge. A short time after

54. *Ibid.*, Pt. 1, p. 914.
55. *Ibid.*, 914–15, 956.
56. This and the following quotation are from *Battles and Leaders*, III, 399. The officer was Captain William E. Miller.
57. *Official Records*, Vol. XXVII, Pt. 1, p. 956.

Gregg received Howard's message, and after the tremendous can-
nonade heralding the charge of Pickett's Virginians had already
begun, he saw a "strong line" of dismounted skirmishers moving
down from Cress's Ridge toward his position. These were the men
of Jenkins' brigade, armed with Enfield muskets, which outranged
and were more accurate than the carbines of his own cavalrymen.[58] However, to Stuart's disgust, Jenkins' brigade had only ten
rounds of ammunition per man.[59]

Earlier in the forenoon, Kilpatrick had been moved once
again. He was ordered to join Merritt's brigade below the left end
of the Union infantry line, south of the Round Tops, to attack the
Confederate right and rear. For reasons not explained in his report, he moved with only Farnsworth's brigade and left Custer
and his brigade behind.[60]

Seeing Jenkins' skirmishers moving toward him, Gregg concluded that "the enemy's cavalry had gained . . . [his right] and
were about to attack, with a view of gaining the rear of . . . [the
Union] line of battle."[61] He decided to meet Stuart's attack with
one of his own and sent forward the carbineers of the 3rd Pennsylvania and 1st Maryland, supported on the right and left by
sections of the 1st New Jersey. At this point, Custer received an
order from Kilpatrick to march south and join Farnsworth and
Merritt. Gregg, however, conscious of the "importance of resisting
. . . [Stuart's] attack . . . which, if succeeded in . . . would have
been productive of the most serious consequences," took the grave
responsibility of directing Custer to ignore the orders of his immediate superior. Custer was eager to cooperate; he told Gregg
that he would be "only too happy" to stay if Gregg ordered him to

58. *Ibid.*, 992.

59. Jenkins had been wounded on July 2, and command of the brigade passed to the senior colonel, M. J. Ferguson, of the 16th Virginia.
Ibid., Pt. 2, p. 698. One of the gunners of Stuart's artillery noted, "We had
a distant view of the [Gettysburg] battlefield, yet we saw nothing but a
vast bank of thick battle smoke, with thousands of shell exploding above
the surface of the white, smoking sea. . . . The artillery fire at one time
was so heavy that the hills shook and the air trembled, and the deep thunder rolled through the sky in one incessant roar." Neese, *Three Years in
the Confederate Horse Artillery*, 188.

60. *Official Records*, Vol. XXVII, Pt. 2, p. 697.

61. *Ibid.*, Pt. 1, 956.

do so. Gregg gave him the order, Custer stayed and was to play a crucial role in the ensuing battle.[62]

The precise sequence of events is unclear, but it is probable that Gregg's decision to keep Custer with him was due to a hitch that developed in Stuart's plans. He intended to have Hampton's and Fitzhugh Lee's brigades move under cover of the woods and out of sight of the Federals to a position from which they could swoop down on Gregg's rear when the Union line was shaken by Jenkins' skirmishers. But Hampton and Lee "debouched into the open ground, disclosing the movement."[63] It may well have been the sight of the two brigades marching toward him that caused Gregg to keep Custer with him, a decision that probably saved him—and perhaps Meade—from a disastrous defeat.

Meanwhile, Jenkins' skirmishers, whom Stuart had reinforced with more dismounted men from Hampton's and Fitzhugh Lee's brigades, had fired off their scanty supply of ammunition and began to retreat before Gregg's skirmishers, who had also been reinforced and whose advance was greatly eased by the fast and accurate fire of their own artillery.[64] Gregg had posted Alanson M. Randol's battery on the left center of his line and Pennington's on his left flank; he said in his report that their fire was the most accurate he had ever seen.

Seeing his skirmishers retreating, Stuart sent forward one of Chambliss' regiments, mounted, to attack the advancing Federals. Joined by the 1st Virginia of Fitzhugh Lee's brigade and the 1st North Carolina and the Jeff. Davis Legion of Hampton's, "the impetuosity of those gallant fellows," Stuart wrote, "after two

62. *Ibid.*, 956; Coddington, *The Gettysburg Campaign*, 521.
63. *Official Records*, Vol. XXVII, Pt. 2, p. 697.
64. *Ibid.*, 688, and Pt. 1, p. 959. This incident illustrates the virtual impossibility of arriving at an accurate picture of these cavalry fights on the basis of participants' reports. In Stuart's version, the *mounted* charge of "one of W. H. F. Lee's regiments," the 1st Virginia, etc., was ordered to check the advance of the Federal skirmishers and to save a part of Jenkins' men from capture. In Captain Miller's version, Gregg's skirmishers, made up of parts of the 3rd Pennsylvania, 1st New Jersey, and 5th Michigan, ran low on ammunition and were being driven back by Jenkins' men, who had been joined by a *"dismounted* regiment from W. H. F. Lee's brigade." The charge of the three mounted Confederate regiments was made, in this version, to capitalize on the opportunity created by the retreat of the Federal skirmishers. *Battles and Leaders*, III, 403.

weeks of hard marching and hard fighting, was not only extra-ordinary, but irresistible. The enemy's masses vanished before them like grain before the scythe. . . . Their impetuosity carried them too far, and the charge being very much prolonged, their horses, already jaded by hard marching, failed under it . . . and the enemy perceiving it, were turning upon them with fresh horses . . . and gradually this hand-to-hand fighting involved the greater portion of the command till the enemy were driven from the field."[65]

Captain William E. Miller of the 3rd Pennsylvania added a Federal cavalryman's tribute to the gallantry of the 1st Virginia, with the comment that "a more determined and vigorous charge than that made by the 1st Virginia it was never my fortune to witness."[66] The charge drove back the 7th Michigan, but was then checked, not by the exhaustion of the Confederates' horses, but by Gregg's artillery and the flank fire of the 5th Michigan and of a portion of the 3rd Pennsylvania; the attackers retreated to their main body. Then came the climax of the battle, recorded in Captain Miller's colorful account:

There appeared moving toward us a large mass of cavalry, which proved to be the remaining portions of Hampton's and Fitzhugh Lee's brigades . . . formed in column of squadrons. . . . A grander spectacle than their advance has rarely been beheld. They marched with well-aligned fronts and steady reins. Their polished saber-blades dazzled in the sun. . . . Shell and shrapnel met the advancing Confederates and tore through their ranks. Closing their ranks as though nothing had happened, on they came. As they came nearer, canister was substituted . . . for shell, and horse after horse staggered and fell. Still they came on. . . . The 1st Michigan, drawn up in close column of squadrons near Pennington's battery, was ordered by Gregg to charge. Custer . . . placed himself at its head, and off they dashed. As the two columns approached each other, the pace of each increased, when suddenly a crash . . . betokened the crisis. So sudden and violent was the collision that many of the horses were turned end over end and crushed their riders beneath them. The clashing of sabers, the firing of pistols, the demands for surrender, and cries of the combatants, filled the air.[67]

65. *Official Records*, Vol. XXVII, Pt. 2, p. 698.
66. *Battles and Leaders*, III, 404.
67. *Ibid.*, 404.

William Brooke-Rawle, a lieutenant in Miller's squadron, wrote an equally vivid account of this fight and added a detail not mentioned by his captain. As the troopers of the 1st Michigan drew their sabers and began their charge, Brooke-Rawle wrote, "the orders of the Confederate officers could be heard, 'keep to your sabers, men, keep to your sabers!' "[68]

When Colonel McIntosh saw the Confederates riding toward him, he gathered up the headquarters staff of his brigade, the buglers and orderlies and all the "scattered men" he could find, and joined in the charge of the 1st Michigan.[69] So did Captain Charles Treichel and his squadron of the 3rd Pennsylvania, every commissioned officer of which was to be wounded in the fight.[70] But the decisive move, for which he was awarded the Congressional Medal of Honor, was made by Captain Miller himself.[71] He and his squadron of the 3rd Pennsylvania were posted facing west, in front of the wooded area near the center of Gregg's line, with orders to "hold [the] position at all hazards." From his flank position, Miller could see, as the Confederate charge swept past him, that the gray mass greatly outnumbered the 1st Michigan and the miscellany of small units attacking the head of their column, and he saw also a great opportunity for his command of a few dozen men. On his own initiative and with a courageous disregard of his orders, he led his men on a charge against the flank of the advancing Confederate column. His momentum carried him right through the enemy's ranks, but he had his men well under control, turned them about, and from the opposite flank charged the portion of the column that his initial attack had separated from the main body and drove it back toward the Rummel farm buildings.[72]

68. Brooke-Rawle, "Gregg's Cavalry Fight," 270.

69. *Ibid.*, 271.

70. *Official Records*, Vol. XXVII, Pt. 1, p. 1051. Captain Miller's account has Treichel charge the right flank, not the head, of the Confederate column. *Battles and Leaders*, III, 405.

71. Miller wrote his brother four days after the battle, "I embrace the first opportunity to say that I am through the campaign safe, with the exception of a slight scratch on my arm, and a want of skin under the seat of my pantaloons." The "slight scratch" was a bullet through his arm. Regimental History Committee, *History of the 3d Pennsylvania*, 305.

72. *Battles and Leaders*, III, 404–405; Brooke-Rawle, "Gregg's Cavalry

Captain James H. Hart's squadron of the 1st New Jersey charged the Confederate right flank at nearly the same time that Miller charged the left. A number of other squadron-strength units joined in these attacks, either on the head of the enemy column or on its right flank, and the Federal batteries kept up their rapid fire until their own men fouled the range. Now the Confederate advance began to lose its momentum; the troopers at the head of the column began to draw rein and veer off to the right and left. Custer, seeing the enemy begin to waver, shouted to the 1st Michigan, "Come on, you Wolverines!" and, with as many of them as heard him in the melee, dashed forward, himself well in advance of his men. Then, at last, the Confederates gave way and retreated to their starting line under the continuous fire of Pennington's and Randol's guns.[73] This ended the battle.

Stuart's losses in this action were 41 killed, 50 wounded (including General Hampton), and 90 captured or missing, but these figures do not include the unreported losses of Jenkins' brigade or of Stuart's horse artillery, both of which suffered severely.[74] The losses of Gregg's own division were relatively light: 1 killed, 26 wounded and 8 captured or missing; however, only McIntosh's brigade of his division was engaged. It was Custer's brigade that sustained by far the greatest number of casualties, with 29 killed, 48 wounded, and 39 captured or missing.[75] The 7th Michigan of Custer's brigade, which had met the charge of the 1st Virginia head on, alone had 13 killed, 48 wounded, and 39 captured or missing, nearly 22 percent of the 461 men it took into the battle.[76]

What was the result of the fight? Stuart's claim that he was only protecting the left flank of the Confederate army is not worth a moment's credence. The course of the battle from its beginning

Fight," 271; Regimental History Committee, *History of the 3d Pennsylvania*, 311–12.

73. Brooke-Rawle, "Gregg's Cavalry Fight," 270, 272. H. B. McClellan courteously disputes Brooke-Rawle's statement that the Confederates were driven back in the final melee, past the Rummel farm and into the woods beyond. McClellan, *I Rode with Jeb Stuart*, 341–45.

74. *Official Records*, Vol. XXVII, Pt. 2, pp. 714–15. McClellan, *I Rode with Jeb Stuart*, 345–46.

75. *Battles and Leaders*, III, 406.

76. *Ibid.*, 406; Isham, *An Historical Sketch*, 28.

makes it evident that his objective was to brush Gregg out of the way and attack the rear of Meade's infantry on Cemetery Ridge, at the same time that it was attacked frontally by Pickett. In this he clearly failed. In the sense that the battle ended with Stuart and Gregg occupying their original positions, it was a draw, but in a wider sense it was a victory for Gregg and, more importantly, for the Union.[77] With one brigade of his own division and Custer's brigade of Kilpatrick's, he had managed to beat back the attack of twenty regiments of Stuart's corps, a force greatly exceeding his own.[78]

In one important respect, this battle was a portent. On the opening day of the main battle, the ability of Gamble's brigade, a relatively small number of dismounted cavalrymen—with the horseholders deducted, Gamble had fewer than twelve hundred men to hold a line a mile long—to withstand the attack of more than twice their number of tough infantrymen, was in a large measure due to the arrival only a few days before the battle of a shipment of Spencer carbines. There were not enough of them to arm the entire brigade, "but probably most of the troopers in the flanking companies were handed the deadly repeater."[79] Then, on July 3, the 5th Michigan, whose flanking fire halted the charge of the 5th Virginia after its sister regiment, the 7th Michigan, had been routed, was also armed with the Spencer. In both cases, the Federal troopers had in their hands a firearm of twice and even three times the rate of fire of units armed with single-shot carbines. Custer's comment on the new weapon, a part of which has been quoted previously, is worthy of repetition: "Colonel [R. A.]

77. Harbord, "Cavalry of the Army of Northern Virginia," 459. Wellman, *Giant in Gray*, 121. Wellman adds that of the twenty-three field-grade officers of Hampton's brigade, twenty-one became casualties during the Gettysburg Campaign. The Federal troopers had no doubts about the importance of what they had accomplished that day. "We cavalrymen have always held that we saved the day at the most critical moment of the battle of Gettysburg." Brooke-Rawle, "Gregg's Cavalry Fight," 274. See also Thomas, *Some Personal Reminiscences*, 12.

78. McClellan, *I Rode with Jeb Stuart*, 346; the numbers were about three thousand actually engaged on the Federal side, opposed to six to seven thousand Confederates. Brooke-Rawle, "Gregg's Cavalry Fight," 284–86.

79. Buckeridge, *Lincoln's Choice*, 55.

Alger, commanding the 5th [Michigan] . . . made such admirable disposition of . . . [his] men behind fences and other defences, as enabled them successfully to repel the repeated advances of a greatly superior force. I attribute their success in a great measure to the fact that this regiment is armed with the Spencer repeating rifle, which in the hands of brave, determined men . . . is in my estimation, the most effective firearm our cavalry can adopt."[80]

The cavalry fight at Gettysburg had another aspect that requires notice. At Kelly's Ford, Brandy Station, Aldie, Middleburg, and Upperville, most of the cavalry on both sides fought as cavalry, on horseback. Indeed, at Brandy Station, and again at Upperville, infantry was added to Pleasonton's command to do the fighting on foot. At Gettysburg, however, there was a change on the Union side. Gamble's brigade on July 1 fought as footsoldiers. Again on the third, large portions of Gregg's forces fought on foot, in appreciably greater numbers than the squadron or two of dismounted skirmishers commonly used in cavalry engagements. This was another portent of things to come, for it foreshadowed the use of cavalry in battle as mobile footsoldiers, a practice that was to become more and more common in the last two years of the war. Here was the beginning of the end, in American military practice, of cavalry on the European model, and the emergence of the employment of cavalry as mounted infantry. The use of cavalry *as* cavalry was not to disappear completely—tactical changes are never so abrupt—and, indeed, some of the most spectacular charges in the traditional mode were yet to come, in the Shenandoah Valley in 1864, and in the Appomattox Campaign in the last few days of the war. Nevertheless, a significant start had been made in the direction of tactics that were to make cavalry in the traditional European sense as obsolete, in General James H. Wilson's words, as the short Roman sword.

This description of the role of the Union cavalry in the preliminaries of Gettysburg and in the battle itself must end on a somber note. On the morning of July 3, Kilpatrick had been ordered to move to the southern end of the Union line, to join Wes-

80. Quoted in Whittaker, *George A. Custer*, 172. The Michigan Brigade was actually armed with the Spencer repeating rifle; it was rearmed with the Spencer carbine in the following spring.

ley Merritt's Reserve Brigade in an attack on the right and rear of
John B. Hood's division (commanded by General Evander Law
after Hood was wounded the previous day), occupying the area
to the west and south of the Round Tops. The terrain on which
Law's men were stationed was similar to the Devil's Den, rough,
broken, heavily wooded, and filled with huge rocks and boulders;
the cultivated area to the west, the southward continuation of the
plain between Seminary Ridge and Cemetery Ridge, was criss-
crossed by stone walls and post-and-rail and worm fences. The
two Federal cavalry commands took position facing generally
north, Farnsworth's brigade in the rough ground on the right and
Merritt's in the more open area to the left.

Just what was intended to be accomplished by attacking the
Confederates at this point, over terrain totally unsuited for cavalry operations, where Law's scanty infantry had every advantage, is unclear. The attack might have had a chance of success
if it had been coupled with a strong frontal attack on Law's division by the Federal infantry of the V Corps, which held the southern end of Meade's line, but no such attack was ordered. To order
the cavalry to attack under such circumstances was an incomprehensible aberration.[81]

Incomprehensible or not, Merritt's brigade had orders it had
to carry out. It attacked dismounted in midafternoon, but could
not make progress against the three regiments of infantry and
two batteries of artillery that Law was able to spare to protect his
right. Despite Merritt's failure, at half past five, Kilpatrick, in
great excitement, gave the 1st West Virginia, his left-hand regiment, the order to charge mounted; a battalion of the 1st Vermont
was ordered to precede the West Virginians as skirmishers.[82] The
charge was doomed from the start and was a total failure. It was
met by the 1st Texas Infantry "behind a rail fence that had been
staked and bound with withes," which the West Virginians were
unable to cross or to tear down. After an initial repulse they tried
again, but for the second time were turned back with great loss.[83]

81. There is an excellent description and analysis of this deplorable
affair in Coddington, *The Gettysburg Campaign*, 523–25.
82. *Battles and Leaders*, III, 394.
83. *Ibid.*, 394.

It was now the turn of the men from Vermont. Kilpatrick directed Farnsworth to order them to charge on the right, where the terrain was even less suited to a cavalry attack than that over which the 1st West Virginia had made its unsuccessful charges. Moreover, if the Vermonters should succeed in driving out of their way the two regiments of Alabama infantry that were directly in their front, they would then have to run the gauntlet of two brigades of Law's infantry on their right. Farnsworth protested, rightly, that to order a charge under such conditions was sheer murder. Kilpatrick then demonstrated his unfitness for high command. As far as he was concerned, he had given an order; consequently, the question of whether or not the charge made sense had become immaterial. He said to Farnsworth, "Do you refuse to obey my orders? If you are afraid to lead this charge, I will lead it."[84] And to his credit be it said that he would most certainly have led the charge had Farnsworth refused. But, after Kilpatrick had spoken there was nothing for Farnsworth to do but to order the charge and lead it himself. The charge overran about a hundred of Law's men, who were taken prisoner, but aside from that its only result was that of the three hundred who rode with Farnsworth, sixty-five good men became casualties, Farnsworth himself, a most promising officer, being among the killed.[85]

84. *Ibid.*, 396.
85. The numbers cited are from *ibid.*, 396. The numbers given in the history of the 1st Vermont are slightly different: twelve killed, twenty wounded (two mortally), and thirty-five missing. Benedict, *Vermont in the Civil War*, II, 602. General Henry L. Benning of Hood's division, who saw the action from the Confederate side, remarked that "the result was that they galloped around and round . . . finding fire at every outlet, until most of them were either killed or captured." Benedict, *Vermont in the Civil War*, II, 600. Kilpatrick's report of the affair is a shabby, disingenuous fabrication from beginning to end; as a corrective, one must read the report of Major Charles E. Capehart, commanding the 1st West Virginia, in *Official Records*, Vol. XXVII, Pt. 1, pp. 993, 1018–19.

XVII

A River to Cross

BY SUNDOWN ON JULY 3 THE BATTLE OF GETTYSBURG was over. There was some desultory firing by nervous pickets in the darkness, but there was no more fighting, just the thousands of dead to be identified if possible and buried in shallow graves, the wounded to be collected, the wrecks of companies, regiments, and brigades to be sorted out, the missing to be accounted for and the survivors counted, sentries posted, caissons and cartridge boxes refilled, rations issued and suppers cooked, and the events of the day to be told and retold. On the Confederate side, in full expectation of a Federal attack the next day, the army—reduced by more than twenty-one thousand casualties—erected rough breastworks and dug rifle pits along the reverse slope of Seminary Ridge.[1] Notwithstanding these preparations for a defense that was never to be tested, a Confederate retreat was inevitable, and on the afternoon of July 4, in a torrential downpour, the retreat began. First to leave was the major portion of the army's wagon

1. Coddington, *The Gettysburg Campaign*, 536, 808n. The Union casualties numbered 23,049, including the 852 casualties of the Cavalry Corps. *Official Records*, Vol. XXVII, Pt. 1, p. 187.

train, many of the wagons and all the ambulances filled with the wounded who could be moved. The train started on the long road back to the Potomac, on a route through Cashtown, Greenwood, Greencastle, and Hagerstown.[2] Escorting the seventeen-mile long line of wagons were six batteries of artillery and Brigadier General John Imboden's cavalry, twenty-one hundred strong but of questionable quality, who, however, were to give an excellent account of themselves in the next few days. As a further protection, Fitzhugh Lee's and Hampton's brigades marched on the column's flanks and rear, and later in the day it was joined by General "Grumble" Jones's brigade also. The retreat of the Confederate infantry, who were to take a shorter, more direct route to the river, began after nightfall on the fourth.

On the morning of the fourth, with the Army of Northern Virginia still much in evidence on Seminary Ridge, Meade ordered Pleasonton to march for the rear and the line of communications of Lee's army and "harass and annoy" them "as much as possible."[3] General Lee had left in position at Falling Waters the pontoon bridge on which his men had crossed the Potomac on their way north.[4] It would have been logical to assume, therefore, that the Confederates would march toward Falling Waters and to the ford a short distance upstream from it at Williamsport, and that the retreat would follow the most direct route, through Hagerstown, to these points. That would have suggested the Hagerstown-Cavetown area for a concentration of the Union cavalry, or at least of a major portion of it. Old sins, however, die hard, and Pleasonton, for reasons not explained in his report, chose to scatter his command. J. Irvin Gregg's brigade was ordered north, to Hunterstown, whence he was to march west toward Cashtown

2. Many of the walking wounded (as well as stragglers) marched along with the train. Lee left behind at Gettysburg 6,802 of his wounded, to be cared for by the Union army. Coddington, *The Gettysburg Campaign*, 537.

3. *Official Records*, Vol. XXVII, Pt. 1, p. 916.

4. Unknown to General Lee until later was the fact that on the forenoon of the 4th, a cavalry detachment of General William H. French's command had ridden out from Frederick and destroyed the pontoon bridge at Falling Waters.

and then south.[5] McIntosh's brigade was to go to Emmitsburg and halt there, in order to protect from a possible attack by the Confederate cavalry the rear of the Army of the Potomac, as it too took up the pursuit. Buford's division, then at Westminster, was ordered to Frederick, twenty-five miles southeast of Hagerstown, and Merritt's Reserve Brigade was ordered to join it there. Kilpatrick's division, reinforced by Pennock Huey's brigade of David Gregg's division, was the only component of the Cavalry Corps ordered to make a direct pursuit; it was to march southwestward through Emmitsburg toward the gaps through South Mountain, through which any retreat directed toward Hagerstown would have to pass.[6]

As was inevitably the case in the closing stages of a long and wearing campaign, the Federal pursuit was gravely hampered by the poor condition of the horses. J. Irvin Gregg, after coming up with the rear of the Confederate retreat on the evening of the sixth, had to halt for the night because his "horses were too much broken down to push" the enemy.[7] The march of the Reserve Brigade to meet Buford at Frederick was "necessarily very slow. Both men and horses were tired and jaded. For five days we had been without forage for our horses, and in almost constant motion. Hundreds of horses dropped down on this march, and were left on the road with their saddles, blankets, and bridles upon them. Men, whose horses 'played out,' trudged along on foot through muddy roads and swollen streams without food."[8]

This situation had, however, been anticipated by Rufus Ingalls, who had received a well-merited promotion to brigadier general. On July 4, he wired General Meigs, "The loss of horses in these severe battles has been great in killed, wounded, and worn down by excessive work. . . . I think we shall require 2,000 cavalry and 1,500 artillery horses, as soon as possible. . . . I hope you have enough to make up deficiencies."[9] Back came General

5. Gregg caught up with the retreat "near Greenwood, and found the road filled with broken-down wagons, abandoned limbers, and caissons filled with ammunition." *Official Records*, Vol. XXVII, Pt. 1, p. 917.
6. *Ibid.*, 916–17.
7. *Ibid.*, Pt. 3, p. 584.
8. Gracey, *Annals of the 6th*, 182.
9. *Official Records*, Vol. XXVII, Pt. 3, p. 524.

Meigs's reply the same day, directing Ingalls to "Stand on no ceremony, but, by purchase or impressment of all serviceable horses
within the range of your foraging parties, refit the artillery and
cavalry."[10] The same day, also, telegrams went out with General
Meigs's signature to his chief quartermasters in Philadelphia, Baltimore, Boston, Detroit, and Indianapolis, directing them to forward horses immediately to the Army of the Potomac.[11] Nor did
General Meigs stop there. He had General Herman Haupt, who
was already performing miracles of organization and drive to restore railroad communications to the army, telegraph the presi-
dents of twelve railroads, "I am informed by the Quartermaster-
General that, in order to reap the fruits of victory, a large number
of fresh horses are most urgently required. They are needed to
remount the cavalry. . . . Extraordinary efforts should be made by
the officers of all railroads over which horses are transported to
push them forward without delay, day and night. Please give this
subject prompt personal attention. In no other way can more efficient service be rendered at this time to the country. The enemy
must not escape if in our power to prevent it."[12]

Pleasonton, perhaps unaware of what Ingalls was already
doing, himself wired Secretary Stanton on the fifth that his "cavalry horses are fast being used up" and asked him to send to Frederick by the following evening the two thousand remounted cavalrymen then in Washington, most of whom, he said, belonged to
the regiments of his corps, and to have them escort to Frederick
the thousand spare horses the Quartermaster's Department had
on hand.[13] And Ingalls followed up his message of the previous day with a telegram in which he declared, "Five thousand
good cavalry horses available to-day . . . would give great additional results to our already important victory."[14] General Meigs
responded the same day with the information that his department
had just remounted two thousand cavalrymen in Washington—
presumably the same two thousand men Pleasonton asked to have

10. *Ibid.*, 524.
11. *Ibid.*, 524.
12. *Ibid.*, 568.
13. *Ibid.*, 543.
14. *Ibid.*, 543.

sent to him—which had taken most of the available supply of horses, but that he would in addition be able within twenty-four hours to start twelve hundred horses for the front. "I have," he went on, "ordered the officers at Harrisburg and Philadelphia to stop all that are coming this way from Indiana, Michigan, New England and New York. I have telegraphed you, by order of the Secretary of War, to stand on no ceremony, but, by purchase, impressment, and seizure, to make every available horse within reach of your foraging parties, useful."[15] Meigs was as good as his word, and even better. He wired Ingalls shortly after noon the next day,

Sixteen hundred horses and over 2,000 cavalry, just mounted or re-mounted, have left this city for Frederick already. I have advice of several trains of cars, from 100 to 275 horses in each, which since the railroads have been opened, are on their way to the Army of the Potomac. By telegraph to various points, all horses *en route* are directed upon Frederick. A few hundred more will be gathered from the trains at this depot. Two hundred and fifty arrived last night, and will be forwarded as soon as shod and fed, and rested for twenty-four hours from their journey. Three hundred start from Detroit to-day and to-morrow; 275 from Boston, by special train, last night.[16]

Later the same afternoon, Meigs was able to send a second message, to inform Ingalls that "Including remounted cavalry . . . I estimate that tomorrow morning there will be about 5,000 fresh horses on their way to you . . . from [Washington], Boston, New York, Philadelphia, Baltimore, Harrisburg, Indianapolis, Detroit, and about 170 will start from Chicago to-morrow. All, if fortunate, will arrive in a very few days."[17]

To mobilize resources and transportation in order to provide five thousand horses on short notice was, by the organizational standards of the day, a major accomplishment in itself. But those horses, and the many thousand more horses and mules the army already had, needed to be fed; for just a single four hundred-man cavalry regiment, this required the daily delivery of nearly five

15. *Ibid.*, 543.
16. *Ibid.*, 568.
17. *Ibid.*, 569.

tons of hay and grain. The Quartermaster's Department was able to rise to the occasion in this thoroughly unglamorous area also. General D. H. Rucker wired Ingalls on July 6 that he had ordered "750,000 pounds of grain and 250,000 pounds of hay to be sent daily, to Frederick. If this is not sufficient, notify me, and more will be sent." And for good measure, he added, "I have collected 800 cavalry horses, in addition to the 1,600 already sent, which I will send to-morrow, if I can get the cars. I would send them by turnpike, if I could possibly raise the men to take charge of them."[18]

These were examples of the growing professional competence of the men in charge of providing the logistical support the Union cavalry needed to remain operational. The skills, energy, and resourcefulness of Generals Meigs, Haupt, Ingalls, and Rucker, and of a host of colonels, majors, and captains who bought the horses, the feed, guns, ammunition, clothing, food, and the multitude of other items needed to keep cavalry in the field and saw to the delivery of these essentials to the armies, contributed as much to the eventual triumph of the Federal cavalry as did the men who rode the horses, fired the guns, and swung the sabers. The Quartermaster's Department had its inefficiencies, its errors of omission and commission, frauds and all the manifold difficulties that are the inescapable concomitant of the operations of a large, rapidly expanded bureaucracy made up mostly of inexperienced newcomers, but it was seldom that any major portion of the Federal cavalry was unable to function for lack of proper logistical support—the extent and quality of which their antagonists had largely to do without.

The first Federal cavalrymen to find the retreating Confederate wagon train were the troopers of Kilpatrick's division. Just at dark on the evening of the fourth, they struck the rear of the train at

---

18. *Ibid.*, 569. As mentioned previously, the prescribed daily ration of a cavalry horse was twenty-four pounds of grain and hay, or ninety-six hundred pounds for a four hundred-man regiment. Obviously, there were many occasions when difficulties of one kind or another prevented the delivery of full (or any) rations for the unfortunate animals.

Monterey Pass, its pace reduced to a crawl by the continuing downpour, which turned the rough, hilly road into a quagmire.[19] The ensuing action, fought until well past midnight in the midst of a wild thunderstorm, in pitch darkness and a driving rain, has lost nothing of its drama in the reports and accounts of the participants. Custer's brigade led Kilpatrick's advance along a road that nullified the effect of numbers, being "too narrow," Kilpatrick wrote, "to reverse even a gun," with a deep ravine on one side and a "steep, rugged mountain" on the other.[20] The rear of the train was protected by a mere handful of men, Captain G. M. Emack's company of the 1st Maryland (Confederate), aided by a detachment of the 4th North Carolina and a single artillery piece. When Kilpatrick's attack developed, General "Grumble" Jones tried to lead his brigade back to reinforce Emack, but the "narrow and difficult way, rendered doubly so by heavy rain ... was so blocked by wagons as to render it wholly impracticable to push ahead the artillery or even the cavalry. With my staff I hastened on, to rally all the stragglers of the train to the support of whatever force might be guarding the road. ... All my couriers and all others with fire-arms were ordered to the front, directed to lie on the ground, and be sparing of their ammunition. . . . For more than two hours, less than 50 men kept many thousands in check."[21]

A trooper of the 6th Virginia described after the war how the situation had looked to the men in the ranks:

I am not familiar with the topography of the country through which we retreated, but all night long we seemed to be in a narrow road, with steep hills or mountains on either side. We had with us a good many cattle with which to feed the army. These got loose in the mountains and hills covered with timber, and between their constant bellowing and the flashes of lightning and crashing thunder the night was hideous in the extreme. Wagons were breaking down, others were getting stalled, and to make matters worse, about midnight we were attacked by the Union cavalry. . . .The cavalry which was stretched along the wagon train was ordered to the front. It was with great dif-

19. Colonel Fremantle wrote that "the road [was] knee-deep in mud and water." *Fremantle Diary*, 221.
20. *Official Records*, Vol. XXVII, Pt. 1, p. 994.
21. *Ibid.*, Pt. 2, p. 753.

ficulty that we could get past the wagons in the darkness . . . but we finally worked our way up to the front and were dismounted and formed in line as best we could on either side of the road among the rocks and trees. . . . The only light we had to guide us was from the lightning in the heavens and the vivid flashes that came from the enemy's cannon.[22]

As Major Charles E. Capehart of the 1st West Virginia saw it from the Union side, "The night was one of inky darkness; nothing was discernible a half dozen paces ahead. As the advance came to the train, they received a heavy volley of musketry, which at once showed the exact position of the enemy. . . . The road lay down a mountain side, wild and rugged. On either side of the road was a heavy growth of underbrush, which the enemy had taken as a fit place to conceal themselves and fire from."[23]

Deciding for some strange reason that his own division was in danger—"No time was to be lost if I wished to reach the train and save my command"—Kilpatrick ordered a charge, to break through the opposition to the train.[24] The charge was made by the 1st West Virginia and a few men of the 1st Ohio, and it reached the wagons in short order. General Jones confessed that the charge of the West Virginians, led by Major Capehart, "swept everything before it. The led horses, wagons, straggling infantry, and camp followers were hurled down the mountain in one confused mass. Ineffectual efforts were made for a rally and resistance, but without avail, until at the foot of the mountain a few joined Captain [W. G.] Welsh's company of Maryland cavalry, stationed at this point, and drove back the advance of the enemy.

22. Hopkins, *From Bull Run to Appomattox*, 104–106. The cattle Hopkins mentions were "bought" by General Lee's quartermasters in Pennsylvania—with Confederate money.
23. *Official Records*, Vol. XXVII, Pt. 1, p. 1018. Willard Glazier wrote that the Confederate artillery "was planted in a position to rake the narrow road on which Kilpatrick was advancing. But the darkness was so intense that the guns could be of little use, except to make the night terribly hideous with their bellowings, the echoes of which reverberated in the mountain gorges in the most frightful manner. To add to the horrors of the scene and position, the rain fell in floods, accompanied with the groanings of thunders, while lightnings flashed from cloud to cloud over our heads, and cleft the darkness only to leave friend and foe enveloped in greater darkness." Glazier, *Three Years in the Federal Cavalry*, 268.
24. *Official Records*, Vol. XXVII, Pt. 1, p. 994.

But this mere handful of men had to yield to the increasing numbers of the enemy."[25]

There are wide discrepancies (understandable, perhaps, under the circumstances) in the testimony on the number of wagons, ambulances, and prisoners captured by the Federal cavalry. Major Capehart reported "the whole train . . . taken—300 wagons, 15 ambulances, together with all the horses and mules attached. The number of prisoners taken was 1,300, including 200 commissioned officers."[26] Colonel Huey's tally was a more modest 150 wagons, but he increased the number of prisoners to 1,500.[27] Kilpatrick agreed with Pennock Huey in recording 1,500 prisoners, but, without mentioning any numbers, laid claim to the capture or destruction of the entire wagon train of General Ewell's corps.[28] Whatever the correct numbers may have been, this was only a portion of the Army of Northern Virginia's wagon train, and General Lee reported merely that "In passing through the mountains . . . the great length of the train exposed them to attack by the enemy's cavalry, which captured a number of wagons and ambulances, but they succeeded in reaching Williamsport without serious loss."[29]

Another attack by the Union cavalry on the Confederate trains was less dramatic than the Monterey Pass affair, but, viewed from the Federal side, had an especially pleasing aspect of its own. Near Greencastle, ten miles south of Chambersburg, detachments of the 1st New York and the 12th Pennsylvania, led by Captain Abram Jones of the New York regiment, caught another section of the Confederate wagon train, moving along under the guard of some of Imboden's cavalry. Jones's attack yielded 300 wounded

25. *Ibid.*, Pt. 2, p. 753. General Imboden's graphic account of the march makes no mention of the attack on the rear of the train during the night. *Battles and Leaders*, III, 422–25.

26. *Official Records*, Vol. XXVII, Pt. 1, p. 1019.

27. *Ibid.*, 970. Most of the prisoners were probably the wounded riding in the captured wagons and ambulances.

28. *Ibid.*, 994. Pleasonton's report credited Kilpatrick with the capture of thirteen hundred prisoners, one battle-flag and a "large number of animals," and with the destruction and capture of "a very large train." *Ibid.*, 917.

29. *Ibid.*, Pt. 2, p. 309. Fremantle, obviously reporting secondhand, states that only thirty-eight wagons were lost. *Fremantle Diary*, 221.

and 345 unwounded prisoners, 90 wagons, and 1 gun.[30] What made this affair pleasurable from the Federal standpoint was that the captured wagons belonged to Fitzhugh Lee's brigade, and Stuart's cavalry was more accustomed to capturing wagons than to losing them. Besides, these wagons may well have been some of those Lee himself had captured at Rockville a scant week before and had marched over much of eastern Pennsylvania since. Stuart, at any rate, showed more annoyance than the loss of a few wagons might have been expected to justify; he wrote in his lengthy report that "a court of inquiry has been convened to inquire into the circumstances of this capture."[31]

At daybreak on July 5, as the head of the wagon train and Imboden's cavalry arrived at Greencastle, still nearly fifteen miles from the river, Buford and Merritt left Frederick on a twenty-five-mile march to Williamsport. It may be assumed that Buford already knew that General Lee's pontoon bridge at Falling Waters had been destroyed and that the torrential rains of the previous day and night had raised the water level of the upper Potomac by more than ten feet, making the ford at Williamsport impassable. Buford's and Merritt's approximately four thousand cavalrymen and the main body of the Confederate train reached Williamsport at about the same time, late in the afternoon, but Imboden had time to organize the best defense he could muster.[32] He posted his

30. *Official Records*, Vol. XXVII, Pt. 2, p. 214. Colonel L. B. Pierce of the 12th Pennsylvania reported the capture of 100 wagons, 5 pieces of artillery, and 500 prisoners. *Ibid.*, 280. The historian of the 1st New York claims as the trophies of this "spirited affair" 134 wagons, more than 600 horses and mules, 645 prisoners, and 2 pieces of artillery, at a cost of 3 killed, a "few slightly wounded," and several disabled horses. Beach, *First New York (Lincoln) Cavalry*, 264–65.

31. *Official Records*, Vol. XXVII, Pt. 2, p. 703. In Stuart's account, the number of wagons lost is given as sixty. There is no further mention in the records of the court of inquiry, and no indication whether or not it ever met.

32. Buford reported that he struck Imboden's pickets at "about 5 p.m." *Ibid.*, Pt. 1, p. 928. Imboden, in his postwar account, wrote that "the enemy appeared . . . about half-past one o'clock." *Battles and Leaders*, III, 427. This is a manifest error, for Buford could not have reached Williamsport from Frederick in nine and a half hours. Chaplain Gracey of the 6th Pennsylvania wrote that the Reserve Brigade, of which his regiment was a a part, "arrived about 4 o'clock on the crest of the hill overlooking Williamsport." Gracey, *Annals of the 6th*, 183.

powerful artillery of twenty-two guns, but with only scanty supplies of ammunition, on the hills to the east of town. To support
the guns, he dismounted all his twenty-one hundred cavalrymen
and put them in the firing line, together with two regiments of
Jubal Early's division of infantry and about seven hundred wagoners, whom he armed with the rifles the wounded had brought
with them from Gettysburg. Buford organized an attack, with his
men dismounted, as soon as he reached Williamsport, and although he was able to force the Confederates back to within a
half mile of the town, that was as near to the wagons as he could
get.[33] At one stage of the fight, a portion of Imboden's force coun-
terattacked at a point where, unfortunately for them, Colonel
Gamble had the carbineers of his brigade "under shelter"; the carbineers held their fire until the attackers were within "short carbine range," when they blazed away with their repeaters, "doing
terrible execution, and driving [the enemy] back into its strong-
hold."[34]

This fight at Williamsport ended in a draw; Buford was unable to break through to the wagons, and Imboden was unable to
drive him away. With a candor none too common in Civil War
action reports, Buford admitted failure. "The expedition had for
its object," he wrote, "the destruction of the enemy's trains. . . .
This, I regret to say, was not accomplished. The enemy was too
strong for us, but he was severely punished."[35] But Buford's fighting this day was not over yet. Kilpatrick, who had taken his command south to Boonsborough after the fight at Monterey Pass,
hastened back north on the morning of the fifth. There is no evidence to indicate that he was aware either of Buford's presence at
Frederick on the fourth, or of his march to Williamsport on the
morning of the fifth. Neither is there any evidence of top-level
coordination by Pleasonton or anyone else of the operations of the
widely separated cavalry commands subsequent to the orders is-

33. With the horseholders deducted, Buford and Merritt had an effective strength of about 3,000 against Imboden's approximately 3,400.
Nevertheless, the Federals thought that they were "greatly outnumbered,
and that by infantry." Gracey, *Annals of the 6th*, 184.
34. *Official Records*, Vol. XXVII, Pt. 1, p. 928.
35. *Ibid.*, 928, 925.

sued to them on the fourth.[36] Hence Gregg, with one of his brigades attached to Kilpatrick's division, another sent on an eccentric march northwestward, and the third guarding the rear of the
army, was in effect without a command, and Buford and Kilpatrick began their operations on the fifth independently of each
other, each in ignorance of what the other was planning to do.

Kilpatrick, at any rate, marched to Hagerstown at the same
time that Buford and Merritt were marching on Williamsport. He
found the town occupied by Chambliss' and Robertson's brigades
of Stuart's corps. Kilpatrick's arrival from the southeast, instead
of from the direction of Gettysburg, apparently surprised and
confused the Confederates, and Kilpatrick succeeded in driving
them out of the town.[37] Then, however, General Alfred Iverson's
infantry brigade arrived and joined in the fight, the Confederate
horsemen rallied, and Kilpatrick was driven out of the town in his
turn.

It was at about this time that Buford, nearing Williamsport,
heard Kilpatrick's guns in the direction of Hagerstown and sent
him word to move his division southward and connect with his
own right, for what would then have been an overwhelmingly
powerful attack on Imboden from two directions, the east and the
north.[38] The concept was excellent, but the attack failed to come
off because, unknown to Buford, by the time Kilpatrick received
the message he was already in serious trouble. For Stuart himself,
portions of two brigades of infantry from Law's division, followed
a short time later by Fitzhugh Lee's brigade, arrived at Hagers-

36. Kilpatrick wrote in his report that he learned of Buford's march
on Williamsport while he himself was marching to Hagerstown; he then
informed Buford of his own plans, "at the same time placing . . . [his]
command at . . . [Buford's] disposal." *Ibid.*, 995.

37. The historian of the 18th Pennsylvania wrote that in Hagerstown
"Sergeant Brown of Company B was shot and killed by a daughter of Dr.
M [sic]. The shot was fired from an upper window in M's house, on the
northeast of the public square." Publication Committee of the Regimental
Association, *History of the Eighteenth Regiment of Cavalry, Pennsylvania
Volunteers, 1862–1865* (New York, 1909), 96.

38. General Buford's report, on which the statement in the text is
based, cannot be reconciled with Kilpatrick's claim, referred to in note
36, that early in the morning he had placed his division at Buford's disposal.

town. Kilpatrick's rear guard, Farnsworth's brigade, now commanded by Colonel Nathaniel P. Richmond, was driven back, and the entire division, attacked from the rear and in flank, was driven into and across the rear of Buford's division, then in position outside Williamsport.[39] With his attack toward the wagons already checked, Buford had no choice but to retreat, which he accomplished in good order, bivouacking near Boonsborough for the night. Some of his men thought that night had come and the retreat had been ordered none too soon; "had the daylight lasted another hour," one of them wrote, "we would have suffered the most disastrous defeat."[40]

The position, when the fighting ended on the evening of the fifth, was that General Lee's wagon train, minus the portions lost in the retreat, had found a haven at Williamsport and was about to be protected by the entire Confederate army, which, as fast as its units arrived, was placed in defensive positions on the hills to the east of, and overlooking, the town. The Potomac remained unfordable, there was no bridge, and the resumption of the heavy rains made it unlikely that a crossing of the river would be practicable for several days to come. Meade's infantry, which had followed the Confederate retreat in what many—and especially the administration—thought was an unduly cautious manner, reached the Potomac on the ninth and was deployed on a line running south from Boonsborough to the river, but about ten miles east of General Lee's lines protecting Williamsport. During the following three days, which Lee's men used to throw up mas-

39. *Official Records*, Vol. XXVII, Pt. 1, p. 1015; see also Stuart's report, *ibid.*, Pt. 2, pp. 701–702. Stuart claimed, with considerable justification, that his attack on Kilpatrick prevented the defeat of Imboden and the capture by the Federals of the "main portion of the transportation" of the Confederate army.

40. Gracey, *Annals of the 6th*, 184. Colonel Gamble wrote in his report that he was delayed until midnight in reaching the camping ground, "the delay being caused by Kilpatrick's division having been driven back in confusion from the direction of Hagerstown, completely blocking the road in our rear, making it impassable for several hours." *Official Records*, Vol. XXVII, Pt. 1, p. 935. There is no hint of this in Kilpatrick's report; indeed, he implies that he retreated only because he received word from Buford that the First Division was about to move back to Boonsborough. *Ibid.*, 995.

sive and well-sited earthworks that would have made a Federal assault on Williamsport costly, if not hopeless, the Army of the Potomac was moved forward slowly to within about two miles of the Confederate position.

While Meade tried to decide whether or not to attack the Confederate position, his horsemen did not remain idle. If they received any directives, either from Pleasonton or from Meade, they are not to be found in the records, and the likelihood is that no such directives were issued. Pleasonton, in any event, was otherwise occupied. General Daniel Butterfield, whom Meade had inherited as chief of staff from Hooker, was wounded at Gettysburg on July 3 and was forced to leave the army two days later. From July 5 to July 9, when the highly competent General Andrew A. Humphreys was appointed to take Butterfield's place, Pleasonton and General G. K. Warren took care of the duties of the post.[41] Their work must have met with General Meade's approval, for on July 10 he wired General Halleck, "In consequence of the very efficient service and the material aid rendered to me by the cavalry during the recent operations, I would esteem it a personal favor if the President would assign Major-General Pleasonton to the command of the Cavalry Corps, the position I found him in when I assumed command."[42] But the assignment was not made. Halleck replied the next day that Meade's telegram had been shown to Secretary Stanton and that although there was no intention to supersede Pleasonton, there was "an objection to any formal order at present" making permanent his status as commanding officer of the Cavalry Corps, instead of having him continue to hold the post as a temporary substitute for Stoneman.[43] What the "objection" was, does not appear in the records; it may have

41. Coddington, *The Gettysburg Campaign*, 558. Pleasonton found time, however, to administer a sharp snub to Kilpatrick, who, when he was hard pressed by Stuart's cavalry on the evening of the fifth, apparently asked General William H. French at Frederick for help. Pleasonton sent him a message asking to "be informed why you have made application to General French for re-enforcement instead of these headquarters." For good measure, Kilpatrick was instructed to "make frequent telegraphic reports of what is going on." *Official Records*, Vol. XXVII, Pt. 3, p. 588.

42. *Official Records*, Vol. XXVII, Pt. 1, p. 90.

43. *Ibid.*, 90.

been an indirect expression of dissatisfaction with Meade, a direct prejudice against Pleasonton himself, or merely a desire to spare Stoneman's feelings; it may well have been a combination of all three.

After their fight with Imboden and Stuart at Williamsport on the fifth, Buford and Kilpatrick encamped for the night to the west of Boonsborough, where they were in a position to protect the right flank of Meade's initial line. The two divisions rested on the sixth and seventh, but Merritt's brigade was sent on a scout northward, toward Hagerstown, and one of its regiments, the 6th United States, had a brush with the 7th Virginia of "Grumble" Jones's brigade. General Jones reported with evident relish that the Virginians availed themselves "of the opportunity to settle old scores. Sabers were freely used, and soon 66 bloody-headed prisoners were marched to the rear, and the road of slumbering wrath was marked here and there by cleft skulls and pierced bodies. The day at Fairfield is nobly and fully avenged. The Sixth U. S. Cavalry numbers among the things that were."[44] The sequel of this fight, omitted, perhaps inadvertently, from General Jones's report, is recorded in that of Lieutenant Colonel Thomas Marshall, who commanded the Virginia regiment. After a running, scrambling chase of four or five miles, the Federals, not yet ready to be numbered "among the things that were," rallied and countercharged their pursuers. As Colonel Marshall reported, "Seeing our only hope was in a quick retreat, we double-quicked it as well as the condition of our horses would allow. I endeavored to rally the men . . . but to no purpose. . . . In this return trip . . . we lost a portion of our laurels."[45]

On the eighth, Buford and Kilpatrick had a far more serious affair on their hands. At five A.M., Stuart advanced against them with his entire command and for several hours pressed them

44. *Ibid.*, Pt. 2, p. 754. The reference to Fairfield is to a fight there on July 4 between the 6th United States and the 7th Virginia, in which the latter was badly worsted. *Ibid.*, 752. On July 7, the 6th United States, a mere skeleton of a regiment, was commanded by Lieutenant Nicholas Nolan, the highest-ranking officer present. His report admits that fifty-nine of his men were killed, wounded, or missing, ten of those being known to be dead. *Ibid.*, Pt. 1, pp. 948–49.

45. *Ibid.*, Pt. 2, p. 761.

back, step by step, to the outskirts of Boonsborough, where the Federals dug in their heels, went over to the attack themselves, and eventually forced Stuart's men back four miles across Antietam Creek, toward Williamsport and Hagerstown. Nearly all the fighting this day was on foot, the "ground being entirely too soft from recent rains to operate successfully with cavalry," as Stuart explained.[46] When the fighting stopped, late in the afternoon, Buford had to confess that he had "had a very rough day of it," but he added proudly that "you never saw the division behave better."[47] Stuart, as was his unfortunate habit, claimed that Buford had a "known superiority in numbers and range of firearms" and ascribed his own retreat in the afternoon to information that had come to him that "the enemy was heavily re-enforced, and that our ammunition, by this protracted engagement, was nearly exhausted."[48]

Colonel Gamble's report of this fight, not Buford's, reveals that at one stage of the battle, Buford personally led the advance line of his skirmishers. Colonel Gamble also makes it clear that Kilpatrick was not the object of his admiration; he writes that "General Kilpatrick, with two squadrons of his command, galloped down the road within a short distance of the enemy, halted, looked at each other, and retired, when the dismounted men of my brigade came up and drove the enemy across Beaver Creek."[49] Indeed, one of Kilpatrick's own dispatches suggests that he became badly rattled in the course of this fight, for in the middle of the day he sent a message to Pleasonton from Boonsborough to tell him, "The enemy has forced General Merritt back near the town. General Buford is about to withdraw to the mountains. . . . I shall hold the town as long as possible, and then retire, fighting, on Buford."[50] But Kilpatrick's heroics were not needed; there is not the slightest hint in the records of any intention on General Buford's part to "withdraw to the mountains."

46. *Ibid.*, 703; see also Kidd, *Personal Recollections*, 178–81.
47. *Official Records*, Vol. XXVII, Pt. 1, p. 925.
48. *Ibid.*, Pt. 2, p. 703. There is no evidence in the records of Buford receiving any reinforcements.
49. *Ibid.*, Pt. 1, p. 936.
50. *Ibid.*, Pt. 3, p. 602. Kilpatrick's own report of the campaign makes no mention of fighting on the eighth.

There was more inconclusive fighting between the two cavalry commands on the ninth, tenth, and eleventh near Funkstown. Buford was invariably the aggressor, but Stuart, although forced back, particularly at Funkstown on the tenth, maintained his screening position in front of the Confederate infantry, who waited in their earthworks for an attack by the Army of the Potomac that never came.[51] Finally, by the thirteenth, the waters of the Potomac had fallen to a point which made the ford at Williamsport passable for infantry, and by the same date Major J. A. Harman, formerly Stonewall Jackson's resourceful quartermaster, managed to put together a pontoon bridge of sorts—a "crazy affair," Longstreet's chief of staff called it—a short distance downstream, at Falling Waters; after nightfall on the thirteenth, the Confederate army began to cross to the south side of the river. The crossing did not go as smoothly or as speedily as General Lee expected, but considering the adverse weather—it was pouring rain once again—the pitch darkness, and the access roads that were deep in mud, it was admirably managed. By three A.M. on the fourteenth, when Kilpatrick learned that the Confederate pickets were withdrawn from his front, the crossing was in full swing.

On the thirteenth, with no sign as yet that the Confederates were to cross the river that night, Buford and Kilpatrick were ordered to attack at seven A.M. the next morning.[52] They moved out promptly when the time came, but found only the Confederate rear guard, the division of Henry Heth, before them. Heth had

51. For the fighting at Funkstown, see the reports of Colonel Gamble and General Buford, *ibid.*, Pt. 1, pp. 936 and 929.

52. David Gregg was ordered on the thirteenth to march early on the fourteenth to Harper's Ferry with two brigades of his division, cross the Potomac, and "move in the direction of the enemy's line of communication from Williamsport to Winchester, to annoy their trains and communication." Gregg did as ordered and got to Shepherdstown, on the direct road between the two towns, on the fifteenth, but the next day he was attacked by three of Stuart's brigades, and his own line of communication back to Harper's Ferry was placed in jeopardy. He therefore decided to retreat to the latter point and did so on the seventeenth. *Ibid.*, Pt. 3, p. 676; Pt. 1, pp. 958–60; and Pt. 2, p. 706. This move might have had a chance of succeeding if the entire Cavalry Corps had been sent, as it should have been.

his two brigades posted behind earthworks on a steep hill flanking the road toward Falling Waters and the pontoon bridge. When Kilpatrick was already engaged with Heth's pickets, Buford sent word that he was about to attack the enemy's flank and rear, in order to cut them off from the bridge; he proceeded to do so with considerable success, capturing a 10-pounder Parrott gun, over five hundred prisoners, and about three hundred muskets.[53] Kilpatrick, however, did not bother to wait for Buford's attack to develop. Two squadrons of the 6th Michigan of his division, led by Major Peter A. Weber, charged the enemy up the hill. Kilpatrick, as well as Custer, to whose brigade the 6th Michigan belonged, mention the charge in their reports, but neither reveals whether it was ordered (and if so by whom) or was made by Major Weber on his own responsibility.[54] J. H. Kidd, who eventually became colonel of the 6th Michigan, wrote in his reminiscences that Custer had ordered Webb to dismount his men (who, Kidd wrote, numbered "less than a hundred") and advance a line of skirmishers to "ascertain what he had to encounter," but that the order was countermanded by Kilpatrick, who ordered Weber to have his men mount and charge the hill.[55] Kidd made no secret of his disapproval of Kilpatrick, whom he described as "brave to rashness, capricious, ambitious, reckless in rushing into scrapes, and generally full of expedients in getting out, though at times he seemed to lose his head entirely when beset by perils which he, himself, had invited. . . . many lives were sacrificed by him for no good purpose whatever."[56] Kidd may have disliked Kilpatrick, but there is no reason to doubt his statement that the senseless order to Major Weber was given by Kilpatrick. It was in the spirit of the order to General Farnsworth a few days before, and it only added to the toll of lives "sacrificed by him for no good purpose whatever"; there were to be many more.

Major Weber, killed in the charge, was unable to turn in a

53. *Ibid.*, Pt. 1, p. 929. Colonel Gamble reported 511 prisoners captured. *Ibid.*, 937.
54. *Ibid.*, 990, 1000. According to Custer, the charge was made by two companies (*i.e.*, by one squadron) of the 6th Michigan.
55. Kidd, *Personal Recollections*, 185–86.
56. *Ibid.*, 164–65.

report of his own. Kilpatrick's version of the charge and of its result is to the following effect: "This charge, led by Major Weber, was the most gallant ever made. At a trot he passed up the hill, received the fire from the whole line, and in the next moment rode through and over the earthworks; passed to the right, sabering the rebels along the entire line, and returned with a loss of 30 killed, wounded and missing."[57] Then there is the version of Colonel Gamble, of Buford's division:

While the brigade was moving around to flank and attack the enemy in rear, to cut them off from the ford and capture them all . . . which we could easily have accomplished, I saw two small squadrons of General Kilpatrick's division gallop up the hill to the right of the rebel infantry, in line of battle behind their earthworks, and as any competent cavalry officer of experience could foretell the result, their two squadrons were instantly scattered and destroyed by the fire of the rebel brigade, and not a single dead enemy could be found when the ground there was examined a few hours afterward. This having alarmed the enemy, he fell back toward the ford before we could get round to their rear.[58]

Buford and Gamble reported with restraint on the action at Falling Waters, which in effect, accomplished nothing. Not so Kilpatrick. Characteristically, he took credit for what in his recital assumed the dimensions of a major victory won by the unaided efforts of his division. "After a fight of two hours and a half," he wrote, "we routed the enemy at all points, and drove him toward the river. When within a short distance of the bridge, General Buford's command came up and took the advance." When, in other words, the battle had already been won by Kilpatrick and his division.[59] Kilpatrick's further claim that he had captured "2 guns, 3 battle-flags, and upward of 1,500 prisoners" was, in an action most unusual for him, disputed by General Lee himself as a gross exaggeration.[60]

57. *Official Records*, Vol. XXVII, Pt. 1, p. 990.
58. *Ibid.*, 936–37. Colonel Gamble was in error in referring to the ford, which was at Williamsport. Heth's division protected the pontoon bridge at Falling Waters.
59. *Ibid.*, 990. Kilpatrick's report was swallowed whole by Pleasonton, who wrote in his own report, "The enemy's rear guard made an obstinate resistance near Falling Waters, but was dispersed by General Kilpatrick." *Ibid.*, 917.
60. *Ibid.*, 991.

With the successful crossing of the Potomac by the Army of Northern Virginia—which can with justice be described as a miraculous deliverance—the last full-scale invasion of the North by the South came to an end.[61] There were to be nearly two more years of fighting, some of it the bitterest, most sanguinary fighting of the entire war, but from July 14, 1863, on, the battles of the Army of Northern Virginia were fought south of the Potomac and were almost without exception defensive in nature.

This volume, after the introductory chapters, has traced the evolution of northern cavalry in the eastern theatre of operations, its painful progress from futility to competence. In July, 1863, its leadership was still of questionable quality, but the rank and file, whose courage and hardihood had never been in question, had learned their trade. At Kelly's Ford, Brandy Station, Aldie, Middleburg, Upperville, at Gettysburg and the pursuit following it, the northern cavalry had held its own, and at times more than held its own, against a tough, skillful, courageous, and exceptionally well led enemy. After the Army of Northern Virginia disappeared from the north bank of the Potomac on July 14, the fortunes of the northern cavalry in the remaining years of war varied; there were to be victories and defeats, successes and failures, but at the end, in April, 1865, it was the cavalry of the Army of the Potomac —the military pariahs of 1861 and 1862—who forced the pace and compelled the surrender of the Army of Northern Virginia.

61. General Jubal Early's march to the outskirts of Washington in the summer of 1864 was of course an exception, but it was more in the nature of a diversionary raid than an invasion.

Appendix

IT WILL BE USEFUL FOR THE READER TO BEAR IN MIND the successive stages in the Table of Organization of a volunteer cavalry regiment. Each step in this process required legislation by Congress. Initially, the War Department wanted volunteer units to adopt the organization of the prewar Regular cavalry regiments. Hence by Act of Congress of July 21, 1861, volunteer cavalry regiments were to consist of three battalions, each of three squadrons, and each squadron of two companies. A company was to have a captain, a first and second lieutenant, five sergeants, eight corporals, two "musicians" (buglers), two farriers, one saddler, one wagoner, and seventy-two privates, for a total of 104 officers and men. Each of the three battalions was to be commanded by a major, who had a staff consisting of an adjutant, a quartermaster, a commissary (all three of whom were commissioned officers), and six sergeants; hence a full-strength battalion had 426 officers and men. In command of the regiment was the colonel, with a lieutenant colonel as second-in-command, and a regimental staff consisting of an adjutant, quartermaster, commissary, surgeon, assistant surgeon, chaplain, and two chief buglers. This made a regiment of 1,278 officers and men. Regimental histories, and the rosters many of them contain, are generally silent on the enlistment of farriers, saddlers, and wagoners. Most companies had at least one farrier (smith), but many of them lacked saddlers and wagoners.

The original purpose of the battalion organization was to make it convenient to split up a regiment into three self-contained, autonomous units, to operate independently at separate posts, a situation common in the prewar Regular cavalry. The volunteer regiments at least in theory were expected to operate as complete units; hence the battalion organization proved cumbersome and over-officered, especially when after a few months of campaigning, regiments were reduced to 400–500 men. An Act of Congress of July 17, 1862, therefore eliminated the battalion staffs and made majors regimental officers; the regimental staff was reorganized by dropping the two chief buglers and adding a regimental sergeant major, two hospital stewards, a saddler sergeant, a chief farrier, and a chief trumpeter; the "squadron" was abolished, the "company" was renamed the "troop," and its roster was changed by the addition of a sixth sergeant, a commissary sergeant, two teamsters, and six privates, and the dropping of the two buglers. The result was a "troop" of 112 officers and men, and a full-strength regiment of 1,361 officers and men. A final change was made by the act of March 3, 1863, which did away with the two teamsters in each troop and the chief farrier, but added a regimental veterinary surgeon and restored the two buglers in each troop.

These successive acts of Congress expressed an intent. They did not describe reality. In no case known to the author did the organization of a regiment, battalion, squadron, or troop conform exactly to the congressional standard. From the beginning, there were regiments with ten companies instead of twelve, independent battalions not combined into regiments, companies lacking the specified number of men, or officers, or noncommissioned officers, or all three. The discrepancy between the legislative standard and actual numbers grew in every regiment with the passage of time. Nothing is more fallacious, when reading of a cavalry charge, than to imagine the advance of nearly thirteen hundred or fourteen hundred men. It was far more likely to be a mere two or three hundred or even fewer, and one case is known of a regiment (unnamed) mustering a mere forty-five men on the firing line at Five Forks, in the spring of 1865.

Bibliography

REGIMENTAL AND OTHER UNIT HISTORIES

Aston, Howard. *History and Roster of the Fourth and Fifth Independent Battalions and Thirteenth Regiment Ohio Cavalry Volunteers.* Columbus: Press of Fred J. Heer, 1902.

Avery, P. O. *History of the Fourth Illinois Cavalry Regiment.* Humboldt, Ill.: Enterprise, 1903.

Barron, Samuel B. *The Lone Star Defenders: A Chronicle of the Third Texas Cavalry, Ross' Brigade.* New York: Neale Publishing, 1908.

Beach, William H. *The First New York (Lincoln) Cavalry.* New York: Lincoln Cavalry Association, 1902.

Beale, R. L. T. *History of the Ninth Virginia Cavalry in the War Between the States.* Richmond: B. F. Johnson Publishing, 1899.

Boudrye, Louis N. *Historic Records of the Fifth New York Cavalry, First Ira Harris Guard.* Albany: S. R. Gray, 1868.

Bowen, James R. *Regimental History of the First New York Dragoons.* N.p.: published by author, 1900.

Britton, Wiley. *The Union Indian Brigade in the Civil War.* Kansas City: Franklin Hudson Publishing, 1922.

Brooks, U. R., ed. *Butler and His Cavalry in the War of Secession, 1861–1865.* Columbia, So. Car.: State Company, 1909.

Brown, Andrew. "The First Mississippi Partisan Rangers, C.S.A." *Civil War History,* I (1955), 371–99.

Brown, Dee A. *The Bold Cavaliers: Morgan's 2nd Kentucky Cavalry Raiders.* Philadelphia: J. B. Lippincott, 1959.

Carter, W. R. *History of the First Regiment of Tennessee Volunteer Cavalry in the Great War of the Rebellion.* Knoxville: Gaut-Ogden, 1902.

Cheney, Newel. *History of the Ninth Regiment, New York Volunteer Cavalry.* Poland Center, N.Y.: Martin Merz & Son, 1901.

Cogley, Thomas S. *History of the Seventh Indiana Cavalry Volunteers.* Laporte, Ind.: Herald Company Steam Printers, 1876.

Committee on Regimental History. *History of the Sixth New York Cavalry (Second Ira Harris Guard).* Worcester, N.Y.: Blanchard Press, 1908.

Comstock, Daniel W. *Ninth Cavalry: One Hundred and Twenty-First Indiana Volunteers.* Richmond, Ind.: J. M. Coe, 1890.

Corliss, A. W. *History of the Seventh Squadron Rhode Island Cavalry, by a Member.* Yarmouth, R.I.: "Old Times" Office, 1879.

Crandall, Warren D. and Isaac D. Newell. *History of the Ram Fleet and the Mississippi Marine Brigade in the War for the Union on the Mississippi and Its Tributaries.* St. Louis: Press of Burchart Brothers, 1907.

Crofts, Thomas. *History of the Service of the Third Ohio Veteran Volunteer Cavalry.* Toledo: Stoneman Press, 1910.

Crowninshield, Benjamin W. *A History of the First Regiment of Massachusetts Cavalry Volunteers.* Boston: Houghton, Mifflin, 1891.

Curry, William L. *Four Years in the Saddle: History of the First Regiment Ohio Volunteer Cavalry.* Columbus, Ohio: Champlin Printing, 1898.

Dacus, Robert H. *Reminiscences of Company "H" First Arkansas Mounted Rifles.* Dardanelle, Ark.: Post-Despatch Print, 1897.

Davenport, Edward A. *History of the Ninth Regiment Illinois Cavalry Volunteers.* Chicago: Donohue & Henneberry, 1888.

Debray, Xavier B. *A Sketch of the History of Debray's (26th) Regiment of Texas Cavalry.* Austin: Eugene von Boeckmann, 1884.

Deibert, R. C. *History of the Third United States Cavalry.* Harrisburg: Telegraph Press, 1933.

Denison, Frederick. *Sabres and Spurs: The First Regiment Rhode Island Cavalry.* Central Falls, R.I.: First Rhode Island Cavalry Veteran Association, 1876.

Deupree, J. G. "The Noxubee Squadron of the First Mississippi Cavalry, C.S.A., 1861–1865." *Publications of the Mississippi Historical Society,* III (1918), 12–143.

Dornblaser, Thomas F. *Sabre Strokes of the Pennsylvania Dragoons in the War of 1861–1865.* Philadelphia: Lutheran Publication Society, 1884.

Duke, Basil W. *A History of Morgan's Cavalry.* Bloomington: Indiana University Press, 1960.

Edwards, John N. *Shelby and His Men, or, The War in the West.* Cincinnati: Miami Printing and Publishing, 1867.

Elwood, John W. *Elwood's Stories of the Old Ringgold Cavalry.* Coal City, Pa.: published by author, 1914.

Ewer, James K. *The Third Massachusetts Cavalry in the War for the Union.* Maplewood, Mass.: Wm. G. J. Perry Press, 1903.

Farrar, Samuel C. *The Twenty-Second Pennsylvania Cavalry and the Ringgold Battalion.* Pittsburg: New Werner, 1911.

Fletcher, Samuel F. *The History of Company A, Second Illinois Cavalry.* Chicago: n.p., 1912.

Foster, Alonzo. *Reminiscences and Record of the 6th New York Veteran Volunteer Cavalry.* Brooklyn: n.p., 1892.

Fox, Simeon M. "The Early History of the Seventh Kansas Cavalry." *Sixteenth Biennial Report of the Board of Directors of the Kansas State Historical Society* (1909), 107–22.

———. "The Story of the Seventh Kansas." *Transactions of the Kansas State Historical Society, 1903–1904.* VIII, 13–49. Topeka: Geo. A. Clark, 1904.

Gillespie, Samuel L. ("Lovejoy"). *A History of Company A, First Ohio Cavalry, 1861–1865.* Washington Court House: Press of Ohio State Register, 1898.

Gilpin, Thomas C. *History of the 3rd Iowa Volunteer Cavalry.* Winterset, Iowa: Winterset News, 189?.

Goodhart, Briscoe. *History of the Independent Loudoun, Virginia Rangers.* Washington, D.C.: Press of McGill & Wallace, 1896.

Gracey, Samuel L. *Annals of the 6th Pennsylvania Cavalry.* Philadelphia: E. H. Butler, 1868.

Guild, George B. *A Brief Narrative of the Fourth Tennessee Cavalry Regiment.* Nashville: n.p., 1913.

Hackley, Woodford B. *The Little Fork Rangers: A Sketch of Company "D" Fourth Virginia Cavalry.* Richmond: Dietz, 1927.

Hancock, R. R. *Hancock's Diary, or, A History of the Second Tennessee Cavalry.* Nashville: Brandon Printing, 1887.

Hard, Abner. *History of the Eighth Cavalry Regiment, Illinois Volunteers.* Aurora, Ill.: n.p., 1868.

Hartpence, William R. *History of the 51st Indiana Veteran Infantry.* Indianapolis: R. Clarke, 1894.

Hinman, Wilbur F. *The Story of the Sherman Brigade.* Alliance, Ohio: published by author, 1897.

Hyndman, William. *History of a Cavalry Company.* Philadelphia: Jas. B. Rogers, 1870.

Isham, Asa B. *An Historical Sketch of the Seventh Regiment Michigan Volunteer Cavalry.* New York: Town Topics Publishing, 1893.

Kelly, R. M., Thomas Speed, and Alfred Pirtle. *The Union Regiments of Kentucky.* Louisville: Courier-Journal Job Print, 1897.

Kirk, Charles H. *History of the Fifteenth Pennsylvania Volunteer Cavalry.* Philadelphia: n.p., 1906.

Lambert, J. I. *One Hundred Years with the Second Cavalry.* Topeka: Capper, 1939.

Lee, William O. *Personal and Historical Sketches of the 7th Regiment Michigan Volunteer Cavalry.* Detroit: Ralston-Stroup Printing, 1901.

Lloyd, William P. *History of the First Reg't. Pennsylvania Reserve Cavalry.* Philadelphia: King & Bard, 1864.

Lothrop, Charles C. *A History of the First Regiment Iowa Cavalry Veteran Volunteers.* Lyons, Iowa: Beers & Eaton, 1890.

Lowes, James H. S. *Unwritten History of the 7th Indiana Cavalry in the War of the Rebellion.* Baltimore: Press of John Cox's Sons, 1899.

McDonald, William N. *A History of the Laurel Brigade.* Baltimore: Sun Job Printing, 1907.

McGee, Benjamin F. *History of the 72nd Indiana Volunteer Infantry of the Mounted Lightning Brigade.* Lafayette, Ind.: S. Vater, 1882.

Mason, Frank H. *The Twelfth Ohio Cavalry.* Cleveland: Nevin's Printing, 1871.

Mead, Homer, *The Eighth Iowa Cavalry in the Civil War.* Carthage, Iowa: S. C. Davidson, 1925.

Merrill, Samuel H. *Campaigns of the First Maine and First District of Columbia Cavalry.* Portland, Maine: Bailey & Noyes, 1866.

Moyer, Henry P. *History of the 17th Regiment Pennsylvania Volunteer Cavalry.* Lebanon, Pa.: Sowers Printing, 1911.

Myers, Frank M. *The Comanches: A History of White's Battalion, Virginia Cavalry.* Baltimore: Kelly, Piet, 1871.

Newcomer, C. Armour. *Cole's Cavalry, or, Three Years in the Saddle in the Shenandoah Valley.* Baltimore: Cushing, 1895.

Nolan, Alan T. *The Iron Brigade.* New York: Macmillan, 1961.

Norton, Chauncey S. *"The Red Neck Ties," or, History of the Fifteenth New York Volunteer Cavalry.* Ithaca, N.Y.: Journal Book and Job Printing, 1891.

Norton, Henry. *Deeds of Daring, or, History of the 8th New York Volunteer Cavalry.* Norwich, N.Y.: Chenango Telegraph Printing, 1889.

Pettengill, S. B. *The College Cavaliers.* Chicago: H. M. McAllaster, 1883.

Pickerill, William N. *History of the Third Indiana Cavalry.* Indianapolis: Aetna Printing, 1865.

Pierce, Lyman B. *History of the Second Iowa Cavalry.* Burlington, Iowa: Hawkeye Steam Book and Job Printing, 1865.

Preston, Noble D. *History of the 10th Regiment of Cavalry, New York State Volunteers.* New York: D. Appleton, 1892.

Price, George. *Across the Continent with the Fifth Cavalry*. New York: D. Van Nostrand, 1883.

Publication Committee of the Regimental Association. *History of the Eighteenth Regiment of Cavalry, Pennsylvania Volunteers, 1862–1865*. New York: Wynkoop, Hallenbeck, Crawford, 1909.

Pyne, Henry R. *The History of the First New Jersey Cavalry*. Trenton: J. A. Beecher, 1871.

Rankin, Richard C. *History of the Seventh Ohio Volunteer Cavalry*. Ripley, Ohio: J. C. Newcomb, 1881.

Reader, Frank S. *History of the Fifth West Virginia Cavalry, Formerly the Second Virginia Infantry, and Battery G, First West Virginia Light Artillery*. New Brighton, W.Va. Daily News, 1890.

Regimental History Committee. *History of the 3d Pennsylvania Cavalry*. Philadelphia: Franklin Printing, 1905.

Robertson, John. *Michigan in the War*. Lansing: W. S. George, 1882.

Rodenbough, T. F. *From Everglade to Canon with the Second Dragoons*. New York: D. Van Nostrand, 1875.

Rose, V. M. *Ross' Texas Brigade*. Louisville, Ky.: Courier-Journal, 1881.

Rowell, John W. *Yankee Cavalrymen: Through the Civil War with the Ninth Pennsylvania Cavalry*. Knoxville: University of Tennessee Press, 1971.

Sanford, W. L. *History of the Fourteenth Illinois Cavalry and the Brigades to Which It Belonged*. Chicago: R. R. Donnelley & Sons, 1898.

Scott, Samuel W. and Samuel P. Angel. *History of the Thirteenth Regiment, Tennessee Volunteer Cavalry, U.S.A.* Philadelphia: P. W. Ziegler, 1903.

Scott, William F. *The Story of a Cavalry Regiment: The Career of the Fourth Iowa Veteran Volunteers*. New York: G. P. Putnam's Sons, 1893.

Sipes, William B. *The Seventh Pennsylvania Veteran Volunteer Cavalry*. Pottsville, Pa.: Miners' Journal Print, n.d.

Slease, William D. *The Fourteenth Pennsylvania Cavalry in the Civil War*. Pittsburg: Art Engraving & Printing, 1915.

Sloan, W. D. "Iowa Cavalry—Sixth Regiment." *Civil War History*, III (1957), 189–98.

Smith, Thomas W. *The Story of a Cavalry Regiment: "Scott's 900,"* Eleventh New York Cavalry*. Chicago: W. B. Conkey, 1897.

Starr, Stephen Z. *Jennison's Jayhawkers*. Baton Rouge: Louisiana State University Press, 1973.

Stevenson, James H. *"Boots and Saddles": A History of the First Volunteer Cavalry of the War, Known as the First New York (Lincoln) Cavalry*. Harrisburg, Pa.: Patriot Publishing, 1879.

Sutton, J. J. *History of the Second Regiment West Virginia Cavalry Volunteers.* Portsmouth, W.Va.: n.p., 1892.

Tarrant, Eastham. *The Wild Riders of the First Kentucky Cavalry (Union).* Louisville: Committee of the Regiment, 1894.

Thatcher, Marshall P. *A Hundred Battles in the West, St. Louis to Atlanta: The Second Michigan Cavalry with the Armies of Mississippi, Ohio, Kentucky and Cumberland.* Detroit: L. F. Kilroy, 1884.

Thompson, B. F. *History of the 112th Regiment of Illinois Volunteer Infantry in the Great War of the Rebellion.* Toulon, Ill.: Stark County News, 1885.

Tobie, Edward P. *History of the First Maine Cavalry.* Boston: First Maine Cavalry Association, 1887.

Trowbridge, Luther S. *A Brief History of the Tenth Michigan Cavalry.* Detroit: Friesema Brothers Printing, 1905.

Vale, Joseph G. *Minty and the Cavalry: A History of Cavalry Campaigns in the Western Armies.* Harrisburg, Pa.: Edwin K. Meyers, 1886.

Walker, Aldace F. *The Vermont Brigade in the Shenandoah Valley, 1864.* Burlington, Vt.: Free Press Assn., 1869.

Weaver, Augustus C. *Third Indiana Cavalry.* Greenwood, Ind.: n.p., 1919.

Wells, Edward L. *A Sketch of the Charleston Light Dragoons from the Earliest Formation of the Corps.* Charleston: Lucas, Richardson, 1888.

Wulsin, Lucien. *The Story of the Fourth Regiment Ohio Veteran Volunteer Cavalry.* Cincinnati: n.p., 1912.

Young, J. P. *The Seventh Tennessee Cavalry, A History.* Nashville: M. E. Church, South, 1890.

National Archives, Washington, D.C.
> Regimental and Company Order and Letter Books. Record Group 94, of the following Volunteer Regiments:
> 8th Illinois Cavalry
> 2nd Iowa Cavalry
> 1st Massachusetts Cavalry
> 2nd Michigan Cavalry
> 5th New York Cavalry
> 3rd Ohio Cavalry
> 7th Pennsylvania Cavalry
> 1st Rhode Island Cavalry
> 1st Vermont Cavalry

AUTOBIOGRAPHIES, MEMOIRS, BIOGRAPHICAL STUDIES

Adams, Charles F. *Charles Francis Adams, 1835–1915: An Autobiography.* Boston: Houghton, Mifflin, 1916.

Adams, F. Colburn. *The Story of a Trooper.* New York: Dick & Fitzgerald, 1865.

Agassiz, George R., ed. *Meade's Headquarters 1863–1865: Letters of Colonel Theodore Lyman.* Boston: Atlantic Monthly Press, 1922.

Alexander, Edward P. *Military Memoirs of a Confederate.* New York: Charles Scribner's Sons, 1907.

Alexander, John P. *Mosby's Men.* New York: Neale Publishing, 1907.

Allen, Stanton P. *Down in Dixie: Life of a Cavalry Regiment in War Days.* Boston: D. Lothrop, 1888.

Alley, Charles. "Exerpts from the Civil War Diary of Lieut. Charles Alley." *Iowa Journal of History*, XLIX (1951), 241–56.

Ambrose, Stephen E. *Upton and the Army.* Baton Rouge: Louisiana State University Press, 1964.

Anderson, Edward. *Camp Fire Stories.* Chicago: Star Publishing, 1900.

————. "Missouri in 1861–1862." *Papers of the Military Historical Society of Massachusetts*, VII, 1–19, 1910.

Anderson, M. W. *Life of General Stand Watie.* Pryor, Okla.: Mayes County Republican, 1915.

Ashby, Thomas A. *Life of Turner Ashby.* New York: Neale Publishing, 1914.

Ashmun, George C. "Recollections of a Peculiar Service." MOLLUS, Commandery of Ohio, *Sketches of War History, 1861–1865*, II, 277–92. 7 vols. Cincinnati: Robert Clark, 1888–1910.

Atkins, Smith D. "With Sherman's Cavalry." MOLLUS, Commandery of Illinois, *Military Essays and Recollections*, II, 383–98. 5 vols. Chicago: A. C. McClurg, 1891–94.

Avirett, James B. *Memoirs of Gen. Ashby and His Compeers.* Baltimore: Selby & Dulany, 1867.

Bartmess, Jacob W. "Civil War Letters." *Indiana Magazine of History*, LII (1956), 49–74, 157–86.

Bayard, Samuel J. *The Life of George Dashiell Bayard.* New York: G. P. Putnam's Sons, 1874.

Baylor, George. *Bull Run to Bull Run, or, Four Years in the Army of Northern Virginia.* Richmond: B. F. Johnson, 1900.

Beale, G. W. *A Lieutenant of Cavalry in Lee's Army.* Boston: Gorham Press, 1918.

Beatty, John. *The Citizen-Soldier, or, Memoirs of a Volunteer.* Cincinnati: Wilstach, Baldwin, 1879.

Beck, Elias W. H. "Letters of a Civil War Surgeon." *Indiana Magazine of History*, XXVII (1931), 132–63.

Berry, Thomas F. *Four Years with Morgan and Forrest.* Oklahoma City: Harlow-Ratliff, 1914.

Blackford, Susan Leigh, comp. *Letters from Lee's Army.* New York: Charles Scribner's Sons, 1947.

Blackford, William W. *War Years with Jeb Stuart.* New York: Charles Scribner's Sons, 1945.

von Borcke, Heros. *Memoirs of the Confederate War for Independence.* 2 vols. New York: Peter Smith, 1938.

Brooks, U. R. "Hampton and Butler." *Southern Historical Society Papers*, XXIII (1895), 25–37.

Bryant, William Cullen, ed. "A Yankee Soldier Looks at the Negro." *Civil War History*, VII (1961), 133–48.

Buell, Augustus C. *"The Cannoneer": Recollections of Service in the Army of the Potomac.* Washington, D.C.: National Tribune, 1890.

Burne, Alfred H. *Lee, Grant and Sherman.* New York: Charles Scribner's Sons, 1939.

Cadwallader, Sylvanus. *Three Years with Grant.* New York: Alfred A. Knopf, 1955.

Carter, Howell. *A Cavalryman's Reminiscences of the Civil War.* New Orleans: American Printing, n.d.

Castel Albert. *General Sterling Price and the Civil War in the West.* Baton Rouge: Louisiana State University Press, 1968.

Castleman, John B. *Active Service.* Louisville: Courier-Journal Printing, 1917.

Catton, Bruce. *Grant Moves South.* Boston: Little, Brown, 1960.

———. *Grant Takes Command.* Boston: Little, Brown, 1968.

Chamberlain, Joshua L. *The Passing of the Armies.* Dayton: Morningside Book Shop, 1974.

Chambers, Lenoir. *Stonewall Jackson.* 2 vols. New York: William Morrow, 1959.

Clark, James Albert. "The Making of a Volunteer Cavalryman." MOLLUS, Commandery of the District of Columbia, *War Papers, No. 70.* Washington, D.C.: Judd and Detweiler, 1907.

Colton, Mathias B. *Column South: With the Fifteenth Pennsylvania Cavalry from Antietam to the Capture of Jefferson Davis: The Civil War Journal and Correspondence of Mathias B. Colton.* Philadelphia: Macrae-Smith, 1931.

Connolly, J. A. *Three Years in the Army of the Cumberland.* Bloomington: Indiana University Press, 1959.

Cooke, John Esten. *The Wearing of the Gray.* New York: E. B. Treat, 1867.

Copp, E. J. *Reminiscences of the War of the Rebellion.* Nashua, N.H.: Telegraph Publishing, 1911.

Cox, Jacob D. *Military Reminiscences of the Civil War.* 2 vols. New York: Charles Scribner's Sons, 1900.

Crane, William E. "Bugle Blasts." MOLLUS, Commandery of Ohio, *Sketches of War History, 1861–1865*, I, 233–51. 7 vols. Cincinnati: Robert Clark, 1888–1910.

Crotty, Daniel G. *Four Years Campaigning in the Army of the Potomac.* Grand Rapids: Dygert Bros., 1874.

Dana, Charles A. *Recollections of the Civil War.* New York: D. Appleton, 1898.

Dana, Charles A. and James H. Wilson. *The Life of Ulysses S. Grant.* Springfield, Ill.: Gurdon, Bill, 1868.

Davies, Henry E. *General Sheridan.* New York: D. Appleton, 1895.

DeForest, John W. *A Volunteer's Adventures.* New Haven: Yale University Press, 1946.

Dinkins, James. *Personal Recollections and Experiences in the Confederate Army.* Cincinnati: Robert Clarke, 1897.

Douglas, Henry Kyd. *I Rode with Stonewall.* Chapel Hill: University of North Carolina Press, 1940.

DuBose, John W. *General Joseph Wheeler and the Army of Tennessee.* New York: Neale Publishing, 1912.

Duke, Basil W. *Reminiscences of General Basil W. Duke, C.S.A.* New York: Doubleday, Page, 1911.

Dyer, J. P. *"Fightin' Joe" Wheeler.* Baton Rouge: Louisiana State University Press, 1941.

Dyer, J. W. *Reminiscences, or, Four Years in the Confederate Army.* Evansville, Ind.: Keller, 1898.

Early, Jubal A. *Autobiographical Sketch and Narrative of the War Between the States.* Philadelphia: J. B. Lippincott, 1912.

Eby, Henry H. *Observation of an Illinois Boy, in Battle, Camp and Prisons, 1861–1865.* Mendota, Ill.: published by author, 1910.

Eggleston, George C. *A Rebel's Recollections.* Bloomington: Indiana University Press, 1959.

———. *Recollections of a Varied Life.* New York: Henry Holt, 1910.

Elliott, C. W. *Winfield Scott: The Soldier and the Man.* New York: Macmillan, 1937.

Emerson, Edward W. *The Life and Letters of Charles Russell Lowell.* Boston: Houghton, Mifflin, 1907.

Ewing, Elmore E. *Bugles and Bells, or, Stories Told Again.* Cincinnati: Press of Curtis & Jennings, 1899.

Ezell, John S., ed. "Excerpts from the Civil War Diary of Lieutenant Charles Alley, Company 'C,' Fifth Iowa Cavalry." *Iowa Journal of History*, XLIX (1951), 241–56.

Fanning, Thomas W. *The Adventures of a Volunteer.* Cincinnati: P. C. Browne, 1863.

Faulkner, J. *The Life of Philip Henry Sheridan.* New York: Hurst, 1888.

Favill, Josiah M. *The Diary of a Young Officer.* Chicago: R. R. Donnelley & Sons, 1909.

Flower, Frank A. *Edwin McMasters Stanton.* Akron, Ohio: Saalfield Publishing, 1905.

Ford, W. C., ed. *A Cycle of Adams Letters, 1861–1865.* 2 vols. Boston: Houghton, Mifflin, 1920.

Forsyth, G. A. *Thrilling Days in Army Life*. New York: Harper & Brothers, 1900.

Freeman, Douglas S. *Lee's Lieutenants: A Study in Command*. 3 vols. New York: Charles Scribner's Sons, 1942–44.

———. *R. E. Lee: A Biography*. 4 vols. New York: Charles Scribner's Sons, 1941.

Freeman, Douglas S. and Grady McWhiney, eds. *Lee's Dispatches to Jefferson Davis*. New York: G. P. Putnam's Sons, 1957.

Fremantle, Arthur J. L. *The Fremantle Diary*. Boston: Little, Brown, 1960.

Gause, Isaac. *Four Years with Five Armies*. New York: Neale Publishing, 1908.

Gibbon, John. *Personal Recollections of the Civil War*. New York: G. P. Putnam's Sons, 1928.

Gilmor, Harry. *Four Years in the Saddle*. New York: Harper & Brothers, 1866.

Gilpin, E. N. "The Last Campaign: A Cavalryman's Journal." *Journal of the United States Cavalry Association*, XVIII (1908), 617–75.

Glazier, Willard. *Three Years in the Federal Cavalry*. New York: R. H. Ferguson, 1873.

Goss, W. L. *Recollections of a Private: A Story of the Army of the Potomac*. New York: Thomas Y. Crowell, [1890].

Govan, G. E. and J. W. Livingood, eds. *The Haskell Memoirs*. New York: G. P. Putnam's Sons, 1960.

Grant, Ulysses S. *Personal Memoirs of U. S. Grant*. 2 vols. New York: Charles L. Webster, 1885.

Grierson, Benjamin H. "Lights and Shadows of Life." Illinois State Historical Society, Springfield.

Guyer, Max Hendricks, ed. "The Journal and Letters of Corporal William O. Gulick." *Iowa Journal of History and Politics*, XXVIII (1930), 194–267.

Hamilton, William D. *Recollections of a Cavalryman of the Civil War After Fifty Years*. Columbus, Ohio: F. J. Heer Printing, 1915.

Hamlin, Percy G. *"Old Bald Head" (General R. S. Ewell): The Portrait of a Soldier*. Strasburg, Va.: Shenandoah Publishing, 1940.

Hannaford, Roger. "Reminiscences." The Cincinnati Historical Society, Cincinnati.

Hardin, Bayliss E. *Brigadier-General John Hunt Morgan of Kentucky*. Frankfort: Kentucky State Historical Society, 1938.

Harris, Samuel. *Personal Reminiscences*. Chicago: Rogerson Press, 1897.

Harvey, Marshall S. *Recollections of 1864–5*. Columbus, Ohio: n.p., 1904.

Haupt, Herman. *Reminiscences of General Herman Haupt*. Milwaukee: Wright & Joys, 1901.

Hay, William H. "James Harrison Wilson." *Annual Report of the As-*

sociation of Graduates of the U. S. Military Academy (1931), 75–83.

Hebert, Walter H. *Fighting Joe Hooker.* Indianapolis: Bobbs-Merrill, 1944.

Henderson, G. F. R. *Stonewall Jackson and the American Civil War.* London: Longmans, Green, 1919.

Henry, Robert Selph. *"First with the Most" Forrest.* New York: Bobbs-Merrill, 1944.

Hitchcock, Ethan A. *Fifty Years in Camp and Field.* New York: G. P. Putnam's Sons, 1909.

Holland, Cecil F. *Morgan and His Raiders.* New York: Macmillan, 1942.

Hood, John B. *Advance and Retreat.* New Orleans: Burke & McFetridge, 1880.

Hopkins, Luther W. *From Bull Run to Appomattox: A Boy's View.* Baltimore: Fleet-McGinley, 1908.

Hosea, Lewis M. *Some Side Lights on the War for the Union.* Cleveland: n.p., 1912.

Hubbard, J. M. *Notes of a Private.* Memphis: E. H. Clarke & Brother, 1909.

Johnson, Adam R. *The Partisan Rangers of the Confederate States Army.* Louisville: Geo. G. Fetter, 1904.

Johnston, Joseph E. *Narrative of Military Operations During the Late War Between the States.* Bloomington: Indiana University Press, 1959.

Jones, J. B. *A Rebel War Clerk's Diary at the Confederate States Capital.* 2 vols. Philadelphia: J. B. Lippincott, 1866.

Jones, Virgil C. *Ranger Mosby.* Chapel Hill: University of North Carolina Press, 1944.

Kearny, Thomas. *General Philip Kearny.* New York: G. P. Putnam's Sons, 1937.

Kidd, J. H. *Personal Recollections of a Cavalryman.* Ionia, Mich.: Sentinel Printing, 1908.

King, G. Wayne. "General Judson Kilpatrick." *New Jersey History,* XCI (1973), 35–52.

Lamers, William M. *The Edge of Glory: A Biography of General William S. Rosecrans.* New York: Harcourt, Brace & World, 1961.

Larson, James. *Sergeant Larson: 4th Cavalry.* Edited by A. L. Blum. San Antonio: Southern Literary Institute, 1935.

Lewis, C. E. *War Sketches: With the First Dragoons in Virginia.* London: Simmons & Botten, 1897.

Lewis, Lloyd. *Sherman: Fighting Prophet.* New York: Harcourt, Brace, 1932.

Liddell-Hart, B. H. *Sherman: Soldier—Realist—American.* New York: Frederick A. Praeger, 1958.

Litvin, Martin, ed. *Sergeant Allen and Private Renick: A Memoir of*

the Eleventh Illinois Cavalry Written by Henry A. Allen. Gales-
burg, Ill.:.Wagoner Printing, 1971.

Logan, India W. P. *Kelion Franklin Pedicord of Quirk's Scouts, Morgan's Kentucky Cavalry, C.S.A.* New York: Neale Publishing,
1908.

Longacre, Edward G. *From Union Stars to Top Hat*. Harrisburg:
Stackpole Books, 1972.

Lytle, Andrew. *Bedford Forrest and His Critter Company*. New York:
McDowell, Obolensky, 1960.

McBride, Robert W. *Lincoln's Body Guard*. Indianapolis: Edward J.
Hecker, 1911.

McCain, Warren. *A Soldier's Diary*. Indianapolis: William A. Patton,
1885.

McClellan, George B. *McClellan's Own Story: The War for the Union*.
New York: Charles L. Webster, 1887.

McClellan, Henry B. *I Rode with Jeb Stuart: The Life and Campaigns
of Major-General J. E. B. Stuart*. Bloomington: Indiana University Press, 1958.

McClurg, Alexander C. "An American Soldier—Minor Millikin." MOL-
LUS, Commandery of Illinois, V, 355–72. 5 vols. Chicago: A. C.
McClurg, 1891–94.

MacConnell, Charles C. "Service with Sheridan." MOLLUS, Commandery of Wisconsin, *War Papers*, I, 285–93. 3 vols. Milwaukee:
Burdick, Armitage & Allen, 1891–1903.

McKinney, E. P. *Life in Tent and Field*. Boston: Richard G. Badger,
1922.

McKinney, F. F. *Education in Violence: The Life of George H. Thomas and the History of the Army of the Cumberland*. Detroit:
Wayne State University Press, 1961.

Mathes, H. Harvey. *General Forrest*. New York: D. Appleton, 1902.

Maurice, Frederick. *Robert E. Lee the Soldier*. Boston: Houghton, Mifflin, 1925.

Maury, Dabney H. *Recollections of a Virginian*. New York: Charles
Scribner's Sons, 1894.

Mercer, Philip. *The Life of the Gallant Pelham*. Macon: J. W. Burke,
1929.

Merington, Margaret, ed. *The Custer Story*. New York: Devin Adair,
1950.

Meyer, Henry C. *Civil War Experiences under Bayard, Gregg, Kilpatrick, Custer*. New York: Knickerbocker Press, 1911.

Michie, P. S. *The Life and Letters of Emory Upton*. New York: D.
Appleton, 1885.

Miller, E. V. D. *A Soldier's Honor with Reminiscences of Major-
General Earl Van Dorn by His Comrades*. New York: Abbey Press,
1902.

Montgomery, F. A. *Reminiscences of a Mississippian in Peace and War.* Cincinnati: Robert Clarke, 1901.

Moore, James. *Kilpatrick and Our Cavalry.* New York: W. J. Widdleton, 1865.

Moore, James B. *Two Years in the Service.* N.p., 186?.

Morton, J. W. *The Artillery of Nathan Bedford Forrest's Cavalry.* Nashville: M. E. Church South, 1909.

Mosby, John S. *The Memoirs of Colonel John S. Mosby.* Bloomington: Indiana University Press, 1959.

———. *Mosby's War Reminiscences: Stuart's Cavalry Campaigns.* New York: Pageant Book Company, 1958.

Mosgrove, George C. *Kentucky Cavaliers in Dixie: Reminiscences of a Confederate Cavalryman.* Jackson, Tenn.: McCowat-Mercer Press, 1957.

Munford, T. T. "A Confederate Cavalry Officer's Reminiscences." *Journal of the United States Cavalry Association,* IV (1891), 276–88.

Myers, William S. *General George Brinton McClellan.* New York: Appleton Century, 1934.

Neese, George M. *Three Years in the Confederate Horse Artillery.* New York: Neale Publishing, 1911.

Nevins, Allan, ed. *A Diary of Battle: The Personal Journals of Colonel Charles S. Wainwright, 1861–1865.* New York: Harcourt, Brace & World, 1962.

———. *The Emergence of Lincoln.* 2 vols. New York: Charles Scribner's Sons, 1950.

Newhall, Frederick C. *With General Sheridan in Lee's Last Campaign.* Philadelphia: J. B. Lippincott, 1866.

Noll, A. H. *General Kirby-Smith.* Sewanee, Tenn.: Sewanee University Press, 1907.

Oates, John B. "John S. Ford: Prudent Cavalryman, C.S.A." *Southwestern History Quarterly,* LXIV (1961), 289–314.

O'Connor, Richard. *Sheridan the Inevitable.* Indianapolis: Bobbs-Merrill, 1953.

———. *Thomas: Rock of Chickamauga.* New York: Prentice-Hall, 1948.

O'Ferrall, C. T. *Forty Years of Active Service.* New York: Neale Publishing, 1904.

O'Flaherty, Daniel. *General Jo Shelby.* Chapel Hill: University of North Carolina Press, 1954.

Opie, John N. *A Rebel Cavalryman with Lee, Stuart and Jackson.* Dayton: Morningside Book Shop, 1972.

Owens, J. A. *Sword and Pen, or, Ventures and Adventures of Willard Glazier.* Philadelphia: P. W. Ziegler, 1889.

Packard, William A. *Joseph Karge: A Memorial Sketch.* New York: Anson D. F. Randolph, 1893.

Parks, J. H. *General Edmund Kirby Smith, C.S.A.* Baton Rougle: Louisiana State University Press, 1954.

Peck, R. H. *Reminiscences of a Confederate Soldier of Co. C, 2nd Va. Cavalry.* Fincastle, Va.: n.p., 1913.

Perry, Bliss. *Life and Letters of Henry Lee Higginson.* Boston: Atlantic Monthly Press, 1921.

Phillips, John Wilson. "Civil War Diary." Ed. Robert G. Athearn. *Virginia Magazine of History and Biography,* LXII (1954), 95–123.

Piatt, Donn and H. V. Boynton. *General George H. Thomas.* Cincinnati: Robert Clarke, 1893.

Porter, Horace. *Campaigning with Grant.* New York: Century, 1897.

Pratt, Fletcher. *Eleven Generals.* New York: W. Sloane Associates, 1949.

Putnam, H. E. *Joel Roberts Poinsett: A Political Biography.* Washington, D.C.: Mimeoform Press, 1935.

Ramsey, George E. "Reminiscences of an Army Surgeon." MOLLUS, Commandery of Michigan, *War Papers,* II, 172–90. Detroit: Ostler Printing, 1888–.

Rea, John P. "Four Weeks with Long's Cavalry in East Tennessee." MOLLUS, Commandery of Minnesota, *Glimpses of the Nation's Struggle,* V, 17–44. 6 vols. St. Paul, 1887–1909.

Robbins, Walter R. *War Record and Personal Experiences of Walter Raleigh Robbins.* Chicago: privately printed, 1923.

Roberts, John N. *Reminiscences of the Civil War.* N.p., 1925.

Rockwell, Alphonso D. *Rambling Recollections.* New York: Paul B. Hober, 1920.

———. "With Sheridan's Cavalry." MOLLUS, Commandery of New York, *Personal Recollections of the War of the Rebellion,* III, 228–39. 3 vols. New York: G. P. Putnam's Sons, 1891–1907.

Rose, V. M. *Life and Public Services of Gen. Ben McCulloch.* Philadelphia: Pictorial Bureau of the Press, 1888.

Ross, Fitzgerald. *Cities and Camps of the Confederate States.* Urbana: University of Illinois Press, 1958.

Russell, William H. *My Diary North and South.* 2 vols. Boston: T. O. H. P. Burnham, 1863.

Sammons, John H. *Personal Recollections of the Civil War.* Greensburg, Montgomery and Son, 1888.

Sandburg, Carl. *Abraham Lincoln: The War Years.* 4 vols. New York: Harcourt, Brace, 1939.

Schofield, John M. *Forty-Six Years in the Army.* New York: Century, 1897.

Schurz, Carl B. *Reminiscences of Carl Schurz.* 2 vols. New York: McClure, 1907–1908.

Seitz, Don C. *Braxton Bragg: General of the Confederacy.* Columbia, S.C.: State, 1924.

Shanks, William F. G. *Personal Recollections of Distinguished Generals.* New York: Harper & Brothers, 1866.

Sheppard, E. W. *Bedford Forrest: The Confederacy's Greatest Cavalryman.* Toronto: Longman, Green, 1930.

Sheridan, Philip H. *Personal Memoirs of P. H. Sheridan.* 2 vols. New York: Charles L. Webster, 1888.

Sherman, William T. *The Memoirs of General William T. Sherman.* Bloomington: Indiana University Press, 1957.

Smith, S. K. *Life, Army Record, and Public Services of D. Howard Smith.* Louisville: Bradley & Gilbert, 1890.

Stanley, David S. *Personal Memoirs of Major-General David S. Stanley, U.S.A.* Cambridge: Harvard University Press, 1917.

Starr, Stephen Z. *Colonel Grenfell's Wars.* Baton Rouge: Louisiana State University Press, 1971.

Swiggett, Howard. *The Rebel Raider: A Life of John Hunt Morgan.* Indianapolis: Bobbs-Merrill, 1924.

Tapp, Hambleton. "Incidents in the Life of Frank Wolford, Colonel of the First Kentucky Union Cavalry." *Filson Club History Quarterly,* X (1936), 82–99.

Taylor, Richard. *Destruction and Reconstruction.* New York: D. Appleton, 1879.

Tenney, Luman H. *War Diary.* Cleveland: Evangelical Publishing, 1914.

Thomas, Clarence. *General Turner Ashby.* Winchester, Va.: Eddy Press, 1907.

Thomas, Hampton S. *Some Personal Reminiscences of Service in the Cavalry of the Army of the Potomac.* Philadelphia: L. R. Hammersley, 1889.

Thomason, John W., Jr. *Jeb Stuart.* New York: Charles Scribner's Sons, 1941.

Tobie, Edward P. *Service in the Cavalry of the Army of the Potomac.* Providence: Personal Narratives Rhode Island Soldiers and Sailors Historical Society, 1882.

Townsend, George A. *Rustics in Rebellion.* Chapel Hill: University of North Carolina Press, 1950.

Treichel, Charles. "Major Zagonyi's Horse Guard." MOLLUS, Commandery of New York, *Personal Recollections of the War of the Rebellion,* III, 240–46. 3 vols. New York: G. P. Putnam's Sons, 1891–1907.

Tremain, Henry E. *The Closing Days About Richmond, or, The Last Hours of Sheridan's Cavalry.* New York: Bonnell, Silver & Bowers, 1904.

deTrobriand, Regis. *Four Years with the Army of the Potomac.* Boston: Ticknor, 1889.

Van Horne, Thomas B. *The Life of Major-General George H. Thomas.* New York: Charles Scribner's Sons, 1882.

Waring, George E., Jr. *Whip and Spur.* Boston: James R. Osgood, 1875.

Watson, William. *Life in the Confederate Army*. New York: Scribner and Welford, 1888.

Weigley, Russell F. "John Buford." *Civil War Times Illustrated*, V (1966), 14–23.

———. *Quartermaster General of the Union Army: A Biography of Montgomery C. Meigs*. New York: Columbia University Press, 1959.

Wellman, Manly Wade. *Giant in Gray: A Biography of Wade Hampton of South Carolina*. New York: Charles Scribner's Sons, 1949.

White, John H. "Forgotten Cavalrymen: General Edward Francis Winslow." *Journal of the United States Cavalry Association*, XXV (1915), 375–89.

Whiting, Frederick, "Diary and Personal Recollections." MOLLUS, Commandery of Iowa, *War Sketches and Incidents*, I, 89–104. 2 vols. Des Moines: Press of P. C. Kenyon, 1893–98.

Whittaker, Frederick. *A Complete Life of General George A. Custer*. New York: Sheldon, 1876.

[Whittaker, Frederick]. "A Volunteer Cavalryman." *Volunteer Cavalry: The Lessons of a Decade*. New York: published by author, 1871.

Williams, John A. B. *Leaves from a Trooper's Diary*. Philadelphia: Bell, Printer, 1869.

Williams, S. C. *General John T. Wilder*. Bloomington: Indiana University Press, 1936.

Williamson, Peter J. "With the First Wisconsin: The Letters of Peter J. Williamson." *Wisconsin Magazine of History*, XXVI (1943), 333–45, 433–49.

Wilson, James H. *The Life of John A. Rawlins*. New York: Neale Publishing, 1916.

———. *Under the Old Flag*. 2 vols. New York: D. Appleton, 1912.

Wilson, Selden L. *Recollections and Experiences During the Civil War, 1861–1865*. Washington, D.C.: n.p., 1913.

Witherspoon, William. "Reminiscences of a Scout, Spy and Soldier of Forrest's Cavalry." Edited by R. S. Henry. *As They Saw Forrest*. Jackson, Miss.: McCowat-Mercer Press, 1956.

Wyeth, John A. *That Devil Forrest: Life of General Nathan Bedford Forrest*. New York: Harper & Brothers, 1959.

———. *With Sabre and Scalpel*. New York: Harper & Brothers, 1914.

Young, B. H. *Confederate Wizards of the Saddle: Being Reminiscences and Observations of One Who Rode with Morgan*. Kennesaw: Continental Book Company, 1958.

ACCOUNTS OF ACTIONS, BATTLES, AND CAMPAIGNS

Anderson, David D. "The Second Michigan Cavalry Under Philip H. Sheridan." *Michigan History*, XLV (1961), 210–18.

Andrews, C. C. *History of the Campaign of Mobile, Including the Co-*

operative Operations of Gen. Wilson's Cavalry in Alabama. New York: D. Van Nostrand, 1867.

Beck, R. McC. "General J. E. B. Stuart at Brandy Station, June 9, 1863." *Journal of the United States Cavalry Association*, XLIV (1935), 5–10.

Belfield, Henry H. "The Wilson Raid." MOLLUS, Commandery of Illinois, *Military Essays and Recollections*, IV, 503–21. 5 vols. Chicago: A. C. McClurg, 1891–1894.

Bigelow, John, Jr. *The Campaign of Chancellorsville: A Strategic and Tactical Study.* New Haven: Yale University Press, 1910.

Britton, Wiley. *The Civil War on the Border.* New York: G. P. Putnam's Sons, 1891.

Brooke-Rawle, William. "Gregg's Cavalry Fight at Gettysburg, July 3, 1863." *Journal of the United States Cavalry Association*, IV (1891), 257–75.

Brown, Dee A. *Grierson's Raid.* Urbana: University of Illinois Press, 1954.

Carpenter, Louis H. "Sheridan's Expedition Around Richmond, May 9–25, 1864." *Journal of the United States Cavalry Association*, I (1888), 300–24.

Catton, Bruce. "Sheridan at Five Forks." *Journal of Southern History*, XXI (1955), 305–15.

Coddington, Edwin B. *The Gettysburg Campaign: A Study in Command.* New York: Charles Scribner's Sons, 1968.

Colby, Elbridge. "Wilson's Cavalry Campaign of 1865." *Journal of the American Military History Foundation*, II (1928), 204–21.

Cox, Jacob D. *The Battle of Franklin, Tennessee, November 30, 1864.* New York: Charles Scribner's Sons, 1897.

———. *The March to the Sea, Franklin and Nashville.* New York: Charles Scribner's Sons, 1886.

Crowninshield, Benjamin W. "Sheridan at Winchester." *Atlantic Monthly*, XLII (1878) 863–91.

Curry, William L. "Raid of the Union Cavalry, Commanded by General Judson Kilpatrick, Around the Confederate Army in Atlanta, August, 1864." MOLLUS, Commandery of Ohio, *Sketches of War History, 1861–1865*, VI, 252–75. 7 vols. Cincinnati: Robert Clark, 1888–1910.

Davis, George B. "The Cavalry Combat at Brandy Station, Va., on June 9, 1863." *Journal of the United States Cavalry Association*, XXV (1914), 190–98.

———. "The Cavalry Combat at Kelly's Ford in 1863." *Journal of the United States Cavalry Association*, XXV (1915), 390–402.

———. "The Richmond Raid of 1864." *Journal of the United States Cavalry Association*, XXIV (1913–14), 362–76.

Deupree, J. G. "The Capture of Holly Springs, Mississippi, Dec. 20,

1862." *Publications of the Mississippi Historical Society*, IV (1901), 49–61.

Dodson, W. C. *Campaigns of Wheeler and His Cavalry*. Atlanta: Hudgins Publishing, 1899.

Downey, Fairfax. *Clash of Cavalry*. New York: David McKay, 1959.

Dyer, J. P. "Some Aspects of Cavalry Operations in the Army of Tennessee." *Journal of Southern History*, VIII (1942), 210–25.

Fiske, John. *The Mississippi Valley in the Civil War*. Boston: Houghton, Mifflin, 1900.

Fox, W. F. *New York Monuments Commission for the Battlefields of Gettysburg and Chattanooga: Final Report on the Battlefield of Gettysburg*. Albany: J. B. Lyon, 1900.

Gilmore, D. M. "Cavalry, Its Use and Value as Illustrated by Reference to the Engagements of Kelly's Ford and Gettysburg." MOLLUS, Commandery of Minnesota, *Glimpses of the Nation's Struggle*, II, 213–25. 6 vols. St. Paul: 1887–1909.

Gregg, David McM. "The Second Cavalry Division, Army of the Potomac, in the Gettysburg Campaign." *Journal of the United States Cavalry Association*, XVIII (1907), 213–25.

Harris, Samuel. *The Michigan Brigade of Cavalry at the Battle of Gettysburg*. Chicago: n.p., 1894

Hay, Thomas R. "The Cavalry at Spring Hill." *Tennessee Historical Magazine*, VIII (1924), 7–23.

———. *Hood's Tennessee Campaign*. New York: Walter Neale, 1929.

Hess, Frank W. "The First Cavalry Battle at Kelly's Ford, Va." *First Maine Bugle, Campaign III, Call 3* (1893), 3–16.

Horn, Stanley F. *The Decisive Battle of Nashville*. Baton Rouge: Louisiana State University Press, 1956.

Hosea, Lewis M. "The Campaign of Selma." MOLLUS, Commandery of Ohio, *Sketches of War History, 1861–1865*, I, 77–106. 7 vols. Cincinnati: Robert Clark, 1888–1910.

Humphreys, Andrew A. *From Gettysburg to the Rapidan*. New York: Charles Scribner's Sons, 1883.

———. *The Virginia Campaign of '64 and '65*. New York: Charles Scribner's Sons, 1883.

Isham, Asa B. "Through the Wilderness to Richmond," MOLLUS, Commandery of Ohio, *Sketches of War History, 1861–1865*, I, 198–217. 7 vols. Cincinnati: Robert Clark, 1888–1910.

Jenkins, Paul B. *The Battle of Westport*. Kansas City: Franklin Hudson Publishing, 1906.

Johnson, Ludwell H. *Red River Campaign*. Baltimore: Johns Hopkins Press, 1958.

Johnson, R. V. and C. C. Buel, eds. *Battles and Leaders of the Civil War*. 4 vols. New York: Century, 1887–1888.

Johnston, William P. "Zagonyi's Charge with Fremont's Body-Guard:

A Picturesque Fol-de-Rol." *Southern Historical Society Papers*, III (1887), 195–96.

Jones, Virgil C. *Eight Hours Before Richmond*. New York: Henry Holt, 1957.

Jordan, Thomas and J. P. Pryor. *The Campaigns of Lieut.-Gen. N. B. Forrest*. New Orleans: Blelock, 1868.

Keller, Allan. *Morgan's Raid*. Indianapolis: Bobbs-Merrill, 1961.

Kennedy, William V. "The Cavalry Battle at Brandy Station." *Armor* (January-February, 1956), 27–31.

Kidd, James H. "The Michigan Cavalry Brigade in the Wilderness." MOLLUS, Commandery of Michigan, *War Papers, No. 11*. Detroit: Ostler Printing, 1888–.

Kniffen, Gilbert C. "Streight's Raid Through Tennessee and Northern Georgia in 1863." MOLLUS, Commandery of the District of Columbia, *War Papers, No. 82*. Washington, D.C.: Judd and Detweiler, 1887–.

Luff, William M. "March of the Cavalry from Harper's Ferry, September 14, 1862." MOLLUS, Commandery of Illinois, *Military Essays and Recollections*, II, 33–48. 5 vols. Chicago: A. C. McClurg, 1891–1894.

Lynne, Donald M. "Wilson's Cavalry at Nashville." *Civil War History*, I (1955), 141–59.

Mason, Frank H. "General Stoneman's Last Campaign." MOLLUS, Commandery of Ohio, *Sketches of War History, 1861–1865*, III, 21–43. 7 vols. Cincinnati: Robert Clark, 1888–1910.

Mies, John W. "Breakout at Harper's Ferry." *Civil War History*, II (1956), 13–28.

Miller, S. H. "Yellow Tavern." *Civil War History*, II (1956), 57–81.

Mitchell, Charles D. "Field Notes of the Selma Campaign." MOLLUS, Commandery of Ohio, *Sketches of War History, 1861–1865*, VI, 174–94. 7 vols. Cincinnati: Robert Clark, 1888–1910.

———. "The Sanders Raid into East Tennessee, June, 1863." MOLLUS, Commandery of Ohio, *Sketches of War History, 1861–1865*, VI, 238–51. 7 vols. Cincinnati: Robert Clark, 1888–1910.

Monaghan, Jay. "Custer's 'Last Stand': Trevilian Station, 1864." *Civil War History*, VII (1962), 245–58.

Monnett, Howard D. *Action Before Westport, 1864*. Kansas City: Westport Historical Society, 1964.

Morrow, Norman P. "Price's Missouri Expedition, 1864." M.A. thesis, University of Texas, Austin, 1949.

Nettleton, A. Bayard. "How the Day Was Saved at Cedar Creek." MOLLUS, Commandery of Minnesota, *Glimpses of the Nation's Struggle*, I, 258–75. 6 vols. St. Paul, 1887–1909.

Pond, G. E. *The Shenandoah Valley in 1864*. New York: Charles Scribner's Sons, 1883.

Rea, John P. "Kilpatrick's Raid Around Atlanta." MOLLUS, Commandery of Minnesota, *Glimpses of the Nation's Struggle*, V, 152–74. 6 vols. St. Paul, 1887–1909.

Robinson, George I. "With Kilpatrick Around Atlanta." MOLLUS, Commandery of Wisconsin, *War Papers*, I, 201–27. 3 vols. Milwaukee: Burdick, Armitage & Allen, 1891–1903.

Steele, M. F. *American Campaigns.* Washington, D.C.: Byron S. Adams, 1922.

Stonesifer, Roy F., Jr. "The Long Hard Road: Union Cavalry in the Gettysburg Campaign." M.A. thesis, Pennsylvania State College, 1959.

———. "The Union Cavalry Comes of Age." *Civil War History*, XI (1965), 274–83.

Toombs, Samuel. *New Jersey Troops in the Gettysburg Campaign from June 5 to July 31, 1863.* Orange, N.J.: Evening Mail Publishing, 1888.

Trowbridge, Luther S. "The Operations of the Cavalry in the Gettysburg Campaign." MOLLUS, Commandery of Michigan, *War Papers, No. 1.* Detroit: Ostler Printing, 1888–.

———. "The Stoneman Raid of 1865." MOLLUS, Commandery of Michigan, *War Papers, No. 7.* Detroit: Ostler Printing, 1888–.

Tucker, Glenn. *High Tide at Gettysburg.* Indianapolis: Bobbs-Merrill, 1958.

Walker, Aldace F. *The Peninsula.* New York: Charles Scribner's Sons, 1881.

Wells, Edward L. *Hampton and His Cavalry in '64.* Richmond: B. F. Johnson Publishing, 1899.

White, Julius. "The First Sabre Charge of the War." MOLLUS, Commandery of Illinois, *Military Essays and Recollections*, III, 25–35. 5 vols. Chicago: A. C. McClurg, 1894.

Wilson, George S. "Wilder's Brigade of Mounted Infantry in the Tullahoma-Chickamauga Campaigns." MOLLUS, Commandery of Kansas, *War Talks in Kansas.* Kansas City, Mo.: Press of F. Hudson, 1906–.

GENERAL AND MISCELLANEOUS WORKS

Abel, A. H. *The American Indian as a Participant in the Civil War.* Cleveland: Arthur H. Clark, 1919.

Barksdale, E. C.: "Semi-Regular and Irregular Warfare in the Civil War." Ph.D. dissertation, University of Texas, 1941.

Barton, John V. "The Procurement of Horses." *Civil War Times Illustrated*, VI (1967), 17–24.

Benedict, G. G. *Vermont in the Civil War.* 2 vols. Burlington, Vt.: Free Press Association, 1886–88.

Boynton, Edward C. *History of West Point.* New York: Van Nostrand, 1871.

Brackett, Albert G. *History of the United States Cavalry.* New York: Harper & Brothers, 1865.

Brooks, U. R., ed. *Stories of the Confederacy.* Columbia: State Company, 1912.

Brownlee, Richard S. *Gray Ghosts of the Confederacy.* Baton Rouge: Louisiana State University Press, 1958.

Bruce, Robert V. *Lincoln and the Tools of War.* Indianapolis: Bobbs-Merrill, 1956.

Buckeridge, J. O. *Lincoln's Choice.* Harrisburg: Stackpole Books, 1956.

Calkins, E. A. "The Wisconsin Cavalry Regiments." MOLLUS, Commandery of Wisconsin, *War Papers*, I, 173–93. 3 vols. Milwaukee: Burdick, Armitage & Allen, 1891–1903.

Carraway, William E. "The Mutiny of the 15th Pennsylvania Volunteer Cavalry." *Denver Westerners Monthly Roundup*, XVII (1961), 5–15.

Carter, William H. *Horses, Saddles and Bridles.* Baltimore: Lord Baltimore Press, 1900.

Commager, Henry Steele, ed. *The Blue and the Gray: The Story of the Civil War as Told by Participants.* 2 vols. Indianapolis: Bobbs-Merrill, 1950.

Cooke, Philip St. G. *Cavalry Tactics, or, Regulations for the Instruction, Formation and Movements of the Cavalry.* Washington, D.C.: Government Printing Office, 1862.

Cory, Charles E. "The Sixth Kansas Cavalry and Its Commander." *Kansas Historical Collections*, XI (1909–1910), 217–38.

Cornish, Dudley T. *The Sable Arm: Negro Troops in the Union Army, 1861–1865.* New York: W. W. Norton, 1956.

Crowninshield, Benjamin W. "Cavalry in Virginia During the War of the Rebellion." *Papers of the Military Historical Society of Massachusetts*, XIII (1913), 3–31.

Cullum, George W. *Biographical Register of the Officers and Graduates of the U.S. Military Academy.* 2 vols. New York: Van Nostrand, 1868.

Cunningham, Frank. *General Stand Watie's Confederate Indians.* San Antonio: Naylor, 1959.

Dale, E. E. and Gaston Little. *Cherokee Cavaliers.* Norman: University of Oklahoma Press, 1939.

Davis, J. Lucius. *The Trooper's Manual.* Richmond: A. Morris, 1862.

Denison, G. T. *A History of Cavalry.* London: Macmillan, 1913.

Doster, Frank. "Eleventh Indiana Cavalry in Kansas in 1865." *Transactions of the Kansas State Historical Society*, XV (1923), 524–29.

Dupuy, R. E. and T. N. Dupuy. *Military Heritage of America.* New York: McGraw-Hill, 1956.

Earle, E. M., ed. *Makers of Modern Strategy*. Princeton: Princeton University Press, 1943.

Forman, Sidney. *West Point*. New York: Columbia University Press, 1950.

Foster, John Y. *New Jersey and the Rebellion*. Newark: Martin R. Dennis, 1868.

French, Samuel L. *The Army of the Potomac from 1861 to 1863*. New York: Publishing Society, 1906.

Fuller, J. F. C. *Armaments and History*. New York: Charles Scribner's Sons, 1945.

————. *The Generalship of Ulysses S. Grant*. Bloomington: Indiana University Press, 1957.

Ganoe, William A. *The History of the United States Army*. New York: D. Appleton, 1942.

Gilmore, D. H. "Cavalry, Its Use and Value." MOLLUS, Commandery of Minnesota, *Glimpses of the Nation's Struggle*, II, 38–51. 6 vols. St. Paul, 1887–1909.

Gleaves, S. H. "The Strategic Use of Cavalry." *Journal of the United States Cavalry Association*, XVIII (1907), 9–25.

Gray, Alonzo. *Cavalry Tactics as Illustrated by the War of the Rebellion*. Fort Leavenworth, Ks.: Army Service Schools Press, 1910.

Halleck, H. Wager. *Elements of Military Art and Science*. New York: D. Appleton, 1863.

Harbord, J. G. "The History of the Cavalry of the Army of Northern Virginia." *Journal of the United States Cavalry Association*, XIV (1904), 423–503.

Harris, Moses. "The Union Cavalry." MOLLUS, Commandery of Wisconsin, *War Papers*, I, 340–73. 3 vols. Milwaukee: Burdick, Armitage & Allen, 1891–1903.

Hazen, W. B. *The School of the Army in Germany and France*. New York: Harper & Brothers, 1872.

Henderson, G. F. R. *The Science of War*. London: Longmans, Green, 1913.

Herr, J. K. and E. S. Wallace. *The Story of the U.S. Cavalry, 1775–1942*. Boston: Little, Brown, 1953.

Higginson, Thomas W. "Regular and Volunteer Officers." *Atlantic Monthly*, XIV (1864), 348–57.

Horn, Stanley F. *The Army of Tennessee*. Indianapolis: Bobbs-Merrill, 1941.

Hutchins, James S. "The United States Cavalry Saddle, McClellan Pattern, Model 1857, in Tojhusmuseet, Copenhagen." *Saertryk af Vaabenhistoriske Aarboger*, XVI (Copenhagen, Denmark, 1970), 146–62.

Ingersoll, Lurton D. *Iowa and the Rebellion*. Philadelphia: J. B. Lippincott, 1866.

Isham, Asa B. "The Cavalry of the Army of the Potomac." MOLLUS,

Commandery of Ohio, *Sketches of War History, 1861–1865*, V, 301–27. 7 vols. Cincinnati: Robert Clark, 1888–1910.

Johnson, James R. and A. H. Bill. *Horsemen Blue and Gray.* New York: Oxford University Press, 1960.

Jones, James P., ed. "'Your Left Arm': James H. Wilson's Letters to Adam Badeau." *Civil War History*, XII (1966), 230–45.

Jones, Virgil C. *Gray Ghosts and Rebel Raiders.* New York: Henry Holt, 1956.

Kempster, Walter. "The Early Days of Our Cavalry, in the Army of the Potomac." MOLLUS, Commandery of Wisconsin, *War Papers*, III, 60–89. 3 vols. Milwaukee: Burdick, Armitage & Allen, 1891–1903.

LaBree, Benjamin. *Camp Fires of the Confederacy.* Louisville: Courier-Journal Job Printing, 1898.

———, ed. *The Confederate Soldier in the Civil War.* Louisville, Ky.: Prentice Press, 1897.

Laugel, Auguste. *The United States During the Civil War, 1861–1865.* Bloomington, Ind., 1961.

Livermore, Thomas L. *Numbers and Losses in the Civil War in America, 1861–1865.* Bloomington: Indiana University Press, 1957.

Logan, John A. *The Great Conspiracy: Its Origin and History.* New York: A. R. Hart, 1886.

Lonn, Ella. *Desertion During the Civil War.* New York: Century, 1928.

———. *Foreigners in the Confederacy.* Chapel Hill: University of North Carolina Press, 1940.

———. *Foreigners in the Union Army and Navy.* Baton Rouge: Louisiana State University Press, 1951.

Luvaas, Jay. "Cavalry Lessons of the Civil War." *Civil War Times Illustrated*, VI (1968), 20–31.

———. *The Military Legacy of the Civil War.* Chicago: University of Chicago Press, 1959.

McClellan, George B. *European Cavalry.* Philadelphia: J. B. Lippincott, 1861.

———. *Regulations and Instructions for the Field Service of the United States Cavalry in Time of War.* Philadelphia: J. B. Lippincott, 1861.

McDonald, Edward H. "Fighting Under Ashby in the Shenandoah." *Civil War Times Illustrated*, V (1966), 29–35.

Mahan, Dennis Hart. *Advanced Guard, Outpost and Detachment Service of Troops, with the Essential Principles of Strategy and Grand Tactics.* New York: Wiley and Putman, 1863.

Maury, Dabney H. *Skirmish Drill for Mounted Troops.* Richmond: Ritchie & Dunavant, 1861.

May, E. S. *Guns and Cavalry.* London: S. Low, Manton, 1896.

Meneely, A. Howard. *The War Department, 1861: A Study in Mobili-*

zation and Administration. New York: Columbia University Press, 1928.

Merrill, Catharine. *The Soldier of Indiana in the War for the Union.* 2 vols. Indianapolis: Merrill, 1866–69.

Morris, Francis. "Cavalry Horses in America." *Report of the Commissioner of Agriculture for the Year 1863: Executive Document No. 91: 38th Congress, 1st Session, House of Representatives.* Washington, D.C.: Government Printing Office, 1863.

Munford, T. T. "A Confederate Cavalry Officer's View on 'American Practice and European Theory.'" *Journal of the United States Cavalry Association,* IV (1891), 197–203.

Naylor, William K. *The Principles of Strategy as Illustrated by the Civil War.* Fort Leavenworth, Ks.: Army Service Schools Press, 1917.

Nevins, Allan. *The War for the Union: The Improvised War, 1861–1862.* New York: Charles Scribner's Sons, 1959.

————. *The War for the Union: The War Becomes Revolution, 1862–1863.* New York: Charles Scribner's Sons, 1960.

————. *The War for the Union: The Organized War, 1863–1864.* New York: Charles Scribner's Sons, 1971.

————. *The War for the Union: The Organized War to Victory, 1864–1865.* New York: Charles Scribner's Sons, 1971.

Newman, James R. *The Tools of War.* Garden City: Doubleday, Doran, 1942.

Oates, Stephen B. *Confederate Cavalry West of the River.* Austin: University of Texas Press, 1961.

————. "Supply for the Confederate Cavalry in the Trans-Mississippi." *Military Affairs,* XXV (1961), 94–99.

Pelzer, Louis. *Marches of the Dragoons in the Mississippi Valley.* Iowa City: State Historical Society of Iowa, 1917.

Quiner, E. B. *The Military History of Wisconsin.* Chicago: Clarke, 1866.

Ramsdell, Charles W. "General Robert E. Lee's Horse Supply, 1862–1865." *American Historical Review,* XXXV (1930), 758–77.

Reid, Whitelaw. *Ohio in the War: Her Statesmen, Her Generals and Soldiers.* 2 vols. Cincinnati: Moore, Wilstach & Baldwin, 1868.

Rhodes, Charles D. *History of the Cavalry of the Army of the Potomac.* Kansas City, Mo.: Hudson-Kimberly Publishing, 1900.

Rodenbough, Theodore H. "Cavalry in the Civil War." Edited by F. T. Miller. In *The Photographic History of the Civil War,* IV, 16–38. New York: Review of Reviews, 1911.

Schaff, Morris. *The Spirit of Old West Point.* New York: Houghton, Mifflin, 1907.

Shannon, F. A. *Organization and Administration of the Union Army.* Cleveland: Arthur H. Clark, 1928.

Smith, Edward C. *The Borderland in the Civil War*. New York: Macmillan, 1927.

Starr, Stephen Z. "Cold Steel." *Civil War History*, XI (1965), 142–59.

Swart, Stanley L. "The Military Examining Board in the Civil War: A Case Study." *Civil War History*, XVI (1970), 227–45.

Thiele, T. F. "The Evolution of Cavalry in the American Civil War, 1861–1863." Ph.D. dissertation, University of Michigan, 1951.

U.S. War Department. Adjutant General's Office. Special Civil War Collection. Horse Books, 1862–1864. National Archives, Washington.

————. *Cavalry Tactics* ["Poinsett Tactics"]. Washington, D.C.: Government Printing Office, 1841.

————. *The War of the Rebellion: A Compilation of the Official Records of the Union and Confederate Armies*. 128 vols. Washington, D.C.: Government Printing Office, 1880–1901.

Upham, Cyril B. "Arms and Equipment for the Iowa Troops in the Civil War." *Iowa Journal of History and Politics*, XVI (1918), 3–52.

Upton, Emory. *The Military Policy of the United States*. Washington, D.C.: Government Printing Office, 1904.

Wasson, R. Gordon. *The Hall Carbine Affair*. New York: Pandick Press, 1948.

Wheeler, Joseph. *A Revised System of Cavalry Tactics for the Use of the Cavalry and Mounted Infantry, C.S.A.* Mobile: S. H. Goetzel, 1863.

Wiley, Bell I. *The Life of Billy Yank*. Indianapolis: Bobbs-Merrill, 1951.

————. *The Life of Johnny Reb*. Indianapolis: Bobbs-Merrill, 1943.

Williams, Kenneth P. *Lincoln Finds a General*. 5 vols. New York: Macmillan, 1949–59.

Williams, T. Harry. *Lincoln and His Generals*. New York: Alfred A. Knopf, 1952.

Wilson, James H. "The Cavalry of the Army of the Potomac." *Papers of the Military Historical Society of Massachusetts*, XIII (1913), 35–88.

Wise, Jennings C. *The Long Arm of Lee*. Lynchburg: J. P. Bell, 1915.

Wood, Evelyn. *Achievements of Cavalry*. London: G. Bell & Sons, 1897.

Index

n, 385 and *n*, 386; Regulars, 1st U.S., Battery E, 434, 437; 2nd U.S., Battery A, 352*n*, 425, Battery B, 352*n*, Battery M, 319*n*, 328, 352*n*, 430*n*, 432, 434, 435, 437; 3rd U.S., Battery C, 405*n*; 4th U.S., Battery E, 352*n*, Battery I, 23, 34

Averell, William W.: commands div'n. under Sheridan, 6; teaches 3rd Pa. horsemanship, duties, 143, 243*n*, 246; dismisses 3rd Pa. officers, 149 and *n*; in Peninsular campaign, 262*n*, 263*n*, 267*n*, 278, 279*n*; allows reporters with command, 293; in Barbee's Cross Roads fight, 320; brigade of, a tactical unit, 325*n*; in battle of Fredericksburg, 325, 326; proposes Suffolk raid, 328 and *n*; halted, 329 and *n*; commands 2nd Cav. Div'n., 339, 352*n*; fails to catch F. Lee, 343–44, 345; at Kelly's Ford, 344–45, 346–50, 347*n*, 348*n*; in Chancellorsville Campaign, 355–56, 362–64, 363*n*

Babbitt, Charles R., 284
Bailey, Ezra H., 72, 73
Banks, N. P.: and Shenandoah Valley Campaign, 222, 249, 279, 280–81; on condition of his cavalry, 282; need of large cavalry force, 283; assigned to Army of Virginia, 288; and John P. Hatch raids, 291; and battle of Cedar Mountain, 294 and *n*; asks for more cavalry, 312; mentioned, 241, 285
Barnes, James, 368*n*, 407, 408
Bartmess, Jacob, 169, 194
Bayard, George: declines 1st N.Y. colonelcy, 72; as colonel of 1st Pa., 84, 131, 134–35; and Shenandoah Valley Campaign, 280 and *n*, 283, 285, 287 and *n*, 291; pickets Rapidan, 294; in battle of Cedar Mountain, 295; and Second Bull Run Campaign, 296, 299 and *n*, 302; suggests cavalry organization, 325*n*; in battle of

Fredericksburg, 325, 326
Beale, G. W., 405
Beale, R. L. T., 387 and *n*
Beardsley, John, 302
Beck, Elias, 378*n*
Benning, Henry L., 441*n*
Binney, Henry M., 305*n*
Blackford, Charles M., 392
Blackford, William W.: on Harper's Ferry escape, 221; on Stuart's "rout" of 6th Pa., 270 and *n*; and battle of Brandy Station, 388, 395*n*; on improvement of Union cavalry, 410
Blair, Austin, 85*n*–86*n*, 128*n*
Blake, George A. H., 276 and *n*, 278*n*
Bliss, Lyman W., 429*n*
von Borcke, Heros: on Stuart's "rout" of 6th Pa., 270 and *n*; on Brandy Station review, 374–75; wounded, 405*n*
Boston, R. B., 402
Botts, John Minor, 376*n*, 388
Boyd, W. H., 71, 75, 206
Brackett, Albert G.: recruits, commands 9th Ill., 85, 131, 137; asks for active service, 205
Bragg, Braxton, 217, 226, 238
Brandy Station (Fleetwood), battle of, 376–95, 403*n*, 415, 417, 461
Brooke-Rawle, William, 436, 437*n*
Brown, John, 210 and *n*
Brown, John, Jr., 203, 263
Brown, Simeon A., 346, 347*n*
Buell, Augustus, 202–203, 329*n*
Buell, Don Carlos, 125, 237
Buford, John: replaces John P. Hatch, 292; career of, 292–93; opinions on ability of, 293; pickets Rapidan, 294; follows Jackson, 296; in Second Bull Run Campaign, 299, 302–303; as Chief of Cavalry, Army of the Potomac, 313; in Antietam Campaign, 314; commands Reserve Brigade, 339, 352*n*; in Chancellorsville Campaign, 353–54, 357, 368; as Hooker's choice to command cavalry, 368*n*; in battle of Brandy Station, 373, 376, 379–

tioned, 54, 184
Thomason, John W., Jr., 390n
Thompson, B. F., 169
Tobie, Edward P., 394
Tod, David, 90, 145
Tompkins, C. H.: as colonel, 85, 157–58, 162–63; and fake capture of Lt. Clark, 148
Torbert, A. T. A., 6, 8n
Town, Charles H., 284
Treichel, Charles, 436, 436n
deTrobriand, Regis: 96–97, 145–46

Upperville, battle of, 407–12, 461
Upton, Emory: career and reputation of, 17–18, 46, 214; destroys mills, collieries, 31; in fight near Montevallo, 34; and attacks at Ebenezer Church, 35; patrols capture Millington, 36

Van Dorn, Earl, 54, 58, 197n, 273
Vincent, Strong, 408–409, 408n

Wade, Benjamin F., 78n, 203
Wainwright, Charles S.: 320
Waltz, Charles, 162
Waring, George E., Jr., 86
Warren, G. K., 272n, 455
Washington, George, 54, 256, 257
Weber, Peter A., 459, 460
Wheeler, Joseph, 58, 60n, 238
White, A. H., 180
White, Frank, 35
Whiting, Charles J., 275–76, 295, 313n
Whittaker, Frederick, 178, 395
Wilder, John T., 23n–24n
Williams, Robert: appointed colonel, 85 and n; as commander,

102, 146, 149, 193–94; reports horses diseased, 312n
Williams, Seth, 412, 413
Wilson, Henry, 91, 111
Wilson, James H.: cavalry commands of, 3, 4, 7; prewar career of, 3; and Wilderness Campaign, 5–6; and Shenandoah Valley Campaign, 6–7; and organization of cavalry, 8, 9, 11, 16, 19, 20–21, 45; in battle of Nashville, 12–13; pursues Hood, 14; and Selma Campaign preparations, 21, 26–27, 29; sends Croxton to capture Tuscaloosa, 31; learns location of Forrest's forces, 35; and victory at Ebenezer Church, 37; and attack on Selma, 39–40, 42; and care of horses, 43; enters Montgomery, 44; evaluates his cavalry, 46; on marauding and pillage, 171–72; and Kilpatrick, 418; mentioned, 18, 24, 165, 214, 439
Winslow, E. F., 19, 44, 45
Wolford, Frank, 83–84, 97
Woodward, John H., 191n
Wyndham, Percy: prewar career of, 95; at Second Bull Run, 95–96; postwar career of, 96n; captured, 285, 286n; commands brigade, 352n; in Stoneman raid, 356; in battle of Brandy Station, 383, 384 and n, 385

Yates, Richard, 65–66, 102, 205

Zahm, Lewis: and horses and supplies, 119, 124n, 132, 138; and Lieut. Goodnow, 149, 151; on saluting, 167–68